NEW ORLEANS UNDER RECONSTRUCTION: THE CRISIS OF PLANNING

NEW ORLEANS UNDER RECONSTRUCTION: THE CRISIS OF PLANNING

Edited by
CAROL McMICHAEL REESE,
MICHAEL SORKIN, and
ANTHONY FONTENOT

ACKNOWLEDGMENTS

The editors wish to thank the following for their generous support of Project New Orleans: the Katrina Fund of the Zemurray Foundation, administered by the Greater New Orleans Foundation; the Tulane Research Enhancement Fund II; the Mary Louise Mossy Christovich Professorship, Tulane School of Architecture; and the Dean's Fund for Excellence, Tulane School of Architecture.

The editors wish to thank the following individuals for their significant contributions: Maureen Long, Ph.D., for Project New Orleans management, research, and editorial assistance; and Lindsey Caruso for text descriptions in the book's project sections.

First published by Verso 2014

"What Should New Orleans Do?" originally published in *Artforum* (December 2005); "Disaster Apartheid: A World of Green Zones and Red Zones" reprinted with permission from Naomi Klein, *The Shock Doctrine: The Rise of Disaster Capitalism* (New York: Henry Holt, 2007); "Beloved Community" reprinted with permission from Rebecca Solnit, *A Paradise Built in Hell: The Extraordinary Communities that Arise in Disaster* (London: Viking Penguin, 2009); "Haunted Housing: Eco-Vanguardism and Eviction in New Orleans" originally published as "Haunted Housing: Eco-Vanguardism, Eviction and the Biopolitics of Sustainability in New Orleans" in *Grey Room* 30 (Winter 2008), 84–113.

1 3 5 7 9 10 8 6 4 2

Verso
U.K.: 6 Meard Street, London W1F 0EG
U.S.: 20 Jay Street, Suite 1010, Brooklyn, NY 11201
www.versobooks.com

Verso is the imprint of New Left Books

ISBN-13: 978-1-78168-272-2 (PBK)
ISBN-13: 978-1-78168-273-9 (HBK)
eISBN-13: 978-1-78168-274-6 (U.S.)
eISBN-13: 978-1-78168-431-3 (U.K.)

British Library Cataloguing in Publication Data
A catalogue record for this book is available from the British Library

Library of Congress Cataloging-in-Publication Data
A catalog record for this book is available from the Library of Congress

Designed by Jessica Fleischmann / still room, with Florian Brożek
Typeset in Atlas Grotesk
Printed in Singapore by Tien Wah Press

TABLE OF CONTENTS

PART IV
Reconstructing Community, Housing (Multiply Considered)

PART V
Reconstructing the Public Sphere

PART VI
Reconstructing Cultural Landscapes

FOREWORD: SITTIN' ON THE PORCH WITH A SHOTGUN
MIKE DAVIS

Where do all the good plans and brave hopes go?[1] Gone to die in books, every one. Buried in the cemeteries of design school libraries where they wait for the Second Coming of a liberal urbanism that never comes. Become torn pages blowing down the dusty hallways of ghost buildings in dead cities like Camden or Detroit. Love letters to an Agency of the Future that never opens its mail. Composted dreams that manure the greed of billionaires with slogans like "Smart growth" and "Urban renaissance."

Whatever curiosity or interest has brought you to this extraordinary book carries with it the responsibility to help keep the conversation alive. Against all odds, the design and planning professions still harbor a formidable minority of dreamers and delinquents who refuse to accept that urban design for the public good must always be a partnership with profit or a negotiation with banks and developers. They understand that more often than not *redevelopment* is a euphemism for the desertification of core cities with African-American majorities and that brightly packaged programs like Hope VI, Clinton's reform of public housing, are little more than gentrification by eviction. For many of the contributors to this anthology, post-Katrina New Orleans—with 40 percent of its population evacuated into exile—was the obvious place to make a last stand for a democratic vision of the American City. And New Orleans claimed a piece of all their hearts, as it always does.

But never innocently. If New Orleans has been a crucible of African-American culture, it has also been the Calvary of racial equality. Set aside Mardi Gras beads and other clichés of the Big Easy: no outsider is morally qualified to join the Second Line unless he or she is prepared to confront the generations of continuous violence committed against people of color in our most fecund and only tropical city. Few Americans, for instance, know that the major events that gave birth to Reconstruction and then brought about its downfall occurred a few blocks from Basin Street. On

1 Some of the observations presented in this essay first appeared in the author's article "Who Is Killing New Orleans?" in *The Nation*, April 10, 2006; it had appeared under the same title online on March 23, 2006.

July 30, 1866, ex-Confederates massacred nearly 250 black Republicans on the front steps of the Mechanics Institute. Congress responded with Reconstruction legislation. Eight years later, a bloody insurrection by the White League deposed the elected Republican government. Faced with the prospect of having to maintain a permanent military occupation of New Orleans and other parts of the South, Republicans instead retreated from the Reconstruction program.

In 1896, a multiracial civil rights alliance, perhaps unique in the South, challenged the introduction of segregation on New Orleans public transport. Homer Plessy was promptly arrested for attempting to sit in a "whites only" section of a local train, and the resulting Supreme Court decision (Plessy v. Ferguson) legalized Jim Crow statutes across the South for three generations. Four years after Plessy's action, the black equal-rights advocate Robert Charles shot a white cop in self-defense, and for days white lynch mobs terrorized neighborhoods of color, while a local newspaper demanded the "extermination" of the city's entire black population. Louis Armstrong was born a year later.

Then there was 1960. Morton Inger described it in his study *Politics and Reality in an American City*:

> When four Negro first-graders entered two previously all-white schools in New Orleans on November 14, 1960, the reaction by the city's extremists was so intense and went unchecked for so long that the city suffered a near catastrophe. Thousands of whites rampaged through the downtown business district hurling bricks and bottles. White children boycotted the two schools for a year, and for months an unruly crowd cursed, shoved, stoned, and spat upon the few white children who continued to attend one of the schools—while the nation watched on television.[2]

Over the next twenty years, white flight to suburban Jefferson, St. Bernard, and St. Tammany parishes emptied mixed working-class neighborhoods, a pattern that was reinforced by the decline of port and manufacturing employment after the end of the Vietnam War. Poydras Street, it's true, sprouted skyscrapers like pumpkins during the 1970s energy boom, but the bust quickly followed, and New Orleans has never reaped real benefits, as Houston as done, from riding the oil, gas, and sulfur roller coaster. Two-thirds of the population had been white in 1960, but just over one-quarter was on the eve of Katrina. Meanwhile black poverty festered in the large archipelago of public housing projects and neglected neighborhoods in the below-sea-level center of the city's topographical "bowl." The fiscal consequences of white flight to the

2 Morton Inger, *Politics and Reality in an American City: The New Orleans School Crisis of 1960* (New York: Center for Urban Education, 1960); excerpt is from the introduction.

suburbs, as well as three decades of job loss, gave New Orleans an economic profile closer to Newark and Detroit than to Atlanta or Charlotte.

From the late 1960s, New Orleans's white elites had identified the city's chief problem not as a deficit of employment but rather as a surplus of poor, underclass black people. Elsewhere, such thoughts might be expressed quietly in country-club locker rooms, but in New Orleans it was shouted from rooftops that the city had to reduce its welfare "burden." Indeed, a generation or more before Katrina, New Orleans was probably the only American city where downsizing the population was seen as a cure, not a problem. But there was a major obstacle: a large, dynamic middle class of color (many still self-identified as Creole) that after the passage of the Voting Rights Act became increasingly skilled at mobilizing the en bloc vote of the housing projects and poorer neighborhoods. The result until the middle 1970s was a stalemate, in which attempts by black Democrats to expand employment and services were frustrated by old-guard whites, whose sweeping plans for urban renewal, in turn, were contested by a growing black electorate.

Mayor "Moon" Landrieu (1970–1978), a white liberal with one foot in Louisiana's unique tradition of Longism (aligning Cajuns and blacks together around public spending for populist goals) and another in the secretive world of Uptown's powermongers, broke the logjam by integrating civil service jobs in exchange for the participation of leading black Democrats in redevelopment planning. This basic deal—public employment opportunities for blacks at the price of supporting the white elite's land-use agenda—was further institutionalized under Landrieu's successor, and New Orleans's first black mayor, "Dutch" Morial (1978–1986), who with Republican developer Joseph Canizaro oversaw the skyscraper renaissance downtown. His son, Marc Morial, mayor from 1994 to 2002, continued the tradition by supporting the expansion of the convention center and targeting spending on historical white neighborhoods, such as the Garden District.

In the years of Morial family rule, moreover, a black nouveau riche stratum, often in junior partnership with major developers and contractors, acquired a substantial stake in the politics of redevelopment. Uptown, where descendants of the White League keep their mausoleums, began to take note of this unexpected form of black power. On the eve of Katrina, therefore, there were even some African-American leaders willing to chant the ancient mantra that the city had become a soul-destroying warehouse for underemployed and poorly educated blacks whose real interests—so it was claimed—might be better served by a Greyhound ticket to another town.

Katrina, providentially, bought several hundred thousand of those tickets. Canizaro, the power behind the scenes of the nominally Democratic Mayor Ray Nagin, was the first to shed crocodile tears. As he told the Associated Press that October after the flood, "As a practical matter, these poor folks don't have the resources to go back to our city, just like they didn't have the resources to get out of our city. So we won't get all those folks back. That's not what I want, it's just a fact."[3]

Or perhaps a dream fulfilled. While sniffer dogs were still finding bodies in muck-filled homes, something like a coup d'état occurred, as an elite, largely white group attempted to wrest control over the debate about how to rebuild the city. Twelve days after the flood walls failed, and as the friends of George Bush—the Shaw Group and KBR, a Halliburton subsidiary—were signing federal contracts to mine gold from the wreckage of New Orleans, Mayor Nagin went to Dallas to meet the city's refugee business leadership, who were holed up there in luxury hotels or second homes. This group was brought together by James Reiss, major real estate investor and chair of the Regional Transit Authority (that is, the official responsible for the buses that didn't evacuate people), mega-developer Canizaro, and Pres Kabacoff, developer-gentrifier and local patron of the New Urbanism.

The summit excluded most of New Orleans's elected black representatives and, according to Reiss as quoted in the *Wall Street Journal*, focused on the opportunity to rebuild the city "with better services and fewer poor people."[4]

The result that emerged from this elite meeting was the Orwellian-named Bring New Orleans Back (BNOB), formed for the strategic purpose of not bringing back the New Orleans of people from the housing projects and poor neighborhoods. Appropriately, Canizaro was appointed chair of its urban planning group. At the end of September the mayor charged BNOB with preparing a master plan to rebuild the city. The highly praised prototype for what life might be like with "fewer poor people" was Kabacoff's 2003 redevelopment of the St. Thomas public housing project as River Garden, a mixed market-rate and subsidized faux-Creole subdivision. Although the commission was racially balanced and included city council president Oliver Thomas as well as jazz musician Wynton Marsalis (telecommuting from Manhattan), the real clout was exercised by committee chairs like Canizaro who lunched privately with Nagin before the group's weekly meeting. This inner sanctum was reportedly necessary because the full-panel meetings did not allow a frank discussion of "tough issues of race and class." Indeed.

At this point it was clear that something like a municipal coup was in progress and that it didn't include most of the city's black political elite. BNOB might have imploded but for a shrewd outflanking movement by Canizaro, who persuaded Nagin to invite the Urban Land Institute to work with the commission. Although the ULI is the self-interested national

3 Associated Press, "Harsh Urban Renewal in New Orleans: Poor, Black Residents Cannot Afford to Return, Worry City Hall Will Exclude Them," October 12, 2005.

4 Christopher Cooper, "Old Line Families Escape Worst of Flood and Plot the Future," *Wall Street Journal*, September 8, 2005, commondreams.org.

voice of corporate land developers, Nagin and Canizaro welcomed the delegation of developers, architects, and ex-mayors as a heroic cavalry of expertise riding to the stricken city's rescue. In a nutshell, the ULI's recommendations reframed the historical elite desire to shrink New Orleans's socioeconomic footprint of black poverty (and black political power) as a crusade to reduce the city's physical footprint to contours commensurate with flood safety and a fiscally viable urban infrastructure. Based on these suspect premises, the outside "experts" proposed an unprecedented triage of an American city, in which low-lying neighborhoods would be targeted for mass buyouts and future conversion into a greenbelt to protect New Orleans from storm surges. As a visiting developer told BNOB: "Your housing is now a public resource. You can't think of it as private property anymore."

Keenly aware that popular resistance was inevitable, the ULI also proposed setting up the Crescent City Rebuilding Corporation, armed with eminent domain and able to bypass the city council, and an oversight board with power over the city's finances. With control of most of New Orleans's public schools already usurped by the state, the ULI's projected trusteeship of experts and elite appointees would spell the end of representative democracy. For veterans of the 1960s civil rights movement especially, it reeked of disenfranchisement pure and simple, a return to the paternalism of plantation days.

The city council, supported by a surprising number of white homeowners and their representatives, denounced the ULI plan. Mayor Nagin, truly a cat on a hot tin roof, danced anxiously back and forth between the two camps, but state and national officials, including HUD Secretary Alphonso Jackson, applauded the ULI scheme, as did the editorial page of the *Times-Picayune*. The BNOB recommendations presented by Canizaro in January 2006 faithfully hewed to the ULI framework. They included an appointed (rather than elected) redevelopment corporation that would act as a land bank to buy out heavily damaged homes with federal funds, wielding eminent domain as needed to retire low-lying neighborhoods to greenbelts or assemble "in-fill" tracts for mixed-income developments à la River Garden.

Canizaro and his colleagues proposed a temporary building moratorium (with Rube Goldberg–like regulations) in tandem with neighborhood planning meetings that would poll home owners about their intentions. Only those neighborhoods where at least half of the pre-Katrina home-owning residents made a commitment to return would be eligible for financial aid. The plight of exiled renters was simply ignored.

Nagin welcomed the report; then, suddenly faced with a potential insurrection, he quickly U-turned and disavowed the building moratorium. "I will sit in my front door with my shotgun," one resident warned at a jammed meeting in the council chambers in mid-January.[5] Another asked,

5 "Displaced Residents Want to Go Home," *United Press International*, January 15, 2006.

"Are we going to allow some developers, some hustlers, some land thieves to grab our land, grab our homes, to make this a Disney World version of our homes, our lives?"[6] The ULI had run afoul of the Fats Domino factor.

Like hundreds of other flood-damaged homes, Domino's house was still structurally sound, and the R&B legend had stuck a defiant sign in the yard: save our neighborhood: no bulldozing! Domino, who had always stayed close to his roots in working-class Holy Cross, knew that his riverside neighborhood and the rest of the Lower Ninth Ward were prime targets of the city-shrinkers. On Christmas Day 2005, the *Times-Picayune*—declaring that "before a community can rebuild, it must dream"—had published a vision of what a smaller-but-whiter-and-better New Orleans might look like: "Tourists and schoolchildren tour a living museum that includes the former home of Fats Domino and Holy Cross High School, a multiblock memorial to Katrina that spans the devastated neighborhood."

"Living museum"—or "holocaust museum" as one activist bitterly observed—sounds like a bad joke, but it was the elite view of what African-American New Orleans should become. In the brave New Urbanist world of Canizaro and Kabacoff, blacks would reign only as entertainers and self-caricatures. The high-voltage energy that once rocked juke joints, housing projects, and second-line parades would be safely embalmed for tourists in a proposed Louisiana Music Experience in the Central Business District. It was the minstrel show version of the city's past for an ethnically cleansed future.

This was also the state-of-play that out-of-town architects and their students encountered when they began to arrive in New Orleans from early 2006 onward—many of them totally innocent of the high-stakes poker being dealt in the name of "bringing New Orleans back." However, the city had more to show them than a history of elite-power dreams. There was also its proud history of grassroots movements, such as ACORN—a national organization of working-class homeowners and tenants, now extinct, that in 2006 had 9,000 New Orleans members, including Fats Domino. There were also dozens of informal neighborhood groups working to stop Canizaro's bulldozers, and a small group of black activists tracing their roots to the city's Black Panther Party of the late 1960s and early 1970s. One had to have a lot of wax in one's ears to remain naïve in the tumultuous atmosphere of 2006 or in the years that followed, which saw the condemnation of perfectly intact public housing projects; the destruction of ACORN (with the complicity of most Democrats); the collapse of the *Times-Picayune*; and the transformation of Louisiana's political scene—where Democrats had held the governorship and U.S. Senate seats—to one resembling Republican Mississippi's, thanks to the storm's evacuation of a huge swath of New Orleans black voters; and the election of "Moon" Landrieu's son, Mitch, the first white mayor in a generation.

6 "Hostility Greets Katrina Recovery Plan," *Washington Post*, January 11, 2006.

There are a number of excellent books on Katrina and the man-made environmental catastrophes threatening southern Louisiana, but for the politics of rebuilding, the best source is David Simon's *Tremé*, the HBO series that with uncanny accuracy chronicles the unequal struggle of local residents against the city-shrinkers and their New Urbanist allies. Indeed, *Tremé* is almost essential viewing for understanding how the burden of the city's racist history has been carried forward into the present, but it is also an evocation of the fierce love for place and culture that continues to resist the elite planners. Is New Orleans back? No, but the story is far from finished.

INTRODUCTION
CAROL McMICHAEL REESE, MICHAEL SORKIN, and ANTHONY FONTENOT

Although this book appears more than eight years after the urban disaster spawned by Hurricane Katrina, the essays that it includes and the urban plans and architectural projects that it illustrates remain vital. They are meaningful not only for New Orleans, providing a way of measuring what has been proposed, what has been accomplished, and what remains to be done, but for any community rebuilding after disaster. We envision our book not simply as a display of creative ideas but also as a medium for stimulating community discussions and for broadening the array of suggestions available as the city rebuilds. It is the intention of the editors to share with the citizens of New Orleans proposals and projects that address the particular concerns of individual neighborhoods, as well as the holistic needs of the city and the metropolitan region, and also to expose, analyze, and circulate to a national and international public the larger concerns and developments that surround urban planning as they have come to the fore in the period of post-disaster reconstruction.

Hurricane Katrina struck the city of New Orleans on August 29, 2005, and the resulting levee breaks and failures flooded 80 percent of the city. The destruction of New Orleans caused by both Hurricane Katrina and the failure of the levees built to protect the city was an experience of horror and revelation. Horror for everyone who experienced the disaster or watched it unfold—in view of the tragic deaths of at least 986 Louisianans, the staggering loss of more than 134,000 residential units in New Orleans (representing 70 percent of the city's occupied units), and the terrible plight of those impoverished and elderly New Orleanians least able to fend for themselves in the chaos that ensued.[1] Revelation—of the shameful racial cleft in the city's social fabric, the virulence of which continues to stun the nation, and of the just as astounding inability of government at the municipal, state, and federal levels to provide aid to desperate citizens. Such was the destruction throughout the metropolitan

1 "Facts for Features: Hurricane Katrina Impact," Greater New Orleans Community Data Center (August 10, 2012), gnocdc.org.

area that those residents who had heeded the mayor's mandatory evacuation order were prohibited from returning until early October 2005. Clearly, the city had to be rebuilt, home by home, business by business, institution by institution, infrastructural system by infrastructural system. In response to the devastation of New Orleans, those who studied and practiced design around the nation and across the globe proffered plans for the reconstruction of the overcome city. Pictured, detailed, and analyzed within this book are many of the undertakings that have propelled the city forward since Katrina struck.

Thinking about how to introduce this book, we began to survey our memories, our giant piles of clippings, and the Big Easy books on our shelves, a long and waxing row to which we ourselves have now added. Doing this, we were struck by the way in which New Orleans has been assimilated into *so many* discourses—both retrospective and prospective—and the way in which these more and more seem to float in relative isolation, unreconciled. Since the storm, the city has been deluged with technical and artistic expertise, with competing and conspiring visions that collectively have come to define the city as a terrain of infinite tractability, a place reduced to some useful zero. New Orleans has become a field of dreams, and not all of them are nightmares. But many are.

In the greatest outpouring of disaster-response design efforts in the history of the United States, hundreds of proposals, ranging from the practical to the visionary, were produced on all scales—of the metropolitan region, the city, the neighborhood, and the individual building. They offered a wide range of hopeful propositions for the process of recovery in New Orleans. This book presents a compilation and review of a number of such responses to Katrina, specifically those that deal with the processes of planning and rebuilding. On the official side, these have, in many ways, simply extended the failures of public-sector reaction to the emergency; hence the book's subtitle: "the crisis of planning." Comprehensive urban planning after Katrina—master planning—went through no fewer than five repetitive and conflicting cycles. Yet even now, and perhaps inevitably, the rebuilding of the city seems more the result of a colluding set of fragments than of a plan finally in hand. Far from a consensus of indifference—given the effort, time, and money expended by citizens, "expert" consultants, and government entities—it has been a reflection of the real distribution and effect of power.

Our book takes a shape that is the outcome of its origins. In the weeks after Katrina, the three editors—two from New Orleans, one from New York—responded to the crisis by direct engagement in planning, by community work, by journalism, by conducting academic design studios, by speaking at events, by expressing perplexity over what might be done. We first came together on a weekend in March 2006 at a symposium, "Regrounding New Orleans," organized by Carol Reese and Joan Ockman, who was then director of Columbia University's Temple Hoyne Buell

Center for the Study of American Architecture. Michael Sorkin served as keynote speaker for the event, which was held at Columbia's Graduate School of Architecture, Planning, and Preservation. Later that same weekend, many of the symposium participants traveled to the School of Architecture at Princeton, where Anthony Fontenot had organized a regional gathering of architecture and planning faculty whose fall 2005 and spring 2006 studios focused on rebuilding New Orleans. As we assessed the impressive body of academic research conducted in the months after Katrina, we three determined to join forces to disseminate whatever work we could gather from the tremendous, though uncoordinated, efforts of architects and planners aross the nation and around the world. We began Project New Orleans in order to compile an archive of physical ideas for the city's reconstruction but also, and most importantly, to make those ideas accessible to those who could potentially use them. Project New Orleans first resulted in an exhibition, held in late 2006 at the New Orleans African American Museum in the city's Tremé neighborhood, and eventually in a website, project-neworleans.org.

We followed these up in late 2009 with a conference, held at Tulane University, "New Orleans Under Reconstruction: The Crisis of Planning," for which we gathered a group of people who had strong ties to the city and had worked on its rebuilding. We knew that the discussion would have an uncertain outcome, but we had high expectations for it, which we now think were justified, given the probing quality of the participants' contributions, which we publish here. We compiled this book to combine and extend the archive and that conference and, we hope, to expand the discussion and the critique. The conference was meant to recapitulate a process that had been under way since Katrina struck. From the moment the levees were breached, questions were bruited of what should be done, who should do it, who should pay for it, and who would ultimately benefit. The "process" is now perhaps perceived to have evolved into a new phase of rebuilding; *The New Orleans Index at Six,* for example, described the city in 2011 as having moved "from recovery to transformation."[2] But the issues that the conference confronted in 2009, which are represented by this book's contents, continue to circle the city like sharks.

The organization of the exhibition and the website mirrored one another and contributed to the way we have organized the book. However, the conference and, ultimately, the book that we built upon it required framing in ways that the exhibition and website did not. The first part of the book comprises four provocative essays that offer strong positions about opportunities and dangers that citizens face as they tackle the city's future. Denise Scott Brown reprises lessons learned from rebuilding London and Rotterdam after World War II; she insists that the key question

2 "The New Orleans Index at Six: Measuring Greater New Orleans' Progress toward Prosperity," Greater New Orleans Community Data Center, August 2011, gnocdc.org.

to be addressed is the role of government—the consideration of possible consequences along a spectrum extending from governmental control to private domination of planning and redevelopment processes. In this regard, we consider that Naomi Klein issued the loudest clarion call of warning, and we excerpt a chapter from her book *The Shock Doctrine* that describes how "government" hurricane aid was delivered by representatives of the same global companies that contracted with the government to rebuild Iraq.[3] She argues that the aftermath of Katrina was viewed as a golden opportunity by the international cabal inspired by Chicago School free-market economics—an opportunity to ride the crest of human and natural disaster by promoting the neoliberal—even fascist—designs of their masters-of-the-universe regime. Rebecca Solnit places in Manichean opposition to this corporate opportunism the selfless mobilization of communal concern and action post-Katrina, which she captures in *A Paradise Built In Hell*, which we also excerpt here.[4] Her book, a work of truly bracing optimism, depicts a series of self-organizing utopias of the kind that have sometimes arisen in the wake of disasters from the great San Francisco earthquake to Katrina. She focuses on the boots-on-the-ground contributions of Common Ground in the Lower Ninth Ward, where Pam Dashiell—a speaker at our conference—figured as a heroine of community-based activism.[5] Solnit finds the communal sunshine in her account of the city's reconstruction, whereas Klein sees the gathering dark clouds of heedless profit-taking.

We close the book's first part with Amy Murphy's argument that New Orleanians must grapple with the seductive dangers posed by their understandable desire to replace what they have lost. But the technological formulas for the control of nature that were developed pre-Katrina and that once bolstered the city's urban expansion are unsustainable, and, in fact, would promote future apocalyptic events. And although the reification of New Orleans's past has contributed importantly to the city's economic health, its future prosperity demands that the racism and classism that have shaped its collective history be addressed. To anchor reconstruction efforts in the quicksand of the past is to build on unstable ground. Murphy finds a number of promising, if fragmented, approaches to transformation that have been undertaken in post-Katrina New Orleans, projects that point the way to achieving urban resilience built on changed attitudes to environmental security and to social diversity.

The work collected in this book does not simply consider the outcomes of the planning process in New Orleans but also seeks to place these

3 Naomi Klein, *The Shock Doctrine: The Rise of Disaster Capitalism* (New York: Henry Holt, 2007).

4 Rebecca Solnit, *A Paradise Built in Hell: The Extraordinary Communities that Arise in Disaster* (London: Viking Penguin, 2009).

5 Sadly, Dashiell died only weeks after the conference; see Katy Reckdahl, "Pam Dashiell, Lower 9th Ward Activist, Dies at 61," NOLA.com.

within the larger framework of what it means *to plan*. The many alternative strategies and discourses stimulated by Katrina and the cultures of recovery that sprang up in the storm's wake suggest that those who envision a unified scheme for reconstruction that attempts to solve all of the problems in the city *at once* must be reconciled to only partial success. The fit between the totality of a plan and the prospects for its realization is one of the critical ways in which that effort must be judged.

Indeed, the diversity of fantasies about, expressions of, and recommendations for a new New Orleans that we reproduce here illustrate the subtext of this book, which is a discussion of the way in which the experience of New Orleans reveals a series of seams and splits in the very idea of planning. Because of long-standing failures of consensus and, in effect, a loss of traditions and skills, the city itself conjures up different portraits of renewal. This surely represents something of New Orleans's anarchic flamboyance—a happy, if not always "efficient," expression of the *genius loci.* There is something extremely constructive in this failure of consensus, this proliferation of alternatives that, like Topsy, just grow. Many vital interests are in serious conflict in New Orleans, so any attempt to "solve" the city's problems will have to confront these conflicts, not simply paper them over with the dream of unified agreement. The central, fundamental idea of the democratic planning process—which must include not just the official plan but also the incredible outpouring of self-organized efforts at mutual aid that have flourished in the city—is that agreement must never be purchased with the suppression of dissent.

Dissent has certainly characterized the planning process in post-Katrina New Orleans, particularly regarding the concept of *triage*. This was brought to bear on the analysis of the effects of differential flooding, whether conceived as an effort, as some feared, to urge shrinking the city's footprint and denying the right of return to residents of certain districts or, in a less ominous and omniscient take, to plan long-, middle-, and short-term prospects for rehabilitation in various areas of the city. The debates concerning *where* and *how* to reconstruct were positioned within a conceptual framework that pitted human and natural history in a duel to the death. These questions—inflected in innumerable ways—lie at the very base of almost everything that has been done and will be done. As the city's "final" master plan—to its credit—recommends, the *whole* city is to remain the terrain of its own reconstruction, a total space of possibility. The idea of a massive, environmentally driven *cordon sanitaire* has been dropped as a matter of planning policy, but the plan is (and perhaps can only be) mute about who, finally, will be able to return.

In the book's second part, we include perspectives on urban planning as it has unfolded since the fall of 2006, taken from inside and outside the process. Christine Boyer provocatively analyzes six "official" plans proffered to guide the rebuilding of New Orleans—each of them a subject of contention—in relation to French philosopher Henri Lefebvre's moral imperative concerning "the right to the city." In this vein, she castigates the federal government's "non-plan"—FEMA's rushed demolitions of storm-damaged properties and HUD's unilateral shuttering, demolishing, and rebuilding of public housing. Melissa Harris-Perry and William M. Harris Sr. further appraise the unequal social effects of relief and reconstruction efforts. They describe Katrina as a "racial disaster" in which first responders who came together to plan for recovery failed to honor principles of collective action, pushing ahead in the absence of those still unable to return to make their voices heard—a disproportionate number of whom were African Americans. Whether acting in good faith under the pressure of emergency response or with an agenda based on race and class prejudice, planners violated an ethical code of inclusive participation, grievously disadvantaging displaced citizens and, eventually, ensnarling the planning process in controversy.

Part II also includes the testimonials of planners associated with three of the plans that Boyer, Harris-Perry and Harris discuss: Ray Manning, who co-led the Bring New Orleans Back (BNOB) commission's planning effort under Mayor Ray Nagin; David Lee, who participated in the City of New Orleans Neighborhood Rebuilding Plan (NONRP or Lambert Plan), which the city council authorized to counter Nagin's; and David Dixon, who led Goody Clancy of Boston's "ultimate" planning effort, which ostensibly wove together the recommendations of the plans that preceded it to create the "Plan for the 21st Century, New Orleans 2030" and which was given "the force of law" with a municipal charter revision and supported by a comprehensive zoning ordinance.[6] Manning is highly critical of what he sees as a conflicted process stymied by insufficiently acknowledged issues: competitive citywide and planning-district visions, lingering and sublimated racial and economic discrimination, and professional self-interest on the part of those charged with producing a comprehensive plan. However regretful he is about the fitfulness of the process, he is nevertheless hopeful about the template that the Goody Clancy plan offers the future.

Michael Cowan argues that although the city needs a master plan to recover effectively, no master plan will succeed unless citizens achieve a shared vision of the social action necessary to create a just city. He finds six inhibiting divisions among New Orleanians that have produced an "intergroup impasse": strategic, socioeconomic, structural, intergenerational, ethnocentric, and ideological—the last being the most damaging, because of its contribution to political paralysis. He believes that con-

6 The BNOB plan was finalized in January 2006, and the Lambert Plan was completed in September 2006. The Unified New Orleans Plan (UNOP), which was substantially funded by the Rockefeller Foundation, was approved by the New Orleans City Council and the Louisiana Recovery Authority in June 2007. In November 2008, the city charter revision giving a master plan the force of law was passed, and in September 2009, the draft Goody Clancy master plan was released, just a month before we held the New Orleans Under Reconstruction conference. The draft zoning ordinance that fleshed out the plan's recommendations was published in January 2010.

sensus must be sought on issues of common concern, as a way out of the "social trap." He judges as real, uplifting progress the post-Katrina efforts of a diverse citizen committee to establish the offices of an inspector general and a police monitor, to bolster municipal accountability and transparency in government. Toni Griffin adds a comparative frame with her analysis of Newark's master plan, "Shifting Forward 2025," adopted in 2009 to propel Mayor Cory Booker's mandate to make Newark "the national model of urban transformation." She warns that planning is too often concerned with physical remedies to urban problems and fails to address social and economic structural inequalities, and she urges planners to expand their purview beyond material rebuilding to encompass sustainable cultural urban restoration. David Lee underscores her concerns, promoting inclusive, broad-ranging educational goals for planners and architects in training who need to "learn to see socially."

David Dixon summarizes the master-planning process that his firm Goody Clancy shepherded in 2008 and 2009, which culminated in the document that was adopted to guide the city's efforts to remake itself. His narrative stresses the preliminary work that the planners staged *before* preparing the document: continuation of a citywide participatory culture of planning; identification of a set of core issues that must be addressed in the document; and recognition of the leadership qualities and skills required to ensure that both the public and city officials adhere to the plan. We have two major criticisms of the Goody Clancy Plan. First, its prescriptions in matters of priority and implementation are too woolly. It shows a tendency to remain distant from the rigorous setting of priorities and a flat-out approach to getting them done. Second, there is a gap between its visionary reach and the (perhaps realistic) fundamental play-it-safe modesty of so many of its recommendations. In attempting to be all things to all interest groups, the plan has been cobbled together, diminishing its overall strength. Nevertheless, as an artifact, the plan is stimulating precisely because of its conceptual insistence that the city's recovery and transformation have predicates that far exceed questions of architecture, planning, and infrastructure. However, it is clear that the utility and impact of the plan are diluted by its extreme apples-and-oranges approach—the fact that it calls for road repairs, Head Start programs, the elimination of plastic bags, and the replacement of lawns with swales. The master plan has *a lot* of plans.

That said, the document is in many ways appropriately comprehensive, and this impossible standard, this setting out of the idea of an elision between physical and social planning, this attempt to have a look at virtually everything—and the truly copious evidence of community involvement in creating this wish list—is something that we think must be admired and served. The city's plan, to its ethical credit, is utopian in its embrace of the dream of doing every virtuous thing that can be thought of. Cities produce far too few such plans, and it is important that New Orleans has adopted a document that stands so squarely against the idea of *triage*, even if it sets the stage for a process of implementation that must rely on a radical mismatch between vision and possibility. Still, the production of an urban plan addressed to dire circumstances must embrace propaganda for raised expectations. Moreover, this is a plan that in many ways reflects what has actually happened in New Orleans, the wide variety of small-scale, community, and individually organized initiatives, groping toward coalescence.

This is not necessarily a bad thing. It certainly shows both the overwhelming voluntarism and the frustration of the process to date as well as highlighting the larger set of debates about how we Americans are to plan our cities, arguments that have been ripe for decades and that for better and worse show few signs of resolution. New Orleans's master plan is impossible, and that is both its problem and its promise. Before we look for what is useful in it, we must ask what forward movement it might propel. Clearly, a Baron Haussmann isn't going to step in, although the sheer vastness of the plan and the fatigue of the citizenry do raise the question of whether one person on a horse can move faster than an army afoot. A more possible, productive, and democratic solution would be to increase the intensity of and—most crucially—the funding for the city's reclamation in increments, so as to enable the completion of discrete, smaller-scale projects. But something is surely lost through this mosaic approach. Potentially, this loss includes great ambitions for the city's common spaces, infrastructures, and purposes. And responsibility devolving upon independent actors who go into divided action would widen the power gap between rich and poor, connected and unconnected. Finally, with responsibility and energy so divided, there is a real risk that nothing much would get done, especially for those who most need help.

As New Orleans began to rebuild, housing was ranked first in order of need, and it seemed self-evident that the focus should be on the single-family house and the multi-unit building, in light of both the extent of home loss and the recognition that density in the city, which had been predominantly built of "singles" and "doubles," would have to be increased on higher and drier sites. We structured two sections of the Project New Orleans website to address the residential domain, and those relate to the book's third and fourth parts, "Reconstructing Domicile, Housing (Singly Considered)" and "Reconstructing Community, Housing (Multiply Considered)." In response to the great need, leading efforts to jump-start residential rebuilding were begun as early as 2006. These efforts included the 2006 competitions sponsored by the *Architectural Record* in partnership with the Tulane School of Architecture: "High Density on the High Ground," which called for designs for a 160-unit apartment complex on a site adjacent to the French Quarter's levee, and "New Orleans Prototype

House Competition."[7] Selected submissions were exhibited at the Ogden Museum of Southern Art in New Orleans in the spring of 2006. In the same year, Global Green staged a competition to rebuild a community anchor in the historic Holy Cross neighborhood of the Lower Ninth Ward, consisting of single-family homes, an eighteen-unit apartment building, and a community center, all complying with LEED (Leadership in Energy and Environmental Design) Platinum standards.[8] In Part IV, we include Anthony Fontenot's interview with the winners of the Global Green challenge, Matthew Berman and Andrew Kotchen, principals of workshop/apd. The Hollywood persona and architectural aficionado Brad Pitt, who served as a judge in the same competition, afterward founded Make It Right, which extended invitations to selected internationally recognized architects to design houses for the decimated Lower Ninth Ward. Make It Right published their invigorating but controversial proposed additions to New Orleans's residential landscape in 2009 in a book about the project's inception and the designs that it offered to returning residents.[9] Currently, Make it Right has completed more than 100 houses and is marching toward its next announced goal of 200.

We also emphasize two efforts to address the overwhelming need for support for returning homeowners, programs funded by competitive HUD grants to teams of researchers in the fall of 2005. One, the still operating Tulane School of Architecture's URBANbuild, focuses on the design and construction of infill housing on lots made available through the removal of blighted and storm-ravaged buildings. In our interview for the book, Byron Mouton, a professor of practice on Tulane's Architecture faculty, who has shepherded the program since its inception, discusses the economic, cultural, and personnel issues URBANbuild has faced in meeting its dual goals of creating prototypical housing models for sale and further development and of providing invaluable educational experiences for Tulane students. The other HUD-funded project for residential reconstruction we include was won by a consortium of faculty from Pratt Institute and New Jersey Institute of Technology. Leading this group were Deborah Gans of Pratt and James Dart of NJIT, who with teams of students examined issues related to rebuilding inundated neighborhoods, such as Plum Orchard in the near northeastern section of the city, where slab-on-grade "ranchers" had been built on low-lying, once swampy terrain and it was critical to propose ideas addressing issues of residential sustainability. Research outcomes from Gans and Dart's project recommended them to the housing corporation run by the Association of

7 James S. Russell, "Designing the Future of New Orleans, *Architectural Record* and Tulane University Host Two Ideas Competitions," archrecord.construction.com.

8 "Holy Cross Project in New Orleans," globalgreen.org.

9 Kristin Feireiss, ed., *Architecture in Times of Need: Make It Right — Rebuilding New Orleans' Lower Ninth Ward* (Munich: Prestel, 2009); see 38–47 for Carol McMichael Reese's essay "From Field of Disaster to Field of Dreams," which focuses on the urban development of the Lower Ninth Ward.

Community Organizations for Reform Now (ACORN), which had received tax-adjudicated properties for redevelopment in Plum Orchard and the Lower Ninth Ward, but ACORN's political troubles put an end to further progress along the lines that Gans and Dart pioneered.

The poignant blocks of lovely houses in Brad Pitt's burg in the Lower Ninth Ward—as well as less-publicized work throughout town, such as that of Global Green, Habitat for Humanity, the Jeremiah Group, and URBANbuild—speak to the beauties of doing what can be done, but they somehow also evoke the specter of tracts of homes still crumbling in subdivisions too far from downtown, in territories perhaps never to be reclaimed because the driving boom of recovery has gone bust (and because "underwater" has new meaning since 2008). But there is optimism in forlorn tenacity. And there is optimism in building.

The latter parts of the book also organize commentary and projects thematically. The centerpiece of Part V, which comprises ideas for developing the public domain, is our interview with Allen Eskew, whose firm Eskew+Dumez+Ripple leads the project Reinventing the Crescent, an endeavor to create a thirteen-mile greenway along the Mississippi River between the Industrial Canal, downriver, and Audubon Park, upriver. An evolving team composed of high-profile architects and landscape architects contributed to the designs, which the community then vetted, but New Orleans is not Chicago, and so far there has been no coalescence of community will and financial backing to embark on a wholesale, Daniel Burnham–inspired rehabilitation of New Orleans's working riverfront, from which the public is largely separated. Nevertheless, the first increment, the farthest downriver section, is scheduled to open soon and should ignite public support.

Part VI includes a number of projects undertaken by architects, landscape architects, and other activists who have worked in tandem with recovering New Orleans communities over many post-Katrina seasons. The scale of the projects ranges from neighborhood chicken coops to the riparian acreage of City Park, New Orleans's largest public park. The communities engaged in restoring their cultural landscapes are as diverse as the Vietnamese immigrant truck farmers of New Orleans East and the African-American homeowners of the city's golf-course suburb Pontchartrain Park. But they share the common goal of resuscitating the urban places that give them a sense of identity, a locus of belonging and a platform for contributing.

The role of urban analysis in reconstruction on the district and regional scales is the theme of Part VII. Yates McKee analyzes the rhetorics of planning and architecture as circulated in the book *New Orleans: Strategies for a City in Soft Land* and the exhibition "Newer Orleans: A Shared Space." He argues that both approaches risk being fetishized through language that is excessively scientistic, in the case of planning, or aestheticized, in the case of architecture.[10] He argues that both approaches neglect disputed political, social, and economic realms and that the antidote must be critical engagement with planning theory and information design. Laura Kurgan presents a case study employing the latter strategy with her justice reinvestment project in New Orleans's Central City area. In order to determine where redevelopment monies might be most productively invested, she mapped incarceration statistics and tracked recidivism rates in Orleans Parish pre- and post-Katrina. Central City emerged as a likely candidate for investment, with a relatively high number of "million-dollar blocks" from which residents have been sent to prison at a cost that has exceeded $1 million a year. Working with nonprofit organizations and community groups, she mapped assets to create an assistance and empowerment network that could leverage services in Central City through four mutually constructed pilot programs. As she explains, this project, based on sociospatial data and participatory programming, represents a "middle-out" approach to planning, in contrast to normative top-down and bottom-up strategies.

In the last part of the book we cover "living with water." We hope the acceptance implied by the phrase acknowledges not only the precariousness of New Orleans but also the cascade of delicate interdependencies that sustain the city. We have been shown with irresistible clarity that the city's life is crucially connected to thriving wetlands along the Gulf, that the excitations of global warming are not just an abstraction, that building and survival are intimately mixed. If nothing else, the thick set of transactions between the "natural" and the built have become at least the theoretical driving force for a very broad collection of decisions and initiatives. Since Katrina, David Waggonner has led the essential, inspiring Dutch Dialogues project that has enabled a cross-fertilized process of planning in relation to the challenges presented by the city's low-lying, flood-prone terrain, inherently soggy soils, and increasing vulnerability caused by coastal erosion. Through a series of workshops, the Dutch Dialogues have brought together experts from the Netherlands—where there is an impressive record of successful interventions in a similarly difficult environment—with planners, architects, engineers, citizens, politicians, and officials from the city, the region, and the state. We include our interview with Waggonner; in it, he emphasizes cognizance of New Orleans's place in a deltaic system, in which the idea of infrastructures is less useful than the concept of networks. If New Orleans is able to

---

10 Joan Busquets, with Felipe Correa, *New Orleans: Strategies for a City in Soft Land* (Cambridge, MA: Harvard Graduate School of Design; Ecuador: Imprenta Mariscal, 2005). This book published the research of a joint design studio mounted pre-Katrina by the GSD and the Tulane School of Architecture in the academic year 2004–2005. The exhibition "Newer Orleans: A Shared Space" was organized by the Netherlands Architecture Institute (NAi), the Tulane School of Architecture, and *Artforum* magazine; it opened in February 2006 in Rotterdam and circulated to the National Building Museum in Washington and the Contemporary Art Center in New Orleans. Three U.S. and three Dutch architectural firms were invited to participate: Morphosis, Huff + Gooden Architects, Hargreaves Associates, Ben van Berkel of UN Studio, MVRDV, and Adriaan Geuze of West 8; see nbm.org.

embrace such a holistic and sustainable point of view at every level of endeavor, then the city will have a real chance to lead from its tragically challenged position.

Where is New Orleans now? The compilers of the *New Orleans Index*—begun in December 2005 by statisticians at the Greater New Orleans Community Data Center (GNOCDC), who since 2007 have partnered with the Brookings Institution—have regularly tracked and updated data for the New Orleans metro area. They position New Orleans comparatively within a set of fifty-seven "weak" U.S. metropolitan areas that includes sixty-five older industrial cities that have experienced long-term economic decline. According to a variety of indicators, New Orleans's metrics show a more robust urban economic and social environment than existed pre-Katrina. Residents earn more; their wages, which for decades were significantly lower than the national average, are now nearly on a par with it; more of their households are middle-income; and they show higher levels of education, with 68 percent of children in 2010–2011 attending schools that met Louisiana's standards, compared to 24 percent in the 2003–2004 academic year. Nevertheless, problems abound. Although the metropolitan area had 90 percent of its 2000 population of 1,316,510 in July 2011, New Orleans's population as a whole has not recovered so rapidly; in 2011, it stood at 74 percent of its 2000 figure—360,740, down from 484,674. The metropolitan area is now more diverse, with gains in Hispanic and Asian residents, but the 2010 census compared with the 2000 census showed that the city had lost 118,526 African Americans. Although African Americans are still in the majority, their proportion has been reduced from 67 percent to 60 percent. The city's economy still relies on "legacy" industries in decline—tourism, oil and gas, shipping and logistics. In 2010, the child poverty rate, 42 percent, was 20 percent higher than the national. Violent crime in 2009 was almost twice the national rate. There is much to be done.[11]

Since the Reagan years, the U.S. has pursued policies that have promoted massive tax cuts, untamed overspending, and huge budget and trade deficits—adding trillions of dollars to the national debt and encouraging disinvestment in social and public infrastructure. As a result, we have seen few policies on urban development based on anything but deregulation. Waking up from a decades-long dream fueled by a belief that free-market economics would automatically solve problems—if only the obstacles of government regulation and social programming were removed—we are now confronted with a disastrous lack of a planning culture, against the backdrop of an endless buildup of social, ecological, economic, and infrastructural urban crises. Given that economics and

11 "Facts for Features: Hurricane Katrina Recovery," Greater New Orleans Community Data Center, August 27, 2012, gnocdc.org.

urbanism are intimately linked, the crisis that we are currently experiencing promises devastating long-term economic and urban consequences. The legacy of deregulation has had a direct impact on the formation of unplanned urban developments across America. Just as deregulated financial markets have proven to be unsustainable, so have many of these deregulated urban developments. The pressing question at hand is what kind of planning is capable of addressing the ingrained complexities of the now deregulated environment?

For a city that has long celebrated the irregular and unexpected, the overweight and confused "Plan for the 21st Century: New Orleans 2030" might be a great and revelatory thing, a strategy capable of finding new ways of being in New Orleans that slight the vitality neither of past nor future. However, it would be a horrible mistake if this plan were not constructively ripped apart to extract the kinds of large and legible projects that can only be implemented by a very large public on its own behalf. Rebuilding the wetlands, providing a house for every refugee seeking to exercise the right of return, demolishing the I-10 corridor through the Central Business District, reconstructing the levees to the highest standard: these are enormous and necessary projects that are not fungible. But it would also be a mistake to set aside the prospect of galvanizing a runaway incrementalism. The question is how, in the environment of reconstruction and transformation, the two strategies can cohabit without prejudice to either and how a return to the kinds of priorities that always favor power can be forestalled. The struggle to find that balance is what this volume is about. While we can dispute the merits of large plans or small, plans centrally or locally conceived, nostalgic or visionary, our expectations and our demands must remain huge.

The plans advanced for rebuilding New Orleans, as well as the rebuilding projects already proposed, under way, or completed, demonstrate a tangled web of approaches and the dilemmas that they raise, whether considered in isolation or in concert with one another. New Orleanians have not been blind to the dangers of opportunism that the infusion of private capital in the rebuilding process presents. And, however grateful they are for the advice and assistance of legions of outsider "experts," they have nonetheless forthrightly criticized these professionals for misreading the historical and contemporary particularities of their city, which has been lauded for its supposed exceptionalism. Furthermore, they have chaffed under and strongly resisted the paternalism of governmental admonition, supported by expert testimony: "We know what's best for you." More than ever, as exemplified by the crisis of planning in New Orleans, we are confronted with an urgent need to reexamine historical and contemporary planning methodologies in order to move beyond the limits of top-down and bottom-up approaches.

Just as Katrina exposed the inequities and imbalances of New Orleans, so the recent financial collapse rendered transparent many contradictions in the larger economy. And, just as the apparatus of planning—in all its complexity—foundered when confronted with Katrina, it faces a similar crisis as it attempts to intervene in the wake of our national economic disaster. New Orleans, because it compactly raises so many vital issues for planning and its future to a flash point, makes an ideal and concentrated example of a set of issues with much wider purchase. As the city and its difficulties increasingly slip from view while the battered national attention fixes elsewhere, this book, *New Orleans Under Reconstruction* seeks to play a pivotal role in defining what a truly democratic and constructive planning practice can be and in deepening the critique of the institutions and habits that stand in its way.

PART I
INTRODUCTORY PERSPECTIVES

WHAT SHOULD NEW ORLEANS DO?
DENISE SCOTT BROWN

After the Great Fire of 1666, England's leading architect, Christopher Wren, made a plan for rebuilding London. Adopting a style fashionable in Europe, he proposed cutting across the city's medieval fabric with broad diagonal avenues that would converge in roundabouts—the *ronds-points* already found on the grounds of the Palace of Versailles and used again in Pierre-Charles L'Enfant's Washington, D.C. Architects ever since have expressed outrage that Wren's plan was not undertaken, but historians point out that the English monarch at the time lacked the power of a Louis XIV and could not stand against the vested interests of property owners and trade institutions—against the stakeholders, as we would call them now. After all, Wren's plan would have been vastly out of character with both the London of his time and the city squares and town houses of the Georgian era that provide perhaps our most pervasive image of the city today. This London was built largely by developers.

Is London's response to urban disaster worth studying as we consider the options for New Orleans? Even if this example and others from history can provide no concrete solutions, they may speed our discovery of the right questions. And speed is of the essence, because billions of dollars are being spent on disaster relief. With some thought, this money could both address present emergencies and be turned toward the future as well. The need now is for good ideas—for proposals more realistic than Wren's yet visionary enough to confront an unprecedented disaster. For in the wake of Katrina, New Orleans faces problems—from the tragic destruction of life and expectations to social dissolution and the breakdown of government control—that challenge all of our ideas of urbanism. Planners, who understand the city as a set of systems, have seen those systems come apart: topography went first, as the flood produced a new water datum (in places ten feet and more above the former ground level), then the infrastructure of transportation and utilities, the local and regional economy, the uniquely vibrant culture, and the myriad patterns and associations of citizens who were drowned or dispersed. After Katrina, architects who knew the city for its Vieux Carré and Jackson Square saw only broken building parts, overturned autos, uprooted trees, shards, driftwood, and mounds of splintered planks. And four months later, the urgent requirements of resettlement still collide with ongoing measures for cleanup, and danger from the natural environment remains. Stopgap mending of levees has left the flood peril far from contained. It's as if the fire in London could at any moment flare up again.

"Vision versus expediency?" should be an early question to ask in the rebuilding of New Orleans. In London after the fire, expediency prevailed. To take another example, as World War II concluded, but well before the last bombs fell, plans were again initiated to rebuild the city; official or unofficial, these were high on vision. For instance, the 1942 Plan for London proposed by the Modern Architectural Research Group (MARS), whose team of architectural visionaries included Berthold Lubetkin, Arthur Korn, Ernő Goldfinger, F.R.S. [Francis Reginald Stevens] Yorke, Maxwell Fry, Denys Lasdun, and, briefly, Walter Gropius, revolved around a concept that—like Wren's—was in line with avant-garde thinking on the continent: London was to become a "linear city," built tightly along new lines of transit strung out from a central urban spine along the River Thames. This plan, no more realistic than Wren's had been, ultimately had no effect on the city's reconstruction (though it probably influenced the postwar, rail-based suburbanism of Scandinavia). Implemented instead was the Greater London Plan, the outcome of work by lawyers and regional planners who were, variously, consultants to the London County Council, members of government-appointed commissions, or civil servants in government agencies and development corporations. Their proposals were based on the nineteenth- and early-twentieth-century idea of the garden city, which was originally conceived to counter the massive urbanization of the Industrial Revolution. Postwar legislation would move bombed-out citizens to a ring of satellite cities built beyond a mandatory greenbelt encircling London. These communities were intentionally located too far from the Great Wen (an old nickname for the London conurbation) to become its dormitory suburbs, and each city was designed to have its own economic base. The results would have to be parsed over decades; the displaced East Enders who were moved to the countryside suffered hardship, their social and support patterns broken by this intrusion of middle-class values about green space. At the same time, the visionary greenbelt sent rents in London sky-high and kept them there. (If, within the city today, a pound behaves like a dollar but costs two dollars, one reason is the greenbelt.) Significantly, this planners' vision of what urban life should be was backed by the fiat of a socialist government. Although the vision was probably shared by a majority of English people, and they perhaps happily paid higher prices to keep their countryside green, I don't believe the question was put to the vote. Yet subsequent generations were well served by the new cities. Why shouldn't they have been? The garden-city pattern is enjoyed by suburbanites everywhere, and how different, in the end, were these new English towns from that archetype of suburbia, Levittown?

As for the inner city, the architecture proposed for its rebuilding was no better than a society still suffering from austerity and the hardships of war could manage. Within London itself, proposals ranged from thoughtful ideas for housing on scattered bomb sites to wholesale urban renewal similar to what would be done for American downtowns in the 1950s and 1960s. The general run of London public housing, or council housing, built to resettle the bombed areas, was ordinary, sensible, and honorable. But here, as after the fire, existing patterns and interests restricted wild-eyed visions. The first rebuilding took place largely within the existing street layout. Medieval property rights—including such concepts as ancient lights[1] and rights-of-way—were preserved, sometimes over cleared bomb sites, and pushed by urgent need, private developers swung into action with gross commercial projects. Where architects prevailed—for example, in the bombed areas around St. Paul's Cathedral—high-design urban renewal projects were constructed. However, these, too, were built only as funding allowed, and they were ill received.

The story of London immediately following World War II offers New Orleans a range of object lessons, from the government-mandated greenbelt and rehousing programs to private commercial development at the center, as well as guidance through the exertion of building and of planning controls over the broader city and region. Cities took diverse approaches to rebuilding after the war. In Rotterdam, for example, the Dutch were already accustomed to strong government action in the building of dikes. After the destruction of the port and the industrial city, businesses accepted the appropriation of private-property rights in bombed areas and the allocation of new rights within replanned industrial and commercial districts. The resulting construction was modest, perhaps dull, but again, arguably the best that could be managed at the time. This particular example might cause New Orleans to consider whether a government's strong directives and involvement will encourage or restrict the establishment of a rich base for the future—and whether, in bad times, a low-vitality environment may result from either private greed speciousness or government conventionality.

But then there is Tokyo, which could be said to rest at the opposite end of the spectrum from Rotterdam, that is, on the lunatic fringe of private pragmatism. In the 1950s, the city's vast center was rebuilt along property lines whose dimensions were derived from the span of the rafters of traditional wooden houses. The result has been a higgledy-piggledy urbanism that, depending on one's philosophy, is the ultimate in exuberance or the final word in bad taste. Tokyo's famous "pencil" or

1 English Ancient Lights law gives property owners the right to easements that will provide light to buildings through fenestration if such has been available for at least twenty years.

"eel" buildings—office buildings sometimes twelve stories high but only twelve feet wide—were a result of this limitation. So were the flush juxtapositions between such buildings and later developments of occasionally overpowering scale. Did this ad hoc rebuilding process allow for a more vital Tokyo than an orderly plan might have?

This might be a crucial question for New Orleans as it rebuilds, given the famed spontaneity and lively cultural heritage that earned the city its nickname "The Big Easy." I believe that, like post-Great Fire London and post-World War II Tokyo, New Orleans will do what it will do. Expediency will prevail. But the scale will not be atomistic. On the one hand, developers and corporations are already descending on the area, with city and state governments courting the opportunities they offer. And although we won't see corporate commercial rebuilding on the scale of Berlin's Potsdamer Platz, for example—or not just yet, because the urban economy, indeed the whole society, is too depleted for that—pencil buildings will not spring up on the sites of former single-family houses, either. On the other hand, the need to condemn and demolish an estimated 25 percent of the houses in the city, and the absolute necessity to protect the new city from floods will, like it or not, mandate a greenbelt or Versailles level of planning and control to deal with select areas and problems.

One might ask what the appropriate scale of rebuilding for local and regional government and private organizations will be. Can New Orleans manage to build the necessary bridge between private pragmatism and government fiat? What is required now, before any large-scale rebuilding, is holistic thought on methods and concepts for realistic environmental protection. If courage is needed, it is the courage to not rebuild the levees as they were (thus courting the same risks) but instead to think strategically about hurricane levels, to evolve new standards for protection against them, and to set out the land-use coefficients of such standards. The people of the city should be shown the meaning of a "500-year flood": There is a one in 500 chance of seeing another flood this year—and next year, too.

Of course, American cities and their state and federal support systems have their own ways of procuring urban infrastructure, and New Orleans is following these now to mend roads and patch up existing levees. But discontinuities and worse in such methods are what caused the tragedy of the recent flood. There must be a change in methods that will allow sophisticated protections on a regional scale to be evolved and to enable the federal government to bring its powers to bear on coordinating, financing, and constructing them with the necessary urgency. This will mean overcoming the political unpopularity of flood-control legislation. No one wants floodplains and floodways declared, and no one wants their boundaries moved inland (until, that is, thousands are killed).

To those who ask, "Why rebuild at all, given the peril of floods?" the answer, I believe, is that the city's strategic location forces the decision. There is no alternative to reconstructing a great port here. Houston,

Miami, and Memphis might pinch hit for a while, but none of these other cities can provide New Orleans's strategic connectivity. From its central saucer on the Gulf at the foot of the Mississippi, this city controls more relationships between the United States and the world than most Americans would imagine. It is still great, still central to us. The renewed city will be modest in scale and based on expedients ready to hand. It will attempt to survive on what remains of its economy; the first starts will be weak, and as people return to neighborhoods where topography allowed least damage, we can envision the direction those will take. In the near future, however, the parts of the destroyed city system that support the regional and national economy, those having to do with the oil industry and the port, will have to be put back.

But will they be set up in the American way, with little reference to one another—transportation planning disconnected from land-use planning, for example—and the whole organized with greater reference to outlying areas than to the city? In the wake of events that altered the most basic relationships among local, regional, national, and global interests, would it be too much to hope that the American revulsion toward regional planning will be overcome enough to allow the economy of the broader region to support the cultural life of the Big Easy? (And if Eastern cities and Los Angeles are learning to help their historic centers and downtowns survive by tapping broader markets in the region, can metropolitan New Orleans do the same?) Possible solutions include building selectively or at some distance, or reforming the landscape before rebuilding the city. But something will be done to revive this city, even if it takes years. And geography and economics, not planners or politicians, will determine the results.

As for the people of New Orleans, many will leave, but some will stay, and the question of how to produce housing for them remains. The trailer houses already provided will suffice only in the short run. I suspect that the housing problem will be solved, U.S. fashion, by developers, merchant builders, and the manipulation of interest and subsidy rates. Direct payments, not a usual method of local government (there is no patronage there), may be needed for those who choose to establish their lives away from New Orleans. Government can't build housing for the diaspora, but it can help people to relocate by providing housing payments and work incentives elsewhere.

But the unique New Orleans culture, having migrated with the city's inhabitants, may not return. The city's scene will reassert itself at a level the new New Orleans can support, but a minimum density will be required to maintain the intense, private-sector zaniness that has long been an important draw for tourists and others. The breaking of the old cultural patterns since many of the people who purveyed them have gone to Texas or Pennsylvania, might become a permanent condition. That raises another issue: In the past, broad population movements caused by war, famine, and oppression—migrations from Eastern Europe or Italy, for example—have pervasively influenced the culture of the United States as a whole. And within the country, earlier dispersions via the Mississippi helped to convey African-American music and culture and Southern industrial and business know-how down the river to the world. What spreading of skills and cultures will be traced out in years to come from the decamping forced by Katrina?

New Orleans today offers an appropriate place and time to reconsider the role of government in urban life. The deadly lack of coordination among levels of government evinced during the emergency should be understood for what it was—a failure of will. In the United States today, few people see government as a resource. Although we may understand how this skepticism developed, we should consider whether it should now be reassessed. Such reassessments occurred during the Great Depression and again with the civil rights movement in the 1960s, when government, especially federal government, defined itself as a friend of the poor and a safety net in times of danger. The pendulum swung back in the 1970s, and today even Democrats question the role of big government—especially when it is in the hands of Republicans. New Orleans reminds us that when great forces hit, when needs are supraregional or beyond the means of state and local government, federal planning and action are essential.

And Katrina calls on architects, environmentalists, and planners to do some rethinking as well. The severity of the disaster forces on us an altered logic in our conception of the city and of our relationships and roles vis-à-vis each other and our society. Few of us are accustomed to considering the city as a broad economic and environmental region or to studying it as a series of overlapping systems and disciplines of thought. We follow what interests us—for architects, it is the physical and the aesthetic, for environmentalists, the natural, and for planners the political and procedural. Planners in particular tend to deal in two dimensions, to consider the city as a "spatial economy" and a series of patterns. Katrina showed that they must learn to understand a third urban dimension in order to save lives, because in some situations topography is death. Planners should make common cause with environmentalists in conceptualizing the vertical dimension of urban topography, and architects and landscape architects must help, because they have been trained to think in terms of section as well as in terms of plan.

There are many roles for the design professional in the aftermath of this catastrophe, from helping rebuild in the private and public sectors to helping city and regional agencies deal with emergency planning and long-term strategizing. Right now, government, too, needs help, in considering how the billions urgently allocated for rescue and clearance can also be used for rational replanning. As we speak, developers are acquiring land and forming architectural teams. How will the public agencies, while still reacting to emergencies, stay on top of the fast-moving private sector? Our work also includes raising questions, as I am doing here.

If, like our European confreres, we are to think joyously of the future New Orleans even while urgent conditions still prevail, then our views must shift. Rather than fret over the plans of our present-day Wrens, we must enter into the muck of cleanup and development and the murk of governmental operations. Our aim should be to help New Orleans do what it will do, but in the best way possible. And we can do this only through cultivating a loving understanding of the mess. We need a measured, realistic approach, while recognizing that even by the criteria of realism, we will have to be in some sense visionary, too. This is what history tells us.

DISASTER APARTHEID: A WORLD OF GREEN ZONES AND RED ZONES

NAOMI KLEIN

> Shelve the abiding fiction that disasters do not discriminate—that they flatten everything in their path with "democratic" disregard. Plagues zero in on the dispossessed, on those forced to build their lives in the path of danger. AIDS is no different.
>
> —Hein Marais, South African writer, 2006[1]

> Katrina was not "unforeseeable" ... It was the result of a political authority that subcontracts its responsibility to the private sector and abdicates its responsibility altogether when it comes to housing, healthcare, education, and even evacuation.
>
> —Harry Belafonte, American musician and civil rights activist, September 2005[2]

During the second week of September 2005, I was in New Orleans with my husband, Avi, and Andrew, with whom I had traveled in Iraq. We were there shooting documentary footage in the still partially flooded city. As the nightly six o'clock curfew descended, we found ourselves driving in circles, unable to find our way. The traffic lights were out, and half the street signs had been blown over or twisted sideways by the storm. Debris and water obstructed passage along many roads, and most of the people trying to navigate the obstacles were, like us, out-of-towners with no idea where they were going.

The accident was a bad one: a T-bone at full speed in the middle of a major intersection. Our car spun out into a traffic light, went through a wrought-iron fence and parked in a porch. The injuries to the people in both cars were thankfully minor, but before I knew it I was being strapped to a stretcher and driven away. Through the haze of concussion, I was aware that wherever the ambulance was going, it wouldn't be good. I had visions of the horrific scene at the makeshift health clinic at the New Orleans airport—there were so few doctors and nurses that elderly

1 Hein Marais, "A Plague of Inequality," *Mail & Guardian*, May 19, 2006.
2 "Names and Faces," *Washington Post*, September 19, 2005.

evacuees were being left unattended for hours, slumped in their wheelchairs. I thought about Charity Hospital, New Orleans's primary public emergency room, which we had passed earlier in the day. It flooded during the storm, and its staff had struggled without power to keep patients alive. I pleaded with the paramedics to let me out. I remember telling them that I was fine, really, and then I must have passed out.

I came to as we arrived at the most modern and calm hospital I have ever been in. Unlike the clinics crowded with evacuees, at the Ochsner Medical Center—offering "healthcare with peace of mind"—doctors, nurses, and orderlies far outnumbered the patients. In fact, there seemed to be only a handful of other patients in the immaculate ward. In minutes I was settled into a spacious private room, my cuts and bruises attended to by a small army of medical staff. Three nurses immediately took me in for a neck x-ray; a genteel Southern doctor removed some glass fragments and put in a couple of stitches.

To a veteran of the Canadian public healthcare system, these were wholly unfamiliar experiences; I usually wait for forty minutes to see my general practitioner. And this was downtown New Orleans—ground zero of the largest public health emergency in recent U.S. history. A polite administrator came into my room and explained, "In America we pay for healthcare. I am so sorry, dear—it's really terrible. We wish we had your system. Just fill out this form."

Within a couple of hours, I would have been free to go, had it not been for the curfew that had locked down the city. "The biggest problem," a private security guard told me in the lobby where we were both biding time, "is all the junkies; they're jonesing and want to get into the pharmacy."

Since the pharmacy was locked tight, a medical intern was kind enough to slip me a few painkillers. I asked him what it had been like at the hospital at the peak of the storm. "I wasn't on duty, thank God," he said. "I live outside the city."

When I asked if he had gone to any of the shelters to help, he seemed taken aback by the question and a little embarrassed. "I hadn't thought of that," he said. I quickly changed the subject to what I hoped was safer ground: the fate of Charity Hospital. It was so underfunded that it was barely functioning before the storm, and people were already speculating that with the water damage it might never reopen. "They'd better reopen it," he said. "We can't treat those people here."

It occurred to me that this affable young doctor, and the spa-like medical care I had just received, were an embodiment of the culture that had made the horrors of Hurricane Katrina possible, the culture that had left New Orleans's poorest residents to drown. As a graduate of a private medical school and then an intern at a private hospital, the doctor had been trained simply not to see New Orleans's uninsured, overwhelmingly African-American residents as potential patients. That was true before the storm, and it continued to be true even when all of New Orleans turned into a giant emergency room: he had sympathy for the evacuees, but that didn't change the fact that he still could not see them as potential patients of his.

When Katrina hit, the sharp divide between the worlds of Ochsner Hospital and Charity Hospital suddenly played out on the world stage. The economically secure drove out of town, checked into hotels, and called their insurance companies. The 120,000 people in New Orleans without cars, who depended on the state to organize their evacuation, waited for help that did not arrive, making desperate SOS signs or rafts out of their refrigerator doors. Those images shocked the world because even though most of us had resigned ourselves to the daily inequalities of who has access to healthcare and whose schools have decent equipment, there was still a widespread assumption that disasters were supposed to be different. It was taken for granted that the state—at least in a rich country—would come to the aid of the people during a cataclysmic event. The images from New Orleans showed that this general belief—that disasters are a kind of time-out for cutthroat capitalism, when we all pull together and the state switches into higher gear—had already been abandoned, and with no public debate.

There was a brief window of two or three weeks when it seemed that the drowning of New Orleans would provoke a crisis for the economic logic that had greatly exacerbated the human disaster with its relentless attacks on the public sphere. "The storm exposed the consequences of neoliberalism's lies and mystifications, in a single locale and all at once," wrote the political scientist and New Orleans native Adolph Reed Jr.[3] The facts of this exposure are well known—from the levees that were never repaired, to the underfunded public transit system that failed, to the fact that the city's idea of disaster preparedness was passing out DVDs telling people that if a hurricane came, they should get out of town.

Then there was the Federal Emergency Management Agency (FEMA), a laboratory for the Bush administration's vision of government run by corporations. In the summer of 2004, more than a year before Katrina hit, the State of Louisiana put in a request to FEMA for funds to develop an in-depth contingency plan for a powerful hurricane. The request was refused. "Disaster mitigation"—advance government measures to make the effects of disasters less devastating—was one of the programs gutted under Bush. Yet that same summer FEMA awarded a $500,000 contract to a private firm called Innovative Emergency Management. Its task was to come up with a "catastrophic hurricane disaster plan for Southeast Louisiana and the City of New Orleans."[4]

The private company spared no expense. It brought together more than 100 experts, and when money ran out, it went back to FEMA for

3 Adolph Reed Jr., "Undone by Neoliberalism," *The Nation*, September 18, 2006.

4 Jon Elliston, "Disaster in the Making," *Tucson Weekly*, September 23, 2004; Innovative Emergency Management, "IEM Team to Develop Catastrophic Hurricane Disaster Plan for New Orleans & Southeast Louisiana," press release, June 3, 2004, ieminc.com.

more; eventually the bill for the exercise doubled to $1 million. The company came up with scenarios for a mass evacuation covering everything from delivering water to instructing neighboring communities to identify empty lots that could immediately be transformed into trailer parks for evacuees—all the sensible things that didn't happen when a hurricane like the one they were imagining actually hit. That's partly because, eight months after the contractor submitted its report, no action had been taken. "Money was not available to do the follow-up," explained Michael Brown, head of FEMA at the time.[5] The story is typical of the lopsided state that Bush built: a weak, underfunded, ineffective public sector on the one hand and a parallel richly funded corporate infrastructure on the other. When it comes to paying contractors, the sky is the limit; when it comes to financing the basic functions of the state, the coffers are empty.

Just as the U.S. occupation authority in Iraq turned out to be an empty shell, when Katrina hit, so did the U.S. federal government at home. In fact, it was so thoroughly absent that FEMA could not seem to locate the New Orleans Superdome, where 23,000 people were stranded without food or water, despite the fact that the world media had been there for days.

For some free-market ideologues, this spectacle of what *New York Times* columnist Paul Krugman termed the can't-do government provoked a crisis of faith. "The collapsed levees of New Orleans will have consequences for neoconservatism just as long and deep as the collapse of the Wall in East Berlin had on Soviet Communism," wrote the repentant true believer Martin Kelly in a much-circulated essay. "Hopefully all of those who urged the ideology on, myself included, will have a long time to consider the error of our ways." Even neocon stalwarts like Jonah Goldberg were begging "big government" to ride to the rescue: "When a city is sinking into the sea and rioting runs rampant, government probably should saddle up."[6]

No such soul-searching was in evidence at the Heritage Foundation, where the true disciples of Friedmanism can always be found. Katrina was a tragedy, but, as Milton Friedman wrote in his *Wall Street Journal* op-ed, it was "also an opportunity." On September 13, 2005—fourteen days after the levees were breached—the Heritage Foundation hosted a meeting of like-minded ideologues and Republican lawmakers. They came up with a list: "Pro-Free-Market Ideas for Responding to Hurricane Katrina and High Gas Prices"—thirty-two policies in all, each one straight out of the Chicago School playbook, and all of them packaged as "hurricane relief." The first three items were "automatically suspend Davis-Bacon prevailing wage laws in disaster areas," referring to the law that required federal contractors to pay a living wage; "make the entire affected area

5 Ron Fournier and Ted Bridis, "Hurricane Simulation Predicted 61,290 Dead," AP, September 9, 2005.

6 Paul Krugman, "A Can't-Do Government," *New York Times*, September 2, 2005; Martin Kelly, "Neoconservatism's Berlin Wall," *The G-Gnome Rides Out* blog, September 1, 2005, theggnomeridesout.blogspot.com; Jonah Goldberg, "The Feds," Corner blog, *National Review Online*, August 31, 2005.

a flat-tax free enterprise zone"; and "make the entire region an economic-competitiveness zone," that is, one with comprehensive tax incentives and waiving of regulations. The group also proposed giving parents vouchers to use at charter schools.[7] All of these measures were announced by President Bush within the week. He was eventually forced to reinstate the labor standards, though they were largely ignored by contractors.

The meeting produced more ideas that gained presidential support. Climate scientists have directly linked the increased intensity of hurricanes to warming ocean temperatures.[8] This connection, however, didn't stop the working group at the Heritage Foundation from calling on Congress to repeal environmental regulations on the Gulf Coast, give permission for new oil refineries in the United States, and green-light "drilling in the Arctic National Wildlife Refuge."[9] All these measures would increase greenhouse gas emissions, the major human contributor to climate change, yet they were immediately championed by the president under the guise of responding to the Katrina disaster.

Within weeks, the Gulf Coast became a domestic laboratory for the same kind of government-run-by-contractors that had been pioneered in Iraq. The companies that snatched up the biggest contracts were the familiar Baghdad gang: Halliburton's KBR unit had a $60 million gig to reconstruct military bases along the coast. Blackwater was hired to protect FEMA employees from looters. Parsons, infamous for its sloppy Iraq work, was brought in for a major bridge construction project in Mississippi. Fluor, Shaw, Bechtel, CH2M Hill—all top contractors in Iraq—were hired by the government to provide mobile homes to evacuees just ten days after the levees broke. Their contracts ended up totaling $3.4 billion, no open bidding required.[10]

As many remarked at the time, within days of the storm it was as if Baghdad's Green Zone had lifted off its perch on the Tigris and landed on the bayou. The parallels were undeniable. To spearhead its Katrina operation, Shaw hired the former head of the U.S. Army's Iraq reconstruction office. Fluor sent its senior project manager from Iraq to the flood zone. "Our rebuilding work in Iraq is slowing down and this has made some people available to respond to our work in Louisiana," a company representative explained. Joe Allbaugh, whose company New Bridge Strategies had promised to bring Walmart and 7-Eleven to Iraq, was the

7 Milton Friedman, "The Promise of Vouchers," *Wall Street Journal*, December 5, 2005; John R. Wilke and Brody Mullins, "After Katrina, Republicans Back a Sea of Conservative Ideas," *Wall Street Journal*, September 15, 2005; Paul S. Teller, deputy director, House Republican Study Committee, "Pro-Free-Market Ideas for Responding to Hurricane Katrina and High Gas Prices," e-mail sent September 13, 2005.

8 Intergovernmental Panel on Climate Change, *Climate Change 2007: The Physical Science Basis*, Summary for Policymakers, February 2007, 16, ipcc.ch.

9 Teller, "Pro-Free-Market Ideas for Responding to Hurricane Katrina and High Gas Prices."

10 Eric Lipton and Ron Nixon, "Many Contracts for Storm Work Raise Questions," *New York Times*, September 26, 2005; Anita Kumar, "Speedy Relief Effort Opens Door to Fraud," *St. Petersburg Times*, September 18, 2005; Jeremy Scahill, "In the Black(water)," *The Nation*, June 5, 2006; Spencer S. Hsu, "$400 Million FEMA Contracts Now Total $3.4 Billion," *Washington Post*, August 9, 2006.

lobbyist in the middle of many of the deals. The similarities were so striking that some of the mercenary soldiers, fresh from Baghdad, were having trouble adjusting. When David Enders, a reporter, asked an armed guard outside a New Orleans hotel if there had been much action, he replied, "Nope. It's pretty Green Zone here."[11]

Other things were pretty Green Zone, too. On contracts valued at $8.75 billion, congressional investigators found "significant overcharges, wasteful spending, or mismanagement."[12] (The fact that exactly the same errors as those made in Iraq were instantly repeated in New Orleans should put to rest the claim that Iraq's occupation was merely a string of mishaps and mistakes marked by incompetence and lack of oversight. When the same mistakes are repeated over and over again, it's time to consider the possibility that they are not mistakes at all.)

In New Orleans, as in Iraq, no opportunity for profit was left untapped. Kenyon, a division of the mega funeral conglomerate Service Corporation International (a major Bush campaign donor), was hired to retrieve the dead from homes and streets. The work was extraordinarily slow, and bodies were left in the broiling sun for days. Emergency workers and local volunteer morticians were forbidden to step in to help because handling the bodies impinged on Kenyon's commercial territory. The company charged the state, on average, $12,500 a victim, and it has since been accused of failing to properly label many bodies. For almost a year after the flood, decayed corpses were still being discovered in attics.[13]

Another pretty Green Zone touch: relevant experience often appeared to have nothing to do with how contracts were allocated. AshBritt, the company paid half a billion dollars to remove debris, reportedly didn't own a single dump truck and farmed out the entire job to contractors. Even more striking was the company that FEMA paid $5.2 million to perform the crucial role of building a base camp for emergency workers in St. Bernard Parish, a suburb of New Orleans. The camp construction fell behind schedule and was never completed. When the contractor was investigated, it emerged that the company, Lighthouse Disaster Relief, was actually a religious group. "About the closest thing I have done to this is just organize a youth camp with my church," confessed Lighthouse's director, Pastor Gary Heldreth.

As in Iraq, government once again played the role of a cash machine equipped for both withdrawals and deposits. Corporations withdrew funds through massive contracts, and then repaid the government not

---

11 Shaw Group, "Shaw Announces Charles M. Hess to Head Shaw's FEMA Hurricane Recovery Program," press release, September 21, 2005, shawgrp.com; "Fluor's Slowed Iraq Work Frees It for Gulf Coast," Reuters, September 9, 2005; Thomas B. Edsall, "Former FEMA Chief Is at Work on Gulf Coast," *Washington Post*, September 8, 2005; David Enders, "Surviving New Orleans," *Mother Jones*, September 7, 2005.

12 United States House of Representatives, Committee on Government Reform—Minority Staff, Special Investigations Division, *Waste, Fraud and Abuse in Hurricane Katrina Contracts*, August 2006, i, oversight.house.gov.

13 Rita J. King, CorpWatch, *Big, Easy Money: Disaster Profiteering on the American Gulf Coast*, August 2006; Dan Barry, "A City's Future, and a Dead Man's Past," *New York Times*, August 27, 2006.

with reliable work but with campaign contributions and/or loyal foot soldiers for the next election. According to the *New York Times*, "The top twenty service contractors have spent nearly $300 million since 2000 on lobbying and have donated $23 million to political campaigns." The Bush administration, in turn, increased the amount spent on contractors by roughly $200 billion between 2000 and 2006.[14]

Something else was familiar: the contractors' aversion to hiring local people who might have seen the reconstruction of New Orleans not only as a job but as part of healing and reempowering their communities. Washington could easily have made it a condition of every Katrina contract that companies hire local people at decent wages, to help them put their lives back together. Instead, the residents of the Gulf Coast, like the people of Iraq, were expected to watch as contractors created an economic boom based on easy taxpayer money and relaxed regulations.

The result, predictably, was that after all the layers of subcontractors had taken their cut, there was next to nothing left for the people doing the work. For instance, the author Mike Davis tracked the way FEMA paid Shaw $175 a square foot to install blue tarps on damaged roofs, even though the tarps themselves were provided by the government. Once all the subcontractors took their share, the workers who actually hammered in the tarps were paid as little as $2 a square foot. "Every level of the contracting food chain, in other words, is grotesquely overfed except the bottom rung, where the actual work is carried out."[15]

According to one study, "A quarter of the workers rebuilding the city were immigrants lacking papers, almost all of them Hispanic, making far less money than legal workers." In Mississippi, a class-action lawsuit forced several companies to pay hundreds of thousands of dollars in back wages to immigrant workers. Some were not paid at all. On one Halliburton/KBR job site, undocumented immigrant workers reported being wakened in the middle of the night by their employer (a sub-subcontractor), who allegedly told them that immigration agents were on their way. Most workers fled to avoid arrest; after all, they could end up in one of the new immigration prisons that Halliburton/KBR had been contracted to build for the federal government.[16]

The attacks on the disadvantaged, carried out in the name of reconstruction and relief, did not stop there. In order to offset the tens of billions

14 Scott Shane and Ron Nixon, "In Washington, Contractors Take on Biggest Role Ever," *New York Times*, February 4, 2007.

15 Mike Davis, "Who Is Killing New Orleans?" *The Nation*, April 10, 2006.

16 Leslie Eaton, "Immigrants Hired After Storm Sue New Orleans Hotel Executive," *New York Times*, August 17, 2006; King, CorpWatch, *Big, Easy Money*; Gary Stoller, "Homeland Security Generates Multibillion Dollar Business," *USA Today*, September 11, 2006. No extensive studies have been conducted on New Orleans labor conditions, but the Advancement Project, a grassroots advocacy group in New Orleans, estimates that 60 percent of the immigrant workforce in New Orleans have not been paid for at least part of their work. See Judith Browne-Dianis, Jennifer Lai, Marielena Hincapie et al., *And Injustice for All: Workers' Lives in the Reconstruction of New Orleans*, Advancement Project, July 6, 2006, 29, advancementproject.org

going to private companies in contracts and tax breaks, in November 2005 the Republican-controlled Congress announced that it needed to cut $40 billion from the federal budget. Among the programs that were slashed were student loans, Medicaid, and food stamps.[17] In other words, the poorest citizens in the country subsidized the contractor bonanza twice—first when Katrina relief morphed into unregulated corporate handouts, providing neither decent jobs nor functional public services, and second when the few programs that directly assisted the unemployed and working poor nationwide were gutted to pay those bloated bills.

Not so long ago, disasters were periods of social leveling, rare moments when atomized communities put divisions aside and pulled together. Increasingly, however, disasters are the opposite: they provide windows into a cruel and ruthlessly divided future in which money and race buy survival.

Baghdad's Green Zone is the starkest expression of this world order. It has its own electrical grid, its own phone and sewage systems, its own oil supply, and its own state-of-the-art hospital with pristine operating theaters—all protected by five-meter-thick walls. It feels, oddly, like a giant fortified Carnival Cruise Ship parked in the middle of a sea of violence and despair, the boiling Red Zone that is Iraq. If you can get on board, there are poolside drinks, bad Hollywood movies, and Nautilus machines. If you are not among the chosen, you can get yourself shot just by standing too close to the wall.

Everywhere in Iraq, the wildly divergent value assigned to different categories of people is crudely evident. Westerners and their Iraqi colleagues have checkpoints at the entrances to their streets, blast walls in front of their houses, body armor, and private security guards on call at all hours. They travel the country in menacing armored convoys, with mercenaries pointing guns out the windows as they follow their prime directive to "protect the principal." With every move they broadcast the same unapologetic message: we are the chosen; our lives are infinitely more precious. Middle-class Iraqis, meanwhile, cling to the next rung down the ladder: they can afford to buy protection from local militias, and they are able to pay off kidnappers to have a family member released. But the vast majority of Iraqis have no protection at all. They walk the streets wide open to any possible violence, with nothing between them and the next car bomb but a thin layer of fabric. In Iraq, the lucky get Kevlar, the rest get prayer beads.

At first I thought the Green Zone phenomenon was unique to the war in Iraq. Now, after years spent in other disaster zones, I realize that the Green Zone emerges everywhere that the disaster capitalism complex descends, with the same stark partitions between the included and the excluded, the protected and the damned.

17 Rick Klein, "Senate Votes to Extend Patriot Act for 6 Months," *Boston Globe*, December 22, 2005.

It happened in New Orleans. After the flood, an already divided city turned into a battleground between gated green zones and raging red zones—the result not of water damage but of the "free-market solutions" embraced by the president. The Bush administration refused to allow emergency funds to pay public sector salaries, and the City of New Orleans, which lost its tax base, had to fire 3,000 workers in the months after Katrina. Among them were sixteen of the city's planning staff—with shades of "de-Baathification," laid off at the precise moment when New Orleans was in desperate need of planners. Instead, millions of public dollars went to outside consultants, many of whom were powerful real estate developers.[18] And of course thousands of teachers were also fired, paving the way for the conversion of dozens of public schools into charter schools, just as Friedman had called for.

Almost two years after the storm, Charity Hospital was still closed. The court system was barely functioning, and the privatized electricity company, Entergy, had failed to get the whole city back online. After threatening to raise rates dramatically, the company managed to extract a controversial $200 million bailout from the federal government. The public transit system was gutted and lost almost half its workers. The vast majority of publicly owned housing projects stood boarded up and empty, with 5,000 units slotted for demolition by the federal housing authority.[19] Much as the tourism lobby in Asia had longed to be rid of the beachfront fishing villages, New Orleans's powerful tourism lobby had been eyeing the housing projects, several of them on prime land close to the French Quarter, the city's tourism magnet.

Endesha Juakali helped set up a protest camp outside one of the boarded-up projects, St. Bernard Public Housing, explaining that "they've had an agenda for St. Bernard a long time, but as long as people lived here, they couldn't do it. So they used the disaster as a way of cleansing the neighborhood when the neighborhood is weakest ... This is a great location for bigger houses and condos. The only problem is you got all these poor black people sitting on it!"[20]

Amid the schools, the homes, the hospitals, the transit system, and the lack of clean water in many parts of town, New Orleans's public sphere was not being rebuilt, it was being erased, with the storm used as the excuse. At an earlier stage of capitalist "creative destruction," large swaths of the United States lost their manufacturing bases and degenerated into rust belts of shuttered factories and neglected neighborhoods. Post-Katrina New Orleans may be providing the first Western-world image of a new

18 Jeff Duncan, "The Unkindest Cut," *Times-Picayune*, March 28, 2006; Paul Nussbaum, "City at a Crossroads," *Philadelphia Inquirer*, August 29, 2006.

19 Ed Anderson, "Federal Money for Entergy Approved," *Times-Picayune*, December 5, 2006; Frank Donze, "146 N.O. Transit Layoffs Planned," *Times-Picayune*, August 25, 2006; Bill Quigley, "Robin Hood in Reverse: The Looting of the Gulf Coast," justiceforneworleans.org, November 14, 2006.

20 Asian Coalition for Housing Rights, "Mr. Endesha Juakali," achr.net.

kind of wasted urban landscape: the mold belt, destroyed by the deadly combination of weathered public infrastructure and extreme weather.

The American Society of Civil Engineers said in 2007 that the U.S. had fallen so far behind in maintaining its public infrastructure—roads, bridges, schools, dams—that it would take more than a trillion and a half dollars over five years to bring it back up to standard. Instead, these types of expenditures are being cut back.[21] At the same time, public infrastructure around the world is facing unprecedented stress, with hurricanes, cyclones, floods, and forest fires all increasing in frequency and intensity. It's easy to imagine a future in which growing numbers of cities have their frail and long-neglected infrastructures knocked out by disasters and then are left to rot, their core services never repaired or rehabilitated. The well-off, meanwhile, will withdraw into gated communities, their needs met by privatized providers.

Signs of that future were already in evidence by the time hurricane season rolled around in 2006. In just one year, the disaster-response industry had exploded, with a slew of new corporations entering the market, promising safety and security should the next Big One hit. One of the more ambitious ventures was launched by an airline in West Palm Beach, Florida. Help Jet bills itself as "the first hurricane escape plan that turns a hurricane evacuation into a jet-setter vacation." When a storm is coming, the airline books holidays for its members at five-star golf resorts, spas, or Disneyland. With the reservations all made, the evacuees are then whisked out of the hurricane zone on a luxury jet. "No standing in lines, no hassle with crowds, just a first-class experience that turns a problem into a vacation ... Enjoy the feeling of avoiding the usual hurricane evacuation nightmare."[22] For the people left behind, there is a different kind of privatized solution. In 2006, the Red Cross signed a new disaster-response partnership with Walmart. "It's all going to be private enterprise before it's over," said Billy Wagner, chief of emergency management for the Florida Keys. "They've got the expertise. They've got the resources." He was speaking at the National Hurricane Conference in Orlando, Florida, a fast-growing annual trade show for companies selling everything that might come in handy during the next disaster. "Some folks here said, 'Man, this is huge business—this is my new business. I'm not in the landscaping business anymore; I'm going to be a hurricane debris contractor,'" said Dave Blandford, at the conference for his "self-heating meals."[23]

Much of the parallel disaster economy has been built with taxpayers' money, thanks to the boom in privatized war-zone reconstruction. The giant contractors that have served as "the primes" in Iraq and Afghanistan have come under frequent political fire for spending large portions of

21 Bob Herbert, "Our Crumbling Foundation," *New York Times*, April 5, 2007.

22 Help Jet, helpjet.us.

23 Seth Borenstein, "Private Industry Responding to Hurricanes," Associated Press, April 15, 2006.

their income from government contracts on their own corporate overhead—between 20 and 55 percent, according to a 2006 audit of Iraq contractors.[24] Much of those funds have, quite legally, gone into huge investments in corporate infrastructure—Bechtel's battalions of earth-moving equipment, Halliburton's planes and fleets of trucks, and the surveillance architecture built by L-3, CACI, and Booz Allen.

Most dramatic has been Blackwater's investment in its paramilitary infrastructure. Founded in 1996, the company has used the steady stream of contracts during the Bush years to build up a private army of 20,000 mercenary soldiers on call and a massive military base in North Carolina worth between $40 million and $50 million. According to one account, Blackwater's capacity now includes the following: "A burgeoning logistics operation that can deliver 100- or 200-ton self-contained humanitarian relief response packages faster than the Red Cross. A Florida aviation division with twenty-six different platforms, from helicopter gunships to a massive Boeing 767. The company even has a Zeppelin. The country's largest tactical driving track ... A twenty-acre man-made lake with shipping containers that have been mocked up with ship rails and portholes, floating on pontoons, used to teach how to board a hostile ship. A K-9 training facility that currently has eighty dog teams deployed around the world ... A 1,200-yard-long firing range for sniper training."[25]

A right-wing journal in the U.S. pronounced Blackwater "al-Qaeda for the good guys."[26] It's a striking analogy. Wherever the disaster-capitalism complex has landed, it has produced a proliferation of armed groupings outside the state. That is hardly a surprise. When countries are rebuilt by people who don't believe in government, the states they build are invariably weak, creating a market for alternative security forces, whether Hezbollah, Blackwater, the Mahdi Army, or the gang down the street in New Orleans.

The emergence of this parallel privatized infrastructure reaches far beyond policing. When the contractor infrastructure built up during the Bush years is looked at as a whole, what is seen is a fully articulated state-within-a-state that is as muscular and capable as the actual state is frail and feeble. This corporate shadow state has been built almost

24 James Glanz, "Idle Contractors Add Millions to Iraq Rebuilding," *New York Times*, October 25, 2006.

25 Mark Hemingway, "Warriors for Hire," *Weekly Standard*, December 18, 2006. One of the most worrying aspects of this industry is how unabashedly partisan it is. Blackwater is closely aligned with the anti-abortion movement and other right-wing causes. It donates almost exclusively to the Republican Party, rather than hedging its bets like most big corporations. Halliburton sends 87 percent of its campaign contributions to Republicans, CH2M Hill 70 percent. Is it beyond the realm of the imagination to conceive of a day when political parties will hire these companies to spy on their rivals during an election campaign—or to engage in covert operations too shady even for the CIA? See Jeremy Scahill, "Blackwater Down," *The Nation*, October 10, 2005; Center for Responsive Politics, "Oil & Gas: Top Contributors to Federal Candidates and Parties," Election Cycle 2004, opensecrets.org; Center for Responsive Politics, "Construction: Top Contributors to Federal Candidates and Parties," Election Cycle 2004, opensecrets.org.

26 Josh Manchester, "Al Qaeda for the Good Guys: The Road to Anti-Qaeda," *TCS Daily*, December 19, 2006.

exclusively with public resources (90 percent of Blackwater's revenues come from state contracts), including the training of its staff (overwhelmingly former civil servants, politicians and soldiers).[27] Yet the vast infrastructure is all privately owned and controlled. The citizens who have funded it have absolutely no claim on this parallel economy or its resources.

The actual state, meanwhile, has lost the ability to perform its core functions without the help of contractors. Its own equipment is out of date, and the best experts have fled to the private sector. When Katrina hit, FEMA had to hire a contractor to award contracts to contractors. Similarly, when it came time to update the Army Manual on the rules for dealing with contractors, the army contracted out the job to one of its major contractors, MPRI—it no longer had the know-how in-house. The CIA is losing so many staffers to the parallel privatized spy sector that it has had to bar contractors from recruiting in the agency dining room. "One recently retired case officer said he had been approached twice while in line for coffee," reported the *Los Angeles Times*. And when the Department of Homeland Security decided it needed to build "virtual fences" on the U.S. borders with Mexico and Canada, Michael P. Jackson, deputy secretary of the department, told contractors, "This is an unusual invitation ... We're asking you to come back and tell us how to do our business." The department's inspector general explained that Homeland Security "does not have the capacity needed to effectively plan, oversee and execute the [Secure Border Initiative] program."[28]

Under Bush, the state still has all the trappings of a government—the impressive buildings, presidential press briefings, policy battles—but it no more does the actual work of governing than the employees at Nike's Beaverton campus stitch running shoes.

The implications of the decision by the current crop of politicians to systematically outsource their elected responsibilities will reach far beyond a single administration. Once a market has been created, it needs to be protected. The companies at the heart of the disaster-capitalism complex increasingly regard both the state and nonprofits as competitors—from the corporate perspective, whenever governments or charities fulfill their traditional roles, they are denying contractors work that could be performed at a profit.

"Neglected Defense: Mobilizing the Private Sector to Support Homeland Security," a 2006 report whose advisory committee included some of the largest corporations in the sector, warned that "the compassionate federal impulse to provide emergency assistance to the victims of disasters affects the market's approach to managing its exposure to

27 Bill Sizemore and Joanne Kimberlin, "Profitable Patriotism," *Virginian-Pilot*, July 24, 2006.

28 King, CorpWatch, *Big, Easy Money*; Leslie Wayne, "America's For-Profit Secret Army," *New York Times*, October 13, 2002; Greg Miller, "Spy Agencies Outsourcing to Fill Key Jobs," *Los Angeles Times*, September 17, 2006; Shane and Nixon, "In Washington, Contractors Take on Biggest Role Ever."

risk."[29] Published by the Council on Foreign Relations, the report argued that if people know the government will come to the rescue, they have no incentive to pay for privatized protection. In a similar vein, a year after Katrina, CEOs from thirty of the largest corporations in the United States joined together under the umbrella of the Business Roundtable, which includes in its membership Fluor, Bechtel, and Chevron. The group, calling itself Partnership for Disaster Response, complained of "mission creep" by the nonprofit sector in the aftermath of disasters. Apparently charities and NGOs were infringing on their market by donating building supplies rather than having Home Depot supply them for a fee. The mercenary firms, meanwhile, have been loudly claiming that they are better equipped to engage in peacekeeping in Darfur than the UN.[30]

Much of this new aggressiveness flows from the fact that the corporate world knows that the golden era of bottomless federal contracts cannot last much longer. The U.S. government is barreling toward an economic crisis, in no small part thanks to the deficit spending that has bankrolled the construction of the privatized disaster economy. That means that sooner rather than later contracts are going to dip significantly. In late 2006, defense analysts began predicting that the Pentagon's acquisitions budget could shrink by as much as 25 percent in the coming decade.[31]

When the disaster bubble bursts, firms such as Bechtel, Fluor, and Blackwater will lose most of their primary revenue streams. They will still have all the high-tech gear and equipment bought at taxpayer expense, but they will need to find a new business model, a new way to cover their high costs. The next phase of the disaster-capitalism complex is all too clear: with emergencies on the rise, government no longer able to foot the bill, and citizens stranded by their can't-do state, the parallel corporate state will rent back its disaster infrastructure to whoever can afford it, at whatever price the market will bear. For sale will be everything from helicopter rides off rooftops to drinking water to beds in shelters.

Already wealth provides an escape hatch from most disasters—it buys early-warning systems for tsunami-prone regions and stockpiles of Tamiflu for the next outbreak. It buys bottled water, generators, satellite phones, and rent-a-cops. During the Israeli attack on Lebanon in 2006, the U.S. government initially tried to charge its citizens for the cost of their own evacuation, though it was eventually forced to back down.[32] If we continue in this direction, the images of people stranded on New Orleans rooftops

29 The corporations on the advisory committee include Lockheed Martin, Boeing, and Booz Allen. See Stephen E. Flynn and Daniel B. Prieto, Council on Foreign Relations, *Neglected Defense: Mobilizing the Private Sector to Support Homeland Security,* CSR No. 13, March 2006, 26, cfr.org.

30 Mindy Fetterman, "Strategizing on Disaster Relief," *USA Today,* October 12, 2006; Frank Langfitt, "Private Military Firm Pitches Its Services in Darfur," National Public Radio, *All Things Considered,* May 26, 2006.

31 Peter Pae, "Defense Companies Bracing for Slowdown," *Los Angeles Times,* October 2, 2006.

32 Johanna Neuman and Peter Spiegel, "Pay-As-You-Go Evacuation Roils Capitol Hill," *Los Angeles Times,* July 19, 2006.

will not only be a glimpse of America's unresolved past of racial inequality but will also foreshadow a collective future of disaster apartheid in which survival is determined by who can afford to pay for escape.

Looking ahead to coming disasters, ecological and political, we often assume that we are all going to face them together, that what's needed are leaders who recognize the destructive course we are on. But I'm not so sure. Perhaps part of the reason why so many of our elites, both political and corporate, are so sanguine about climate change is that they are confident they will be able to buy their way out of the worst of it. This may also partially explain why so many Bush supporters are Christian end-timers. It's not just that they need to believe there is an escape hatch from the world they are creating. It's that the Rapture is a parable for what they are building down here—a system that invites destruction and disaster and then swoops in with private helicopters and airlifts them and their friends to divine safety.

Contractors are rushing to develop alternative stable sources of revenue, and one of them is disaster-proofing other corporations. This was Paul Bremer's line of business before he went to Iraq: turning multinationals into security bubbles, able to function smoothly even if the states in which they are functioning are crumbling around them. The early results can be seen in the lobbies of many major office buildings in New York or London, with their airport-style check-ins complete with photo-ID requirements and x-ray machines, but the industry has far more ambitious plans, including privatized global communications networks, emergency health and electricity, and the ability to locate and provide transportation for a global workforce in the midst of a major disaster. Another potential growth area identified by the disaster-capitalism complex is municipal government: the contracting out of police and fire departments to private security companies. "What they do for the military in downtown Fallujah, they can do for the police in downtown Reno," a spokesperson for Lockheed Martin said in November 2004.[33]

The industry predicts that these new markets will expand dramatically over the next decade. A frank vision of where these trends are leading is provided by John Robb, a former covert-action mission commander with Delta Force turned successful management consultant. In a widely circulated manifesto for *Fast Company* magazine, he describes the "end result" of the war on terror as "a new, more resilient approach to national security, one built not around the state but around private citizens and companies ... Security will become a function of where you live and whom you work for, much as healthcare is allocated already."[34]

33 Tim Weiner, "Lockheed and the Future of Warfare," *New York Times*, November 28, 2004.
34 Information in the next two paragraphs is also drawn from John Robb, "Security: Power to the People," *Fast Company*, March 2006.

Robb writes,

> Wealthy individuals and multinational corporations will be the first to bail out of our collective system, opting instead to hire private military companies, such as Blackwater and Triple Canopy, to protect their homes and facilities and establish a protective perimeter around daily life. Parallel transportation networks—evolving out of the time-share aircraft companies such as Warren Buffett's NetJets—will cater to this group, leapfrogging its members from one secure, well-appointed lily pad to the next.

That elite world is already largely in place, but Robb predicts that the middle class will soon follow suit, "forming suburban collectives to share the costs of security." These "armored suburbs" will "deploy and maintain backup generators and communications links" and be patrolled by private militias "that have received corporate training and boast their own state-of-the-art emergency-response systems."

In other words, a world of suburban Green Zones. As for those outside the secured perimeter, "they will have to make do with the remains of the national system. They will gravitate to America's cities, where they will be subject to ubiquitous surveillance and marginal or nonexistent services. For the poor, there will be no other refuge."

The future Robb describes sounds very much like the present in New Orleans, where two very different kinds of gated communities emerged from the rubble. On the one hand were the so-called FEMA-villes: desolate, out-of-the way trailer camps for low-income evacuees, built by Bechtel or Fluor subcontractors, administered by private security companies, who patrolled the gravel lots, restricted visitors, kept journalists out, and treated survivors like criminals. On the other hand were the gated communities built in the wealthy areas of the city, such as Audubon and the Garden District, bubbles of functionality that seemed to have seceded from the state altogether. Within weeks of the storm, residents there had water and powerful emergency generators. Their sick were treated in private hospitals, and their children went to new charter schools. As usual, they had no need for public transit. In St. Bernard Parish, DynCorp had taken over much of the policing; other neighborhoods hired security companies directly. Between the two kinds of privatized sovereign states was the New Orleans version of the Red Zone, where the murder rate soared and neighborhoods like the storied Lower Ninth Ward descended into a postapocalyptic no-man's-land. A hit song by the rapper Juvenile in the summer after Katrina summed up the atmosphere: "We livin' like Haiti without no government": failed state U.S.A.[35]

35 Juvenile, "Got Ya Hustle On," on the album *Reality Check*, Atlanta/WEA label, 2006.

Bill Quigley, a local lawyer and activist, observed,

> What is happening in New Orleans is just a more concentrated, more graphic version of what is going on all over our country. Every city in our country has some serious similarities to New Orleans. Every city has some abandoned neighborhoods. Every city in our country has abandoned some public education, public housing, public healthcare, and criminal justice. Those who do not support public education, healthcare, and housing will continue to turn all of our country into the Lower Ninth Ward unless we stop them.[36]

The process is already well under way. Another glimpse of a disaster apartheid future can be found in a wealthy Republican suburb outside Atlanta. Its residents decided that they were tired of watching their property taxes subsidize schools and police in Fulton County's low-income African-American neighborhoods. They voted to incorporate as their own city, Sandy Springs, which could spend its taxes on services for its 100,000 citizens and not have the revenues redistributed throughout the larger county. The only difficulty was that Sandy Springs had no government structures and needed to build them from scratch—everything from tax collection, to zoning, to parks and recreation. In September 2005, the same month that New Orleans flooded, the residents of Sandy Springs were approached by the construction and consulting giant CH2M Hill with a unique pitch: Let us do it for you. For the starting price of $27 million a year, the contractor pledged to build a complete city from the ground up.[37]

A few months later, Sandy Springs became the first "contract city." Only four people worked directly for the new municipality—everyone else was a contractor. Rick Hirsekorn, heading up the project for CH2M Hill, described Sandy Springs as "a clean sheet of paper with no governmental processes in place." He told another journalist that "no one in our industry has done a complete city of this size before."[38]

The *Atlanta Journal-Constitution* reported that "when Sandy Springs hired corporate workers to run the new city, it was considered a bold experiment." Within a year, however, contract-city mania was tearing through Atlanta's wealthy suburbs, and it had become "standard procedure in north Fulton." Neighboring communities took their cue from Sandy Springs and also voted to become stand-alone cities and contract out their government. One new city, Milton, immediately hired CH2M Hill for the job—after all, it had the experience. Soon, a campaign began for

36 Bill Quigley, "Ten Months After Katrina: Gutting New Orleans," CommonDreams.org, June 29, 2006, commondreams.org.

37 Doug Nurse, "New City Bets Millions on Privatization," *Atlanta Journal-Constitution*, November 12, 2005.

38 Annie Gentile, "Fewer Cities Increase Outsourced Services," *American City & County*, September 1, 2006; Doug Nurse, "New City Bets Millions on Privatization."

the new corporate cities to join together to form their own county, which would mean that none of their tax dollars would go to the poor neighborhoods nearby. The plan has encountered fierce opposition outside the proposed enclave: politicians say that without those tax dollars, they will no longer be able to afford their large public hospital and public transit system; that partitioning the county would create a failed state on the one hand and a hyperserviced one on the other. What they were describing sounded a lot like New Orleans and a little like Baghdad.[39]

In these wealthy Atlanta suburbs, the three-decade corporatist crusade to strip-mine the state was complete: It wasn't just every government service that had been outsourced but also the very function of government, which is to govern. It was particularly fitting that the new ground was broken by CH2M Hill, a multimillion-dollar contractor in Iraq paid to perform the core government function of overseeing other contractors. In Sri Lanka after the tsunami, it had not only built ports and bridges but was "responsible for the overall management of the infrastructure program."[40] In post-Katrina New Orleans, it was awarded $500 million to build FEMA-villes and put on standby to be ready to do the same for the next disaster. A master of privatizing the state during extraordinary circumstances, it was now doing the same under ordinary ones. If Iraq was a laboratory of extreme privatization, the testing phase was clearly over.

39 Doug Nurse, "City Hall Inc. A Growing Business in North Fulton," *Atlanta Journal-Constitution*, September 6, 2006; Doug Gross, "Proposal to Split Georgia County Drawing Cries of Racism," *Seattle Times*, January 24, 2007.

40 United Nations Office for the Coordination of Humanitarian Affairs, "Humanitarian Situation Report—Sri Lanka," September 2–8, 2005, reliefweb.int.

BELOVED COMMUNITY
REBECCA SOLNIT

PITCHING A TENT

Thanks to Katrina, the Bush administration lost its mandate of heaven. Perhaps the president and his team should have lost it in the chaos of September 11, 2001, but they cannily framed that situation in a way that led to a surge of patriotic fear and deference and defined the administration as decisive, powerful, unquestionable—until the summer of 2005. Only then did the media and public begin to criticize the administration with the fearlessness that should be part of every era, every democracy. Many reporters standing in the ruins of the Gulf voiced unscripted outrage over the incompetence, callousness, and cluelessness of the federal government during the catastrophe. After Katrina, people who had been afraid to criticize the administration were emboldened to do so. It changed the tone nationwide, and Bush soon became the most unpopular president in American history.

On September 1, the president said, "I don't think anyone anticipated the breach of the levees." The media later obtained videotape of him being warned of that possibility on August 28. The public, too, began to speak out more fearlessly that summer. Poverty and race became issues again. MSNBC commentator Keith Olbermann was so outraged by Katrina that on September 5, 2005, he launched into a furious, widely circulated tirade against the Bush administration, the beginning of his Special Comments that were routinely the most hostile critique of the president in the mainstream media and one of the most noted. "It wasn't Iraq that did George Bush in—it was the weather," he said in 2007. Bush's own pollster, Matthew Dowd, said later, "Katrina to me was the tipping point. The president broke his bond with the public ... I knew when Katrina—I was like, man, you know, this is it, man. We're done." By then a liberal black man with a background in community organizing had become a serious contender to succeed that president in the 2008 election—an unimaginable possibility not long before; and another Democratic contender for the White House launched his campaign in New Orleans and made poverty its central issue. The nation shifted, not only from deference to the president but from fealty to the politics of the far right, and Katrina was the turning point

Bush had been on a five-week vacation at his ranch in Crawford, Texas, when the hurricane hit, and he waited a few days before deciding to return to work in the nation's capital. On the way, he had Air Force One swing low over New Orleans. Being photographed sitting comfortably looking out an airplane window at a city in which people were still stranded did not help his image. His vacation had been disrupted already, though. Cindy Sheehan, the mother of a soldier killed in Iraq a year earlier, had camped outside the presidential expanse to demand that Bush meet with her. Harrowed by grief at her son's death, she tried to make sense of it by demanding the president tell her "for what noble cause did my son die?" She thus became a major voice in the antiwar movement, a surprising role for a suburban mother of three and devout Catholic who had hitherto led a quiet life, surprising most of all to her.

At that moment in August 2005, the rangy blond mom with her unstudied, heartfelt, and sometimes outrageous speech became the narrow point of a wedge opening up room to debate the war. She set up a tent in a ditch by the road to the presidential ranch in Crawford on August 6, and supporters began to gather, bringing their own tents and vehicles and building an impromptu village around what began as a small vigil. They named it Camp Casey, after her dead son whose image was everywhere. During a slow news month, this standoff between a bereaved mother sitting at the gates and a president who wouldn't show his face became a huge story. Her son's death had been her disaster; that she made something remarkable of her response to it was clearly her salvation.

I stopped by Camp Casey the day that Hurricane Katrina hit the Gulf and found a big camp and an extraordinary community akin in many ways to disaster communities. The rolling green landscape studded with small groves of oak trees was beautiful. The sky was strange, huge white clouds swelling overhead, the air stifling. A field of crosses, one for each American soldier dead in the war, stood in front of the huge shade tent with open sides and in which all the meetings, meals, and conversations were held. Someone had come the day before and decorated the crosses with roses of all colors that were wilting in the steamy air. Retired colonel Ann Wright—the career diplomat who resigned on March 19, 2003, the day the U.S. war against Iraq began—strode around making sure everything was going well at the camp. Tough, sweet, and enormously competent, she had directed the evacuation of the U.S. presence in Sierra Leone when that nation erupted in conflict and helped establish the embassy in Afghanistan in 2001. She radiated the same joy many others there did: that this was exactly the meaningful work they had always wanted, and the heat and disarray and discomfort mattered not at all compared to this great sense of arrival. Everywhere people were having the public conversation about politics and values a lot of us dream about the rest of the time, average-looking people of all ages from all over the country, particularly the heartland.

I met a woman who lost her teaching job in Indiana for saying something against the war to elementary-school kids and who was terribly worried about her Navy son; a twenty-five-year-old from Kansas City, Missouri, on his honeymoon with a wife who pushed his wheelchair everywhere, because an explosion in Iraq had paralyzed him; an old man from Slater, Missouri, who had been in the Marines from 1957 to 1963 and had been sleeping in his Ford pickup with 300,000 miles on the odometer during the encampment; four elders from the American Indian Movement, who said what everyone said, "I heard about it and I had to come." The dozen or so clean-cut, serious young veterans of the unfinished war were restless that day, worried that much of the Louisiana National Guard and its equipment was stationed in Iraq when their state needed them desperately. Immediately afterward, the camp broke up, and the group Veterans for Peace drove busloads of supplies to the Gulf, becoming one of the earliest relief efforts to arrive, responding directly from outside the gates of the president's vacation home while inside everything was stalled and confused.

Sheehan herself moved through the camp, giving interviews, hugging veterans, receiving gifts, seemingly inexhaustible, as though grief had hollowed out all usual needs and left her nothing but a purity of purpose. She said to me at the end of that day, August 29, "This is the most amazing thing that has ever happened to me and probably that ever will. I don't even think I would even want anything more amazing to happen to me."

RECONCILIATIONS

Early in his work with the civil rights movement, Martin Luther King Jr. began to talk about the "beloved community." The movement was against discrimination, segregation, and other manifestations of racism. In King's eyes, it was not only against but also *for*—for a larger vision, a utopian ideal of fellowship, justice, and peace. Every activist movement begins by uniting its participants in important ways, giving them a sense of purpose drawn from the wrongs they seek to right and the shared vision of a better world. In 1957, King wrote that the ultimate aim of the Southern Christian Leadership Conference, a key player in the movement, was "to foster and create the 'beloved community' in America where brotherhood is a reality ... Our ultimate goal is genuine intergroup and interpersonal living: integration." Integration was no longer merely a practical matter of buses, schools, lunch counters, and workplaces. It was a metaphysic of solidarity and affinity, a condition of hearts rather than laws and facilities. The same year, he declared that the nonviolent activist in this movement "realizes that noncooperation and boycotts are not ends themselves ... The end is redemption and reconciliation. The aftermath of nonviolence is the creation of the beloved community." Of course, that was a movement that came out of the black churches of the South, and so it was religious from its roots on up. Other groups took up the term, notably the

Student Nonviolent Coordinating Committee, which organized Freedom Summer and introduced ideas about participatory democracy rather than charismatic leadership to the activists of the 1960s.

What begins as opposition coalesces again and again into social invention, a revolution of everyday life rather than a revolt against the system. Sometimes it leads to the kind of utopian community that withdraws from the larger society; sometimes, particularly in recent decades, it has generated small alternatives—cooperatives, organic farms, healthcare projects, festivals—that became integral parts of this society. One of the fundamental questions of revolution is whether a change at the level of institutions and systemic power is enough or whether the goal is to change hearts, minds, and acts of everyday life. Someone like King wanted both: the end of the official apartheid and discrimination in the United States and the transformation of spirit and imagination in each and every citizen.

When we talk of social change, we talk of movements, a word that suggests vast groups of people walking together, leaving behind one way and traveling toward another. But what exists between these people is not movement but a settling in together that is the beginnings of community. (Though in other cases, notably that of the civil rights movement, a community quite literally got up and began moving, through streets, across states, into diners and voting places.) This is one of the major rewards of activism—a new community offering a new sense of shared purpose and belonging, and honoring the principles for which it fights, the conditions so palpable among the people at Camp Casey that August. Again and again, antiwar, environmental, social justice, human rights, and other movements generate new communities, often transcending old divides, and in the process bringing something of that urgency, purposefulness, suspension of everyday concerns, fellowship, and social joy also found in disaster. This, of course, is not always what happens: dysfunctional organizations with bad internal dynamics are legion, but much of the activism of the 1980s in particular focused on cleaning up the process—working toward egalitarianism, nondiscrimination, and accountability from the inside out.

The affinities with disaster communities are obvious: activist communities come into being in response to what is perceived as a disaster—discrimination, destruction, deprivation—and sometimes generate a moment or fragment of a better world. As Temma Kaplan, a New Yorker who had been part of that movement in the American South, said, "For a short time, during the first few days after 9/11 I felt that Beloved Community that we talked about in the civil rights movement."

After Katrina, existing communities had been devastated both by the physical damage that scattered residents to the corners of the country and also by the traumas of the social and political catastrophes. The volunteers who came from outside the area did something to restore those existing communities and in the course of doing so generated an ephemeral series of communities all their own. Religious groups played a huge role in the resurrection of New Orleans. In terms of sheer might, Catholic Charities and the Methodist Church did the most. (A Mennonite call to retired RV owners to congregate in the Gulf listed among the benefits of volunteering, "Becoming the 'hands and feet' of Jesus offers a very rewarding retirement activity; fellowship with other persons of a like mind as you become part of a team; bring back hope to those who have lost it; enjoy social times, potlucks, eating out together, accepting local invitations for meals." Though the Mennonites I saw were mostly in their prime and fiercely good as construction crews.) The tight-knit community around Mary Queen of Vietnam Church in New Orleans East organized the congregation whose early return and effective mutual aid made it possible for others in the Vietnamese American community to return as well.

And then there were the groups descended from the countercultures, the not-always-beloved communities of resistance of the 1960s, the Black Panthers and the Rainbow Family, as well as a lot of young anarchists connected to more recent movements around economic and environmental justice and human rights. Often while the big groups were still sorting out their business or entangled in bureaucracy, the small groups these radicals begat were able to move faster, to stay longer, to sink deeper, to improvise more fitting responses to the needs of the hour. The volunteers became their own culture. And much of the positive experience of disaster seemed to belong to them, not to the residents.

Six months after the hurricane, I stopped in at the Made with Love Café, in St. Bernard Parish, just across the line from the Lower Ninth. The dining room was a big tent where volunteers served three hot meals a day to hundreds of returnees. New Orleanians called it "the hippie kitchen." Behind a young woman in a bandanna and undershirt serving up food, a sign painted on cardboard in bright colors read, TO EMERGENCY COMMUNITIES MADE WITH LOVE CAFÉ & ALL THE AMAZING RESIDENTS: WE WILL NOT FORGET YOU! A black woman and white man were singing and playing music as people sat at long tables talking and eating. Around the main pavilion was a collection of tents, trailers, temporary buildings, and other tarp-covered structures, a packaged food giveaway, a yoga site, and various other amenities. I struck up a conversation with one of the volunteers, Roger, who was walking his two elderly greyhound rescue dogs around the back of the complex. A white-haired white retiree with a thick Boston accent, Roger seemed almost transfigured by joy when he spoke of his work in this little community. He and his wife worked in the supplies site, handing out free stuff. They had found the volunteer opportunity on the Web, driven down to participate, and were, when I met them, six weeks into an eight-week stay.

Half an hour later, I met an African-American man who'd been in New Orleans all his life. We were standing at the site where the infamous barge bashed through the levee to flood the Ninth Ward. Looking downcast, this substantial middle-aged man told me he had grown up at the levee breach in a house that had become a pile of splinters and rubble, though after Hurricane Betsy in 1965, his family had moved uptown. This day six months later was the first time he felt ready to come and look at the devastation. He had been evacuated from New Orleans, spent three months in Houston, come back, but he said it didn't feel like home anymore, and it never would. He was grieved and embittered by the way people like him had been treated in the eventual evacuation and upon their return. If he could win the lottery, he told me, he would leave New Orleans for good. This spectrum, from Roger's joy to the local's despair, was New Orleans early on.

The out-of-town volunteers were often very different from the locals, emotionally and culturally. But the groups weren't necessarily at odds. I asked Linda Jackson, a former laundry owner who became a key staff person at NENA, the Lower Ninth Ward Neighborhood Empowerment Network, how the community felt about the assistance pouring in from around the world. She replied in her whispery voice, "They're stunned. They never thought the world would reach out the way they did. I'm not going to say that it makes up for [the initial, official Katrina response], but the help that we've been given from throughout the United States and the world, it makes us work that much harder. We say, You know what, if these people can come down here and take off of work, drop out of school for a couple weeks, there's no way, there's just no way we can have a negative attitude."

Over and over again I met volunteers who told me they initially came for a week or two but who three months, six months, a year later were still at work in New Orleans. One morning in June 2007, I stopped at the Musicians' Village that Habitat for Humanity was building in the Upper Ninth Ward—a whole neighborhood of small, tidy row houses raised well off the ground and painted in bright colors. I struck up a conversation with a small, dark man of unclear ethnicity and a very distinct Harley-Davidson motorcycle, Brian from Monterey, California. He told me that ten months earlier, in August 2006, he had taken a detour to New Orleans from his journey to watch the leaves change in Vermont, "And I was going to stay for a month, but after a couple weeks they realized that I was the only trim carpenter they had. So they asked me to stay."

Habitat for Humanity was founded by a wealthy couple who realized that their money wasn't giving them purpose or joy; it is a Christian group and one that has a strategy for integrating volunteers and locals. They call it "sweat equity": the future homeowners must work on the houses—though in New Orleans the houses were going up in such numbers that the homeowners would sometimes be chosen only later. Brian said that for him, it wasn't about saving New Orleans or social justice, "At first I thought it was, or I just wanted to help because it was such a mess. In New Orleans East, this elderly couple had been in this house thirty-five or forty years, very elderly, they couldn't get anybody to tear it down, they had no insurance, they had to get the lot leveled, so every day they would burn. They would tear off part of their house and burn it in the front yard. You see stuff like that and you just get angry. The money's there. The money is there, and like I said, at first I thought I was doing it for an idealistic reason, but I get more out of it than I put into it, a lot more. I get letters and postcards from people that have been here, and a lot of them just can't wait to get back. I'm doing it for the people here, the people I'm working with, and the volunteers. That's where I get my love from."

FINDING COMMON GROUND

It started out with shotguns on a front porch, transformed into young medics bicycling through the streets offering assistance to anyone and everyone who wanted it, and it ended up as dozens of relief and reconstruction projects around the city and thousands of volunteers. Malik Rahim, the former Black Panther who reported to anyone who listened that vigilantes were murdering African-American men in Algiers, recalls, "Right after the hurricane I got into a confrontation with some white vigilantes in Algiers, and when I got into them I seen that I was overmatched. I had access to a couple of weapons, and maybe enough ammunition that I could withstand maybe two, three firefights with them, and that's about it. I made a call for some help. Scott Crow and Brandon Darby came to assist us."

Crow and Darby were white activists from Texas who had worked with Rahim on the case of the Angola Three—former Black Panthers who had endured decades of solitary confinement on questionable charges. One of them, Robert King Wilkerson, had been exonerated and released, and the young Texans came to check in on him. Their adventures in eluding the authorities, launching a boat, exploring the city by water, and eventually being united with King were considerable, and at the end the two young white activists, the two older ex-Panthers, and Rahim's partner, Sharon Johnson, sat together in Algiers and talked.

As Rahim, a substantial, powerful, deep-voiced man with long dreadlocks, remembers it, "Scott on the morning of the fifth of September, he said it was time that we organize. And when he told us this, we sat down at my kitchen table and we started organizing Common Ground. The name came from Robert King Wilkerson. King said that what we have to do—because our main discussion was upon how come social movements, all social movements, in America start off with a bang and end with a fizzle—what he said was that we allow all our petty differences to divide us. And King said what we have to find then is that common ground that's going to bring everybody together. So with that we said, 'Hey, that's it, Common Ground, let that be the name.'" The response brought up another King, the one who had popularized the term "beloved community" and had declared, "Hate cannot drive out hate, only love can do that."

Rahim continued, "After that I had twenty dollars, Sharon put up thirty dollars, and with that we financed Common Ground." Millions of dollars would follow. "And from there we was blessed that our phones were still working, so from there we started getting on the phone. We started calling around the country to everyone we knew, and started asking them for some assistance. After that here comes Veterans for Peace. The first to come up was the Veterans for Peace from Florida, and they brought up a bunch of supplies. The next thing you know people start coming. Cindy Sheehan came. And with her came a lot of help. By then we had opened up our health clinic, at least it was a first-aid station by then. A group from France came and helped us make the transition. We organized Common Ground Relief on the fifth of September, and on the ninth we organized a first-aid station. And then maybe three weeks later we made the transition from a first-aid station to a bona fide health clinic. But when it was a first-aid station, it was open 24–7; we must have been serving at one time from 100 to 150 people a day. Again, like I said, I'm a spiritual person and I truly believe that the Most High casts no burden on you greater than you could bear. My life has been a life of community activism, so I was always able to call upon some of the things that he had blessed me with to provide, to use now in this time of need. A food distribution center was easy for us to start with because this was what I learned how to do when I was in the Panther Party. The health clinic or the first-aid station: again, what we did in the Panther Party."

The Panthers had started out as an oppositional group to fight police brutality and discrimination in the inner city. The rhetoric of the Panthers was fiery, and the images of young African Americans with weapons and of spectacular shoot-outs with the police (and ambushes by police in which Panthers died) were all too memorable. Much of the rest of the Panthers' achievements have been overshadowed by their outlaw glamour and "Off the pigs" rhetoric. The year of its founding, 1966, the Party had come up with a "ten-point program" whose last point was, "We want land, bread, housing, education, clothing, justice, peace, and people's community control of modern technology." As the party spread to cities across the United States, the members went about providing some of those things. They fed breakfast to schoolchildren, tested for sickle-cell anemia, and escorted elders to the bank to cash their checks safely. They called these "survival programs." The term underscores how much the inner city felt like a disaster zone.

Common Ground started out with its own survival programs. And the truth of the organization's name was borne out by a clinic that immediately began offering medical services to everyone on the West Bank—including some of the vigilantes who confessed about the murders to the medics while receiving care. Rahim credits the medics who bicycled around the area with preventing an all-out race war in the volatile area. They went door-to-door checking on people, offering care, and softening the divides and fears. At first Common Ground was run largely out of Johnson and Rahim's modest one-story house, and then the storefront clinic nearby in Algiers was added.

In the Lower Ninth Ward, Common Ground set up a tool-lending station, and as the volunteers began to flood in, some were put to work gutting houses ruined by the floodwaters. Others began to work on bioremediation, on a soup kitchen, and on other projects. It was an ambitious organization that planned, in addition to basic survival programs, to replant the cypress swamps killed off by the salt water of the MR-GO canal on the north side of the Lower Ninth, to try to take over a big apartment complex on the West Bank to lodge many of Katrina's displaced, and to publish a small newspaper for a while. Sometimes its reach exceeded its grasp: the housing project fell through, after a lot of time and money were squandered on it.

The organization was sometimes criticized for bringing white people into black communities, for attempting to make policy as well as practical change, for the ambitious scope of its plans and programs, for its sometimes turbulent internal politics. Thousands of volunteers cycled through, bringing fresh energy—and chaos. A lot of the activists needed to be oriented on how to work across cultural and racial differences. Many came from groups that operated by consensus and wanted that form of direct democracy to be the modus operandi at Common Ground. Allowing transient volunteers to make major decisions without living with the consequences didn't make sense to Common Ground's leadership, and so a lot of friction resulted.

Still, the extremely informal methods often worked, and they allowed improvisation in constantly changing circumstances. Emily Posner, a white volunteer who came early on and stayed a long time, recalled, "After the disaster, it was amazing; the Red Cross had a hundred warehouses all over the place and their stuff was just sitting there. Sit, sit, sit, and then we would befriend some Red Cross workers and say: 'Come on, we need to drive our trucks in here.' So we would just get the stuff and get it out and distribute it all over the community. And we did this in not just Red Cross warehouses but all kinds of groups. We had a network of grassroots people working together all over the Gulf. 'We have all this chicken and no electricity yet—can we send a truck over to your community?' And that way the most amount of people would get something.

"There's all kinds of communities within Common Ground. When you work with eleven thousand people [the number of volunteers who had passed through by early 2007], hundreds of people have taken up, at a certain point, long-term roles. While it's an informal thing, there are friendships that have been made that will last forever, and those friendships will be needed in the future for sure. We're a network of people now that if a storm happens we know what to do. And we'll all call each other." When it worked well, people on both sides of the old racial divides went away with changed perceptions. The volunteers mitigated the racial violence and demonization of the first days after the storm. And they went back to their homes and communities around the country, often transformed in some ways by the experience, and spread the word. This kind of social change is incalculable but important. When he studied Common Ground's beginnings, disaster scholar Emmanuel David thought of Freedom Summer, the movement to register Mississippi voters in 1964, which brought a lot of college-age youth from around the country down to witness and combat racism and poverty. They then went home again bearing stories of what they had seen, galvanized to keep working toward some version of the beloved community. Freedom Summer is a landmark in American history, but the actual number of participants in rebuilding New Orleans is far, far larger—certainly in the hundreds of thousands at this point, but no one is counting. Of course, what transpired also made visible who had abundance and who was destitute—a nation of haves and have nots.

Rahim says the encounters his organization fomented "showed blacks that all whites are not evil or oppressors or exploiters because here that's the only thing that we ever had. And it showed the whites that all blacks here are not criminals, that there are good God-fearing people here." Volunteers stayed in rough barracks in the community, often in reclaimed buildings. "We work with solidarity. That means that if you work here, you going to have to stay here. You going to have to keep your presence in the community, and it breached those gaps. We was the first organization to reach out to the Native American community in Houma, we was the first organization to reach out to the Vietnamese community here." Common Ground's motto is Solidarity, Not Charity, an emphasis on working *with* rather than *for* that sets it apart from many national relief groups, however messy its realization of its goals. Projects begat projects. The clinic split off to become a separate organization, Common Ground Clinic, which begat the Latino Health Outreach Project, which for a few years provided outreach and aid to the hordes of mostly undocumented immigrants who arrived to do the hard work of demolishing and rebuilding the city.

Aislyn Colgan, the young medic who had told me about vigilantes confessing to her about the murders, reflected on her nearly two years on and off with the Common Ground Clinic, "I was only twenty-five when I came down here, and I was in the middle age range. There were very few people over the age of forty, so no one had any experience and we were all learning how to be a leader without being forceful, and a lot of people had different ideas about that. I use the excuse all the time: it was so life and death, that chaos and crisis was propelling a lot of our actions. It took a long time for the clinic to transition. I don't think it was until right when I was leaving that we realized that we have to keep that spirit alive, the spirit that it was created in, that 'we have to just give everything we can.' We were open twelve hours a day, seven days a week the first three months and giving, giving, giving because that was the spirit that it was created in and how do you institutionalize that? How do you make it sustainable?

"It is so rare that you get an opportunity to put into action what maybe you've sat around the coffee table and talked with someone about. When do you ever see that the powers that be are failing at their duty, and when do you ever get the chance to move beyond being angry about it and actually do something very concrete and tangible and immediate? Like, you can't provide these people with healthcare, but we're here and we can do it. We would get calls from the Red Cross asking us if we had any gloves because they were out of gloves. You're the Red Cross, you just got billions of dollars donated to you and you don't have gloves? And here we are getting everything donated to us through all of these informal networks of organizations, and the National Guard was referring people to us. The systems that you'd expect to be in place were just not, and we were able to provide, to fill that gap. I was really surprised by—I don't know if the right word is *empathy*—but I was really surprised by just how far down you go with someone. I really built my life around the struggle the last year and a half. I gave every ounce of my attention to this city and it really has changed my whole way of thinking about things and viewing the world.

"On one level I'm a lot more scared that the government isn't going to come through. I don't have faith in the government, or even large organizational city bodies or anything to come through in a natural disaster, and I live in the Bay Area, so I'm really scared about earthquakes. I don't believe that anyone is going to come save me and that really freaks me out. Then also on a personal level I feel like the further down—I don't know how to describe it, but there's a depth to my understanding of pain and a depth to my understanding of joy. I was never a person who cried about happy things, but I find that I cry more often. I feel like I have a much stronger sense of the harshness of life and also the beauty. It's like they're one and the same."

WELCOME HOME

After the 1906 earthquake, San Francisco became a landscape of ruin, but also of improvised outdoor community kitchens, tents, odd piles of salvaged stuff, lavish giveaways in a largely nonmonetary gift economy, lowered social boundaries, and humorous signs—and heartfelt signs, such as the Mizpah Café's ONE TOUCH OF NATURE MAKES THE WHOLE WORLD KIN. As one of the witnesses described the scene, "When the tents of the refugees, and the funny street kitchens, improvised from doors and shutters and pieces of roofing, overspread all the city, such merriment became an accepted thing. Everywhere, during those long moonlit evenings, one could hear the tinkle of guitars and mandolins, from among the tents." It resembles the campouts that have become a major part of counterculture gatherings since the 1960s, notably the biggest and longest-lived of them all, the Rainbow Gatherings held annually since the early 1970s.

Rainbow Gatherings bridge the gap between utopian experiment and traditional carnival, incorporating costuming, dancing, music, festivity, ceremony, and large-scale mingling. In creating an infrastructure to maintain weeks of communal life, the gatherings recall utopian communities, but in producing nothing practical and instead relying on resources garnered in the outside world, whether by Dumpster diving or putting it on a credit card, they are more like a festival. If you regard mainstream society as a disaster—some Rainbows call it Babylon—it makes sense to create the equivalent of a disaster community as an alternative and refuge from it. This is one of the arenas in contemporary society where revolution, disaster, and carnival converge into something namelessly new. The first Rainbow Gathering was in 1972, and it's said that Vietnam vets with experience in setting up field kitchens, latrines, and hospitals were instrumental in creating the infrastructure. This emphasis on autonomous systems of survival—as the back-to-the-earth movement, among other things—is one of the overlooked legacies of the 1960s, arising from a sense that the mainstream was already a disaster (and maybe from childhoods spent amid scenarios of post-atomic survival). The right-wing survivalist equivalents are notably less gregarious, focusing on pioneer-style nuclear-family units holed up alone and armed against everyone else.

Rainbow Gatherings, which now bring together about thirty thousand people to a different national forest location each year, build a functioning temporary society quite literally from the ground up. Each site is chosen for access to potable water, and an often elaborate piping system brings waters from source to camp. A group arrives early to set up, laying out the grounds and digging latrines, hugely important in preventing disease from spreading and fulfilling the commitment to leave behind an undamaged landscape. Another group stays behind to do cleanup. There is no formal structure or hierarchy, but a great deal of informal organizing—all decisions are by consensus, anyone may participate, and volunteer groups perform all tasks. (Those who have been around a long time and done a lot of the work accrue power, but it is hard to call this hierarchy.) In addition to the national gathering in the United States each July (with a day of prayer and meditation on the Fourth), regional gatherings, a worldwide gathering, and gatherings in Canada, Europe, New Zealand, and Australia are now established. I have been to a regional Rainbow Gathering, and my response was mixed—I'm not big on clouds of pot smoke, hugs from strangers, hybridized religious appropriations, and grubby personal style—but I saw the desire and partial realization of a goal of creating a mutual-aid gift-economy society and an impressive and moving atmosphere of sweetness, openness, and generosity.

A crucial aspect of Rainbow Gatherings that was not true of Woodstock in 1969 or Burning Man now is that they truly exist as far outside the monetary economy as possible. Burning Man, the huge annual desert gathering, charges a steep admission, patrols to keep the nonpaying out, hires a company to supply and maintain hundreds of chemical toilets, contracts a local hospital to set up a clinic on site, and leaves all major decisions to the staff of the limited-liability corporation it has become. (Many of the paying attendees, however, create their own gift communities within their camps or with offerings of music, dance zones, drinks, and spectacle to the general public.) The Rainbow Family passes the hat, charges nothing, admits everyone, and food, sanitation, and medical care are all collective volunteer efforts (though the quality of care and cooking can be erratic). The kitchens are the hubs, and many Rainbows are devoted to their annual intensive of cooking and giving away food to strangers. It is a fuzzy but functioning version of the beloved community, an intentional version of disaster's inadvertent communities, and arrivals at gatherings are routinely greeted with "Welcome home."

When Katrina hit the Gulf region, the 2005 national gathering in West Virginia's Monongahela National Forest had been over for more than a month. But many participants kept in touch and some converged on the disaster zone. One named Hawker wrote on September 22 of that year, "As the magnitude of the disaster began to sink in I started receiving phone calls from around the country from my Rainbow friends suggesting we go down and feed folks. What a great idea, I thought. If anyone knew about keeping people healthy in a primitive setting and dealing with creating refugee camps it was Rainbow. Add to that that we knew each other already and we seemed like a natural." His group settled in Waveland, Mississippi.

Hawker continued, "The whole town was wiped out by a thirty-foot wave that took the town out completely. Almost nothing salvageable was left. Katrina was the great equalizer for this town, making poor and rich equals in the struggle for basic food, shelter, clothing, and survival ... We arrived in the parking lot of a Fred's food store and met a local Christian relief group from Bastrop, Texas called Bastrop Christian Outreach Center. They were down there, as they said, 'to just love on everyone as much as we can.' That sounds like Rainbow to me. We joined forces in a common goal to serve and help as much as we could. We were two totally different groups united by a common cause. The relationship couldn't have been better. We set up a common serving area but two kitchens, one of BCOC and one Rainbow. After time Rainbows went to the BCOC kitchens and BCOC folks came and helped in the Rainbow Kitchen. We become one together. We cooked, set up a 'wall-less mart' where people could get basic food, camping gear, clothing, and other needs. We provided medical needs in our first aid tent (up the road Carolina Medical from Charlotte, North Carolina set up a larger mobile field hospital for more serious needs). But mostly we tried to give the town the love and support they needed. One of my favorite tasks was to sit down and eat dinner with locals each night. They usually couldn't wait to tell you their stories. The days were long and the heat tremendous. This was the hardest I have ever worked as I got up at 7:00 a.m. to work till midnight each night with sweat pouring down me all day in the 95- to 103-degree sun. Yet the faces who came each morning and thanked us for giving them hope made it all worth it."

They were serving as many as 4,000 meals a day, much of the food donated by the Organic Valley cooperative, in a geodesic-dome tent donated by people from Burning Man. That a bunch of latter-day hippies found common ground with evangelical Christians is in some way typical of disasters; the crisis created circumstances in which their common goals mattered a lot and their divergent beliefs and lifestyles didn't. Some of the churches were doing good works a century ago and may well be doing them a century from now. Their stability has value. So does the instability of the counterculture groups, the ability to improvise and adapt. Disaster scholars like to talk about emergent organizations, organizations that arise in response to the needs of the moment. *Emergent* suggests one round of response—and often such groups appear to fulfill one task or one urgent round of needs and then dissolve. But Common Ground evolved from addressing something as urgent as medical care to something as long-term as wetlands reconstruction and still exists years later (and it is itself in some sense an outgrowth of the Black Panthers forty years before). What began as the Waveland kitchen would move from location to location, wherever the need was most urgent, broaden its offerings, adapt to its community, and shift both toward a formal nonprofit organizational structure on the one hand, and giving over the roles and resources to the communities themselves on the other, and then dissolve.

Some volunteers had been doing such work for decades before Katrina and as American Rainbow Rapid Response would continue doing it in other sites around North America afterward, from the U.S.–Mexico border to Wisconsin, where small towns and farmers working with the Organic Valley cooperative were flooded in the summers of 2007 and 2008. The ability to metamorphose adaptively may be as valuable as the ability to survive as a distinct entity or agenda. Both churches and counterculture groups have been able to work small-scale and improvise with the communities they serve, rather than dispensing the one-size-fits-all aid that often issues forth from the largest organizations. Government disaster planning often presumes that volunteer efforts would work better with more centralized coordination, but the opposite is often true.

After Katrina, Rainbow Gathering regular Felipe Chavez was tending another kitchen, the Welcome Home Kitchen that set up in Washington Square Park just east of the French Quarter in New Orleans shortly after Katrina and was soon driven out. Nearly two years later, I ran into him in the Upper Ninth Ward at St. Mary's of the Angels, cleaning the grill of a salvaged restaurant stove. St. Mary's had allowed Common Ground and other volunteer groups to set up a base there, and a lot of people were moving through.

Chavez, a Yaqui Indian from Tucson, Arizona, told me, "It's unfortunate it takes disasters to bring people together, but in a way I feel like it was a miracle, and good things happen after that. One example of that is all these people coming to help and showing compassion. And in New Orleans, there's a lot of people walking the streets that need shelter, that need help. There's people that are off their meds and maybe dangerous, and there's no place for them to be, so they need help and they just end up in jail. There's still a lot of healing that needs to come to New Orleans." The Rainbow Gathering had given Chavez that sort of help decades before. He was an alcoholic whose friend took him to a Rainbow Gathering in the late 1970s. There he was overwhelmed, burst into tears, was comforted by strangers, and turned his life around, both by reconnecting with his own indigenous heritage and by beginning a life of service.

On December 1, 2005, the New Waveland Café closed down, and much of the equipment and many of the crew moved to St. Bernard Parish, just across the line from the Lower Ninth Ward, to establish the Made with Love Café. Like the New Waveland, it was a community center where meals drew people in to receive everything from washing machines to social support. One of the Waveland volunteers, Mark Weiner, had taken it upon himself to organize it as a nonprofit, so that as the free supplies dried up they could apply for funding, and so that as the goodwill and energy of the disaster aftermath slackened, he could maintain a viable structure. A stocky, red-haired, earnest young man who had recently graduated from Columbia University, Weiner told me that he and the other young man who formalized the organization had not been part of the Rainbow Family but had been impressed by what they were doing—and many Rainbows came with them to the new project. Two years later, none remained, but their influence lived on. For Weiner, the key idea was a kitchen as the hub of a community space that could offer other practical and intangible forms of aid.

So in December 2005, Weiner created a registered nonprofit called Emergency Communities. The name "was our third choice, and the other two were taken by bands. It has various meanings, it could be a noun in the sense that we are building an emergency community, each site is an emergency community. Or it can be the creation of a community from an emergency. But the idea is to blur the lines between those that are helping and those that need help into a single community." It was a goal along the lines of Common Ground's Solidarity, Not Charity. The Made with Love Café moved in January 2007 across the line to the Lower Ninth, where there were finally enough people to make use of such a facility, and the Comin' Home Café opened. It was housed in a church building that had been gutted to a concrete floor, bare walls, and a roof, but it was on the main thoroughfare, St. Claude Avenue, and it had washers, dryers, computers, phones, and a big-screen TV on which Saints games were shown. In front were big oaks, full of screaming parrots, and a hand-painted comin' home sign. In the back were two refrigerator trucks, a screened kitchen made to be disassembled and taken to the next volunteer site, and various vehicles in which volunteers lived. There was a small library, bright murals of a marching band of alligators and an alligator in an Emergency Communities apron, cheerful tablecloths on all the tables, and young volunteers moving purposefully around the building and the visitors.

Weiner was good at the art of the possible. Because a group of local youths got out of hand and intimidated other community members, EC hired security services from a large corporation, a step not in keeping with a lot of radical ideas of community. The actual guards, however, were locals who got on well with both community members and volunteers. The anarchic consensus model of the Rainbow Family didn't last, either. As with Common Ground, entrusting major and lasting decisions to transient members was problematic. Weiner thought that efforts like Emergency Communities had an ongoing future anywhere disaster hit. He wasn't so sure its internal organization was such a model. He called it a benign dictatorship and added, "I'm more into democracy than that. I just happen to be the benign dictator." Even so, his goal was to just provide aid and perhaps a catalyst for devastated communities to get back on their feet and take care of themselves—to give power away, not accumulate it. Emergency Communities also ran a community center in Buras, down on the peninsula south of New Orleans that got hammered as hard as any place by Katrina, and by the middle of 2007, the center had been handed back to the community to run, and St. Bernard had its own organizations in place. The Comin' Home Café ran through late 2007.

When I first met Weiner, I thought he represented a move back to the mainstream from what the Rainbow Family had launched—until I found out he was the son of Maoist revolutionaries from the 1960s. He didn't retain all his parents' beliefs, but he did keep a critique of the mainstream and a sense of the malleability of society and its radical possibilities. Emergency Communities went through a remarkable evolution during its more than two years after Katrina, from a Rainbow Family project in a rural area to a new nonprofit in an urban one, from one in which the volunteers shared a background to one marked by diversity. It was an extreme example of the improvisation disaster brings, the ability to respond to changing circumstances in ways the larger nonprofits rarely can. It comes out of both the emergency that generated it and the long legacies of the unrest of the 1960s. That it ceased to exist is also a response to changing circumstances; but the thousands who came through to give or receive support were in many cases changed by the interactions. Dispersed throughout the world, they continue their activist work.

As sociologist Emmanuel David wrote to me, "What seems so beautiful about these groups is that many of them emerged spontaneously out of the specific conditions of the event. Now that the organizational structures are in place, the groups can enter (and some plan to and have entered) into other disasters. But the question is: can these emergent groups turned established groups function with the same level of improvisation/creativity that once characterized their actions? Or will these groups formalize, create policies and procedures, the same kind of mechanisms that bogged down the Red Cross, FEMA, and other organizations?" The answer varies from organization to organization.

WEIGHING THE BALANCE

The volunteers are evidence that it doesn't take firsthand experience of a disaster to unleash altruism, mutual aid, and the ability to improvise a response. Many of them were part of subcultures, whether conservative churches or counterculture communities, that exist as something of a latent disaster community already present throughout the United States and elsewhere. Such community exists among people who gather as civil society and who believe that we are connected, that change is possible, and who hope for a better earth and act on their beliefs. They remind us that though disasters can be catalysts to bring out such qualities, disasters do not generate them; they are constructed by beliefs, commitments, and communities, not by weather, seismology, or bombs. Some of these groups explicitly advocate for another kind of society; some are happy to repair and augment the existing one.

Years later, it is hard to weigh the balance. The original catastrophe of Katrina—the lack of an evacuation plan for the poor and frail, the ill-maintained levees—was the result of abandonment of social ties and investments. Yet despite the dire consequences of this social withdrawal, the answer to Katrina on the part of New Orleans Mayor Ray Nagin and many others has been more abandonment, more privatization. They made of the catastrophe an opportunity to further conservative goals: they fired every public school teacher in New Orleans and reinvented the school system as, largely, privatized charter schools less accountable to parents and taxpayers; they closed public housing in the city at a time when the need for homes was desperate, rents were escalating, and the huge projects were some of the most intact housing left in many neighborhoods; they let Charity Hospital, for generations the source of most healthcare for the poorest, stay dead; reduced public transit by 80 percent; and through lousy management increased the burden of returnees by such acts as demolishing Holy Ground Baptist Church without bothering to contact the pastor or congregation, who were in the process of rebuilding the church. Some of these were fiscal decisions on the part of a hard-hit city, but the desire to privatize the system and shut out the poor was an ideological choice. In countless ways the state and federal government magnified and expanded these losses. In 2008, the billions of dollars of aid supposed to be available to rebuild were just beginning to be released. These were not responses to disaster, but expansions of it.

In the wake of Katrina, New Orleans was full of contrasts. There was a marked one between the volunteers who were free to come and go from the disaster zone and those who were trying to resettle it. But there was a more dramatic conflict between those who believe in civil society and the possibility of a beloved community and those who, along with Hobbes, Le Bon, and a lot of elites who panic, believed that their own selfishness was justified by a selfish world.

As the dictionary defines it, a *crisis* is "the point in the progress of a disease when a change takes place that is decisive of recovery or death; also, any marked or sudden change of symptoms, etc." Almost every disaster is a clash between opposing forces and visions of society. Even Mexico City had losses as well as wins; the ruling party proved as resilient as the communities that organized. And even New Orleans has victories. Some of them are as small as a friendship or a rebuilt church, some as large as new awarenesses and preparedness across the continent.

People were caught unprepared by Katrina—both by the material damage and by the enormity of the elite panic—in ways that will not happen again anytime soon. The disaster discredited a regime at the height of its powers. Citizens and outside volunteers together won many victories, though victory sometimes meant nothing more than keeping at bay the more destructive schemes to reinvent the city for the few. Friendships and alliances were formed across old divides, of which Brad Pitt's involvement with the Holy Cross Neighborhood Association and the Lower Ninth is only the most extreme example. Much that was tangible and important was achieved, from the clinics in the first days of the disaster to the ongoing reconstruction efforts. But the events of Katrina left many scars—Malik Rahim, for example, was so dismayed by the racism he encountered in the first days after the storm that three years later he was planning to leave the country. He feared a pandemic could bring an even worse response. Beyond that, Katrina's effects are still unfolding, in a devastated city and its citizens but also in the hearts of the hundreds of thousands of volunteers and in the new coalitions that arose.

This has been a book about disaster's recent past, but it also has a future, a future where knowledge matters and so do desire and belief.

NEW ORLEANS, NATURE, AND THE APOCALYPTIC TROPE

AMY MURPHY

PRELUDE TO AN ARGUMENT

It is 2004. George Bush has just announced that he will be targeting up to $12 billion of new and existing NASA funding to restart efforts to go to the moon again. A few days later, stand-up comedian David Cross enters a packed auditorium: "Let's do this, Washington, D.C.!" Taking his place at the microphone, he continues, "It is cool, man, we are going to the moon. *We are going to the moon!*" Cutting through the cheering, a man in the back of the auditorium heckles loudly. Cross replies, "Hey man, let me say something. People are upset about this, but I think it is great. I think we have to sink all the rest of the money into the moon." The crowd chuckles. "First of all (A), I didn't know there was oil up there; apparently there is… " The audience howls. "A lot of people think that is ridiculous, and it's a waste of money and all this. But I disagree. I strongly disagree." His voice registers equal measures of sarcasm and conviction. "I mean, if you are going to single-handedly subvert the Kyoto accord, and if you are not going to really invest any money into alternative energy sources, and you are going to roll back every environmental protection, and you are going to implement a law that allows corporate polluters to police themselves, and you are going to leave your children and your grand-children a trillion-dollar deficit, you know, *You better have a backup plan!*" The audience claps and cheers. "Seriously, this is what is going to happen. We are all going to go along with it. We are going to plunge into a horrific deficit, but we are going to have a beautiful, beautiful space station up on the moon. But *then* we are going to find out," Cross mimics an apologetic but condescending government official, "Oh! No, no, no. It is only for rich people. Did you all think you all were coming? No, no, no … the *meek* inherit the *earth*!"[1]

1 David Cross, "Track 10: Going to the Moon," *It's Not Funny* (Seattle, WA: Sub Pop Records, compact disc recorded live January 2004, Washington D.C., original release date May 4, 2004).

Dorothy, Toto, and Katrina

THE APOCALYPTIC TROPE

> Tragedy conceives of evil in terms of guilt ... Comedy conceives of evil not as guilt, but as error.
>
> —Stephen O'Leary[2]

Although Hurricane Katrina was an extreme act of nature, we know that much of the destruction of New Orleans was caused not only by natural forces, but also by human error. Popular films like *WALL-E* or comedy sketches like the one above can make light of several centuries of mistaken decisions regarding nature, but rendering Katrina as a comedy will never be an option. Though some might want to assign the guilt for human failures during the storm to a single individual or political party, the decisions that set up this particular tragedy were put in play centuries ago. It might be hard for us to admit now, but catastrophes like Katrina are collective tragedies and are built into our culture's own ideological narrative. Avoiding future disasters of this scale and type requires that not only the few people with means to have a "backup" plan but all of us together start imagining a whole new plan, a plan based on a new and different relationship with nature.

The apocalyptic trope has proven to be one of the most complicit, resilient, and powerful metaphors used throughout our history to manipulate human behavior. It has been a centralizing rhetorical element, connecting a multitude of conservative agendas—religious, military, and

2 Stephen D. O'Leary, *Arguing the Apocalypse: A Theory of Millennial Rhetoric* (Oxford: Oxford University Press, 1994), 68.

industrial—for the full extent of the recorded history of our common quest to control nature. In ironic contrast, the apocalyptic trope has also been one of the most relied upon and productive rhetorical devices in the almost as ancient environmental movement, which some say dates back as far as 1200 B.C.E., from the writings of the Iranian prophet Zoroaster.[3]

Lawrence Buell writes in his seminal work *The Environmental Imagination*,

> The apocalypse is the single most powerful master metaphor that the contemporary environmental imagination has at its disposal ... The rhetoric of apocalypticism implies that the fate of the world hinges on the arousal of the imagination to the sense of crisis. It presupposes that "the most dangerous threat to our global environment may not be the strategic threats themselves but rather our perception of them, for most people do not yet accept the fact that this crisis is extremely grave."[4]

From the first publishing of *Silent Spring* by Rachel Carson in 1962, it is hard to find any contemporary environmental argument that does not cite this metaphor directly or indirectly, including Paul Krugman's opening statement in "Building a Green Economy," his recent cover article for the *New York Times* magazine:

> If you listen to climate scientists ... It is long past time to do something about emissions of carbon dioxide and other greenhouse gases. If we continue with business as usual, they say, we are facing a rise in global temperatures that will be little short of apocalyptic. And to avoid that apocalypse, we have to wean our economy from the use of fossil fuels.[5]

Many current scholars argue that the reality of this particular crisis will only be accepted after an actual apocalypse has occurred. Yet several significant apocalypse-like events *have* already occurred in our time, not as a result of greenhouse gases but rather because of the actions we have taken and the presumptions we have made regarding our relationship to nature and our desire to continue controlling and manipulating it.

Cities such New Orleans, Hiroshima, and Chernobyl that have experienced devastation from man and/or nature soon come to know, once the immediate tragedy has ended, that there is *unfortunately* no single apocalypse, or an ultimate apocalypse. Our traditions and desires are knitted deeply into our built environment. Because we will continue to have as many successes as failures in our continued attempts to control

3 Greg Garrard, *Ecocriticism* (London: Routledge, 2004), 85.

4 See Lawrence Buell, *The Environmental Imagination* (Cambridge, MA: Belknap Press of Harvard University Press, 1995), 285, later quoting Al Gore's *Earth in the Balance: Ecology and the Human Spirit* (Boston: Houghton Mifflin, 1992), 36.

5 Paul Krugman, "Building a Green Economy," *New York Times* Magazine, April 11, 2010, 34.

nature, avoiding a subsequent, perhaps even worse, disaster might prove close to impossible unless there is a significant rethinking of our culture's relationship to nature. As Buell suggests:

> Since the old dream of bending nature to our will (through genetic technology, for instance) also continues to run strong in late twentieth-century American culture, we may expect the oscillation between utopian and dystopian scenarios that began in the last century to continue unabated into the next as the switch flicks back and forth depending on whatever scientific breakthrough or technological foul-up dominates public attention ... there is no question of it disappearing anytime soon as plot formula.[6]

In truth, looking at the city's complete history, one could argue that Katrina has not been the most destructive apocalyptic event to affect New Orleans and it won't necessarily be the last one.[7]

That being the case, it seems that New Orleans must now choose what to do next. It must decide if this tragedy was significant enough to warrant exploring alternative attitudes toward nature and the city's relationship to it or if the traditions and ideologies that created the rich but complicated existing relationship must continue regardless. On the one hand, it is clear that from the beginning to the present day New Orleans has embraced to an almost unprecedented level a desire to control nature. A settlement first established as a military outpost surrounded by swampland, built on the mouth of America's most heavily-used industrial river, and socially organized through a diverse group of religious institutions, the city has a historical fabric that supports the triadic synergy that has traditionally existed among the industrial, military, and religious factions of society. Yet, on the other hand, in the wake of Katrina and the subsequent failure of the established authorities and their resources to protect the inhabitants fully from nature's return or revenge, New Orleans and its citizens must now ask whether, in fact, the kind of control long promoted in the interest of these factions is possible, and—an even more profound question—whether the desire for total control of nature in and of itself significantly contributes to apocalyptic destruction.

Those prophesying from either "side" of the current debate regarding our future relationship with nature sincerely argue for a stronger sense of security for their community's future—economic, moral, social, and biological. So this argument is about more than a sincerity of purpose. At its most basic level, it is about which model best manages risk and

6 Buell, *The Environmental Imagination*, 308.

7 One could also argue that, though occurring at a snail's pace relative to Katrina (and thus not media-packaged for immediate consumption), the decline of need for a Caribbean trade route in the nineteenth century, our shift from an industrial to an information economy in the twentieth century, and global warming in the twenty-first century have all led or will lead to more significant devastation.

better enables resiliency. The issue of victimhood, particularly when one contemplates the further allocation of national and local resources to the city, looms indirectly over almost any discussion regarding the reconstruction of New Orleans. Should we understand the people of New Orleans to be merely the most recent unfortunate victims in the age-old battle against nature, reinforcing a historically justified sense of the need to battle nature as an archrival of mankind with all the technology at our disposal? Should we categorize the city as a victim of poor engineering, and lay the blame for our lack of oversight on corruption, rather than critiquing our desire for such control? Or should we believe that New Orleanians brought this calamity upon themselves, constructing them as victims of an act of God, foretold by prophets of righteousness?

Thankfully, most Americans discount with disgust John Hagee's incendiary comments suggesting that Katrina was a punishment from God for New Orleans's sins.[8] Most Americans understand that earthquakes, hurricanes, and tornados happen and therefore understand that the nation needs to contribute to the reconstruction of any city that is significantly damaged by such an event. Additionally, most Americans also understand New Orleans's vital role in the nation's energy economy as well as in our historical-cultural economy. If rebuilding those two components (the city's energy and tourism infrastructures) were the only question, the debate would be over. But there is also an actual city to be rebuilt. New Orleanians need to arrive at their own answers for how to rebuild it so that it can thrive with a certain level of self-reliance, independent of its connection to the global energy economy or identity as a tourist destination. They must use this "horrible opportunity" to redress not only the rising tides of global warming but also the common issues plaguing many urban centers nationwide: continued racial divisions, postindustrial blight, and stagnation.[9]

One of the most compelling stories in the aftermath of any natural disaster is the spontaneous agency of ordinary people where the traditional authorities are not properly equipped to deal with the disaster's magnitude. New Orleans has provided a profound lesson for all communities in how important local self-determination can be in stabilizing and rebuilding neighborhoods and various communities. This issue of agency is a central theme in several recent fictive apocalyptic narratives in both print and on film that explore the consequences of various natural and man-made

8 John Hagee made this point on "Christian Zionism, Katrina," an interview by Terry Gross on *Fresh Air*, National Public Radio, September 18, 2006. Hagee stated, as he had on many other occasions, "I believe that New Orleans had a level of sin that was offensive to God, and they are—were—recipients of the judgment of God for that ... I believe that the Bible teaches that when you violate the law of God, that God brings punishment sometimes before the Day of Judgment. And I believe that the Hurricane Katrina was, in fact, the judgment of God against the city of New Orleans."

9 This refers to comments from several interviews of various local government officials in the short film *After Katrina: Rebuilding St. Bernard Parish*, directed by Adam Finberg, 2006, available on the DVD *The Katrina Experience: The Power of Culture to Heal*, Full Frame Documentary Film Festival and IndiPix, 2006.

disasters. This is particularly common in many Asian "postapocalyptic" anime films such as Hayao Miyazaki's *Nausicaä of the Valley of the Wind* (1984); Katsuhiro Otomo's *Akira* (1988); *Appleseed,* directed by Shinji Aramaki (2004); and *Sky Blue*, directed by Kim Moon-saeng (2003).[10] Like the people of New Orleans after Katrina, the protagonists of these films, made in the indelible shadow of Hiroshima and Nagasaki, are forced to question their own agency as they try to decide whether they should rebuild without making any significant changes to their cities' social and spatial practices, some of which, they know, have contributed to the apocalypse.[11]

In American natural disaster films, such as Michael Bay's *Armageddon* (1998) or Roland Emmerich's *Day after Tomorrow* (2004), the narratives (like the TV coverage of Katrina), deal only with the protagonists' choices during the event itself and do not confront "what to do in the next moment." The Japanese anime productions, on the other hand, begin their stories after the apocalypse has already occurred. In its chaotic, toxic, dystopic aftermath, the protagonists are immediately thrust into some form of leadership as a result of the limits of traditional authority. The heroes and heroines that emerge are typically young adults in a liminal state between losing their innocence and gaining a sense of their own power. Unlike the authorities or older citizens, who are more invested in previous regimes and ideologies, they can imagine a future distinct from the past.

In his online article "Recovering New Orleans," Thomas Campanella states that after any significant disaster there is often a certain degree of "regressive resilience," meaning that the citizenry immediately want to resurrect exactly what was there before, including the city's social order and political culture: "Just as the built environment is commonly reconstituted as before, the power structure and social hierarchy of a city can quickly replicate itself in the wake of a catastrophe. Divisive pre-disaster inequalities and injustices are resilient, too."[12] Eventually, though, the impulse to repeat may be reconsidered, when new information is literally unearthed from the destruction itself. Citing the work of Diane Davis on the 1985 Mexico City earthquake, Campanella notes that "the tremors not only shook up the city's buildings but the very legitimacy of the political system and its leadership," exposing "a raft of official corruption and abuses." Once they'd collapsed, new government buildings were found to be of substandard construction quality, and exposed cellars

10 See also *Origin: Spirits of the Past,* dir. Keiichi Sugiyama, 2006. Interestingly, in contrast to American apocalyptic films, where a middle-class male—that is, the common man—is often thrust into saving the world, the main heroes in Asian anime often have an implied connection to traditional power—the murdered father of Princess Nausicaä, the heroine of *Nausicaä of the Valley of the Wind,* was king of their village; the mother of Deunan Knute, the heroine of *Appleseed*, was the country's most important scientist, prior to being killed by a government soldier.

11 Thomas J. Campanella, "Recovering New Orleans," September 21, 2005, planetizen.com/node/17448. See also the related book edited by Campanella and Lawrence J. Vale, *The Resilient City: How Modern Cities Recover from Disaster* (Oxford: Oxford University Press, 2005).

12 Campanella, "Recovering New Orleans."

of ruined police stations "contained evidence of torture. These revelations galvanized the capital's 'resilient citizens' to demand political accountability and a reordering of reconstruction priorities."[13]

The events of Katrina as revealed by the 24–7 media feeds offered a more explicit indictment of impotent political authority, humanity's vain attempt to control nature, and the persistent divisions of society based on race and class than anything film directors in either Tokyo or Hollywood have yet imagined for the screen. Katrina exposed the fact that our beliefs about nature, technology, and authority can in fact be as destructive as nature itself, by indirectly creating what economists refer to as a set of negative externalities.

Traditionally, cornucopian free-market economists and demographers have argued that "the dynamism of capitalist economies will generate solutions to environmental problems as they arise and that increases in population eventually will produce the wealth needed to pay for environmental improvements."[14] After a number of catastrophes, from the toxic dumping at Love Canal in the 1970s to present-day events such as Katrina, our culture has been forced to adopt a more consequential logic. As Paul Krugman explains:

> The logic of basic economics says that we should try to achieve social goals through aftermarket interventions. That is, we should let markets do their job, making efficient use of the nation's resources, then utilize taxes and transfers to help those whom the market passes by. But what if a deal between consenting adults imposes cost on people who are not a part of the exchange? When there are negative externalities—costs that economic actors impose on others without paying a price for their actions—any presumption that the market economy, left to its own devices, will do the right thing goes out the window.[15]

In our more industrial landscapes, such as New Orleans, where the control of nature is exercised relatively uncritically for the sake of our larger cultural and economic progress, there can be clear consequences for those affected when things fail as they did during Katrina.

The issue is not whether New Orleans is worth the hundreds of billions of dollars we have collectively spent since Katrina to rebuild the city, or whether that expense can be justified through the logic of capitalist risk. Rather, the issue is the terms by which the city protects itself going forward. A choice now has to be made as to whether to use public and private funds to become more resilient (by embracing new technology as well as planning strategies which are in better balance with the

13 Ibid.

14 Garrard, *Ecocriticism*, 17.

15 Krugman, "Building a Green Economy," 36.

inevitable cycles of nature) or to remain resistant toward adopting such strategies (and thus continue to expose the city to equivalent future disasters due to miscalculation and human error).

RESILIENT OR RESISTANT

> To the average child of the United States in the present day Nature is indeed a great mystery, not insofar as it is incomprehensible but insofar as it is virtually nonexistent to his perceptions.
>
> —Harold Fromm[16]

Although much of New Orleans looks verdant and lush, and the Big Easy is an impressive force of nature in its own right, the landscape of New Orleans is generally considered more a resource than a life source. Built on a malarial swamp in the delta of our nation's most powerful and mercurial river, the city in its dealings with nature has always been prone to extremes as a tactical necessity. New Orleans has always been more susceptible to the literal ebbs and flows of the natural world than most cities. Humanity's control of nature and presumed rank at the top of the natural order has been one of the central tenants of the whole of Western culture over millennia, and New Orleans pre-Katrina provides one of the world's most complete historical examples of this position. The ideological structures that help rationalize the extreme control of nature are kin to the ideological structures that support the culturally rich, technologically facilitated, and socially layered city of New Orleans itself.

Jhan Hochman points out that in the most general sense, living close to nature has been typically seen as "a kind of poverty"; we view "nature as the past" or as evidence of a certain "immaturity of culture."[17] In a vast number of cultural representations (from millennium-old religious parchments to contemporary popular pulp), women, youths, and people of color are often rendered as being closer to nature and lower in the social order of things. Not only is this type of classification reinforced in many visual narratives, it is also deeply established even in our colloquial language, through well-worn binaries categorizing, for example, primitive versus advanced cultures, the lower versus the upper classes, and our mother earth versus our celestial father. Hochman states,

> Because world nature is routinely and reductively constructed as unconscious raw material, any entity associated with nature stands to lose its rights to ethical culture and gain admittance into culture only or primarily as a material, aesthetic, recreational, or suffering

16 Harold Fromm, "From Transcendence to Obsolescence: A Route Map," *The Ecocriticism Reader*, Cheryll Glotfelty and Harold Fromm, eds., (Athens, GA: University of Georgia Press, 1996), 33.

17 Jhan Hochman, *Green Cultural Studies: Nature in Film, Novel, and Theory* (Moscow, ID: University of Idaho Press, 1998), 7.

David Metraux

Nature as both female and negative

> object. People of color, women, the lower classes, and youth, all reduced to labor, gain admittance into culture predominately as means to another's profit and leisure.[18]

There is equal evidence that leftist/Marxist/communist constituents have developed just as poor an environmental record as the right, often justifying industrialization and exploitation of the land as "a necessary step for proletarian liberation."[19] Thus, it is clear that the issue is not limited to any one period of time or single political ideology in New Orleans or in the United States or any other Western nation.[20]

As Greg Garrard suggests, as we move forward, "Environmental problems can not be clearly divorced from things more usually defined as social problems, such as poor housing or lack of clean water."[21] Nature worldwide is now caught between satisfying our economic desires and providing for our biological needs. Karl Marx stated in the nineteenth century that every culture sees its land according to its own desires; today, we are forced to see something more complicated than past societies have seen. Like no other generation before us, we must now view nature not only as property but also, once more, as part of us: a vessel made of the same matter from which we are created. In a text written before World

18 Hochman, *Green Cultural Studies*, 8.

19 For a discussion of the limitations and blind spots of both left and right politics in their relation to the environment, see Kate Soper, *What Is Nature?* (London: Wiley-Blackwell, 1995).

20 Simone Birgitt Hartmann, "Feminist and Postcolonial Perspectives on Ecocriticism," in *Nature in Literary and Cultural Studies: Transatlantic Conversations on Ecocriticism,* Catrin Gersdorf and Sylvia Mayer, eds., (Amsterdam: Rodopi, 2006), 96.

21 See Garrard, *Ecocriticism*, 28–29 and 167, discussing how environmental groups such as Worldwatch aim to ensure that the burden of sustainability should not fall disproportionably on the Third World or the underclass.

War II, *Seibutsu no Sekai* ("the world of living things"), Japanese biologist Kinji Imanishi struggled to reconcile the hierarchism of Darwinism with traditional Eastern philosophies and science:

> It may seem incredible that the earth, originally detached from what is now the sun, which further nourished it with light and warmth, gradually developed into the ship filled with passengers ... Part of the earth became the materials for the ship and eventually took the form of the ship. The remaining parts became the passengers. Thus the ship did not precede the passengers, nor the passengers the ship. The ship and the passengers originally differentiated from a single thing. Moreover, they did not differentiate haphazardly. The ship became a ship in order to take passengers, and the passengers became passengers in order to board the ship. This is a natural conclusion, as we cannot conceive of the ship without passengers, nor the passengers without the ship ... the various things in this world are in some kind of relationship, and the reason for this is that the world has a structure and a function, which derive from the growth and differentiation from one thing.[22]

Here, man is not made in the image of a god as separate from nature or banished from it, but instead continues to be part of it. The Western theory of evolution is based on a hierarchy of species, but "differentiation" includes the nonliving world as well.

Our society of a half-century later is relatively more accommodating of nature, but we still do not place ourselves in it. We, in fact, do not see nature per se; we see objects that refer to nature. For Garrard, in our current media, "the way the relationship of the viewer to the wildlife is constructed may be highly problematic, narrowing our experience of nature from full sensory, intellectual, and political engagement to a purely visual relation that is further distorted by overemphasis on violence and sex. Nature programming, in other words, may be little better than 'eco-porn.'"[23] One might argue that some of the coverage of Katrina, as a type of return of the repressed dominatrix, was a kind of extension of this way of seeing nature. Now that the storm and its corresponding media furore are spent, and the city's displaced population has not been able to return, a different type of nature has begun to reinstate itself, turning parts of the city into real-time illustrations from a chapter of Alan Weisman's best-selling book *The World Without Us* or images from an episode of the History Channel's documentary *Life After People*.[24]

22 Kinji Imanishi, *A Japanese View of Nature: The World of Living Things*, Pamela J. Asquith, Heita Kawakatsu, Shusuke Yagi, and Hiroyuki Takasaki, trans. (London: Routledge Curzon, 2002), 2.

23 Garrard, *Ecocriticism*, 151.

24 Alan Weisman, *The World Without Us* (New York: Thomas Dunne Books, 2007); *Life After People*, History Channel, 2008.

Interestingly, rather than dismissing or denying this return of nature entirely—on both the conceptual and practical level—some groups in New Orleans, as well as whole communities, such as Greensburg, Kansas, devastated in 2007 by an F-5 tornado, and Detroit, Michigan, devastated by a shift in our economic base, have begun to redefine prosperity as dependent on a more sustainable notion of ecology.[25] This is a radical change in the perception of ecology, which has been more typically couched as the politics of "no" or, as Andrew Ross suggests, rendered as a politics of restriction that limits economic growth.[26] The entire town of Greensburg was able to rally around this new perception, but a larger city, such as New Orleans, rallies mainly at the grassroots, neighborhood level. Wayne Curtis wrote in the *Atlantic* about the rebuilding:

> In the absence of strong central leadership, the rebuilding has atomized into a series of independent neighborhood projects. And this has turned New Orleans—moist, hot, with a fecund substrate that seems to allow almost anything to propagate—into something of a petri dish for ideas about housing and urban life. An assortment of foundations, church groups, academics, corporate titans, Hollywood celebrities, young people with big ideas, and architects on a mission have been working independently to rebuild the city's neighborhoods, all wholly unconcerned about the missing master plan. It's at once exhilarating and frightening to behold.[27]

Yet when one looks beyond these individual interventions, seeking to find a more collective response, any examples of such experimentation at a broader cultural level are hard to find.

Ambitious attempts to move past the "regressive resilience" of rebuilding have, for the most part, failed or been rejected. One example is the city's early negative reaction to the Urban Land Institute's report soon after the storm. This report proposed returning "its most devastated low-lying areas to wetlands and concentrating more housing on higher ground," in order to "among other things, reduce the burden on the levees and canals that protect the city from storms."[28] As reported four years later by *New York Times* architectural critic Nicolai Ouroussoff, the local community became upset at the necessary relocation of its residents:

> The idea of adjusting the city's footprint in any way became politically toxic, and Mayor C. Ray Nagin quickly made it clear that the city's

25 See summaries of sustainable post-tornado rebuilding efforts in Greensburg, Kansas, greensburggreentown.org and planetgreen.discovery.com.

26 Quoted by Hochman in *Green Cultural Studies*, 11.

27 Wayne Curtis, "Houses of the Future," *The Atlantic*, November 2009.

28 Quoted in Nicolai Ouroussoff, "Reinventing America's Cities: The Time Is Now," *New York Times*, March 29, 2009.

redevelopment would be left in the hands of private interests ... many of the city's low-lying areas are as barren now as they were a week after the storm. And it's still possible to imagine a more sustainable, socially inclusive city, one that could serve as a model as powerful and far-reaching as the American subdivisions of the 1950s. For that to happen, however, a range of government agencies would need to work together to come up with a more coordinated plan.[29]

The truth of the matter is that there are many cities worldwide that have been trying to recover from the decline of their population and their economy for decades longer than has New Orleans. Many of these communities have begun to rethink the virtues of scaling down and shifting the metrics of long-term sustainable success to a basis not of population growth but of quality of life, following the "tenets of the burgeoning, European-born Shrinking Cities movement. The idea: If cities can grow in a smart way, they can also shrink smartly."[30]

In a study published in 2009, a coalition of landscape architects, academics, activists, and local institutions attempted to weave together several of the threads discussed here into a plan for the rehabilitation of Pontilly, the adjacent Pontchartrain Park and Gentilly Woods neighborhoods. The joint endeavor of Longue Vue House and Gardens and the Pontilly Disaster Collaborative produced the *Pontchartrain Park + Gentilly Woods Landscape Manual*, a volume of speculative interventions for this historic area of the city. The manual focused on planning for future resiliency against another Katrina; reinstating nature in the foreground of New Orleanians' daily lives; and strategically aligning traditional restoration priorities with economic incentives geared toward long-term stability.[31]

The manual points out that Pontilly not only is emblematic of New Orleans neighborhood development in general but also stands as a clear example of the twentieth century's faith in technological progress, as well as our determination to control nature. It is a classic example of American postwar, urban open-space design for low-density suburban landscapes, as well as a national example of segregation-era progressivism. In the coalition's view, rehabilitation is going to be impossible without change: "Pumps and levees are never infallible, and the infrastructure failures that devastated the low areas of New Orleans could happen again. To reconstruct the area just as before would invite the next disaster." The group proposes simply that "the places that community members value for their image must also act as infrastructure to slow and hold water."[32]

29 Ibid.

30 Haya El Nasser, "As Older Cities Shrink, Some Reinvent Themselves," *USA Today*, December 27, 2006.

31 Jane Wolff and Carol McMichael Reese, eds., *Pontchartrain Park + Gentilly Woods Landscape Manual* (New Orleans: Longue Vue House and Gardens, 2009), 2–4. See also Wolff and Reese's essay in this volume.

32 Ibid., 2.

Design: Whitney Jayne Hoffman Cooper, Robert Reich School of Landscape Architecture, Louisiana State University

Student proposal for a "water explorative island" in Pontchartrain Park, showing the boardwalk from the neighborhood to the outdoor classroom

Within the plan, each house and garden is considered as an autonomous unit that collects water and so mitigates the overall assault on the city's stormwater drainage system and decreases overall flood failures. The group also proposes planting boulevards with mature cypress, which can absorb up to 200 gallons of water daily and would also help mitigate wind damage during storms; redesigning existing infrastructure such as the Dwyer Canal, Pontchartrain Park's historic golf course, and public rights-of-way as water and pedestrian pathways; and the substantial regrading of the local Coghill School as an emergency refugee site for the most extreme future natural disasters. Both at the school and other locations, the landscape would provide a didactic narrative to children and other residents, making clearer the inherent interdependencies between the land and its inhabitants. Seeking a way to incentivize the economic interests to support the ecological, the designers propose that any new "hydrologically sound strategies for landscape rehabilitation may also become ways to argue for insurance and tax abatements. If, for instance, homeowners can demonstrate that their gardens absorb enough water to prevent damage to their houses, they may qualify for lower risk premiums than they would otherwise."[33] Although many of the its proposals were only speculative, the Pontilly landscape manual and similar emerging projects represent in the broadest sense a desire to balance the forward march of human progress with the cyclic temporality of the natural world.

33 Ibid., 5.

THE FOUNDATION OF THE DILEMMA: A CRISIS IN CONCEPTUALIZING TIME

> Postmodernism is what you have when the modernization process is complete and nature is gone for good.
>
> —Fredric Jameson[34]

Apocalyptic events are almost always seen in relationship to time and space, as we have witnessed with 9/11 at Ground Zero. This holds true for Katrina as well. The entire episode has become understood in terms of time and location: when and where the hurricane changed from level 2 to 3 to 4, when it struck the city, how the authorities waited to respond, and so forth. This point was recently illustrated in an NPR story told by David Bianculli about *Treme*, the new HBO series set in New Orleans. He notes that the first thing that you see in the opening sequence are the words *Three Months After*. No more than that is provided to explain the show's context, and no more is necessary.[35] Katrina is to New Orleans as a murder is to the beginning of a noir film; it represents an end and a beginning all in the same shot. And as with any noir film, the "story" that the city creates after Katrina will become the context in which the entire past will be understood. So there is a crisis in New Orleans that, I would argue, transcends the crises of economy and politics: It is the city's relationship to time. If the city can productively solve that, it has the potential to solve the many other questions about its future, including its relationship to nature.

Historically, New Orleans's own sense of its exceptionalism originates from a sense of time quite distinct from that of the rest of the United States. This operates on many levels. First and foremost, there is musical time: The city has always been considered a distinguished place of "origin" for the development of jazz. There is also cyclical time: yearly, the city is deeply tied to a centuries-old religious and secular ritual, Mardi Gras. And there is the special cycle of day and night: After dark, the city becomes more Vegas than the "real," atemporal Vegas, where all your troubles are magically suspended so that you can have the "time of your life."[36] During the day, the city's pace slows down to Big Easy speed, in strong contrast to the hustle and bustle of the rest of urban America. Lastly, and most germanely, the city, unlike most others, has always lived with a much longer cycle, the kind that shapes geography: the time of the next 100-, 200-, or 300-year storm (although, as this paper has argued,

34 Fredric Jameson, *Postmodernism, or, the Cultural Logic of Late Capitalism* (Durham, NC: Duke University Press, 1991), ix.

35 David Bianculli, "*Treme*: A Haunting Snapshot Of Life After Katrina," *Fresh Air*, National Public Radio, April 5, 2010.

36 Michael Sorkin, "Telling Time," in *Anytime*, Cynthia Davidson, ed., (Boston: MIT Press, 1999), 234–41.

Still from *The Curious Case of Benjamin Button*

Still from *Home*

a strong belief in technology largely muffled the ticking of this time bomb for most of the city's recent history).

When Katrina struck, any real sense of time in the city stopped somewhat literally, a condition depicted in several popular media renditions of New Orleans. It is interesting how consistent this metaphor of "stopped time" became in representing the city after Katrina. Whether in the big-studio film *The Curious Case of Benjamin Button* or the short experimental film *Home* (well known on the festival circuit), the traditional temporality of old New Orleans is wonderfully depicted, showing with great accuracy the city's poetically layered reality organized through an elliptical structure that creates an inseparable connection between the present and the past.[37] Whereas the narrative of *Curious Case* pushes the rewind and forward buttons of time simultaneously, creating a

37 *The Curious Case of Benjamin Button*, dir. David Fincher, 2008; *Home*, dir. Matt Faust, 2008.

Möbius-like flow between then and now, *Home* skillfully intercuts a series of home movies with current footage of a single home destroyed by Katrina to depict that often ineffable axis of time conditioned by recollection. However, the conclusion of each film is strikingly similar, with not an inch of narrative or film supplied to help the viewer imagine the future of the city after the storm. The intentional eerie silence and rupture shown at the end of both is truly haunting and speaks directly to a sense of general crisis on the part of a city unable to imagine its own future as distinct from its past.

Though some residents claim that New Orleans has adopted a "frontier town" spirit since 2005, there are still few official or widespread examples of transformative approaches emerging after the disaster, beyond those demonstrative projects mentioned earlier.[38] There are many reasons why returning to the city might prove difficult for some, yet one has to wonder if going "back" to New Orleans might signify to some going back in time. Katrina unveiled a city that was more complex and multifaceted than perhaps most of the outside world, and even New Orleans, understood or cared to acknowledge. New plans for the city should make use of the Wittgensteinian logic that "what is torn is torn" and emphasize a transformation in understanding. It is hard to imagine the city moving forward without clearly embracing and better representing its spatial, cultural, economic, and temporal diversity, as well as reinstating a more present, less-contained nature—and the diaspora of still unreturned residents—in a more direct way.

Interweaving the city's diachronic (or linear) notion of time and space with a more nuanced concept of synchronic (or simultaneous) time and space would allow the city a means to incorporate a range of simultaneous realities, as well as its vision for the future, within its larger cultural narrative or official history. To do otherwise would be to force the entire city to return to its reduced, unsustainable, race-plagued identity for the sake of luring tourists and maintaining tradition.[39]

One could argue that the temporal DNA of every city worldwide develops out of some particular relationship between these two dimensions, the diachronic and the synchronic. New Orleans pre-Katrina was almost solely diachronic in that the city prioritized a singular historically time-based narrative (often ignoring its synchronic potential), whereas at the other extreme, a city such as Los Angeles has traditionally been much more interested in its synchronic dimension, made up of many concomitant realities (each one mostly about only the present; Los Angeles in fact often seems to ignore its diachronic value by not preserving its historical fabric or planning for the future).

38 Guy Raz interviewing Tom Piazza, author of *City of Refuge*, in "Author: New Orleans Slowly Reclaiming Itself, Katrina and Recovery," on *All Things Considered*, National Public Radio, August 29, 2009; Carrie Kahn, "Population in Flux Redefines New Orleans," *Weekend Edition*, National Public Radio, August 26, 2007.

39 Bernard Tschumi, "DiaSync," *Anytime*, 168–75.

Yet New Orleans has not always reduced its narrative to mainly the diachronic thread. Looking broadly at its past, one can see that the city has always been at its strongest when its synchronic identity has been more present. For example, it was connected to global time in the twentieth century through its energy, entertainment, and sports economies as well as its traditional shipping economy, and in the nineteenth through its very population—in 1850 (unlike in 1950) 40 percent of its very diverse citizens were first-generation immigrants. In fact, the Mississippi was the Internet of its day, making New Orleans one of the first examples of "glocality"—that product of an intense alchemy, which many cities seek, between local character and global reciprocity.[40] Kermit Ruffins, a local musician who appears in *Treme*, said on a recent NPR program that he feels rooted when he plays his trumpet in Congo Square, the plaza where slaves once gathered on Sundays to eat, play drums, and dance: "Congo Square is the heartbeat of America as far as I'm concerned."[41] Vintage postcards of the fifty states commonly show, in place of location names, icons of invention, history, and industry—an oil rig for Oklahoma City, a movie camera for Los Angeles, the Liberty Bell for Philadelphia, an automobile for Detroit— and the iconic jazz musician is almost always the metonym for the city of New Orleans, suggesting that historically, at least, the city was connected to the rest of country, acting as one node of many, by which any American might access a unique thread of history, geography, and progressive and creative culture.

In the recent decades prior to Katrina, though, New Orleans was struggling to keep that synchronic dimension in play. Once disaster struck, this disconnection became even more palpable—prompting one New Orleans official when interviewed in a documentary short about life after Katrina to remind the viewers that the people down there were still part of America.[42] And in a more troubling example, this sense of New Orleans being out of "sync" relative to other places was problematically inferred during the media coverage during Katrina, when people leaving the city were commonly called "refugees" rather than "evacuees," as if these victims were from another place and time altogether.[43]

Since Katrina, however, a very distinctly new "cognitive map" of the city has begun to emerge, one that is much more diverse, spontaneous, and inclusive. In the unscripted use of the Internet during the storm to connect citizens to each other outside the traditional channels of authority,

40 Andrew Curtis, a colleague who has done extensive work in New Orleans on disease prevention, notes that one has to remember that not all synchronicity is positive: it also plays a role in the spreading of viruses and other problems provoked by global flows of people and products.

41 Deborah Elliot, "New Orleans Locals Put Their Stamp On HBO's *Treme*," *Morning Edition*, National Public Radio, April 8, 2010.

42 "After Katrina: Rebuilding St. Bernard Parish," dir. Adam Finberg, 2006, in the DVD *The Katrina Experience: The Power of Culture to Heal*, Full Frame Documentary Film Festival and IndiPix, 2006.

43 Mike Pesca, "Are Katrina's Victims 'Refugees' or Evacuees?" *Day to Day*, National Public Radio, September 5, 2006.

in the periodic practice of collective representation through the city's distinct religious leaders working together on common issues, there are signs that the city has begun to embrace a "both/and" identity rather than "either/or" dichotomy. In this model, the parts can make up a sense of the whole, and the past and future can coexist more dynamically in relation to their simultaneous presences. In essence, the city's vision of itself has the potential to become organized as more of a Google-like search-engine structure rather than remaining a singular, grand historical narrative.

The festival Prospect.1 New Orleans is another interesting example of this new cognitive mapping of the city's synchronic potential. In 2008, its inaugural year, the biennial dispersed art throughout the city instead of centralizing it in one tourist spot in the French Quarter or in the concentrated arts enclave along Julia Street in the central business district. Dan Cameron, the festival's founder and artistic director, selected eighty-one local, national, and international artists, representing thirty-six countries and five continents. The work was exhibited in twenty-four locations throughout the city, which importantly and chiefly included the more diverse and often unvisited neighborhoods of New Orleans. This citywide show represented the largest biennial of international contemporary art ever organized in the United States, with 42,000 individual visitors, and produced an estimated $23 million in general economic activity between November 2008 and January 2009.[44]

The interactive social media site Open Sound New Orleans, which displays voices, music, and ambient noises found across the city on a collective map, is a similar organization that has also emerged since Katrina. Under the direction of Heather Booth and Jacob Brancasi, the organization provides the technology for the citizens of New Orleans to represent themselves through both sound and location. By tying the particular sounds of each community to a map, this project in many ways clearly advocates a more synchronic, participatory vision of New Orleans, encouraging people to become involved in creating a more cognitive understanding of their city's diversity and simultaneous presentness.[45] Through articulating such new synchronic impulses and sharing them collectively, the project offers the promise of a future city where citizens are stronger agents of their own fate and the acceptance of their diversity is more visible.

As for the larger-scale official planning strategies being proposed for the city, it is my hope that this attitude or shift in our view of space and time could lead to new ways of envisioning and programming tomorrow's New Orleans, self-consciously creating a more productive balance between historical linearity and present simultaneity, progressive development and cyclical nature, global connection and local autonomy. New catalytic programs should be strategically inserted throughout the urban

44 See prospectneworleans.org.
45 See opensoundneworleans.com.

fabric to complement the city's historical dimension. Its intellectual capital, the universities, the health sector, and the arts, should be supported in equal balance with its industrial capital—traditional manufacturing and production and big-box retail development.[46] Public schools, churches, and other program elements that are already naturally dispersed throughout the city should be given new transformative potential through hybrid programming and other appropriate mixed-use strategies, to stand in contrast to the stable urban elements in the historic core. Planners should create distinct places for multiple types of populations, from youth to senior citizens, identified throughout the web of the city, rather than solely focusing on inserting new destinations for tourists.[47]

This both/and attitude is in direct contrast to the apocalyptic mindset, in which all mankind and nature are controlled through a single historical narrative of progressive climactic crises and in which (although we know the end of the story at the beginning and although we win) it isn't paradise on earth. As Greg Garrard writes, "To use the narratological term, [the apocalyptic] is always 'proleptic' ... in this dialectic ... apocalypticism both responds to and produces 'crisis.'"[48] In a city where so much of nature has been shaped by humankind, there is much to do in terms of retooling the city so that both the "ship" and the "passengers" are not forever locked in a game in which to win is actually to lose.

As with "victims" of other past and current social ills such as racism, misogyny, and ongoing class division, the only way to achieve redress is for those invested in the rewards of change to dedicate themselves to that progress. There is so much in the news today about the "end of nature," that environmental battle fatigue, or ecological resignation, is in fact one of the most challenging aspects of the latest crisis of global warming, and perhaps in the rebuilding of New Orleans as well.[49] In her article "Afterglow: Chernobyl and the Everyday," Ursula K. Heise states, "The question of how an awareness of environmental deterioration and technological risk can become part of everyday life without leading to apocalyptic despair, reluctant resignation to a new state of normalcy, or bored indifference has become an urgent issue for environmentalists and ecocritics."[50] Building on Frederick Buell's work examining the rising expectation of crisis that emerged during the

46 Edward Glaeser, in his lecture "Reinventing Cities: What Experience of Global Cities Tells Us," delivered at Harvard University on March 9, 2009, stated, "Apart from climate, human capital is one of the best predictors of a city's growth. Cities survive only by adapting their economies to new technologies, and it is human capital that enables cities to adapt successfully to change." See also Richard Florida, "Where the Brains Are," *The Atlantic*, October 2006.

47 For a city like New Orleans, it is probably equally crucial to recognize the many "informal" or below-the-radar economies that operate in the micropopulations and communities not well mapped by standard means such as tax records, census information, residency applications, and public health statistics. Many of these economies are interwoven with other locations outside of New Orleans, creating their own synchronic reality.

48 Garrard, *Ecocriticism*, 86.

49 See Bill McKibben, *The End of Nature* (London: Penguin, 1990).

50 Ursula K. Heise, "Afterglow: Chernobyl and the Everyday," in *Nature in Literary and Cultural Studies Studies: Transatlantic Conversations on Ecocriticism*, Catrin Gersdorf and Sylvia Mayer, eds., (Amsterdam: Rodopi, 2006), 181.

1960s and 70s, Heise argues that from this point on, "People no longer fear environmental disasters in the future so much as they 'dwell in crisis,'" as Buell puts it: that is, they live with an awareness that certain limits in the exploitation of nature have already been exceeded, that past warnings were not heeded, and that slowly risk scenarios surround them on a daily basis.[51]

However, successes give hope. The few projects I have outlined above could become milestones in the road that moves us past the destructive dichotomies of man versus nature or technological progress versus environmental catastrophe. The Greek *apokalypsis* means a disclosure or the lifting of a veil covering something that has been hidden through deception or misguidedness. In this sense, an traumatic event such as Katrina, like the earthquake in Mexico City, is apocalyptic, for it ultimately reveals a great deal about our society as well as our human "nature," offering to all of us a new starting point for alternative approaches.

POSTSCRIPT

On April 20, 2010, the *Deepwater Horizon* drilling rig exploded in the Gulf of Mexico, killing eleven workers and injuring seventeen more. Now better known as the BP oil spill, this ecological and human disaster released almost 5 million barrels of crude oil into the ocean and is considered the largest oil spill in the history of the petroleum industry. While the physical destruction was not within the boundaries of New Orleans per se, there is no doubt of the profound impact on the region economically, emotionally, and, to some, existentially, following so closely on the heels of Katrina. Though much could be added in terms of the relationship between the spill and the arguments stated in this essay, what is most important is to circle back to the simple point introduced at the beginning: These disasters should not be blamed on any one person, party, or company, as it is far more productive to see them as the inevitable consequence of our widely endorsed, several-millennia-old ideology of resourcism, which is supported by a stable set of assumed interrelational hierarchies among different global human groups and nature herself.

Special thanks to my three wonderful USC graduate research scholars, Ashley Margo, April Sommer, and Jennifer Choi, for their help with collecting sources, and to my colleague, Heather Galles, for her opinions and edits.

51 Ibid. Heise is making reference here to Frederick Buell's *From Apocalypse to Way of Life* (New York: Routledge, 2003).

PART II
PLANNING PERSPECTIVES

THE ONCE AND FUTURE NEW ORLEANS OF PLANNERS MILTON MEDARY AND HARLAND BARTHOLOMEW, 1920–1960

CAROL McMICHAEL REESE

Hurricane Katrina struck New Orleans on August 29, 2005, and the flooding that followed forced the wholesale evacuation of the city's residents. It took more than seven weeks to drain the water from the city, and in that period authorities did what they could to prohibit residents from returning. By early October, "look and leave" missions lasting only a few days were allowed, and in later October the checkpoints along major highways were abandoned. As soon as significant numbers of us who had been displaced returned to stay, we began to meet to make plans. We wanted to join forces in rebuilding our lives and our city.

One month after the storm, Mayor Nagin had established the first citywide planning effort, Bring New Orleans Back. In November, BNOB participants held a public conference in collaboration with the Urban Land Institute.[1] Neighborhood organizations that had existed before the storm or had formed in response to the widespread destruction of residential districts also met during these early months of recovery.[2] New Orleans is often described as a city of neighborhoods; many of the neighborhood groups that mobilized post-Katrina became remarkable agents for rehabilitation and change, and they continue in that role today.[3] In our neighborhood forums we planned how schools could be reopened, municipal services reinstituted, health and safety insured, streets repaired, and claims for damages to homes and personal property most rapidly executed. We took part, as we were able or inclined, in citywide recovery planning, such as the mayor's Bring New Orleans Back and the city council's Neighborhoods Rebuilding (Lambert) Plan, which were competi-

1 November 12–15, 2005. "Experts," many from elsewhere, led this conference, which included politicians and citizens. A report on its findings guided the next phase of planning; see Urban Land Institute, *New Orleans, Louisiana: A Strategy for Rebuilding* (Washington, D.C., November 12–18, 2005), uli.org. Consult the timeline in the back matter of this volume for the unfolding of events related to recovery and rebuilding.

2 One of the new groups was the Neighborhoods Planning Network (NPN) now the Neighborhoods Partnership Network, which continues its efforts; seenpnnola.com.

3 The Greater New Orleans Community Data Center defines the boundaries of seventy-two neighborhood statistical areas, based largely on census tracts. The boundaries are drawn for the purpose of "the organization and presentation of data," with the disclaimer, "these are not to be confused with neighborhood association boundaries or boundaries that are self-identified by residents," gnocdc.org.

tive from the outset and ultimately contentious and divisive.[4] Not until the Unified New Orleans Plan (UNOP) process got under way in the spring of 2006, funded by the Rockefeller Foundation, did we truly begin to grapple with the idea that our end goal should be a community vision for the future of the city. The three community congresses that UNOP staged between October 2006 and January 2007 created a general planning ethos. Our recovering neighborhoods would form the building blocks of a holistic plan—what professionals call a comprehensive or master plan. In June 2008, the City Planning Commission selected Goody Clancy of Boston to lead the process of preparing a master plan that would combine previous post-Katrina efforts with further public participation solicited from the city's thirteen planning districts. In August 2010, after two years of discussion and preparation, Goody Clancy presented our "Plan for the 21st Century: New Orleans 2030," and the city council adopted it.[5] It took three more years to develop the Comprehensive Zoning Ordinance (CZO), which dictated land-use regulations to ensure that the plan would be followed. The public meetings to debate the CZO's restrictions and guidelines concluded just as this book was going to print.

In the fall of 2005, desperately picking up the pieces of our lives, few of us imagined that it would take eight years for our community to achieve a master plan, a comprehensive zoning ordinance, and a city charter amendment (passed in November 2008) that positioned the master plan as the ultimate authority guiding land-use decisions. These were the hard-won outcomes of the community planning process that followed the city's devastation, and only time will tell whether they will play a significant role in New Orleans's resurgence. Some of us believe that indeed they will.

David Dixon, who led the City Planning Commission's master-planning process for Goody Clancy, hailed it as a step that had never before been taken in New Orleans. Professional planners, officials, and citizens unaware of New Orleans's urban history greeted our recent comprehensive planning effort as a novel activity, but in fact it was not. In the previous century, the city's civic leaders did in fact try to create a master plan, leaving us with an important—and thought-provoking—legacy. But the history of urban planning in New Orleans has received little professional or scholarly analysis and is generally unrecognized, so earlier work did not inform the plans made for the city's post-Katrina future. Nevertheless, those historic phases of urban planning have much to teach us as we move forward with reconstruction. Above all, we can learn the ways in which planning in Jim Crow–era New Orleans created a separate and unequal urban environment for black and white citizens and bequeathed

4 See Christine Boyer's essay in this part for an analysis of the post-Katrina planning process.

5 "A Plan for the 21st Century: New Orleans 2030," communicationsmgr.com. On the development of the plan and its fundamental principles, see David Dixon's essay in this part.

to us segregated, stigmatized zones that must be understood in their historic complexity in order to be restored and fully incorporated into the life and benefits of the city.

New Orleans's first foray into comprehensive planning began in 1919, spearheaded by commercial elites who hired Philadelphia architect and planner Milton Bennett Medary as an adviser and public relations consultant to those who supported the master-planning effort, though he did not contribute a plan per se. In 1926, following Medary's consultancy and landmark legislation at the federal and state levels that supported the rights of municipalities to regulate land use and to exercise eminent domain, the city hired St. Louis planner Harland Bartholomew to produce an actual master plan.[6]

Bartholomew's first New Orleans consultancy resulted in a comprehensive zoning ordinance and a series of reports intended to be compiled into a master plan. However, the economic effects of the Depression precluded the city's ability to extend its four-year contract with Bartholomew, and a definitive plan was not reached. New Orleans's progressive mayor deLesseps Story "Chep" Morrison (who served four terms, from 1946 to 1961), brought Bartholomew back to New Orleans in 1948, under very different national and local conditions, to renew his efforts to produce a master plan. Once again, Bartholomew produced a series of studies toward the compilation of the plan. Although the city adopted a number of independent "chapters" of Bartholomew's proposal between 1951 and 1954, a complete master plan was never attained. Nevertheless, Bartholomew continued to advise the city about planning matters until the late 1960s and into the mayoral administration of Morrison's successor, Victor Schiro (1961–1970).

Bartholomew's voluminous studies of New Orleans—issued under such headings as Report, Ordinance, Manual, Regulations, Master Plan, Comprehensive Plan, Development Program, and Renewal Program—document not only current conditions in the city but also the urban characteristics that he and his clients envisioned as optimal for its future.

Bartholomew's plans for New Orleans persist as rarely opened artifacts—yellowing volumes in weakening, dusty file boxes on the shelves of libraries and archives.[7] Yet, for all of us, practitioners and laymen alike, they offer valuable insights not only on the key role that Bartholomew's firm played in the national development of the planning profession but also on local intersections of geography, race, economics, and politics in Jim Crow New Orleans. From our early-twenty-first-century perspective,

6 For the most comprehensive overview of Bartholomew's career, see Eldridge Lovelace's *Harland Bartholomew: His Contributions to American Urban Planning* (Urbana, IL: University of Illinois, 1993). Lovelace, a student of Bartholomew's at the University of Illinois, joined the firm immediately after he graduated, in 1935, became a senior partner in 1961, and continued there until his retirement in 1981. His book, however, makes no reference to Bartholomew's work in New Orleans.

7 The firm's archives are preserved in the Department of Special Collections of Washington University Libraries, St. Louis; see the finding aid at library.wustl.edu. Tulane University Libraries and the New Orleans Public Library hold copies of many of the commissioned projects delivered to municipal and private clients in New Orleans.

we must judge them as sadly and shamefully lacking. Relying on pumps and outflow canals, the plans failed to address the inherent dangers of the city's below-sea-level topography. And those prepared between 1926 and 1930, taking for granted the city's Jim Crow traditions, were silent about most of the deplorable human effects of racial oppression and segregation. However, the plans do show that some of Medary's and Bartholomew's clients were at least taking steps toward a more equitable, inclusionary future for all of New Orleans's citizens, no matter how tentative and incomplete those steps appear in hindsight.

In this essay, hoping to interest those who would analyze New Orleans's planning history in order to influence its planning future, I sketch Medary's and Bartholomew's contributions. There are those who assert that knowledge of the urban past may aid in avoiding missteps in the present and future. From this point of view, Medary's recommendations and Bartholomew's plans can serve as critical guides, not only in tracing New Orleans's path from the past to the present, but also in offering exemplars, providing benchmarks, and uncovering pitfalls. It's not too late to scrutinize these documents for every shred of intelligence to be gained. New Orleans's new "Plan for the 21st Century," contains provisions for writing and adopting changes; the plan is designed to evolve, particularly in relation to the Comprehensive Zoning Ordinance completed late in 2013. And subsequent master plans will be prepared. Instead of assigning New Orleans's earlier planning eras to the dustbin of history, we who evolve and create new plans should learn more about them: such knowledge could well transform the process, now and for the future.

RAISING CIVIC AWARENESS OF PLANNING ISSUES AND PROCESSES IN NEW ORLEANS, 1919–1921: MILTON B. MEDARY OF PHILADELPHIA

In 1919, civic leaders in New Orleans decided that the preparation of a comprehensive plan would advance the city's reputation and pave the way for growth in its commercial and industrial sectors. The city planning committee of the New Orleans Association of Commerce, founded in 1913 to promote the city and its port as hospitable environments for business, manufacturing, and shipping, hired Milton Medary in 1919 to advise them, for a fee of $5,000.[8] City planning as a profession was in its infancy, but by the time Medary came to New Orleans, several prominently published examples of urban plans had captured the interest of America's competitive municipalities. The comprehensive McMillan Commission Plan of 1902 for Washington, D.C., which envisioned a revitalized Mall at the heart of the national capital and a new metropolitan

8 See Blaine A. Brownell, "The Commercial-Civic Elite and City Planning in Atlanta, Memphis, and New Orleans," *Journal of Southern History* 41 (August 1975): 339–68. Medary's consultancy fee of $5,000 would be approximately $57,000 in 2013 dollars.

park system extending beyond the District of Columbia, had been promoted nationally by civic groups through magic-lantern slide shows. In 1909, Daniel Burnham's beautifully illustrated *Plan of Chicago* appeared in a lavish publication.[9] The same year saw the first national conference on city planning, held in Washington, D.C., as well as the first university course on the subject, offered by Frederick Law Olmsted Jr. in Harvard's School of Landscape Architecture. In 1913, the nation's first professorship in civic design was established at the University of Illinois (Urbana-Champaign) for the renowned Charles Mulford Robinson, who had built a national career as a planning consultant on the popularity and strength of his essays and lectures concerning urban improvement. The first issue of the journal *City Plan* appeared in 1915, and the American City Planning Institute was formed in 1917 as a professional organization for those with university training and practical experience.[10]

Prominent urban planners in the first two decades of the twentieth century pursued their commissions based on varied academic preparation and professional practice: Burnham (1846–1912) was an architect, Olmsted (1870–1957) a landscape architect, Robinson (1869–1917) a journalist, and Bartholomew (1889–1989) a civil engineer—he had studied at Rutgers, although he took no degree. Undoubtedly the work that planning consultants had accomplished in other aspiring U.S. cities inspired the New Orleans Association of Commerce to hire an adviser; Robinson had prepared plan reports for Denver and Los Angeles in 1906 and 1907, respectively, and Bartholomew had prepared his first plan for Newark in 1913, while in the employ of Ernest P. Goodrich and George B. Ford. Milton Medary (1874–1929) was not widely known as a planning consultant, and how he came to the attention of the association's committee is unknown. His architectural firm, Zantzinger, Borie, & Medary, was nationally recognized, and he had possibly established local relationships in New Orleans during the time that his firm worked on the 1911 competition for the design of the H. Sophie Newcomb Memorial College for Women (today incorporated in Tulane University's Newcomb-Tulane College). Zantzinger, Borie, & Medary lost the Newcomb commission to James Gamble Rogers, but their entry was judged among the five best of the twenty-seven submissions.[11] By 1919, Medary himself had garnered a number of honors and had become a leading figure in the architectural profession. He joined the board of directors of the American Institute of Architects (AIA) in 1912, and in 1918, he was appointed chair of the U.S. Housing Corporation, which was charged with building housing for war-industry workers. New

9 Daniel H. Burnham and Edward H. Bennett's *Plan of Chicago* (1909), reprinted by Princeton Architectural Press (1996).

10 Jon Peterson, *The Birth of City Planning in the United States, 1840–1917* (Baltimore, MD: Johns Hopkins University Press, 2003).

11 Warren Powers Laird served as consultant for the competition and as a member of the jury, philadelphiabuildings.org.

Orleans greeted him as an "expert" and a "city planning specialist."[12]

Medary's work in New Orleans proceeded in two phases. The research period began in 1919 and continued into 1920. During it, Medary and members of the Association of Commerce studied existing conditions in the city, collecting data about such concerns as population dispersion, land use, and distribution of functional building types. This preliminary phase accorded with what Medary described as the "generally accepted underlying principles of City Planning." Armed with information about the city's demographics, business and industrial districts, transportation networks, and civic amenities, Medary then began to report to the public. On August 22, 1920, the second phase of his consultancy was initiated when he published the first of a year-long series of "papers," newspaper articles that ran to several columns in length and appeared almost weekly, duplicated in the morning and afternoon dailies under different headlines.[13] The multiple publication venues of Medary's articles produced loud echoes of the public campaign to promote a planning enterprise. Medary's first piece appeared in the morning *Times-Picayune* under the banner "New Orleans to Begin Work on City Plan; Gigantic Undertaking Inaugurated Soon, Is Sponsored by Association of Commerce." The afternoon *States* published the same piece under the headline "Plan of Growth to Be Urged Here, Association of Commerce to Open Drive for Planning Board." However, the *States* gave the piece even greater heft, prefacing it with the editorial explanation that New Orleans, the "port market for deposit and exchange of the Mississippi Valley" needed to embark on city planning "to reach the world's new markets of promise in Latin America and the Orient."[14] This preamble also included the text of the Association of Commerce's resolution to pursue city planning in New Orleans through "the passage of any and all laws that may be necessary to put it into effect." The legal implications of comprehensive urban planning were as paramount then as they would be in the post-Katrina planning process a century later.

In the 1920s, New Orleans had to wrest from the state legislature the legal right to enforce zoning laws before a city plan could be put into effect. Clearly, those who paid the piper were the city's business elites,

12 In Philadelphia, Medary was a member of the City Planning Bureau; see Milton B. Medary Jr., "New Orleans Will Benefit from Other Cities' Mistakes," *Times-Picayune*, August 22, 1920, and "Plan of City Growth To Be Urged Here," *States*, August 22, 1920. For biographical information see Sandra L. Tatman, "Zantzinger, Borie, & Medary (fl. 1910–1929)," philadelphiabuildings.org; "Brief Biographies of American Architects Who Died Between 1897 and 1947," sah.org; and Jeffrey S. Eley, "Milton Bennett Medary," thesis for the degree of master of architectural history, University of Virginia, 1982.

13 In 1920, New Orleans's three major newspapers were the *Times-Picayune*, the *New Orleans States*, and a second afternoon journal, the *New Orleans Item*. A scrapbook containing copies of Medary's articles compiled by the Association of Commerce is in the Louisiana Division of the New Orleans Public Library.

14 *Times-Picayune* and *States*, August 22, 1920. See also "N.O. Must Plan to Meet Problems of Modern City Life Says City Planner," *Item*, June 17, 1920, and Meigs O. Frost, "Ounce of Zoning Now Is Worth Millions to N.O.," *Item*, September 5, 1920. Frost, a journalist, wrote a number of columns published in the *Item* further explaining Medary's calls for zoning legislation at the state level and his proposals for managing growth in New Orleans. On the development of the port, see John Wilds, *James W. Porch and the Port of New Orleans* (New Orleans: International Trade Mart, 1984).

but they needed political allies to change state laws on the municipality's "power to police" and right to exercise eminent domain. Medary's articles, therefore, served as campaign literature targeted at voters and their elected representatives.

Medary continued his column-of-sorts through July 1921, with the goal of raising civic consciousness concerning the potential of planning to direct urban development for the benefit of all. Assuming that his public had little knowledge of the subject of municipally supported planning, he discussed the broad array of issues involved. He explained the advantages of zoning for managing land use to ensure the highest possible land values, and he described recent legislation passed by other cities and states that enabled the establishment of zoning districts and building codes, urging New Orleans and Louisiana to follow suit. He continued to make trips to New Orleans during the year that his articles appeared, giving lectures to such civic groups as the Rotary Club and the Housewives League, lectures that he illustrated with magic-lantern slides depicting the "before" and "after" conditions of cities that had engaged in comprehensive planning and enacted zoning laws.[15]

The geographic reach of Medary's articles was expansive and his tone instructive; he sought to make citizens aware of the successful urban planning ventures undertaken elsewhere, citing examples of U.S. cities such as Chicago, Philadelphia, New York, Cincinnati, and Washington, D.C., and of international cities including London, Paris, Rome, and Canberra. Although some of his commentary was generic and could have been published with few changes about other port cities, Medary also wrote of his impressions of New Orleans, gathered on numerous trips, and analyzed the findings of surveys that he and the New Orleans Association of Commerce had undertaken. His prose was strongly boosterish—as the association undoubtedly expected it to be—not only in promoting New Orleans, but also in stating a case for the growth and physical improvement of U.S. cities. The 1920 federal census counted more than 50 percent of U.S. citizens living in cities—a watershed in urban growth—and with a population of just over 387,000, New Orleans was the South's largest city. A prosperous postwar era for U.S. cities seemed to be dawning; it was an opportune time for a concerted effort to enhance New Orleans's regional and national standing through planned growth.

New Orleans was the seventeenth-largest U.S. city. Among the fifty largest it had the fifth-highest land area, at 178 square miles, but the second-lowest population density (the lowest was Los Angeles), an average of 2,175 inhabitants per square mile. Thus, the city of New Orleans—geographically synonymous with Orleans Parish—controlled a relatively vast amount of territory. Much of this terrain was swampy, but the recent expansion of the city's pumping system made urban development and

15 "Civic Beauty Talk by Expert Medary," *Times-Picayune*, February 24, 1921.

densification seem an achievable and lucrative goal.[16] Those businessmen, industrialists, and politicians who stood to gain from the city's growth were undoubtedly receptive to Medary's suggestions about how that growth could be planned to produce the greatest successes and rewards.

Medary's first article espoused the commercial and industrial "upbuilding" of the city through municipally sanctioned planning that would provide for the "comfort and health" of New Orleans citizens, clarify the "confusion" of public and private interests (particularly in terms of unregulated expansion), and propose public improvements in relationship to one another—all in order to achieve "the greatest amount of good for the greatest number as against the material interest of any individual or class."[17] Nevertheless, in the first six months of publication, Medary's articles emphasized transportation issues, presumably because of the Association of Commerce's interest in promoting the movement of goods into and through New Orleans. He addressed rail, highway, street, and river transportation systems to explain how New Orleans might better accommodate commercial transit. He emphasized the urgency of accommodating newly expanding truck transport as well as the construction of Louisiana's first bridge across the Mississippi River, a project then still in the planning stage. His concentration on the free flow of traffic across the city and on the ground connections that linked the city with the region underscored the importance of New Orleans's port and its position at the nexus of the Mississippi and the Gulf of Mexico.

Although Medary's recommendations took into account development endeavors that had been begun or proposed previously, he also offered his clients visionary projections of his own. For Medary, the organization and simplification of rail lines in the city was paramount, and so was their relationship with the nascent highway system. He argued for the grouping of rail lines around two emerging industrial nuclei that were understood to have key roles to play in New Orleans's development: one to the west of the city center, near the site of the planned bridge, and the other to the east of the city, near the canal then under construction to link the Mississippi River with Lake Pontchartrain.[18] Another defining

16 On the development of New Orleans's drainage and flood-control systems in the early twentieth century, see Craig E. Colten, *An Unnatural Metropolis: Wresting New Orleans from Nature* (Baton Rouge, LA: Louisiana State University Press, 2005). Colten deals provocatively with the inequitable distribution of drainage, sewerage, and water systems in terms of the city's racial geography.

17 Milton Medary, "New Orleans Will Benefit from Other Cities' Mistakes." See also Medary, "Getting Ready for the City of the Future, First Zoning Step Is To Map All Data," *Times-Picayune*, September 12, 1920: "The Association of Commerce of the city of New Orleans has been at work on the preparation of these data for more than a year and now has completed a series of maps and diagrams and has compiled and tabulated information showing conditions as they exist in the city at the present time."

18 Both projects were authorized by the state in 1916. The Huey P. Long Bridge, in Jefferson Parish near the Harahan railroad yards, opened in 1935. The Industrial Canal, located in the Ninth Ward of Orleans Parish, opened in 1923. Its later connections with the newer Gulf Intracoastal Waterway and the Mississippi River Gulf Outlet proved catastrophic for tangential neighborhoods when the storm surge propelled by Hurricane Katrina led to breaches in the canal's floodwalls and the subsequent flooding of huge sections of the Upper (upriver) and Lower (downriver) Ninth wards. More lives were lost in the Lower Ninth Ward than anywhere else in the city.

aspect of Medary's traffic and transit planning was his recommendation for the construction of a main passenger terminal in the Central Business District, a "union" railroad station in the urban discourse of the early twentieth century. Medary and his clients assumed that such a project would, in turn, create opportunities for building an impressive new node of civic structures. Indeed, when plans for the Union Station and civic center were realized in the 1950s under deLesseps Morrison's mayoralty with federal urban renewal funds, Medary's outline for the improvement of the CBD materialized. However, although his clients embraced some of his suggestions, others, such as his proposal for an elevated street railway, failed to gain proponents.

Despite Medary's insistence in his first paper that comprehensive planning would benefit all New Orleanians, he did not address the social conditions in the city that comprehensive planning might ameliorate until March 1921, seven months after his series began. In "Suburban Areas Orleans Problem," he decried the deleterious effects of overcrowding and argued that planned, controlled residential expansion could prevent them. In his estimation, the passage of building codes limiting population per acre would discourage real estate speculation predicated on increased density in new districts and preserve the city's "open gardens and trees ... what is best in older districts." Addressing new residential developments in "outlying districts," Medary described two distinct types: those that might be built near industrial zones, to provide housing giving workers close proximity to jobs, and those in more exclusively suburban residential zones—that is, areas lacking industry. Both types of districts were to include "local centers" as venues for commerce, recreation, culture, and worship, and they were to be connected to other commercial, recreational, and civic nodal points by means of a planned network of streets.[19] Medary's suggested inclusion of these centers in neighborhood developments would become standard U.S. planning practice, promoted especially by architect and planner Clarence Perry (1872–1944).[20] In the New Orleans of the early 1920s, however, the implementation of such a proposal across the city's social spectrum was limited by segregationist attitudes and practices. For example, developers of new residential sections for whites along the lakefront, which was ripe for development, designed landscapes with curving streets and neighborhood recreational areas, but developers of new subdivisions for blacks offered lots in gridded blocks at the far reaches of the city limits, and included no neighborhood amenities.[21]

---

19 Medary, "Suburban Areas Orleans Problem," *States*, March 6, 1921.

20 See excerpts from Perry's "The Neighborhood Unit: A Scheme of Arrangement for the Family-Life Community" (1929) published in *The City Reader*, Richard T. LeGates and Frederic Stout, eds. (New York: Routledge, 2011, 5th ed.), 488–98.

21 See Harland Bartholomew, "Prosperity through Protection, New Orleans," a report for the Board of Commissioners of the New Orleans Levee District, May 15, 1928. In 1920, there were 100,930 African Americans in New Orleans, 26.1 percent of the city's population.

Not until he had been writing his column for nine months did Medary take up what he termed the housing problem:

> The term "housing" which has come into general use is unfortunate and has a sinister sound, suggesting something in common with the terms employed in connection with commercial and industrial commodities ... suggests the mere finding of space and shelter and the human aspect of the problem is not implied, although the individual home is the cradle and nursery of the whole population of the country and of the succeeding generation, and cannot fail to have a vital influence upon the morale of the nation as a whole ... It has been a problem from time immemorial in old centers and much legislation, known as housing legislation, has been advocated and some of it enacted with the hope of establishing some minimum standards below which living conditions should not be permitted to descend ... Very little housing legislation in the past, however, has interested the public as a whole, and it has rarely been the subject of newspaper discussion ... Treated purely as an economic problem, the housing situation must be traced back to the use of the land on which houses are built ... The individual owning the land may crowd it to almost any density without being responsible for the human product. Housing, therefore, becomes a community problem and a national problem, for the community and the nation are vitally interested in the problem which represents the next generation of American citizenship.[22]

In the column that followed, Medary described slum clearance as a solution for dealing with the community sanitation issues and health risks posed by crowded tenement conditions, citing such an undertaking in London as an example. But he failed to carry through the emphasis on the human element of his previous article, for he offered no solution for rehousing those displaced in the slum clearance process.[23] From 1919 to 1930, when Medary and Bartholomew served as consultants, the most deplorable slums in New Orleans were in areas directly adjacent to the Central Business District, in neighborhoods that Mayor Morrison would redevelop for a new civic center, and in the district "back of town" known as Central City.[24]

Medary explicitly addressed the issue of race in New Orleans's master-planning enterprise only as his consultancy was drawing to a close, in

22 Medary, "Expert Discusses Housing Problem," *States*, May 8, 1921.

23 Medary, "Zoning Works to Prevent Overcrowding," *Times-Picayune*, and "Zoning Prevents Home Crowding," *States*, both published May 15, 1921.

24 On post-Katrina rebuilding in Central City, see Bradford Powers's essay on the Jericho Road housing initiative (Part III) and Laura Kurgan's essay on the justice reinvestment proposal (Part VII). The area in which the Central City neighborhood developed was swampy, and in the mid nineteenth century, it became home to free persons of color as well as recently freed slaves; see Richard Campanella, *Geographies of New Orleans, Urban Fabrics before the Storm* (Lafayette, LA: University of Louisiana, 2006), 309–10.

July 1921, when he published an article on recreational facilities, "Park Facilities for Workers Held N.O. Need, This Is Particularly True in Case of Negro Population, Medary Says." Medary's tacit agreement with segregation policies, which established separate parks for "both white and colored population," permeated his piece, but he stressed the paucity of park space for the latter group: "There is one park only for the colored race, one square in area, The Thomy Lafon Park." Although he praised New Orleans's larger parks (whose golf courses and other recreational facilities were not open to blacks), he urged the distribution of smaller parks "for the recreation of the large number of workers in the city." He made no specific recommendations about establishing new parks for black citizens, but he urged that the park system, which had been proposed in 1920 by the Park and Parkway Extension Committee, "should not be planned in final form without first planning to meet the needs of the whole city by providing such additional parks and open spaces as are needed to proportion park facilities to the whole population in its present and future distribution ..."[25] It is unclear whether by proportional distribution Medary meant an aggregate appraisal of the population—white and black—in its citywide geographic dispersal or the particulate analysis of racial clusters in neighborhoods. We will likely never know Medary's personal position regarding civic equality for blacks or have any inkling of client discussions he might have had in Jim Crow New Orleans. Nonetheless, in this article he seems to have taken a stand, however veiled, for some sort of racial equity in urban planning.

In his writings for the papers, Medary spoke most directly to whites, because in that segregationist period the dailies that published them represented New Orleans's white community. Not until the *Louisiana Weekly* began publication in 1925 did the black community have its own daily, in which the issues that Medary's planning series raised could at least be aired with the interests of a black readership and electorate in mind.[26] African Americans would not find actual seats at the tables of civic power in New Orleans for several more decades.

The lone existence of Thomy Lafon Park, which Medary noted in his commentary, and the subsequent history of its development in the Central City neighborhood are instructive for those who are working today to break down New Orleans's enclaves of economic and racial segregation.[27] One must trace the 150-year social marginalization of Central City to understand the intractability of its downward spiral over generations and the difficulties that planners now face in proposing solutions. The

25 Medary, *Item*, July 3, 1921.

26 Beginning in 1862, a number of black newspapers were founded in New Orleans but they were relatively short-lived; of these, the *Weekly Louisianan* had the longest run, 1872–1882; lib.lsu.edu. The *Louisiana Weekly* continues publication.

27 Thomy Lafon Park was inaugurated on August 16, 1915, "New Orleans Parks and Squares, Openings, Name Changes, Etc.," City Archives, New Orleans Public Library, nutrias.org.

district lies below sea level, and New Orleans's rainy subtropical climate made stormwater flooding a frequent problem there until the early twentieth century, when the city's pumping system was installed. In the nineteenth century, this disadvantageous topographical condition produced low land values; this was where the city established Locust Grove Cemeteries 1 and 2 for indigents in 1859 and 1876, respectively, in an area bounded by Sixth, Magnolia, Seventh, and Locust (now Robertson) streets. The city remedied this unwise decision in 1879, replacing Locust Grove, which had become known as the burial place for indigent blacks, with the new Holt cemetery on City Park Avenue, along the higher ground of Metairie Ridge.[28] The old cemetery site was then open for development, and in 1905, the city built an elementary school for blacks at Seventh and Locust, naming it in honor of Thomy Lafon, a free man of color who had amassed a substantial fortune in business and real estate, which he invested philanthropically in educational, medical, and social service institutions.[29] The siting of Thomy Lafon School exemplified Jim Crow–era attitudes and development practices, which stigmatized various urban locales as being "for Negroes." In 1915, the city underscored the racial profile of Central City by opening Thomy Lafon Park, adjacent to the school at Sixth and Magnolia streets. In 1941, the Thomy Lafon School became the center of the Magnolia public housing project, also for blacks, which was developed according to the prevailing superblock concept, with traffic routed around the complex. In this way, the school and the residential community that it served were emphatically isolated from white New Orleans.

In 1954, during the mayoralty of deLesseps Morrison, the old Lafon School was replaced by a new school; its architects, the New Orleans firm Curtis and Davis, won a national award for the design.[30] This architecturally distinguished building should have brought some measure of civic distinction to the deteriorating neighborhood; instead, it was engulfed by the bitter struggle to end school segregation and by the aura of poverty, degradation, and crime that settled on the Magnolia (later C.J. Peete) complex and all the rest of New Orleans's public housing, which was shamefully administered by the Housing Authority of New Orleans. HANO demolished some sections of C.J. Peete in 1998, but when Katrina struck in 2005, rebuilding had not yet begun. After the storm, led by

28 See Leonard V. Huber, "New Orleans Cemeteries: A Brief History," in *New Orleans Architecture: Volume III, The Cemeteries*, ed. Mary Louise Christovich (Gretna, LA: Pelican, 1974), 60.

29 On Thomy Lafon, see the description of "African Americans in New Orleans: *Les Gens de Couleur Libres*," an exhibition mounted in the Louisiana Division of the New Orleans Public Library in 1999, nutrias.org.

30 In the 1930s, Nathaniel Curtis led New Orleans's design professionals in recognizing the desperate housing needs of the city's poor and offering architectural solutions; see his papers "Slum Clearance" (1935) and "An Architect Looks at Housing" (1938) in the Nathaniel Curtis Collection, record 5, folders 5–8, Louisiana Research Collection, Special Collections, Howard-Tilton Memorial Library, Tulane University. The school received an American Institute of Architects (AIA) Honor Award.

HUD and supported by local prejudice, national and local powers that favored the shuttering of most of New Orleans's public housing triumphed. The sturdy brick C.J. Peete complex was demolished, and the 1,400 units that it had contained at its maximum size were replaced by 460. These were built in traditional New Orleans architectural styles and met Hope VI, New Urbanist guidelines for a mixture of units to be offered at both subsidized and market rates.[31]

Meanwhile, the architecturally—and socially—significant Thomy Lafon School at the center of C.J. Peete (renamed and rebranded as Harmony Oaks) was assailed by forces lobbying for the reconfiguration of New Orleans's embattled and underperforming public schools. Ironically, historical research undertaken in an effort to preserve the school, which was eligible for National Register listing, revealed that not all of the bodies interred in the Locust Grove cemeteries had been removed before the original Lafon School was built. So in 2011 the demolition proceeded, because contemporary Louisiana law prohibits inconsistent use of former cemetery sites, and it was determined that the school, if preserved, could not be reopened and that the only permissible use of the site would be for a park.[32] Theoretically, the new mixed-income residences of Harmony Oaks will bring this section of Central City more fully into the civic circle of New Orleans.[33] Moreover, the post-Katrina master plan potentially enhances the area's future by linking it with newly configured commercial corridors, recreational sites, and civic nodes.

The approach to master planning taken in post-Katrina New Orleans has been an altogether more holistic and balanced one than that which Medary advocated almost a century ago. In the scant attention that he paid to issues of racial inequity, he mirrored the prevailing social ethos of the majority of those who held power in the city. In his focus on transportation planning and zoning legislation, he was likely responding to the needs that his clients expressed. Fulfilling the mission at hand, he emphasized New Orleans's image as a machine for commerce and produc-

31 The Magnolia complex was also familiarly known as Nolia. Its subsequent namesake, Cleveland Joseph Peete, managed the complex from 1952 to 1978. On Harmony Oaks, see Katy Reckdahl, "New C.J. Peete Not as Social, Some Residents Say," *Times-Picayune*, August 21, 2011, NOLA.com; "Then and Now, a Run Down of the Projects," April 18, 2011, noprojects.blogspot.com; and Doug MacCash, "Harmony Oaks Apartments, at a Glance," *Times-Picayune*, February 13, 2011.

32 Raised on piers, Thomy Lafon School did not flood after Katrina, but it suffered extensive wind and water penetration damage. The acts affecting the disposition of the school are the Louisiana Unmarked Burial Sites Preservation Act and the Louisiana Cemeteries Act; see Lindsey Derrington, "Thomy Lafon Headed for Demolition; Hope Remains for Salvage and Documentation," April 12, 2010, docomomo-nola.blogspot.com.

33 Post-Katrina redevelopment strategies for remaking the city's troubled public housing followed those that HUD and HANO undertook before the storm and resulted in the similar, disturbing outcome of a low replacement rate for fully subsidized units. Troubling issues remain for New Orleans's former public housing projects "under reconstruction": (1) the displacement of residents who lived in them before the storm and now reside outside of New Orleans or elsewhere in the city (in Section 8 housing, for example), and (2) the downsizing of the number of subsidized, below-market-rate units (including both public housing and low-income units) available to economically stressed citizens. In the case of Harmony Oaks, by 2011, only 15 percent of the households residing before Katrina in the old C.J. Peete had returned and only 193 of the 460 new units were characterized as public housing.

tion, but largely neglected consideration of urban aesthetics and civic amenities such as the beautification of the city's lake- and waterfronts, the hallmarks of the City Beautiful plans that Daniel Burnham and Charles Mulford Robinson had published. For Medary's clients, the demands of business and industry were paramount.[34]

LEGALITIES AND POLITICS OF PLANNING IN NEW ORLEANS, 1918–1926

Given Medary's success as an architect, it does seem curious that he concentrated his efforts on the rhetoric of his weekly "papers" and did not produce a handsomely illustrated report or design portfolio—work products that the pioneers of U.S. urban planning such as Robinson and Burnham routinely prepared.[35] In the rapidly expanding field of postwar planning, Medary and his New Orleans clients may well have asked themselves what forms the recommendations of a planning consultant should best take. The decision of New Orleans planning advocates to invest initially in a public relations campaign was undoubtedly politically strategic. In Louisiana, political pressure to give local zoning decisions the force of law resulted in the passage in 1918 of the state's first zoning enabling act, Act 27, and so Medary and his clients could foresee an increasingly hospitable environment for the zoning measures on which Medary's recommendations depended. Act 27 faced legal challenges, but it was further supported by a provision in the new state constitution of 1921, passed on June 18 while Medary's articles were appearing. In 1923, the act was strengthened by a court decision in its favor. Also in that year, New Orleans's Commission Council created the City Planning and Zoning Commission, whose role was to serve as official adviser to the council on planning and zoning matters.[36] Both of these newly adopted functions of municipal government were reinforced in 1926 with the passage of two acts in the Louisiana legislature: Act 240, the State Zoning Enabling Act, and Act 305, the City Planning Enabling Act. The latter gave municipalities the authority to establish planning commis-

34 Following Medary's consultancy in New Orleans, President Harding named him to the U.S. Commission of Fine Arts, on which he served from 1922 to 1927, and in 1928, he published "The Aesthetic Value of City Planning in the National Capital." This essay appeared in a report of the National Conference on City Planning titled *The Development of the National Capital and Its Environs* (Philadelphia: Fell, 1928). Medary also served as president of the AIA from 1926 to 1928, and shortly before his death the organization awarded him its Gold Medal for his 1927 design of the Bok Tower in Mountain Lake Sanctuary (today Bok Tower Gardens), Lake Wales, Florida.

35 See, for example, Charles Mulford Robinson, *The City Beautiful: Report of the Municipal Art Commission for the City of Los Angeles, California* (1909).

36 Act 27 of 1918 gave municipalities with populations of more than 50,000 the authority "to define and regulate the kind, style and manner of construction of buildings and other edifices which may be erected on certain designated streets and thoroughfares and to permit or prohibit the establishment and operation of businesses and trades within designated limits." The Louisiana constitution of 1921 contained the provision "All municipalities are authorized to zone their territory; to create residential, commercial and industrial districts, and to prohibit the establishment of places of business in residential districts." See Jefferson B. Fordham, "Legal Aspects of Local Planning and Zoning in Louisiana," *Louisiana Law Review* 6 (May 1946), 501–2.

sions, to be appointed for ten-year terms by a city's mayor and approved by its commission council.[37] Therefore, when the City Planning and Zoning Commission of New Orleans offered Harland Bartholomew & Associates a consultancy in 1926, the way was clear, as it had not been during Medary's consultancy, for legal enactment of any proposals that the firm might make.

Medary's planning consultancy should also be analyzed in relation to the political milieu of municipal government, which was in many ways influenced by political machinations at the state level. Athough Medary was hired by the city's commercial elite and therefore not immediately responsible to those who held political office, he was working in a city dominated by machine politics. The mayor, Martin Behrman, first elected in 1904 and now serving his fourth term, helmed a group known as the Ring within the Old Regulars of the Democratic Party. In his first and second terms, the Ring fielded mostly winning candidates in the city's wards and commandeered the majority of seventeen alderman's seats on the city council. After Luther E. Hall was elected governor of Louisiana in 1912, the Reform contingent of the Democratic Party in the state legislature engineered the change of New Orleans's governmental structure from a ward-based system to a commission council system—with five commissioners elected at large—in order to undermine the power of the state's boss politicians.[38] Strategically, the Behrman camp made the best of this tactical change by nominating well-respected citizens to run for election to the commission posts—besides mayor, these were commissioner of public finance, commissioner of public safety, commissioner of public utilities, and commissioner of public property. Behrman and his slate retained the mayoralty in 1916 for a fourth term, and Medary began his work in a stable municipal political environment that promoted commercial enterprise as well as physical reform. During Behrman's mayoralty, the city's sewer and potable water system was expanded and the Public Belt Railroad and docks developed. Behrman was defeated for reelection in 1920 by the ascendant Reform faction and their mayoral candidate, Andrew McShane. In the following election, however, he regained his position and, no doubt influenced by Medary's studies and empowered by the city's new zoning and planning powers, entered his fifth term in office, in May 1925, with an ambitious plan for civic improvement.

Charles A. Favrot, chair of the City Planning and Zoning Commission, led the drive to complete a zoning plan, warning Behrman of the "danger"

37 Harland Bartholomew & Associates, "Preliminary Major Street Report" (New Orleans: September 1926), 42, in the Louisiana Research Collection, Special Collections, Howard-Tilton Memorial Library, Tulane University.

38 Mary Lou Widmer, *New Orleans: 1900 to 1920* (Gretna, LA: Pelican, 2007), 58–9, and Hermann B. Deutsch, "New Orleans Politics—The Greatest Free Show on Earth," in *The Past as Prelude, New Orleans 1718–1968*, ed. Hodding Carter, (New Orleans: Pelican, 1968), 315–22.

of past "piecemeal zoning" and urging that "immediate steps be taken by the Commission Council to budget sufficient funds in order that the complete zoning of the city may be quickly effected and the city as a whole planned so that all future improvement may be reconciled to the eventual developments of a city plan."[39]

Behrman died unexpectedly on January 12, 1926, and was succeeded in office by the commissioner of finance, Arthur O'Keefe, according to the procedure specified by state legislative reforms.[40] However, the city's contract negotiations with Harland Bartholomew & Associates were well advanced, and on January 16, 1926, the Planning and Zoning Commission signed a four-year contract with Bartholomew to produce a master plan.

COMPLETING A COMPREHENSIVE ZONING ORDINANCE AND UNDERTAKING A MASTER PLAN, 1926–1930 AND 1948–1951: HARLAND BARTHOLOMEW OF ST. LOUIS

Harland Bartholomew's reputation was well advanced when the New Orleans Planning and Zoning Commission hired him as their consultant. His first professional job had been for the New York District of the U.S. Army Corps of Engineers, and he subsequently worked for Ernest P. Goodrich, who received the commission to create a city plan for Newark, New Jersey in 1911. Goodrich sent him to represent the office in Newark, and although Bartholomew did not initially welcome the assignment, it launched his career as one of the most prolific U.S. urban planners of the twentieth century. He delivered the preliminary plan to Newark in 1913, and in 1914 the city's planning commission hired him as their engineer and secretary, making him "the first full-time municipal planning employee in the United States."[41] In 1915, the St. Louis planning commission offered him a job, which he began in January 1916; he would remain the St. Louis commission's engineer for forty-eight years, until 1954. When Charles Mulford Robinson died, in 1918, the University of Illinois offered Bartholomew Robinson's professorship in civic design on a "non-resident basis," a position he held until 1956. He founded Bartholomew & Associates in 1919, and by 1926 he had produced comprehensive plans for at least eleven U.S. cities, including St. Louis, Omaha, Memphis, Wichita, Schenectady, and Cedar Rapids.[42]

Upon signing a contract for a city plan, Bartholomew would dispatch a "resident engineer" to live in the client city through at least the research phase of the project. Supported by employees in the St. Louis office, such

39 Annual Report of the Planning and Zoning Commission, September 1, 1924–June 30, 1925, catalog record AQ200, City Archives and Special Collections, Louisiana Division, New Orleans Public Library.

40 Louisiana Division, New Orleans Public Library, "Administrations of the Mayors of New Orleans, Martin Behrman (1864–1926)," nutrias.org.

41 Lovelace, *Harland Bartholomew*, 6, 12.

42 Ibid., 6–12, 56.

as other engineers and statisticians, the resident engineer then hired researchers and draftsmen locally.[43] The Bartholomew firm followed a particular working method that left a remarkable paper trail. They compiled a city plan from the disparate studies that they identified as appropriate to the particular urban context—for example, on zoning and land use, population, major streets, recreational facilities, transit, and housing. They circulated these studies to their clients as preliminary reports for comment and refinement and then revised the reports, which became draft chapters of the final plan. In their practice, the preparation of a city plan required two to three years.

Moreover, the firm insisted that the best results from comprehensive planning would be obtained by considering that a master plan would have a useful shelf life of twenty to thirty years. Because unforeseen occurrences would always intervene, they suggested that a master plan should be updated at roughly its half-life mark, ten to fifteen years after adoption. In this regard, the firm offered a flexible approach to decision-making related to urban development, with the adopted plan providing a potentially fungible framework. Clearly, and strategically in terms of business acumen, they encouraged their clients to consider long-term relationships at the signing of initial contracts.

In New Orleans, the Planning and Zoning Commission supervised the work of Bartholomew's team. Between 1926 and 1930, they conducted eleven studies of conditions in the city, which they published as reports "all for the general betterment of city development." As was Bartholomew's custom, he issued the reports singly, as drafts for discussion and revision; six of the studies he completed after closing his local office in 1931. The subjects were major streets (1926, adopted 1927); freight and railroad transportation (1927); zoning (1927, adopted 1929); street traffic (1928); transit (preliminary 1928, completed 1929); recreation (preliminary 1929, completed 1930) and civic art (1931); the port (1931); industry (1931); regional planning (1931); factors involving the carrying out of city plans—economic, legal, and educational (1931); and subdivision and platting (1931). It is not known how the city and Bartholomew's firm negotiated priorities for the scheduling of these studies, but we can assume that the order in which they were undertaken indicates local opinion about their urgency and importance. Indeed, Medary's articles of 1920–1921 seem to have provided the agenda for Bartholomew's work, as transportation surveys and the

43 Information on the work of Bartholomew's New Orleans team from 1926 to 1930 can be found in the files of the City Planning Commission (Boxes 1–5), City Archives and Special Collections, Louisiana Division, New Orleans Public Library; see the bound Comprehensive Zoning Ordinance (1929) for explanations of the team's goals and research methods. Bartholomew employees contributing to the published reports were H.W. Alexander, S.M. Bate, C.W. Baughman, Lawrence H. Conrad, William D. Hudson, Earl O. Mills, and L. Deming Tilton. Mills and Tilton were partners in the firm when Bartholomew accepted the New Orleans contract, and Hudson became a partner shortly thereafter. The title page of the draft Civic Manual (December 11, 1929), on which the master plan was to be based, lists Conrad as author (Box 3, Item 4). Within the city archives, the annual reports of the City Planning and Zoning Commission are catalogued as AQ200. For a retrospective account of Bartholomew's work in this period, see Morrison Papers, miscellaneous subject files, S-1, Advisory Committee (1946), also in the New Orleans city archives.

preparation of a comprehensive zoning ordinance took precedence and occupied three of the four years of his contract. However, Bartholomew also included detailed reports on recreation and public space, subjects that Medary had treated summarily and only at the end of his consultancy.

By the end of 1930, as their contracted consultancy period was drawing to a close, Bartholomew's team consolidated the eleven studies in a final report, which they delivered for the Commission Council's consideration and adoption, the next steps toward producing a master plan. However, the city government did not renew the firm's contract, a decision made necessary by the economic downturn of the Great Depression, and did not bring the master-planning process to a definitive conclusion.[44] Nevertheless, the two Bartholomew reports that the Commission Council did adopt—those on major streets and zoning—guided planning decisions in the years that followed and persuaded Mayor deLesseps Morrison to renew Bartholomew's consultancy in 1948.

The preparation and passage of New Orleans's first comprehensive zoning ordinance was the most important outcome of Bartholomew's initial consultancy in the city. Astonishing efforts were made over an eighteen-month period to ensure that this ordinance would be approved. The Planning and Zoning Commission held a citywide essay contest on "The Value of a Comprehensive City Plan to New Orleans" and awarded twenty prizes on June 8, 1927, as a prelude to Bartholomew's presentation of a draft ordinance to the commission on June 22, 1927. The commission subsequently placed notices of public hearings on the ordinance in the four daily newspapers, illustrated with draft zoning maps, and held thirty general hearings between June and October 1927 to solicit comments. After releasing a revised draft to the public in late October, the commission staged ten more hearings in eight zoning districts, concluding the first phase of hearings on the draft in January 1928. In July and August 1928, city council and commission members met with Bartholomew's resident engineer in executive sessions to discuss another iteration of the draft ordinance. Between September 1928 and January 1929, the commission organized a second phase of hearings—eleven general and eight district meetings. On June 1, 1929, two years after Bartholomew delivered the first draft, the commission council passed New Orleans's first comprehensive zoning ordinance. It became law at midnight on June 11, 1929, culminating the decade of work put into its preparation and enactment.[45]

44 The Planning and Zoning Commission's Annual Report for calendar year 1930 noted, "Mr. Bartholomew offered to keep in close contact with this Commission until after the completion of the Revised City Plan Report and Civic Manual for New Orleans, and to come to the City at such times as his services might be needed on work not in final shape at the termination of his contract ..."

45 The Planning and Zoning Commission kept copious records of the 1927–1929 vetting process; in the city archives, see catalog records AQ305 1927-28, "Report of Public Hearing Districts No. 1–8" and AQ305 1928–29d, "Brief Digest of Public Hearings." The Comprehensive Zoning Ordinance 11,302-CCS (Cal. 11,105) listed twelve categories of land use: A and B, for residences; C and D, for apartment districts; E, F, and G, for commercial; H, a special district for the Vieux Carré; I, J, and K, for industrial; and L for heavy industry/unrestricted. Later in 1929, the creation of a zoning board of appeal followed the passage of the ordinance.

Of all the reports prepared for the final plan between 1926 and 1930, "Report on a System of Recreation Facilities, New Orleans, Louisiana (October 31, 1929)" is of particular value for understanding how attitudes about segregation configured the urban landscape. In it, we see not only the city's contemporary but also its future urban territory, as well as its social future, characterized unequivocally by separation and inequality. Bartholomew urged that the number of small parks or playgrounds associated with public schools should be increased throughout the city, but especially in relation to schools attended by blacks. He acknowledged the dearth of facilities for black children: "Thomy Lafon Playground is the only playground for colored children in the city. It contains 2.00 acres. The playground is located at Magnolia Street and Sixth Street in the heart of the congested colored section. It has a swimming pool in addition to the regular playground apparatus."[46] Plate IX in the report "Present & Proposed Recreation Facilities For Colored Population" mapped the city's African American population and the schools designated for them, including those with small parks. On the same plate, Bartholomew noted locations for new neighborhood parks, which he placed both in areas with a high density of black residents and in districts with sparser black populations. Thus, in this singular illustration, we confront not only the impetus to improve urban conditions for the city's blacks—without providing true equality—but also the desire to plan for future segregation.

In the Planning and Zoning Commission's annual report for 1929, one commissioner, General Allison Owen, expressed particular support of Bartholomew's proposal for three new relatively large parks for blacks, to be developed in more distant sections of the city.[47] These were a twenty-acre park east of the city center, between Claiborne and Florida Avenues near the St. Bernard Parish line; a fifty-acre park in Algiers, across the river from the city center, and a lakefront recreational area of unspecified size near the Industrial Canal. Were the areas for the two parks chosen as appropriate for black occupation because of their low-lying topography, relative remove from the city center, and proximity to

46 One version of Bartholomew's "Preliminary Reports on a System of Recreation Facilities and Civic Art, New Orleans, Louisiana" contains forty-nine original photographs taken by E.K. Stores of St. Louis; it is in the photographs collection of the city archives.

47 Allison Owen (1869–1951) studied architecture at MIT and had a distinguished professional career in New Orleans. He was prominently involved in efforts to improve the urban environment and served as vice-chair of the Planning and Zoning Commission in 1926, when the Commission Council hired Harland Bartholomew. He was an active member of a number of civic organizations, including the Association of Commerce and the Park and Parkway Commission. In 1928, the *Times-Picayune* awarded him its Loving Cup, an honor still given annually to New Orleanians who significantly contribute to the city's welfare. Owen's papers are in the Louisiana Research Collection, Special Collections, Howard-Tilton Memorial Library, Tulane University: specialcollections.tulane.edu. Recently I was surprised to learn that my house (constructed in 1920–1921), connects me to this man. The previous owner was his granddaughter, William Miller Owen III—named for his son, who died in 1919 in military service before her birth in 1920, but called Miller. In 1926, Miller's maternal grandparents bought the house, and after they died, in 1942, Miller and her mother took possession.

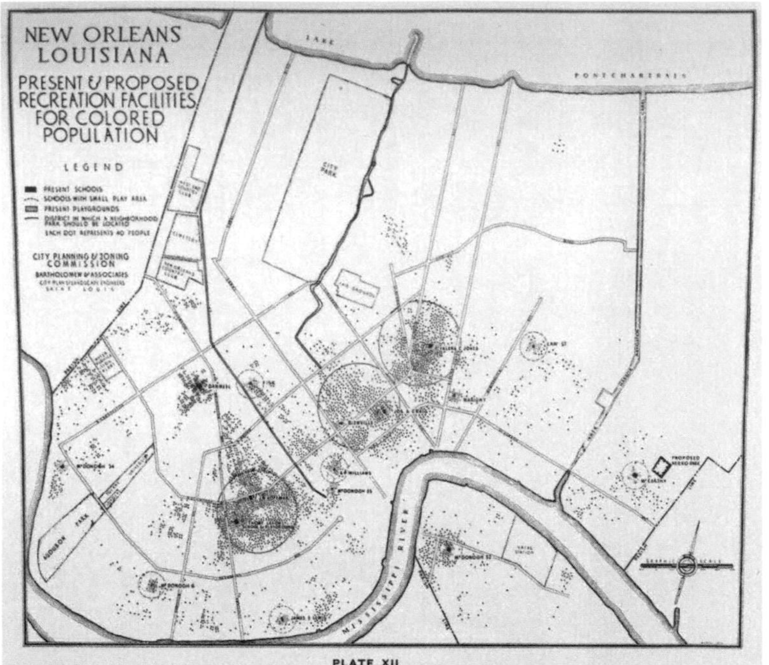

Harland Bartholomew and Associates, "New Orleans, Louisiana, Present & Proposed Recreation Facilities for Colored Population," Plate XII in Report on a System of Recreation Facilities, New Orleans, Louisiana (typescript), submitted March 27, 1929, revised October 31, 1929, by the Recreation Committee of the City Planning and Zoning Commission.

Louisiana Research Collection, Special Collections, Howard-Tilton Memorial Library, Tulane University

zones that the new CZO had designated for industrial use?[48] How should we understand Bartholomew's proposal and his clients' response? Did he inspire them to envision facilities for New Orleans's underserved citizens that they would not have imagined without his recommendations? Were Bartholomew and the commission complicit in offering plans that would draw blacks farther away from the center of the city? We may never be able to answer such questions, but we do know that the white ideas about black spaces that were recorded in 1929 continued to determine the city's racial geography. In the late 1940s, Mayor Morrison's administration developed the Pontchartrain Park subdivision for middle-class black home buyers at the lakefront near the Industrial Canal, in the section that General Owen described as appropriate for a new black recreational area; he also built the Desire housing project for blacks just north of the area proposed as the site for a twenty-acre black park.[49]

Shortly after Morrison took office in 1946, Brooke H. Duncan, the "coordinator" of Morrison's all-white advisory committee, described to Morrison the current state of affairs in relation to the four-year master-planning effort that Bartholomew had led from 1926 through 1929:

48 See Michael Sorkin and Terreform's proposal for "New Algiers" in Part VII of this volume.

49 See Jane Wolff's and my "Pontchartrain Park + Gentilly Woods Landscape Manual" in Part VI of this volume.

> The only planning, other than Major Street and Zoning, that has occurred in the past sixteen years has been more or less sporadic and executed by active and interested officials or public bodies acting from an individual viewpoint without any regard or care of consequences to an over-all plan. Such plans that were approved, were on the basis of friendship or the political power of those interested ... Failure to officially adopt the remaining nine plans has caused costly mistakes and confusion, and these plans should be revised and adopted as soon as possible in order to complete a master plan or pattern to which all future planning should conform.[50]

Morrison heeded Duncan's advice and included a line item in the city's 1948 budget to hire Bartholomew to complete the master plan. The Planning and Zoning Commission issued a three-year contract, renewable annually, to Bartholomew, who once again formed a work team in New Orleans headed by a "resident engineer" from his St. Louis office.[51] As Bartholomew explained in his introduction to the first report from his renewed consultancy, "Scope of the Master Plan," a number of significant changes in urban conditions and in ideas about the benefits of urban planning necessitated a reworking of the recommendations that Bartholomew's firm had made at the end of the 1920s. Growth in air travel required airport planning. Automobile traffic had exceeded projections of earlier decades, placing demands on streets and parking facilities that were not being met. Cities nationwide were addressing the problems of substandard housing and blighted neighborhoods with plans for large-scale redevelopment. Recreational and educational facilities were being planned according to new conceptions of their contribution to physical and mental health. Comprehensive planning could no longer ignore the relationship of burgeoning cities to their metropolitan areas.

The reports that Bartholomew issued during his second New Orleans consultancy were very different in tone, focus, and content from those of his first. Initially, Bartholomew's team imagined that the master plan would be written on the basis of sixteen studies, listed in the preliminary scope report: "Scope of the Master Plan" (presented, September 1948; released to the public, 1948); "Character of the City" (presented, October 1948; released to the public, March 1949); "Population" (presented, November 1948; released to the public, June 1949); "Major Street Plan" (presented to the commission for study, April 1949; adopted, August 1951); "Land Use" (combined with Zoning); "Parking Facilities" (presented,

50 Brooke H. Duncan to Mayor deLesseps Morrison, Morrison Papers, S1, Advisory Committee (1946), City Archives, New Orleans Public Library.

51 The Bartholomew team included resident engineer William H. Singleton, assistant resident engineer H. Alden Deyo, and research analyst Julia Y. Maddox. Millard Humstone replaced Singleton in June 1949. In that year, Bartholomew made four trips to New Orleans to consult with the commission, and his partner Russell H. Riley made eight trips.

September 1949; adopted 1951); "Zoning" (presented with "Land Use," December 1949; released, 1952); "Housing" (presented, 1950; adopted 1954); "Transit Facilities"; "Transportation: Truck, Rail, Water, and Air"; "Parks: Playgrounds and Recreational Facilities and Public Schools" (presented 1950); "Public Buildings and Publicly Owned Lands"; "The City's Appearance"; "Capital Expenditure Program"; "Administrative Policy and Practice"; and "Legislative." Bartholomew added a report on subdivision regulations, which was presented in 1949 and adopted in 1950. Eventually, he consolidated the sixteen projected studies into twelve "chapters," but a definitive, bound publication seems not to have appeared. In 1952, Bartholomew referred to the project as the Twenty-Five-Year Development Program. Certainly the Bartholomew team's copious research and the resulting reports that appeared regularly between 1949 and 1952 influenced the trajectory of urban improvement and development during Morrison's administration.

In many ways, Morrison made the urban environment a priority in his administration. He formed a Planning Advisory Committee with membership composed of "technicians" from various city agencies so that they could be made aware of and discuss progress on the preparation of chapters of the master plan. He welcomed the support of the Citizens' Planning Committee, organized in 1951 of representatives of various civic associations "to carry on the public information and education without which the Master Plan is not likely to serve as the economical guide it is designed to be." Morrison published yearly a heavily illustrated annual report, edited by his public relations officer David McGuire, that prominently focused on urban accomplishments: newly surfaced streets and improved drainage to new recreation centers, public housing complexes, and separate residential subdivisions for whites *and* blacks; an international airport in Jefferson Parish; a Union Station in the CBD; an international trade mart; and a civic center, including a city hall, courts building, and central library. Morrison was the only New Orleans mayor to take Bartholomew's reports on conditions in New Orleans as a guide for concerted action. During his administration, from 1946 to 1961, New Orleanians, informed by Bartholomew's team, planned and realized the potential benefits of that planning, even though *the* plan was not yet signed, sealed, and delivered.

Bartholomew consulted irregularly with New Orleans after Morrison left office in 1961 (to become the U.S. ambassador to the Organization of American States in Washington) and also worked with private development clients. In 1959, he produced "A General Plan, New Orleans East"

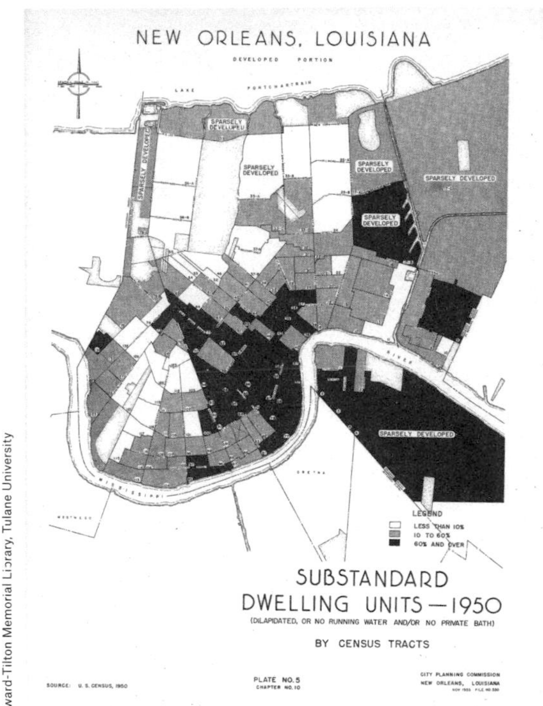

Howard-Tilton Memorial Library, Tulane University

City Planning Commission, "Substandard Dwelling Units—1950," Plate 5 in *The Comprehensive Plan for New Orleans: Housing*, Chapter 10, adopted June 22, 1954, first edition September 1954.

for the consortium of developers New Orleans East, Inc.[52] Under Mayor Schiro's administration, he prepared the "Manual for Community Renewal" for the newly renamed Planning Commission in 1965, followed by reports on "Community Goals and Existing Environmental Conditions" in 1966. A Community Renewal Program Grant from HUD partially financed the latter, under Title I of the Housing Act of 1949, amended in 1959, which was designed to secure additional funds for housing and urban renewal. Bartholomew's final contribution to comprehensive planning in New Orleans was the completion of the Revised Zoning Regulations in 1967.

New Orleans's population peaked during Morrison's administration: the 1960 census counted 627,525 inhabitants. Bartholomew's twenty-five-year development plan had predicted that the city would grow to 700,000 by 1970, but the white flight that followed federally mandated integration, the port's loss of competitive advantage over Houston's port, increased competition from Miami's port, and Houston's ascendance as the control center of the Gulf Coast oil and gas industry all dealt severe blows to New Orleans's economic development and halted its growth

52 This area, far from the city center but still within the city limits, presents significant problems for secure post-Katrina rebuilding, as it contains some of the lowest-lying terrain in Orleans Parish. On the politics and economics of its development, see J. Mark Souther, "Suburban Swamp: The Rise and Fall of Planned New-Town Communities in New Orleans East," *Planning Perspectives* 23 (April 2008), 197–219.

trajectory. Even so, New Orleans's subsequent loss of faith in planning as a tool to achieve urban improvement should not be ascribed only to economic contraction and the social upheavals of the 1960s and 1970s. Although Bartholomew's studies were prepared during years of optimistic anticipation about the future and expectations of prosperity—albeit not for all—those reports from the early 1950s and the mid-1960s squarely faced the city's environmental problems, including the drastically disparate qualities of neighborhoods, the paramount need for drainage and water management, the widespread blight in historic areas, and the danger of unregulated subdivision. A half-century later, we still face these problems. Bartholomew drew the road map, but the city moved off course.

I have written this essay to remind New Orleanians that we have a century's worth of planning experience on which to build as we reconstruct our city. I have described only the outlines of former planning ventures here because an analysis of them would require much more thorough study than the format of this book allows. However, I hope that as we plan in the present we *will* analyze the ways in which New Orleans planned in the past. One of the strengths of Bartholomew's approach was to acknowledge continual change in the urban environment and the need to be responsive to change. His repeated collection and analysis of data at discrete points in time established a comparative methodology that can continue to serve us well. I believe that studying what we envisioned, what we achieved, and what we failed to achieve in the last century is key to today's critical planning process. In the crisis post-Katrina, we achieved a new master plan, but we cannot stop planning.

ACKNOWLEDGMENTS

I am indebted to research assistants Lindsey Caruso, doctoral fellow in Tulane's "City Culture Community" Ph.D. program, and Hee Young, master of architecture student in the Tulane School of Architecture, for sleuthing, scanning, and organizing archival materials, thereby contributing importantly to this essay, and to Thomas F. Reese for his (always) insightful comments.

NEW ORLEANS UNDER RECONSTRUCTION: A CRISIS IN PLANNING AND HUMAN SECURITY

M. CHRISTINE BOYER

> Climate change is a far greater threat to the world than international terrorism.
>
> —Sir David King, chief scientific adviser to the United Kingdom, 2000–2007

THE "RIGHT TO THE CITY" AND HUMAN SECURITY

In 1967, Henri Lefebvre in his famous treatise "The Right to the City" proclaimed that all citizens segregated in ghettos and condemned to live in substandard housing have the right to return to the city. By this—because space is political and under control of the state—he meant they had the right to a decent urban life, to freedom, to education, to participation in decisions affecting them, and to appropriate space as a vehicle of human security. He noted, "This requires an integral theory of the city and of urban society, using all the resources of science and of art."[1] Lefebvre's concept of the right to the city involved not only a discourse on the contemporary conditions of the city but also a self-reflective theoretical discourse about the urban as an abstract concept. He ended his book *The Urban Revolution* with the following comment: "[T]his kind of discourse can never be completed. Its incompletion is an essential part of its existence."[2]

"Human security" is now an emerging paradigm for studying global vulnerabilities; it supplants the idea of national security with a people-centered view and focuses on nonmilitary threats to human welfare. In a humane world, people should live in security and dignity, free from poverty and despair, with an equal opportunity to develop fully their human potential.[3] Issues of this kind of security involve serious risks to

---

1 Henri Lefebvre, reprinted as "The Right to the City," Christian Hubert, trans., in *Architecture Culture 1943–1968*, eds. Joan Ockman and Edward Eigen (New York: Rizzoli, 1993), 436.

2 Henri Lefebvre, *The Urban Revolution*, Robert Bononno, trans. (Minneapolis, MN: University of Minnesota Press, 2003; originally published in 1970 under the title *La Révolution Urbaine*), 166.

3 Taking into consideration the immense damage to the Gulf of Mexico's oil platforms, rigs, pipelines, refineries, and petrochemical plants—accounting for a quarter of U.S. oil extraction—as well as the damage wreaked on New Orleans's port facilities, where most of the United States' bulk agricultural commodities are exported and bulk commodities of industrialism imported represents a huge threat to U.S. economic security. See "A Perspective on Human Security: Chairman's Summary" (First Ministerial Meeting of the Human Security Network, Lysøen, Norway, May 20, 1999). For Port of New Orleans information, see "Port of New Orleans" Wikipedia page.

humanity that decision makers need to prioritize and act upon. All citizens have the right to be safe from chronic threats of hunger, disease, and insufficient shelter and from harmful disruption to the pattern of their daily lives in their homes, jobs, and communities. The United Nations Development Programme (UNDP) in its "Human Development Report" (1994) goes further, securing "freedom from want" and "freedom from fear" for all persons as the basis on which human security must rest. Conflict and deprivation are interconnected; violence and inequality are the root causes of insecurity, and when things spin out of control, the urban problematic explodes.[4]

This paper examines Lefebvre's unfinished discourse on how the right to the city is linked to the issues of human security. It assesses whether the UNDP's 1994 goal of human security has been attained with respect to decent living conditions and open opportunities for all in the process of planning New Orleans's reconstruction. As one plan metamorphoses into another, as segmented proposals split up or merge, are there principles of urban segregation, spatial fragmentation, and neighborhood triage at work?

SECURITY FROM HARMFUL DISRUPTIONS IN THE PATTERN OF DAILY LIFE

In his book, Lefebvre warns against what he calls blind fields—"blind in the sense that there is a blind spot on the retina ... and negation of vision. A paradox. The eye doesn't see; it needs a mirror."[5] The media aids this blindness, making the hurricane tragedy, for example, more than visible—represented in real time—and then forgetting it as soon as the spectacle is eclipsed by yet another newsworthy event. Lefebvre asks how and why there are blind fields and answers his own question: "Bad faith, misunderstanding, and a failure of recognition (false awareness and possibly false consciousness) play a role ... To understand [blind fields] we must take into account the power of ideology ... and the power of language."[6]

Urbanism, Lefebvre explains, is not really a scientific or technical discipline—as architects and planners are wont to believe—but an evolving epistemology.[7] It requires theoretical treatment, or conceptual formulations, that would lead eventually to a new urban practice, a new science of the urban totality. Without such development, urban ideologists are left to exaggerate the importance of their so-called planning activities, offering an impression that urbanism manages things and people in innovative and positive ways, which, he notes, is merely a mythology that architects promulgate. Urbanists claim that their doctrine tends toward

4 United Nations Development Programme, *Human Development Report 1994* (New York: Oxford University Press, 1994), hdrnet.org.

5 Lefebvre, *The Urban Revolution*, 29.

6 Ibid., 31.

7 Ibid., 6.

Ted Jackson, *Times-Picayune*/Landov

As tens of thousands of evacuees waited without food or water, the convention center in New Orleans became an epicenter of despair. Angela Perkins aroused the world with her cry, "Help us, please."

unity, but in fact it harbors things unsaid and contains many blind fields. It also contains a will that tends toward efficiency regardless of the problems it must address: "Urbanism is doubly fetishistic."[8] There is its fetishizing of satisfaction: For each perceived need it supplies an object, yet meanwhile there is a range of social needs it simply ignores. And there is its fetishizing of space: It fails to resolve conflicts between use value of land and exchange value of land. Space is the raw material it controls by setting boundaries and internal frontiers, dividing it into compartments, arranging it into hierarchies of exclusivity.

Disasters often enhance the spatial politics of planning. For example, Hurricane Katrina destroyed much of the southeastern region of the United States. On August 31, 2005, 80 percent of New Orleans was flooded, with some parts under fifteen feet of water. By Federal Emergency Management Agency (FEMA) estimates, 107,000 occupied housing units were flooded, and an additional 27,000 sustained wind damage, making the event and its subsequent damage the worst residential disaster in U.S. history.[9] Yet in the post-Katrina political climate, many cried out, "Let the city go; its government is inept and corrupt, its school system is failing, a good percentage of its population is on welfare." Even more said, "No one should live in a city below sea level!" For others, the question wasn't whether New Orleans could survive. Technologically it could; witness the Dutch, who have been able to hold back high water from their cities. Rather, the issue was "whether the gumbo city has the gump-

8 Ibid., 159.

9 The Brookings Institute Metropolitan Policy Program and the Greater New Orleans Community Data Center, *The New Orleans Index: Tracking the Recovery of New Orleans and the Metropolitan Area* (2009).

tion to make it ... Will [New Orleans] use the disaster to find itself a new reason for being and rebuild itself as a sustainable, thriving city of the twenty-first century?"[10] New Orleans is currently a shrinking city and has been since 1960. In many of its neighborhoods, where there is widespread blight and crumbling infrastructure, resettlement has slowed to a trickle. In 2009, there were by one accounting some 65,888 unoccupied addresses in New Orleans.[11] (Throughout the discussion "New Orleans" should be understood as the New Orleans metropolitan region, which contains seven parishes. One, Orleans Parish, is coterminous with the city.) By the most optimistic estimates in the fall of 2009, the city had merely half of its peak population of 627,525 measured by the 1960 census.[12] Public healthcare, public education, and public housing are all less available and less affordable and are being privatized.

Louisiana's wetlands, the essential line of defense against a hurricane's storm surge, have been reduced by 1,875 square miles since 1900, and are expected to lose another 673 square miles by 2050. The Army Corps of Engineers's risk maps suggest that many parts of the city remain at risk for floods of up to eight feet from a storm that has a one percent chance of occurring in any given year.[13] Allowing development in the coastal wetlands and reengineering the flow of water routes has frayed New Orleans's natural safety net to the point that losses from another catastrophe are considered inevitable.

In spite of all of these difficulties and the reality of a shrinking city, six different city-driven plans and one federal "non-plan" for the reconstruction of New Orleans have been created since 2005. In most plans that are grandiose, promises made are not kept, and the schemes themselves end up on a shelf full of dust. Recovery cannot be achieved overnight;

---

10 Peter Coy, "The New New Orleans," *Businessweek*, September 12, 2005.

11 A figure compiled by William Quigley and Davida Finger in their statistical publication "Katrina Pain Index—2009," marking the four-year anniversary of the devastation. Quoted by Terry Keleher, "By the Numbers: Katrina Families Still Wait for Justice," *Colorlines*, September 2009.

12 In March 2009, the population of New Orleans topped 300,000 for the first time since Hurricane Katrina, according to U.S. census estimates, but four of the seven parishes in metropolitan New Orleans had shrunk since 2007, according to population estimates made on July 1, 2008. Maggie Merrill, Mayor Ray Nagin's director of policy, called the March 2009 estimate a milestone. Louisiana State University sociologist Troy Blanchard proclaimed, "The pace of the rebuilding process can vary ... The fact that it has continued at this rate almost three years after the storm shows it's not tapering off. People are continuing to come back." See Matt Scallin, "New Orleans population tops 300,000 for the first time since Katrina," *New Orleans Metro Real-Time News*, March 19, 2009, NOLA.com.

13 The *Times-Picayune* published nine articles in 2004–2005 pointing out that federal funds supposed to go to New Orleans for hurricane protection were diverted by the Bush administration to the Iraq War instead. Thus, the Corps of Engineers, who are responsible for building canals, maintaining levees, building dikes, etc., received only 20 percent of the funds allocated to protect the city. The Corps warned the *Picayune* in 2004 that the levees were sinking and that flooding from Lake Pontchartrain was a threat. The poorly built levees of insufficient height were breached fifty times in the aftermath of Hurricane Katrina: three main ones at key junctures around the city, including the 17th Street Canal levee, the Industrial Canal levee, and the London Avenue Canal flood wall. According to a June 2007 report by the American Society of Civil Engineers, these breaches were responsible for most of the flooding. Yet George W. Bush, interviewed by Diane Sawyer, on ABC's "Good Morning America," September 1, 2005, stated, "I don't think anybody anticipated the breach of the levees." See Brookings Institute, *The New Orleans Index* (2009) and "Is Bush to Blame for New Orleans Flooding?," published by the Annenberg Public Policy Center of the University of Pennsylvania in September 2005.

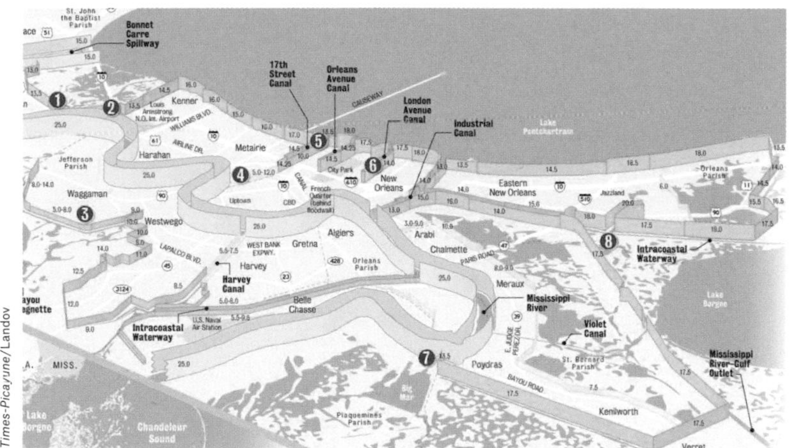

Times-Picayune/Landov

Breaches in the city's levees, which had been designed and built by the United States Army Corps of Engineers, were responsible for most of the flooding, according to a June 2007 report by the American Society of Civil Engineers.

thus, there are always new plans being proposed. Lefebvre claims that planning sees space as a homogeneous empty medium: a place to house objects, people, machines, industries, communication flows, and networks. He calls this a "logistics of restricted rationality" that destroys differential spaces of the "urbanity" and of "habitation" by reducing them to neutral zones.[14] "As for the architect, he condenses (in the sense in which the term was used by Soviet architects between 1920 and 1925, referring to the architect as a social condenser)."[15] The architect builds with respect to financial constraints, norms, and values; his schemes, determined by class criteria, result in segregation even when his intention is to bring about integration and interaction; he is caught in the world of commodities without recognizing it as a world.

Not surprisingly, many planners in New Orleans set out to condense the shrinking city, making overt choices about who had the right of return and who did not, playing games with economic developers and neglecting the human security rights of ordinary citizens. Televised images shot from helicopters captured individuals stranded on their rooftops waiting for relief efforts in the days after the levees broke. Images shot from motorboats traveling across the flooded parts of the city, particularly the Lower Ninth Ward, as well as images shot from roaming vehicles on the ground once the waters receded, captured the spectacle of wrecked automobiles, crushed and ruined houses, and debris scattered along streets where humble homes once stood. All of these images—the spectacle of the storm's violence and the spectacle of massive class inequalities—were beamed around the globe by satellite television. The cameras were there and then gone, displaying the inevitable hit-and-run

14 Lefebvre, *The Urban Revolution*, 48.
15 Ibid., 90.

nature of a media frenzy. Once the spectacle was normalized, bulldozers demolished wrecked homes, cleared away uprooted trees, and removed rotting refrigerators and trashed vehicles—whatever debris there was. Once the cameras were no longer looking, fields were leveled and cleared.

Five years after the storm, the Lower Ninth Ward, having taken the brunt of actual loss of life, appears strangely, eerily beautiful. In this semitropical environment, tall grass has sprung up in fields everywhere, erasing most of the last visible scars of flood damage. Only an occasional driveway or cement foundation from a house remains. Even the high-water marks on still-standing structures have been removed. An entire community is gone. Signs of new human life are springing up like the grasses, slowly: a few defensive, raised houses; an array of architectural offerings commissioned by Brad Pitt's Make It Right organization. No dramatic relics of pain are left, no marks of the spectacular dismemberment in these grassy fields. There are even plans afoot to plant hundreds of bald cypress in Bayou Bienvenue near the Lower Ninth Ward to help bolster the wetlands' ability to absorb storm surges. But the former citizens of the ward—the New Orleans diaspora—who were ejected from the security of their old homes, are still scattered in other cities across the U.S. How did all this clearance and severed redevelopment come about? Who exactly controls these beautiful fields of grass? Has the Lower Ninth Ward been hijacked? Who might be dictating that some lands lie fallow and that other parcels be traded to developers? Who might have the right to select those citizens who can return and those who are "better off" banished from the fields of the Lower Ninth Ward? Is this void of belonging—are these ejected and scattered citizens, these fallow lands and enclave economies—the work of social condensers? As Lefebvre might ask of the planners, from what place do they speak, and for whom?

William Quigley, a public interest lawyer in New Orleans, has claimed that in the wake of the hurricane "New Orleans is a developer's dream, and a resident's nightmare." And Nicolai Ouroussoff, architectural critic for the *New York Times*, referring specifically to the demolition and rebuilding of the city's public housing, called the reconstruction of New Orleans "one of the most aggressive works of social engineering in America since the postwar boom of the 1950s, and architecture and urban planning have become critical tools in shaping that new order."[16]

BRING NEW ORLEANS BACK COMMISSION PLAN

"Action Plan for New Orleans: The New American City" was the city's first reconstruction plan; it was sponsored by the Bring New Orleans Back Commission (BNOBC), which Mayor C. Ray Nagin assembled. The

16 William Quigley is a human rights lawyer and law professor at Loyola University New Orleans. Quoted by Tram Nguyen in "A Game of Monopoly," *Colorlines* 38 (May/June 2007); Nicolai Ouroussoff "Ideas & Trends: Unbuilding—Architecture, All Fall Down," *New York Times*, November 19, 2006.

plan was delivered to him on January 11, 2006.[17] It called for neighborhood planning teams to begin work by February 20 and to complete their plans within a brief three months, by May 20, with a citywide consolidated draft plan to be finished by June 20, 2006.[18] BNOBC called this plan an attempt to create "a smaller, more manageable footprint," with rebuilding planned for higher, drier ground in the city rather than for the lower, more flood-prone areas. To use Lefebvre's term, it would "condense" the city. The plan recommended that large parts of flooded neighborhoods be replaced with parks and that a four-month moratorium be imposed on building permits in neighborhoods with the worst flooding, in order to keep residents from reinvesting in areas that would later be charted for demolition. In general, it recommended that the city take a go-slow attitude in rebuilding low-lying areas.

Recognizing publicly subsidized housing as an asset, the plan nevertheless allowed this issue to be addressed by the U.S. Department of Housing and Urban Development (HUD) where appropriate, effectively washing its hands of the responsibility for housing low-income inhabitants and allowing them to be rejected as a negative problem, one that Katrina had miraculously solved. In order to propel quick action, a new city agency, the Crescent City Redevelopment Corporation (CCRC), was proposed. It was to be empowered to undertake buyouts with funds received from FEMA, the Community Development Block Grant program (CDBG), or other redevelopment sources and to exercise powers of eminent domain "when health and safety issues exist or adequate public facilities and services cannot be provided."[19] The BNOB plan called for a new master plan for the city, to be given the force of law with revised zoning and development codes designed in conformity to its guidelines. It recommended, as well, the complete reorganization of the school system, the construction of a fifty-three-mile light-rail system crisscrossing and looping the city, and the creation of a new jazz district in the old Storyville section north of the French Quarter (an idea promoted by trumpeter Wynton Marsalis, a member of BNOBC and cochair of its culture committee), and, of course, the provision for a levee protection system "better and stronger than ever"—as President George W. Bush put it.[20]

Thousands of evacuees, as well as New Orleans residents, were furious over this first recovery plan, which assumed that population and revenue would be severely and permanently reduced, requiring a new approach to the city. It was a plan, in their eyes, for "us not to return," essentially a

17 The Bring New Orleans Back Commission engaged the Philadelphia-based firm Wallace, Roberts & Todd, LLC—Master Planners; they delivered the "Action Plan for New Orleans: The New American City" on January 11, 2006, npr.org/documents. See also Wallace, Roberts & Todd, "Urban Planning Committee: Action Plan for New Orleans Executive Summary," January 30, 2006, columbia.edu.

18 Wallace et al., "Urban Planning Committee," 17.

19 Ibid., and Wallace, "Action Plan for New Orleans," 49.

20 Quoted in Wallace, "Action Plan for New Orleans," 21.

developer's dream of a new American city that labeled "immediate opportunity areas" all those with little or no flood damage and that left areas with deeply flooded and heavily damaged properties facing an unknown future. It allowed only one month for each neighborhood to complete the identification of displaced residents who were "committed" to return. Many evacuees, in fact, were ready to return and to begin the long process of recovery, but the plan ignored too many of their needs. They were angry over the obstacle to recovery that a four-month moratorium on building permits imposed on flooded neighborhoods during the same period when neighborhood plans were supposed to be developed. What about the delivery of city services and the repair of public infrastructure and utilities? Would schools, retail facilities, and worship and health centers be close enough to service-damaged neighborhoods? What was the guarantee that they would not be allowed to invest their money in areas that might be condemned?[21]

On January 16, 2006, Nagin predicted that New Orleans would become a "chocolate city," with black residents fewer but nevertheless prominent, and always "colored" by racial admixture. (He also claimed that God was mad at America, a remark that he called inappropriate the next day.) In line with many of his constituents, he disavowed the plan that his appointed commission had produced. Residents aimed their anger at BNOBC members and particularly at Joseph C. Canizaro, a key architect of the plan who promoted the go-slow policy. They feared that recovery investment would be wasted on properties in neighborhoods that would eventually fail the BNOBC's "viability" test, which required assurance that half of a given neighborhood's evacuated population planned to return and rebuild. Under the plan, an area that failed this test would be reduced in size or plowed under and allowed to revert to swampland or green space. The BNOBC's land-use committee allocated $12 million for "buyouts." Canizaro declared, "If we don't get a reconstruction authority in place right away, we won't have a chance with implementation." One city resident, Harvey Bender, pointed his finger at Canizaro during a BNOBC hearing and declared, "I don't know you, but I hate you. You've been in the background scheming to take our land." Canizaro responded, "There's no question if you have 200,000 less people [in the city], there's going to be shrinkage ... People don't want to hear that."[22] (See the illustration of the plan in Melissa Harris-Perry's essay in this volume, on page 159.)

The public was outraged by the reconstruction map, which showed large green patches spread over most low-lying neighborhoods of all income strata. Major portions of Gentilly, Mid-City, Lakeview, and the Lower Ninth Ward would be excluded from the immediate process of recovery. The plan's division of the city into three kinds of areas—

21 Kim Cobb, "New Orleans Residents Are Enraged over Recovery Plan," *Houston Chronicle*, January 12, 2006.
22 Ibid.

"immediate opportunity areas," "neighborhood planning areas," and "infill development areas"—also brought storms of protest. Nor did New Orleans residents like the moratorium on rebuilding imposed on two thirds of the city, a moratorium slated to begin on January 20, 2007.[23] The plan itself focused on neighborhood rebuilding around the proposed new light-rail stops, and it called for consolidation of those areas with insufficient population in order to support "equitable and efficient service delivery." Rebuilding would start in "immediate opportunity areas," those dry areas that had suffered little or no flood damage and already evidenced repair activities. Other areas that not been so lucky were designated "neighborhood planning areas."[24] Here, residents would decide their future based on facts presented on revised FEMA Base Flood Elevation (BFE) maps after these maps had been prepared.[25] In spite of uncertainty over maps yet to be seen, the planning process was supposed "to level the playing field for recovery, regardless of the internal resources in any neighborhood."[26] Some New Orleanians were not convinced; to them, the plan looked like a calculated and cruel scheme to permanently depopulate middle- and low-income areas of the city and to rebuild only the wealthy areas and tourist districts.[27]

Each neighborhood's plan would recommend land uses (according to their location and density), public facilities and services, phasing of development, a property acquisition plan, and guidelines for new construction. Next, these plans would be glued together, after tough decisions had been made and desires given equal consideration, into a citywide development plan. "Infill development areas"—vaguely described as blighted and disputed properties, brown fields, underutilized sites, and sites requiring demolition and clearance—would be consolidated to accommodate urban development. One of these areas was the Lower Ninth Ward, where it would be necessary to demolish a large number of buildings to protect the "health and safety" of the entire city, which in many cases would trigger the process of property turnover. The city plan seemed to get things terribly mixed up: neighborhood plans would have to respect the guidelines on "city capacity" (influenced, no doubt, by the ULI's earlier findings of October 2005) that preceded them.[28] The outcome—which many feared was intentional—would be exploitation:

23 Kate Randall, "City Residents Denounce 'Bring New Orleans Back' Rebuilding Plan," *World Socialist Web Site*, January 14, 2006.

24 Each neighborhood planning district would consist of neighborhood residents, a planner/urban designer, a historic preservation expert, a City Planning Commission representative, an environmental/public health consultant, a mitigation planner, a finance expert, administrative/technology support, and community outreach. The group would reach out to displaced residents through the Internet and by other means. See Wallace, "Urban Planning Committee," 14, and Wallace, "Action Plan for New Orleans," 44.

25 Eventually, on April 12, 2006, Advisory Base Flood Elevation maps were released by FEMA.

26 Wallace, "Urban Planning Committee," 13.

27 Randall, "City Residents."

28 Wallace, "Urban Planning Committee," 17.

real estate developers buying up vacant land at fire-sale prices.[29]

Babatunji Ahmed, a New Orleans craftsman, complained, "The smaller footprint means you don't want my mamma back! You don't want my grandchildren back!" Lower Ninth Ward resident Tanya Harris told the *New York Times*, "I'm not seeing that laid-back New Orleans character right now. I'm seeing a fighting spirit. I mean, my grandmother would chain herself to that property before she allowed the city to take it."[30] "I don't think it's right that you take our properties. Over my dead body ... Like I said, I didn't die with Katrina," cried out Lower Ninth Ward resident Caroline Parker during BNOBC hearings.[31] Robyn Brags from New Orleans East said the timetable was too short: "I don't think four or five months is close to enough time given all we would need to do." Families with school-age children, although they might want to return, would not be able to do so and thus would not be counted until the summer. Harvey Bender proclaimed, "I'm ready to rebuild and I'm not letting you take mine. I'm going to fight, whatever it takes, to rebuild my property ... I'm going to suit up like I'm going to Iraq and fight this."[32]

Running for reelection in May 2006, Mayor Nagin put himself at some distance from this unpopular plan. Lifting the moratorium, he offered to let residents rebuild anywhere, but warned that they did so in flood-prone neighborhoods at their own risk. He recommended revamping schools, building a new light-rail system, undertaking new riverfront development, and demanding better flood protection. Some twenty or so neighborhoods of New Orleans were to establish planning teams to investigate whether their areas were sustainable or not. And, again, these plans were to be completed by May 2006.[33] When BNOBC's smaller-footprint condenser plan failed to gain FEMA's support, the city council inaugurated another plan.

CITY OF NEW ORLEANS NEIGHBORHOODS REBUILDING PLAN (THE LAMBERT PLAN)

Another proposal, implementing Lefebvre's "democratization of the management of the city," was titled the Neighborhoods Rebuilding Plan, also known as the Lambert Plan for its project manager, Lambert Advisory of Miami. Funded by the New Orleans City Council, it was presented to the mayor's office in October 2006.[34] The planners reported that all flooded neighborhoods—those with more than two feet of water—wanted to rebuild their housing stock, restore streets and other infrastructure,

---

29 Randall, "City Residents."

30 Quoted by Jordan Flaherty in "Glossary of the Struggle for New Orleans," on the Web publication *A Katrina Reader*, March 21, 2006, katrinareader.org.

31 Quoted by Randall in "City Residents."

32 Ibid.

33 For early evidence of the mayor's revisions and additions, see Wallace, "Urban Planning Committee."

34 City of New Orleans, "Neighborhoods Rebuilding Plan Summary" (October 2006), 4–5.

reopen schools, and bring back supermarkets and pharmacies. In fact, the plan urged that neighborhoods be enhanced to exceed their condition in August 2005, and that the unique qualities of specific neighborhoods be retained. Many low-income neighborhoods feared not only "improvement"—the euphemism for "displacement" or "gentrification"—but also the city's deployment of eminent domain, which would force them from their homes.[35] Forty-seven neighborhoods developed plans under the city council–sponsored project; thirteen of these were communities where more than 50 percent of children under the age of five lived in poverty; in eleven of them, the level was 66 percent. Thus, a second yardstick for improvement was how far these neighborhoods could make improvements in the quality and stability of life part of the overall recovery plan for New Orleans.[36] In other words, "human security" issues and "the right to return" were placed front and center in this neighborhood-by-neighborhood plan.

More dramatically, the Lambert Plan specifically focused on flooded areas of the city, because early in October 2005 the Urban Land Institute (ULI) and some members of Congress had begun to advocate policies to ensure that flooded sections of the city would not be rebuilt.[37] Their recommendations had influenced the plan suggested by the BNOBC. In reaction to this, the New Orleans City Council provided residents with a planning process that would allow them a voice in deciding what would become of their communities. The neighborhoods were divided into seven groups encompassing ten of the thirteen planning districts in Orleans Parish; each group was assigned planning teams to assist individual neighborhoods, in order to coordinate plans across groups, planning districts, and city-wide work on infrastructure and other projects already in progress.[38]

Communities believed, naively, that funds that provided core support of the rebuilding process through the CDBG program were to be used in areas of "concentrated distress"—those flooded areas where a majority of homes had suffered severe damage from the storm. Nonflooded areas suffering minor problems, such as poor trash service or job loss, were expected to recover on their own over time. Constituents assumed, as well, that the federal government would keep its commitment to provide an adequate flood protection system and would provide housing assistance to encourage not only the reconstruction of damaged homes but also the construction of new residential units for both owner- and renter-occupied housing. Moreover, they believed that there would be adequate nonhousing funds to address infrastructure, public facilities repair, and other public improvements.[39] However, the planning process itself caused an unforeseen

35 Ibid., 4.
36 Ibid., 5.
37 Ibid., 7–9.
38 Ibid.
39 Ibid., 11–12.

dilemma: the number of meetings began to spiral out of control. It had been assumed that three meetings per neighborhood would be sufficient to complete each neighborhood's plans. The "executive" summary of the Neighborhoods Rebuilding Plan document explained, "Because the stakes were so high and emotions so deep, and because many neighborhoods had begun planning with little to modest direction on their own, in order to 'prove their viability,' it quickly became apparent that three very structured meetings were insufficient to build a rapport and trust with the neighborhood groups."[40] It was essential that neighborhoods not be afraid of the planning process, so planning consultants began to meet neighborhood groups "in homes, under tents, on the street, in playgrounds, and most importantly in houses of worship."[41] The planners brought information and gathered information, helped define communities' needs, provided strategies for implementation, and outlined which barriers had to be removed before implementation efforts could begin. The planners were trying to develop trust—which the two previous plans, the ULI's and the BNOBC's, had not gained—even holding three meetings for displaced residents in Baton Rouge, Atlanta, and Houston to accommodate evacuees who wanted to make their voices heard. To be legitimate, a plan would have to be perceived by the neighborhoods as the result of their own efforts.

Although New Orleans was determined to construct its own recovery, it was becoming apparent that the city was developing a patchwork of proposals riddled with uncertainties. Urban proposals, Lefebvre warns, don't go very far; they are a form of class urbanism, a strategy papering over the fact that space harbors ideology.[42] This ideological urbanism is caught between special public interests and private interests; it promotes a compromise between a neodirigist organization, in which free enterprise is ascendant, and a neoliberal position that calls for voluntary or consensual planning activities, that is, citizen participation. The urbanist slips into the crack between developers and power structures, accepting fragmentation of the urban terrain and even contributing to it. The citizens of New Orleans, those who remained behind in the stricken city, were drawn into a planning process that over the years became a series of empty decision-making sessions, and eventually these worthy citizens were exhausted by an excess of meaningless debate. In the meantime, a developer's game of triage was given free reign.

This developer's game has been played elsewhere with great success. "Urbanism," Lefebvre claims, "is a mask and a tool."[43] In 1971, Anthony Downs, a real estate adviser, suggested to American municipal managers how to handle cuts in federal spending in the wake of the dramatic reduction of federal categorical grants, as focus shifted from obsolete and blighted

40 Ibid., 12.
41 Ibid.
42 Lefebvre, *The Urban Revolution*, 157.
43 Ibid., 180.

areas of a city to the entire city. Community development funds might be used, he noted, to "leverage" private investment dollars by spending the government's money in "moderately or marginally" deteriorated neighborhoods that displayed the following strengths: historic value that could attract middle-class residents back to the city; proximity to downtown districts that had already undergone renewal activity and could support nearby residential recycling; the presence of hospitals, universities, museums, and other institutions that might create local housing markets for their employees as well as attract other reinvestors. Following his advice, many cities implemented this planned policy of triage.[44]

The nonprofit ULI can be criticized for just such tactics. The organization provoked outright fury when it suggested only a few months after Katrina that, in effect, the same concept of triage should be put into practice in New Orleans. Divide the city into three, ULI advised: areas that will recover with aid, those that will recover without aid, and those that will never recover. Concentrate the delivery of services in "viable" areas and forget about the areas that are hopeless. Their report, released in mid-November 2005, included recommendations to leave vast, mostly poor areas of the city without services, giving the stamp of approval to a vision of New Orleans rebuilt by prioritizing the demands of corporations and developers.[45]

On July 19, 2006, John McIlwain of the ULI criticized the city's planning efforts and the mayor's lack of leadership in the *Times-Picayune.* He wanted the city to follow ULI's recommendations to shrink the city's footprint, eliminating—intentionally or not—dozens of low-income neighborhoods. Thomas Murphy, former mayor of Pittsburgh (January 1994–January 2006) and also of the ULI, expressed frustration that New Orleans had not used eminent domain aggressively enough to seize privately owned blighted properties in order to sell them to generate funds for reconstruction. City Council President Oliver Thomas retorted that the ULI had made "incorrect assumptions about New Orleans from the outset" and had proposed elimination of some neighborhoods that were not even below sea level. In spite of the council's awareness of ULI's position, by 2007 the city had put a triage system into effect, focusing on struggling areas such as Gentilly Boulevard and Elysian Fields Avenue and renewing areas that could benefit from investment, such as Canal Street. One of the chief leaders of this effort was Edward J. Blakely, Nagin's "recovery czar," director of the mayor's new Office of Recovery Management from January 2007 to July 2009. Meanwhile flooded and destroyed low-income areas saw no reconstruction at all, except those few homes built by philanthropic organizations. By late March 2007, $1.1 billion in redevelop-

44 *Triage* comes from the French verb *trier*, meaning to separate, sort, sift, or select. It was first applied to the process of prioritizing medical patients based the severity of their condition, and it works effectively when resources are short and treatment is needed immediately. For notes on Anthony Downs, see M. Christine Boyer, *The City of Collective Memory* (Cambridge, MA: MIT Press, 1994), 407–8.

45 Randall, "City Residents."

ment monies from state and local funds had been allocated for infrastructure repair and other projects with the hope of leveraging private investment in new businesses and recovery projects.

The ULI kept up their criticism of New Orleans recovery efforts over the years. They targeted Mayor Nagin for failing to deliver on his ambitious plans to bring back an impoverished city, claiming that he was an inept leader who allowed nonprofits to take the reins and who tended to switch about on his support for programs. For example, he unexpectedly shifted funds from a second-mortgage program that targeted moderate-income renters—"the group least likely to return to the city due to a severe shortage of affordable housing," according to the ULI—to a program that assisted owners of damaged homes, leaving renters high and dry. The ULI also argued that the Office of Recovery Management Nagin established did not have sufficient power to control all the agencies involved in his development projects, including those working to secure financing and acquire land.[46] In other words, Nagin's market strategies were insufficient to implement ULI's vision of a New Orleans recovery.

THE UNIFIED NEW ORLEANS PLAN

Meanwhile, as a condition for releasing federal recovery funds, the Louisiana Recovery Authority (LRA) mandated that a plan for New Orleans must address comprehensively the entire city—not only the areas that had flooded but also those that had not. Backed by funds from the Rockefeller Foundation, and with the approval of the LRA and the City Council, the Unified New Orleans Plan (UNOP) was initiated to achieve this goal, and their work culminated in another plan, the "Citywide Strategic Recovery and Rebuilding Plan," meant to incorporate not only those plans previously undertaken but also newly accomplished planning efforts in the thirteen planning districts of Orleans Parish. Delivered in June 2007, UNOP called for an additional $14.3 billion for New Orleans's recovery.[47]

UNOP began its planning in September 2006, when architects, city planners, and neighborhood residents organized to address the city's seventy-three officially recognized neighborhoods. The process it provided was two-tiered: forty-seven neighborhood plans (achieved in the Lambert Plans) would be integrated into thirteen new district plans, and these would be merged with the work of another set of planners who were detailing a comprehensive citywide plan. Planning districts, for example, might have a list of sites and structures in need of repair, such as neighborhood schools, parks, libraries, and streets. These local projects would only achieve citywide significance, however, when grouped together into a larger project such as "Repair, Renovate, or Construct New District/Neighborhood Parks."

46 Cory Dade, "Grassroots Put New Orleans Back on its Feet," *Wall Street Journal*, August 19, 2009.

47 City of New Orleans, "The Unified New Orleans Plan: Citywide Strategic Recovery and Rebuilding Plan," June 2007, unifiedneworleansplan.com.

Sidestepping or abetting the lengthy process of planning, depending on your point of view, UNOP developed an extensive communications network: a website (unifiedneworleansplan.org), newsletters, media relations, call centers, and rounds of neighborhood weekend meetings with simulcasts in New Orleans, Houston, Dallas, and Atlanta. Again, the planners gathered information, assessed progress, surveyed needs, reviewed past plans, and established population benchmarks, and eventually published a Recovery Data Atlas on the UNOP website.

Since the BNOBC's map had been so controversial when it was unrolled in January 2006, UNOP decided to forgo the politically divisive map format and offered instead an "illustrative framework":

> Maps of recovery planning policy areas ... must be done as part of the implementation phase, when funding is secure. Also all maps will change, as the rate of population return within neighborhoods and the risks of future flooding in those neighborhoods are constantly changing. A map drawn six months ago would be very different from one drawn today or one drawn six months from now.[48]

The plan highlighted the word *recovery*, pointing out this was not a master land-use plan or a comprehensive plan. Instead, it focused on capital projects and programs to correct or repair the effects of disaster, including preventive measures to assure that a similar disaster would not reoccur: "Time is of the essence when lives have been disrupted, when businesses have been destroyed and communities torn apart."[49] It set the limit for such recovery within a span of ten years. Although the plan recognized that people were still living in every one of the neighborhoods of the city, that every citizen had the right to return to New Orleans, and that all neighborhoods of the city must eventually be rebuilt, the report also argued that the city had been given a grand opportunity to reinvent itself in a smarter, stronger, and safer manner with a higher quality of life.[50] However, accomplishing all this remained a challenging target.

UNOP, like other plans before it, divided the city in three: a policy area A with "less flood risk and/or higher repopulation rates," a policy area B with "moderate flood risk and/or moderate repopulation rates," and a policy area C "with highest flood risk and slowest repopulation rates."[51] Strategies, policies, programs, and projects were tailor-made to each type of area, and all recovery strategies were contingent on the rate of return

48 Ibid., 19–20.

49 Ibid., 10.

50 Ibid., 2–53, 56. The right to return, plus the right to return to a safer, more secure city, was a mantra throughout the report.

51 Laurie A. Johnson, "Recovery and Reconstruction Following Large-Scale Disasters: Lessons Learned in New Orleans," paper presented at the second International Conference on Urban Disaster Reduction, November 27–29, 2007, 6, ncdr.nat.gov.tw.

of population and a diminished risk of future flooding. Indeed, the report devoted a good deal of space to outlining flood-protection policies.

The encompassing citywide plan proposed a "Neighborhood Stabilization Program" in areas hardest hit and with the fewest people returning, that is, policy area C; here, remaining and returning residents could relocate to planned "cluster developments," where there would be upgraded infrastructure, social and commercial services, and, most importantly, neighbors. This strategy, the plan argued, would help the city and other agencies focus investments and upgrade public services and infrastructure in targeted areas, inevitably attracting residents and businesses to sites near one another. Clustering—or social condensing—would reduce guesswork for residents and businesses about a community's viability, and by restoring quality of life, it would stimulate additional investments. Two programs would assist property owners in abandoned parts of policy area B to raise their homes as a flood protection: Elevate New Orleans and Slab-on-Grade Remediation. To influence those rebuilding the city, UNOP recommended that developers follow the guidelines of the *New Orleans Pattern Book* developed by New Urbanism advocates—guidelines HUD accepted as de facto housing policy. For some, this meant the expansion of a "beloved small-scale lifestyle" replicating that of the city's older neighborhoods. For others, it signaled approval for dreary taupe- and putty-colored apartment complexes, decorated with florid ornamentation and organized around little-used green spaces, or of Disneyesque Creole cottages in populated enclaves.

The plan outlined three recovery scenarios, explaining that "scenarios" were different from "vision plans," which ask, "What do you want to happen?" or "What would you like to see?" Scenarios, it noted, are based on uncertainties, strategic opportunities, conflicts, and challenges.[52] The first scenario was called Re-pair and was based on the current amount of disaster funding, allowing no additional improvement in flood protection; it assumed that public services and facilities would be repaired along with housing but not improved beyond their pre-Katrina levels. Population growth in this scenario would be incremental but slow and not expected to reach pre-Katrina levels, so that the city's tax/consumer base would not allow for a higher quality of life or service delivery. The second scenario, Re-habilitate, assumed a moderate increase in funding, enabling the improvement of systemic infrastructure problems and providing means to leverage other investments and projects. Additional flood-protection defenses would aid rebuilding and resettlement, allowing the city to regain its pre-Katrina population levels. Quality of life would be moderately improved. The third scenario, Re-vision, was the most optimistic. It assumed that significant new funds would be available, allowing many quality-of-life enhancements, including state-of-the-art schools and

52 UNOP, 51–56.

healthcare facilities. Many structural and community assets would be elevated or relocated out of harm's way. The population would fully recover or exceed pre-Katrina levels, and the city would be well on its way to achieving its greatest economic, social, and cultural aspirations.

After considerable public discussion, establishing a list of priorities, the Re-pair, Re-build, and Re-vision scenarios were blended into a comprehensive vision and framework for the city's recovery.[53] Seven recovery goals were set: Multilevel flood protection must be integrated with all rebuilding plans; limited funds for infrastructure recovery must be efficiently and effectively allocated and strategically invested to stimulate neighborhood revitalization and accommodate an influx of new population; an adequate supply of affordable rental housing must be made available and offered especially to public-housing residents who wanted to return; a more rational pattern of resettlement must be fostered by concentrating community services and commercial activity in areas of higher elevation, providing an incentive for relocation into clustered development; key facilities that would generate employment, such as the Louisiana State University/Veterans Administration Medical Complex, must be retained and expanded, and new growth industries must be developed; investment in community facilities must be maximized, their locations planned to enhance revitalization; and, finally, New Orleans culture and historic architecture must be preserved.

UNOP promoted whole neighborhoods coming back, rather than just individuals.[54] Joe Butler, a spokesperson for the planning coordinators, promised, "What you won't see in the plan [are] directives that prioritize certain neighborhoods or districts." In rather vague terms, he continued, "We are not in any position to select how they are brought back [or] the timeline [on which] they are brought back."[55] So, after an eighteen-month planning process, New Orleans received its most comprehensive and detailed plan yet, one with district-by-district wish lists of projects—but with no priorities set, no timelines established, and no budget allocated. Some New Orleanians were getting worried. They still believed their opinions should be considered in the planning and budgeting process, but it was becoming apparent that citizen participation could also be a colossal waste of time and energy and that plans incorporating their input might be nothing but paper dreams.

2007 REDEVELOPMENT PLAN (BLAKELY PLAN)

In late March 2007, while UNOP was undergoing review and revision, another recovery plan was unveiled, this one promoted by Edward J. Blakely, whom the mayor had appointed executive director of the Office

53 Ibid., 57–9.

54 Ibid., 70–1.

55 "All About The Shouting," Urban Conservancy, January 16, 2007, urbanconservancy.org.

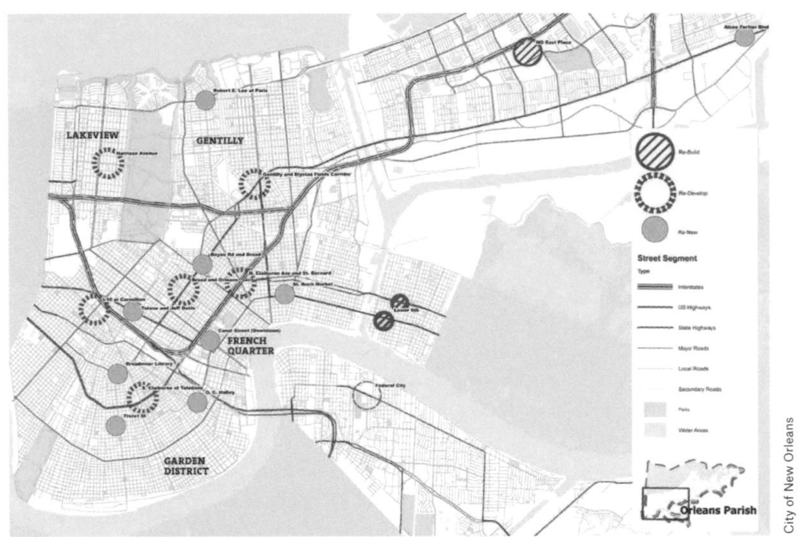

City of New Orleans

City of New Orleans Recovery Plan, March 2007. Blakely focused on seventeen recovery areas, dividing the city into three categories by strategy: rebuild, redevelop, and renew.

for Recovery Management in January of that year.[56] His plan focused on seventeen "hub sites"—zones approximately a half mile in diameter—located around the city to act as magnets for commercial development. Blakely proclaimed, "If I could pump life back into these places, you might pump life back into the entire city."[57] Each hub was a high-visibility site, with sufficient land and other assets to attract investors and with adequate resources to catalyze other developments, such as schools and libraries. These hubs were all centered on the old markets, "on which the city was built in the first place."[58]

Blakely had arrived in New Orleans spewing forth a stream of outspoken pragmatic realism. New Orleans, he said, had a culture of domination, not participation: Whatever group receives something then tries to take over the whole turf. He added that New Orleans had a paper-thin economy mainly based on T-shirt sales.[59] But plans, he said, are powerful; they give people hope. "The last person who had a big idea was Huey Long ... Big ideas are hard to swallow here." A bit of realistic finger-pointing might bring success and permit New Orleans to "once again become a trade and travel gateway to Latin America."[60]

"Modestly" budgeted at $1.1 billion, this plan—or so it was hoped—would not suffer from the lingering, do-nothing fate of all previous plans. "We're not sitting around waiting for anybody any longer," Mayor Nagin

56 Bradford McKee, "New Orleans Recovery Plan Released," *Architect Magazine* (May 2007), also posted May 7, 2007, on architectmagazine.com.

57 Adam Nossiter, "Steering New Orleans's Recovery with a Clinical Eye," *New York Times,* April 10, 2007.

58 Adam Nossiter, "New Orleans Proposes to Invest in 17 Areas," *New York Times,* March 30, 2007.

59 Nossiter, "Steering New Orleans's Recovery."

60 Wayne Curtis, "The Savior of New Orleans," *Architect Magazine,* August 6, 2007.

proclaimed in his news conference unveiling the Blakely plan. "We're going to move this city forward with the resources that we can generate creatively, and everybody who wants to join us later, you're welcome to come on board." Blakely claimed, "By September, we hope to have cranes on the skyline."[61] Some funds would be used as loans, others would be offered as "incentives" to private developers, and some would be allocated for the renewal of public works such as clinics and libraries. But, once again, an implicit and refurbished triage strategy was put into effect: Fifteen of these selected sites either had not been hit by Katrina's flood waters or had already begun to rebuild on their own. Blakely selected only two devastated areas for targeted redevelopment: a site in the Lower Ninth Ward and a section surrounding the Lake Forest Plaza shopping center near the Lake Pontchartrain shore. The city once more was divided in three: "re-build areas" that had experienced severe destruction and required major rebuilding or significant public and private investment in order to recover; "re-develop areas" where recovery efforts and resources were already in place and could act as catalysts for further recovery; and "re-new areas" that required modest public intervention to supplement work already being done (Blakely's hubs).[62] The plan's ultimate goal, like UNOP's, was to attract private investment to higher, safer neighborhoods by concentrating services and funds in these areas as a lure to developers. Nine of the seventeen targeted zones fell into re-new areas. "These areas are doing fine and were doing fine before," Blakely said. "With just a little bit of touch-up, paint-up, and spruce-up, they'll do very well."[63] Only two of the areas were "re-build" areas—the two mentioned above—but the supposed rationale for focusing on "re-new" areas was that people needed action; they were tired of planning and meeting; they were "planned out."

City councilwoman Cynthia Willard-Lewis eagerly accepted this plan as a crucial step in New Orleans's lagging recovery. "This is the summer of decision making," she said. "Many of our families will be returning, and to add to their personal investments, it is significant that they see our police officers moving out of FEMA trailers and into buildings, that our public libraries are opened and that the green space for recreation ... is put into place."[64] This was a strange reply to a plan promoting commercial revitalization. Jane S. Brooks, professor and chair of the Planning and Urban Studies Department at the University of New Orleans was more realistic: "People can start to see where this targeted reinvestment is going to occur." She attributed the wide acceptance of the Blakely plan to the broad public participation that led up to it: "People are ready to understand that this is the first wave of investment ... If this works, maybe

61 Russell McCulley, "New Orleans Unveils Katrina Recovery Plan," *Reuters*, March 29, 2007.
62 Michelle Krupa, "LRA Approves New Orleans Recovery Plan," *Times-Picayune*, June 25, 2007.
63 Curtis, "The Savior of New Orleans."
64 Krupa, "LRA Approves."

there will be another wave of investment. There's no miracle here. What he's trying to do is use public money to attract private money."[65] But as Lefebvre noted, planning based on class criteria results in segregation even when the intention is to bring about integration and interaction.[66]

Controversy continued to swirl around Blakely's head. Giving an interview to the *New York Times*, he bluntly criticized those foregrounding the "right to return" as using people for political gain. The fact had to be accepted: The lower-income population, now relocated outside the city, might not be coming back. Of course this meant that when the dust settled, New Orleans would be different and would have a new population, perhaps one with more energy. He characterized pre-Katrina New Orleans as a "third-world country" and the new energetic population as its salvation.[67] Arrogant or pragmatic, Blakely saw himself in the role of an urban renewal surgeon: "I'm like the doctor, going into surgery. I'm putting my best thing there. The patient, I hope, lives. But post-surgery, the patient, if they start eating hog maws again and not exercising, what can I do? I approach all my urban planning projects that way."[68]

Yet despite all the bravado about new energy and newcomers, one year after the plan's announcement there were no construction cranes looming over the city, no Parisian boulevards refurbished, and little in the way of real redevelopment. In April 2008, Adam Nossiter reported:

> There has been nothing to signal a transformation in the sea of blight and abandonment that still defines much of the city. Weary and bewildered residents, forced to bring back the hard-hit city on their own, have searched the plan's 17 "target recovery zones" for any sign that the city's promises should not be consigned to the municipal filing cabinet, along with their predecessors. On their one-year anniversary, the designated "zones" have hardly budged.[69]

Blakely was gradually given broad authority—ultimately a staff of more than 200 and control over eight other agencies—yet his recovery plan was stuck in the mud. "They come up with these plans that look great and sound great," Sheila White, a Mid-City resident said. "They give people hope. Then, they fall into the background. Promises are made, and they are not kept."[70] After a year, most of the seventeen target areas were still designated on a municipal website as in "preliminary design" or "planning," with only a few labeled under "construction." Blakely conceded that progress to date consisted of "still light stuff. I think people

65 McKee, "New Orleans Recovery Plan Released."
66 Lefebvre, *The Urban Revolution*, 90.
67 Nossiter, "Steering New Orleans's Recovery."
68 Ibid.
69 Nossiter, "Big Plans are Slow to Bear Fruit in New Orleans," *New York Times*, April 1, 2008.
70 Ibid.

were expecting they'd wake up one morning and it would be nirvana. But little things are happening, cleanups, fix-ups, and so on."[71]

THE FEDERAL GOVERNMENT'S "NON-PLAN"— FEMA DEMOLITIONS AND THE U.S. DEPARTMENT OF HOUSING AND URBAN DEVELOPMENT'S INTERVENTIONS IN DISASTER RECOVERY AND PUBLIC HOUSING

Soon after Katrina's impact became clear, HUD Secretary Alphonso Jackson predicted that New Orleans was "not going to be as black as it was for a long time, if ever again." He then worked to make that prediction come true. While human rights lawyers admit there are no precise figures on the racial breakdown of poor and working people from New Orleans who were displaced, no one challenges the strong indications that evacuees were overwhelmingly African American. Immediately following Katrina, the black population of New Orleans plummeted by 69 percent, whereas the white population fell only 39 percent, according to a study by the Center for Constitutional Rights.[72] Areas that began to recover more quickly were more affluent and predominately white. In 2008, New Orleans, which had been 66.7 percent African American in 2000, was estimated to be no more than 60.7 percent African American.[73] Of course these statistics do not give a complete picture: They do not calibrate for the shrinking population base, leaving out most of the city's former residents, most of whom were poor and black, and so they fail to explain what is actually being measured.

Meanwhile, the federal government's "non-plan" for addressing hurricane-spawned destruction and resultant blight was put into operation, making debris removal and demolition a growth industry. FEMA announced it would pay for demolition of properties that the city listed for removal before August 29, 2007; after that date, the city would have to cover the costs.[74] Properties scheduled for demolition were published in lists in the *Times-Picayune*. These properties were supposed to move through the city's normal code and health adjudication process, and their owners were supposed to receive blight citations and to be granted a hearing if they desired one. At the same time, FEMA paid for teams of consultants to conduct historical surveys of neighborhoods in order to identify structures that ought not to be demolished, because of their historic character and significance. Between April 2006 and August 2007, about 3,800 properties were demolished by contractors hired by the Army Corps of Engineers. "Do Not Demolish" signs began sprouting on the front porches of homes in the knock-down fields. Officials argued that for the sake of public safety,

---

71 Ibid.

72 Center for Constitutional Rights, "International Human Rights Obligations and Post-Katrina Housing Policies: Briefing Paper to the Technical Experts for the Advisory Group on Forced Evictions United States Mission," July 26–31, 2009.

73 Bruce Eggler, "Census Population Estimate for New Orleans for 2008 Too Low," *Times-Picayune*, October 2, 2009.

74 This program was renewed into 2009 and restarted in the spring of 2011.

M. Christine Boyer, October 2009

The rebuilding of New Orleans has been an overwhelming task. The storm left 22 million tons of garbage to be hauled, according to state estimates—about fifteen times the debris removed after the September 11 attacks on the World Trade Center.

moldy, rat-infested houses on the edge of collapse and unkempt yards full of trash had to go. Although many property owners willingly took advantage of the FEMA-financed demolition program, mistakes were made: Properties were misidentified; displaced owners could not be located. Confusion reigned as the 2007 deadline neared; houses that were merely damaged, already gutted, and ready for repair ended up on the list of 1,700 condemned properties.[75] Davida Finger, a staff attorney at the Katrina Clinic of Loyola Law School, sued the city over its demolition process, pointing out that adjudication hearings that were legally required seldom occurred in practice.[76] By 2008, the clear-cutting of whole neighborhoods seemed out of control: New Orleans may have had trouble attracting investment money to implement any of its well-publicized plans, but the $11.1 million that the federal government had offered to local contractors through FEMA had created a lucrative demolition industry.[77] While all eyes were on the planning process, FEMA and the Army Corps of Engineers had demolished thousands of damaged homes before the city took over with an estimated 20,000 derelict homes remaining.

Still another program, the "Road Home Homeowner Assistance Program," implemented to at least partially compensate property owners for their losses, also disadvantaged sectors of New Orleans's population, often those that were poor and black. Financed by HUD's Community Development

75 "New Orleans Demolition List Draws Criticism: Katrina Survivors Fighting to Save Their Homes," NBC News, August 12, 2007.

76 Jason Beaubien, "New Orleans's Wrecking Ball Levels Healthy Homes," National Public Radio, January 22, 2008.

77 Alan Gutierrez, "The New Orleans Demolition List and 'Accidental' Demolitions: Grand Conspiracy or Hard-Charging Can-Do Incompetence?" thinknola.com, February 15, 2008.

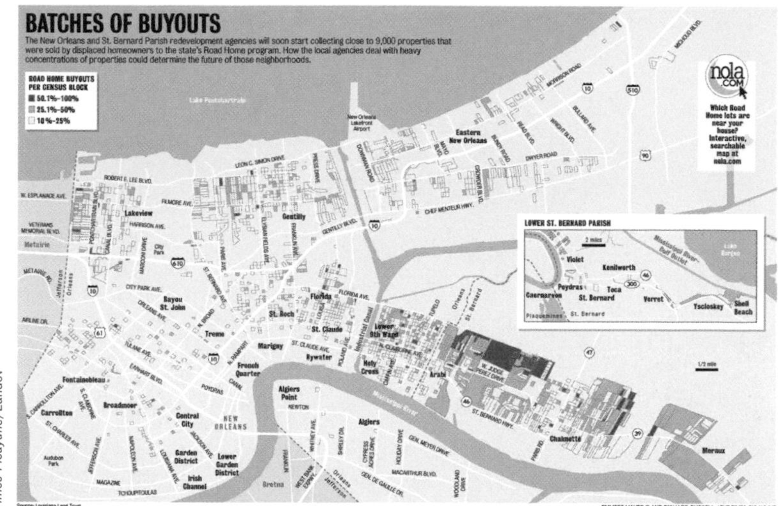

Times-Picayune/Landov

"Batches of Buyouts"

Block Grant Recovery Assistance program, the publically chartered nonprofit Road Home Corporation, conducting business as the Louisiana Land Trust (LLT), was empowered to take title to properties purchased by the Road Home program and to dispose of them, as well as to lease, renovate, improve, or expand buildings, not limited to housing stock, on them. The stated rationale was that abandoned derelict properties must not be allowed to drag down the entire recovery process.[78] With $11 billion in federal funds, the Road Home program became the largest housing redevelopment program in U.S. history. It also became highly controversial. A class-action suit filed in 2008 on behalf of more than 20,000 African-American homeowners and two fair-housing organizations claimed that the program did not take into account the systematic assessment of low property values to black neighborhoods, a legacy of the racial discrimination in New Orleans's housing market. These lower assessed values figured into the Road Home program's calculations of compensation settlements, leaving these homeowners without sufficient funds for rebuilding. Their settlements contrasted demonstrably with those granted to homeowners in largely white neighborhoods, and the suit demanded that such disparity be rectified.[79]

In *The Urban Revolution*, Henri Lefebvre warns of blind spots in the process of planning. "The blinding is the luminous source (knowledge or ideology) that projects a beam of light that illuminates *elsewhere*."[80] The dazed and blinded planners stare at what is left in the shadows; they

78 Mark Waller, "Jefferson Hopes to Auction off Road Home 'Buy Outs,'" blog.NOLA.com, November 12, 2007; Chris Kirkham, "In St. Bernard, Concrete Slabs Will Be Turning into Grass," *Times-Picayune*, January 17, 2010.

79 "Suit Alleges New Orleans's 'Road Home' Program Discriminates Against Blacks," *Louisiana Weekly News Report*, November 29, 2008.

80 Lefebvre, *The Urban Revolution*, 31.

cannot see crucial facts and so manipulate in the dark a limited set of indicators and indexes. Their language is biased as well: Some homes are described as "derelict structures," for example, and other houses as "properties." Erroneous, if not illegal, demolitions and payouts based on historic racial bias can hardly bear scrutiny in face of the international respect for Lefebvre's right to the city or human security.

A second flash point ready to blind the planners and thwart the security of low-income residents loomed large on New Orleans's post-Katrina horizon. In 2006, James Glassman writing in the *Wall Street Journal*, openly declared, "It was planning—specifically, the horrifying housing projects, largely destroyed in Katrina; the stultifying school systems, the Superdome and other wasteful public-works projects—that held the city back." He applauded the Katrina "tragedy" for providing the nation with "the most exciting urban opportunity since San Francisco in 1906."[81] Despite a critical shortage in housing, the Housing Authority of New Orleans (HANO) proposed to demolish New Orleans's "Big Four" public housing projects. HUD, which had taken control of HANO several times in its checkered history—a history marked by inefficiency, incompetence, and corruption—essentially mandated the demolition. A new city council, voted into office by a reduced, demographically wealthier and whiter electorate, approved the demolitions in December 2007. But a plan for rehousing the 20,000 individuals who would be displaced was not immediately forthcoming. Moreover, the architectural integrity of the housing to be taken down, which had been constructed mostly in the 1940s and was ranked among the nation's best, was ignored. HUD (and HANO) wanted a fresh start; they considered public housing to be a failed social policy and the housing projects to be dead-end ghettos of poverty.[82] Even though there was considerable protest, 4,500 units of public housing scattered across the city were marked for demolition in the summer of 2008.[83]

At the public hearing on demolition procedures, a woman called out to city council members standing at the back of the room while they waited for protesters to calm down: "Why y'all standing behind the curtains? ... This ain't no stage show! Get out from behind those curtains and tell us why you want to demolish our homes."[84] Meanwhile protesters outside battled with the police, who used pepper spray and stun guns to tame the

81 James K. Glassman, "Cross Country: Back to the Future," *Wall Street Journal*, January 12, 2006; also quoted in Randall, "City Residents."

82 Nikolai Ouroussoff, "High Noon in New Orleans: The Bulldozers Are Ready," *New York Times*, December 19, 2007, and Tram Nguyen, "A Game of Monopoly," *Colorlines* 36, May/June 2007.

83 Shortly after Katrina, Congress allocated $10.4 billion in Community Development Block Grants to Louisiana for housing recovery. The state got another $1.7 billion in low-income housing tax credits, called the Gulf Opportunity Zone Act or GO Zone, aimed at offering incentives for developers and nonprofits to build affordable rental housing. HANO and, by extension, its receiver HUD, applied for funds to redevelop the four public housing complexes that were demolished. See Nguyen, "A Game of Monopoly"; K. Chandler, "Demolition of 4,500 of New Orleans's 6,000 public housing units to be razed despite massive protest," *Westside Gazette*, December 27, 2007.

84 Jenny Jarvie, "Fury in New Orleans as Housing Demolition OK'd," *Los Angeles Times*, December 21, 2007.

Craig Morse, 2006, culturesubculture.com

"Stop Evicting Katrina Survivors!"

crowd. As the six-hour meeting commenced, SWAT teams stood between council members and the heated audience who had come to voice their opinions about renovating and reopening the sturdy brick public housing structures, some of which had barely been damaged by Katrina. Some spoke of a conspiracy to purge the city of its poorest residents, noting that no plan existed to rehouse those who would be displaced. Others were in favor of mixed-income communities, something better than public housing. "It's about being able to walk into a little house and be able to say, This is a house, it ain't a project. What we've got to demand," said Donna Johnigan, a former tenant of the B.W. Cooper project, "is better housing."[85]

Before Katrina, renters and low-income residents were in the majority in New Orleans, but the storm destroyed more than half of the city's rental units. The housing advocate Davida Finger commented:

> What we saw after the storm was an emphasis on property owners all around, treating renters as second-class citizens ... To be forward-thinking, we have to take into account all that's happened to renters. There is no quick fix policy, but there has been ... recognition that so much of what determines a family's outcomes turns on housing.[86]

Sheila Crowley, president of the National Low Income Housing Coalition, speaking at a Washington, D.C. hearing in 2007, put it this way, "Katrina is about wrenching hundreds of thousands of people from homes to which most will never return. Katrina is about the sudden and complete

85 Ibid.
86 Tram Nguyen, "They Can't Go Home Again," *Colorlines* 51, July/August 2009.

loss of all that homes mean—safety, respect, privacy, comfort, and security."[87] As Lefebvre puts it:

> Habiting should no longer be approached as a residue, as a trace or result of so-called superior levels ... What I would like to attempt here is a reverse decoding of the habitual situations, but taking habiting rather than the *monumental* [architecture] ... as the point of departure. The dialectical and conflicted movement between habitat and habiting, simultaneously theoretical and practical, moves into the foreground.[88]

The situation in New Orleans prompted United Nations officials to call for an immediate halt to the demolition of public housing, which it described as a violation of human rights that was forcing mostly African-American residents into homelessness. The joint statement issued by UN experts on housing and minority issues declared, "The spiraling costs of private housing and rental units, and in particular the demolition of public housing, puts these communities in further distress, increasing poverty and homelessness." Despite these calls for justice and human security issues, demolitions continued to deny citizens of New Orleans the right to the city. Blind to the meaning of "habitat," even calling the UN experts "misinformed," HUD demolished intact public housing apartments, spending nearly $1 billion on new mixed-income development, with the result that New Orleans ended up with much less affordable housing. It was left to nonprofits, such as ACORN Housing, Global Green, Habitat for Humanity, and Make It Right, to build houses for the poor, a few at a time.[89] Yet nothing seemed to mitigate the "high-rent/low-wage housing squeeze" in New Orleans. By 2009, many of the displaced were living in extended families and another 4,600 were living in FEMA trailers, while an increasing number were squatting in the city's 71,000 abandoned buildings.[90]

REINVENTING THE CRESCENT RIVERFRONT PLAN

Seeking to promote the interests of private developers, particularly of those owning parcels on the high ground along Mississippi River's natural levee who might benefit from public investment, Mayor Nagin favored the 2006 "Reinventing the Crescent" riverfront plan. Under an agreement between the board of commissioners of the Port of New Orleans (also known as the Dock Board) and the board of directors of the New Orleans

87 Ibid. See also the testimony of Sheila Crowley, president of the National Low Income Housing Coalition, presented to the Financial Services Committee, U.S. House of Representatives, February 6, 2007, at nlihc.org.

88 Lefebvre, *The Urban Revolution*, 85.

89 James S. Russell, "U.S. Bureaucrats Start Bulldozing Landmark New Orleans Housing," *Bloomberg Report*, December 18, 2007.

90 Rents increased by 4 percent between 2008 and 2009, and rents in 2009 were 52 percent higher than before Hurricane Katrina, according to the *New Orleans Index*; see Nguyen, "They Can't Go Home Again."

Building Corporation (NOBC), the entity that controls land owned by the city (or by the corporation), Nagin's administration proposed pouring as much as $300 million into improvements on the approximately six-mile stretch of riverfront extending upriver from the Industrial Canal (at Poland Avenue) to the Jackson Street wharf. Most of this money was intended to finance the removal of disused or underutilized docks and wharves and to build parks, but the plan also called for residential towers that could attract wealthier people to shore up the city's tax base.[91] Opponents and competing interests soon surfaced in response to the Reinventing the Crescent plan, which was initially developed by a multidisciplinary team of architects, landscape architects, and urban designers that included Alex Krieger of Chan Krieger Sieniewicz (Cambridge, Massachusetts); George Hargreaves of Hargreaves Associates (Cambridge, New York, San Francisco, and London); Enrique Norton of TEN Arquitectos (New York and Mexico City); and Allen Eskew of Eskew+Dumez+Ripple (New Orleans). Politicians representing hard-hit areas protested that those living in or hoping to return to struggling sections needed the help more than the riverfront developers did. New Orleans Cold Storage, a poultry exporter and a generator of local jobs, argued that it ought to be granted a warehouse site near the foot of Elysian Fields Avenue, where the existing Mandeville Wharf's shed was to be retrofitted as a pavilion and performance space.[92] But others, notably the Dock Board, argued for rezoning selected properties from light industrial to recreational, in order to create more land use, arguing that the sites offered extraordinary views of the city and were a stone's throw from the lucrative tourist quarter. There was something "authentic" and visually exciting about watching passing ships and barges: "New Orleans is about this rich legacy of a port city. We want this mix."[93]

As Lefebvre notes, urbanists slip into the cracks between the demands of developers and of those in political authority, and even when they think they are uniting the city they tend to increase its fragmentation.[94] A riverfront plan for New Orleans had been proposed first in 2004, but it was put on hold by Katrina; the Reinventing the

91 "New Orleans Building Corporation Records," City Archives, New Orleans Public Library, nutrias.org (accessed May 28, 2011) state: "The New Orleans Building Corporation was incorporated as a public benefit corporation in May 2000. It was formed for the purpose of owning, leasing, developing, and operating properties owned by the City of New Orleans or by the Corporation, including but not limited to planning, renovating, constructing, leasing, subleasing, managing, and promoting such properties. The direction and administration of the Corporation is vested in a seven-member Board of Directors comprised of the Mayor, the Councilmembers-at-Large, one district Councilman, and three members appointed by the Mayor with Council approval. The Directors elect a President, Vice-President, Treasurer, and Secretary. The concept of setting up a clearinghouse to oversee the city's real estate is a direct outgrowth of a fifty-six-year lease signed in 1963 between Mayor Victor Schiro and the International Trade Mart, the precursor organization to the World Trade Center. The lease led to the construction of the office tower at the foot of Poydras Street. As part of that agreement, the Schiro administration established the New Orleans International Trade Building Corp. to act as the city's landlord for the World Trade Center project."

92 Jen DeGregio, "Reclaiming the River," *Times-Picayune*, April 5, 2008.

93 Ibid.

94 Lefebvre, *The Urban Revolution*, 158.

Crescent plan was approved in January 2008, with the first redevelopments scheduled to open in 2011 along a one-and-a-half-mile strip bordering the Marigny and Bywater neighborhoods. A projected $30 million in improvements was to transform a gritty industrial zone marred by burned-out cargo docks into a verdant green space replete with bike paths, pavilions, two piers, and even electricity-generating windmills.[95] Like all the other plans, this one has not escaped controversy. In a city slow to rebuild affordable housing and make basic infrastructure improvements since 2005, some citizens ask why there should be high-rises on the waterfront and why those who own waterfront property are leading the planning process.

A PLAN FOR THE TWENTY-FIRST CENTURY: NEW ORLEANS 2030

In 2007, an activist coalition supporting a new master plan ordinance gave impetus to the creation of a "master plan" for New Orleans, intended to consolidate the post-Katrina planning efforts of citizens and professionals alike. An amendment to the city charter, giving legal status to whatever master plan document voters approved, was prepared, and in April 2008, the New Orleans City Council voted in support of this amendment. Two months later, in June, the City Planning Commission formally announced their support for a master plan to guide the city's development.[96] Goody Clancy & Associates of Boston, which during the UNOP process had led planning teams in three districts—CBD/Warehouse/French Quarter, Gentilly, and Bywater/Marigny—were chosen as consultants to lead the endeavor. They believed that this represented a first for New Orleans (see David Dixon's essay on page 179), but in fact the city's planning and zoning commission had engaged in "master planning" as early as the 1920s (see Carol McMichael Reese's essay on page 97). In relatively short order, Goody Clancy commenced work on its plan, holding citizen meetings aimed at informing voters and reaching consensus. On November 4, 2008, voters passed the charter amendment giving the yet-to-be-finalized master plan the "force of law," but not without significant opposition, particularly among African Americans who feared that the

95 Jen DeGregorio, "Architects Present Concept for Redeveloping New Orleans Riverfront," *Times-Picayune*, January 14, 2009; Shawn Kennedy, "New Orleans Riverfront Plan Gets Green Light," *Architectural Record*, January 14, 2008.

96 Goody Clancy prepared the "Plan for the 21st Century: New Orleans 2030," which was approved by a seven-zero vote of the city planning commission with little discussion. The city allocated $2 million of recovery money for this master plan. See Bruce Eggler, "New Orleans Master Plan Wins Approval of City Planning Commission," *Times-Picayune*, January 26, 2010, and "New Orleans Master Plan Proposal Polished with 147 Amendments" *Times-Picayune*, January 12, 2010. Before the finalization of the plan, the Neighborhood Partnership Network published the "Residents' Guide to the Draft of the 21st Century Plan for New Orleans" in July 2009; see communicationsmgr.com. On September 15, 2009, Goody Clancy published a second draft, "Draft Plan 21st Century New Orleans Master Plan, Executive Summary." For all master plan documents analyzed herein, see nolamasterplan.org. Under the heading "January 2010, Plan for the 21st Century: New Orleans 2030" are PDF files of "Volume 1, Executive Summary," and "Volume 2, Implementation."

amendment would "rubber stamp" a plan that neglected their interests.[97] On September 5, 2009, the City Planning Commission released Goody Clancy's draft, "A Plan for the 21st Century: New Orleans 2030."

The next stage of the planning process was the completion of a comprehensive zoning ordinance (CZO). Goody Clancy and the planning commission presented the completed master plan and the accompanying CZO in January 2010. Henceforth, according to the Master Plan Ordinance, all land-use decisions and zoning codes would be required to conform to the master plan and CZO. No capital improvement program, nor any annual capital budget, could interfere with its stated goals, policies, and strategies. Once a year, the plan could be amended to allow capital improvements not mentioned in the plan but consistent with it, and every five years it could be updated as well.[98] Such a detailed legal process of master planning has seldom been tested or tried in the United States over the past fifty years: the test, however, requires specific and well-argued outlines and policies, not a wish list of envisioned dreams.[99]

Unfortunately, New Orleans's master plan is in fact a "vision" plan, a set of goals to be achieved under ideal circumstances.[100] Like most of the plans before it, this one fails, as well, to provide implementation policies or to set priorities among different proposals. Although the CZO determines land-use classifications, the master plan itself neglects to offer detailed plans such as urban design projects, maps, or criteria for the future physical development of the city.[101] Nor does it discuss how to change the perception that New Orleans is not a safe place for investment as long as it remains at risk of another catastrophic flood.

The plan appears to be a grab bag of everyone's needs and desires. It offers lists of suggestions: improving the city's website; recruiting multilingual firefighters; providing better training for the 311 system, to improve reports back to citizens on enforcement actions; and banning plastic bags in stores.[102] It envisions that, over the coming years, key decisions will be made by nearly twenty new groups and twenty new plans or studies from newly formed commissions on housing, historic preservation, heritage tourism, cultural activities, pedestrian and bicycle access, climate change, etc. It calls for a "rehabilitation-friendly building code" using tax credits and other incentives to achieve "higher-value reuse" of old buildings. It advocates moving away from the "curatorial" approach to preservation to one that promotes "historic character" as a valuable contribution to con-

97 Bruce Eggler, "New Orleans City Charter Amendment Would Give Master Plan Force of Law," *Times-Picayune*, October 27, 2008.

98 Goody Clancy, "Volume 1, Executive Summary," 2.

99 California, which has experience with master planning, is an exception.

100 See Chapter 1, "A Vision and a Plan for Action," in Goody Clancy, "Volume 2, Implementation," 1–7.

101 For detailed criticism of the draft "Master Plan for New Orleans," see Bureau of Governmental Research, "In Search of the Master Plan: Making the New Orleans 2030 Draft Plan Work," October 2009, bgr.org.

102 Goody Clancy, "Volume 1, Executive Summary," 84–6.

temporary life.[103] It proposes urban-agriculture zones and describes an accelerating resettlement of neighborhoods "with innovative land assembly" plans and density levels that can provide "the critical mass needed to support vibrant commercial districts, walkable streets, convenient transit, lively parks, and similar amenities."[104] It has, in other words, adopted many of the visions presented in preceding plans has and also added its own.

By this writing in 2010, the citizens of New Orleans have grown cynical, after being organized to participate in the planning processes for five long years but without seeing much transparency, instead being kept in the dark about the specific goals in plan after plan. They are not optimistic about more participation, on commissions not yet established, with major decisions postponed for the coming years. This, even though the plan proclaims, "Once divided by competition over a 'shrinking pie' as the city lost people and jobs, New Orleanians can now work together to nurture growth and share its benefits." The plan cites several reasons why its authors think New Orleans's "turn has come!"[105] It even states an explicit condition for ensuring that its prediction comes true: there will be guaranteed "neighborhood participation in decision making about land-use action."[106]

David Dixon, head of the Goody Clancy team who produced the master plan, boasts that when the Army Corps of Engineers finishes levee improvements by 2011, the city will be protected from the potentially disastrous outcomes associated with a 100-year storm. New Orleans will no longer be a city of "wet" and "dry" neighborhoods, but one in which all sections can plan confidently for the future. One might add: "those sections still remaining, not bulldozed under with their terrain stripped clear, and those citizens, mostly white, who remain or will come to reap the harvest of a shrunken city." For it is just this middle-class clientele that the plan invites to New Orleans: "The share of Americans who want to live in walkable urban neighborhoods will grow for the next fifteen to twenty years," and those people "are increasingly choosing amenity-rich mixed-use communities," such as those the master plan envisions for New Orleans. In short, the dreams of New Urbanism advocates have won out: dreams of a pedestrian-friendly city as an alternative to a car-oriented city. At the same time, poor black communities have lost out, their eradicated homes replaced by visions of a sustainable, green city—resource-efficient, environmentally healthy, and resilient. The plan predicts that gated and exclusive enclaves with landscaped canals, parks with water features, and shady tree-lined streets will be the new norm. The plan points out that while New Orleans has a well-established "stake" in energy and trade, there is a new constellation of emerging industries, and these

103 Ibid., 3.

104 Ibid., 42, and Bruce Eggler, "Draft of Ambitious Master Plan for New Orleans Goes Online Today," *Times-Picayune*, March 20, 2009.

105 Eggler, "Draft of Ambitious Master Plan."

106 Goody Clancy, "Volume 1: Executive Summary," 2.

will be the drivers of its future prosperity. In addition, energizing entrepreneurs are expected to flow into this city of rising opportunities.[107] As the *New York Times* observed in the aftermath of Katrina, there was an urge to rebuild "that is as primal as the force that pushes grass up through the cracks in the sidewalk." However, the *Times* did not push an analysis of their homily asking what forces are doing the pushing and where in the city the grass would be coming up.[108] "How do you build a city with equity? There is no manual," a community organizer observed way back in 2005.[109]

To base land-use decisions on such a vague document as the 2010 master plan is to beg for future conflict. The master plan, now invested with the force of law, enables the Planning Commission to stop any development it deems not in compliance, but the document does not specify what development is allowed and where. At the end of *The Urban Revolution*, Henri Lefebvre comments, "As a form of representation, urbanism is nothing more than an ideology that claims to be either 'art' or 'technology' or 'science,' depending on the context."[110] There are vested interests that must be satisfied, and these interests are known because they have been either openly stated or studied by experts. The case of real estate, "where capital flows in the event of a depression, although enormous profits soon slow to a trickle," is an important example.[111] Urbanism is unwittingly involved with real estate capital and thus "implies the intervention of power more than that of understanding. Its only coherent, its only logic, is that of the state—the void. The state can only separate, disperse, hollow out vast voids, the squares and avenues built in its own image—an image of force and constraint."[112]

THE RIGHT TO THE CITY AND HUMAN SECURITY REVISITED

A joke that circulated after Hurricane Katrina claimed that if the people of New Orleans had wanted the federal government to come to their rescue right away they should have blamed the storm on Al Qaeda.[113]

"Human security," meaning the guarantee of well-being and human dignity for all individuals, were words never deployed in the aftermath of Hurricane Katrina. Yet freedom from fear and freedom from want are essential to the provision of human security—an effort that focuses attention on human beings rather than on states, governmental policies, and planning bureaucracies. Seeing the effects of environmental change

107 Ibid. See especially sections "How We Live" and "How We Prosper."

108 The *New York Times* quoted (without reference) in the Rockefeller Foundation's report "New Orleans Planning for a Better Future" (September 2006), 4.

109 Ibid., 3.

110 Lefebvre, *The Urban Revolution*, 158–9.

111 Ibid., 159.

112 Ibid., 160–1.

113 Michael Renner and Zoe Chafe, "Hurricane Katrina in a Human Security Perspective," *World Watch*, September 1, 2006.

through the lens of human security connects issues such as rising seawaters and the occurrence of lethal storms to the issues of poverty, vulnerability, equity, and conflict. Environmental factors were known to have dramatic impact on migration flows long before the displacement of New Orleans's post-Katrina diaspora. Nonlethal destruction, such as the erasure of ecosystems, had degraded New Orleans's environmental safety net for decades previous to Katrina, making the city increasingly vulnerable, and all the while dire warnings were issued. Clearly, environmental disasters can be as destructive as military invasions, and in the case of New Orleans, the economically marginalized population living in low-lying neighborhoods prone to flooding and without an economic safety net, suffered the most. Plans to reconstruct New Orleans have continued to show bias against the poor; whether planners admit it or not, they have implemented a triage strategy in every one of their proposed redevelopment and recovery schemes.

In post-Katrina New Orleans, racial and economic factors inhibit the ability of the most vulnerable citizens to return to their homes, to participate in redevelopment plans, and to rebuild their neighborhoods. They are excluded—they are given no right to the city, no right of return to their homes, no right to be protected from discrimination. Yet the right to housing, which includes residential stability and security of tenure, is contained in the UN Guiding Principles on Internal Displacement, and the United States has accepted this policy in international situations but has failed to apply it at home. Discriminatory post-Katrina plans have all prioritized economic viability over residents' needs, economic incentives over crime prevention. Homelessness rates, which in 2008 were nearly four times higher in New Orleans than in other American cities, remain problematic as reconstruction produces higher rents and creates shortages of affordable housing, resulting in continued displacement. Only meager assistance has been offered through a rental repair program, and none of the redevelopment plans have mentioned implementing affordable rental units. Undoubtedly, reconstruction plans for New Orleans represent a clear retrogression with respect to human security issues. These plans need to be radically rethought, and greater focus trained on the recipients' end; otherwise, the power invested in planning authorities is far from legitimate, as their proposed actions deploy yet more violence against the most vulnerable. If the new New Orleans is not rethought, it will continue to be a blind spot of racism in the eyes of the nation, and the "urban" as a problematic will remain unsolved. Lefebvre, speaks of what is involved in planning in accordance with industrial rationality:

> A reduction that is both social and mental, toward trivialization and toward specialization ... Blindness, our not-seeing and not-knowing, implies an ideology. These blind fields embed themselves in representation. Initially, we are faced with the *presentation* of the facts and groups

of facts, a way of perceiving and grouping. This is followed by a *re-presentation*, an interpretation of the facts [with all of its misinterpretations and misunderstandings] ... The blinding (assumptions we accept dogmatically) and the blinded (the misunderstood) are complementary aspects of our blindness.[114]

114 Lefebvre, *The Urban Revolution*, 30.

ETHICAL DILEMMAS IN POST-KATRINA NEW ORLEANS PLANNING

MELISSA HARRIS-PERRY and
WILLIAM M. HARRIS SR.

> They talk that "freedom matters" but didn't even leave a ladder ...
> I knock on the door; hope isn't home
> Fate's not around and the luck's all gone.
> Don't ask me what's wrong; ask me what's right.
> —Lil Wayne, "Tie My Hands"[1]

Rebuilding is a messy process that introduces important ethical questions about achieving the right balance between community participation and efficient policy implementation. With the benefit of perspective gained over more than five years, this is a useful moment to question how successful local planning efforts in post-Katrina New Orleans have been in striking such a balance. This essay illuminates a key ethical challenge facing the urban planners in contemporary New Orleans: how to meet the need for decision-making efficiency while honoring the democratic responsibility to allow participatory processes. We begin with the assumption that planners are motivated by a desire to efficiently and fairly produce a fully recovered New Orleans but that they face structural constraints and competing professional and political values that limit the effectiveness of their work. We are not naïve about the fact that some policy makers are aggressively uninterested in pursuing egalitarian ends; nevertheless, we begin with this assumption of just intentions in order to demonstrate that sticky ethical problems persist even when planners and elected officials attempt to pursue fairness and equity.

Many skilled researchers and activists have already identified the readily apparent injustices in post-Katrina New Orleans; our goal is somewhat different. We do not offer a comprehensive (or even cursory) review of how key decision makers made their planning choices in the city after the storm. Instead, we offer an overview of the principles of collective action, government process, and policy making that are meaningfully present in the case. Because we are writing about broad ethical

1 New Orleans hip-hop artist Lil Wayne, "Tie My Hands," on *Tha Carter III*, Cash Money Records (2008).

concerns, we often present our arguments at a level of abstraction that obscures the vital human reality of the Katrina experience. This analytic abstraction should not diminish the reality of the ethical dilemmas confronting decision makers in post-disaster New Orleans. These are concrete problems about how to fairly distribute scarce resources among vulnerable populations. The choices made by those charged with solving them determine whether citizens can return to their neighborhoods, whether families will have shelter, whether children will learn to read, whether workers will have fair wages, and whether businesses can earn a profit. In short, the principles are abstract, but their consequences are quite real.

First, we review several philosophical approaches governing a polity, in order to identify a set of guiding principles that create the shared norms of American policy making. This gives us a framework for adjudicating New Orleans's responses to crisis planning. Second, we demonstrate that Hurricane Katrina was not only a natural disaster but also a racial disaster, with specific consequences for African-American citizens. Next, we situate Hurricane Katrina within the racial and political moment in which it occurred in order to illuminate how contemporary American government understands itself in relation to African Americans. Finally, we argue that the racial dimensions of the disaster coincided with the violation of key ethical principles. This leads us to conclude that much of the continuing racial injustice in New Orleans results from the difficult effort of trying to balance efficient planning with participatory processes in the aftermath of Katrina.

PHILOSOPHICAL APPROACHES TO POLICY MAKING

Hurricane Katrina caused unprecedented damage to public infrastructure, commercial enterprises, and personal property.[2] The storm temporarily displaced every resident of New Orleans and permanently dispersed nearly half the population. In a city that was already wrestling with violent crime, decreasing population, and concentrated poverty, the August 2005 levee failures created a catastrophic event of nearly unimaginable proportions. In the aftermath of an exogenous shock of this magnitude, American policy makers and planning professionals are faced with a dilemma that goes to the heart of the American political system. The task of rebuilding requires centralized decision making, quick administrative choices, clear bureaucratic processes, and disciplined, dispassionate planning. Restoration of multiple interdependent systems requires specialized technical knowledge and decisive choices. Centralized, hierarchal, authoritarian systems appear well equipped to create and employ the systematic processes so desperately needed in a disaster context. If such efficiency were the only standard for

2 See Mark Burton and Michael Hicks, "Hurricane Katrina: Preliminary Estimates of Commercial and Public Sector Damages," a report produced by the Center for Business and Economic Research of Marshall University (Huntington, WV, 2005); see also Sheila Jasanoff, "Beyond Calculation: A Democratic Response to Risk," in *Disaster and the Politics of Intervention*, ed. Andrew Lakoff (New York: Columbia University Press, 2010), 14–40.

judging the quality of recovery, an authoritarian system of planning would be required following a disaster. Massive disaster tempts us to vest all authority in a single, size-limited, expert, and benevolent decision-making body.

There is a philosophical as well as practical basis for this yearning for authoritarianism as a response to disruption and uncertainty. In Western political theory, it was most clearly explicated by the seventeenth-century political philosopher Thomas Hobbes: Human beings originally exist in a state of nature that offers them perfect freedom but little security. In this natural condition, each person must fend for himself, and although each is free to behave as he likes, he is never safe from those who are bigger, stronger, and more powerful. This kind of freedom leads to a human existence that is "brutish, nasty, and short."[3] Therefore, mankind chooses instead to live in communities ruled by governments. These governments provide security, predictability, physical infrastructure, and opportunities to accumulate private property. These governments also require men to give up some of their natural freedom. In *Leviathan*, first published in 1660, Hobbes argues that it is preferable to relinquish the brutish life of absolute freedom for the limited but secure liberty of civilization, and that the best form of government for the protection of human interests is a powerful monarchy. The benevolence of the system's central decision maker—the monarch—derives from his self-interest: he maintains his own strength by crafting a just community. Hobbes argues further that monarchs are best suited to address complex problems because, as sole rulers, they can act quickly and rationally without having to balance multiple competing interests and egos.[4]

A cursory review of early planning efforts in New Orleans reveals a Hobbesian response. In the days immediately following Hurricane Katrina, national media presented the hurricane-damaged city as a lawless place of unrest, violence, and disintegrating civic institutions.[5] In the first days of disaster coverage, television news reported roving, armed gangs of young black men opportunistically profiting from the tragedy, suggesting that these men were stealing from electronics stores, raping women trapped in the evacuation centers, and trying to assassinate relief workers.[6] Later evidence showed that most of these young black men were organizing to assist other survivors who were unable to find supplies: the elderly, the sick, and women with children.[7]

---

3 Thomas Hobbes, *Leviathan* (New York: Oxford University Press, 2009 reissue edition).

4 Ibid.

5 Sociologists Kathleen Tierney, Christine Bevc, and Erica Kuligowski argue that this crime framework has roots in "disaster myths" in their article "Metaphors Matter: Disaster Myths, Media Frames, and Their Consequences in Hurricane Katrina," in *Shelter from the Storm: Repairing the National Emergency Management System after Hurricane Katrina*, Annals of the American Academy of Political and Social Science 604 (March 2006), 57–81. "Following Hurricane Katrina, the response of disaster victims was framed by the media in ways that greatly exaggerated the incidence and severity of looting and lawlessness."

6 Michael Eric Dyson, *Come Hell or High Water: Katrina and the Color of Disaster* (New York: Basic Civitas, 2006).

7 Havidán Rodríguez, Joseph Trainor, and Enrico L. Quarantelli, "Rising to the Challenges of a Catastrophe: The Emergent and Prosocial Behavior Following Hurricane Katrina," in *Shelter from the Storm*, 82–101.

The effects of the initial framing were pernicious. Post-Katrina New Orleans was reported to the nation as though it were in a Hobbesian "state of nature" requiring the aggressive authoritarianism of a powerful leader to bring it back to civilization. The enormous structural challenges imposed by the flooding combined with a sense that the city's residents were out of control to propagate centralized, authority-driven solutions. In many instances, government interventions in New Orleans followed authoritarian models.[8]

Although no one advocated for New Orleans to appoint a monarch, the idea of centralized authority for recovery decisions was seductive. For example, New Orleans Mayor C. Ray Nagin appointed Dr. Edward James Blakely as the city's "recovery czar" in January 2007, transferring unprecedented authority to this unelected official. Blakely had an impressive résumé of experience coping with post-disaster contexts. As an expert in urban planning and economic development and a respected national figure, he came to the job with the right credentials, expertise, and contacts. He also came with a clear plan to encourage private development and craft a denser city built on a smaller footprint primarily in high-ground neighborhoods. But despite his official authority, his professional expertise, and his clear ideas, Blakely ultimately accomplished little during his tenure.

Blakely was a mismatch with New Orleans, the consummate outsider in a city where people trace their residence by generations and centuries rather than by decades.[9] He maintained a house and employment in Australia and never made New Orleans his permanent home. In a context when thousands were fighting desperately to return to their city, many citizens balked at the idea that its reconstruction should be directed by someone who seemed uninterested in it as a place to live. Further, Blakely's comments to the press about New Orleans life and culture were often politically tone-deaf. This czar may have had official authority, but because he was so broadly vilified by New Orleanians, he was without real power.[10] For effective and just planning to go forward in a contemporary American city, official authority must be accompanied by meaningful public support.

8 For example, sociologist and disaster expert Eric Klinenberg points to the "militarization of social support programs" as a key component of the post-disaster response to the deadly 1995 Chicago heat wave; see *Heat Wave: A Social Autopsy of Disaster in Chicago* (Chicago: University of Chicago Press, 2002). He argues that there is a fundamental and dangerous mismatch between the needs of stranded citizens and the paramilitary style of containment and confrontation that was used by government responders. For Joel Bleifuss's interview with Klinenberg discussing parallels between Hurricane Katrina and the Chicago heat wave, see "Disasters: Natural and Social," *In These Times*, September 26, 2005. D'Ann R. Penner and Keith C. Ferdinand collected a series of first-person accounts from African-American survivors of Hurricane Katrina in *Overcoming Katrina: African American Voices from the Crescent City and Beyond* (New York: Palgrave Macmillan, 2009). Several of them tell compelling stories of how military personnel deployed to New Orleans to assist in rescue and evacuation treated survivors as though they were enemy combatants rather than citizens in need of relief.

9 In the 2000 census, New Orleans recorded the highest native-born population of any American city: more than 75 percent of New Orleans residents had been born in Louisiana.

10 It is easy to follow the brutal relationship between Blakely and the city of New Orleans by reviewing coverage of his tenure through the *Times-Picayune*. For a taste of the dislike between the city and its would-be leader see David Hammer, "Ed Blakely Lambastes New Orleans," *Times-Picayune*, November 2, 2009.

This need for public support was readily apparent in Mayor Nagin's first attempt at generating a post-storm restoration plan. Mayor Nagin's Bring New Orleans Back (BNOB) commission, established in September 2005, convened panels of local leaders in the months that followed to create a plan for land use, infrastructure, transportation, housing, education, culture, and economic renewal. Through the auspices of the Urban Land Institute (ULI), the commission's efforts were aided by national experts who came to the city just weeks after the storm, long before many New Orleanians themselves were able to return. They gathered information through site visits, documents, historical analysis, economic forecasting, and personal interviews. Using econometric models, they considered population loss, the environmental sustainability of existing neighborhoods, and the likely commercial future of the city. In relative isolation, this small group applied their combined professional expertise to the problems at hand. On November 18, 2005, they staged a conference in the ruined city and presented their preliminary findings.[11]

We presume that most planners in the ULI group came to New Orleans with good intentions. Some may have had personal economic interests attached to the recommendations, but for the most part, the group was composed of people who were stunned and saddened by the destruction in New Orleans. They took their jobs seriously and worked hard to apply their professional tools to the task of creating a vision and a plan for a city many of them loved and all of them respected. Judged solely by standards of efficiency and sustainability, the ULI team's comprehensive report offered a rational, dispassionate, achievable, reasonable plan for rebuilding the city. According to one Hobbesian theory, this plan should have been swiftly implemented. However, the reality of New Orleans does not conform to strict technocratic planning standards, nor does it fit a seventeenth-century philosophical model of governing. In fact, the effects of the ULI effort were disastrous for the top-down planning model and instructive about the role of democratic decision making in crisis circumstances.

On January 11, 2006, the Urban Planning Committee of the BNOB commission released to the general public a final report on its work, which included the ULI's land-use recommendations.[12] On the same day, in anticipation of the unveiling of the BNOB report, the *Times-Picayune* published an interpretive article, "4 Months to Decide, Nagin Panel Says Hardest-hit Areas Must Prove Viability." The article was illustrated with

11 Professor Harris-Perry (then Harris-Lacewell) was in New Orleans conducting university research during the November 2005 meetings shepherded by the ULI. There she observed both the BNOB commission's processes and the initial reactions of community members to the recommendations. For a ULI news item about the outcomes of the meetings, see "Moving Beyond Recovery to Restoration and Rebirth: Urban Land Institute Makes Recommendations on Rebuilding New Orleans," November 18, 2005, uli.org. This webpage also contains a link to the PDF of the sixty-five page report "A Rebuilding Strategy, New Orleans, LA."

12 A PDF file of the sixty-nine page report "Action Plan for New Orleans: The New American City" can be found at columbia.edu.

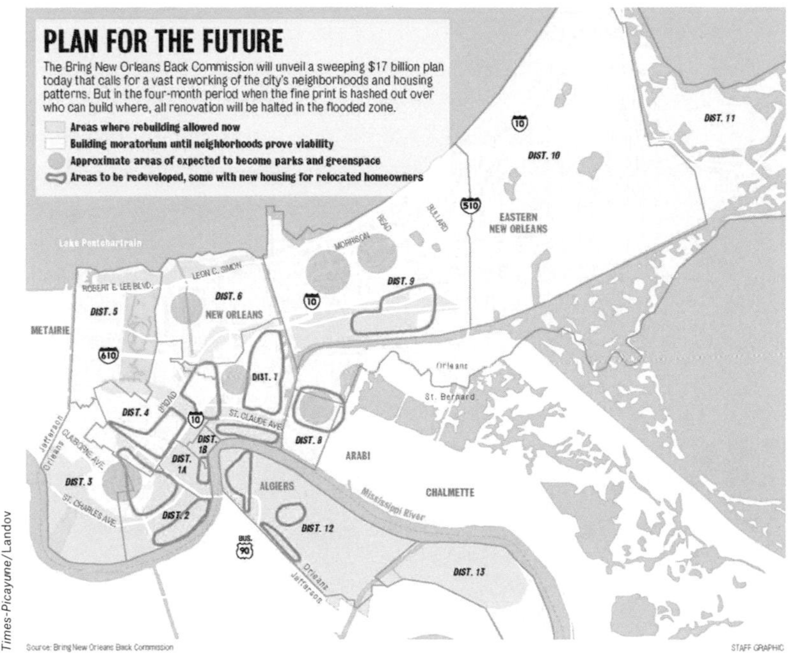

Times-Picayune/Landov

"Plan for the Future"—the so-called green-dot map—a staff graphic published in the *Times-Picayune* on January 11, 2006, with its source identified as the Bring New Orleans Back Commission.

a staff-produced graphic captioned "Plan for the Future." It showed six large green circles that designated the areas "expected to become parks and green space." The green circles were drawn directly over existing neighborhoods, homes, schools, churches, and businesses. Having assessed the land, the economy, and the environmental impact of rebuilding, ULI and BNOB planners had apparently decided that many of these existing communities should not be rebuilt on the terms of their pre-Katrina use. As a result of this recommendation, the BNOB/ULI plan came under heavy criticism; it was derided and associated in the public's mind with the green-dot diagram, although, ironically, neither the preliminary nor the final report of the BNOB commission contained that particular illustration.[13]

It is beyond the scope of this essay or the capacity of these authors to adequately capture the absolute fury with which the people of New Orleans received this plan. Few events in the post-disaster city more completely unified disparate neighborhoods, which banded together to resist the idea that their own beloved areas of the city would not be rebuilt. The green-dot graphic came to represent centralized, top-down decision making and was labeled as antidemocratic, disenfranchising, class-biased, and racist. The green-dot map so powerfully dominated public discourse about the ULI

13 Frank Donze and Gordon Russell, "4 Months to Decide, Nagin Panel Says Hardest-hit Areas Must Prove Viability," *Times-Picayune*, January 11, 2006.

proposals and, by extension, the BNOB reports that few other elements were discussed or debated. Whatever virtues existed in the proposals were largely ignored in the public eruption against an authoritarian process that seemed to strip individuals of their right to return.

The BNOB/ULI green-dot fiasco is illustrative of the central ethical dilemma faced by crisis planners in the American political system. The ULI planners came to New Orleans to engage in a planning process that the mayor initiated. They came in good faith and with substantive experience and expertise. Yet in the end their plans were met with disdain and distrust. These planners learned, as recovery czar Ed Blakely did later, that Americans expect and demand the right to participate in policy making. It is foolish and impossible to judge the ULI plan solely by a set of technical standards about a hypothetical city. We cannot decide if the ULI plan was a good plan based exclusively on how it made use of land and how that land use compares to an abstract, ideal model. New Orleans is not hypothetical. It is a real city, with living, breathing, suffering, displaced residents. Those residents have participatory rights and expectations that emerge from the undergirding philosophical guidelines of American politics. The United States may owe an intellectual debt to Thomas Hobbes, but the nation's founding principles depart from the *Leviathan* prescription in dramatic ways. Unlike the authoritarian vision of Hobbes, American founding documents convey a strong respect for participatory decision making and divided authority and show a preference for procedural equality over efficiency. In short, the American version of the social contract is more the descendant of the eighteenth-century philosopher Jean-Jacques Rousseau than it is the child of seventeenth-century Thomas Hobbes.

Rousseau, unlike Hobbes, did not believe that a benevolent ruler was sufficient to secure human freedom. People could only be free when they themselves had the inalienable and indivisible capacity for self-rule. In his 1762 text *The Social Contract*, Rousseau advances this idea of self-rule, that people must be able to choose the laws and policies by which they will live and that they must retain the right to alter the government if it ceases to meet their collective needs.[14] It is toward Rousseau that Thomas Jefferson gestures in the Declaration of Independence, when he declares the self-evident nature of man's inalienable right to "life, liberty, and the pursuit of happiness" and when he asserts that governments are instituted among men for the purpose of securing these rights. American revolutionaries were unconvinced that they must submit to the central authority of a king. Instead, they renegotiated the social contract to require that the state derive its authority from the consent of the governed. This philosophical legacy of popular sovereignty and self-rule provided the

14 Jean-Jacques Rousseau, *The Social Contract, Or Principles of the Political Right*, (1762), and Thomas Hobbes, *Leviathan*.

guiding principles for American policy making and lies at the heart of the ethical dilemma facing New Orleans planners.

A dispassionate, data-driven, hierarchal planning process might produce results that are reasonable from the perspective of abstract best practices. One might even argue that moving forward aggressively with the ULI's proposals or acting swiftly to implement Blakely's vision would have created a beautiful, safe, sustainable city. But even if these outcomes had occurred, implementation of these plans after such scant public participation could never have produced a truly just outcome. In our democracy, process is often just as important as outcome. No matter what the final choices, participation by the people in their own planning is a linchpin of fairness. Without this participatory basis, even the most technically proficient plan cannot be a just plan.

Yet despite American insistence on participation, the historical realities of the United States belie any idea that this nation has been perfect in rendering its Rousseau-inspired ideal. America's founders had to balance the principle of direct participation against the reality that the country was too large and too complex, even in 1787, the year of the Constitutional Convention, to be governed by a system of direct democracy. These founders, while seeking freedom and autonomy for all men of their own class, were content to draft a constitution that disfranchised those who did not own property, that codified women as noncitizens and declared slaves nonpersons. Structural and legal inequality are deeply embedded in the fabric of the American state. Even after nearly 230 years, the legacy of this inequality marks the basic realities of citizenship for all those who were excluded from the United States' first social contract.

This legacy of deeply embedded race and class inequalities was at the heart of New Orleans's swift and angry reaction to the green-dot plan. ULI's green space proposal would have had disproportionate negative effects on the poorest, most vulnerable, and most African American–concentrated areas of the city. Black and poor residents lived in these often ecologically marginal areas because decades of racialized policy choices and private lending decisions had relegated the least powerful residents to the most vulnerable areas of the city. These were the same residents who were least able to return to the city in November 2005, and they were therefore the most silent in the early planning process. The green-dot plan reinforced these existing inequalities in a manner that raised immediate concern among African Americans and racially conscious white activists throughout New Orleans. These concerns were already heightened because Hurricane Katrina was a disaster with explicit racial meaning. To emphasize this point, let us pause for a moment to review the ways in which Hurricane Katrina was a racial disaster in addition to being a natural disaster.

KATRINA AS RACIAL DISASTER

A hurricane is a force of nature. A hurricane has no political, social, economic or historical allegiances. In this sense, a hurricane cannot and does not discriminate. But much of the Katrina disaster was caused not by the storm but by massive and multiple breaches in the levees that released torrents of water into the city, and it is false and dangerous to believe that those breaches can be blamed on neutral forces or that the burdens they left behind have fallen on all citizens equally.[15] The failure of the levees means that Hurricane Katrina is as much a man-made tragedy as a natural one.[16] Levee construction is the responsibility of the federal government, and levee maintenance falls under the auspices of states and localities. When levees break, it is an indication that these policy systems have failed. Unlike storms, governments make conscious choices, and those choices are rooted in political, social, economic, and historical contingencies.[17] Katrina was a color-blind storm, but it was a racialized disaster whose consequences were felt most brutally by the poor, the elderly, the infirm, and people of color. Race is a key factor in predicting those most likely to have been trapped in the city, those most likely to have been involuntarily relocated a significant distance from their families, and those most likely to have experienced continued loss of income and quality of life in the years following the storm.[18] The storm caused greater proportionate property loss and greater permanent displacement for black New Orleans residents.[19] African Americans directly victimized by the storm labored under both geographic and social vulnerability.[20]

Not only were the storm's effects racially unequal, but they also provoked significantly different reactions from black and white Americans who viewed the unfolding disaster through the media. Public opinion research shows that both black and white Americans watched significant media coverage of the storm and its aftermath. Yet despite the immediate and overwhelming visual evidence it offered that African-American residents were more likely to be stranded in the city, more likely to experience catastrophic property loss, and least likely to have a path to return in subsequent years, black and white Americans formed vastly different

15 See Robert C. Lieberman, "The Storm Didn't Discriminate: Katrina and the Politics of Color Blindness," in *Du Bois Review: Social Science Research on Race* 3 (Spring 2006), 7–22.

16 See Adolph Reed Jr., "Introduction," *Unnatural Disaster: The Nation on Hurricane Katrina*, ed. Betsy Reed (New York: Nation Books, 2006).

17 See Jasanoff, "Beyond Calculation," 14–40.

18 Arloc Sherman and Isaac Shapiro, "Essential Facts about the Victims of Hurricane Katrina" (Washington, D.C.: Center on Budget and Policy Priorities, 2005), katrinaresearchhub.ssrc.org.

19 Ibid. See also Susan L. Cutter, Bryan J. Boruff, and W. Lynn Shirley, "Social Vulnerability to Environmental Hazards," *Social Science Quarterly* 84 (June 2003), 242–61, and Thomas Gabe, et al., *Hurricane Katrina: Social-Demographic Characteristics of Impacted Areas*, Congressional Research Service Report RL33141, 2005.

20 Cutter, "The Geography of Social Vulnerability: Race, Class, and Catastrophe"; Social Science Research Council, "Understanding Katrina: Perspectives from the Social Sciences," June 11, 2006, understandingkatrina.ssrc.org.

opinions about the racial meanings of these images.[21] Nearly all respondents to a survey funded by the Pew Charitable Trusts conducted immediately after the storm were discontent with the government's response to the emergency.[22] But the Pew data revealed that while 71 percent of African Americans believed that Katrina proved that racial inequality remained a major problem in the country, a majority of whites (56 percent) felt that racial inequality was not a particularly important lesson of the disaster. Seventy-seven percent of African Americans felt the federal government response was poor or only fair; a much smaller majority of whites—55 percent—agreed. In a stunning racial disjuncture, 66 percent of African-American respondents believed that if most of the victims had been white the response would have been faster, whereas 77 percent of whites believed that race had made no difference in the speed of government response. Most white Americans believed that Hurricane Katrina's aftermath was tragic, but they understood it primarily as a natural disaster followed by technical and bureaucratic failures. Conversely, most black Americans saw the aftermath of Katrina as a racial disaster.

It is from this vantage point of racial disaster that we must view the ethical dilemma of post-storm planning. Katrina's racially disparate impact means that participatory planning processes were even more important than they would have been under normal circumstances. To underscore this point, let us return to our discussion of political philosophy. American policy making is far too complex to be executed by means of direct democracy, but input from the public remains an ethical standard. Participation is critically important, and race and class inequalities are still the primary barriers to achieving that ideal. Those who have the resources (time, money, education, influence) to participate are as a group systemically different from those who lack these resources. In New Orleans, as in many other American cities, race is the single most definitive and systemic determinant of inequality. In the context of a massive catastrophe in which the legacy of racial injustice played a

21 Kathryn A. Sweeney, "The Blame Game: Racialized Responses to Hurricane Katrina," *Du Bois Review: Social Science Research on Race* 3 (March 2006), 161–74. In the same issue, see also Leonie Hurdy and Stanley Feldman, "Worlds Apart: Blacks and Whites React to Hurricane Katrina," 97–113, and Tyrone Forman and Amanda Lewis, "Racial Apathy and Hurricane Katrina: The Social Anatomy of Prejudice in the Post-Civil Rights Era," 175–202.

22 "Two in Three Critical of Bush's Relief Efforts," Pew Research Center, September 8, 2005. The Hurricane Katrina Survey, sponsored by the Pew Research Center for the People and the Press, obtained telephone interviews with a nationally representative sample of 1,000 adults living in continental United States telephone households. The survey was conducted by Princeton Survey Research Associates International. Interviews were done in English by Princeton Data Source, LLC, September 6–7, 2005. Statistical results were weighted to correct known demographic discrepancies. The margin of sampling error for the complete set of weighted data was ±3.5 percent. The oversample of African Americans was designed to allow a sufficient number of interviews for reporting results of this demographic group. The national sample of telephone households was supplemented with an additional 103 interviews with African Americans whose households had been recently contacted for past Pew Research Center national surveys. Demographic weighting was used to ensure that the survey results reflected the correct racial and ethnic composition of national adults, based on U.S. Census information.

critical role, the creation of racially inclusive planning processes is an ethical responsibility. All commitments to professional and technical aspects of planning must be balanced against this fundamental principle that people have an inalienable right to self-government and therefore cannot be shut out of a civic rebuilding process, especially if race plays a key role in determining who is shut out. The commitment to full inclusion must obtain even when public participation makes planning processes less efficient. This principle of racial justice is not just a preference of the authors; it is a broadly articulated position of U.S. policy makers. In fact, the months preceding the disaster in New Orleans were an extraordinary moment in American racial history, when several levels of U.S. government unambiguously reinforced the nation's commitment to participatory democracy and racial justice.

RACE, RECONSTRUCTION, AND GOVERNMENT RESPONSIBILITY

Despite the continuing reality of racial inequality, the past fifty years can easily be called the most hopeful decades of black citizenship in American history. In this half-century, African Americans have rolled back voting restrictions, asserted the right to fair and equal treatment under the law, and made real gains in education, access, and visibility. The summer of 2005 was a surprising culmination of many of these struggles. On May 3, 2005, the state of Illinois exhumed the body of slain black teen Emmett Till. Till's kidnapping, torture, and murder in 1955 galvanized the modern civil rights movement. The exhumation of his body was ordered by the Justice Department in an effort to reopen the case and offer some semblance of justice after more than fifty years. Less than a month later, on June 21, 2005, a Mississippi jury convicted Edgar Ray Killen on three counts of manslaughter for the 1964 slaying of three civil rights workers: James Earl Chaney, Andrew Goodman, and Michael Schwerner. Killen, eighty years old on the date of the verdict, was sentenced to serve sixty years in prison. By pursuing both the Till case and the Killen conviction, government agencies reconfirmed the critical importance of racial justice, even when the terms of that justice have been shamefully delayed. The renewed Till investigation and late Killen prosecution were public statements that repudiated a time in American history when whites who dared to raise their voices against racial injustice, and blacks who dared to raise their voices at all, were silenced with terror and murder. These actions were both substantive and symbolic.

Perhaps the most profound and unlikely moment of racial reconciliation in the summer of 2005 came on June 13. On that date the United States Senate apologized for failing to act to halt lynching in America. Between 1890 and 1960, nearly 5,000 Americans were murdered through acts of lynching. Most of victims were African-American men and women living in the South, murdered by white mobs who acted with the full knowledge and tacit consent of their communities and local law enforcement.[23] During these decades of domestic terrorism, more than 200 pieces of antilynching legislation were introduced in the United States Congress. The most famous and successful was the Dyer Anti-Lynching Bill, introduced in 1918 by Missouri Republican Leonidas C. Dyer. After aggressive lobbying by the National Association for the Advancement of Colored People, citizen-led efforts throughout the nation, and reporting by courageous black journalists in the South, the Dyer Bill finally passed the House of Representatives in 1922.[24] The bill proposed prison sentences and steep fines for those who participated in lynching. If this bill had passed into law, it would have restored one aspect of Reconstruction by forcing the federal government to assume responsibility for human rights violations occurring in the South. The bill was filibustered by Southern Democrats, and it died on the Senate floor.

In June 2005, just six weeks before Hurricane Katrina devastated the city of New Orleans, the U.S. Senate reversed this shameful history and apologized for its decades of inaction. The resolution was proposed and shepherded through the Senate by the Democratic senator from Louisiana, Mary Landrieu.[25] It is both a stunning achievement and a bitter irony that a Southern Democrat who represents the city of New Orleans gave the impetus to this resolution. The apology indicated a profound understanding that American lawmakers cannot ignore the need to directly confront the life-threatening realities of racial inequality if they hope to fulfill their basic responsibility as policy makers.

Before the ink on this powerful resolution was dry, Hurricane Katrina revealed just how utterly unjust America's racial caste system remains. Relegated by income and housing inequities to housing on dangerously low ground, and abandoned by their government in the face of a storm that flooded it, black New Orleanians embodied the vast and continuing disparity between the American promise and American reality. The men, women, and children whose starvation, dehydration, suffering, displacement, and deaths were captured on the evening news were the constituents of the same Senator Landrieu who just weeks before had spearheaded a powerful articulation of the need for racial justice.

23 See Philip Dray, *At the Hands of Persons Unknown: The Lynching of Black America* (New York: Random House, 2002).

24 Patricia Sullivan, *Lift Every Voice: The NAACP and the Making of the Civil Rights Movement* (New York: The New Press, 2010).

25 The language of the resolution is unprecedented, direct, and unflinching. It reads, in part: "Resolved, That the Senate—(1) apologizes to the victims of lynching for the failure of the Senate to enact anti-lynching legislation; (2) expresses the deepest sympathies and most solemn regrets of the Senate to the descendants of victims of lynching, the ancestors of whom were deprived of life, human dignity, and the constitutional protections accorded all citizens of the United States; and (3) remembers the history of lynching, to ensure that these tragedies will be neither forgotten nor repeated." U.S. Congress, Senate, *Apologizing to the victims of lynching and the descendants of those victims for the failure of the Senate to enact anti-lynching legislation*, 109th Cong., 1st sess., 2005, S.RES.39.IS.

Although it is a bit of a departure, we believe it is worth remembering that Hurricane Katrina occurred in this specific racial, political context, a context that dramatically highlights the ethical dilemma that planners faced in the disaster's wake. In the months leading up to the storm, the United States had reaffirmed its commitment not only to Rousseau's insistence on participation but also to Rousseau's concept of the general will. Rousseau's theories sought to limit individual preferences in favor of the latter.[26] The general will, he wrote, is created out of popular sovereignty and rests on the assumption that individuals, while they must always be free to express their desires, must willingly submit to what is best for the whole. Not even a monarch can ignore the general will; all must be subject to it, because the good of the whole must be counted more valuable than the needs of any single citizen. In the summer of 2005, policy makers in multiple arenas of American life reaffirmed that the collective good was violated when black Americans were subjected to second-class citizenship. When Illinois reopened the Till murder case, when Mississippi prosecuted Edgar Ray Killen, and when the United States Senate apologized for its inaction on lynching, each affirmed that African Americans should be full participants in America's social contract.

Yet although the disaster in New Orleans came immediately after these strong, clear, public renegotiations of the racial terms of that contract, when the time came to make decisions about the disposition of the city, its neighborhoods, and its people, the first impulse was not to embrace the democratic, participatory, general will–focused model proposed by Rousseau, but instead to impose a Hobbesian, autocratic process. This is where the ethical dilemma was resolved into a racial injustice. If we accept the premise that black and poor New Orleanians have a fundamental right to meaningful participation in forming the general will, or public consensus, that is to govern their lives, then a number of the most prominent planning efforts in New Orleans immediately following the storm were moral violations of that right. Technical proficiency alone, no matter how great, could not justify a process that excluded the majority or even a significant number of the public from participation. Instead, the city needed planning processes that offered multiple, repeated, fair opportunities for citizens of all racial and social backgrounds to contribute meaningfully to the policy making that would shape the city's future.

NO EASY SOLUTION

It would be simple but inaccurate to end our analysis of the planning process with a critique of the lack of community participation in the months immediately following the storm. In these early months, Hobbesian impulses encouraged planners to engage in practices that violated their ethical responsibility to allow meaningful, inclusive public participation.

26 Rousseau, *The Social Contract*.

But post-Katrina planning efforts changed dramatically in 2006. Having been battered by the early planning failures, elected officials in New Orleans took a sharp turn toward direct democracy–style community participation. This began with the city council's (and Mayor Nagin's) almost immediate repudiation of the BNOB commission's plan and countervailing support for a new effort that fundamentally altered the planning process. The council commissioned a group of planning experts, led by the Lambert Advisory, and the planning teams that they sponsored were required to hold multiple community-based meetings to gauge the interests and preferences of both returned and still displaced residents.

This strategy was built on the assumption that each neighborhood had a right to self-governing autonomy regarding its renewal, an assumption that also characterized the competing and contemporaneous planning process that produced the Unified New Orleans Plan (UNOP), which was funded, in large part, by the Rockefeller Foundation. Concerted and repeated efforts were made to meet with and otherwise involve displaced residents in cities like Houston and Atlanta, where many New Orleanians had been involuntarily relocated. These meetings, like their counterparts in New Orleans, were open forums of often unorganized but passionate input from those directly impacted by the disaster. Citizens asked questions, demanded answers, expressed preferences, and challenged the expertise of architects, planners, and elected officials. Repeatedly these citizens rejected plans for a smaller city footprint and demanded efforts to protect homeowner property rights as the primary, inviolate concern of policy making. This new direction in planning was a dramatic reversal of early attempts to impose a hierarchal process on redevelopment, but it was a reaction so powerfully oppositional to authority and expertise that its results offered little significant improvement in producing racially just outcomes for New Orleans.

Recall that Rousseau's primary political concern was with the maintenance and protection of the general will. He was deeply concerned that autocratic leadership would undermine this general will, but he also suspected that jealous protection of private property would easily distract citizens from their commitment to the same general will. This protection of individual interests at the expense of the collective good was readily apparent in many of the planning and policy choices that emerged in the months and years following Hurricane Katrina. Legislation presumably designed to protect homeowners has allowed an already vast residential blight to worsen throughout the city. Choosing to keep the city's existing footprint has led to an overburdened municipal infrastructure forced to serve neighborhoods with populations too reduced to maintain their former tax contribution. Privileging the input of citizens with the access and resources to participate allowed the massive destruction of public housing, against the interests of the most marginal and vulnerable community members. Participatory planning may be fair in the sense that it is a democratic process, but citizen input does not guarantee substantively fair and just outcomes.

Post-Katrina planning is a stark reminder that there is no easy answer to this basic ethical dilemma. Urban planners have a responsibility to offer solid participatory opportunities to communities and citizens. They simultaneously have a responsibility to employ their professional expertise and experience to manage discord, give meaningful advice about land use, and offer policy leadership based in technical expertise. It is not a reasonable solution to simply eschew those professional responsibilities under the veil of giving people what they demand. This is particularly true when racial justice is one of the outcomes at stake.

It is interesting to note that many have described post-Katrina policy making as a project of reconstruction. In one sense this term describes the need to build again the city's infrastructure, property, and population. But read in the light of the racial injustices of the Katrina disaster, "reconstruction" evokes a second important meaning. The post–Civil war years 1864–1877, known as Reconstruction, formed a brief but critical period in American history that established the federal government's supremacy and articulated a national commitment to the equality of all citizens regardless of race.[27] Political expediency, the legacy of states' rights, and lingering attachment to white supremacy brought an early end to the era. Once the federal troops that had supported Reconstruction programs were withdrawn from the South, the programs were abandoned and replaced by Jim Crow policies promoting racial segregation, enforced by the terror of lynching. Black citizens of the American South endured nearly a century of struggle for equality. In the summer of 2005, Hurricane Katrina forced yet another confrontation with that post-Reconstruction legacy. What happened in Mississippi, Illinois, and the United States Senate that summer suggested that America was moving toward acknowledging and correcting the wrongs of its past. The levee failure in New Orleans revealed just how powerfully those historic wrongs continue to shape contemporary realities.

We now find ourselves embarked on a new period of reconstruction, one that, like its predecessor, raises profound questions about the norms by which we govern our nation. Urban planners are only one small part of this contemporary reconstruction, but they are being called upon to directly confront its ethical conundrums in their work as experts, advisers, and decision makers. In this brief chapter we have not offered any neat answers as to how to incorporate meaningful input from the community while simultaneously crafting reasonable, sustainable plans for post-Katrina New Orleans. Instead we have flagged what we perceive as a serious and ongoing dilemma for planners, one in which historical racial

27 Eric Foner, *Reconstruction: America's Unfinished Revolution, 1863–1877* (New York: Harper & Row, 1988).

injustice is starkly present and must be mitigated. It is clear that benevolent and expert but disengaged policy making is insufficient. It is equally clear that a purely participatory process can result in suboptimal outcomes. Public participation is essential, but it, too, is insufficient without the partnership of expertise. Participation does not absolve urban planners from the responsibility to meaningfully engage in and contribute to the ongoing struggle for human justice and restoration in New Orleans.

LESSONS LEARNED: OBSTACLES TO IMPLEMENTING A RESILIENT VISION FOR NEW ORLEANS

WM. RAYMOND MANNING

Five years after Katrina, there is a collective effort among those involved to identify the obstacles that have slowed rebuilding and the advancement of future visions for New Orleans, and to explore the general role of planning in making a reconstructed city possible. When progress to date is viewed critically as a comprehensive urban strategy, it is apparent that the holistic vision necessary for the city has not developed at a rate corresponding to the urgency of city's need for it. A well-envisioned plan would have created the infrastructure not only for immediate recovery but also for sustained and sustainable, resilient continuing development in all parts of the city, development that included all urban constituents and their individual and collective needs. The obstacles to comprehensive land-use planning following the disaster ranged from the failure of government and official planning entities to discern their responsibilities for recovery, to the misappropriation of resources and the failure to prioritize their use, to the overreliance on short-term consultants. At different stages of the planning process, these shortcomings varied in importance, but all weighed heavily on the process in their turn.

Moreover, the layered influences of politics, race, and class created a range of conflicts that impeded the implementation of a comprehensive strategy. The many planning processes undertaken since August 29, 2005, including both sanctioned plans and unofficial efforts, have revealed the subtle and not-so-subtle ways in which race, class, and professional competitiveness have impeded progress. Certainly, the professional class could have played a more significant role in advancing the progress of recovery, had they viewed their individual and collective efforts as collaborative solutions rather than as a means to control the implementation process or pursue self-interest and future professional assignments.

Most important, who would have known what to do? Prior to the storm, the city lacked a strong planning model, and there was not a formal culture in which to engage citizens politically. As a result, the post-storm recovery and mitigation processes were developed and constructed as reactions rather than overarching solutions. Now, five years later, we need an analysis of these fundamental flaws that have stymied the recovery planning process, in order to move forward in constructing a long-term master city plan that includes disaster preparedness.

In the aftermath of the 2005 flooding, there was a cry for large-scale planning to address both the devastation and the opportunities it created. The federal process of emergency management and recovery planning was acknowledged, but it lacked force to deal with the magnitude of the urban situation. Professional organizations, such as the American Planning Association (APA), Urban Land Institute (ULI), American Institute of Architects (AIA), and others brought the "best and brightest" to New Orleans to inaugurate what are now viewed as exemplars of disaster planning, through a series of lectures, discussions, and community programs. One of the first forums to propose a framework for active community participation in recovery planning was "Reinhabiting NOLA," a conference sponsored by the Tulane/Xavier Center for Bioenvironmental Research in November 2005. In my own remarks at that conference, I quoted what then–Secretary of State George Marshall said in 1947: "The most important action to be taken was to reestablish confidence based on a singular clear plan that could be faithfully executed." The Marshall Plan, officially called the European Recovery Program, was designed to help reconstruct the cities of war-torn Europe. The plan reestablished and developed urban centers by addressing immediate needs such as housing while establishing a resilient future with provisions for industry and business. With this focused infusion of funding over five years, between 1947 and 1952, targeted cities were not only able to recover but also to thrive and develop prosperous economies. London and Berlin are now world-class, vibrant, and important urban centers; this was not so immediately following their near destruction during World War II. They have become what they are as a direct result of a clear vision that concentrated planning efforts and prioritized massive economic aid.

The initial response and planning efforts in New Orleans failed to yield one focused plan that the citizens of the city could see being executed and proudly claim as *their* plan for the future of their city. The lack of coordination between various planning efforts and teams resulted in confusion about disparate components, especially at the neighborhood level—what would be implemented versus what was merely recommended, what would or could be funded, and how resources would be prioritized. In "An Overview of Post-Katrina Planning in New Orleans" (October 18, 2006), Jedidiah Horne and Brendan Nee noted a "poorly defined relationship between planning and implementation, [giving] residents unrealistic expectations about what can be delivered to their neighborhoods," and described the plans as "a perplexing bundle of short- and long-term public and private projects, the logical results of processes which do not distinguish between planning for trash pickup and planning for light rail." Excluding for a moment the current Master Plan (developed by a team of consultants in which I was a participant and led by the Boston firm Goody

Clancy), there were four main recovery-planning initiatives, various aspects of which have been adopted overwhelmingly as discrete projects and without a larger framework to direct the appropriation of limited resources.

These four initiatives ranged in scope, but they can all be critically measured against the same standard: a comprehensive, interdisciplinary, and sustainable strategy. The first local recovery plan was proposed by the Bring New Orleans Back (BNOB) Commission, formed in September 2005 to oversee development of a rebuilding plan for the entire city.[1] The commission team was appointed by the mayor and included volunteer participants from the Urban Land Institute (ULI). The first draft of the BNOB plan, issued in November 2005, was heavily debated, particularly in regard to its proposal to shrink the built footprint of the city and prioritize the allocation of resources. The ULI issued an independent report that similarly proposed shrinking the city and prioritizing the distribution of resources to what were considered more viable neighborhoods. The controversy this provoked was complicated by local and national newspapers that published interpretive material misrepresenting the planning documents, leading stakeholders to believe that many of the flooded neighborhoods would not be rebuilt at all. The largely negative response from New Orleans residents, who rallied around collective neighborhood and racial identities, arose from this misunderstanding of the intentions of local government in promoting the BNOB process, of the resulting reports, and of the implications of the experts' suggestions that they contained.

In the beginning of 2006, I was asked, along with Reed Kroloff, dean of the Tulane School of Architecture, to chair the BNOB Urban Planning Committee, which led intensive neighborhood-based work. This pro bono process included more than 100 public meetings within the city's thirteen planning districts, with the goal of assisting communities as they developed individual viability plans. We endeavored to develop strategies that would allocate resources in a comprehensive way, but this planning process was halted when FEMA withdrew funding.

In light of the debate over the BNOB results, the New Orleans City Council initiated a separate (and competing) neighborhood planning process in February 2006, hiring the Miami-based firm Lambert Advisory. The New Orleans Neighborhoods Rebuilding Plan, more commonly known as the "Lambert Plan," was developed to promote strategies for all flooded neighborhoods. It was a direct response to the BNOB plan, which had been criticized as designed only for those neighborhoods found viable by the commission's preliminary assessments. The Lambert Plan focused on forty-six Orleans Parish neighborhoods that were significantly flooded, but in many cases the neighborhoods as defined by

1 See the nolaplans.com, developed by Horne and Nee, for links to websites and published plan documents, including further information about the timing and funding sources of the individual plans, and for documentation of the planning process through January 2007. Each of the four plans are represented by a series of phased documentation.

the plan did not correspond to the more informal boundaries recognized by local and active neighborhood associations. Although Lambert expanded on the BNOB plan's identification of viability, reassessing and revising the BNOB's recommendations for less viable portions of the city, it failed to develop a comprehensive strategy that would guide prioritization and allocation of resources citywide.

Parallel to both of these plans was FEMA's Emergency Support Function #14 (ESF-14), which was never incorporated into other planning processes. ESF-14 was invoked shortly after Katrina, with the intention to promote "long-term community recovery" across nineteen hurricane-affected parishes. ESF-14 employed a workforce comprising FEMA staff, local experts, and national consultants. As confusion mounted over the BNOB and Lambert plans, ESF-14 was largely ignored within the local community, but it filled a valuable need for hurricane-affected parishes other than Orleans that were without resources or capacity to develop their own independent plans. The Louisiana Recovery Authority (LRA) required a comprehensive plan for any parish that was seeking federal Community Development Block Grants (CDBG). For many smaller parishes, ESF-14 was this plan.

By midsummer 2006, the three plans, BNOB, Lambert, and ESF-14, were under scrutiny not only from local members of the community but also from key stakeholders at the state level. The New Orleans City Planning Commission responded by developing yet another plan, the Unified New Orleans Plan (UNOP), which would also satisfy LRA requirements to receive infrastructure funding. By this time, the BNOB Commission had been effectively terminated, but because Reed Kroloff and I continued to participate through the Louisiana Recovery Authority and the Greater New Orleans Foundation, the strategy that we developed and the scope of work that we defined were instrumental in securing funding initiatives for the state-sanctioned planning process for the entire city. This subsequently brought in $3.5 million in funding, which was directed to the UNOP effort.[2] UNOP hired a team of planning firms, hoping that if their endeavor were directed by a nongovernmental entity, the political confusion that scuttled earlier plans would be avoided. UNOP included work from the BNOB and Lambert plans; indeed, it ultimately absorbed the Lambert Plan, which was approved by the city council in October 2006. UNOP also responded to citizen input gathered at citywide public meetings, called community congresses.

Ultimately, UNOP also presented challenges: it considered fine-grained issues specific to individual neighborhoods and to the larger

2 The UNOP funding, administered by the Greater New Orleans Foundatation (GNOF), was largely supported by a grant from the Rockefeller Foundation (RF). Working closely with GNOF, the RF helped created the New Orleans Community Revitalization Fund, a critical resource for the long-term viability of implementing UNOP. The RF also provided strategic support for two government agencies, the New Orleans Redevelopment Authority and the Office of Recovery Management. See the Rockefeller Foundation, "Rebuilding New Orleans," rockefellerfoundation.org.

planning districts but neglected to consider citywide strategies; as previous plans had, it failed to provide a framework within which to prioritize the deployment of resources. Each neighborhood and planning district selected different components and amenities, developing separate ideas about its future removed from the logistics of the needs of the city as a whole and without a budget or resources to fund the projects it proposed. Despite these shortcomings, the city council approved UNOP as New Orleans's official recovery plan in June 2007.

As these plans unfolded over the course of nearly two years of citizen response to the damage inflicted by Katrina, each caused more confusion for the residents of New Orleans. All four—the BNOB plan, the Lambert Plan, the Orleans Parish ESF-14 Recovery Plan, and UNOP—focused on the planning districts, ignoring the urban issues of the entire city. At the same time, many of their efforts were led by nationally renowned—and based—experts, rather than local planners. This set up a "fly-in" planning process that was not sustainable, especially considering the length of time necessary to implement effective citywide solutions. The resulting response and recovery plans were unable to identity citywide priorities and resources that met the needs of the city as a whole as well as the specific needs of each neighborhood.

Little has been written regarding the cost of planning in post-Katrina New Orleans, and I submit that the four recovery plans I've analyzed were costly in ways that we do not fully understand. These plans certainly brought state and federal resources, such as additional infrastructure funding, to the city, but can we assess their cost in terms of expenditures toward a sustainable and resilient vision for the city? When their rosters of volunteers, committees, and professionals are enumerated and the hours expended by those participants are calculated according to published meeting schedules, it can be argued that the four primary recovery studies have an aggregate value of at least $80 million, using a straightforward compensation figure of $100/hour as an average for all participants. With the proper research, we might find that we have spent in human energy and time almost $100 million in planning for the recovery of New Orleans. Since these processes have been "authentically democratic," the question becomes: Did they result in a comprehensive framework and priorities that are restoring vibrancy to all parts of the city? I would suggest that they did not.

Also largely omitted from almost all of the planning efforts to date is an analysis of the long- and short-term negative effects of a storm-ravaged city on its citizens, effects both psychological and physical. Since most of the planning efforts were spatial plans driven by project-centered approaches, it stands to reason that social considerations were given no priority in the distribution of resources. Almost two years after the storm, the American Medical Association published a study by Dr. Kevin Stephens, director of the New Orleans Health Department, that stated, "The post-

Katrina mortality rate for the first six months of 2006 was approximately 91.37 deaths per 100,000 ... Compared to the pre-Katrina population mortality rate of 62.17 deaths per 100,000 population, this represents an average 47 percent increase from the baseline mortality." When viewing these startling statistics in relation to FEMA ESF-14 recovery projects for Orleans Parish, we find that of the $2.2 billion value of recommended projects, the single highest-value project for healthcare was the full restoration of Tulane and LSU medical schools, with an estimated value of $100 million or 4.6 percent of the total.[3] These figures suggest that recovery planning must consider the effects of trauma on survivors. Any holistic planning team must include healthcare providers and social workers who can guide the conversation on these hidden effects of storm damage. The BNOB plan included teams with social and cultural experts, but subsequent plans did not; as a result, much residual trauma has not been addressed. We cannot truly estimate the social and cultural cost of post-disaster trauma demonstrated by the citywide increase in homelessness, incarceration, suicide, and mental health issues. Viewed through the lens of comprehensive urban systems, the recovery plans advanced for the city can be understood not to have been very synergistic. Rather, they were conceived from the points of view of disparate disciplines and proposed projects that separated urban spatial needs from social and cultural needs, privileging the former over the latter.

Building on this finding, we can identify other issues that have become apparent within the "democratic" recovery planning processes over the past few years. Although there is great cultural diversity in New Orleans's own architectural and planning community, the leadership in professional planning organizations and firms nationwide is predominately white and male. Despite efforts to sprinkle teams with available African-American and female professionals, the drivers and leaders of the various planning commissions did not resemble the community for which their planning was conducted, and none of their good intentions or words could change that fact.

New Orleans has a legacy of segregation, and the identity of many neighborhoods has been shaped by this reality. There were professionals in the city who were supportive and excited about my role in the Urban Planning Committee; however, having seen the reaction of other colleagues when I was asked to co-lead the BNOB neighborhood planning process in 2006, I can tell you that their reluctance to accept my leadership [as an African-American professional] helped prevent the process from gaining momentum. Reflecting on my thirty-year experience of design practice and civic engagement in New Orleans, I also realize that many practitioners hesitated to participate in a planning strategy that would be guided by an interdisciplinary leadership team and suppress recognition of individuals

3 Kevin Stevens et al., "Excess Mortality in the Aftermath of Hurricane Katrina: A Preliminary Report," *Disaster Medicine and Public Health Preparedness* (2007), dmphp.org.

and their contributions. Opportunistic professionals who hoped to be awarded individual projects were averse to a collective vision, and that hindered the immediate recovery planning process.

In sum, the city planners undervalued the real needs of the city's people. If the city had been truly planning for them, recovery expenditures would have been prioritized to promote the general "health, safety, and welfare" of all citizens. We would now be on our way to establishing a truly sustainable and resilient culture of community had all of the major planning efforts valued and dealt with basic human needs, had planning models been based on the need to create consensus as well as confidence, and more than anything, had those in leadership roles sought to heal a wound made in our city more than 100 years ago.

In 1892 Homer Plessy, a New Orleans activist, deliberately provoked his own arrest by boarding a whites-only train car in the Bywater neighborhood and refusing to move to a car for colored passengers, as required by the Separate Car Act. Plessy's arrest enabled him and his Committee of Citizens to plead before the United States Supreme Court that the "separate but equal" laws were unconstitutional, in that they denied equal protection of the law and perpetuated the features of slavery.[4] Plessy lost his case, but his argument resonated in the civil rights movement of the twentieth century and helped decide the case of *Brown v. Board of Education of Topeka* in 1954.[5]

The social and legal traditions of segregation pervade the history of land-use and settlement patterns in the city of New Orleans. Acknowledging the historical urban effects of racism, especially as enacted by white flight from the city proper and the successive development of neighborhoods, that were physically, if not socially, segregated, and overlayering that over what is now known about neighborhood viability in terms of topography and safety, would most likely lead to different decisions about our urban footprint and what is considered suitable land for the development of a community. Too often, we understate the reality of persistent racism and the segregation of neighborhoods in our city relative to their topography. Clearly this argument is complicated by the culture of collective identities that characterizes New Orleans neighborhoods, and, looking forward, a comprehensive vision for the city must consider the resiliency of culture and community, including all citizens, in synergy with urban and spatial planning.

During the urgent planning responses, I was often asked to be patient and told that rebuilding was a marathon, not a sprint. Additionally, I was told that I should be more positive about the results that were being achieved at the time, however minor they seemed in relation to what needed to be done. Today, I can see the enormous progress made by a

4 *Plessy v. Ferguson*, 163 U.S. 537 (1896).

5 Keith Weldon Medley, *We as Freemen: Plessy v. Ferguson* (Gretna, LA: Pelican, 2003), 222.

bottom-up process of citizen engagement that has paved the way for future rebuilding. When we examine the level of that engagement throughout successive planning efforts, we begin to realize the resiliency of New Orleans. In the face of a complete failure of the federal and state governments, individuals crafted ways to rebuild their homes and lives. They did this in spite of the roadblocks thrown up in their path. These grassroots efforts are unparalleled; they are the reason for the recovery of New Orleans to date. Tourism has rebounded to such a degree that New Orleans got top ranking in 20 percent of the categories of the *Travel + Leisure* magazine's 2009 "America's Favorite Cities" survey—receiving the more "firsts" than any of the thirty cities surveyed.[6]

However, the conflict between neighborhood-scale, grassroots rebuilding efforts and citywide planning processes has taken an enormous toll on the lives, structures, and communities that have been rebuilt on a case-by-case basis. That conflict is nowhere more evident than at the sixty-seven-acre site for the new Veterans Administration hospital. The U.S. Department of Veterans Affairs and Louisiana State University chose a site in the Mid-City neighborhood. The planned medical complex shares a footprint with a neighborhood whose residents have been rebuilding and restoring their community independent of, or lacking, a comprehensive recovery plan to assist and guide their process. The twenty-five city blocks comprising Mid-City house more than 160 historic structures, most of them private homes, that have been repaired and rebuilt since the storm. Under current plans for the medical facilities, these buildings must be removed. Meanwhile, in the adjacent Central Business District (CBD), the abandoned Charity Hospital, a 1939 Public Works Administration project, sits dormant, deemed unsafe and unusable by the Louisiana State University medical system. In 2008, a feasibility study was conducted to assess the reuse of Charity Hospital as an alternative to the Mid-City "urban renewal" strategy of replacing a rebuilt neighborhood with medical facilities. The study concluded that adapting Charity Hospital would not only be feasible, it would also be cheaper and would be completed more quickly, providing an important civic node within the existing medical district of the CBD, which includes the Tulane University medical complex. In September 2010, groundbreaking commenced on the Mid-City site after U.S. District Judge Eldon Fallon rejected arguments by the National Trust for Historical Preservation that there was not sufficient study of harm to the community, historic buildings, and surrounding environment, saying that the state and federal governments had done the required reviews.[7]

Reflecting on the past five years, I believe that had we developed our

6 See travelandleisure.com/afc/2009/city/new-orleans.

7 For more about the attempt to save Charity Hospital, see the National Trust for Historic Preservation's webpage, preservationnation.org.

recovery framework under a singular priority, to confidently create a comprehensive plan, we would not now be faced with the kind of decision between competitive visions that the Mid-City VA Hospital debate exemplifies. But rather than listing all of these overlaps or competing activities, I would like to close by looking forward to the City of New Orleans Master Plan.[8] Developed by a team of consultants led by Goody Clancy, a team of which I was a vocal member, the Master Plan builds on preceding recovery and rebuilding schemes but also establishes a long-term vision for the future of the city, along with a zoning code to guide implementation. Approved in August 2010, the Master Plan was adopted and given the force of law, along with a comprehensive zoning ordinance. The Master Plan creates a framework to guide decision makers and members of the community in the development of a twenty-first-century New Orleans consistent with the historic, physical, cultural, and social identity of the city. This long-term, integrated citywide approach to balanced growth and urban systems begins to answer the call for a culture of community development that is sustainable and resilient.

Alison N. Popper acted as a research and editorial assistant in the adaptation of this paper for publication.

8 The City of New Orleans Master Plan ensures that the city will grow in a way reflective of our community's vision and goals for the future, the policies that we want to follow, and the strategies that we decide to pursue to achieve the vision. See nolamasterplan.org and David Dixon's essay in this part.

THE PLAN FOR THE TWENTY-FIRST CENTURY: NEW ORLEANS 2030

DAVID DIXON

OVERVIEW

When Hurricane Katrina flooded New Orleans in 2005, it piled biblical destruction on two decades of stagnation, decades that had left a long list of very real challenges: a legacy of blighted and vacant land almost unmatched in any other American metropolis, an outmoded and failing infrastructure, a narrow economic base without the diversity that could generate more and better jobs, and a disproportionate number of residents without the skills or education to compete in a twenty-first-century economy.

In 2008, three years after the hurricane, New Orleans launched an effort to address these problems with the first citywide master plan in its history.[1] The City Planning Commission chose my firm to lead the master-planning effort. This essay addresses three aspects of what followed: the New Orleanians' struggle to build a culture of *citywide* discussion about planning before master planning itself could begin; the core issues that the master plan then had to address to make a substantive difference; and the kind of robust city leadership that this diverse community will need to embrace over the twenty-year lifespan (and beyond) of the plan that we prepared in order to solve the city's problems and take advantage of new dynamics that could lead to an era of renewed prosperity.[2]

DEVELOPING A CITYWIDE PLANNING CULTURE

New Orleanians had for decades battled to shape and control City actions along lines defined by race, neighborhood, income, and other factors of difference.[3] Economic stagnation during the 1980s cemented this inclination, as citizens struggled to maintain their share of a shrinking economic pie. This tradition of turning every planning or land-use decision into a pitched political battle was undermining efforts to col-

1 For the history of master planning in New Orleans between 1920 and 1960, see Carol McMichael Reese's essay in this part.

2 Master plan documents and zoning ordinances that were the outcome of the process described in this article can be found at nolamasterplan.org.

3 This essay adopts the convention of capitalizing "City" when the term refers to the municipal government and using the uncapitalized "city" to describe New Orleans as a whole.

laborate—a key to rebuilding the city after Katrina—including early efforts funded by national organizations and foundations. Our planning team quickly discovered the need to create a culture of discussion about citywide planning, one marked by a willingness to talk directly about difficult questions, to make decisions based on data, to accept tradeoffs, and to respect the importance of an inclusive and transparent public process. This new attitude toward planning would have to supplant the ingrained habit of political infighting and encourage people to cross lines of separation in order to develop a shared vision and strategies that would serve the interests of the entire city.

Following Hurricane Katrina, New Orleanians took a first critical step in a new direction when they turned to each other to begin restoring their homes and launched intensive neighborhood-based rebuilding initiatives under the Lambert and UNOP planning processes.[4] Although very successful at the neighborhood level, these processes neither framed a citywide plan nor even shared perspectives on the issues facing New Orleans. In part, this failure grew from the fact that these efforts were not sponsored or led by the City itself; in part, it reflected the lack of any comprehensive planning precedent. The national backers of the UNOP process, despite excellent intentions, could not speak for city government or commit it to adopt or implement the recommendations that the process produced. Without a belief that the City would carry out planning recommendations, neighborhood residents had little incentive to abandon familiar perspectives and the well-understood tradition of fighting for local interests in order to work together as members of a wider community.

As New Orleanians moved further into this unfamiliar territory, divisive cleavages became glaringly apparent. A fundamental test of a planning culture, however, is whether people are willing to work together to resolve tough issues, and as the master plan process moved forward, New Orleanians had plenty of opportunities to demonstrate an increasing commitment to do just that. Three issues stood out:

Racial and economic inequalities. Less than one month into the process, the challenge of creating a plan that would carry legitimacy citywide took on real immediacy. A widely respected planning and preservation advocate introduced a referendum measure to revise the city's charter and give key elements of the master plan "the force of law." Long-established racial tensions shaped the reaction of many African-American neighborhood leaders to this proposal. Changing the charter, they argued, would undermine their ability to secure a fair share of City investments for their neighborhoods and to protect those neighborhoods from onerous development projects (for example, proposals to site trash-recycling facilities near New Orleans East and Gentilly). Following narrow voter

4 In her essay in this part, M. Christine Boyer discusses the planning initiatives that preceded the master-planning effort that David Dixon led.

Goody Clancy

The Master Plan is dedicated to the memory of the Reverend Marshal Truehill IV, Ph.D., former chair of the New Orleans City Planning Commission, who devoted his life to helping New Orleanians cross lines of race and class to work together to address the city's deep-rooted economic and social challenges.

approval of the amendment (51/49), many of these opponents began to refer to "the Master's Plan" and asserted that it would dilute the political clout of African-American leaders; a former mayor led a nearly successful effort to derail the master-planning process in the state legislature.[5]

Bridging the city's racial and economic divides became an urgent priority, which our planning team addressed on three fronts. We brought the former planning director of Birmingham, Alabama, to a citywide forum, where for several hours he answered pointed questions about how that city had used a transparent planning process to empower lower-income African-American neighborhoods both by making information generally available and by ensuring participation in decision making. We met informally with African-American leaders and revised the outreach process to enable all neighborhood leaders to invite planners to their neighborhoods to resolve issues directly with their constituents. Most important, our team added social equity as a priority to the emerging plan, linking workforce readiness and the economic enfranchisement of all residents to the goal of providing New Orleans with a better-trained, more competitive workforce. This last effort, accomplished through another series of informal meetings, which we sponsored in conjunction with African-American and white leaders, played a critical role in building an understanding of how crossing boundaries to plan together could benefit the entire community.

The future of New Orleans East. Issues around rebuilding heavily flooded New Orleans East (the low-lying section extending east of the Industrial Canal to the city/parish limits), which was predominantly

5 Tim Morris, "Panel Deadlocks on New Orleans Master Plan Bill," *Times-Picayune*, June 10, 2009.

African-American, divided the community early in the master-planning process and threatened to persuade three city council members to oppose any citywide plan. Almost immediately after Katrina, national observers proposed the idea of "reducing the city's footprint" as a strategy for preparing New Orleans to withstand devastating future storms. Several community leaders took up this call and argued that the master plan should address the risks and costs of recovery investments in "the East," which they suggested was too sparsely populated and too vulnerable to future flooding to rebuild. The African-American councilwoman who represented these neighborhoods—as well as two African-American council members who aligned with her—responded that "reducing the footprint" was code for undermining the middle-class neighborhoods into which African Americans had moved beginning in the 1960s. The issue stirred political passions, but our planning team believed that credible data could provide a foundation for productive discussion.

We undertook the first public mapping of flood hazards following the closing of the Mississippi River Gulf Outlet channel and the completion of the Army Corps of Engineers improvements. The resulting maps helped demonstrate that the East would be better able to withstand flooding than most areas of the city outside of the historic crescent. Moreover, a repopulation analysis determined that more than 50,000 people had returned to the East, and no credible options for resettling them existed. An economic-development assessment indicated that demand for commercial redevelopment in the East could create an important asset for New Orleans, which earns roughly one third of its revenues from sales tax. This information resolved the debate and helped build a broader awareness that planning, when rooted in hard data and analysis, empowers people by enabling them to make informed judgments. At the same time, participants witnessed the paralysis that ensues from conflict, and the concept of a "master plan for every person and every place" emerged.

The institutionalization of community participation. The charter amendment required that the master plan include a formal program of community participation to be adopted by the city council. Although many neighborhoods had long had active associations with strong ties to city council members, others did not, and there was no formal process for collecting neighborhood feedback on development projects and related issues. A coalition of community activists had worked for several years to implement a citywide program without success, in part because many business leaders interpreted their initiative as an effort to stymie development and investment.

We waited to propose a formal participation program until the end of the planning process, when almost two years of bringing stakeholders together to engage in compromise and to resolve thorny dilemmas had built consensus around many issues. We formed a broad-based task force, inviting representatives of the business and development communities to participate and help identify goals and key objectives for a formal program. The task force designed a program, which neighborhood activists accepted, to insure that review of development proposals would include citywide as well as neighborhood perspectives and that reviews would be conducted in the spirit of improving, not blocking, proposals. Although the debate continues, these efforts helped reframe the discussion: All participants ultimately acknowledged the value of a more inclusive, transparent, and accountable community process. One important byproduct was recognition of the value of assigning city planners to work with specific districts as technical resources and as facilitators for the review and revision of development proposals.

DEVELOPING A MASTER PLAN THAT ARTICULATES A CITYWIDE VISION

As New Orleanians began to plan together, they learned that collaboration while addressing difficult issues can have value in its own right: A plan that integrates the aspirations and needs of the entire community generates in turn the citywide political will essential to meeting significant challenges. While many Americans assumed that New Orleans's ability to survive future storms dwarfed other issues, New Orleanians were confronting three fundamental challenges: (1) diversifying and growing an economy after several decades of stagnation; (2) translating renewed economic growth into refilling or reusing more than 60,000 vacant and blighted parcels across "dry" and "wet" neighborhoods; and (3) fostering the kind of resilience that all river-delta cities require in era of global warming and rising sea levels.[6] As planning progressed, participants debated controversial topics—insufficient affordable housing, an intrusive elevated expressway, endangered wetlands—but in each case they found the resolution to create a vision of a city of enhanced economic opportunity, higher livability standards, and stronger environmental resilience, which would be characterized by a spirit of inclusivity, respect for differences, and the acknowledgment of shared responsibility.

Expanded economic opportunity to which everyone contributes and from which everyone benefits. The decades of economic stagnation that followed the oil and gas bust of the 1980s taught many New Orleanians to think of their city as a Southern outpost of the Rust Belt—impoverished, shrinking, and far removed from a golden past it could never recapture. Yet as residents began to plan together and to focus on data, they discovered that New Orleans possessed significant economic potential that effective planning and implementation could unlock. They learned that despite common conceptions to the contrary, median household income

6 Any section of New Orleans, even those lying above sea level, can flood during a rainstorm if the pump and drainage system cannot move water into the outfall canals rapidly enough. "Dry" and "wet" are used here to distinguish those areas that lie, respectively, above sea level or below. Those of the latter category experienced devastation in the aftermath of Katrina, when water remained in them for days and even weeks.

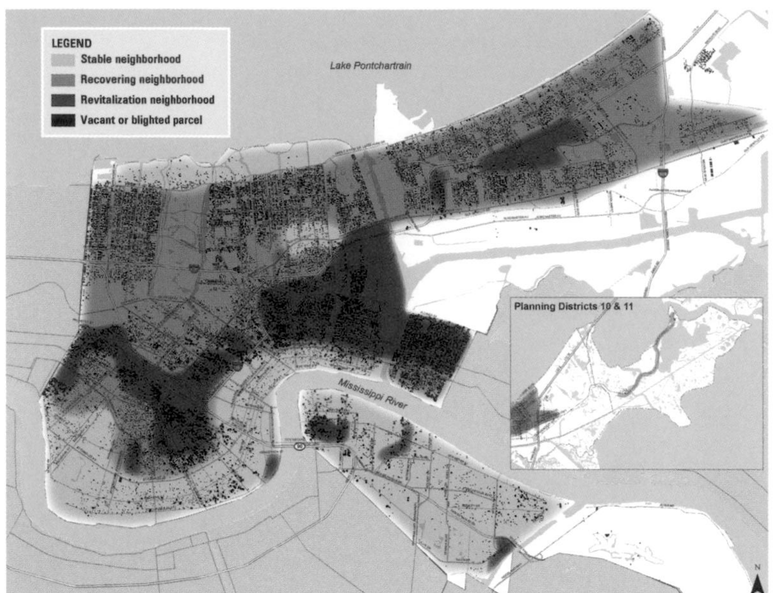

Goody Clancy

There are 60,000 vacant and blighted houses and lots across New Orleans—roughly two-thirds are the product of the city's decline following the oil bust in the mid-1980s, and one-third are the product of Hurricane Katrina. With strong city leadership, New Orleans can attract a new generation of residents who could refill most of these houses and lots. To accomplish this task, the city will need to tailor specific strategies to revitalization (significant subsidies, site acquisition), recovery (mix of subsides, site acquisition, and other strategies), and stable neighborhoods (growing market demand).

had risen faster than the national norm since the mid-1990s. By 2008, the city's poverty rate had fallen below rates in "comeback" cities such as Baltimore and Memphis, and new "creative" industries represented the strongest source of job growth.

The master plan recommended citywide strategies that would tangibly accelerate this recovery and growth. Robust economic development policies, with a particular emphasis on stronger regional collaboration, could produce an additional 100,000 jobs by 2030, yielding a regional growth rate that could match or exceed national norms. Establishing New Orleans as an effective partner in regional economic development would require creation of a well-funded and well-staffed public-private partnership. This partnership would take the lead in producing economic diversification—New Orleans's number-one task—in addition to giving continued support to mature industries, such as the port. Investments in education, expanded job training, workforce preparedness, and similar programs would be needed to build the kind of educated and skilled workforce that the city would require in order to compete for twenty-first-century industries. New Orleans could then aim to take national leadership in alternative-energy and coastal protection and restoration technologies. At the same time, New Orleans could build on its natural strengths—architecture, art, music, and other amenities that have proven so attractive to the professionals who drive growth in creative industries, from the arts to digital media, and in life science research.

Enhanced standards of livability that preserve the city's character and enrich the quality of life it provides. With the right public policies in place, New Orleans would be poised for growth. The master plan urged aggressive efforts to address blight and stimulate neighborhood revitalization in order not only to reverse decades of neighborhood disinvestment but also to return the number of households roughly to the figure of the 1960 census, after which New Orleans's population had declined. This effort would require coordination among agencies to assure restoration of both "dry" and "wet" neighborhoods. It would also require City-led initiatives to promote vitality in neighborhood commercial districts, expand public transportation, and encourage development of high-quality housing options. Mixed-use neighborhoods would replace faded shopping centers and long-vacant industrial sites. A strong focus on enhancing livability in neighborhoods from Audubon to New Orleans East could aid in slowing or reversing regional sprawl. Within the Downtown Development District, the residential population could double, enriching the CBD as a center of intensified urban living, business, and culture and as a "common ground," drawing people from across the city as well as visitors from around the world.

Increased-sustainability measures that give resilience priority and provide a better fit with the city's natural setting. The analysis of potential flood impacts associated with "500-year" storms, undertaken early in the planning process, indicated that with new measures in place New Orleans would be far safer in the future. The current round of Army Corps of Engineers improvements represents only a first step, however, and the Corps's strategies represent only a small fraction of those that the city and region should pursue. New Orleans's universities house leading researchers who study promising approaches to resilience, ranging from reclaiming regional wetlands to "hardening" utilities and individual buildings. Collaborating with these visionaries, City leadership could make New Orleans a global center of knowledge about how to make low-lying cities more resilient in this period of global warming.

New Orleans's most critical step will be to take direct charge of planning for its future by establishing a new, strong environmental department. This department would set the agenda for a safer, more resilient city, a potential model of urban sustainability. Adherence to the new comprehensive zoning ordinance and associated city policies could make New Orleans a leader in green planning and design. A new "blue system" of canals and water parks could retrofit New Orleans in concert with its natural setting, reducing subsidence and helping manage storm water.

DEVELOPING A NEW SENSE OF SHARED DESTINY THAT PROMOTES AN ERA OF ROBUST CITY LEADERSHIP

The New Orleans city council unanimously approved the final version of the master plan in August 2010. In doing so, it set the stage for the City to move into implementation. But an underlying issue continues to

Landscaping of the city's many canals offers an opportunity to store water during heavy rains and reduce periodic flooding while also adding a new "blue signature" system of parks.

raise concerns throughout the community—skepticism about the City's will and capacity to lead. If New Orleanians are not confident that city government will step forward to train people for jobs, to provide adequate services to all neighborhoods, and to conduct thorough analyses of development projects and their impacts, then the citywide planning culture that they nurtured during two years of master planning could atrophy.

Mayor Mitchell Joseph ("Mitch") Landrieu, elected on February 6, 2010, has taken promising first steps toward restoring confidence, even in the face of a fiscal crisis and other major challenges. His appointment of a deputy mayor to coordinate agencies charged with implementing planning decisions and of a nationally respected director of place-based planning represent his commitment to the master-planning process and to the recommendations contained within the plan itself.

In order to move forward the city's vision, which the plan articulates, city government should establish leadership to pursue these priorities:

- Creating a new ethos of partnership on the regional, state, and federal levels, in which all partners recognize their shared stake in the city's welfare and contribute to tackling long-standing challenges.
- Establishing a City department to devise and advocate strategies for promoting environmental resilience.
- Crafting an integrated mission and work program for the New Orleans Redevelopment Authority, the Department of Code Enforcement, the City Planning Commission, and related municipal agencies to devise and implement innovative approaches to land assembly, which will enable the City to bring back multiple blocks at a time, rather than single houses, in blighted neighborhoods.
- Building a public-private economic development partnership to spearhead economic diversification, to tap the region's competitive

strengths in creative industries, cultural tourism, green industries, healthcare, and other industries of the mind, to develop regional economic cooperation, and to provide every citizen with the skills needed to contribute to and benefit from a modern economy.

- Devising an integrated transportation strategy that makes a compelling case for state and federal support for a twenty-first-century network of roads, utilities, and technologies—beginning by replacing the deteriorating I-10 Claiborne Expressway.
- Launching a program of municipal district planners, who will add planning capacity and equip the City to take full leadership on all projects that affect New Orleans and its neighborhoods.
- Chartering a broadly representative task force to rethink affordable housing, one that would seat housing providers, neighborhood leaders, housing advocates, bankers, developers, and other stakeholders at the same table.
- Establishing a formal program for community participation in the urban planning process.
- Conserving and reinforcing the historic character of New Orleans's traditional neighborhoods.
- Responding to untapped market demand by supporting redevelopment of underutilized "opportunity" sites and corridors as new neighborhoods that celebrate New Orleans's traditions of mixed use and walkability.

All of this hard work could bring impressive rewards to a city whose physical environment would nurture a uniquely rich quality of life. New Orleans could become a national model showing how preserving and celebrating heritage can attract and inspire innovative investment. By 2030, the city could offer a choice of neighborhoods—dating from the eighteenth to the twenty-first century—whose tree-lined streets would invite walking and whose lively commercial districts would encourage lingering and meeting friends. Vibrant new mixed-use neighborhoods could replace strip malls, and underutilized industrial corridors could be refashioned with the tree-lined character and human scale of the city's historic streets and parks. A network of streetcars, bicycle paths, and other transportation choices could tie the city's neighborhoods together. Neutral grounds, filled with thousands of trees, could take on a park-like quality and restore the tree canopy to shade 50 percent of the city during hot summer months. A renewed network of "Main Streets" in diverse districts could attract thousands of people on weekends to sample the city's cultural richness. Landscaped canals, rain gardens, and water-filled parks could add a signature layer of twenty-first-century design to this historic city.

Economic recovery could enrich every aspect of the city's life. Exciting new small businesses could convey the unique spirit of individual neighborhoods. Downtown's offerings could expand with the addition of new mixed-use neighborhoods on South Rampart and along the river near the

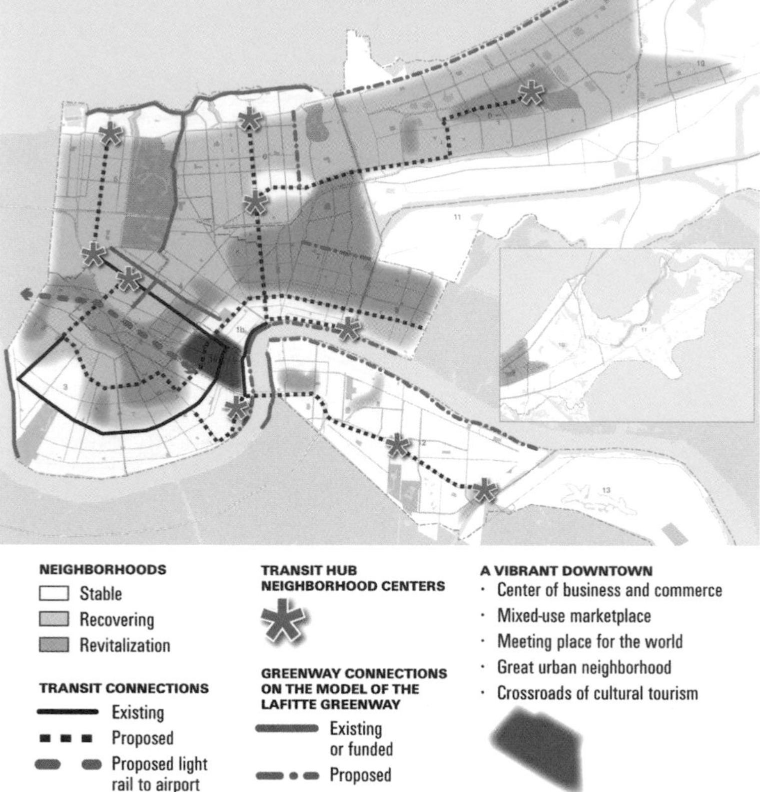

A new generation of transit-served, mixed-use neighborhoods and a revitalized downtown will bring New Orleans's historic tradition of walkability, vibrant public spaces, and living heritage into the twenty-first century and make the city highly competitive as a place to live, work, play, and innovate.

convention center. Thousands of new residents would energize downtown streets, supporting restaurants, cafés, shops, and galleries. Across the city, the new medical district and revitalized university campuses and neighborhoods could add a twenty-first-century chapter of architectural and urban design quality. A more affluent city could invest in riverfront parks and lakefront beaches that would draw together people from every walk of life to enjoy the city's natural setting.[7] As New Orleans nears its 300th birthday, the master plan stands as an invitation for New Orleanians to continue to come together and engage each other with energy and shared civic commitment to make their city's fourth century its proudest.

7 Allen Eskew discusses the post-Katrina development of a riverfront park for the Reinventing the Crescent Project in Part V.

CITIZEN ADVOCACY AND PLANNING POLICY
JEANNE P. NATHAN

Since arriving in New Orleans in 1972 from New York City, Jeanne Nathan has devoted her career to expanding opportunities for artists of all disciplines and developing the creative economy. From 1973 to 1978 Nathan worked as a broadcast reporter, producer, and managing editor for the NBC affiliate WDSU in New Orleans, covering government, urban issues, and the economy and producing weekly artist profiles. In 1976 she cofounded the Contemporary Arts Center in New Orleans, an alternative space for the visual and performing arts. As head of her own marketing company, she developed numerous award-winning cultural initiatives as part of her marketing strategy for clients. She worked for three mayors and served on a number of transition teams, most notably creating and implementing the Office of Tourism, Arts and Entertainment for the Mayor's Office in New Orleans and the New Orleans Arts Tourism Partnership. Most recently, Nathan founded the Creative Alliance of New Orleans (CANO), a network of cultural and creative producers and businesses, and now serves as its executive director. CANO's mission is to provide training, education, and information for creative artists, cultural producers, and the community while promoting the revitalization of the city as a cultural and economic center. Key CANO initiatives include arts tours and experiences, marketing for artists of all disciplines, and Creative Futures, a program that helps students learn about and pursue educational and career opportunities in the creative industries. Nathan led community outreach initiatives during the various phases of post-Katrina planning, and coordinated the development of joint green and cultural municipal policy platforms. She presently hosts a weekly radio program, *Crosstown Conversations*, that promotes dialogue between different sectors of the city on urban planning, environmental, and cultural development issues. The program was fostered during her seven years working on all phases of the recovery, rebuilding, and rezoning for the City of New Orleans. Anthony Fontenot conducted this interview on August 20, 2011.

FONTENOT: Given that you have been involved with practically all of the planning phases since Katrina, I think you are in a very interesting position to comment on the political and planning processes and the various roles that neighborhood organizations, planning groups, architects, and citizens have played in the reconstruction of New Orleans. I would like to begin by asking you to reflect on developments in New Orleans since Katrina and present what you think are some of the key issues that the city has grappled with since the storm. Also, can you describe your involvement with the official and unofficial planning processes in the city, extending from your involvement with the mayor's office to neighborhood organizing?

NATHAN: Perhaps I should set the stage by offering some pre-Katrina background. In the capacity of a marketing and public relations person, I've been involved in community outreach for many projects over the years, including outreach for commercial projects that required public coordination, such as the New Orleans Center next to the Superdome, the 1984 Louisiana World Exposition, and the restoration of the St. Charles Avenue streetcar line, as well as with political campaigns and neighborhood initiatives. Previously, as a broadcast reporter I covered urban issues, city planning, economic development, tourism, the city council, and the city and state administrations. Also, I tracked my husband Robert Tannen's work with numerous projects, including the creation of the Historic District Landmarks Commission, the selection of a location for the second bridge over the Mississippi River [Crescent City Connection, formerly the Greater New Orleans Bridge], a plan for a festival marketplace, and one for a downtown mall.

FONTENOT: How would you characterize the attitude toward planning before and after Katrina?

NATHAN: Two key things happened. Before the storm—with the exception of the Downtown Neighborhoods Improvement Association, which I founded here in the Tremé area—most neighborhood organizations were run by property owners whose main concerns were the value of their properties and the quality of life as it affected their homes. Our organization was formed to address broader issues of social equity, economic development, and quality of life. After the storm, some neighborhood organizations dramatically broadened their perspectives beyond the usual NIMBY focus of articulating what they did not want, i.e., a Walmart, a bar, or a coffee shop. Instead, they became ombudsmen on behalf of their neighborhoods, because immediately after the storm they were faced with a profound paralysis on the part of government at all levels. That paralysis was a product of incredibly complicated processes resulting from attempts to recreate government after the storm. Essentially, everything had to be recreated. There was a tremendous amount of confusion and finger-pointing, as well as efforts to restructure relationships at all levels, and the neighborhoods were more or less left to their own devices in figuring out how to come back. There was a fear immediately after the storm that certain neighborhoods might not—in fact, there was enormous uncertainty about the fate of the entire city. So people responded by saying, "Well, I'm going to make damn sure that *my* neighborhood will come back." Historically, an enemy helps rally the troops. In this case the enemy was anyone who questioned the viability of a neighborhood that suffered great damage from the storm, that was in greater jeopardy because of its topography. The lower the sea level, the greater the damage and the problems associated with return. So in neighborhoods such as Lakeview, Broadmoor, and the Lower Ninth Ward, the level of organization and determination was greatest.

FONTENOT: The scenario that you have just outlined describes a shift in society from endorsing negative rights, expressed as "We do not want this or that to occur" to positive rights, which is to say, "We demand that redevelopment happen" or "Services must be provided." This raises interesting questions about the relationship between citizens and their government in the history of American politics and the activation of a publicly involved citizen. To what degree do you think that this political shift, from "government should not interfere with private affairs" to "government must provide for the community," was a result of the calamity that was unfolding during that time, and how far does it represent a new direction in political activism?

NATHAN: I would rephrase that somewhat. I don't think that the role of government historically in America was to keep things from happening.

FONTENOT: Well, at least since the end of World War II a more libertarian *laissez-faire* attitude took root in the United States that was increasingly suspicious of the role of the state and supported a deregulated market economy while rejecting federally sponsored programs and various government regulations.

NATHAN: But that libertarian stance, expressed by a broader constituency, is a more recent phenomenon in American history. What had been much more characteristic up until and throughout most of the twentieth century is a more proactive perception of what government's role was—except in the South. Here there was, in fact, a very strong states' rights point of view, shaped in part by the slave economy and then by post–Civil War resistance to Northern principles, especially on racial issues. Fundamental Jeffersonian principles dating back to the founding of the nation also lingered longer in the South. As a result of that, a philosophy evolved that wanted government to just stay out of the way, and there was a demand for it to be minimized. I think that contributed to the lack of accountability that is still evident. I can only speak about New Orleans and Louisiana, not having lived elsewhere in the South. And my views are informed by having grown up in New York City, where government is evaluated on the basis of performance: effective provision of services, problem-solving, economic development, and action on issues of social equity. Here, it seems people are most interested in corruption, and in government facilitating business. (In New Orleans, ironically, government is blamed for the lack of economic and business progress.) It shouldn't be entirely surprising that even while public officials praised local organizations for their role in helping their neighborhoods, and indeed the entire city, to come back, they developed policies and strategies that were in conflict with what many neighborhood and grassroots organizations and residents wanted to happen in various parts of the city. The processes for deciding how rebuilding funds were used were often not transparent, not reflective of neighborhood preferences, and frequently resulted in funds promised to local projects being moved to others preferred by public officials. Even though these officials made a show of engaging the public, too often they talked the talk but didn't walk the walk, especially in cases where the officials had already taken a position that was different from neighborhood leaders'. And, further, there were many issues where conventional wisdom was the basis of public policy, as opposed to thorough research, analysis, and consideration of alternatives. This was particularly true of the decision to demolish 4,000 units of public housing, and of the planning for the medical district.[1] The conventional wisdom held that the "housing projects" were characterized by "concentrated poverty, crime, and low quality of life." The further assumption was that tearing them down was the only solution. Numerous statistics demonstrating that the crime rate in the projects was no higher than in other neighborhoods and that 95 percent of project tenants had jobs were ignored. And studies by major universities, architects, and engineers, including one from MIT, demonstrating that the projects could be renovated—bringing tenants back faster—to create attractive housing in a fraction of the time and cost that demolition and rebuilding would require, were ignored.

I often speak of the yin and yang of the recovery and redevelopment process. While public officials were too often making decisions based on inadequate consideration of the issues, neighborhood leaders, organizations, and residents were engaging in a sequence of planning phases through which they were becoming more and more expert at viewing urban development issues, with greater understanding of a range of options, and becoming more effective advocates for programs and policies that would help the rebuilding of their neighborhoods. We now have many more community leaders who are capable and informed advocate-planners than before Katrina. They worked with national, regional, and local urban planners through five city planning phases that helped secure funding for projects and will ultimately result in a much more cogent, relevant, and useful Comprehensive Zoning Ordinance for New Orleans

1 The Greater Orleans Biosciences Economic Development District spans 1,500 acres adjacent to downtown New Orleans and is situated in the neighborhoods of Mid-City and Gert Town. Neighborhood groups were concerned about the extensive demolition required to clear the area. See "Neighbors Concerned about BioDistrict in New Orleans: A Letter to the Editor," NOLA.com.

than has ever existed before.[2] They also worked several years on master planning for the school system that has been contentious and complicated, with much resistance to change, and chagrin over the fate of teachers who lost their jobs in the process. These efforts may very well bring about a phase where citizen and parent involvement in the schools will rise to play a more decisive and sustained role in assuring that the charter-school reform movement results in improved schools and greater community engagement and oversight.

Currently, as we move beyond recovery into a new era of long-term rebuilding under a new administration, with an infusion of intellectual capital and experienced bureaucrats, we are expanding efforts to explore alternative strategies and programs. The pressure to achieve results, however, is also driving political choices that may not be best for the city in the long run, but do address irksome conditions that citizens are anxious to change, including blight and a high crime rate compared with other major and midsize American cities.

FONTENOT: To pick up on one of your main points about how decisions are being made, how should research be used to make an argument for one policy over another and how does it become part of an open and transparent process? It would seem reasonable to require officials to present a coherent and logical argument to the public indicating what alternatives they have examined and how they came to their conclusions about key issues.

NATHAN: There was a profound disconnect between the dialogue going on within the walls of City Hall and the dialogue occurring at the community level during the first several years after the storm. Citizens put a great deal of time, thought, and consensus-building into the five phases of planning post-Katrina. The master plan for New Orleans, approved by the city council in August 2010, reflects the city that citizens want to project and grow. The plan is an effective foundation for the new zoning ordinance presently being reviewed, which should be refined and approved by next spring.[3] I do expect the ordinance to dramatically change the way the city does business—reducing horse trading between elected officials, developers, and citizens and establishing clearer principles based on "place-based" delineations of neighborhoods in relation to land use and development patterns. And I do think the administration and council are trying harder to reconcile community preferences with their own views, but there still is a continuing disconnect between planning principles, the preferences of the community, and the decision-making

2 The Urban Land Institute's "A Strategy for Rebuilding New Orleans," the city council–backed "Lambert Plan," Bring New Orleans Back (BNOB), Unified New Orleans Plan (UNOP), and the "Plan for the 21st Century: New Orleans 2030."

3 As this volume goes to print, the Comprehensive Zoning Ordinance still has not become law. In October 2013, the City Planning Commission held the final round of planning district meetings for public discussion of the updated draft of the CZO, culminating two years of review by the commission, consultants, and citizens.

processes of public officials with regard to certain issues, such as the medical district. That project, which essentially flattened seventy acres in the heart of the city, including many homes that had been restored after the storm, was opposed by an unprecedented coalition of more than fifty neighborhood and citizen organizations. Consultant studies provided viable alternatives that would have reduced the footprint of the district without hurting its viability and attractiveness. Alternative plans, in fact, might have created a more concentrated and walkable district. In this case, the determination of Louisiana State University to execute its own plan blocked any serious consideration of alternative concepts for use of the land and preexisting buildings, such as the Charity Hospital building, which consultants demonstrated could be easily renovated into a contemporary and effective hospital.

FONTENOT: In your opinion, what would be some of the best strategies for holding the mayor and other city officials accountable to precisely the kind of "local intelligence" often produced in collective discussions during the planning processes? Given how extremely limited resources are in New Orleans, particularly in these dire economic times, this resource, information, would seem to be invaluable. What would be the best way to incorporate this knowledge into the official decision-making processes of the city?

NATHAN: The master plan for the city was supposed to include provisions for a community-participation infrastructure. The discussion of how this might work has been flawed by a combination of inexperienced leadership, community apathy on the issue, and administrative resistance to creating an additional bureaucracy. I don't favor a highly structured and hierarchical way of doing things, but I am afraid that if we don't have some kind of independent process for sustained community engagement and input, we could return to the combative, unproductive process of conflict between developers and communities that was typical before the storm. I am most familiar with the community boards in New York City. Although some developers might prefer the boards didn't exist, since their positions on projects have influence, if not the final say, the boards have successfully provided a systematic and predictable process for community input on projects from the beginning. It was understandably hard to get the attention of citizens who were dealing with rebuilding their own homes and neighborhoods. The concept of community participation in planning for the future was just too intangible to capture sustained interest. It will be unfortunate if this essential ingredient in realizing the promise of the master plan is scrapped in favor of an outreach process internal to city government.

FONTENOT: What do you think are some of New Orleans's greatest accomplishments in planning since Katrina? Has the city accomplished anything of great significance that other cities might learn from?

NATHAN: I think that one of the greatest accomplishments has been approval of the master plan, and the preparation of the new Comprehensive

Zoning Ordinance. There was a great deal of suspicion about the plan, since preservationists pushed for giving it the "force of law" at the ballot box at a time when most people were unfamiliar with the concept. Some communities feared it was another strategy to prevent the redevelopment of downtown neighborhoods. The plan allows for annual amendments, but that was not well known initially. Anyone who is really unhappy with some of the principles that are in it can initiate a process to change it. Having a master plan that basically endorses the underlying concept of New Orleans as a "human-scale" city of single-family and double-shotgun homes, with plenty of green space, pedestrian-friendly neighborhoods, a system of bike paths, opportunities for neighborhood-based cultural facilities and economic development, and very neighborhood-based energy is a great thing. I really have to credit the City Planning Commission and its consultant team, led by Goody Clancy, for being deliberate in an approach that encouraged, respected, and integrated neighborhood input into the plan. I have to say that all of the citywide planning initiatives—from the mayor's first commission, the Bring New Orleans Back effort, the city council's "Lambert Plan" in the "wet" or heavily damaged neighborhoods, the Unified New Orleans Plan [UNOP], the master plan and its accompanying Comprehensive Zoning Ordinance—all of the phases have really been very diligent and sincere in soliciting involvement of not just community organizations but also citizens in general, and integrating their recommendations into the final documents. UNOP generated a recommendation, for example, to take down parts of I-10. This came straight from the citizens of the surrounding neighborhoods.

There was substantial debate over planners' recommendations for multifamily housing. Some neighborhoods wanted to see it anywhere but in their area. Others had had bad experiences with poorly planned and managed multifamily housing. Finding ways to make the integration of such housing, as well as identifying areas that could absorb retail, commercial, institutional, and industrial uses, was also controversial. It is a credit to the planners and residents alike that they were able to identify places to accommodate these kinds of land uses, which will allow for much-needed growth in the city without jeopardizing the city's underlying human scale. This was a major achievement.

The Comprehensive Zoning Ordinance now in review is an impressive document. Again, it endorses the fundamental nature of this city that we love, the way we interact between our neighborhoods, and a more robust and varied use of our central business district. It is a place-based plan that strives to be true to the character of different parts of the city. The city previously tried to create a zoning ordinance and master plan at least twice in the past couple of decades and did not get through the process. Earlier unapproved plans sat on shelves. This one will be finished, and it will be smart, easy to read, and easy to work with, reduce confusion and ambiguity, and avoid endless variances that now clog our ordinance.

FONTENOT: Now that there is this new planning framework, do you have any thoughts about the impact that this new "culture of planning" has had on the way people think about planning, their relationship with the city, and the mechanisms by which change occurs in the city? Also, do you think that the basic achievements in citizen participation in planning will be sustained in the future?

NATHAN: I had a conversation this morning with a gentleman who has been working with the city during all this planning, and we were talking about a streetscape project that we started three years ago that is just now being put out to bid. And from what I understand, a lot of hard-fought decisions about financial commitments to projects that came out of the planning are very much now being reconsidered. And so the question is, Will the commitments made to community-supported and requested projects in the early months and years after the storm actually go forward, or will funds for them be diverted to projects that city officials feel are more important? Another concern is the Darwinian nature of neighborhood project funding. Some neighborhoods—because of celebrity involvement, leadership capacity, or funding opportunities—have been able to secure much greater commitments than others. So while all neighborhoods have become more engaged in advocacy planning, some are benefiting disproportionately. I worry about the long-term impact of the neglect that certain neighborhoods are experiencing, which may erode their commitment to planning.

FONTENOT: Has there been some sort of mechanism put in place to encourage investment in neighborhoods, such as the large key projects that accompany the plan for the redevelopment of the riverfront? Is there a strategy, whether in the form of policies or incentives, to encourage particular kinds of new development in neighborhoods? What I am trying to get at is how does the city hope to manifest the ideals of the master plan? It seems to me that planning and investment would need to go hand in hand. Otherwise, one runs the risk of developing a master plan that lacks practical means for channeling funds to various neighborhoods to encourage development in particular ways with neighborhood partners.

NATHAN: I guess the most significant source of funding and initiatives for new development is the U.S. Department of Housing and Urban Development. HUD provides funding through various programs. The funding is funneled through the state's Department of Community Development and then through the city's Department of Facilities, Infrastructure and Community Development. There are several public/private entities whose mission it is to encourage new development: the New Orleans Business Alliance, Greater New Orleans Inc., the Business Council of New Orleans, and the Downtown Development District. The city also has its Department of Economic Development. These agencies and organizations aim to promote general business growth, not so much real estate-based development. There is no agency such as the Boston

Redevelopment Authority or the Empire State Development Corporation that specifically promotes development.

FONTENOT: I remember years ago an event that you organized at Tulane University to discuss the role of contemporary architecture in New Orleans. I presented a series of studies on new housing typologies for New Orleans. I would like to reflect on those discussions we had before Katrina, on the need for fresh and innovative ideas about architecture in New Orleans and for more international engagement with local issues. Those ideas we talked about in 2000 seem to have manifested at an astonishing speed, less than five years in most cases. Besides the architectural trends in New Orleans, I'm curious to know what you think about all the projects that have been designed and built, many by international offices, since Katrina—everything, from the Tulane University URBANbuild houses to the Make It Right houses to the Global Green project in Holy Cross. All of these have brought in international firms as well as local progressive offices to design and build in a contemporary idiom.

NATHAN: I think these projects are islands.

FONTENOT: Do you think they play a significant role in changing the way the people of New Orleans think about architecture and the city? Do you think they influence new types of progressive development in New Orleans?

NATHAN: Yes. First of all I would say that the Global Green project's first house, a LEED platinum house functioning now as a visitor center, gets many visitors every week who enter it to see what the inside of a "green house" can be like, what it can include. It is actually quite homey, but the green elements are very explicit and easier to understand in reality than in technical documents. So I think there is no doubt that in encouraging people to think about green building, the Global Green projects have had an important impact. I think that the Make It Right project is exciting. It is like a huge playground or stage set filled with quite extraordinary architectural ideas, and there are people living there now who—based on their previous lives in shotgun or ranch-style houses—would *never* have imagined living in houses like that. They have learned how to live in these fairly radical, contemporary houses, so their experience has to have a value and it probably has an impact on their friends, relatives, and neighbors. As for it having an impact on the construction of buildings throughout the city, I don't see a lot of evidence of that yet, but that does not mean that it will not happen. What is interesting and important to ask is whether the demolition of blighted housing that is now creating empty lots all over the city will provide an opportunity for more new architecture, or will it turn New Orleans into another Detroit? Given this process, many of us would really rather see a lot of the houses be rebuilt than torn down. If you look at the new public housing that was recently built, it is not "new" architecture. It is very much "traditional" New Orleans architecture—and I don't think that is a terrible thing, because having just spent time in the Northeast, I think traditional New Orleans architecture is pretty extraordinary. I'm totally in favor of the most adventurous new architecture in the universe, but I don't see the point in demolishing viable property. I'm for homesteading. I've been trying to catalyze a homesteading program that would give some of the retrievable properties to people who will fix them up, live in them, and help restore neighborhoods.

FONTENOT: I agree with you on both of those points. I think we should encourage homesteading and I also think we should encourage working with what exists while introducing new elements into the historical urban landscape. In fact, I believe we need to perfect that kind of urbanism in New Orleans as a way of developing a new character for the city in the twenty-first century. The challenge would be to understand the context well enough that we could hold on to some of the basic urban principles as we developed a new type of architecture capable of evolving in response to a range of cultural, technological, economic, and aesthetic concerns. It would be unfortunate if we were not able to fully take advantage of the great stock of historical houses while opening up opportunities for architectural and urban experiments. Any closing thoughts on where New Orleans is now in the planning process and where you hope this process will lead?

NATHAN: My mantra is twofold. First, there has been a process for holding community meetings and listening to people, but not as strong a process for integrating those recommendations into public policy and actual funded projects. This is a critical area that has to be addressed. Second, I think there has been a failure to do the research and analysis on various strategies and then pick the best one to move the city forward. There has been a tendency to jump on an approach rather than analyze the various options. The LSU hospital plan is a case in point. LSU had a plan and held public hearings. Hundreds of people came out to those hearings to oppose a huge suburban-style campus, but afterward LSU did not spend one single second that I know of, and I could be wrong, to make any real adjustment to that plan in response to this overwhelming neighborhood opposition, which some fifty neighborhood organizations joined. I found that utter disregard for the public's concerns appalling. I have never seen fifty organizations come behind anything in my almost forty years in New Orleans. I also feel that the architectural and preservation communities have been largely absent from the debate on the city's future. Angela O'Byrne attempted to open a dialogue with the nonprofit City Works. But once architectural firms got back in gear, most of the energy behind that and similar efforts dwindled. Understandably, many have had to rebuild their own businesses and lives. Virtually no local architects opposed or encouraged dialogue about the destruction of our public housing. And we are not talking about behemoth high-rise buildings. We are for the most part talking about garden apartments that could have been renovated, much as Pres Kabacoff renovated some of the older buildings in the former St. Thomas project.[4] The architects bemoaned the demolition of numerous iconic Modernist buildings since the storm but put up no really effective opposition to it.[5] The destruction of these buildings combined with the demolition of blighted traditional residential buildings constitutes a kind of third or even fourth Katrina. We've lost Modernist schools, churches, office buildings, and residences. There is even talk of tearing down Edward Durell Stone's 1959 International Trade Mart on the riverfront. A lot of money will be wasted on demolition and rebuilding when a new skin could bring out the best of the existing building, which offers spectacular views of the city. Post-Katrina, there has simply not been an architectural or urban planning conscience expressed by the professional architects or planners in New Orleans. They seem to be afraid to buck the system in a city that is essentially a small town.

FONTENOT: The destruction of publicly financed buildings across New Orleans in the years following the storm, is apparently part of a much larger phenomenon. This idea is very close to Naomi Klein's *Shock Doctrine*, which argues that those who wish to "implement unpopular free-market policies now routinely do so by taking advantage of certain features of the aftermath of major disasters, be they economic, political, military, or natural." While citizens are still in shock and local government is disorganized, policies are put in place that would otherwise be very difficult to impose. This theory was demonstrated in post-Katrina New Orleans, first when the public school system was dismantled and replaced with charter schools, and second when public housing and many schools were demolished en masse. These irreparable losses represent the other side, the "dark side," of reconstruction. And now, as you mentioned, mass demolition of blighted privately owned housing stock will further erode the fabric of the city. Is demolition really the only or the most viable solution for reconstructing New Orleans? Is New Orleans a model of reconstruction? Since Katrina, have intelligent

4 The St. Thomas Housing Project in New Orleans, built between 1938 and 1941, was the first public housing project to receive funding following the Wagner Housing Act of 1937. In 2001 most of the buildings were demolished and the "River Garden," a mixed-income development, was constructed by Pres Kabacoff of HRI Properties. This pattern of demolishing "modern" public housing and replacing it with "traditional" New Orleans typologies, loosely modeled on the principles of New Urbanism,in order to create "mixed-income" developments, was followed throughout the city of New Orleans after Hurricane Katrina.

5 The Louisiana chapter of DOCOMOMO, an international organization for the documentation and conservation of buildings, has attempted to preserve the modern architecture in New Orleans, with limited success. Given that significant examples were demolished in the city's recent past—for example, the 1968 Rivergate Convention Center, designed by Curtis and Davis Architects, torn down in 1995—it is all the more unsettling to witness continued, widespread obliteration of modern buildings such as Hoffman Elementary (1954), designed by Charles Colbert; St. Frances Xavier Cabrini Elementary (1954), designed by Curtis and Davis Architects; and Phillis Wheatley Elementary School (1954), designed by Charles Colbert. Wheatley, which served the historic New Orleans African-American neighborhood of Tremé, survived the storm relatively undamaged but through political maneuvering was subsequently demolished. Although New Orleans was a pioneer in the preservation movement and developed a strong appreciation of its eighteenth- and nineteenth-century history, this destruction illustrates the city's limited appreciation of its twentieth-century architectural legacy. Many exceptional modern buildings in New Orleans were acknowledged worldwide and won major national awards for their regionally-specific and innovative approaches to modern design.

decisions been made about what should be demolished and what should be redeveloped?

NATHAN: I think the preservation community has been as stymied as the public and the city government during this phase. Preservationists have a history of retrieving housing and neighborhoods throughout the city. But I don't sense that they ever came to terms with the enormity of the impact of Katrina or of the post-storm redevelopment policies that put our housing stock and neighborhoods in further jeopardy. The city sends out notices about the next hearing on buildings that are slated for demolition, listing dozens and dozens of houses that will be torn down, without offering an effective blueprint or guidelines for dealing with the process as a whole. There is no preservation policy or plan I know of that addresses the magnitude of the housing being destroyed. I give preservationists enormous credit for preventing the demolition of buildings in the Central Business District in the 1970s; for preventing the destruction of the riverfront in the French Quarter; for jump-starting the revitalization of the Garden District, Holy Cross, and parts of Tremé. But as for meeting the challenge of a city that was washed away in a cataclysm and is being further cleansed by post-storm policies, I hope they—all of us—find a way to stop the carnage.

FONTENOT: Can you offer any insight that you've gained working and living in New Orleans after Katrina that may be useful for thinking about politics, activism, and the formation of new communities in the twenty-first century?

NATHAN: There is some kind of revolution afoot in the world related to the frustration our citizens have felt when their voices had no impact on major policy decisions. At the heart of the frustration is a realization that democratic institutions are no protection against injustice and tone-deaf politics and governance. The relationships between the Arab Spring, the occupation of Wall Street, and our dissatisfaction with the handling of New Orleans's redevelopment is where I seek guidance for fashioning a better way for government and the governed to work together with more understanding of the underlying realities of our economy—our challenges and our opportunities.

FONTENOT: Should other cities look to New Orleans to find new ways of thinking about urban development and city government?

NATHAN: I think there has to be more research and policy development regarding the process of rebuilding after disasters. I don't think New Orleans is a poster child for post-disaster planning. I think a more in-depth study of how things worked and didn't will be useful in devising better strategies.

FONTENOT: What do you think about the two different mayors' administrations that have governed the city since Katrina? Can you offer some thoughts about the different ways in which the Nagin and Landrieu administrations have approached the question of planning and reconstructing of the city?

NATHAN: Mayor Landrieu has a lot of really smart and capable people in his administration. He has made quite an effort to put together a brain trust, much as his dad, Moon Landrieu, did when he was mayor in the 70s. More than any of the other administrations that I have worked with here, Landrieu has been bringing in some big thinkers. He talks about building the future city and not so much about the past one. He is determined to make things happen. I just hope that he uses his brain trust to full advantage and allows for the kind of debate, inside and outside his offices, that will help identify creative and effective strategies to build that city of the future. I actually think that Nagin will ultimately get more credit for what he accomplished, despite his stumbles. The days, months, and years immediately after Katrina were extraordinarily difficult for everybody. And other public leaders share the blame for the initial chaos and inadequately thought-out policies. The state and federal governments, too, as endless news reports have noted. Ironically, despite the bungles at the federal level, the federal requirement for planning as a condition of reconstruction funding deserves credit for one of the most positive outcomes of the storm: the development of better-informed, planning-savvy community leaders and residents. I hope they will remain engaged in the rebuilding of a city too great to perish in a flood.

BENEATH THE UNDERDOG: URBAN DESIGN AND THE SOCIAL CONTRACT

M. DAVID LEE

Beneath the Underdog, the title of the autobiography of the late jazz bassist and composer Charles Mingus, is an apt metaphor for the proposition I make in this essay.[1] Hurricane Katrina exposed to the world in a dramatic fashion the failings of New Orleans's physical and social infrastructure. There were dangerous cracks in that infrastructure long before Katrina, and many were well aware of it. The fact is, that although Katrina got the attention of the world, if only for an agonizing moment, any number of inner-city neighborhoods in this country are being slowly overwhelmed by similar, if less dramatic, failures. This is not a new story, simply one that is for the most part ignored, except when extraordinary events, usually negative, suddenly thrust these neighborhoods onto the front pages.

Design schools, which once devoted considerable studio energy to addressing real-world problems—urban blight and the need for affordable housing and basic public facilities—have been preoccupied, instead, with creating fantasies, buildings that some would even call bizarre. And outside the academy, professional city planners have seemed less driven by thoughtful design strategies informed by place and cultural precedent than by faith in the "Bilbao effect"—the construction of a signature, high-style building such as Frank Gehry's Guggenheim Museum in that city—or in an Olympic designation as the bright paths to revitalization. Someone said, "In crisis lies opportunity." The near crash of the U.S. banking system has had a sobering effect everywhere, but nowhere more sobering than among the design professions. The kinds of high-profile, eccentric, and in many cases self-indulgent projects celebrated by the media have ground to a halt. Now large firms are "throwing elbows" and competing for commissions that would have not drawn a sniff of interest from them in the past. Unfortunately, too, experienced professionals and newly minted graduates alike are without jobs in the design fields.

Where, then, is the opportunity? I offer a modest proposal: We need a design-centered, updated model of the storied Civilian Conservation Corps

1 Charles Mingus, *Beneath the Underdog: His World as Composed by Mingus*, ed. Nel King (New York: Knopf, 1971).

(CCC) that employed so many during the Depression, building a wonderful countrywide infrastructure of roads, bridges, and dams and making improvements to our national parks that still serve us today. The fight to slow global warming and to live more sustainably is cited as this era's equivalent of the civil rights struggle. Whether or not that is an overstatement, the threat of global warming is real and design professionals have tangible roles to play in its mitigation. We cannot, however, limit our thinking to the familiar zones of form, technology, and an abstract theoretical dialogue that is often provocative to no end. Real progress toward a more sustainable future will be made only if we approach this crisis holistically and on multiple fronts—political, social, economic, and physical.

There is general agreement that the most sustainable thing we can do right out of the box (pun intended) is to preserve as much of the rational built environment as we can. Ironically, some of the most distressed neighborhoods in the country have the bones to become the most environmentally sustainable. These were once the most fashionable portions of our cities, with grand boulevards and iconic public buildings, churches, and historic parks, which still recall a faded glory. Though much of it needs work, substantially constructed historic building stock remains in these areas and in many cities it enjoys excellent proximity to downtown business districts, hospitals, and cultural facilities

That's the good news. The flip side is that in the inner city, schools are underperforming and often in poor physical shape; a culture of drugs and violence threatens and drives out solid residents; and good jobs are missing or far removed. Nevertheless, it only makes sense and is simply good public policy to invest the resources to make these neighborhoods thrive again. It will take tremendous political will and (stimulus) capital to do so, but not to do so is patently foolish and frankly threatens the well-being of the entire country. I believe that if the design professions are to be relevant in this task, we need to employ not only imagination but also accessible language and design tools that will allow us to work productively with those in the social services sector to repair both the physical and social infrastructure in ways that are mutually reinforcing. At a design jury at Yale years ago, someone commented, "You architects need to learn to see socially." Several weeks later at a talk that I gave to a gathering of social service organizations, I countered that social service workers needed to learn to see spatially.

That is, both sides must learn to plan and design in ways less driven by formal dogma and familiar precedents. Instead, we will need to work across not only our own design fields but also other professional disciplines. We must plan and build informed equally by socioeconomic considerations (how 60s!) and by the particulars of place, culture, and traditions. One size does not fit all.

As difficult as such an effort promises to be, we cannot limit ourselves to addressing only the "technology" of sustainability while ignoring its

David Lee

North Philadelphia

social dimension. To be sure, the social problems to be faced are tough and seemingly intractable, but as the song says, "It's not easy being green." We must be willing to rethink everything: for example, we must challenge the ubiquitous refrain that every attempt to improve the physical environment will result in gentrification, which is by definition a bad outcome. But if "gentrifying" means renovating crumbling buildings, agitating for improved city services, gaining a voice in city hall, and lobbying for better-performing schools, even at the risk of rising property values, then perhaps the more salient issue to be addressed is not how to fight gentrification but rather how to forge an *inclusive* gentrification. Living in neighborhoods exclusively defined by poverty, violence, and despair—even if they are affordable—is not good for anyone and especially not good for our children.

I have spoken about these issues for years, incorporated them into my teaching, and sought to incorporate them into my practice. Across the country, I have seen evidence of the successful transformation of some neighborhoods, but many more remain in distress. Recently, I drove around Chicago's South Side, where I spent some of my formative years. While it was depressing to see what had happened since those days, I could also see evidence of resurgence. It would be easy for anyone working in city planning and design to become cynical, but I have always maintained that it is the job of designers always to see the glass as half full. After watching a broadly diverse, enthusiastic, and hopeful crowd in Chicago's Grant Park on an unseasonably warm November 2008 election night, I began to hope that perhaps now, more than in any recent time, we can allow ourselves to believe that we are capable of summoning the will to reverse decades of decline and disinvestment, and to reimagine

David Lee

New Orleans

even our most troubled inner-city neighborhoods as sustainable, beautiful, and inclusive jewels in our national urban fabric.

CODA

At the time that I delivered this paper, October 2009, no one anticipated another disaster to New Orleans and the Gulf region on the scale of the BP oil spill. As resilient as New Orleanians and the New Orleans diaspora have proven to be, this was and is a hard blow to take. That said, I have no doubt that the city will survive, but the question remains how will it also thrive. Clearly, nature will challenge and test the city as she always has and will continue to do so. That phenomenon we have little ability to thwart. What we can do, though, is function in ways that mitigate the man-made actions that enable and exacerbate the destruction wrought by natural occurrences. With intelligent planning, New Orleans and, indeed, the region and the country can strike a better balance between the preservation and enhancement of natural systems and how we build and rebuild our cities and towns.

The BP disaster exposed an unholy connection between our addiction to oil and the economic, social, and physical consequences of its production. Too few of us in other parts of the country fully appreciate how much we benefit from and depend upon the petroleum generated in the Gulf, nor do we realize how much of the seafood industry is centered there. The acrimonious debate on whether to place a moratorium on further offshore drilling until inspections could be made exposed a dilemma poised between our need to protect the natural environment and our insatiable demand for oil. Whether we like it or not, we will need to drill for oil and we will also need to have clean waters in which to fish, both for the foreseeable future. The challenge we need to address as a nation, and this is not news, is the scale of our dependency and the difficult prospect of "drastically" reducing that dependency in the near future and for the long term.

In this essay, I have made a case for the active preservation of the existing built fabric and infrastructure in our cities as an investment in sustainability. Our dependence as a country on New Orleans and the Gulf region to supply the rest of us disproportionately with oil—and seafood—dictates that, in fairness, we owe the city and region a commitment to reduce the demand for oil and the problematic infrastructure it requires. But as we wean ourselves away from our oil dependency, we must simultaneously put in place initiatives and strategies to redirect lost jobs into double-bottom-line endeavors that provide good employment and lead us to a more sustainable national lifestyle.

I believe that a commitment to rethink and rebuild cities and towns at greater densities with better connectivity through improved infrastructure is the direction to pursue. Such a strategy preserves our physical history, generates local jobs and protects open-space resources. At the risk of seeming self-serving on behalf of the planning and design professionals, I would argue that construction jobs have a huge multiplier effect, because the work for the most part must be done in situ. Construction activity also generates jobs at multiple skill levels, and it impacts the economy vertically, from Wall Street to Main Street. We once made a plan to put a man on the moon; we have "been there, done that." Now, how about putting men and women to work building a more sustainable and independent nation?

ELBOWS TOGETHER, HEARTS APART: INSTITUTIONAL REFORM, ECONOMIC OPPORTUNITY, AND SOCIAL TRUST IN POST-KATRINA NEW ORLEANS

MICHAEL A. COWAN

> A "social trap" is a situation where individuals, groups, or organizations are unable to cooperate owing to mutual distrust and lack of social capital, even where cooperation would benefit all.
>
> —Bo Rothstein[1]

I. THE SOCIAL TRAP NAMED NEW ORLEANS

If you have a taste for the sheer dazzling differences of humanity, the music, food, dialects, arts, architecture, and worship of New Orleans spread a feast for the spirit every day. If you can stand to face the mixture of good and evil in America's soul, that is also daily in plain sight here. I write these words after a day that began with the chairman of our city council's criminal justice committee informing me that only one place in the world now lives with more murders than New Orleans, and ended with the weekly rehearsal of Shades of Praise, the joyful interracial gospel choir that has become a living symbol of bridging the racial divide.[2] Such lows and highs make up the days of New Orleanians. On August 29, 2005, this wonderful, terrible city was plunged into chaos when Katrina's winds brought down the poorly built walls between us and brought in the water all around us. This contemporary morality play was staged for the whole world, our shameful brokenness and lack of leadership put on display for all to see and judge—harshly.[3]

Contrary to popular local and national opinion, the fundamental problem facing New Orleans is not poverty or geographic vulnerability.[4] Nor is it racism.[5] Those are symptoms of a deeper social malady. The underlying dynamic that has kept our city in steady decline for the past fifty years is a "social trap"—the inability of government, business, and

---

1 Bo Rothstein, *Social Traps and the Problem of Trust* (New York: Cambridge University Press, 2005).

2 shadesofpraise.org.

3 James Zogby, "Shame of Katrina Is Still With Us," *Gulf News*, April 24, 2006.

4 Juan Williams, "Getting Past Katrina," *New York Times*, September 1, 2006, A17; Christopher Drew and John Schwartz, "Storm and Crisis: The Levees; Floodwall Anchors and Soil Gain New Focus as Suspects," *New York Times*, October 27, 2005, A28.

5 Alex Jung, "How Black Is New Orleans? New Census Figures Don't Tell the Whole Story," *Colorlines*, May 1, 2008, 8.

civic leaders to negotiate with integrity across racial, religious, and class lines to bring into being a city that works better and more equitably for all groups. In New Orleans, groups divided by ethnicity and class are caught up together in a downward spiral of chronic conflict over where we should be going and how to get there. Both locals and outsiders typically misattribute our social dilemma to racism, the indifference of the wealthy, or pathology in poor black families, but in fact an intergroup impasse over goals and action is the underlying social trap in which New Orleans continues to be caught.[6] The long years since Katrina drew an indelible line in New Orleans's history have done us the painful service of keeping a bright public spotlight on that social trap. And although the uniqueness of the Crescent City is legendary, and rightly so, what plagues our body politic is by no means our challenge alone: The incapacity of elected, business, and civic leaders to compromise and act across cultural and class lines for the common good is *the* American dilemma.[7]

A visible thread weaves its way through the fabric of complexity-bordering-on-chaos that is post-Katrina New Orleans: We see progress when enough members of different groups partially escape the inertia of our social trap by achieving a measure of consensus about what to do on concrete matters like criminal justice reform and then acting on that agreement, and we see paralysis when they do not. I begin this essay by retrieving an image of the world as it should be, forged in the crucible of America's finest hour (so far), an image with a powerful message for those caught in traps of mistrust. Then I describe the conflicts underlying the process of understanding problems, selecting goals, and choosing methods of change, conflicts that continue to plague the recovery of New Orleans and limit her future. I next present three ways of thinking strategically about how to free a city from a social trap. And finally I recount the most promising attempts that New Orleanians have ever made to move beyond our divisions toward shared social action, through an emerging network of diverse leaders and citizens who are basing our strategy for change on one of those three strategic models.

Out of and because of the devastation that Katrina brought, New Orleans stands on the threshold of becoming for the first time more than the sum of her extraordinary parts: a city where government serves all citizens efficiently, ethically, and fairly; where the economy affords opportunity to all who are willing to work and learn; and where intergroup trust transforms crippling divisions into powerful unity for the common good. The well-being of the whole city, and therefore of the members of all her differing groups, hangs in the balance. And a powerful lesson for

6 Rothstein, *Social Traps*, 4–5 and 17–18.

7 Gunnar Myrdal, *An American Dilemma* (New York: 1962), lxix–lxxi; Stephen Graubard, "An American Dilemma Revisited," in *An American Dilemma Revisited*, ed. Obie Clayton Jr., (New York: Russell Sage Foundation, 1996), 1–24.

America about diminishing the social killer named poverty and banishing the social fiction named race awaits the outcome.[8]

II. ELBOWS TOGETHER, HEARTS APART

In Nashville two days after Christmas in 1962, with Jim Crow dying but not yet dead, Dr. Martin Luther King Jr. issued a prophetic challenge:

> When the desegregation process is one hundred percent complete, the human relations dilemma of our nation will still be monumental unless we launch now the parallel thrust of the integration process ... In the context of what our national community needs, desegregation alone is empty and shallow. We must always be aware that our ultimate goal is integration, and that desegregation is only a first step on the road to the good society ... Integration is creative, and is therefore more profound and far-reaching than desegregation. Integration is the positive acceptance of desegregation and the welcomed participation of all in the total range of human activities. Integration is genuine interpersonal, intergroup doing.

Then he went on to declare his foreboding about an America desegregated but not integrated:

> We do not have to look very far to see the pernicious effects of a desegregated society that is not integrated. It leads to physical proximity without spiritual affinity. It gives us a society where ... elbows are together and hearts are apart. It gives us spatial togetherness and spiritual apartness.[9]

Where do we New Orleanians find ourselves today? Exactly where Dr. King feared we might: Racial segregation and discrimination have been illegal for the past half-century, yet the human relations dilemma of our very diverse city is indeed monumental. In post-Katrina New Orleans, as elsewhere in America, our elbows may be legally together from 9:00 a.m. to 5:00 p.m., but, with the notable and not insignificant exception of Saints games in the Superdome, our hearts remain largely apart.

Dr. King dreamed, worked, and died for an America in which members of all groups would engage in acts of "genuine interpersonal, intergroup doing." *Inter-* means "between" or "among;" *doing* means "acting." So "genuine interpersonal, intergroup doing" means members of diverse

---

8 See Ivan Hannford, *Race: The History of an Idea in the West* (Baltimore, MD: Johns Hopkins University, 1996); and Winthrop Jordan, *White Over Black: American Attitudes Toward the Negro, 1550–1812* (New York: Norton, 1977), for compelling historical accounts of the social creation of the construct of race.

9 Martin Luther King Jr., "The Ethical Demands for Integration," in *A Testament of Hope: The Essential Writings of Martin Luther King, Jr.*, ed. James M. Washington, ed. (San Francisco: Harper & Row, 1986), 118.

groups not ignoring or shouting at each other, not just analyzing racism, classism or other -isms, but rather reasoning, compromising, and acting wisely and justly together on concrete matters of common interest such as safe streets and good public schools. Dr. King's vision of the America that should be was people acting together with integrity for the benefit of all, building a world where we judge others and are judged on the content of our character, as revealed by our actions.[10] His cherished name for that American dream, which he discovered in the writings of the American philosopher Josiah Royce, was "the Beloved Community."[11]

The experience that Royce's biblically resonant phrase captured for Dr. King came from lifelong membership and ordained service in the bible-centered African-American church. In that milieu, his vision of the world as it should be was deeply shaped by the Jewish prophets. How often and how powerfully did we hear him retrieve for us the troubling words of Amos: "Let justice roll down as waters, and righteousness as a mighty stream."[12] The vision of "righteousness" from the great Jewish tradition shaped Dr. King's moral compass and holds particular meaning for New Orleans and other divided communities right now. According to the biblical record, in times of trial, when gathering clouds of external threat filled the horizon of the Chosen People with despair and there seemed no way out, God's spirit would come upon His people through anointed leaders.[13] Under their spirit-filled leadership, three things happened. First, the system of justice was restored to reliable and proper functioning for all. Second, mercy, understood not just as helping those in need but also providing for fuller participation of the marginalized—the widow, the orphan, the outsider—was undertaken as obligatory. Third, those who had renewed their commitment to the communal practice of justice and mercy had a renewed and powerful experience of God's presence among them.[14]

The same three Beloved Community challenges—creating just public institutions, opening the door to full participation by all who are willing to do their part as workers and citizens, and learning to recognize each other as fellow creatures of the same God and fellow citizens of the same democracy—are the very ones facing New Orleans (and America) today. The genuine interpersonal, intergroup doing that we must undertake to address those challenges now is not a replay of the movement politics of the civil rights era, although it will likely require its movement moments. Nor is it simply an exercise in individuals pulling themselves up by their own bootstraps, although individual rights and responsibilities are at the heart of social change in a democracy.

10 Martin Luther King Jr., "I Have a Dream," in Washington, *Testament of Hope*, 219.

11 Charles Marsh, *The Beloved Community (*New York: Basic Books, 2006), 49–50.

12 Amos 5:24, *American Standard Bible*.

13 Michael Welker, *God the Spirit,* trans. John Hoffmeyer (Minneapolis, MN, Fortress Press, 1994), 52–3.

14 Ibid., 113 and 123–4; Michael Lodahl, *Shekhinah/Spirit* (New York: Paulist Press, 1992), 42–7.

Instead, the key to surmounting today's challenges is bridge-building leaders convening government-business-civic partnerships that embrace the maximum degree of diversity possible without losing their capacity to act effectively on specific matters of common interest.[15] These partnerships must create concrete plans for addressing these issues based on demonstrated successes elsewhere, and then mobilize a broad and deep constituency to see that they are implemented. Every plan of action should include specific ways of holding government officials, business and civic leaders, and ordinary citizens accountable for doing their respective parts. Every group willing to cooperate and compromise in this public work will contribute to and benefit from the genuine interpersonal, intergroup doing required for success.

III. WITHOUT A SHARED VISION: LIFE IN THE BIG UNEASY

Why have New Orleanians both before and after Katrina been unable to create plans for the future that will benefit all, and then see to their implementation? In the ancient book of wisdom called Proverbs, we read, "Where there is no vision, the people perish."[16] A people's vision cannot be separated from its interests and those of the others with whom its members share a world. Political philosopher Hannah Arendt notes:

> The language of the Romans, perhaps the most political people we have ever known, used the words "to live" and "to be among men" (*inter hominess esse*) or "to die" and "to cease to be among men" ... as synonyms.[17]

To be political is to have interests (the word is from the Latin "*inter*" plus "*esse*"), and that means to share a world with others who have other, and differing, interests. Without a clear-eyed grasp of how their interests are interrelated, members of diverse ethnic, religious, and socioeconomic groups living in the same place are stuck in the trap of paralyzing social mistrust—caught in divisions that limit, damage, and kill.

Good quality of life for all in New Orleans requires fair and feasible plans to fix the many things that are strained or broken here. The shared vision we lack is not a master plan, or an agreement on some set of abstract principles, but rather a pragmatic commitment to the just and efficient rebuilding of a broken city, with the details to be negotiated in an ongoing series of compromises. Our failures of leadership, endless delays, and lost opportunities post-Katrina have only confirmed what observant New Orleanians knew before the storm: Our elbows are together but our hearts are apart, and we are perishing. Beneath the shallow surface of *laissez-*

15 Clarence Stone, *Regime Politics: Governing Atlanta, 1946–1988* (Lawrence, KS: University of Kansas, 1989), 210–12.

16 Proverbs 29:18, *King James Bible*.

17 Hannah Arendt, *The Human Condition* (Chicago: University of Chicago Press, 1958), 7–8.

les-bons-temps-rouler New Orleans, what is most evident to us and the world is our deep, demoralizing divisions. These chasms prevent trust in fellow citizens and investment in shared public life. They also create the incentive for those who can do so to secede from public involvement and make private arrangements for their own health, education, and safety. That leaves those without the financial resources to go private nevertheless having to fend for themselves in a city and state where waste, fraud, and abuse have long prevented all citizens, especially poor and working-class families, from receiving what they pay for and deserve from government. The result is a city where in varying degrees all live with declining opportunities in a climate of growing fear and distrust.

Like its pre-storm incarnation, I find post-Katrina New Orleans divided in six ways. The first division is *strategic*: Since the civil rights era, our predominantly black political officials and mainly white business leaders have failed to come to agreement on policies and plans for making the changes needed for the well-being of all; meanwhile, the leaders of our faith-based, nonprofit, neighborhood, and educational institutions have been too segregated from each other and inwardly focused to push political and business, leaders into such an agreement. The second division is *socioeconomic*: The gap between rich and poor grows while the middle class declines. The third is *structural*: The citywide efforts of elected, business and civic leaders are not well aligned with the efforts of neighborhood-based leaders. The fourth is *intergenerational*: A new generation of business and civic leaders attempting to find its voice in New Orleans is not being actively recruited and mentored by senior leaders. The fifth is *ethnocentric*: In their obsessive preoccupation with each other, black and white New Orleanians have consistently failed to acknowledge the presence and seek the participation of the Hispanic, Asian, Arab, and other cultural communities at the table of public life, to their own detriment and the whole city's; in a similar vein, Christian faith communities have been loosely connected if at all to other denominations, let alone to their Jewish, Muslim, and Buddhist counterparts. Our sixth division is *ideological*: Leaders and citizens of New Orleans disagree profoundly about what to do about the continuing effects of racism and poverty.

While New Orleans has continued to sink ever deeper into the decrepitude produced by these six mutually reinforcing divisions over the past half-century, Southern cities that not long ago were her minor rivals economically and socially—including Atlanta, Houston, and San Antonio—have moved, imperfectly but decisively, to embrace a multiracial political economy.[18] The proof that a community's political institutions both make possible and limit its economic vitality, as I will argue below, can be found in the pudding of the vibrant regional economies of those three areas, which produce

18 Stone, *Regime Politics* Chapter 9; Mark Warren, *Dry Bones Rattling* (Princeton, NJ: Princeton University, 2001), 47–57 and 62–5.

steadily expanding opportunities for businesses and individuals and a deeper tax base to support necessary public services.[19] That social and economic vibrancy stands in stark and sobering contrast to the steady regression of New Orleans from a national economic powerhouse to a tourist destination with wasteful, corrupt, and discriminatory political institutions and chronically unrealized regional economic potential. As New Orleanians prolong our "racial" fight over a shrinking pie, diverse urban communities whose leaders and citizens have fashioned a good enough political consensus face the much preferable challenge of negotiating over what to do with a growing pie. As the African-American middle class of New Orleans continues to diminish because of the lack of economic opportunity for well-educated young adults, Atlanta has become what Ambassador Andrew Young calls, only partly in jest, "African-American heaven." The Big Easy, caught in the regressive web of strategic, socioeconomic, structural, intergenerational, ethnocentric, and ideological divisions I have described above, is being left in the dust by that "City Too Busy to Hate"—and many others.

IV. CLASHING IDEOLOGIES, POLITICAL PARALYSIS

Among the six divisions outlined above, the ideological one—our endless, fruitless, divisive debate about race and poverty—is the most intense and polarizing, and also the most potent in feeding the others. Those working in good faith to change our city for the better while disagreeing fundamentally about race and poverty typically end up treating each other as enemies or maneuvering behind each others' backs, instead of seeking common ground from which to oppose those whose agenda is to restore the dysfunctional pre-Katrina balance of political and economic power to serve well-connected insiders, black and white. Because I see repeated polarizations on issues like affordable housing, public schools, and community-police relations stemming directly from unacknowledged differences in perspective on race and poverty, I want to try to shed some light on what is keeping us stuck by identifying six groups with conflicting views on what to do about race and poverty in New Orleans. I regularly see proponents of these views engaging in polarizing confrontations or attempts at mutual avoidance in the city council, city planning, and school board meetings where New Orleans's future is being contested, while those intent on restoring the *status quo ante* operate unopposed against the commonweal. The conflicting groups are:

- White racists, like Louisiana's own David Duke, who hold to the ideology of white superiority.[20]
- Black and other ethnic bigots, like Minister Louis Farrakhan, who

19 Bureau of Economic Analysis, U.S. Department of Commerce, Regional Economic Accounts, bea.gov.

20 David Duke, "Black Population Welfare Bomb Ticks," davidduke.com; Anti-Defamation League, "David Duke Update: Extremism in America," adl.org.

publicly profess hatred for the "white devils."[21]

- Antiracists who are convinced that institutional (or structural) racism—defined as political, economic, and cultural power used to limit the life chances of people based on skin-color prejudice—is *the* underlying social problem. They are certain that any effort at social change that does not take undoing institutional racism as the starting point will make racism and poverty worse, no matter how well intentioned its participants may be.[22]
- Individualists who assume that people need to pick themselves up by their own bootstraps and take advantage of the opportunities already available to them. They believe that the antidiscrimination and voting rights laws passed in the 1960s leveled the playing field so that all who are willing can compete and win. They are convinced that people who insist on bringing up race are looking for advantages, that is, "playing the race card." For them, race-based policies are racism in reverse.[23]
- Black nationalists who conclude that African Americans and other peoples of color must always fend for themselves and are foolish to expect any real help from whites. Their conviction, born of 400 years of experience in America, is that their survival is, and always has been, in their own hands. They have learned that power concedes nothing willingly.[24]
- Pragmatists who believe that the way forward is not talking about race and poverty but rather working together side by side, reaching across ethnic and class lines to heal our destructive history: making the public schools work for all children regardless of race or class; fighting the corrupting effects of government waste, fraud, and abuse; and ensuring that police treat members of all groups with professionalism and respect.[25]

These six groups and their defining positions are generalized categories or "ideal types."[26] Although some people belong almost entirely to just one category, most show characteristics of several, for example, pragmatic individualists or antiracist black nationalists.

The first two positions, white racism and black bigotry, feed cancerous

21 Mattias Gardell, *In the Name of Elijah Muhammad* (Durham, NC: Duke University, 1997), 151–3.

22 Keith Lawrence, et al., *Structural Racism and Community Building* (Washington, D.C.: The Aspen Institute), 8–19.

23 Stephan Thernstrom and Abigail Thernstrom, *America in Black and White* (New York: Simon & Schuster, 1997), 436–40.

24 Frederick Douglass, "The Significance of Emancipation in the West Indies," in *The Frederick Douglass Papers*, ed. John W. Blassingame, vol. 3 (New Haven, CT: Yale University Press, 2004).

25 Edward T. Chambers and Michael A. Cowan, *Roots for Radicals* (New York: Continuum, 2005), 66–8; William Julius Wilson, *The Bridge Over the Racial Divide* (Berkeley, CA: University of California, 1999), 85–93.

26 Max Weber, *The Theory of Social and Economic Organization*, trans. Talcott Parsons (New York: Free Press), 12–14.

divisions in our social body and must be opposed by those who uphold the sacred dignity and inalienable rights of all human beings. The other four views each hold an important grain of truth. The antiracists are correct that the ongoing history of race in America has created systematic and cumulative disadvantages for African Americans and others that to this day cause suffering and limit people's life chances based on the color of their skin.[27] The individualists are correct that people are endowed with certain inalienable rights, are responsible for their actions and have opportunities available to them, which they choose to take or ignore.[28] The black nationalists are correct that African Americans, like members of any cultural group, need to do the "organic work" of building the economic and political institutions that give them the power to decide on and act in their own interests.[29] The pragmatists are correct that at some point those who are serious about addressing racism and poverty have to get busy building diverse coalitions aimed at changing what race and poverty have done, such as fixing district attorney's offices, public schools, and adult literacy programs, and reforming mismanaged and corrupt city government.[30]

In my experience of communicating with people who see the world predominantly through those four filters in New Orleans and elsewhere over the past seventeen years, I have found that each single perspective, although partly true, leaves its proponents with a predictable blind spot that limits their effectiveness as agents of change by leaving them unable to identify potential allies with shared interests. Antiracists can offer no credible strategy for reversing the effects of institutional racism by addressing critical social issues, and they regularly alienate others by insisting that *their* way is the way and that anyone who doesn't see it *that* way is (take your pick) naïve or racist. Individualists do not recognize that there is no such thing as a human being unaffected by society, and, more pointedly, that millions still are born, live, and die burdened with accumulated social and economic disadvantages tied to the color of their skin and other characteristics.[31] Black nationalists fail to identify and recruit nonblack allies who can and would collaborate with them for the well-being of all, based on enlightened group interest. Pragmatists can be so impatient to get things done that they unnecessarily alienate those who have understandable reasons for wanting the historic effects of racism or other prejudices to be acknowledged by prospective partners before they agree to collaborate.

27 Michael Brown, et al., *White-Washing Race* (Berkeley, CA: University of California, 2003), 226–8.

28 David Boaz, *Libertarianism* (New York: The Free Press, 1997), Chapter 3; Bill Cosby and Alvin Poussaint, *Come on People* (Nashville, TN: Thomas Nelson, 2007), Chapter 8.

29 Frank Wright, *Northern Ireland: A Comparative Analysis* (Dublin: Gill and Macmillan, 1987), 2–3.

30 Michael A. Cowan, "Beyond Single Interests: Broad-based Community Organizing as a Vehicle for Promoting Adult Literacy," in *Review of Adult Learning and Literacy*, eds. John Comings, Barbara Garner, and Cristine Smith (Mahwah, NJ: Lawrence Erlbaum Associates), 241–3, 245–50, and 253–9; Jonathan Sacks, *The Home We Build Together* (New York: Continuum, 2007), Chapter 15.

31 Charles Tilly, *Durable Inequality* (Berkeley, CA: University of California, 1998); George Lipsitz, *The Possessive Investment in Whiteness* (Philadelphia: Temple University, 1998), vii–xx.

Leaders and ordinary citizens in post-Katrina New Orleans still see each other through the lenses of these differing ideological perspectives, just as we did before the storm that would upend our lives. Like all human beings, we have come to the present moment with a set of assumptions about what is and should be happening based on our past experience. Those assumptions both make possible and limit how we understand what is occurring right now and what the realistic possibilities of the moment are. That understanding is our interpretation of the situation. It is not simply dictated by what appears outside of us, nor by what is transpiring in our minds, but rather in the meeting between the world and our minds. Our interpretation of the situation enables and limits the action that we can take within it. Apart from dumb luck, no person's action in a situation can be any better than his or her interpretation of it.[32] My point is this: *The* underlying problem blocking recovery, prosperity, and equity in New Orleans is the chronic inability of antiracists, individualists, black nationalists, and pragmatists to reach compromises of ideological integrity that would allow us to act together against white racists, black (and other) bigots, and amoral opportunists of all colors, who have their own plans for the future of our city.

This failure to collaborate serves the interests only of unscrupulous opportunists of all colors. Repetitive, polarizing public fights in city council, planning commission, and school board meetings among those who see the same city through different filters keep New Orleanians from compromising and acting together fairly and wisely to undo gradually the continuing damage done by racism and poverty. Before and after Katrina, New Orleanians have consistently demonstrated veto power, a capacity to polarize and organize *against* anything, typically along racial lines.[33] What is more difficult, and what we have thus far been unable to accomplish (with a few notable exceptions that I will present below) is organizing *for* the changes that will make New Orleans whole for the first time. Six years after surviving as extreme a crisis as any American city has ever faced, when New Orleanians must either make critical decisions or default to state or federal government or the market, we typically polarize, stop local progress, and leave our future in the hands of others because we find it very difficult to agree and act together on basic matters affecting us all—including strengthening the levees between us and the water surrounding us, repairing breaches of trust between citizens and police, providing quality education for all of our children, and creating the conditions that would allow our regional economy to thrive.

32 Michael A. Cowan, "The Heart of the Human Condition," delivered at the Common Good Seminar at Loyola University, and "The Sacred Game of Conversation," *The Furrow* 44.1 (1993), 30–4.

33 George Tsebelis, *Veto Players* (New York: Russell Sage Foundation, 2002), 17–18; See Frank Donze and Bruce Eggler, "Bitter City Council Meeting Ends with Grants Deferred, Nagin Administration Takes Brunt of Blame," *Times-Picayune*, October 17, 2008, A-1; Mark Ballard, "Entergy Sparks Shouting," *Baton Rouge Advocate*, October 16, 2008, D-1; and Charles Lussier, "School Take-over Concerns Aired," *Baton Rouge Advocate*, October 17, 2008, B-1.

V. MOVING BEYOND IDEOLOGICAL DIVISIONS: NEGOTIATION, COMPROMISE, AND MUTUAL ACCOUNTABILITY

So what must we do to escape the inertia of our ideological divisions, to release ourselves from the trap of crippling social mistrust? We can start with the recognition that diverging views need not be conflicting ones. Practical compromises on specific matters negotiated with integrity by those who differ yield plans with strengths that advocates of any single view could not produce alone, as well as buy-in from the differing groups that forge them. A divided "we" becomes a diverse united constituency capable of genuine interpersonal and intergroup doing: not by having "stakeholder" planning sessions led by people with no real relationship to the city, or by creating artificial "vision statements," or by dwelling too much on the past, or by avoiding different "others," but rather by engaging in collective actions with a common purpose based on overlapping group interests. Our challenge, then, is to convene and sustain conversations leading to compromises on specific plans for seeking the well-being of the whole city, across the lines of race, class, and religion, on concrete matters like public safety, health, and education. Such compromises can only be fashioned by those who understand that their group's basic interests—safety, health, equity, prosperity and peace—cannot be achieved unilaterally but only by taking account of the basic interests of others. Whatever the particular issue at hand, our challenge is to replace our paralyzing ideological standoffs with pragmatic agreements on matters of common interest. We will only achieve successes on this road when proponents of the four approaches stop dismissing and demonizing those who hold other views. Progressive members of all four groups do indeed have enemies—racists, bigots and opportunists—but they are not the enemies of one another. Rather, they—we—are potential allies with unique assets to bring to the process of change who have not yet been able to make common cause by focusing on shared interests.

We will pick up the pace and extend the scope of the recovery of New Orleans, and do some bridging of ethnic and class divisions in the process, when proponents of all four valid but limited positions on race and poverty work at the discipline of listening to, learning from, and compromising with people of good faith who hold other views, as they all work together on issues of concern to all. In addition to broadening and deepening the base of organized citizens available to push together for change, such an approach has the uncomfortable but liberating effect of making all of us more aware of the limitations of our own views. There is plenty of potential common ground in post-Katrina New Orleans, but we will not find our way to it unless we are willing to stop fueling unproductive, disrespectful controversies and start identifying and building on mutual, or at least compatible, perspectives and interests. When a city is caught in a social trap, shared vision will not be present and cannot be dialogued into existence at the beginning of a process of social change. Like social trust, a shared vision can only emerge as a byproduct of concerted deliberation and action on matters of shared concern.

A very important benefit we as a body politic will gain by breaking through the impasse of chronically clashing perspectives on race and poverty is that in order to do so we must first grow out of our biracial ethnocentrism, our narrow obsession with black/white conflict, which is what most people in New Orleans are thinking about when the subjects of race and poverty are raised. Members of the other cultural groups making up our city don't appreciate being treated like a distraction from someone else's fight, and rightly so.[34] As in ancient biblical communities in crisis, the livability of the whole city depends upon the recognition of all of its groups and the opportunity for all of them to fully participate.

So what strategic courses of action are available to elected, business, and civic leaders and their followers who intend to act together, bridging ethnic, religious, and class divisions, to set their divided and devastated city on the path to a decent life for all?

VI. PUBLIC INTEGRITY, ECONOMIC OPPORTUNITY, AND SOCIAL TRUST

Comparative research on societies around the world demonstrates that when most citizens believe that public officials do their jobs fairly and efficiently and that economic opportunity is available to all who are willing to learn and work, they are also more likely to trust fellow citizens and cooperate for the common good.[35] Conversely, when most citizens believe that public officials routinely engage in or condone waste, fraud, and abuse, or that economic opportunity depends on insider connections, they will mistrust each other and refuse to cooperate even when doing so would benefit all. Social trust, economic inclusion, and good government are circularly related. When the circle moves negatively, public institutional integrity, economic opportunity, and social trust spiral downward together; when it moves positively, the three elements strengthen each other. Social scientists have made a compelling case that economic opportunity, honest and efficient public institutions, and social trust go together for better and for worse; however, they offer three contending recommendations about where to start if we intend to move the circular relationship among the three factors in a positive direction.

34 Human Relations Commission, City of New Orleans, "We Believe in One New Orleans Listening Session #3," transcript from March 27, 2008, 50–1. On file with author; available at cityofno.com. The Human Relations Commission held various listening sessions, convened expressly to hear from different communities and ethnic groups and to "come together and thoughtfully look at those themes and make recommendations perhaps for policy, perhaps for certain problematic issues to promote more inclusion in the life of New Orleans" (5–6).

35 Rothstein, *Social Traps*, 106–17.

STARTING WITH TRUST

Those who start with social trust believe that if you want to build the public institutions necessary to support the creation of economic opportunity, you should unite people who have been politically, economically, or racially divided by encouraging them to form groups together based on shared interests, geographic proximity, social concerns, hobbies, etc. A civil society rich in "voluntary associations" provides the social glue that makes it possible for governmental and business institutions to function properly.[36] This approach to building social trust is direct: Members of historically alienated groups must meet face-to-face in voluntary associations in order to create the social trust required for good government and economic growth.

STARTING WITH ECONOMIC OPPORTUNITY

Those emphasizing economic opportunity believe that markets left free to function will reward competence, create a growing pool of economic opportunities, and generate a stronger tax base to support necessary government services.[37] They are convinced that government attempts to create economic equality by forced redistribution schemes involving taxation of businesses and individuals, or social policies like affirmative action that give advantages to some people based on ethnicity or gender to make up for past discrimination, interfere with and can destroy the market's job-creating power by distorting the dynamics of economic competition and chasing businesses into jurisdictions with transparent, consistent ground rules applied evenhandedly to all.[38] When local economies flourish, more households build assets, local governments have the resources to address public concerns, and social trust rises. But when business owners must "pay to play," that is, bribe local officials directly with cash in envelopes or indirectly with campaign contributions in order to get contracts or permits, or when public decisions are "steered" based on nepotism, ethnicity, or political affiliation, the economic base and the employment opportunities only it can generate, the tax revenues it produces, and social trust all spiral downward together.[39] From this perspective, public institutions play a limited but crucial role in economic development; they establish and enforce transparent rules and norms for all, starting with property rights and equal treatment under the law, without which businesses and individuals will not invest in local communities and underlying inequalities cannot be addressed.

36 Robert D. Putnam, Robert Leonardi, and Raffaella Y. Nanetti, *Making Democracy Work: Civic Traditions in Modern Italy* (Princeton, NJ: Princeton University, 1993), 181–5, and Robert D. Putnam, *Bowling Alone* (New York: Simon & Schuster, 2000), 134–7.

37 Boaz, Chapter 8.

38 Ibid., 228–42.

39 Eric Uslaner, "The Bulging Pocket and the Rule of Law," paper presented at the "Quality of Government" conference, November 17–19, 2005, Quality of Government Institute, Gothenburg University, Sweden, 15–16; Bo Rothstein and Eric Uslaner, "All for All: Equality, Corruption, and Social Trust," *World Politics* 58 (October 2005), 47–8.

STARTING WITH THE INTEGRITY OF PUBLIC INSTITUTIONS

Those whose starting point is the integrity of public institutions believe that assuring that those institutions are truly universal, that is, that they serve all citizens efficiently (not wastefully), honestly (limiting corruption and cronyism), and fairly (without regard for ethnicity, wealth or connections) is the single most powerful way to create social trust in a community.[40] First, a definition: "Institutions [create] the rules of the game in a society or, more formally, [embody] the humanly devised constraints that shape human interaction."[41] That is, society is the game, its institutions provide the formal and informal rules of play and the mechanisms to enforce them, and individuals and organizations are the players.

When public entities play by the rules of efficiency by not wasting public resources, of honesty by eliminating corruption, and of fairness by treating all as equally entitled to their services, they increase social trust indirectly, by creating the ground rules necessary to give all their citizens good value for their tax dollars and generate economic opportunity for more people.[42] Especially in circumstances where there have been significant ethnic, religious, or class conflicts and divisions, the likelihood that people in general will trust each other goes up when members of all groups experience the elimination of waste, corruption, and discrimination from public institutions like planning commissions, school boards, and city halls. When those institutions function universally, that is, efficiently, honestly, and fairly for all, belief in "the system" fuels economic opportunity for all and breeds trust in other people in the community. When and insofar as public institutions fail to meet the standards of universality, legitimate government services and benefits are denied to taxpayers, economic opportunity is limited, and mistrust blocks and fractures relationships among people, reinforcing histories of division. A community's public institutions both make possible and limit its economic vitality and opportunity, which in turn affects levels of trust among its various groups.

VII. BUILDING SOCIAL TRUST FROM ABOVE IN POST-KATRINA NEW ORLEANS

As an active citizen leader in New Orleans since 1991, and as one fully engaged in the effort to rebuild since Katrina, I am convinced that the future of our city hinges on whether or not our diverse leaders and citizenry will continue coming together to make public institutions—including but not limited to city government and the local criminal justice system—accountable for efficiency, ethics, and fairness, because without a framework of trustworthy public institutions, economic opportunity for all businesses and citizens will be severely limited, and without eco-

40 Bo Rothstein, *Just Institutions Matter* (New York: Cambridge University Press, 1998), 106–17.

41 Douglass C. North, *Institutions, Institutional Change, and Economic Performance,* (Cambridge: Cambridge University Press, 1990), 3.

42 Ibid., 27–35; Rothstein, *Social Traps*, 108–9.

nomic opportunity for all, we will never transcend our race and class divisions. The road to enhanced social trust is indirect. It runs through reforms of our public institutions that are necessary in order to create equity of economic opportunity for all.

In the words of political scientist Bo Rothstein, "Social trust comes from above and is destroyed from above."[43] Rothstein adds:

> If it proves that I cannot trust the local police, judges, teachers, and doctors, then whom in society can I trust? The ethics of public officials become central here, not only with respect to how they do their jobs, but also to the signals they send to citizens about what kind of "game" is being played in the society.[44]

The actions of mayors, city council members, district attorneys, police chiefs, judges, criminal sheriffs, sewer and water board members, and inspectors general send the most powerful signals that businesses and individuals receive about the rules of the game in a community. The behavior of these public leaders determines whether people feel that they can trust their government, members of other groups as well as of their own, and even themselves.[45] Progress on economic inclusion and racial reconciliation can be realized most powerfully and quickly in New Orleans and elsewhere when leaders and members of different groups take the indirect route of reforming public institutions and then holding them accountable.

When public officials waste or steal taxpayers' money or favor particular individuals or groups with insider deals at the expense of others, that activates the vicious spiral of bad government, inequality of economic opportunity, and diminished social trust. As I noted above, New Orleans has been caught in that downward spiral for half a century. In the previous section, I argued that if we want to see greater economic opportunity for all businesses and citizens and build social trust among groups that have been divided, our most promising strategy for change is diverse citizen partnerships working to make public institutions operate efficiently, ethically and fairly. Now I'd like to describe the well-advanced efforts by such networks of citizen leaders to do just that by initiating the reform of two critical public institutions in post-Katrina New Orleans: city government and the police department.

Waste, corruption, and discrimination in local and state government have been millstones around the neck of New Orleans. In January 2006, the Government Efficiency and Effectiveness Committee of the Bring New Orleans Back Commission (BNOB) recommended the establishment

43 Rothstein, *Social Traps*, 199ff.

44 Ibid., 122.

45 Ibid., 121–2; Wilson, *The Bridge Over the Racial Divide*, 82–3.

of an inspector general's office to detect and prevent waste, fraud, and abuse in the expenditure of public funds.[46] New Orleans needs such an office: most local citizens and business owners, as well as many state and national elected officials and private investors, rightly perceive our city government as poorly managed, including financially, and contaminated by patronage, corruption, and discrimination. Unless this perception is changed, local and national investors, private and public, will continue to be reluctant to place their bets on the future of New Orleans. During the post-Katrina work of BNOB, former Mayor Stephen Goldsmith of Indianapolis warned members of the government reform committee that city government's basic role is to make businesses and individuals believe that it is in their interest to invest in the city's future.[47] The future of the city hinges on those investments. A powerful, effective inspector general's office offers New Orleans the best opportunity the city has ever had to interrupt the waste, corruption, and discrimination that have always diminished economic and political opportunity for all but insiders while reinforcing mistrust among outsider groups.

New Orleans faces a second complex challenge, that of creating a just and efficient criminal justice system. National experts who conducted a recent intensive study of the New Orleans police department recommended strongly that the city recommit itself to a community policing approach.[48] By "community policing" they meant not simply an alternative patrolling technique to be applied unilaterally to neighborhoods by police officers, but a change in the culture of policing and being policed, a culture that requires and creates a relationship of trust between citizens and police officers that allows them to solve problems together. In neighborhoods throughout New Orleans, police officers and community leaders would begin to build the working relationship they need to cooperate actively in apprehending and indicting criminals and in preventing crime. At present, levels of trust between the police department and residents and leaders of some of the city's neighborhoods are extremely low. Many residents are unwilling to report criminal acts or testify against indicted parties in court because they feel that the police have treated them disrespectfully or because they fear that the police will not protect them from the thugs who threaten to harm them if they cooperate. In such a climate of pervasive distrust and fear, community policing has no chance of sustainable success. Around the nation, the most successful approach to the problem of antagonism and mistrust between citizens and police is an independent police monitor to investigate, report, and

46 Committee on Government Efficiency and Effectiveness, "20 Steps in the Right Direction," Bring New Orleans Back Commission, cityofno.com; Association of Inspectors General, *Principles and Standards for Offices of Inspector General* (Philadelphia, 2001), inspectorsgeneral.org.

47 Commitee on Government Efficiency and Effectiveness, "20 Steps," 2.

48 Brown Group International, *A Strategic Plan of Action for the New Orleans Police Department* (New Orleans: New Orleans Police and Justice Foundation, 2007), 28–43.

make specific recommendations for improving the way the police force treats citizens and visitors.[49] Mistrust between the neighborhoods and their law officers is among the most significant challenges New Orleans faces in effectively addressing crime. An independent monitor could play a major role in building the bridges of trust and cooperation that would make strong community policing possible and our streets safer for all.

Challenged by BNOB's January 2006 recommendations on city government reform, city council members and the most broadly representative network of civic and business leaders that New Orleans has ever seen have aligned interests and worked together steadily for six years to authorize, fund, and implement the offices of inspector general and police monitor.[50] That work involved creating a diverse and informed constituency for both offices; actively supporting the city council members who introduced the necessary ordinances and budget proposals for both; encouraging the appointment of independent members of the ethics board, charged with hiring the city's first inspector general; lobbying the state legislature for a law strengthening the inspector general's powers; introducing the founding inspector general to the city in an ongoing series of public meetings; and changing the city charter to protect the inspector general and independent police monitor from political interference by future mayors or city councils. *Who* did the sustained work to establish these two critical institutional reforms is as important as *what* was done. Without elected leaders, these reforms would not have happened. Without business leaders, they would not have happened. Without civic leaders, they would not have happened. Without elected, business, and civic leaders representing the ethnic, religious, and economic diversity of New Orleans working together, these pivotal reforms would not have happened. And without our ongoing cooperative vigilance, they will not be sustained.

The most promising change in the social fabric of New Orleans resulting from the devastation of Hurricane Katrina is the emergence of expanding and deepening networks of diverse business and civic leaders working in active partnership with government officials to change specific things, such as the establishment of the inspector general and independent police monitor. Those two accomplishments are not our only success stories. Similar efforts by other action networks have also led to reforms in regional levee boards, property-tax assessment, the district attorney's office, the courts, and the public defender's office. These partially overlapping networks are not operating from a master plan or guided by one group

49 For an overview of a model police auditor system, see Samuel Walker, *The New World of Police Accountability* (Thousand Oaks, CA: Sage, 2005), 135–170.

50 Gary Solomon chaired the Committee on Government Efficiency and Effectiveness of the Bring New Orleans Back Commission; Kevin Wildes, S.J.; Janet Howard, and Una Anderson chaired subcommittees on ethics, taxing, and restructuring respectively; C. Daniel Karnes was legal counsel and researcher; the author served as chief of staff and principal author of the committee's report. Stephen Goldsmith of the Kennedy School of Government gave technical assistance. Kenneth Ferdinand, Robert Montjoy, Bob Brown, Mark Drennan, Jackie Clarkson, Yvonne Mitchell-Grubb, and Jim Brandt were committee members.

of government, business, or civic leaders. Instead, they focus on their respective interests but share a strategic and pragmatic commitment to getting important things done by seeking allies, including those with different perspectives and interests; compromising without loss of integrity; implementing the best practices from around the country and the world; and exercising the public discipline of holding each other as well as public officials accountable for keeping the promises made to one another.

Since its founding in 2007, the Office of Inspector General of the City of New Orleans has issued numerous audits, reviews, inspections, and evaluations of the finances and performance of city government, covering city vehicles, city purchasing, accounts payable and fixed asset control, city collection of hotel and motel taxes, sanitation contracts, and private management of major post-Katrina infrastructure rebuilding projects. It has also produced thirteen public letters calling the attention of the mayor, city council, chief administrative officer, and police superintendent to administrative practices that leave the city vulnerable to waste and corruption in areas that include the awarding of city contracts, procurement of goods and services, expense reimbursement, electronic monitoring of parolees, disadvantaged business enterprises, and contract proposals for remodeling the municipal auditorium. The office's investigations of the New Orleans Public Belt Railroad, the French Market Corporation, and the city's crime surveillance cameras led to criminal indictments, resignations, and cessation or major modification of these programs' operations. And although some still attempt to delegitimize the office by portraying it as an effort by whites to curb black politicians, the broad gist of public opinion, across lines of race, class, and geography, is that the office of inspector general has become an effective catalyst in the movement to end the waste, fraud, and abuse in New Orleans's city government. It has done this by creating the transparency that allows city administrators, legal authorities, and citizens, for the first time in the city's history, to hold elected and appointed officials accountable for their stewardship of public resources. The inspector general's office has introduced something new to the political culture of New Orleans, namely, a growing public expectation that waste, fraud, and abuse by elected or appointed officials is likely to be exposed, with timely and serious consequences for those who misuse the public trust for personal gain.

The effort to reform our local criminal justice system has also continued and strengthened. Strong public support from the networks of engaged citizens described above has led to the New Orleans Police Department's initiation of community policing, along with several other major reforms. The Office of Independent Police Monitor is now fully established and functional. It has executed a joint agreement with the newly restructured Public Integrity Bureau of the police department that allows the monitor timely access to information on incidents involving use of force by police officers. These reform efforts have helped reduce the Orleans Parish

Prison population from a former high of 7,500 inmates, a total that made it the eighth-largest prison in the United States, to a number much closer to national standards for a city jail. Citizen advocacy has also led to significant city funding for indigent defense and, for the first time, for citizen monitoring and reporting on criminal courts. The post-Katrina criminal justice action partnerships have developed a working knowledge of the local criminal justice system as a system, including all of its component agencies and their interrelationships. That shared knowledge allows them to choose leverage points wisely. Significant movement toward reform is now observable in all elements of the local criminal justice system and also in their integration. The level of change under way in this system, like the change in city hall catalyzed by the Office of Inspector General, would have been unimaginable (and, therefore, impossible) prior to the hurricane, which undid business as usual in New Orleans.

Diverse networks of civic collaboration leading significant, sustainable institutional changes on this scale are new to the historically divided city of New Orleans, and in truth, they are unusual anywhere.[51] The underlying commitment that animates and orients the work of our reform networks is to work together to build a city where public institutions do the business of all the people efficiently, ethically, and fairly; where economic opportunity grows for all who are willing to work and learn; and where social trust replaces division, in a positive spiral benefiting all. Building that city together will be a struggle for years to come, but the effort is seriously under way, thanks in part to the radical disorganization and deep suffering wrought by Katrina. Building on these promising beginnings will require that we sustain and strengthen the kind of genuine interpersonal and intergroup doing by elected, business, and civic leaders that has given New Orleans an independent inspector general and a police monitor. Lying immediately ahead of these new and vulnerable social action networks is a minefield of potentially polarizing conflicts, as the groups attempt to support the deep transformations of our public schools now ongoing and to open the governance of the sewerage and water board and airport authority to public scrutiny, assure the provision of affordable healthcare and housing, and promote agreement on a legally binding master plan to govern future development in the city.

VIII. POSTSCRIPT— GENUINE INTERPERSONAL AND INTERGROUP ACTION: THE ROUTE TO ONE NEW ORLEANS

In the six years since Katrina struck, those who live and work here have continually had to field one question from those who do not: How

51 John Alderdice and Michael A. Cowan, "Metaphors for One Another: Racism in the United States and Sectarianism in Northern Ireland," *Peace and Conflict Studies* 11.1 (2004), 31–6; also available at shss.nova.edu. This article draws a parallel between racism in the United States and sectarianism in Northern Ireland and argues for broad-based cross-community organizing focused on matters of common concern as the preferred approach to dealing with both.

is your recovery going? My short answer is: The leaders and citizens of the city of New Orleans have been unable so far to achieve a working consensus about how to prioritize the rebuilding of our city; that failure has delayed and limited our recovery and added immeasurably to the disruption and suffering that all have endured, albeit not equally. With billions of dollars in public and private investment in the pipeline, we will eventually rebuild our physical structures and systems. New flood protection, schools, police and fire stations, hospitals and community healthcare clinics, shops and stores will be forthcoming. As our "recovery" inches forward, vulnerable annually to another disastrous storm until Category 5 hurricane protection is in place (which itself depends on bridging our divisions), a key question remains for our government, business, and civic leaders and our citizenry to answer: Will the differing groups that make up the body politic of New Orleans act together so that our political and economic institutions are governed by rules of efficiency, integrity, and fairness, or will we allow these bodies to continue to be riddled with waste, corruption, and discrimination? As challenging as the massive physical reconstruction we face is, the far more difficult rebuilding that confronts New Orleans is the same one that badly strained the social fabric of our city before the storm. In sustained acts of genuine interpersonal, intergroup action, we must make our public institutions serve members of all groups efficiently, ethically, and fairly, because that is the route to economic opportunity and social trust.

Like all Americans, the citizens of post-Katrina New Orleans must choose between remaining in physical proximity without spiritual affinity —elbows together and hearts apart—and coming together in a "mighty stream" of genuine interpersonal and intergroup action for the common good. Just as all mighty streams have their source, so will the healing of New Orleans: in public institutions that are efficient, ethical, and fair. The diverse action partnerships of elected, business, and civic leaders, through sustained, collective acts, have given New Orleans an independent inspector general, a police monitor, and other critical institutional reforms. In doing so they have initiated what I believe history will one day judge to be the most important contributions ever made to our historic city, allowing it to become a place of equal treatment and opportunity for all, a place where social trust bridges race, class, and religious divisions. That new New Orleans will be a more wonderful place to visit, and a magnificent place to live. Where there is no shared vision, the people perish, but with elbows and hearts together in the service of the common good, they flourish.

ACKNOWLEDGMENTS

I want to thank Edward Chambers of the Industrial Areas Foundation for mentoring me in public life and leadership and expanding my social imagination; Kevin Wildes, S.J., of Loyola University; Ben Johnson, Professor Ludovico Feoli, and Richard Freeman of the Greater New Orleans Foundation; Byron Harrell, of Baptist Community Ministries Foundation; and Gary Solomon, of the New Orleans Business Council, for their constant financial and personal support of the post-Katrina experiment in social change called Common Good; Dr. John Lord Alderdice of Belfast for twenty-five years of transatlantic conversation and inspiration on the holy subject of peacemaking; Professor Clarence Stone of the University of Maryland, for educating New Orleans leaders on the strengths and limitations of Atlanta's biracial governing regime; Professors Ludovico Feoli of Tulane University and Bo Rothstein of Gothenburg University, Sweden, for calling my attention to the relevance of the "new institutionalism" in political science to the rebuilding of New Orleans; Professor William Julius Wilson of the Kennedy School of Government, for pioneering analysis and personal encouragement on bridging the racial divide, and Professor Stephen Goldsmith, director of the Innovations in American Government program, and Maureen Griffin, also of the Kennedy School, for three years of prompt responses to my requests for information on national best practices in government reform; New Orleans city council members Shelley Midura and James Carter and inspector general Christopher Mazzella, of Miami/Dade County, and inspector general Robert Cerasoli of New Orleans, for pioneering work in the establishment of the first offices of inspector general and independent police monitor in New Orleans; Rick Heydinger, Beverly Stein, Jim Chrisinger, and Babak Armajani of the Public Strategies Group, for wise counsel on reforming public institutions; and Kathleen Hurstell Riedlinger, John Comings, Jay Lapeyre, Dan Karnes, Richard Albares, Fred Aigner, Michael Sartisky, Ben Johnson, Tom Fiutak, and Mike Gecan, for critical readings of previous versions of this essay.

HURRICANES, CIVIL UNREST, AND THE RESTORATION OF THE AMERICAN CITY: LESSONS FROM NEWARK FOR A NEW PLANNING RESPONSE

TONI L. GRIFFIN

In the summer of 2007, Newark, New Jersey was preparing for the fortieth-anniversary commemoration of the 1967 riots, or "civil unrest," as most local cultural historians are quick to reframe it. Why would a city commemorate a riot, an event that eradicated pride of place and community within a matter of days? Perhaps it was because, even today, parts of this community's landscape remain scarred and contested, the memories of injustice there are fresh, and the lack of progress is apparent.

The level of public commemoration seen in Newark that summer of 2007 was reminiscent of what we now watch annually on television around August 29, when we are reminded of the devastation of Hurricane Katrina. Of course, Newark's disasters came not at the hands of Mother Nature but at the hands of Americans increasingly frustrated by national and federal policies that seemed to belie our nation's sense of humanity, equity, and justice. Enraged citizens waged a ground war with police in neighborhoods where people felt persistently disadvantaged and deliberately isolated from economic prosperity.

Both the Newark civil disaster of 1967 and the New Orleans ecological disaster of 2005 received nationwide media attention and forced Americans for a brief moment to sit and uncomfortably confront some of our country's most challenging urban problems. In 1967, we watched the gush of fire hoses pushing men and women down to their knees; in 2005, we watched walls of water fill spaces where block parties and backyard barbecues were once held. In Newark, rioters were packed into police wagons; in New Orleans, disoriented poor and elderly citizens were packed into a sports arena. The causes of these events may differ, but the planning responses to their aftermaths are similar. In both Newark and New Orleans, the federal government mobilized to take action at the local level. Post-riot Newark saw various iterations of urban renewal initiatives that brought unprecedented resources to the inner city with a specific mandate to assemble, clear, and rebuild—and perhaps even make amends for the negative impact of previous federal programs that had failed to serve the inner city and our most vulnerable populations.

In post-Katrina New Orleans, planners and policy makers quickly created federal triage and infrastructure rebuilding programs alongside city- and neighborhood-scale plans in an effort to recover both real estate and population. But the infamous mapping exercises that proposed "build" and "no-build" areas of the city, though they may have been an appropriate response to the city's natural ecology, were not a sensitive one to the needs of preexisting human systems of community and mobility.

Whether devastation is caused by a natural storm or a burst of civil fury, the planning response aimed at healing the urban landscape seldom addresses the economic, social, and civic ills that were already deeply embedded there. We often do not acknowledge in our city recovery efforts that most of the destroyed neighborhoods were already contested spaces, in part because they were without a civic culture informed by comprehensive or inclusive planning. Public officials, developers, planners, and designers have been quick to remedy the physical landscape with grand plans for rebuilding, including projects designed to secure greater economic returns. Yet rarely in practice have we integrated a candid public policy discourse about whom the recovered city will be for or how the rebuilding process might address the city's most long-standing as well as its urgent challenges in a more culturally and economically sustainable manner.

It is important to remember that in 1967 Newark was already shrinking, losing population to the surrounding suburbs and rapidly becoming another "chocolate city," where poverty, unemployment, and newly elected black leadership were all on the rise. Over the past thirty-seven years, Newark has lost nearly 38 percent of its population and the population of New Orleans has declined by 33 percent. The destruction of Hurricane Katrina only exacerbated the chronic problems that many of the city's hardest-hit neighborhoods were already experiencing because of stagnant or deteriorating social and economic conditions.

This is not to suggest that no progress has been made in these cities since their respective disasters hit. Within the last half-century, we can point to urban revitalization models that have repositioned downtowns and redesigned the footprint of public housing. In Newark between 1980 and 1990, projects such as the Gateway Center office complex and the New Jersey Performing Arts Center were developed and now stand in the downtown as symbols of urban renaissance, but they have little economic or physical connection to the communities most devastated by the summer of 1967. More recently in New Orleans, development in the French Quarter and parts of the downtown has reignited the local economy, but tough environmental, ecological, social, and economic challenges still remain. All of these efforts were essential to bolstering the mainstream economies of their cities; however, we still lack strategies for moving our most vulnerable populations and their communities to the next level of economic stability. As public officials, planners, and designers, we must admit that we have not always learned from the hard consequences of public policy systems that promote institutional racism and reflect indifference to the needs of those on the margins of our community. We would be smart to be more self-critical and seriously review past practices, when we have intentionally shut out diverse voices, enacted public policy without balanced social objectives, ignored the growth and influence of black and Hispanic populations, and placed private interests above equitable public benefits.

The election of the nation's first African-American president suggests that the time has come to stop talking in muted tones about race, class, and urban redevelopment. In *More than Just Race: Being Black and Poor in the Inner City* (2009), noted Harvard University sociologist William Julius Wilson suggests that poverty is not longer framed as a condition of economic downturn but as a condition of personal responsibility—and our cognitive memory has now recorded the face of poverty as a black or brown one. During this paradigm shift, we have allowed generations of American families in many of our country's greatest cities to live in the same concentrated and contested spaces of social and economic isolation. Similarly, we have continued to create physical remedies to address inner-city decline separately from meaningful strategies addressing the social and cultural breakdowns that are now so finely intertwined with space and place.

Perhaps we should stop trying to "rebuild" and "reconstruct" our cities and neighborhoods, terms that so vividly imply that "redevelopment" applies only to the built environment. Instead, we should be seeking to "restore" our cities in ways that include mending our civic culture; restoring the resiliency of our built, natural, and social systems; and committing to provide sustainable and equitable access to opportunity. We must be deliberately and consciously concerned with what our planning policies will leave for the next generation—we must imagine how urban life will be for the ten-year-old in 2011 who will be thirty in 2031. If we do not keep this image at the forefront of our thinking, television programs such as HBO's critically acclaimed *The Wire* will continue to be the only media that illuminate the complex ways structural inequalities and cultural isolation play themselves out in a persistent cycle of social and spatial decline.

So many of our urban communities have continued to struggle in a post-disaster context. To move our cities and our practice forward, we must embrace a transracial, transpolitical, and transdisciplinary approach to planning that is values-based, placing resident advancement, rather than physical intervention, at the core of land-use policy. Over the past four years, Newark has been tackling these issues head-on. In 2006, newly elected Mayor Cory A. Booker set as his mandate making Newark "the national model of urban transformation." An ambitious and seemingly untimely task, but the mayor took on his own call to action as a challenge: Reframe the question of urban revitalization and transform the cycle of decline into a cycle of sustainable urban restoration. And though he knew that issues of crime and education would need to be a top priority of his inaugural term, he also committed to restoring the function of professional planning within city hall and updating the city's master plan, a task that had not been undertaken in two decades.

A brief snapshot of Newark at the end of the last decade shows a city of 281,000 people, 25 percent of them foreign-born and 25 percent children under eighteen, where households headed by single women with children represent almost 50 percent of families, 31 percent of children live in extreme poverty, and only 35 percent of residents have a high school diploma. Newark's employment crisis serves as a major barrier to resident prosperity: the unemployment rate was 12 percent at the last census, and 40 percent of the city's eligible adults, among whom are 1,900 parolees who return each year, are not participating in its labor force. Seventy-five percent of the workforce commutes outside the city for work and 40 percent of residents do not own a car. Seventy percent of Newark has a tree canopy of less than five percent. Obesity is reported in 34 percent of Newark residents. Newark loses more than $600 million in retail spending to surrounding cities because it lacks quality shopping options, and over 30 percent of households spend nearly 50 percent of their family income on housing. The city has placed these prevalent inner-city indicators at the center of its master-planning process to remind us that we must restore the *people* of Newark in order to fully restore the city.

Shifting Forward 2025, Newark, NJ, the reexamined and re-envisioned master plan adopted in 2009, proposes a sustainable urban restoration model, through which at the scale of the neighborhood a closed-loop system of interrelated social, economic, environmental, and spatial targets and measures can be established. The plan positions Newark to move beyond the "cycle of disinvestment" that has plagued the city for much of the past fifty years to achieve a "cycle of success." With vision and strategic planning, Newark will *shift forward* to create a clear model for growth, a culture of civic engagement, and an environment of strong leadership and accountability. The plan prioritizes three themes and related goals for success.

By 2025, increase family wealth and cut Newark's unemployment rate in half by creating access to up to 25,000 jobs. The strategies recommended below best align the skills of Newark's current workforce and projections for growth:

- Maximize growth at air and seaports, with an increase from 22 to 33 percent in the proportion of port and port-related jobs going to Newark residents.
- Recapture Newark's share of regional retail and retail spending, putting it on par with top retailing cities in the region, through an increase in the number of residents in the retail sector with access to up to 4,000 jobs.
- Retain land for job-creating enterprises and creating opportunities for up to 4,000 jobs through the expansion and incubation of businesses

in light-industrial and commercial zones within the city and region.

- Improve resident mobility to jobs with support for long-range transit projects and policies that improve resident access to employment opportunities and stimulate community and business development.
- Increase freight mobility with improvements in regional waterborne and rail freight infrastructure to promote more job-intensive uses and employment opportunities for Newark residents.

By 2025, increase family health, leveraging regional growth to create visible and self-sustaining environmental improvements in Newark's neighborhoods. During past planning efforts and in public conversations, residents have often cited the need to concentrate on four essential ingredients for safe and healthy neighborhoods:

- Safe, active, and connected places, created by prioritizing public investments throughout our neighborhoods that help prevent crime and improve pedestrian safety.
- Access to quality housing choices, promoted by creating approximately 20,000 new housing units.
- An adequate and accessible system of parks and recreation that ensures that all Newark residents live within a 10-minute walking radius of safe and attractive green space and recreation facilities.
- Quality public facilities and services provided by identifying opportunities to upgrade, co-locate, and/or transform the city's community facilities from places of service delivery to true neighborhood centers.

By 2025, increase family choice, building a city where a diverse range of people will want to live, raise their families, visit, and run businesses. This means promoting Newark as a sustainable city that offers a broad range of commercial, educational, cultural, and social choices for all residents, regardless of their race, income, or age:

- Facilitate a "living downtown" by making that area more attractive to people who are interested in living and working in walkable, vibrant places and to businesses seeking a competitive location.
- Promote a "city of learning": make Newark more innovative, creative, desirable, and prosperous, especially by expanding the reach and role of learning institutions, students, graduates, and faculty in the city.
- Make the Passaic River a regional asset by building a continuous, redeveloped Passaic Riverfront for the benefit of all residents and the region.
- Promote historic and cultural assets by doubling the number of arts, cultural, and entertainment visitors to the city and doubling their spending in the city to increase revenue and vibrancy.
- Create and sustain a greener and healthier urban environment for

all Newarkers—high- or low-income, current or future—that will be an essential factor in creating and maintaining Newark as a city of choice, where residents and businesses decide to invest and grow.

In past years, for reasons of expediency, both political and economic, Newark, like many cities, reduced its funding and staffing capacity and therefore strayed from practicing planning in a comprehensive manner through a regulatory review body. Development decisions were too often made on an individual, ad hoc basis without proper consideration of how projects would affect the city as a whole. And more often than not, planning, when it was undertaken, was a government-directed, top-down process, resulting in a lack of continuity between day-to-day planning decisions, adversely affecting the city's growth and its community-driven goals.

Unanimously approved for adoption in 2009, Newark's reexamined and revised master plan provided an opportunity to advance a new framework in which planning could inform and coordinate government activity and through which government, residents, and other stakeholders could work together. Newark's leadership considered good planning essential to providing not only a holistic approach to decisions about the city's future but also to placing immediate concerns in the context of broader opportunities. They believed that building a consensus vision for the city through a transparent and inclusionary process would encourage a sense of shared responsibility, seating the community at the table with city government officials and developers in a partnership for progress.

Advancing a more interdisciplinary approach to planning practice and institutionalizing a more inclusive and participatory civic engagement culture are imperatives for repositioning urban communities. However, it is essential to note that the effectiveness of any planning process and resulting plan requires identifying and cultivating enlightened, proactive, and forward-thinking urban leadership. Changing how we plan and restore our cities requires us to strengthen our collective voices and diversify the positions from which we as professional planners and designers practice. Designers and planners must collaborate with social scientists, economists, environmentalists, and educators, and perhaps even seek leadership positions in the public policy–making arena.

However, planning and design professionals cannot lead this charge alone. Our political and civic leaders must provide a strong voice for planning reform. These leaders—elected, grassroots, and corporate—must be bolder and braver in their rhetoric and actions in order to ensure real and measurable progress in urban transformation. In our era of great innovation and expansion, we have viewed our land and financial resources as abundant, and therefore we have often discarded our urban communities as dross-scapes. We must view this new century of planning as an opportunity for reclaiming, recapturing, and restoring that which has made American cities great.

PART III
RECONSTRUCTING DOMICILE, HOUSING (SINGLY CONSIDERED)

RESTORING THE REAL NEW ORLEANS, RETAINING THE CULTURE

ANDRÉS DUANY

FRAMEWORKS OF HOPE: EARLY THOUGHTS, NOVEMBER 2006

More than a year into the supposed recovery of New Orleans, it is clear that very little has been built. The only thing that may have been achieved is a distillation of hope—by this, I mean the mental frameworks by which individuals, organizations, and their leaders hope to effect the recovery of the city. By what means do people think the city will be brought to life? There are three frameworks of hope. The first may be called foreign aid; the second, the magic bullet; and the third, the long road.

Most faith is put into foreign aid: federal programs that send down the money. Billions have been allocated, principally through the Road Home program, which promises distribution of some $4 billion to be used for rebuilding by households. This is tangible help, but it can also be argued that the federal government has, in fact, been the great hindrance to recovery.

To understand why, look at the book *The Resilient City: How Modern Cities Recover from Disaster*, edited by Lawrence J. Vale and Thomas J. Campanella. The essays it contains chart the recovery of some fifteen cities that were devastated by various events: San Francisco after the 1906 earthquake, Chicago after the great fire of 1871, Berlin after the World War II bombardment, and even early modern London after its great fire in 1666. Interestingly, this book was published just before Katrina struck, and therefore its examples do not include New Orleans. The book is replete with insights, but perhaps the most interesting is shown in the timeline that traces a recurrent pattern for the rebuilding—certain events occur within days, others within weeks, others within months, and there is a sense of completion within a surprisingly short number of years. Chicago, for example, was rebuilt within three years. The book shows a pronounced coincidence across the centuries, across types of devastation, and across cultures. If New Orleans's recovery were analyzed using the same techniques, it would be off the chart. In comparison with all cities studied, New Orleans has done nothing.

One explanation for this dismal performance is that New Orleans has been retarded precisely because of a massive federal intervention. The feds prevented the residents from returning for three months—even if their houses were in habitable condition. Much was lost in this period. FEMA took an incredible nine months to establish the flood elevation to which houses must be rebuilt. This suppressed rebuilding activity by any but the most desperate or irresponsible.

And now, fifteen months after the event, the Road Home program is just beginning to write the federal checks that were promised as the basis of reconstruction a year ago. In the meantime, most people have been waiting for their payments to be determined, and that process is even now going so slowly that it will be years before the last of them are provided. Looking at the stories of the resilient cities, one can see that this degree of expected government help is unprecedented, and it arguably has stifled activity. In fact, almost the only sign of reconstruction in New Orleans has been among the Vietnamese Catholic community. In a manner particular to a culture that is self-reliant, they went ahead using the resources of their own community, under the leadership of their priests. Months ago, they had already rebuilt their homes, businesses, and civic buildings. The contrast with the rest of the city could not be more brutally clear.

In further confirmation, take the last comparable event before Katrina, Hurricane Andrew. I was involved in that reconstruction, which took place thirteen years ago. Overall, in the very poor community of Florida City where I worked first and then in South Dade County, I don't remember the presence of the federal government. The National Guard was there to keep the peace, but FEMA employees were just the people at the margins who provided the trailers and, much later, funding for the debris hauling. It was up to the community to rebuild for themselves, because the government was not in the picture. Can one conclude anything but that the feds have been the great impediment in New Orleans, lagging in their response time and making promises they have not kept? Perhaps those who base their hope on foreign aid will get something—but only after feeling righteous anger over the delays.

The second framework of hope, the magic bullet, can be defined as the reliance on a spectacular urban project. A magic bullet, as we know, is that special missile that, although expensive, is expected not to miss its target. The history of the deployment of this American urban planning phenomenon in New Orleans is, in fact, typical. Among the magic bullets volleyed in New Orleans were the rotating restaurant atop the World Trade Center building (planners in the 1960s dropped rotating restaurants all over the United States, from the Seattle Needle's to the Atlanta Centennial Tower's), three enclosed shopping malls in the central business district (post-Katrina, one of them is closed, one is on artificial respiration, and one is just barely surviving), an interstate highway through downtown to make it more accessible to suburbanites, a casino, a convention center, the Superdome sports arena, and the Audubon Aquarium of the Americas. In 1984, New Orleans even implemented that most extravagant of magic bullets, a world's fair. None of these bullets did the job. All of them financially succeeded or failed individually, but New Orleans itself continued its linear decline.

Now, after Katrina, the latest generation of magic bullets is being deployed: Witness Thom Mayne's project for a new city hall that would demolish the perfectly good existing one and create a flying leap of a park over Poydras Street. Other "starchitects"—Rogers, Hadid, Libeskind, Gehry—have been asked to build on the waterfront. I, who own a house on the waterfront of the Marigny, personally look forward to having one of these spectacular buildings to view from my front window (I really do). I wish them success, but under no circumstances should one be under the illusion that this particular generation of magic bullets will save New Orleans any more than the others did. They are an amusement, a welcome distraction, but also a false hope. It is ironic that these structures are pitched at tourism—the idea having emanated from that selfsame concerned group of architects who spent the first six months post-Katrina wringing their hands in worry that New Orleans would be reduced to a less-than-authentic tourist destination. Plans for a new waterfront are fine, unless they come at the expense of that old golden goose of tourism, the French Quarter. We must be vigilant.

The third framework of hope is the long road. This one has received scant attention, except perhaps from the creators of the Unified New Orleans Plan. This hope rests on the building-by-building, block-by-block restoration of a city to its former quality of life. It involves the provision of massive amounts of affordable and middle-class housing, as well as a design for the public realm, which is to say a design that encourages the street life that makes New Orleans preeminent among American cities as a place capable of attracting people who have the means and talent to be elsewhere and who contribute so significantly to the lifeblood city's cultural vibrancy.

This incrementalism is receiving attention from the professionals, but there seems to be little understanding from political or cultural leaders that it requires their support. The day-to-day municipal administrators, the volunteer groups, the nongovernmental organizations, and the bottom-up community leaders deserve more attention. These range from the Vieux Carré Commission, routinely bypassed; ACORN, routinely reviled; the Bureau of Governmental Research, routinely ignored; and the very many talented small builders—people who can work with their hands, one house at a time, and for whom so little is being done as they slog through negotiations to secure the provision of reasonable insurance, electrical rates, and mortgages and through the processes of permit-granting and inspection.

Let us be clear: All three of the frameworks of hope are marvelous. Foreign—that is, federal—aid will perhaps become something other than the impediment that it has been. The magic bullet, the riverfront scheme, is what it is—spectacular. It will succeed in drawing attention, but it is not the cure for New Orleans. One hopes that it doesn't become a distraction or a surrogate for real achievement. The third, the long road of incremental restoration of quality of life, is the most likely to have a substantial effect. Ironically, it is the avenue that was most neglected prior to the hurricane and it will require the greatest cultural change to adopt. After all, well before Katrina New Orleans had tried the other two; the city has been the national champion at extracting federal aid, and it can boast one of the most complete collections of magic bullets actually implemented by any American city. So we know that those solutions didn't stem the city's long, long, long slide. Let us not be distracted.

LATER THOUGHTS, 2008

Like so many others, I have long been a visitor to New Orleans. In my case, this goes back to 1979, when we studied the city design of Seaside, Florida. I have often been back because New Orleans is one of the best places to learn about architecture and urbanism in the United States. My emphasis on design might seem unusual, but it shouldn't. The design of New Orleans has a quality and character comparable to its music and cuisine, although those receive most of the attention.

In all those visits, I regret to admit, I did not get to know the people—not really. Such is the experience of the tourist. This all changed when Katrina brought me back in the role of planner. Engaging the planning process brought me face to face with the city's reality.

Apart from the misconceptions of the tourist, I had also been predisposed by the media to think of New Orleans as a charming but lackadaisical and fundamentally mismanaged place that had been subjected to unwarranted devastation, with a great deal of anger and resentment as a result. That is indeed what I found at first. But as I engaged in the planning process, I came to realize that the anger I witnessed was relative. It was much less intense, for example, than the bitterness one encounters in the typical California city plagued with traffic. The people of New Orleans have an underlying sweetness and a sense of humor, irony, and graciousness that is never far below the surface. These are not hard people.

Pondering this, I had an additional insight. I remember specifically when, on a street in the Marigny, I came upon a colorful little house framed by banana trees. I thought, "This is Cuba"—I am Cuban myself. New Orleans came to feel so much like Cuba that I was driven to buy a house in the Marigny as a surrogate for my inaccessible Santiago de Cuba.

I came to realize that New Orleans is not really an American city, but rather a Caribbean one. And seen through the lens of the Caribbean, New Orleans is not among the most haphazard, poorest, and misgoverned American cities, but rather among the best organized, wealthiest, cleanest, and competently governed Caribbean cities. This insight was fundamental, because from that moment I understood New Orleans and truly began

Duany Plater-Zyberk & Company

Bywater Cottages, corner of Dauphine and Gallier streets

to sympathize with it. But the government? Like everyone, I found the city government to be a bit random; I thought that if New Orleans were to be governed as efficiently as, say, Minneapolis, it would be a different place—but not a place that I could care for. Let me work with the government the way it is. It is the human flaws that make New Orleans the most human of American cities.

When understood as Caribbean, New Orleans's culture seems even more precious—and vulnerable to the effects of Katrina. Anxiety about cultural loss is not new. There has been a great deal of anguish regarding the diminishment of the black population and how, without it, New Orleans would ever be able to regain itself. Just so. But I fear that the situation is direr and less controllable. I am afraid that even if the majority of the city's former population does return to reinhabit its neighborhoods, that will not mean that New Orleans, or at least the culture of New Orleans, will be restored. The reason is not political but technical. The lost housing of New Orleans was quite special. Entering the damaged and abandoned houses, one can still see what they were like before the hurricane. They were exceedingly inexpensive to live in, built by people's parents and grandparents or by small builders paid in cash or by barter. Most of these simple, pleasant houses were owned debt-free. They had to be because they did not meet any sort of code and therefore did not qualify for mortgages by current standards.

It was possible to sustain the unique culture of New Orleans because housing costs were minimal, liberating people from debt. One did not have to work a great deal to get by. There was the possibility of leisure. There was time to create the fabulously complex Creole dishes that simmer forever; there was time to practice music, to play it and listen to it live. There was time to make costumes and to parade; there was time to party and to tell stories; there was time to spend all day marking the passing of a friend. With a little work, a little help from the government, and a little help from family and friends, life could be good! This is a

Bywater Cottages, Gallier Street elevation

typically Caribbean social contract: one to be understood not as laziness or poverty but as a way of life.

This ease, which has been so misunderstood in the national scrutiny following the hurricane, is the Caribbean way. It is a lifestyle choice, and there is nothing intrinsically wrong with it. In fact, it is the envy of some of us who work all our lives to attain the condition of leisure only after retirement. It is this way of living that will disappear. Even with the federal funds for housing, there is little chance that new or renovated houses will be owned without debt. It is too expensive to build now. The higher standards of the new International Building Code are superb but also very expensive. There must be an alternative, or there will be very few paid-off houses. Everyone will have a mortgage that will need to be sustained by hard work—and this will undermine the culture of New Orleans.

What can be done? Somehow the building culture that created the original New Orleans must be reinstated. The hurdle of blueprints, permits, contractors, inspections—the professionalism of it all—eliminates self-building. Somehow there must be a process allowed whereby people can build simple, functional houses for themselves, either by themselves or through barter with professionals. There must be free designs for houses that can be built in small stages and that do not require an architect, complicated permits, or inspections; there must be commonsense technical standards. Without all this there will be the pall of debt for everyone. And debt in the Caribbean doesn't mean just owing money—it means elimination of the culture that arises from leisure.

To start, I would recommend an experimental "homebuilt" area where one "contracts out" of the current North American system, which consists of the nanny state raising standards to the point where it is so costly and complicated to build that only the state can provide affordable housing—solving a problem that it created in the first place. However it may sound,

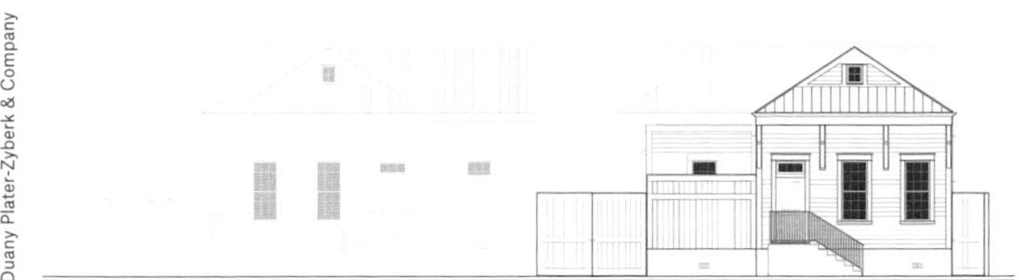

Duany Plater-Zyberk & Company

Bywater Cottages, Dauphine Street elevation, May 2008

this proposal is not so odd. Until recently this was the way that this country was built, from the Atlantic to the Pacific. For three centuries Americans built for themselves. And they built well enough, so long as what they built was theirs. Individual responsibility could be trusted. We must return to this as an option. Of course, this option is not for everybody. There are plenty of people in New Orleans who follow the conventional American eight-hour workday. But the culture of this city does not flow from them; they provide the backbone of New Orleans, but not its heart.

AN ACT CREATING THE "HOMEBUILT HOUSING ZONE" OF THE CITY OF NEW ORLEANS

WHEREAS among the historic rights of New Orleanians has been the construction of their own dwellings;

WHEREAS the great majority of the smaller houses characteristic of New Orleans have been built though the action and responsibility of their owners;

WHEREAS such houses have proven over many decades to be durable, economical, pleasant to inhabit, and environmentally appropriate;

WHEREAS the damage done by Hurricane Katrina requires that tens of thousands of such self-built houses be expeditiously rebuilt or replaced;

WHEREAS governmental staff is overstretched to the point of inability to process plans and provide inspections expeditiously;

WHEREAS an accretion of restrictive codes, mandatory reliance on licensed architects and contractors, highest construction standards, and complex permitting protocols have increased very substantially the cost of house building;

WHEREAS, even with the substantial government subsidy that is available, housing remains out of reach of most New Orleanians;

WHEREAS for the sake of economy and cultural continuity it should be possible to reuse surviving foundations and to salvage material that may not meet the new codes and standards;

WHEREAS self-help and bottom-up decision making are the stated intentions of the Unified New Orleans Plan;

WHEREAS all attempts to deliver economical housing on the requisite scale having failed, the plight of the citizens of New Orleans justifies the exploration of unconventional methods, including traditional ones;

THEREFORE, by action of the City Council, A HOMEBUILT HOUSING ZONE (HH Zone) is hereby created and added to the City of New Orleans Zoning Code. The Staff of the Planning Department is directed to draft an HH Zone that incorporates the following provisions:

- The HH Zone shall operate as a contract between the City of New Orleans (The Municipality) and the owner of the Lot (The Owner).
- The HH Zone shall be an overlay zone applicable within current R-2 Residential Zones.
- The HH designation shall be available by right upon request by the documented Owner. Each Owner shall have a one-time right to an HH Zone designation.
- The HH designation shall be available only to single- and double-family houses intended exclusively for residential use, with an internal area no more than 1,600 square feet per unit and no more than two stories.
- The HH designation shall exempt the Owner from the requirements of current permitting procedures, applicable building codes, the employment of licensed professionals, and the protocol of inspections with the exception of the filing of a Request for Commencement of Construction (the required information regarding location, etc., is to be developed by The Staff) and Notification of Completion of Construction.
- As a condition of receiving the HH designation, The Owner shall agree by contract to hold The Municipality harmless for injury and death as a consequence of the construction and the habitation of the house as well as the consequences of fire, wind, water, and theft.
- As a condition of receiving the HH designation, The Owner shall acknowledge by contract that housing built under the standards of the HH designation may not qualify for insurance and mortgage and shall hold the municipality harmless for these consequences.
- The Owner shall agree by contract for the sake of neighborhood harmony to abide with the setback, height, and other form-based aspects of (a) the R-2 Residential Zone, (b) the building preexisting on the lot, and (c) the average metrics of the two houses closest to either side of the lot and the three houses on the opposite side of the street.
- The Owner shall agree to comply with the standards and health and safety codes for all applicable utilities.
- The Owner shall agree to complete the work of construction within two years of the filing date of the Request of Commencement.
- The Homebuilt Housing Act shall sunset within three years of its incorporation to The Code unless it is extended by action of the New Orleans City Council.[1]

1 See Doug MacCash, "Urban Planner Andrés Duany Shows Off His Bywater House Prototypes," January 31, 2009, blog.NOLA.com.

RECOVERY CHAOS: URBAN NEIGHBORHOOD REDEVELOPMENT AFTER DISASTER

BRADFORD POWERS

INTRODUCTION

I served as the founding executive director of the nonprofit Jericho Road Episcopal Housing Initiative from January 2006 to March 2012.[1] Jericho Road was established post-Katrina, to work effectively for the redevelopment and revitalization of Central City, a primarily African-American, low-income neighborhood. Specifically, Jericho Road sought to provide housing options for Central City families earning less than the median income for the metro area.[2] Our organization worked to improve the quality of life in the neighborhood using three related and reinforcing strategies: we directly developed and broadly supported affordable, healthy, and high-quality housing; we created neighborhood organizations to link residents so that they could articulate, prioritize, and implement their own redevelopment goals; and we provided technical assistance—not only to residents but also to government entities—supportng productive, locally informed strategies to reduce urban blight.

The timing of Jericho Road's foundation and its initial success in fundraising efforts owed much to the local and national focus on recovery from the destruction caused by Hurricane Katrina in 2005. The section of Central City where Jericho Road decided to work had flooded in the aftermath of the storm but was not so damaged that residents and philanthropic donors judged it to be irrecoverable. Flood damage aside, Central City was like a ship that had been long lost at sea. Many of the issues that the neighborhood faced were the result of decades of disinvestment in New Orleans's urban core that had resulted in a failed education system,

1 The name Jericho Road comes from an image Dr. Martin Luther King Jr. used in the famous "Beyond Vietnam: A Time to Break Silence" speech he delivered on April 4, 1967 at Riverside Church in New York City: "A true revolution of values will soon cause us to question the fairness and justice of many of our past and present policies. On the one hand, we are called to play the Good Samaritan on life's roadside, but that will be only an initial act. One day we must come to see that the whole Jericho Road must be transformed so that men and women will not be constantly beaten and robbed as they make their journey on life's highway. True compassion is more than flinging a coin to a beggar. It comes to see [that] an edifice which produces beggars needs restructuring." See Stanford University's Martin Luther King Jr., Research and Educational Institute, mlkkpp01.stanford.edu.

2 HUD annually determines median income for metro areas in the United States. In 2011, $56,552 was the median income for a family of four in the New Orleans metro area; see huduser.org.

a tenuous low-wage economy, epidemic rates of violent crime, low family savings, and inadequate public housing infrastructure. Jericho Road's mission was to work with Central City residents to address the historic and systemic negative outcomes of disinvestment and to reduce their impacts. However, Central City residents generally viewed nonprofits that relied on government funding as extensions of the political machine. Moreover, the community suffered from a culture of corruption involving elected government officials, centered on the activities of two city council members and a member of the U.S. House of Representatives. All three were in office at the times they were accused of racketeering and bribery.[3] When Central City needed partners to aid in its post-Katrina recovery, residents were highly distrustful of those who claimed to be able to help or were interested in doing so. Certainly Central City was a tough place for a new nonprofit to start.

At the time of the storm, most of the neighborhood's buildings were one- and two-story wooden residential structures, the majority containing one to four units. Most of them had been built in the first half of the twentieth century. When Katrina struck, there were more renters than homeowners in Central City, and approximately 30 percent of the properties there were either vacant or contained blighted structures. Blight was especially prevalent along the once vibrant commercial corridors of the neighborhood.[4] During my time at Jericho Road, we built and sold twenty-five single-family, energy-efficient affordable homes on scattered sites for individuals and families whose earned income ranged from 65 percent to 100 percent of the median income in the New Orleans metro region. We envisioned and then helped to create a partnership that developed New Orleans's first LEED New Construction Multi-Family Development.[5] In addition, Jericho Road cleared the titles and took legal and physical possession of more than seventy-five blighted and tax-delinquent properties in our targeted neighborhood. We elimi-

3 New Orleans City Councilman Oliver Thomas pled guilty to bribery charges and served a three-year sentence. United States Representative William Jefferson was convicted of bribery and is serving a thirteen-year prison term. Former New Orleans City Councilwoman Renee Gill-Pratt was convicted of racketeering and received a seven-year sentence, which she is currently appealing; see Frank Donze, "Oliver Thomas Enters Prison Today," *Times-Picayune,* January 2, 2008, NOLA.com; Greg Stohr, "Convicted Ex-Representative Jefferson Loses at High Court," *Bloomberg*, November 26, 2012, Bloomberg.com; and Frank Donze, "Renee Gill-Pratt Sentenced to Seven Years in Prison," *Times-Picayune,* November 2, 2011, NOLA.com.

4 I stress the distinction between "neighborhood" recovery and "citywide" recovery because these are two very different activities. Those of us who worked on the neighborhood scale of redevelopment felt a certain disdain for the continuously incomplete and contradictory citywide plans that press release after press release promoted but that failed to gain any traction with various city agencies, especially at the neighborhood level. I acknowledge that my colleagues, who concentrated on larger-scale redevelopment efforts, expressed disdain for us neighborhood activists, who were intent on gaining whatever benefits we could for the particular neighborhoods in which we worked. But the tensions between these two redevelopment scales are real and have made recovery processes much less efficient than they might have been.

5 Leadership in Energy and Environmental Design (LEED) is a project of the U.S. Green Building Council (USGBC), which is a 501(c)(3) nonprofit organization committed to promoting a prosperous and sustainable future for the nation through cost-efficient and energy-saving green buildings; see usgbc.org.leed. For further details on the project, see themusesapartments.com.

nated the blight on these properties by clearing debris from the sites, rehabilitating existing structures, and building new homes or neighborhood amenities such as community gardens. We also provided advice and resources to others throughout the city about how to do the same.[6] We both started new neighborhood organizations and supported existing ones, and we founded, constructed, and operated the Saratoga Street Fruit Tree Orchard and the Faubourg Delassize Community Garden.[7] Sometimes we were successful in seeing policy changed so that more money flowed to our target area; at other times, we fought hard for change but lost. We created jobs, helped start careers, and established a place where innovative strategies in urban redevelopment could hatch. All of Jericho Road's Central City projects were within fifteen blocks of one another.[8] We were joined by residents, other nonprofits, businesses, and governmental agencies. We had some great successes and, as in life, many failures.

I write to share the insights that I gained regarding one aspect of this work, the development and sale of affordable, infill, single-family homes. I describe the urban context of New Orleans at the time of the storm, state the guidelines we used to develop the geographic boundaries of our target area, discuss the challenges of land acquisition and our contributions to facilitating that process for the entire city, identify significant design elements of the houses that we built, and review some of the general challenges we faced. I conclude with some larger insights on the chaotic process of recovery, and why that process made planning, acquiring, designing, and building so damn difficult.

JERICHO ROAD'S SINGLE-FAMILY HOMES

Under the leadership of Christ Church, New Orleans's Episcopal cathedral, I was hired to help move an idea forward. The cathedral had obtained an exploratory grant in the fall of 2005 from Episcopal Relief and Development, an international aid organization based in New York City.[9] The purpose of the small seed grant was to start an organization that would work to ensure equality in the rebuilding of New Orleans, addressing the fear that when property values increased as a result of privately funded high-end redevelopment, low- and moderate-income families would be priced out of the housing market.

6 Jericho Road and the City Center of Tulane University's School of Architecture collaborated on a booklet outlining strategies to achieve blight reduction. The City Center's Scott Bernard, Dan Etheridge, and Seth Welty were our invaluable partners; see tulanecitycenter.org/news/228.

7 We were fortunate to have amazing fellows from Grinnell College and AVODAH, the Jewish Service Corps, who worked with Central City residents over the course of their fellowships to form two neighborhood organizations, Faubourg Delassize and Faubourg Livaudais. Jericho Road also supported the growth of an existing neighborhood organization, Faubourg Lafayette.

8 Louisiana Avenue, St. Charles Avenue, Clio Street, and Simon Bolivar Avenue/LaSalle Street formed the boundaries of Jericho Road's target area.

9 Episcopal Relief and Development is an international agency that seeks to mount compassionate responses to human suffering on behalf of the Episcopal Church of the United States; see episcopalrelief.org.

As it turned out, very few high-profile projects were actually undertaken; most of the sexy new post-storm condo towers never made it past clamoring headlines and highly stylized renderings. However, the pressure to rehabilitate and rebuild low- and moderate-cost housing was real. New Orleans's housing stock had been deteriorating for decades. Humidity, rainfall, and time wreaked havoc on the city's wooden homes. Before Katrina, applying a thick coat of paint was an accepted housing rehabilitation strategy, and these superficially tended buildings were especially vulnerable to the storm's ravages. Renters were particularly at risk post-Katrina. Small-time landlords did what they could to complete repairs, but many simply did not have the funds.[10] Paychecks were interrupted or simply vanished.[11] Many folks could not pay the old rents, and rents for rehabilitated properties were rising fast. Supply and demand is not pretty in post-disaster settings.

The first six months after the storm was a chaotic time. Volunteer labor and donor dollars generously provided water, food, and other basic needs for those who were "gutting" flooded homes, a task that became a central focus for many volunteer workers.[12] A house must be gutted before it can be rebuilt; however, rebuilding obviously cannot follow if no funds for it are available. Many homeowners who undertook to gut their houses themselves or who were the beneficiaries of the labors of volunteer gutting teams could not subsequently secure the resources to rebuild them and endured a second heartbreak.[13]

In late winter of 2005–2006, I pitched six points to my executive committee to guide us in determining our specific goals and target area. We developed a vision statement that called for building a network of solid homes, which we hoped would lead to more resilient streets and neighborhoods and a more resilient city. The points were:[14]

10 Gouging and profiteering became commonplace. While we were building our first homes, I heard about a landlord who was renting a two-bedroom house to sixteen people and charging them each $150 a month. The house was for sale, so I called the realtor and went to see what was what. I counted eleven air mattresses in the house, but saw no other furniture. The bathtub had been pulled out, and it appeared the landlord expected the tenants to use the outside hose as a shower. The folks living in the house were not day laborers taking advantage of new employment opportunities, but rather two families who had been neighborhood residents for many years. In my experience this was not an isolated incident.

11 For the most accessible data on the damages sustained in the wake of Katrina and the progress of New Orleans's recovery, see the Greater New Orleans Community Data Center, gnocdc.org.

12 Gutting a house can entail a broad range of activities, depending on the extent of water damage. Basically it requires removing all personal property and building materials other than the frame, exterior wall, and roof. It is difficult and dangerous work, physically and emotionally draining.

13 The reasons that some folks found themselves with gutted homes that they could not rebuild were varied. The responses of private insurance companies were uneven and especially inadequate for higher-value homes. The federally financed and state-administered Road Home Program paid homeowners the assessed value of their property, not the cost of rebuilding; on this program see road2la.org. The Greater New Orleans Fair Housing Action Center provided invaluable help to many during this process; on their programs see gnofairhousing.org.

14 Board members Ellen Ball and Julie George were particularly instrumental in supporting these guidelines over the years by asking tough questions that kept us on track.

- Let us choose a small area of New Orleans to support so that our resources will be better targeted and we can support resident leaders. Let us choose one neighborhood or even a portion of a neighborhood in which to work.
- Let us focus our assistance in a neighborhood in which there was minimum flooding and which has a minimum likelihood for future flooding.
- Let us focus on a neighborhood that is well situated near jobs and served by New Orleans's public transport system.
- Let us focus on a neighborhood that abuts relatively undamaged high-value real estate, so that Jericho Road's efforts can leverage success and new homebuyers will have confidence in the prospect of investing.
- Let us choose a neighborhood where the residents have articulated both need and desire for affordable high-quality housing.
- Let us choose a neighborhood where there has been massive disinvestment. Let us choose a neighborhood of opportunity.

Jericho Road's board accepted these parameters, which led us to the Central City area, where the organization still operates.[15] After an examination of the many needs revealed by the storm and after speaking to resident-led organizations, we decided to focus on providing high-quality and affordable housing. We also decided to market the homes that we built to homeowners, rather than selling them to prospective landlords or renting them ourselves. The board made a funding request to Episcopal Relief and Development and in early spring 2006 received a $2,200,000 grant, to be paid over three years. The funds were to cover operations, land purchases, design services, legal fees, construction costs, and, finally, housing subsidies at time of sale.

Low-income wage earners needed financial assistance to qualify for loans to purchase Jericho Road's houses: "soft" second mortgages underwritten by the federal government and subsidies that we, the developers, provided and for which we had to raise substantial funds. Here is how a typical deal would look: The average cost of one of our houses, excluding our operational costs, was about $160,000; this included the purchase price of the land, the construction cost of the house, and additional costs for fencing, landscaping, and the purchase of appliances, including clothes washer and dryer. The sale price for our houses was approximately $125,000; the developer subsidy was about $35,000. A soft second mortgage was available to buyers who did not qualify to borrow enough to cover the asking price of $125,000; such a mortgage usually carries no interest rate and the principal

15 Bishop Charles Jenkins, Dean David Duplantier, and Chris Beary served as the board's executive committee during the search for our area of focus.

Jericho Road

Stick-built Jericho Road houses in Central City under construction

amount of the loan is forgiven after a stipulated period of time, so long as the buyer remains in the house and makes mortgage payments. If a potential buyer could afford a $90,000 mortgage, a soft second mortgage of $35,000 would be needed to meet the purchase price of $125,000.[16]

Thus, each home that Jericho Road sold represented a minimum investment of $70,000 that would not be recouped, and we had other expenses as we set about community building. We cleared lots of illegally dumped tires, helped to fix neighbors' fences, and even helped the guy who cut the grass on our lots obtain better insurance so that he could qualify for a Small Business Administration loan and grow his business. We tried to leverage every opportunity to stimulate positive change in Central City.

As we began our work, we came to realize how important it was to support potential homebuyers and networks of neighbors. Our goal was to make sure that every house we built was a place where a healthy rhythm of family life could thrive.[17] We envisioned this rippling through the neighborhood, attracting other investments small and large. The chairman of Jericho Road's board, Bishop Charles Jenkins, said often, "Let us build homes, not simply houses." This would become our core strategy in Central City: to consider that everything we undertook there, no matter its scale, could help to weave the communal fabric.

Jericho Road's successes depended on the team we put together. I was the sole employee for the first year, but I had a strong and diverse

16 The federal government funds this type of mortgage product, but those federal agents disbursing soft second mortgages in New Orleans failed miserably during the early, critical years of rebuilding. In fact, the buyers of our first homes obtained theirs from another local nonprofit, Neighborhood Housing Services, which paid them out of a grant received from Qatar.

17 Abagail Nelson, Jericho Road's extraordinary program officer from Episcopal Relief and Development, brought this general concept to our endeavor.

board of directors who were trusted, successful, and committed leaders from across the city.[18] In January 2007 Holly Heine joined me as second employee and director of operations. Heine had run the Episcopal Diocese of Louisiana's massive volunteer management effort for the first year and a half after the storm. At Jericho Road, her energy, sense of order, and strategic thinking complemented my more chaotic methods of problem solving and management style. We next added Chris Ross, a seasoned developer of affordable homes, as our director of housing programs. We hired Michael Robinson, a youth "street" minister, as our lead community organizer. Grinnell College and AVODAH, the Jewish Service Corps, supported our efforts with fellowships that enabled incredibly talented and energetic service-oriented youth to join us, greatly contributing to our work.[19]

LAND ACQUISITION

Acquiring land for redevelopment became a big problem for developers throughout post-Katrina New Orleans. Although a significant number of the tens of thousands of flooded or previously blighted properties had little value, they were not easy to purchase, because it was difficult to obtain "clear" titles for which title insurance could be provided. Obtaining a clear property title free of liens and other legal encumbrances as well as the attendant and requisite title insurance is key in the formal legal process of property transfer that ensures a property's future value and salability. As an attorney, I understood this. As soon as I began to search for properties that Jericho Road might buy, I recognized the extensive problems posed by the informal local conventions of land transfer processes posed, especially in our disaster recovery situation, with its intense time pressures and the rigid paperwork requirements for federally funded rebuilding programs. The properties that we were looking to buy represented a number of problematic categories, most difficult of which was the tax-adjudicated property.

One of Jericho Road's most important successes was its positive impact on the efficiency of the city's tax-adjudicated property title transfer program. Length constraints for this essay and my respect for readers' sanity prohibit me from describing in full New Orleans's complicated system for dealing with tax-delinquent properties. In short, a party who wishes to buy a property on which taxes are outstanding may pay them and may obtain title to said property after a certain number of years have passed and certain rigid administrative details are satisfied. This arrange-

18 One key asset that Jericho Road possessed was access to legal advice. I am a lawyer, lawyers in the bishop's office were available to help us, and two lawyers served on our board of directors. We were not afraid to enforce contracts or sue for proper relief. A nonprofit working in a low-income neighborhood needs to partner with lawyers representing two distinct arenas of practice: the strong, well-financed firm and the small firm or solo practice with expertise in fighting hard in city court.

19 We hired Alison Ecker to stay on after her Grinnell fellowship ended to implement the blight reduction strategy that we had developed with Tulane University's City Center.

ment ostensibly benefits the city, because it can produce tax revenues from a formerly nonproductive property.[20]

In the spring of 2006, Mayor Ray Nagin announced his administration's intent to emphasize this program, which brought focus to the redevelopment effort, even though the city government did not immediately make the list of tax-adjudicated properties publicly available. Mysteriously, however, a photocopy of the list appeared at my office door one day in a brown bag—this is the truth!—and we scoured it for properties that we might want to purchase. Jericho Road's real estate attorney Scott Simmons (another hero on our team) and I examined the records of each property in our target area, looking for additional liens that would slow the purchase process; we studied the sizes of lots and photographed surrounding buildings; we mapped the properties in relation to public transit and schools. We then contacted the title company writing title insurance on each of these properties and learned about the problems they presented, which largely had to do with the enforcement of the regulations concerning notifications to property owners—what types of notices had to be sent, by whom and to whom. We realized that in order to move forward with our purchase plans, we needed to clarify the steps for removing legal impediments and completing the process. We also realized that other developers seeking to do the same would benefit from our analysis of the process and our strategies to manage it successfully. We presented our findings to the city agency in charge of the program, which accepted and circulated them. We benefited because we were offered the adjudicated lots that we had hoped to pursue, but others benefited as well, because our clarification of the process made it more transparent, improving developers' access to adjudicated properties and moving the properties back into commerce.[21] Unfortunately, a year later the program was put on hold by turf battles between the city attorney's office and the New Orleans Redevelopment Authority. This was another example of the insanity of system conflict at a critical time of rebuilding.[22]

There were other city programs meant to return properties to productive status that also stumbled. In 2006, New Orleans implemented the Good Neighbor Program, somewhat oddly named because it encouraged

20 This concept was formulated to promote property transfers and blight remediation. In practice, property transfers could be delayed or stopped altogether if the required advisory notices had not been properly administered or if more than one potential purchaser had paid the outstanding taxes; both situations created legal snafus. The system employed to realize the concept was not working and was making post-Katrina redevelopment difficult. Its failure exemplified the "anti-commons" idea developed in Michael Heller's *The Gridlock Economy* (New York: Basic Books, 1998). Heller describes how the fractured ownership that often results from tax sales creates gridlock, making it difficult for individuals to use, care for, and exchange land.

21 Jericho Road also recommended to the city that tax-adjudicated properties not be sold at tax sales, since selling them piecemeal made it more difficult for developers to assemble critical masses of properties. In areas that were struggling, rebuilding in clusters was the only sensible approach.

22 Assistant City Attorney Brenda Breaux should receive credit for bringing the two entities together and restarting this program that was so important to the city's recovery efforts.

neighbors to submit forms documenting blighted properties belonging to others. Thinking Jericho Road could take advantage of this initiative, I drove around Central City for days filling out forms for lots on block after block after block. Sometimes I grabbed an intern to go with me; other times I went alone, clipboard in lap, maps and street addresses taped to my dashboard. I was stopped twice by police and successfully explained to interested officers what I was doing.[23] I submitted 156 forms to the councilperson's office. A month or two later I was told that the program had been canceled. There were many other redevelopment projects that we were disappointed not to engage in, among them the Salvation Army's EnviRenew, the Katrina Cottage project, and the New Orleans Redevelopment Authority's various Central City RFPs.[24]

Recovery efforts also suffered from a lack of transparency in the disposition of city-controlled property. Before the storm, blighted properties had remained largely unchallenged, and citizens viewed the New Orleans Redevelopment Authority, to whose portfolio these properties were relegated, with distrust. Suspicion of inside dealing was so strong and pervasive that when our first homes were under construction, Central City residents assumed that they were being built for folks with "connections." Jericho Road's mission was best communicated when neighbors saw our new homeowners sitting on their front porches or unloading their groceries and remarked in excited disbelief, "That's the owner? I work with her, and she isn't anyone special," meaning anyone connected to city hall.

DESIGN FOR, BUT "DON'T EXPERIMENT ON," THE POOR![25]

During my time at Jericho Road we built *and* sold twenty-five single-family homes clustered in our target neighborhood.[26] We used five different contractors and three different architects. Overall, it was a difficult set of relationships. All of these partners both thrilled and disappointed us. And I am sure that Jericho Road was a stubborn and unreasonable client. Local architect Kim Finney was a stalwart contributor to Jericho Road; she and her husband provided advice not only on building but also on government regulations. Their real-time knowledge was key to our success, and other architects advised us as well early on. By 2007, Jericho

23 The positive outcome of my encounters with police was that Sergeant Yolanda Jenkins of the police department became a member of Jericho Road's board.

24 I cannot discuss here what I experienced as the problematic general lack of accountability for both public and private initiatives in post-Katrina rebuilding efforts. However, I urge planners working in post-disaster situations to address and outline optimal levels of oversight and accountability; this is essential in a recovery environment where project funding and dependent deliverables are conditional and results may be minimal.

25 Between 2005 and 2010, everyone who was anyone in the community redevelopment world came through New Orleans. I was lucky to meet many of these folks. Among them was Gus Newport, former mayor of Berkeley, California, and a nationally recognized community development expert, who gave me guidance, courage, and specific advice. His central message to me was "Don't experiment on the poor." This became a guiding principle for Jericho Road. We always tried to work "for" rather than "upon" the residents of our target area. We were not always successful.

26 Although it is very difficult to build a home, it is twice as hard to build and then sell it!

Road was able to begin construction on a new house approximately every six weeks. We hoped to attract additional architects to the project and that they might deeply discount their fees, given that construction was rapidly advancing. But the architects we contacted seemed wary of becoming involved. They were looking for larger projects, and since we had settled on traditional design solutions, they saw little opportunity in our project for innovative practice.

We had decided to build three- and four-bay shotgun houses, the historical style prevalent in our area, because feedback from realtors and potential homebuyers convinced us that Central City residents not only associated shotguns with warm memories of home but also wanted to restore the neighborhood fabric that had been so damaged in the storm. Our clients had grown up in shotguns, visited their grandparents in shotguns—rented and owned. They wanted their own grandchildren to grow up visiting them in shotguns. Further, Jericho Road's board of directors had decided that they did not want to experiment with design in the low-income market. Nevertheless, our traditional-looking houses had been updated with modern appliances, foam insulation, and a plan that included a side hallway running the length of the house, so that rooms opened into it rather than into one another, as had been common in the old shotgun plan.

We had to balance our decision to configure the exteriors of our houses according to traditional shotgun patterns with careful attention to building codes, energy efficiency, rainwater management, and crime prevention. We knew that our clients might want to add burglar bars, since theft was a problem in the neighborhood, and we designed the windows so that iron bars could easily and attractively be added. We placed air conditioning units atop ten-foot-high platforms to thwart theft. We mounted gutters on four-inch overhangs to separate them from exterior walls. Our decisions about construction details departed from tradition, for better or worse, as the design critics whom we invited to advise us on improving our houses were quick to inform us. From them we learned, for example, that traditional front porches were four feet deep, whereas ours were six feet deep. We continued to build the deeper porches, hoping residents would think of them as outdoor rooms. We wanted to encourage folks to be on them, with their eyes on the street, to help reduce crime and build community.

Basically, these three-bedroom, two-bath homes were long skinny boxes with pretty smiles—the front porches. The average lot was 29 feet wide and 110 feet long, and the floor area ranged from 1,200 to 1,400 square feet. We wanted our houses to look qualitatively different from the poorly built affordable housing in the city, and we decided to invest in the highest-quality materials that we could afford for the details of the front façades, leveraging the largely fixed costs of our solidly built

Jericho Road

Stick-built house inspired by the traditional three-bay shotgun model, with solid wood front door and solid brick front stairs

standard construction.[27] This strategy, unique in New Orleans at the time, was envisioned and implemented by Chris Ross, our director of housing. Every detail was critical—the scale of the front windows, the materials of the front door, stairs, porch rails, and walkway. For example, Chris insisted on solid wood doors, which cost an additional $450 but attracted the attention of funders, buyers, and neighbors. In employing this strategy, we signaled that serious long-term investments were being made in the neighborhood and that other investors should join us.[28]

Jericho Road's first five homes were modular, or prebuilt. Originally we had planned to build houses designed by Miami architect Andrés Duany employing structured insulated panels (SIP). In 2006, Duany had offered to design a group of houses for Jericho Road if we could obtain contiguous lots. Although this was a difficult request to fill so early in

27 Using superior products for some of the houses' most visible elements meant possible lower maintenance costs and longer life, preserving the "curb appeal" of our homes. We were aware that Jericho Road's houses were among the highest priced ever marketed in the neighborhood, making us the area's highest-end developer. To resolve the tension between our two goals, building high-quality affordable houses and serving the needs of the neighborhood, we focused our efforts on assisting buyers who had strong connections to the area, which helped us succeed at both. By 2012, however, the sales price had risen to $150,000.

28 When two or more of Jericho Road's houses were completed on a block, other investors became interested, which was our goal. From our perspective, ideal investors were former neighborhood residents who had left the area but who were paying attention to what was happening there and considering return. Investors seeking to develop properties for rent were less than ideal, but we attempted to work with them, too, with uneven results.

Jericho Road

Stick-built Jericho Road house, inspired by the four-bay shotgun type but with an added bay; decorated for Christmas by the new owner

the recovery, I was able to secure five lots. Duany produced three designs and connected us with a builder who had access to the SIP manufacturer in Florida that Duany wanted us to use. We reviewed the plans and the contract and set a price for construction. I was very excited; Jericho Road was barely five months old, and we were going to build three homes designed by the internationally acclaimed architect Andrés Duany! I was also aware that our partnership had potential fund-raising possibilities; some of our New York–based funders would love it.

On the day that the builder was to sign the contract, he failed to show up. After fielding his excuses for a week, we began to look for a new builder. Meanwhile, we learned that the city planning department had changed the procedures for subdividing the lots to accommodate Duany's plans.[29] The new procedures would require months to follow, and my board, feeling the pressure to break ground, decided against subdivision and Duany's scheme. I was brokenhearted, but I was under pressure to build. We located a modular home provider who promised quick results. The transition from working with Duany to signing with a slick-talking modular provider (who went bankrupt a year after our first houses were constructed) was tough.

When we decided to buy our first three modular homes from a manufacturer in Texas, the Louisiana Manufactured Housing Association informed me that we did not have a proper license to buy and sell modular homes. I found a legal opinion that seemed to put in doubt their claim that we needed a license, and we went forward, telling them that they would have to present an injunction to stop us. We never heard from

29 For Duany's demonstration project in the Bywater neighborhood, multiple houses sited in a group around an interior patio, see his essay in this part.

Jericho Road

Driving wooden piles to support the cement foundation of a Jericho Road modular house

them again. When innovators activate plans to enter well-established systems, those comfortably ensconced within the challenged systems look for ways to stymie innovation. This is a predictable response—and another factor that planners must consider.

Our modular houses were solid, but the process of preparing for and installing them was frustrating, if not wild, and more expensive than the manufacturer claimed it would be. Before taking delivery of the modulars, we had to hire local contractors to prepare foundations and supply utility lines, but only after "setters" had put the houses in place could we hire local electricians and plumbers to connect the electrical and water service. A setting schedule gone off track could be costly, since plumbing and electrical contractors threatened to move to other jobs if they were not paid for the work as scheduled—another example of post-disaster supply-and-demand economics. I remember clearly the evening the first modular rolled into the neighborhood, trucked in from Texas. The transport firm wanted us to take delivery, but we told them that we had contracted for the house to be set upon delivery, by another firm who were to bring in a crane or a bulldozer, and that we could not take delivery until the setting was accomplished. This "discussion" went late into the night and was eventually resolved in our favor, thanks to the lawyers on our team. In another instance, we had to raise the modular unit forty-five feet in the air, where it literally spun in the wind, in order to set it without cutting down a mature tree on the skinny lot. On another lot, we had to wait three months for a water meter to be installed before we could set the house that had been delivered. We finally turned from modular to stick-built housing because we could not realize the savings in time and money that we expected. The modular industry was simply not well enough integrated.

Jericho Road

Jericho Road's first modular house arriving in the neighborhood to be set on the lot from which the photograph was taken

LANDSCAPING

Many of our decisions about Jericho Road's investments in landscaping came down to questions of what future maintenance homeowners would want or be able to undertake. There was not much space to landscape on our lots. The front yards were small, perhaps twenty-nine by ten feet; there were two six-foot-wide strips of land on each side of the houses; and the backyards measured approximately twenty-nine by twenty feet. We decided to fence the backyards for privacy and the added feeling of safety. The questions then were "Shall we plant a traditional lawn? Will the homeowner want to maintain the grass?" Or, "Do we want to plant a wild grass or even a vine?" We decided "yes" to traditional lawns and explored both seeding yards and laying sod. For a while, we even used grant funding to provide new homeowners with push mowers, hoses, and sprinklers. Another design idea that elicited many opinions was a picket fence in front of the homes. We decided to invest in wrought-iron fences instead, and they seemed to make the houses really pop. We always had to replace or build new sidewalks, and when there were no curbs on the blocks, we struggled to provide them, although construction and maintenance of curbs should have been the city's responsibility.

The following anecdote about our efforts to help "green" the neighborhood reveals something of the ups and downs we faced.[30] I spoke to the residents of a block on which we were about to begin building, asking

30 A simple way to determine the wealth of a neighborhood is to assay the number of trees. Viewing on Google Earth the neighborhood where Jericho Road's projects are, one sees that there is no tree cover. Properties of higher value just blocks away have lush green canopies.

them if they wanted us to plant some shade trees.[31] The residents, who were all elderly, said, "Sure." Borrowing a pickup truck and a trailer, I collected twenty-two crape myrtles from the nonprofit Parkway Partners and placed them in a storage area at the cathedral. I promised the clergy they would remain there one week, but I knew that the process would take a "bit" longer. In fact, it took about six weeks of work to get those trees planted: obtaining approval from the city and utility company took five weeks, and the actual planting required an additional week. As I began to plant the trees, which were four feet tall, some of the older residents refused them, explaining that they had agreed to *trees* and that when I had made the offer, they had imagined mature crape myrtles, which reach at least fifteen feet. I won a few over, but I eventually moved about one third of the young trees to other locations.

FRUSTRATIONS AND HEARTBREAKS

Building a home and then selling it to a qualified first-time homeowner is an amazing experience. Sitting in the closing attorney's office with our new buyers, we could get pretty emotional, for them and because we believed that we were helping to revitalize our beloved city. But closing the sale on one of our houses did not mean that we ceased to be involved with the purchasers. In fact, our single most difficult task was supporting the new homeowners' efforts to make repairs while encouraging them to undertake routine maintenance independently. We addressed issues that were our responsibility, but we also provided new filters for air-conditioning units and showed homeowners how to install them. Eventually extracting ourselves from their ownership process was a complicated dance, but one that brought them—and therefore us—incredible rewards.

Home building in a low-income, high-crime neighborhood also had its heartbreaks, professional and personal. One beautiful day, just before Thanksgiving, we heard shots half a block away and rushed over to join a small crowd around a dying boy—a new homeowner's son. We later learned that the shooting had been over a girl. Banks would ask us not to send our "type of client" for prescreening. Tools were stolen out of our trucks while we were working fifteen feet away. Hundreds of tires were dumped on our lots. We unknowingly used contaminated drywall from China in four of our homes, and we had to replace it at great expense. Builders walked away from jobs that were half finished. Backlogs in the city's building permits department and a shortage of water meters cost us months in construction delays. Building inspectors intimated that payments to them would accelerate the permit process. We never paid.

31 This was the same block on which we built our first home. I spent hours there pretending to sweep or measure, hoping to meet residents on the block. This turned out to be an important and successful strategy. When neighbors saw thieves taking copper pipe or other materials from our construction sites, they called me, because they had developed a vested interest in Jericho Road's success. These were the best worst calls I got: I told myself that although we were being robbed, we were also building networks.

Jericho Road

The Coltons and their Jericho Road house

A potential funder offered us significant support *if* we agreed to build houses that the organization favored but were not appropriate for our mission. We passed. While news reporters interviewed me, and with 100 volunteer carpenters on site, I watched as two police detectives searched drainpipes on the block for a weapon they believed had been used the night before. In many different ways, these sorrows cut deep.

Revitalization is work that necessarily challenges community power dynamics, however functional they may be. In the neighborhood where I worked there were strong class and racial tensions and they flared up often as post-Katrina rebuilding became more chaotic or power relationships changed. Overall, the community that Jericho Road was trying to serve supported us well.[32] But we did encounter people who tried to bully us by playing race and class cards. We won battles with neighborhood bullies in the courts, in the councilperson's office, and, most powerfully, in community meetings. Without strong neighborhood partners whose trust we had earned and maintained, we would not have been able to counter those who felt their power bases threatened by our work. One example illustrates well the neighborhood support that was critical to our success. During our blight campaign, a woman accused Jericho Road of pressuring the city to demolish her property for reasons she claimed

32 As an outsider working in this predominantly black neighborhood, I was occasionally the focus of anger or frustration, and some of it was probably justified. There were residents who called me "white devil," yet outside the neighborhood I was sometimes called "nigger lover." My front porch was doused with a flammable liquid and set on fire; the flames reached fifteen feet, consuming my porch. I add this personal and unsettling detail to emphasize that folks who do community redevelopment work face risks. It is important that helping organizations understand these risks and know how to face them; Jericho Road did. Most often the worst one risks is professional or personal slander. I lost some friends but gained others.

were related to class and race; she was loud, and the confrontation was ugly. We invited her to come to a community meeting so that she could make her case. She was confident of winning, until one resident asked her why she had let the disrepair on her lot endanger the neighborhood—pieces of her building were literally falling into the street. She had no answer and left the meeting after apologizing to those present.

One final comment concerning the framing of the recovery context in New Orleans: In many of the debates about what to fix, how to undertake fixes, and who would get paid to do the work of fixing, locals opposed national and even international players. In many ways, New Orleans is a very cosmopolitan city, and in others it is powerfully parochial—particularly when it comes to deciding who is a New Orleanian. Before Katrina, to be considered a local you had to have been born here and have family here. After the storm, at least for some years, you could join the ranks of locals, regardless of your origin, if you were here during the storm and could tell a Katrina survival story. Nonlocals, however, came to play a significant role in the rebuilding process, since the money to rebuild came largely from outside sources and guidelines for program expenditures were often written elsewhere. Tensions between locals and outsiders over the control of recovery funds often sabotaged efforts to move forward. Some outsiders who arrived to participate in the rebuilding process brought expertise in their fields that was badly needed, and some insiders with whom they interacted understood how best to position their efforts for the best outcomes. Successes came when each group recognized the importance of the other's contributions and a collaborative process was the result.

CONCLUSION

In *Rebuilding Urban Places After Disaster: Lessons from Hurricane Katrina*, Eugenie Birch and Susan Wachter write,

> Disasters have a disproportionate effect on urban places. Dense by definition, cities and their environs face major disruptions in their complex, interdependent environmental, economic, and social systems. Weaknesses not readily apparent in pre-disaster times surface as long-standing structural and substantive problems become prominent: environmental abuses are exposed; the local economy falters; municipal services collapse; social places disappear. The post-Katrina plight of New Orleans and several smaller cities on the Gulf Coast exemplifies this phenomenon.[33]

I agree with these observations, but I would suggest a further qualifier with regard to New Orleans. The weaknesses that Birch and Wachter

33 Eugenie L. Birch and Susan M. Wachter, eds., *Rebuilding Urban Places After Disaster: Lessons from Hurricane Katrina* (Philadelphia: University of Pennsylvania Press, 2006), 1.

highlight were readily apparent in New Orleans before the storm. Therefore, a key question should be: Have we—"we" defined as all of us who would claim citizenship—taken enough responsibility for the city's condition pre-Katrina? Despite the euphoria and pride that have accompanied our successes in post-Katrina recovery, we must examine critically our current redevelopment efforts, in order to ensure that the New Orleans of the future will be better governed and more socially equitable, economically productive, and environmentally sustainable than it was before the storm.

Lawrence Vale and Thomas Campanella conclude *The Resilient City* with twelve "Axioms of Resilience" that ring true to me after my experience in New Orleans.[34] In a similar spirit and as a practitioner, I offer three axioms that may help frame how we analyze New Orleans's recovery and, possibly, the past and future recoveries of other cities:

- Nothing that happens in relation to a disaster is fully understandable in the moment, including what happens in the recovery phase. There are simply too many moving parts and too many unintended and unexpected consequences. Uncertainty and tension were always present during the more than six years that I worked in New Orleans's recovery community.
- Recovery priorities are driven by power, and so in all cities recovery development will be inequitable, just as normal development is inequitable. In New Orleans, flooded neighborhoods that were apparently similar in terms of pre-Katrina social and economic conditions received extremely varied levels of support. For example, Central City was the beneficiary of hundreds of millions of dollars in recovery aid, while Hollygrove was almost completely overlooked.
- Recovery is highly dynamic in its direction, momentum, and ultimate achievement as power shifts. In New Orleans, the ever-changing conditions for federal and state monies and large private foundation support contributed significantly to the dynamism of recovery efforts. The private foundations with which I spoke were especially concerned that the formulation of a master plan for rebuilding the city was so slow. They wanted to know that the city had a "plan" before making commitments, and I had to respond again and again that there was not yet a plan. The recovery process was manic and painful.

A natural disaster produces a potent opportunity for communal introspection. New Orleans was nearly broken, shrinking, and sinking before Hurricane Katrina made landfall on August 29, 2005. Yet locals did not widely acknowledge the city's fragile condition. Katrina exposed

34 Lawrence J. Vale and Thomas J. Campanella, eds., *The Resilient City: How Modern Cities Recover From Disaster* (New York: Oxford University Press, 2005), 35, 339–53.

the inequities and pervasive failures of New Orleans's infrastructural systems and civic institutions, and the city must continue to address the fundamental problems that the storm exacerbated. Recovery and redevelopment will always be contingent on the state of an affected community when disaster strikes. Certainly it is helpful to analyze the needs of a post-disaster community with regard to the type of disaster that it experienced—hurricane, foreclosure wave, earthquake, or civil collapse—but in undertaking recovery work it is equally important to understand the challenges that the community faced and the capacities that it manifested *before* disaster struck.

Working with Jericho Road was the hardest, most joyous, and most distressing thing I had ever been lucky enough to do. We were able to deliver on some projects and not on others.[35] We never foresaw the worst hurdles, and that's a good thing, because we might not have stayed the course if we had known how difficult it would be.

35 My biggest defeat was in failing to finish the cleanup of a brownfield site into which I had put enormous time and effort. I still hope to see rebuilding there one day.

STILL SEARCHING FOR HIGHER GROUND

BYRON MOUTON

The editors' discussion with Byron Mouton addressed issues of neighborhood revitalization on the scale of "domestic infill," focusing on the work of URBANbuild, the program he directs at the Tulane School of Architecture, and on the work of his office bildDESIGN. Residential projects completed since Katrina have offered Mouton the opportunity to explore pedagogical techniques involving the overlap of academic research and professional practice. As of 2011, six years post-Katrina, the URBANbuild program has designed and built six houses in various neighborhoods of New Orleans in collaboration with the nonprofit Neighborhood Housing Services. Mouton hopes these will serve as prototypes in further community redevelopment citywide. Anthony Fontenot, Carol McMichael Reese, and Maureen Long conducted this interview on August 19, 2010.

FONTENOT: What was the original mission that URBANbuild set out to accomplish?

MOUTON: When we started the program [in 2005], the goal was to give students an opportunity to build a house. In the most basic sense, we wanted to teach them how to build a house and give them a chance to realize a design project. The week Katrina hit, the program was on its way. I was helping Doug Harmon with it; he really initiated the idea.[1]

REESE: To what extent was the first iteration of URBANbuild dependent on the HUD grant?[2]

MOUTON: It was very dependent on it. The HUD grant gave us some credibility and provided us with some resource funding for purchasing

1 Doug Harmon is an adjunct associate professor and the director of the Graduate Architecture Program in the School of Architecture at Tulane University.

2 HUD awarded $300,000 to URBANbuild in 2006 through its Universities Rebuilding America Partnership Community Design program. The stated goal of the grant was to "provide quality affordable housing to traditionally underserved communities and [to] create solutions to rehabilitate and revitalize areas of the city historically dominated by blight and abandonment." See Kathryn Hobgood, "Tulane Receives $300,000 HUD Grant," Tulane Office of Public Relations, March 15, 2006, tulane.edu. See also Deborah Gans's essay on page 293, which describes a collaborative venture involving faculty from the Pratt Institute in Brooklyn and the New Jersey Institute of Technology to rebuild the Plum Orchard neighborhood of New Orleans East. This venture was funded in March 2006 by the same HUD program.

tools. It covered small portions of the salaries for some of the people. Really, what makes the program successful is our collaboration with the nonprofit, federally funded Neighborhood Housing Services (NHS). There is no way we could do this without that collaboration. And last year we collaborated with Make It Right (MIR). These organizations have the ability and skills to acquire lots and match families with subsidized funding. They are successful and are proving to work quite well, and the collaboration among nonprofits—the university, NHS, and MIR—allows us to run the operation fairly smoothly. They trust us. They take some risks. They let us do things that aren't familiar, they are willing to listen, and they are interested in participating in the investigation. They provide the funding for what we fabricate.

FONTENOT: When you were setting up URBANbuild, what were the some of the precedents and models you were looking at?

MOUTON: There were the other well-known design-build programs, such as Sam Mockbee's Rural Studio and Studio 804 in Kansas. But, for me, I've always liked building things. I remember finishing my formal education in undergrad, leaving school, and then realizing that I had no idea what I was doing. I was fortunate enough to work on construction projects that were well designed and interesting—and with good people. I saw the program as an opportunity to share that experience.

FONTENOT: How has URBANbuild's mission changed from its inception to the present?

MOUTON: During the first year [the fall semester of 2006 through the spring semester of 2007], I realized that the program forced students to work on a single project collectively, act professionally, and respectfully hold each other accountable. So what I am really excited about now with the program is not that we can make interesting projects—let's just assume that is what is going to happen no matter what—but that through this process students learn to be diplomatic. The students learn how to negotiate differences while bargaining and challenging each other in an effort to get what they want. Most important, in a school where, typically, strong designers are, let's say, praised, set on a pedestal, and admired, it is really interesting to see a group of students work collectively on a project and watch some of them realize that there is more to this mission, this profession, than just being a great designer. Some of them are fantastic at managing people, some are great with marketing, and some of them are great with detailing. Frankly, what is really great about the URBANbuild program now is that it has become a leveling field. With each project, we begin with a new group of students. Some of them are used to being in the limelight, and it is interesting to watch them struggle with unfamiliar territory. You also watch people who have not always been the center of attention rise to the top, and that aspect has been really nice. From a teacher's point of view, that has been incredibly rewarding, and it was not expected. Based on my previous experience of teaching design studio, I assumed that we would begin by establishing the perimeters and then pushing the students to get them to think about various aspects, and that they would learn through a familiar method of comparing ideas. I was surprised to discover that it was not at all like that with this program. They really are forced to collaborate responsibly.

REESE: In the beginning, there was one particular set of course scenarios, and I wonder how that has changed over time?

MOUTON: Actually there were two studios that were happening simultaneously: One was called the Macro Studio and the other was the Micro Studio, so there were simultaneous investigations occurring at different scales.

REESE: Was any of the research that was developed in the Macro Studio brought into the Micro Studio? How did those interface? Has URBANbuild lost anything, given that the Macro Studio is no longer taught?

MOUTON: In my opinion, they were never properly fused. There was separation from the very beginning, but not in a negative way. The directors of the macro research were very interested in global urban ideas, while not always giving attention to the very rich quality of some of the local ideas about the urban fabric. Because the macro study was happening in a very amorphous way on a larger scale, it did not readily influence what we were doing in concentrating on the making of a home. On the other hand, the homes that were being developed with the micro research did in fact influence and infiltrate the macro research, primarily because it was easier to take the parts and pieces that we were developing and then inventively assemble them. In other words, they could make neighborhoods using our parts and components. In fact, now there is a discussion among some faculty members who suggest that we should move away from the single-family prototype and move toward the multifamily prototype. I think it is a great idea, but we can't build those with students in the same way.

The URBANbuild Micro Studio has been developed in response to very real limitations regarding time. In the fall semester, students develop several prototypes; then they vote and select one. They then develop drawings for review by the city, and a site is determined. We break ground in early January, and the house is constructed by the end of May using unskilled labor. We do have some people out there who help us, but it would not be easy to take on larger projects that venture into the macro territory with those same limitations. So although the macro research was great, insofar as the studio developed content-rich ideas, I have to say that its work never really infiltrated the Micro Studio. We were always doing something different. The macro researchers were interested in their agenda, and we micro directors were very interested in our agenda.

As someone who is trying to maintain a practice in the city and satisfy my responsibility at Tulane as a professor of practice, I like very much the fusing of what I am doing in my office with what I am doing with

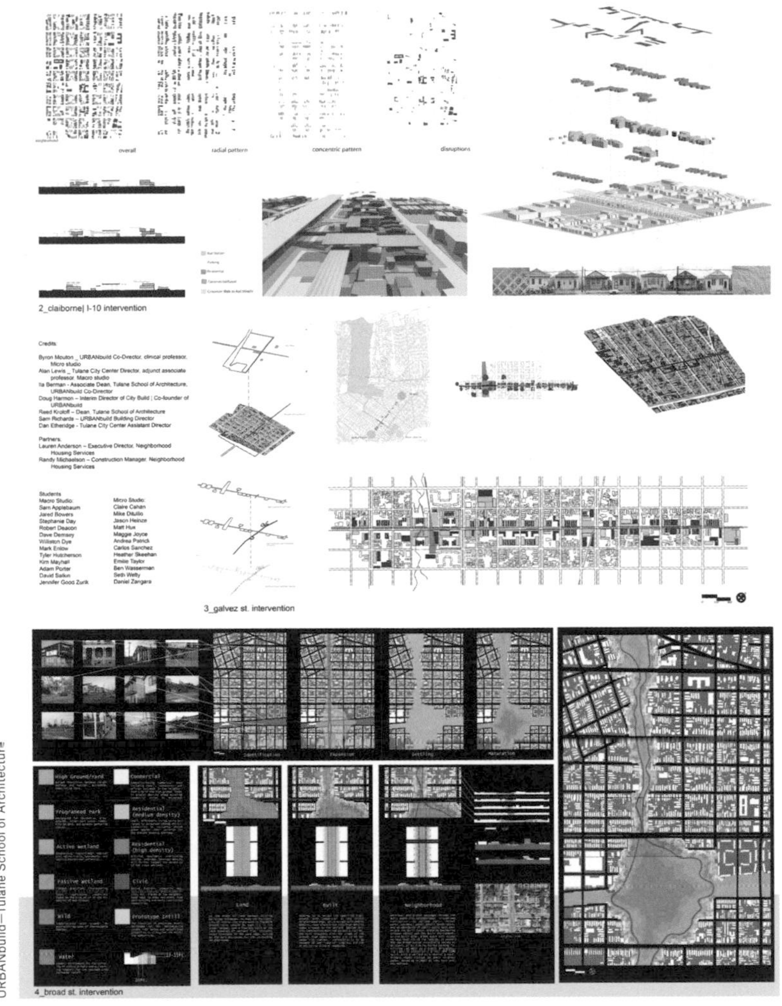

Tulane URBANbuild, Spring/Summer 2006

students in the field. I think it is great, and the students enjoy it. In my opinion, it decreases what used to be a very large gap between professional and academic research, and it appears that the gap is being reduced more and more. If we take into account new technologies that decrease the effort to go from what is drawn to what is made, we are already talking with fabricators in a much more immediate way. And I think that is the future of professional education. Students will be introduced to construction methodology earlier rather than later, and I think that will allow them to be better and more inventive at what they do.

FONTENOT: In the past in architectural education, many believed that students should learn about architecture through a direct exposure to construction. This idea of valuing practice and the "craft of making" distinguished itself from a more academic approach.

URBANbuild—Tulane School of Architecture

URBANbuild #1, front (street) facade, 1922 Dumaine Street

MOUTON: *Craft* is a funny word. With that term comes all this history. It is a nostalgic term. We can't afford to make these prototypes for "underprivileged" neighborhoods in a highly crafted way. We've got to rely much more upon off-the-shelf standards. With the exception of some parts and components, I refer to these projects as Home Depot houses. We really try to get all the material and components from local vendors.

REESE: As editors, we are interested in the instigation of endeavors and projects post-Katrina and in questioning how sustainable they are over time.

MOUTON: What potentially threatens the program is how to find funding for the educators. The HUD money was used to pay people who, like me, spent quite a bit of extra time getting the houses built. That extra time was covered by the HUD grant, so that is a little tricky at the moment, now that the HUD money is gone.

REESE: So what you are saying is that this program, which requires that you break ground in January and finish construction in May, requires more time, much more time, than you would be paid for if you were simply teaching an option studio. In terms of sustainability, is there currently a problem of how to pay you for all the time that you spend?

MOUTON: Yes, and not just me, but two other people as well who help with construction and budget management.

FONTENOT: Outside of those three main people, are there other external contractors and workers?

MOUTON: There are. I am the architect of record, and Tony Christiana is the contractor of record. He is the contractor I do most of my office projects with. In addition, we have our subcontractors: licensed electricians, plumbers, and mechanical and HVAC consultants. Outside of that, the students do every single other thing except hang and float the drywall.

URBANbuild—Tulane School of Architecture

URBANbuild #5, exterior on Make It Right (MIR) site, 1724 Deslonde Street

To give you an idea, we work Monday through Saturday. If we don't meet the deadline of the week by the end of Saturday, then we work Sunday. That is just the way it is. Now in fairness I am not there all day every day. Some days I need to be there all day, and other days I get the students set up and then leave.

FONTENOT: What amount of time are the students spending on site?

MOUTON: They are there at least fifty hours a week, and they love that. All the work is complete by sunset, and then they go home. They try to trick themselves into believing that they can go out and have a good time, but they realize pretty quickly that, as young as they are, their bodies are not really prepared for that kind of work; they are exhausted. It is really interesting, because they begin to develop a real work ethic.

REESE: How many hours of credit do they get? Do they take other classes?

MOUTON: They get twelve hours of credit [per semester], plus they get their community service credit.[3] They also get IDP credit [from the Intern Development Program of the National Council of Architectural Registration Boards]. Some of them take classes at night. I've had students who absolutely needed a class to graduate, and so they would have to leave the site one day a week, for example. It has been pretty flexible, and it works.

REESE: So in the sustainability equation for continuing the URBANbuild program, do you feel that the academic environment's ability to fund educators and their pedagogical goals is more an issue than the nonprofit community partners' ability to fund their operations?

MOUTON: Fortunately, we have been able to make it work. Last year

3 Post-Katrina, Tulane instituted a public service requirement for graduation; see tulane.edu.

[academic year 2009–2010] was the most difficult so far, because Neighborhood Housing Services had moved from their old facilities to a new facility, and they were working to get settled. All of a sudden it was time to start the URBANbuild project, but given that business operations don't run according to an academic calendar, they did not have the funding ready to go, because two of the previous URBANbuild projects had not sold. So, at the last minute Dean [Kenneth] Schwartz and I seized an opportunity for the students to collaborate on the development of a project that had been started in my office. It was a duplex project that MIR had asked bildDESIGN to develop.

This is interesting because it raises a question that is often asked: Are these projects really student-run, or are they heavily influenced by the teacher? It is always blurry and, quite frankly, the answer is yes to both. No matter how we look at it, I'm responsible for the budget and the safety and the performance of the building. There are times when I have to say, "Don't do that." Or I will suggest, "Maybe you should think about this." I'm pretty persuasive and sometimes demanding, because I have to be. At a certain point it is no longer an academic exercise; it is a professional exercise, and I am liable.

I was nervous about engaging the students in bild's MIR project; I did not know how students would feel about continuing to develop a scheme that I had initiated in my office. MIR proposed to team us up with one of their selected general contractors, because their projects are twice the scale of the projects we typically do, and they offered us access to systems and technology that we had never been able to afford. We decided to go for it, and it worked out pretty well, because we had developed just a preliminary scheme, so there was room for student development and involvement.

There is a side story, too. NHS did offer us an opportunity to renovate and restore a house they had. I thought that could be pretty interesting, but when I went to see the house, I was not convinced. My response professionally and academically was that it made no sense to restore that house. It really was not worth restoring, and we are not training students to be repair people. In my opinion, that is something the preservationists should be initiating. I'm not interested in teaching our students to be carpenters. I'm not interested in their finishing school so that they can work as electricians or repair moldings and scrape off paint. We are training architects to think about issues and execute those thoughts through the production of physical form. Often we talk about the difference between replication and design. It is a pretty loaded conversation. So that is why we chose to work with MIR.

MIR was really cool, and they asked if we could help them with other issues. So the students were asked to deal with the landscape problem associated with Bayou Bienvenue, the old cypress swamp that was killed by saltwater intrusion. One group of students took an interest in that, and they looked into methods of revitalizing that body of water. A second group addressed the issue of urban agriculture. MIR wanted to purchase a herd of goats, hire a goatherd, and use the animals to maintain the terrain, which is common practice in other places. So they asked us to design a goat house! We talked about having a little fun with the idea, and then we noticed that there were flatbed trailers left all over the site from the modular homes that had been delivered. I suggested that they let us build a goat house on a trailer, and then they could decide where to park it later. So that was the project that allowed the students to do something that they felt they had authored from the beginning.

REESE: Did the students build the duplex?

MOUTON: We were building the house as a duplex, but it sold while it was under construction to a couple who wanted it as a single. Fortunately, our scheme was designed to be easily convertible into a single-family dwelling with the removal of the party wall. We drew it and marketed it that way. When this couple saw it in the brochure, they decided it was the one they wanted. He is a musician, and she studied at Savannah College of Art and Design (SCAD). They were going to live on one side, and the wife, the mother—they have two children—was going to use the other side as her painting studio. They are an interesting couple from the Lower Ninth Ward who made the decision to come back. I don't think many people like that would return if MIR were not happening here.

In terms of the house's design, many things were changed from the preliminary bild plan, and the students got to use solar systems as well as new cooling and heating systems. The house is LEED platinum certified. We could not have afforded those achievements without the MIR collaboration—we were able to gain access to all sorts of new technologies and vendors. The students met an incredible range of product providers. I learned a lot from that project. It was a phenomenal, priceless educational experience.

At the same time, the students were also able to be quite critical of the way things are happening in the city. All of a sudden we were in the middle of the MIR zone working on a house, amid many other houses that were being fabricated in an effort to rebuild a neighborhood. That was the first time that a macro discussion encroached upon the micro world—a great contrast to the context of our previous URBANbuild projects. The first four houses we built were infill houses, and we couldn't lose, because there was already a great existing fabric that was working. It was neglected, but it was working. The MIR experience allowed the students to realize that making a house doesn't always equate to making a part of a neighborhood.

FONTENOT: What is the difference in the URBANbuild and MIR budgets? What is MIR's current definition of affordability?

MOUTON: In the beginning, they didn't have one. Let's face it, even they will admit this. The program has a star at the top who attracts much attention, and because of that, many donations are provided. The staff were are all originally laymen, and they were hired to produce a certain quantity of buildings in a certain amount of time, so they hit the ground running with very little planning and preparation. Step one was to get something built to gain recognition. So for the first round of design proposals, star architects were invited to participate. For the second round, they explained that they wanted to incorporate what they had learned from the first phase, and they gave us designers stricter limits on cost per square foot.

Regarding the definition of affordability, there were two considerations in evaluating MIR's success: (a) how inexpensively could a house be built and (b) how inexpensively could it be operated? MIR succeeded with (b), but they failed tremendously with (a). The high-design houses were expensive to build. They knew that from the beginning, but they were committed to getting it done. So, when they began to replicate the first houses, they stripped them down. MIR did this independently without consulting the architects, and that rightfully upset many of them. MIR now realizes that was a mistake; they really do. And so, for example, after our scheme was built, another family wanted the same house, but they wanted it for single-family occupancy, not as the original duplex design. MIR consulted me and asked me to help them with the revisions and reductions, whereas in the past they'd just done it themselves. It was a huge step for them to ask the architects to help them prioritize what should be kept and what should be eliminated.

REESE: Was this a one-off experience, both for MIR and URBANbuild?

MOUTON: MIR asked if we would be interested in running another studio with students, and I had to say, No, because that is not our business. We are not here to provide a service; it is not fair to our local colleagues. One should pay an architect to do that. But it was an interesting dilemma, because they were not making that offer as a way to save money—they offered to pay us. Apparently, they enjoyed the energy of the youthful minds and the care that was provided. So to answer your question, I don't think it will be a one-off. I think this will grow into something else. They would like to maintain a relationship. I'd rather say that the experience has allowed us to realize that URBANbuild could establish productive relationships with many organizations. That really is the point, and that really is what we have to do.

FONTENOT: What are the similarities and differences between URBANbuild and other rebuilding programs, not only MIR but also the Global Green project in the Holy Cross neighborhood? What could you learn from these other programs that might be helpful in order to move forward with URBANbuild?

MOUTON: MIR claims to be trying to develop a neighborhood, and when it is all done and filled, they will have a neighborhood. But they started by thinking about houses as independent, freestanding, autonomous

Will Crocker. URBANbuild—Tulane School of Architecture

URBANbuild #3, exterior from street corner, 1900 Seventh Street

objects. They could have established height restrictions; they could have asked for front porch and stoop conditions. They could have made some effort to develop consistency from the very beginning. That did not happen. But when I compare URBANbuild—to be self-critical and reflective—I see that we are guilty in some of the same ways. It is true that we always ask the students to start by looking at what is there. And every one of our schemes has a front porch and stoop in relationship to the street. There is always a place for someone to sit outside and have an exchange with the neighbors. But frankly, we are now beyond the point of being timid or bashful about trying to introduce unfamiliar architectural language. We have been criticized for that. We get as much hate mail as we do love mail. Frankly, I think that the older neighborhoods can handle progressive design on infill lots, because there is such a strong, authentic stock in them. Before we start replicating stylistically what is there, we should fix what is there. In all fairness, MIR doesn't have an existing fabric to rely on.

I like the Global Green projects in Holy Cross very much, because they were first invested in community.[4] From the get-go, the message

4 For a description of the Global Green project, see the interview with Matt Berman and Andrew Kotchen in Part IV of this book.

of that program was "Here is a very special place on higher ground in a neighborhood that is worth revitalizing. Let's start with what we have." That is very similar to what we are doing in Central City with NHS.

REESE: Are there other nonprofits that are willing to partner with these types of programs? Tulane has a wonderful partnership with NHS, but have others come forward?

MOUTON: I've approached some. I've spoken with a representative from Jericho Road [the Episcopal Housing Initiative], and he seemed to like our work. He discussed the possibility of a collaboration with his board, but they would rather do things that are a bit more conventional, and I think their reasoning is based on respect for the existing, historic residential fabric. They don't want to be viewed as treating the "underprivileged" members of society as guinea pigs, which is a criticism that we get sometimes. The people who contact us and who love what we are doing tend to be younger people, some of whom are from the neighborhoods where we have worked and some of whom are not—it is fifty-fifty now. Global Green is a nice mix. They've got the funding, they've got the access to the technologies, they are working in an older neighborhood, and, interestingly, I don't think people have been so critical of what they have done stylistically. It has been fairly well accepted.

FONTENOT: Why do you think that is the case?

MOUTON: Because I don't think they appear to be stepping on anyone's toes. Or let's put it this way, I don't think anyone reads their investment there as taking what is not theirs. What has happened there in terms of rebuilding is similar to what has happened in Central City; the difference is that Central City has been struggling with more extreme issues of poverty and crime. I keep waiting for major improvements to occur, but the area is still struggling. It's a tough part of town.[5]

REESE: Has NHS been able to sell all its URBANbuild projects?

MOUTON: Yes. They've actually sold pretty quickly. People have been interested in them immediately, but to qualify for the subsidies is not easy. People applying for help have to show proof of employment with the same employer, I think, for the past three years. And they must be within a certain income bracket, and—this was the shocker—they have to have an almost perfect credit score, which is almost impossible. So what NHS does is help people improve their scores. They put people through training.

FONTENOT: Does URBANbuild develop a new model for each project? Do you aspire to reproduce your models?

MOUTON: It has always been an aspiration. We set out to develop prototypes, but not one has yet been reproduced. The idea was to give these schemes to NHS and let them reproduce them. But NHS says—and

---

5 Laura Kurgan's essay in Part VII deals with urban planning responses to crime and recidivism rates in Central City.

they are right—that the fancy parts such as the moving shutters make them unaffordable to reproduce. My response is that the schemes would work just as well if some of the extras were removed. For example, the box with the polycarbonate hurricane shutters could be provided with salvaged shutters. In the "S" scheme, the one that was featured on the Sundance Channel documentary *Architecture School*, it would be possible to reduce the cantilevers. So my attitude is that the ball is in their court.[6] If they want to reproduce the prototypes, then the best idea would be to get a contractor involved and build four of a particular type in a three-block radius at the same time to gain some efficiency and affordability.

FONTENOT: What does URBANbuild need in order to successfully reproduce these prototypes? In other words, what is currently lacking that would enable the program to fully realize its goal of multiple reproductions?

MOUTON: The obvious answer is always funding. But if we had the grant funding, what would we do with it? We would need a facility in which to tool up and produce these houses rain or shine. I think Studio 804, run by Dan Rockhill at the University of Kansas, is the best program out there. They have invented ways to make homes with an assembly of parts, and they produce impressive projects. They make and store the parts in their facility, and then they assemble them onsite. Three of the five URBANbuild houses have been made using prefabricated panelized systems. Finding a way to specialize in the fabrication of manageable parts that could be easily transported would be the next step.

REESE: Your pedagogic aim, it seems to me, has been to continually generate creative ideas. So if you were to engage in the process of reproduction, would that still qualify as an URBANbuild project?

MOUTON: We would love to continue producing prototypes, with the hope that they would be picked up by a producer and replicated.

FONTENOT: With or without the involvement of URBANbuild, as in a full team of students building them?

MOUTON: With a changed involvement. Some of the schemes that the students developed that were not built consisted of pieces that could be rearranged on a site in different ways. We call these core pieces. So let's say that we develop a scheme that relies on the use of core elements and that could fit on a lot thirty feet wide by 120 feet deep and also on a lot forty feet wide by sixty feet deep—substandard lots. If we could design these core components in such a way that they could be efficiently produced, then the students could be responsible for creating master plans and rearranging these components on various sites. Recently we gathered all the projects we've done so far and made a little booklet. The idea was that we could use the booklet to go after more support and

6 Robert Lloyd, "'Architecture School' on the Sundance Channel," *Los Angeles Times*, August 20, 2008.

Will Crocker. URBANbuild—Tulane School of Architecture

URBANbuild #4, exterior showing rear porch, 2036 Seventh Street

funding. In retrospect, the first semester of URBANbuild produced a really great assortment of custom homes. We did not end up with prototypes, and that was criticized. The second year we decided to think about what it means to develop prototypical ideas. The schemes composed of core pieces are good examples. The components are solid, private, and secure, and they also contain "wet" areas—bathrooms and kitchens. A thin lightweight fabric groups these components together in various configurations on diverse sites. Stacked vertically, they produce a scheme with a reduced footprint. After five years, we have a body of work that we can use to get more attention. We have built almost a million dollars' worth of homes: that is amazing!

FONTENOT: What is the average price per square foot?

MOUTON: We are building them for about 100 bucks a square foot. That is not market rate; the labor is free. The market rate would probably be about $125 a square foot. But we could reduce that in a number of ways, with simplification.

REESE: What is the advantage to the community of URBANbuild? In other words, I see a clear advantage to the Tulane School of Architecture, to its students, and to you as a faculty member and as a practitioner. But what is the contribution to the community?

MOUTON: I think it is education, exposure to ideas. I talk to students about this: When you are young and trying to convince clients to pursue a design path but don't yet have a body of work to show, you can only show them drawings. Yet no matter how wonderful your representation techniques are, the drawings are not reality. At some point, you are lucky enough to get something built, and that's step one. Eventually you have a small body of work. That is why many architects are not successful until they are in their forties, because it takes that much time to have

URBANbuild—Tulane School of Architecture

URBANbuild #6, exterior, 1821 Toledano Street

enough work to convince people to have confidence in the proposed ideas.

What is interesting about how this body of work affects the community—and I am referring to the neighborhoods where we have built—is that it allows younger people to become invested. Now there is the threat of gentrification. Three of the five URBANbuild houses have been sold to people who are not from the neighborhoods where they were built and who do not belong to the community's racial majority. And that has been criticized.

But there is another community out there that URBANbuild has been helping, and it is the architectural community. Many young or small firms are bringing their clients or potential clients to see these examples of new ideas and new materials that are being used. That has been a discovery. Some may say that is self-serving, and I don't know how to respond to that.

REESE: Is the program sustainable for you as an individual?

MOUTON: I would hope that the next step for me would be that I'm able to share what I have learned with a younger generation. As with any academic program, as some faculty members move on, part of their responsibility is to bring in the next generation and let them run with it. I'm not saying that I want to do that now, but it's going to happen. It is not as easy for me to run up a ladder as it was ten years ago—that is just the way it is. But I can definitely help. I would always be willing to help with fund-raising and things like that.

FONTENOT: Do you think that this type of architecture would be being built in New Orleans if Katrina had not struck?

MOUTON: We imagined the program before Katrina, so I think something would have happened. Would it have been received in the same way? No. I think that Katrina has forced members of this community to realize that what they have maybe isn't so good. Maybe we need certain things that are better. As a practitioner, I've had an enormous number of people contact bild who are interested in new ideas. More people now want to live in homes that appear to be a little bit different, and I think that is only because of Katrina. It has been five years since Katrina hit and we have built, from the ground up—between bildDESIGN and URBANbuild—fifteen new houses. Without the hurricane, we would not have built so many houses so quickly, and perhaps I would have continued to work on commercial projects. But I love building houses.

PROJECTS
SINGLE-FAMILY HOUSING

Not surprisingly, much of the imaginative and physical effort to recuperate New Orleans has focused on the question of the house. The single-family dwelling is the characteristic residential type in New Orleans and represents a fundamental increment of investment and tractability: houses are being repaired and rebuilt not simply because they must be but because they can be. This is the ur-form of recovery: attention paid directly to individuals, to families.

Reconstruction has also offered designers an opportunity to propose improvements to the nature of the New Orleans house and to riff on its condition. In general, this commentary has engaged two specific paradigms. First is the shotgun, the type that expresses both a sense of local architectural and domestic traditions and an apt modesty in a city that has been overwhelmingly poor. The second type is the slab-on-grade typical of the great wave of suburbanization that became such a dominant feature of New Orleans's postwar morphology. This architecture was completely indifferent to the possibility of flooding, an embodiment of the distortions of sprawl that had come to characterize the city, and it was an embrace of modernization—locally understood as Californiaization—that residents across the U.S. readily adopted as a generic form of spatial consumption.

The proposals gathered here have in common at least four concerns: the elevation of houses to resist flooding, the laying in of an apparatus of sustainability, a sense of practical economy (sometimes realized through prefabrication or factory assembly), and the channeling of a cultural vibe that speaks to the question of New Orleans-ness. There is a certain radicalism in the concerted application of common sense in most of these proposals, and considerations of style—so central to architects—become relatively trivial. To be sure, the construction of numerous units of architectural singularity as demonstration projects raises the question of aggregation, the character of a neighborhood in which each unit is unique. But this concern, too, seems minor. This is not likely to become the uniform paradigm—most of the projects are for infill situations—and the constraints of the small envelope of most of these houses (a typical lot is 40×100 feet) have the effect of muting the visual cacophony. And, as always, formal cavils about the solution recede in the face of the magnitude of the problem.

It is also the case that many of these proposals offer a sense of locality that transcends narrow questions of appearance, investing instead in ideas about climate, materiality, durability, organization, and distribution. These considerations redefine the idea of the indigenous: it is no longer a matter of style only but, even more, a resonance with bioclimatic conditions and operational needs. This is perhaps the most hopeful message of this work, which, in its thoughtfulness and ecological understanding, stands as a rebuke to the typical American housing McProduct.

TARPON HOUSE

COLLEGE OF ARCHITECTURE + PLANNING
+ LANDSCAPE ARCHITECTURE
University of Arizona, Tucson

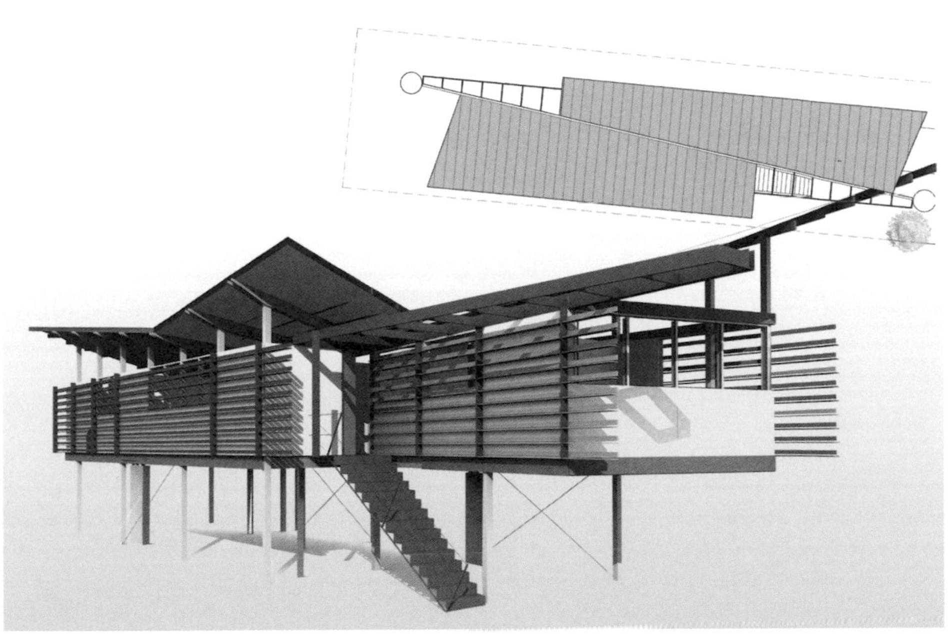

Instructor: John Messina
Designer: Earl Larrabee

Like its fish eponym, *Tarpon House* is designed to breathe in the moist New Orleans atmosphere. Adjustable louvers along the sides of the house allow for controlled natural ventilation, and an inverted roof channels rainwater, which collects in runoff cisterns at each end. The home is elevated above the height recommended for security from flooding.

L9 PIL-AFT: SUBURBAN GERMINATION

GRADUATE SCHOOL OF ARCHITECTURE, PLANNING, AND PRESERVATION

Columbia University, New York City

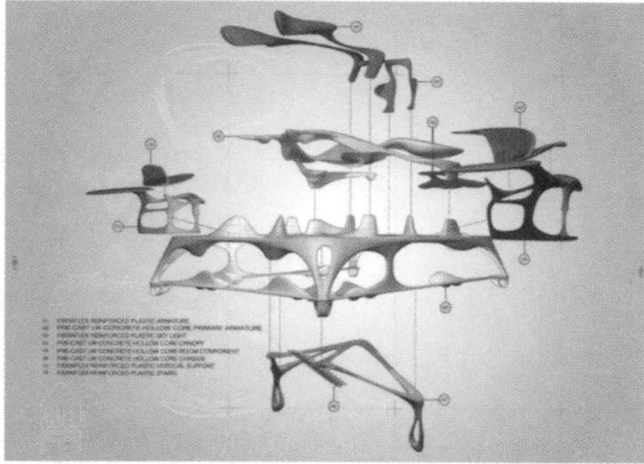

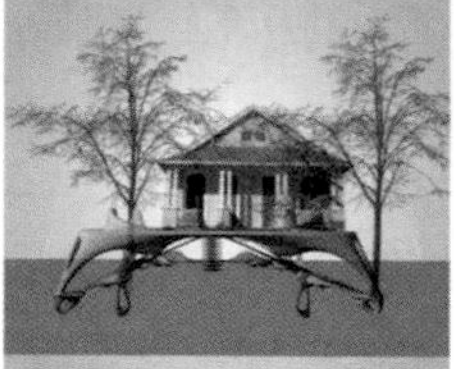

Foundation Elevation with Existing Housing

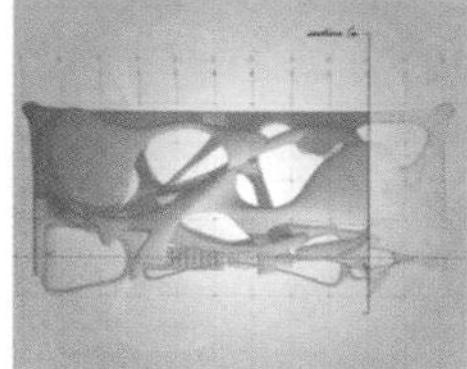

Second Level Plan View

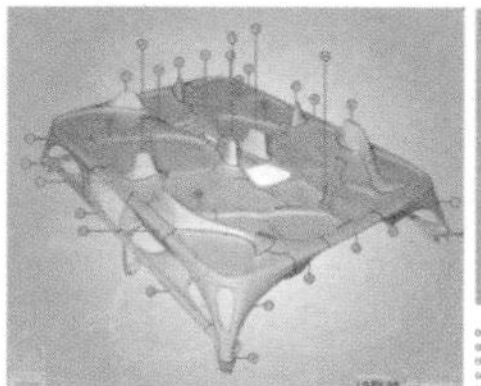

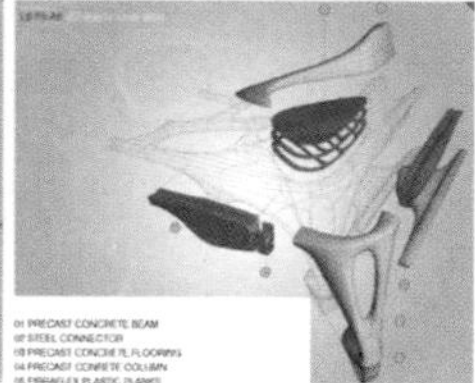

Single Unit Foundation Infrastructure Component

Instructor: Laurie Hawkinson

Designers: Adam N. Hayes, Robert J. Mezquiti

This proposal reimagines the foundational system as one of the publicly provided amenities for the single-family house. The designers present a version created specifically for New Orleans's Lower Ninth Ward, a foundation that elevates the building to a safe height above sea level and protects the home's essential utilities. This raised foundation, visible from the street, also creates new usable spaces at grade.

FLOAT HOUSE

MORPHOSIS

Culver City, California

Designed in collaboration with UCLA's Department of Architecture and Urban Design and built in New Orleans's Lower Ninth Ward neighborhood for the Make It Right Foundation, *Float House* draws its design from the shotgun house, a style predominant throughout New Orleans. In a flood, this single-family home built on a mass-produced chassis will securely float in water rising as high as twelve feet. The house can be manufactured cheaply and generates and sustains all of its own water and energy needs.

BREEZE HOUSE

COLLEGE OF ARCHITECTURE, DESIGN AND CONSTRUCTION
Auburn University, Auburn, Alabama

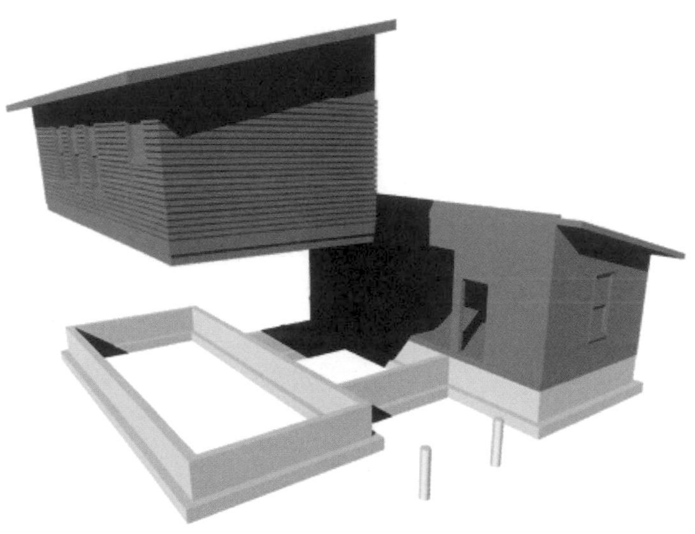

Modular units placed on foundations

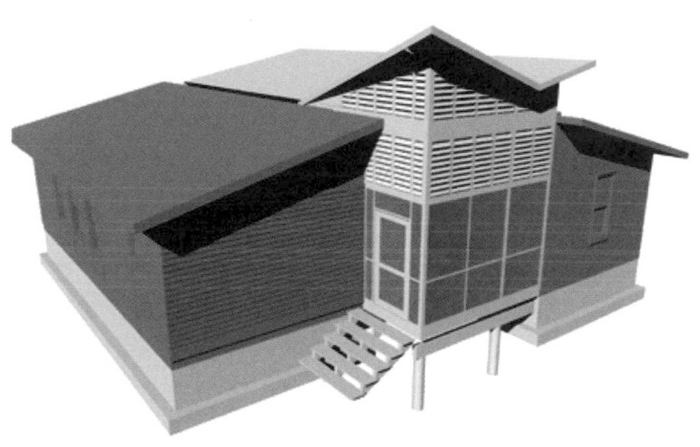

Site built center section

Instructors: Stacy Norman, David Hinson
Designers: Joey Aplin, Samuel Bassett, Cayce Bean, David Davis, Danielle Dratch, Joey Fante, Betsy Farrell, Russ Gibson, Jennifer Givens, Simon Hurst, Walter Mason, Bill Moore, Matt Murphy, Ryan Simon, Mackenzie Stagg

Breeze House, designed in collaboration with Habitat for Humanity and built in Greensboro, Alabama, is a quickly constructible, low-cost, energy-efficient prefabricated single-family home, available to be built in areas where need is significant and volunteer resources are limited. Two separate modular units are connected by a breezeway, each with rooms arranged on either side of a central open hallway. The design promotes cross ventilation for cooler interior spaces in a hot climate.

ecoMOD2: preHAB

SCHOOL OF ARCHITECTURE
University of Virginia, Charlottesville

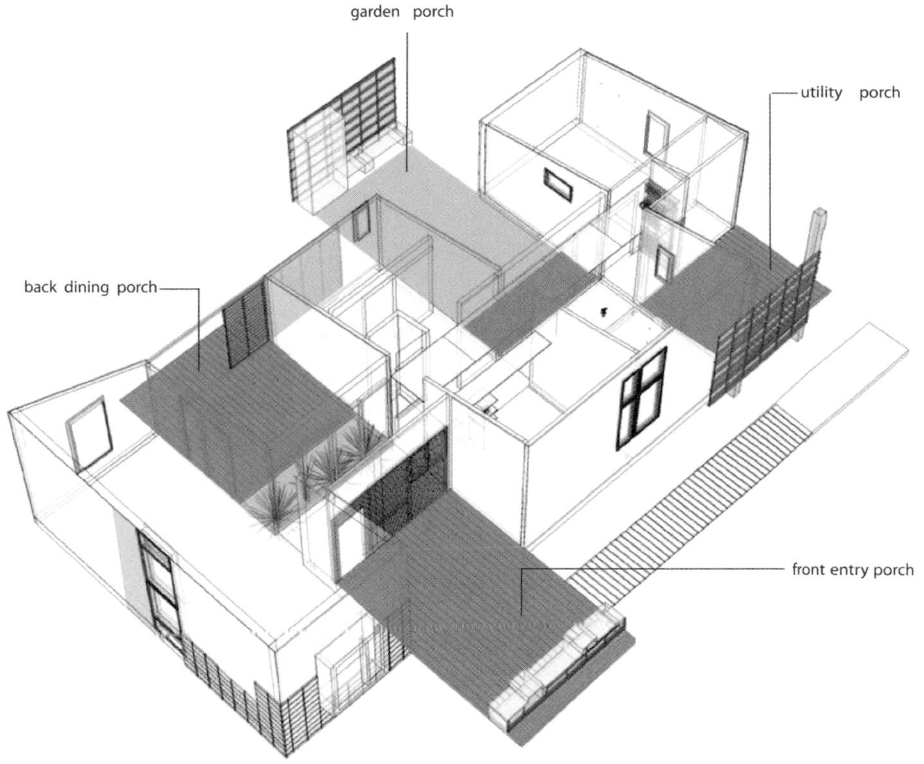

Instructor: John Quale
Designers: Sara Anderson, Maria Arellano, Kelly Barlow, Rasheda Bowman, Brian Hickey, Adrienne Hicks, Nikita Johnson, Benjamin Kid, Ginger Koon, Emmy Lewandowski, Jamie Norwood, Michael Pilat, Greg Redmann, Carol Shiflett, Jessica Soffer, Tommy Solonon, Ginny Wambaugh, Joy Wang

Created through a partnership between Habitat for Humanity and the University of Virginia schools of architecture and engineering. This prefabricated house can be adapted to the needs and preferences of individual single families. The prototype, built in Gautier, Mississippi, uses space and energy efficiently and is constructed with a unique steel-and-foam panel system that is resistant to mold and hurricane-force winds.

MAKE IT RIGHT HOUSES

MVRDV

Rotterdam

MVRDV proposed these three house designs, reproduced here from a set of five, to the Make It Right Foundation as overtly political provocations representing the risks of rebuilding in the Lower Ninth Ward, where structures are dependent on levees for flood protection. The traditional long, narrow New Orleans shotgun house served as the model for each design. In *Bent House,* living room and bedrooms are lifted above the federally mandated base flood elevation (BFE), and shaded spaces are provided for a carport in front and a garden in back. The kitchen and dining area are at the center of the house on the lowest level. *House on the Lift* is a cantilevered shotgun that provides tree canopy views and an open lot below for gardening. *House on the Ramp* is also lifted above the BFE, and its entrance ramp (enclosed at ground level to create storage space) is wheelchair accessible.

SAY YOO-HOO TO THE BUNGALETTE

GRADUATE SCHOOL OF ARCHITECTURE, PLANNING, AND PRESERVATION

Columbia University, New York City

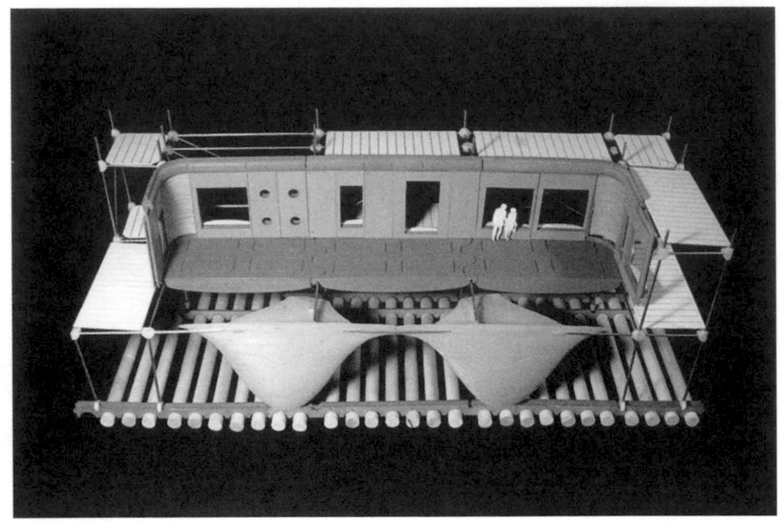

Instructor: Laurie Hawkinson
Designer: Lee Ping Kwan

This storm-proof cottage represents a new take on movable housing units like the trailer. Perched on pontoons that allow it to float during floods, the home includes cisterns to collect water, a filtration system for water treatment, and solar panels to meet energy needs both during normal usage and in an emergency. The *Bungalette* is a secure and self-sufficient shelter that is able to take itself "off the grid" for several months should the need arise.

PART IV
RECONSTRUCTING COMMUNITY, HOUSING (MULTIPLY CONSIDERED)

PLUM ORCHARD, MON AMOUR
DEBORAH GANS

The title of this paper is an homage to *New Orleans, Mon Amour* by Andrei Codrescu, but also a witness to the absence of Plum Orchard and similar neighborhoods from his book and from other political frameworks.[1] As part of a larger consortium of consulting experts, faculty, and students from Pratt Institute and New Jersey Institute of Technology, the three authors presented here, James Dart, Denise Hoffman Brandt, and I, came to know this neighborhood of New Orleans East through the Association of Community Organizations for Reform Now (ACORN) Housing, our local partner in an academic United States Department of Housing and Urban Development Rebuilding America Partnership grant awarded in the wake of Katrina.[2] ACORN historically had large constituencies in the Lower Ninth Ward and in portions of New Orleans East.

The charge of the grant was to provide the community planning, design, and development expertise needed to bolster the local capacity to rebuild, and in so doing to develop strategies for future like events in the age of global warming. The extended suburbs of New Orleans East and, indeed, of so much of the U.S. coastline are an abundant product of officially sanctioned, privately financed postwar development, built when the popular mindset held that technology could triumph over natural conditions and that government was the conceptual center of this technocratic power. Over the past thirty years, an emerging consciousness of the vulnerability of low-lying coastal territory has shifted demographics so that the suburbs most susceptible to coastal flooding and erosion are

1 Andrei Codrescu, *New Orleans, Mon Amour: Twenty Years of Writings from the City*, (Chapel Hill, NC: Algonquin Books, 2006). See Gans's related "Below the Sill Plate, New Orleans East Struggles to Recover," posted on the *Places* section of the Design Observer Group's website, June 27, 2011. This essay also appears in *Beyond Shelter, Architecture and Human Dignity*, ed. Marie J. Aquilino, (New York: Metropolis Books, 2011).

2 The participants and disciplines of the consortium were: from New Jersey Institute of Technology, Professor Darius Sollohub, infrastructure planning, and Professor James Dart, architecture and urban design; from Pratt Institute, professors Deborah Gans and Lawrence Zeroth, architecture and urban design, and Vicki Weiner, Brad Lander, and Ronald Shiffman, planning; and from City College, Denise Hoffman Brandt, landscape architecture. Consultants included David Drew Burner of the New York Botanical Gardens, Dr. Robert Dresnak of the NJIT School of Civil Engineering, and Steven Handel of the Rutgers Center for Urban Restoration Ecology.

now often the poorest. To allow Plum Orchard to survive and reinvent itself is therefore to begin to address a larger future.

I remember the first time we drove across the Industrial Canal—the fault line in the present mishap—into a territory beyond the cultural pale. There the cloudless sky, made bluer by its seeming reflection in the occasional blue tarp, set off the profiles of tidy ranch houses along curving streets. Even the absence of kids, cars, and dogs could not shake the illusion of normalcy, for after all, the American bedroom suburb on a weekday is an abandoned vessel—dad at work, mom at supermarket, kids at school. In this uncanny suburb, we witnessed the deep linguistic connection between *solstitium*, the solstice, and the *iustitium*, the Roman state of exception: the first, the standstill of the sun; the second, the standstill of the law.[3] In the absence of the neighbor there was the writing on the walls to tell the story—floodwater elevation etched onto each facade, emotion-laden graffiti scrawled on the amenable surface of garage doors: we will be back; house for sale; see you soon. In the absence of the state, the people had spoken and accomplished the tactical holding of the neighborhood, with a house on every block marked or under renovation. Mardi Gras ritually enacts festivals of disorder and anarchy descended from French medieval *charivari*, but Katrina had produced, at least in this neighborhood, an authentic state of exception in which the law was suspended for the common good during a state of siege.

Initially we asked ourselves what was the attachment to this "anywhere" suburb that could bring people back to invest their last dollar while both national media and "word on the street" pronounced it doomed to be wiped off the map. Portrayed in the news as an *arriviste* landscape, too new, too simple, too remote to belong to the "real" New Orleans, it in fact has deep claims to its New Orleanian paternity. In contrast to the further reaches of Orleans Parish, projected to be developed between 1959 and the early 1980s first as New Orleans East and subsequently as Pontchartrain New Town in Town and Orlandia by Dallas oil tycoon Clint Murchison Sr. (owner of Six Flags Over Texas, and with ties to both J. Edgar Hoover and the mob), his son Clint Murchison Jr. (owner of the Dallas Cowboys), and their partners, Plum Orchard has a veritable historical patina and upright pedigree.[4] It is not a subdivision at all but an incremental resettling of territory by upwardly mobile African Americans who refurbished and expanded, tore down and rebuilt their fishing shacks and country cottages at the end of World War II. It is old enough to produce the same kind of genealogy found on high ground. A resident described his house as "my

3 Giorgio Agamben makes this point with a quote from Aulus Gellius, "So the sun stood as in the cessation of the law," in *State of Exception*, trans. Kevin Attell, (Chicago: University of Chicago Press, 2005. The argument made throughout this essay in relation to a state of exception owes much to Agamben's book.

4 On the suburban development of New Orleans East, see J. Mark Souther, "Suburban Swamp: the Rise and Fall of Planned New-town Communities in New Orleans East," *Planning Perspectives* 23 (2008), 197–219.

mother's, where she was born, though her parents were from the Lower Ninth, where we still own a house that was her great-grandmother's." His genealogy moves the neighborhood seamlessly from the older city across the rift of the Industrial Canal and the boundary of the Chef Menteur Highway and back again. Even the further reaches of New Orleans East can lay some claim to this narrative, for city residents have been moving eastward along the natural high ground of Chef Menteur (Gentilly Ridge) and building fishing cottages on streets named "Trout" and "Bass" since 1850, a full seventy-five years before the Industrial Canal separated the eastern stretches of Orleans Parish from the city proper.

The political dimension of the design of New Orleans as a whole is nowhere more evident than in Plum Orchard, in the standoff between community and ecology. On the initial Urban Land Institute (ULI) maps that considered shrinking the city to high ground, Plum Orchard appeared as one of the infamous "green dots" to be eliminated.[5] The wholesale erasure of a neighborhood, a measure that the city presented as ecologically correct, confronted the wholesale immobility of individuals as community. In researching ways out of this crippling dialectic, we looked for new understandings of "local" that would embrace both ecology and community. On the website of the United States Department of Agriculture, one of our students found the National Resource Conservation Service urging that multiple small plots of modified wetland can be as effective a water-management device as a major march.[6] This suggested that the amassing of individual gestures over time could take on the outline and force of a master plan: "many" as an alternative to "extra large." That alternative was our starting point in a search for strategies of many sizes that could effect environmental good without exacting a huge social price. The plans and methods we developed over the next few years, working closely with a small group of residents, reimagined not only the individual yard and concomitant retrofitting of the remaining houses, but also the shared landscape of the block, the ganged logics of housing and social utilities for a group of twelve blocks that we called the Model Block, and the connection of such model blocks to each other and the city at large.

STEP 1: THE BROCHURES

The situation we found upon our arrival in New Orleans with our students in the winter of 2005 was one of spontaneous individual rebuilding within a landscape of civic inactivity. Citizens' actions included some old practices that increased vulnerability. The scattered site development secured blocks but reduced the possibilities for alternative land

5 A reproduction of this map appears in Melissa Harris-Perry and William M. Harris Sr.'s essay in Part II of this volume.

6 Maria Plater-Zyberk, in the seminar led by Deborah Gans, Pratt Institute, Spring 2006.

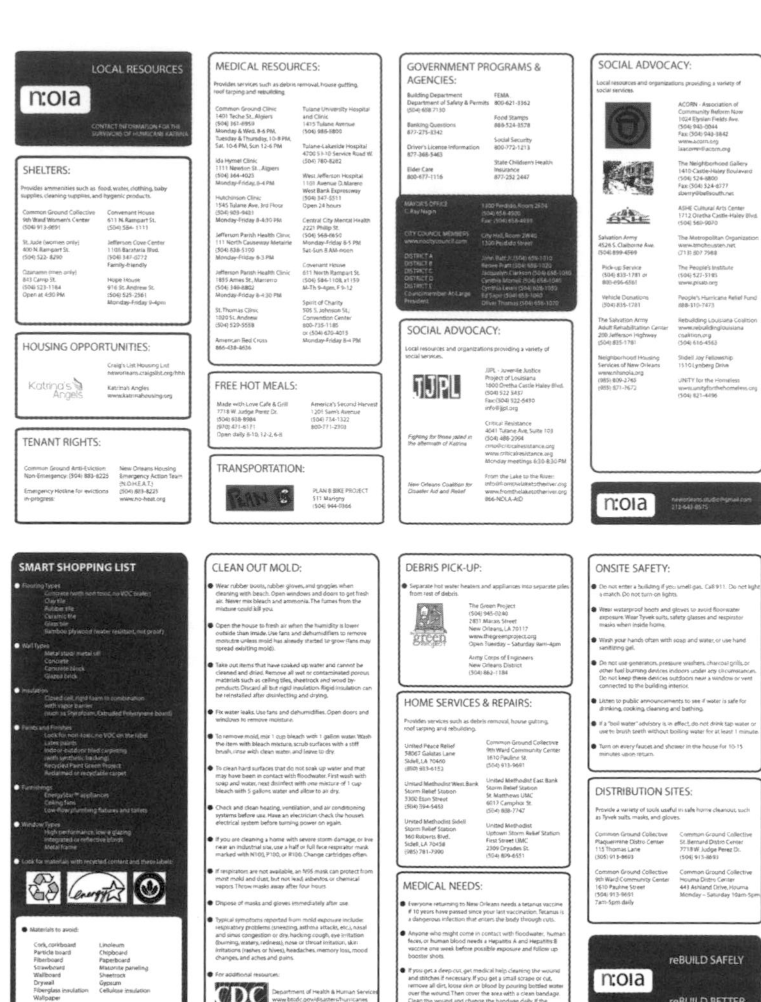

Gans Studio

Rebuilding Brochure

use. We needed to act fast, and so we came up with our first propositional tactic—the brochure. The brochure is an alternative to the very thick book: immediate, distributable, and short. We began with brochures addressed to those in the middle of rebuilding, brochures dealing with local services, directions for cleaning and demolition, and lists of environmentally sound and flood-resistant building materials and methods. The "Retrofitting the Rancher" brochures addressed individual houses that we had surveyed. They went beyond home improvement to visualize the environmental transformation of a neighborhood through devices that could be implemented within private properties, such as attic areas of refuge, solar roofs, cisterns, green walls, and porches for shade and ventilation. The students illustrated these devices in drawings of actual homes in the neighborhood, so that the residents could imagine such transformations concretely and aspire to them—as they did. When the drawings were exhibited at a citywide rebuilding event held in the summer

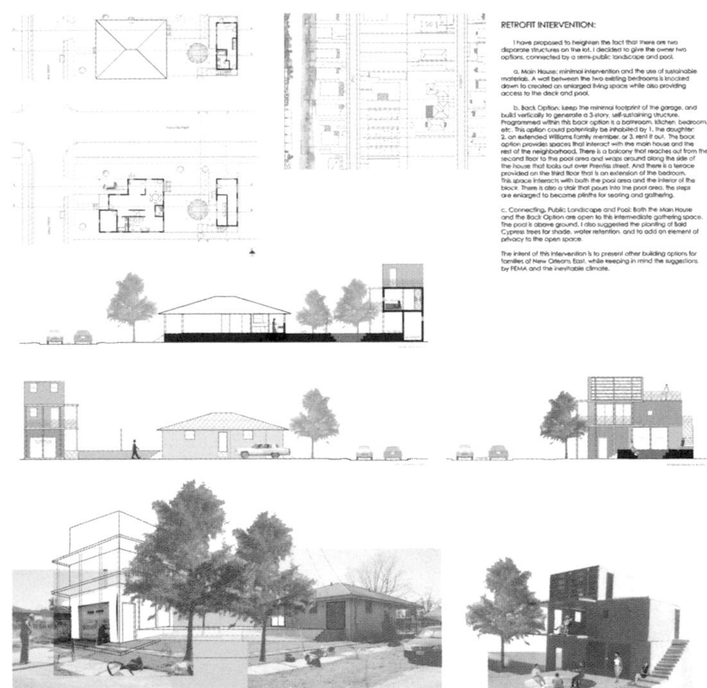

Gans Studio

Retrofit the Rancher brochure for 4661 Dale Street. Pratt student Emily Levy proposed using a backyard pool as a water management device and a new two-story "pool cabana" as a raised refuge.

of 2006 at City Park, strolling passersby recognized their neighbors' houses and asked how similar proposals could be applied to their own. Our brochure "Project Backyard: An Alternative to Mowing" was the first of several brochures and posters of increasing sophistication that addressed water management through local gardening, an idea that had enormous neighborhood appeal.

Because so much of the population was absent, our initial survey of 6,000 houses and households—several of which the students emptied and stripped down to the salvageable stud walls—was largely physical. But as a stronghold of the ACORN membership, the neighborhood was a strategic choice, because it provided a way to disseminate information by word of mouth and mailing lists. Through a combination of ACORN databases and geographic information systems (GIS), we were able to create maps of local and far-flung refugees that became our organizational base for contact with the neighborhood diaspora, including our outreach efforts to Houston and other cities of displacement where there were connections with the national structures of ACORN. A group of planning students scouted for residents at the Camp Renaissance refugee center outside of Baton Rouge and recorded interviews with the displaced about their experiences and their aspirations for life after the storm. These documentation processes were intended as immediate resources to accelerate community organization and rebuilding, but they also produced an oral history project and a record of the effects of the storm over a period of a year, as we periodically updated the surveys.

To empower the stable core of locally situated neighbors who finally emerged, we created a brochure titled "What Is Planning and What Is A Plan," as well as a "Facilitators Handbook" based on a previous text that team member Ronald Shiffman had used in New York City after 9/11 with great success. The establishment of community organizations within New Orleans East was critical, given that all of the successive official plans—from the ULI's to Bring New Orleans Back (BNOB), the Lambert Plan, and the Unified New Orleans Plan (UNOP)—called for the determination of the city's footprint according to the strength of community self-assertion, so that silence meant elimination. Germinating community organizations in a bedroom suburb immediately ensured that the community would survive in the short term and also supplied it with its first governing structure for fielding larger aspirations and political strategies over time.

STEP 2: THE MODEL BLOCK

Our neighborhood visioning sessions, mappings, socioeconomic modeling, and environmental analysis together resulted in the proposal for what we called the Model Block, an intermediary scale of "the local," that covered twelve square blocks or 100 acres, with a pre-Katrina population of 740 families. In order to define its reach, we used standard community-based planning determinants, such as the ten-minute walk to public transportation and the location of schools and markets, but we also included extended family networks, natural drainage patterns in relation to the existing sewer systems and pumps, routes of evacuation, and potential sites of refuge. As we continued our work in the neighborhood, natural boundaries emerged: I-10, to the west, is a major raised highway and an evacuation route to Baton Rouge; Chef Menteur, to the south, is the old commercial artery on naturally high ground that connects the east to the downtown; Dwyer Road, on the north, provides major drainage infrastructure at the lowest edge of the site; and the convent of the Sisters of the Holy Name provides a defined green space to the east. Most importantly, the inhabitants identified with these boundaries, having historically labeled the area "the Goose" and having experienced it as a social and a physical enclave.

For us, the Model Block was a planning unit; but it was also a social covenant based on the argument that no individual should reclaim a territory alone, that a neighborhood is the smallest sustainable unit, and that a cluster of at least three houses should be the fundamental unit of a neighborhood. This covenant mirrored the informal principles of our neighborhood clients, most notably the Alexanders, who settled there in the 1940s and have sustained their stake in it throughout the anarchy of Katrina and the absence of the state by using their elaborate social and economic family network. Their ploy of house swapping among their

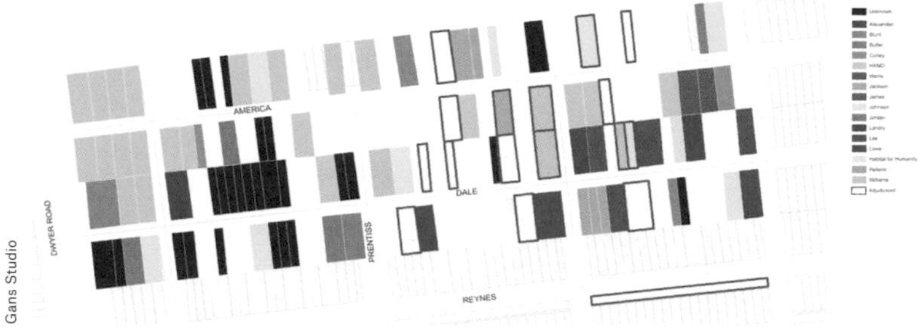

Gans Studio

Family networks: Each color represents an extended family group. Blocks outlined in red are properties adjudicated before the storm.

multiple properties according to family needs appears in our proposal as the swapping of low-liers for high-grounders, sacrificing flooded property to expanded wetland and increasing density uphill. In other words, the neighborhood "repositions itself in place," as James Dart describes the process.

The families also employed a land-use pattern based on this repositioning. In distinction from the usual subdivision formula of ownership based on homogenous income bracket, Plum Orchard is characterized by a mix of renter- and owner-occupied properties as well as single- and multifamily homes. Indeed, the richer suburbs of New Orleans East have resisted the introduction of exactly this economic mix, which they consider lowers real estate values. Residents of Plum Orchard understand that the mix allows for families to move up rather than out and to remain in the neighborhood even when young, old, or unemployed. These micro economies inform the Model Block: in the rent-to-own, in which a family pays rent toward eventual home ownership; in the mix of typologies that include double and even triple houses throughout; and in apartment buildings along the high ground of Chef Menteur that are equipped with rental, assisted-living, and income-generating commercial spaces.

The physical support of this socioeconomic map is a multiscalar network of "local" infrastructure, from paths, cisterns, and off-the-grid services to through-streets, sewers, and city pumping stations. Each element performs multiple functions, one of which is always water management, as described in the work of Darius Sollohub and his students. East-west cross streets internal to the neighborhood are a slow system of porous surfaces with underground flood storage basins. Taking advantage of their low traffic volume and modeled on the Dutch *woonerf*, they are designed as "living room streets," with street furniture but no signs or curbs. Each terminates in a dead end that is reclaimed as a lagniappe of community, economy, and amenity, housing, for example, an off-the-grid power canopy, recycling depot, or community garden. The faster, dominant north-south streets that run downhill from Chef Menteur have subsurface drainage that carries water out of the neighbor-

Gans Studio

Section of site showing, center, a live oak with its extensive root system and a soft-paved street with gravel underlayment and, left and right, proposed designs for raised houses, with a small, lower-set fishing cottage representing original built fabric. Plantings depicted include elephant ears, monkey grass, a banana palm, crape myrtle, and a southern red oak. The red line is 0-0 Base Flood Elevation (BFE), as determined by calculating the flood level that would have a one percent chance of being exceeded in a given year; this is also known as the "100-year flood level." The federal government sets BFEs for insurance and regulatory purposes.

hood into the city system and to the Dwyer Pump Station, which, propitiously, has been reconstructed at increased capacity for a 100-year storm. At two feet above the 100-year flood, Chef Menteur is the obvious path of evacuation and commercial corridor, and a Bus Rapid Transit has been proposed for it.

The fundamental infrastructure, the ground itself, underlies all these devices as a continuous field that extends far beyond the boundaries of the Model Block and even of the city. Its layered wetland ecology of saltwater, brackish water, and freshwater historically engendered a layered architectural response—raised-cottage, Creole, shotgun, slab-on-grade—that has recently been mismatched, with tragic consequences in light of the storm. Within the Model Block we have rematched the house type to the terrain, as James Dart discusses in his essay, and have also reshaped the relationship between nature and the culture of the neighborhood, a process elaborated by Denise Hoffman Brandt and her students in their work on rear gardens, front yards, driveways, streetscapes, and even fences. The domestic planting of the field alone can manage the first 150,000 gallons dumped by a storm that may occur once every ten years, as calculated by Sollohub. By extrapolation, such a tactic could have a similar impact on a much larger field. To illustrate the Model Block as a fragment of a larger field, we have drawn it as a series of plans taken at key heights in relation to the Base Flood Elevation (BFE), each describing a terrain. At the upland Field Condition BFE 20-0, for example, the map exhibits the clusters and increased densities of housing versus the land reserved as wetland, while at 0-0 BFE, the Model Block appears as a continuous landscape of swales and surface drywells punctuated only by piles, porches, and stairs.

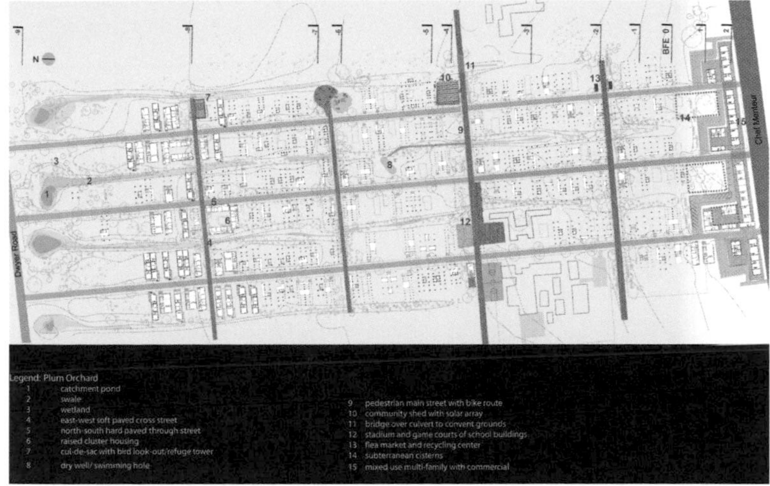

Gans Studio

The Model Block at 0-0 BFE: social and water infrastructures. At this elevation the site appears to be a continuous field of pilotis of raised houses and the ground below them.

In sum, the Model Block is less a master plan than it is a fine-grained remapping of a locale in terms of its environmental features and hazards, its social networks and other previously invisible assets. This remapping frees the analysis of neighborhood terrain from gross nomenclatures such as "flooded" and "toxic," indicating precise zones that can be viably resettled and recommending precise tactics for doing so. As calculated by the Rational Method,[7] if all the proposed field conditions and instruments of the Model Block, including the Dwyer Road pump improvements, are implemented, the neighborhood would not flood at all in a 10-year storm scenario and would flood only at street level during a 100-year flood. Moreover, because the water reserved by the Model Block is the first several hundred thousand gallons, the margin of safety for the community expands in time and so transforms the nature as well as the degree of risk.

The Vietnamese population of Village de l'Est in New Orleans East has also pursued a plan that redefines not just the level but also the very nature of risk.[8] With strong connections to the watery landscape, which is reminiscent of their homeland's, they fish the lake for a living and plant gardens by the bayou with rice and vegetables. They were undeterred by Katrina and have returned with plans for a new neighborhood center replete with traditional Vietnamese water gardens, housing for the elderly, and a community/evacuation center. They have addressed the paralyzing conflict between ecology and community by asking the root question of what it means to be safe. Their answers are subtle scenarios in which their proposed

7 The Rational Method is the engineer's standard means of quantifying runoff as the inverse consequence of the ability of material or structure to absorb and hold water.

8 See Elizabeth Mossop's essay in Part VI of this volume.

safe haven includes new (or perhaps old) ways of living with water, climate, and landscape and of living in their houses while planning for potential evacuation. They suggest an approach to coastal development that requires nothing less than a new phase in the U.S. environmental movement, in which the burden of controlling nature will expand from an approach that depends both on setting aside vast tracts of reserved land and on the "security" provided by equally vast civil engineering projects to one that creates a tighter weave of managed yet inhabited resources.

In comparison, as a third-generation suburb without the linguistic and cultural homogeneity of Village de l'Est, Plum Orchard is in some regards merely typical, but as such it is also important. The returning refugees from Plum Orchard and their neighbors, formerly regarded as banal suburbanites, have become a decisive factor in the future of New Orleans by asserting the difference between political and physical safety. It was our ambition to help them envision their marginal piece of New Orleans East as an equally significant place.

ACKNOWLEDGMENTS

Members of the Pratt architecture studio, led by professor Deborah Gans, were: Benjamin Armas, Jennifer Bishop, Morie Bustler, Omar Calderon, Leslie Eggers, Jocelyn Elliot, Alex Gryger, Randall Horning, Alana Jaroworski, Zachary Joslow, Jessica Kao, Aimee Keefer, Emily Levy, Stanley Mayerfield, David Meinhart, Maria Plater-Zyberk, Joshua Plourde, Neil Price, Maria Salazar, Sean Slemon, Gillian Sollengberger, Marly Sutton, Stephanie Thomas, and Palmer Thompson-Moss.

Members of the NJIT NOLA studios were the Spring 2006 undergraduate options studio, with James Dart, faculty, and students Chad Coronato, Astra Freet, Thomas Jardim, Hyung S. Kang, Andy Kim, Viren Patel, John Rago, Thomas Reynolds, Richard Rush, Patricia Sabater, and Matthew Schott; the Fall 2006 undergraduate options studio, with James Dart and students John W. Anthal, Amanda E. Bossen, Adam B. Brillhart, Justin M. Foster, Asuka Hayashi, Cliff Chan Lau, Ninett N. Moussa, Supredee Parichan, Andre W. Pause, Joshua D. Prol, Austin J. Sochocky, and Marc Joseph SoHayda; the Fall 2006 master of infrastructure planning studio, with Darius Sollohub, faculty, and students Joseph Cosenza, Anthony D'Agosta, Joseph Fassacessia, Siiri Julianus, Maryam Katouzian, Kelli Miller, Chuks Nwanesi, Laura Parks, Madhvi Patel, Ha Pham, Sean Quinn, Kelley Sander, Don Sharp, Chetasee Trivedi, and Trupti Vedak; and the Spring 2007 undergraduate comprehensive studio, with James Dart and Robert A. Svetz, faculty, and students Marlon Alexander, Hedi Allameh, Thomas L. Anderson, Amanda Bossen, Chad Coronato, Isabel DeSousa, Anisha R. Gulrajani, Eric Evan Gumbs, Richard Jecmen, Sonia Parada, Viren Patel, Jeff Potter, Sameh Salmon, and Alex Voronovsky.

LANDLOCKED
DENISE HOFFMAN BRANDT

Backyard Biome, a first-year graduate landscape studio at the City College of New York (CCNY) held in the spring of 2007, was conceived to examine the potential within the *new* New Orleans East for recovering neighborhood and domestic landscapes in a way that would allow them to better adapt to and withstand a gamut of challenges. These included recurring flood damage in low-lying areas, soils toxicity caused by deposits of industrial sediments, and the prospect of unabated hurricane disturbances. The cross-disciplinary initiative was undertaken in coordination with Pratt Institute and New Jersey Institute of Technology architecture studios, which were working with funding from HUD and in partnership with the ACORN Housing. City College landscape students collaborated with the Pratt architecture students in a neighborhood-planning charrette and incorporated the Pratt students' designs for building typologies into their proposals. The studio projects speculated across a range of scales, from the delta to the yard, in order to construe the complex environmental and social ecologies that were the context for Hurricane Katrina's disruption of the city. The studio objective, to consider strategies for reviving the neighborhood of Plum Orchard, in part through the creation of experientially compelling and ecologically viable public and private spaces, reflected the goals of the Model Block project. This essay presents our studio discourse and our conception of the Plum Orchard domestic landscape as an arena providing for everyday public and private social engagement and an infrastructure on the "family" scale designed to mitigate ongoing environmental disturbance.

On my last visit, in the summer of 2009, two years after the conclusion of our studio work, a scatter of high-fenced yards with new lawn defined the latest iteration of domestic terrain in Plum Orchard. Security—protection from criminal trespass along streets that no longer have "eyes"—had become the dominant post-Katrina neighborhood landscape ideal. One resident told me she did not go out after nine o'clock at night. Resettlement was proceeding at a creeping pace, and this devolution of neighborhood territory stemmed from both nonexistent top-down planning and overwhelming (yet understandable) bottom-up angst about losing land rights in any municipally driven land-swap scenario—an idea that was advanced early on but not incorporated into the Louisiana Recovery Authority's Road Home process. When asked if she would be willing to relocate to a more populated area on higher ground, an eighty-seven-year-old woman—awaiting LRA assistance while living in an isolated trailer—she had virtually no neighbors within a two-block radius—responded that the piece of land on which she stood was hers, and no one could make her leave it. Plum Orchard's transformation from neighborhood to patchy frontier zone is collateral damage in an escalating war against the dynamic environmental systems that have defined life in New Orleans for centuries. New Orleanians have always dealt with the downside of their subtropical climate, from the daily annoyance of mosquitoes to the yearly threat of floods. Framing Katrina as an epochal event obscures the ecological continuum. John McPhee compellingly describes New Orleans in *The Control of Nature*:

> Torrential rains fall on New Orleans—enough to cause flash floods inside the municipal walls. The water has nowhere to go. Left on its own, it would form a lake, rising inexorably from one level of the economy to the next. So it has to be pumped out. Every drop of rain that falls on New Orleans evaporates or is pumped out. Its removal lowers the water table and accelerates the city's subsidence. Where marshes have been drained to create tracts for new housing, ground will shrink, too. People buy landfill to keep up with the Joneses. In the words of Bob Fairless, of the New Orleans District [U.S. Army Corps of] Engineers, "It's almost an annual spring ritual to get a load of dirt and fill in the low spots on your lawn." A child jumping up and down on such a lawn can cause the earth to move under another child, on the far side of the lawn.[1]

Through their daily activities and spatial habits, the residents of New Orleans take their place among the many interrelated organisms perpetuating the reciprocal processes that create the eco-region of the lower Mississippi. In Plum Orchard, domestic terrain is valued less for its capacity to connect the home with the natural realm than for its use as a tool to oppose natural forces.

Other New Orleans neighborhoods, with different socioeconomic perspectives, do not take the same approach to inhabiting their yards. The layers of climate adaptation embedded in the Plum Orchard landscape—a preference for paved surfaces (to move water away from homes and into storm sewers quickly), unease with a lot of large trees (they might fall on your house), and annual attention to filling low land to eliminate standing water—are domestic defensive tactics in climate

1 John McPhee, *The Control of Nature* (New York: Farrar, Straus, and Giroux, 1989), 210.

combat. And they are class-based. For a cash-strapped population, these family-scale design responses are necessitated by the prohibitive costliness in both money and labor of repeated cycles of property repair. The ability or inability to pay for repairs determines suburban yard use, and yard use determines social standing in New Orleans East.

Before Katrina, the almost seamless fit of domestic landscape responses to climate with Plum Orchard's suburban subdivision format hid a grounded engagement with local environmental systems. Hardened surfaces for water management were apparent extensions of the 1970s subdivision aesthetic. Yet, despite tacitly accepting that macro-engineered structures would hold—the storm sewers would remain effective and the levees would be structurally sound—these microscale practices instrumentalized domestic terrain as stormwater management infrastructure, a zone of private guerilla warfare against a liquid adversary. When the big guns failed, after the Army Corps of Engineers ultimately proved ineffectual at fighting off even a Category 3 storm, the ad hoc apparatus of everyday battles against the water was damaged. The former carpet-condition of contiguously managed yards no longer existed. To make recovery possible, the water management infrastructure of Plum Orchard domestic landscapes would have to be revamped. In undertaking the studio research project, we understood that we had to reconsider both the motives for and the methods of controlling environmental processes in order to propose adaptations to this new, sparsely occupied terrain.

FRONT YARDS

In July 2006, I toured New Orleans East with Deborah Gans and the Pratt students, trying to get a sense of what its life had been like before the storm, in order to gain a frame of reference for what the district might become. Encounters with residents of Pines Village (a neighborhood near Plum Orchard) and descriptions of the local pre-Katrina front-yard landscape made clear that although the distance from sidewalk to stoop varied, it was "talkable." Whether residents were seated on the steps of a shotgun or in lawn chairs on the entry slab of a brick ranch, their front walks were conduits to the *goings on* out front. We chatted with a few people sitting outside near the street—their stoop wasn't usable—as if they wanted to be there to welcome returning neighbors in order to reanchor themselves in the *new* neighborhood. In fact, one year after our studio surveyed Plum Orchard, a landscape architecture student based a project on returning residents' situation as tourists in their own altered neighborhood.

Pre-Katrina, many yards in Plum Orchard were surrounded by low fences that did not obstruct views into "private" property. It was evident early on in our project, however, that there would be a shift in priorities from neighborly interface to security as residents returned to a paradoxically *alien* home territory. During our photo survey of Plum Orchard street frontage, we encountered former residents returning to check in on their property, residents living off-site while repairing their homes, and residents living in trailers on their lots while awaiting financial assistance. Discussions with these denizens of Plum Orchard revealed consistent loyalty to their land as a defining right and to their neighborhood as home, as well as an equally consistent fear of the danger inherent in its depopulation. The eighty-seven-year-old woman at Pressburg and Ray Streets stood in front of a trailer, behind a low fence, as she described both her isolation and her allegiance to her plot of land.

Little had changed by the summer of 2009, when a resident of America Street recounted to me how she returned to New Orleans from Houston, motivated by her sense of responsibility to her community to repair and maintain her house and lot. She described the paradoxical feeling of being simultaneously at home and estranged that seemed characteristic of post-Katrina Plum Orchard. She expressed her regret that the neighborhood she returned to was not the neighborhood she had left, that she knew very few people there, and that the streets were now frightening after dark. A comprehensive plan for clustering resettlement could have eased the minds of these isolated returning residents, as well as moving them upslope out of the lower, flood-prone zones.

The phenomenon of dissociation from the home landscape was never dominant, however, in the discourse of rebuilding. Yet within the framework of rethinking a model block, the need to recover the social envelope of the front yard, activated by the stoop or landing, was profoundly felt. The yard is not only a marker of the "Joneses'" position in the neighborhood economic spectrum, it is also a mechanism for the Joneses to establish a relationship with other members of their community—that is, it supports relations among people as social organisms and between those organisms and their environment: the recovery of the yard is critical to the recovery of a neighborhood's ecology. While everyone waited for the verdict on whether or not houses would have to be elevated further above the flood level, besides concerns for building costs and building form, many questions were raised: How could a vital eye-to-eye social connection be retained with a possible vertical difference of three to eight feet between the parties engaged? How would the houses be connected to the ground? A vision of the yard as an armature for the house and also its public interface became a focus for civic design in the studio. This was a situation distinctly different from the pre-Katrina conception of the front yard as a privately engineered public display of the homeowner's position within a social hierarchy.

During discussions with returning residents over the course of the HUD project it became clear that eliminating fences in order to enhance the sense of civic connection was not going to be an option. Desolate tracts with abandoned homes and overgrown lots were not conducive to a sense of security. Practically considered, the frontier character of the new Plum Orchard mandated fences. Studio design discussions, therefore, focused on the importance of mitigating the visual impact of the fences. Several students proposed matrices to establish flexible guidelines for house-to-street spatial relationships. Fixed setbacks were not required, so students were able to formulate setbacks that varied according to different house elevations; they studied view lines to determine optimal lines of sight over lower fences. Yard-planting strategies were assessed for their ability to buttress the front fences while keeping the stoop-street interface open.

I am disappointed, and perhaps this reflects a romantic turn of mind, that in 2009, instead of a recovered Plum Orchard community making eye contact across front yards, most neighbors kept their houses behind tall fences. Not only were the fences high, but some new ones were constructed to be completely opaque screens between the house and the street. These fences required a substantial financial investment, and it seemed unlikely they would be removed when/if the neighborhood repopulated to a safe density. Katrina's destructive aftermath extends beyond property damage; there is a legacy of socially damaging reconstruction as well.

Most Plum Orchard yards were dominated by lawn and concrete, and the stark (but easily maintained) surfaces seemed at once visually oppressive and psychologically reassuring. These yards-as-drainage-ways stood in sharp contrast to the surrounding overgrowth on uninhabited, unmanaged properties. The potential for explosive plant growth called for a "max-bio" (maximizing biota) strategy, in which plant water-uptake, permeable surfaces, and soil drainage are optimized to reduce neighborhood stormwater flow rates. We offered this approach as an alternative to the prevailing practice of using hardened ground surfaces to move water into the sewer system. The reimagined front yards retained the practical function of pre-Katrina yards as domestic-scale water infrastructure, but by engaging hydrologic processes rather than deflecting them—by co-opting the environment rather than confronting it with force. The plantings could also cool homes (lowering air-conditioning costs) by creating shade, and could provide a physical barrier between the home and the street or adjacent abandoned property that improved both soil quality and the scene of neighborly interactions.

BACKYARDS

The Plum Orchard backyards that we encountered were more diverse than the front yards; they seemed to function as unique private arenas. This was strikingly evident in Pines Village, where we were taken to see a stable—complete with horse—built against the back of a structurally damaged shotgun house. The house belonged to the mother of the horse-owner. She was still living wherever she had evacuated to, but the horse remained *in situ* and was doing fine. Subsequent studio research indi-

Hoffman Brandt Landscape Design

Plum Orchard front yard in 2009, and after "max-bio" planting

cated that the stable represented an extreme end of the spectrum of backyard land use, which commonly tended toward small garden plots, the occasional barbecue (more often these were located in the side or front yards), and storage and workshop areas. Departing from the typical suburban ideal, the backyards were not generally configured as built-out play areas dedicated to leisure activities.

Two possibilities for reimagining backyard spaces emerged: connecting the front and rear yards, taking advantage of the new ground condition that elevated houses provided and optimizing homeowner programming, and re-creating underused, undervalued backyards as systemic, local-scale stormwater management systems. In the latter case, the yards would be incrementally integrated into swales and retention areas, decreasing the amount of stormwater running into the sewer system, in order to delay or even reduce peak flows. This soft, collective drainage infrastructure would have to be negotiated into private property around personal and family yard activities.

Several of the CCNY landscape architecture students took on the second option as a design investigation, and the discussion around their proposals highlighted the need to calibrate theory with practice. The clear attachment of residents to specific parcels of land as an expression of their inalienable human rights triggered an important debate over how much land it was reasonable to co-opt for stormwater management—given that just because land seemed underused to the students did not mean it was not valued by its owners. The misguided idea that the only way we can express a connection to land is by "using" it is a byproduct of discriminatory land practices historically aimed at revoking the property rights of Native Americans, who did not "use" the land in a manner legible to European-Americans accustomed to processes of resource extraction. European-Americans who seized the land with this justification visibly registered their ownership by comprehensively transforming its environmental systems. The students understood that taking land for bio-swales and retention areas for the collective good would still be just that, taking land, and still the functional operation of this common land would be largely invisible.

Therefore, the students became more focused in their proposals—perhaps too focused. Calculating exactly the amount of water that could be collected in rills was a challenge. Digging deeper to contain more water with less of a footprint opened the potential for hazardous drops and continuous wetland conditions. Would the neighborhood appreciate the return of the bayou to their backyards? What about mosquitoes? Could we really suggest that they install bat houses for mosquito control? The communal water management strategies undertaken in Viet Village provided, unfortunately, an inappropriate paradigm.[2]

The mix of renters and homeowners that had made Plum Orchard a model for low-density subsidized housing undermined its ability to act collectively in the recovery process. Certainly after Katrina there was no strong community structure in place to channel individual land management actions for the common good. In order for an organization like ACORN to take on the implementation of collectively managed, neighborhood-scale soft infrastructure, it would first have to achieve an extraordinary level of neighborhood buy-in.

2 For a description of water management strategies undertaken post-Katrina there, see Elizabeth Mossop's essay in Part VI of this volume.

Hoffman Brandt Landscape Design

Rendering of Plum Orchard backyard in 2009, and after bio-swale implementation

Domestic landscapes present powerful opportunities, as interfaces of the public and private realms, but these benefits are not easily accessed through top-down agency; on the contrary, they require bottom-up organization and in some cases coordinated physical labor. How could water-management infrastructure at the block scale be designed incrementally and in a manner that allowed the residents themselves to implement and maintain it? What if a group of residents refused to participate, leaving a gap in the linear flow system? Although it was a broad planning objective, the challenge of designing such a system without a clear agency for implementation, or even a majority of stakeholders present, required a different approach. The virtue of the domestic-scale water management apparatus that predated Katrina, although it was limited in impact, was that it took the battle onto home terrain. Individual residents decided when and how to mediate between the social space of the home landscape and its mechanics for moving water based on personal agency and a sense of traditional practices.

The student proposals for backyard bio-swales were notable for their consideration of these issues. Strategically placed collection ponds were shifted to lower elevations, on the assumption that these properties would ideally be less densely reinhabited (although that was not necessarily being borne out by the ongoing resettlement process). Students attempted to diagram a phased implementation of the swales to deal with potential disconnects at nonparticipating lots, and they conceived planting the swales as a way of boosting the experiential capacity of the backyard and bringing out a common neighborhood identity. Facilitating residents' reattachment to native and locally adapted plant systems was also considered critical for successful collective bio-swale management. Design proposals contained features to enable discreet yard-by-yard, family-by-family opportunities for occupation of the *community* home territory. Children's play areas; shady spots to sit, talk, and watch birds; connecting paths where they might be desirable and fences where the residents simply wanted privacy all became part of the bio-swale design. The HUD design team advanced a proposal that considered all of these issues, and a schematic plan was rendered as an idealized condition to encourage neighborhood participation. In the end, however, a plan for neighborhood-scale stormwater management proved too complex for ACORN to implement.

THE "HOME DEPOT" POSTER

Landscape studios generally investigate context—social and environmental—as the milieu for performance of the design. Yet often the site to be transformed is interpreted as open, unoccupied, in a state awaiting habitation. Plans, sections, and views represent projected images of future occupation. Formalization of those images is predicated on acceptance of unified, top-down stylings. In converging a normative design process with an already actively occupied zone, bottom-up, ad hoc conditions are either accommodated or overridden. In Plum Orchard, we saw that the most opportunistic approach would be to enable evolving spatial habits and to dispense with a holistic design gesture. We realized that planning for this domestic landscape might actually mean not planning as we think of it at all.

One outcome of this realization was "Plant Yourself," a poster produced by the HUD team aimed at returning residents and hung in local home-building supply stores. Designed to communicate an expanded repertoire of domestic-scale apparatuses for environmental engagement, the poster would reframe the neighborhood's common enemy—that is, the phenomena characteristic of a subtropical climate—as merely the context within which homeowners operate. The poster offered five tips for replanting New Orleans East. Given that homeowners were rebuilding their houses as extended do-it-yourself projects, it made sense to appeal to their aspirations as they looked over the building and yard displays. The first tip, "Just Plant" pointed out the benefits of planting to improve not only the environment but also property values—and lighten the overworked home rebuilder's mood. Making clear the practical uses for domestic landscaping is basic in helping a homeowner to reevaluate the property's less legibly used spaces. Other tips made the case for layered plantings (from ground covers to canopy trees) and low-maintenance native plants, in order to optimize thermal benefits for the home, maximize neighborhood rainwater uptake, and reduce investment in yard maintenance. A range of plant-layer options was laid out in a matrix keyed to soil moisture and demonstrating a spectrum of soil-moisture conditions viable for beneficial planting. This approach emphasized a decision-making response to specific local ground conditions without suggesting that the hydrological, thermal, or experiential benefits need be diminished in any situation. The poster listed easily attainable, locally supplied plants, framing them as immediately available tools for recovery.[3] Images of the plants were included to display their ornamental appeal and make them more desirable—homeowners would, after all, be designing their yards as emblems of their own recovery.

The poster's messages, like so much else in the discourse of recovery, were overwhelmed by the greater imperative to rebuild houses. ACORN displayed "Plant Yourself" in their offices, but it was never distributed to the commercial venues for which it had been designed. ACORN administrators understood that creating a community context—to make homes as opposed to houses—was essential for community revival; however, they lacked the resources and organizational force to address neighborhood recovery. On a beautiful day in July 2009, there were no children "jumping up and down" in the yards or on the streets of Plum Orchard. The "empty subdivision with both parents at work on a school day" quiet seemed to be the new norm.[4] Proliferating security fences that drew scant household resources away from the production of *working* yards were also undermining social connections that could otherwise have sparked a renewal of neighborly collective action. Although many "empty" yards appeared to be intermittently mowed (not least to limit rat habitat),

3 David Dew Bruner, a graduate of Louisiana State University and a faculty member at the New York Botanical Garden, provided expertise in the area of native plants.

4 The Greater New Orleans Community Data Center's website showed that 61 percent of Plum Orchard addresses were receiving mail in June 2010, well under the average of 81 percent for New Orleans as a whole. See gnocdc.org.

Hoffman Brandt Landscape Design with David Dew Bruner

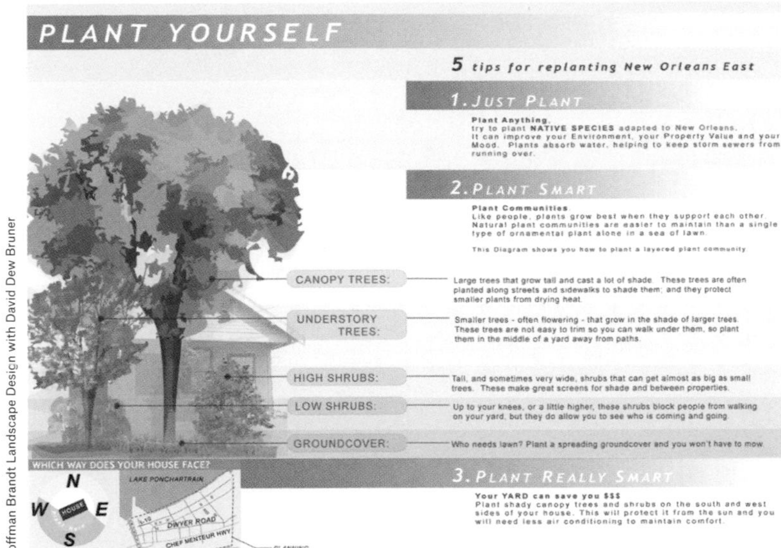

"Home Depot" poster (upper section)

Hoffman Brandt Landscape Design with David Dew Bruner

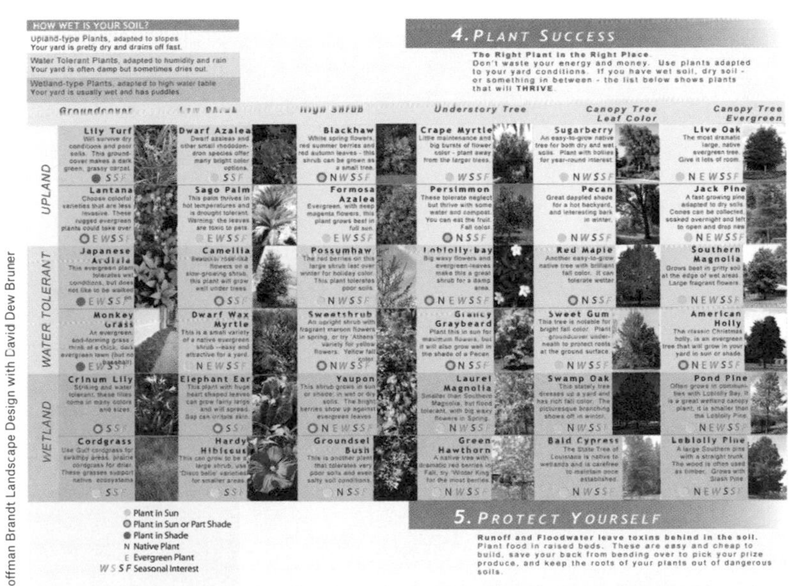

"Home Depot" poster (lower section)

many were simply left to the weeds. Paved surfaces showed large areas of collapse, heaving, and cracks, and on this dry day, there were standing pools, evidence that underlying soil remained compacted from the weight of floodwater.

The Army Corps of Engineers insists that it is now on the right track and that the Sewerage and Water Board has improved the pumps. The city's ongoing confrontation with its climate is increasingly dominated by the large weaponry of macroengineering, which seeks to confine dynamic environmental systems, often with deleterious consequences. And so New Orleans's new normal is more of the same old, same old.

ACKNOWLEDGMENTS

Members of the CCNY landscape architecture studio, led by Professor Hoffman Brandt, were Amanda Bayley, Sara Duarte, Adrian Hayes, Michael Payton, Kelli Rudnick, Sabrina Tropper, and Tisha Vaaska.

REPOSITION IN PLACE, NO BIG PLANS: THE ADJUDICATED PROPERTIES PROJECT FOR THE LOWER NINTH WARD AND NEW ORLEANS EAST

JAMES DART

The HUD-funded community planning work described by Deborah Gans had a continuing afterlife in a redevelopment project for housing on tax-adjudicated properties, which were primarily in the Lower Ninth Ward and partially within Plum Orchard in New Orleans East. ACORN Housing Corporation, a not-for-profit housing developer based in Chicago (an affiliate of ACORN, the community activist organization until recently based in New Orleans), was awarded an initial 150 lots by the city of New Orleans in the fall of 2006. The inherent conflict between these two "siblings"—activist community organization and not-for-profit developer—presaged the project's limited outcomes long before the recent ACORN imbroglios.[1] Other challenges quickly appeared.

We shifted from working as academic advocates for rational, integrated planning and reconstruction, high-minded and above the fray, to participating as professionals charged with building a limited number of houses, scattered across neighborhoods where nearly every house had been destroyed and the entire population dispersed. Our nearest new neighbor was Brad Pitt with Make It Right; Global Green was down the street across St. Claude Avenue in Holy Cross. Our task was to design individual houses rather than the field in which they would sit, and although these houses would often be close to one another, they would not be clustered. Moreover, they were to be financed and sold individually, without the economic benefit of traditional subdivision development or the social benefit of family networks. However, having conceptualized the genetic code of the Model Block, we resolved to implant it in the project on an ad hoc basis by slotting contiguous sites on higher elevations to sell first, and by investing the architecture with the potential for clusters and field conditions.

1 Kenneth M. Reardon et al., "Commentary: Overcoming the Challenges of Post-Disaster Planning in New Orleans, Lessons from the ACORN Housing/University Collaborative," *Journal of Planning Education and Research* 28 (2009): 391–401.

DARCH/Gans Studio

HOUSE 4B, MoMA "Home Delivery" submission

ABOVE THE SILL PLATE: PROTOTYPES + PREFABRICATION

We organized a series of focus groups during late 2006 and into 2007 made up of neighborhood residents likely to be interested in moving back to the Lower Ninth Ward. We presented preliminary design work, and after feedback from the groups we modified the program for each prototype to produce more fully developed house designs. Concurrently with the focus group meetings, and as a way of testing our assumptions about the design possibilities of modular prefab, we submitted the project to Manhattan's Museum of Modern Art (MoMA) for inclusion in its 2008 exhibition on prefabrication, "Home Delivery."[2] Having established a general range of prototypes, some inspired by our students' studio work, our research for the "Home Delivery" submission led us to a series of modules, which we called combines, that could be assembled to form a variety of plan configurations. Nice idea, but we soon learned that the "module" in modular housing referred not to the optimal dwelling unit components, shop-fabricated and trucked to a site, but to the dimensional capacity of the truck itself. For in-plant construction, if you maximize the area of the module to fit the available truck bed, or platform, you minimize cost. The module *is* the truck; the house *is* the flatbed. We

2 "Home Delivery: Fabricating the Modern Dwelling," on view at MoMA in New York City, June 20–October 20, 2008.

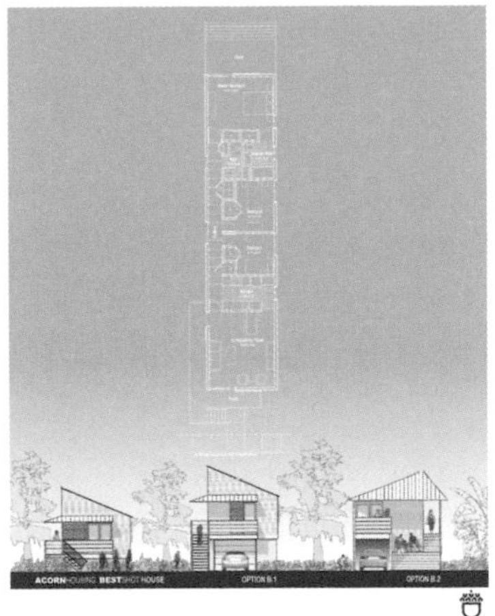

DARCH/Gans Studio

FirstShot/BestShot House, L9W Rising, sales tear sheet

also learned, in due course, that maximum truck/platform dimensions vary across the country given interstate highway regulations, distance traveled, overhead clearances, and so on. And we came to understand (and admire) the sophisticated fabrication process of the modular house even as we despaired over the banality of the typical design product, its details and materials.

By the Mardi Gras season of 2007, we had developed five basic house prototypes responding to available lot sizes and various family needs: the one-truck FirstShot or Aging-in-Place 960-square-foot, two-bed, two-bath starter; the one-and-a-half truck models (three trucks bring two houses) BestShot, 1,120-square-foot, three-bed, two-bath family; CourtYard, 1,420-square-foot, three-bed, two-bath family; and Mother-in-Law 1,780-square-foot, three-bed, two-bath family with separate rental/suite; and the two-truck TwoStory A + B, 1,600-square-foot + 1,750-square-foot, three-bed, two-bath family. In design intent, these houses channel traditional elements of pre-air-conditioning subtropical domestic architecture, including crawl spaces, high ceilings, cross-ventilation, deep shading, and deployable jalousie shutters, with as many sustainable practices as our "state-of-shelf" budgets and ambitions could accommodate: high-performing wall and roof systems, rainwater catchment, solar panel–ready roofs, and lawn-free lots planted with water- and wind-loving native plants and trees. Of paramount importance, too, were the requirements of affordability and replicability.

BELOW THE SILL PLATE: CONSTRUCTION + COMMUNITY

Costs for each house ranged from $140,000 and $150,000, for the FirstShot and BestShot, to $240,000 for the Mother-in-Law. Even at this modest price point, these costs pushed the limit of the area's Mean Affordability Index. Red flags went up. In what proved to be a vain attempt to wish down costs, we took our simplest three-bedroom model, the BestShot, and priced it three different ways: conventional wood-framed

DARCH/Gans Studio

Mother-in-Law House, L9W Rising, sales tear sheet

modular by Haven Homes in South Carolina; Structural Insulated Panels (SIPs) modular by the now defunct Louisiana System Built Homes (LASBH) in St. Martinsville, Louisiana; and stick- or site-built construction by several local general contractors. Costs for construction varied very little among these scenarios because the one-off strategy precluded any economy of scale. Prefabrication without mass production meant quality control and speed did not result in appreciable savings.

MISSING THE MARK

More significantly, the prices of these houses built one at a time, or even many at a time, failed to attract any but a handful of qualified buyers. Even as ACORN Housing investigated subsidies and soft seconds, lenders, funders, and the architects realized that housing units financed and sold individually could neither build community on any viable scale nor meet

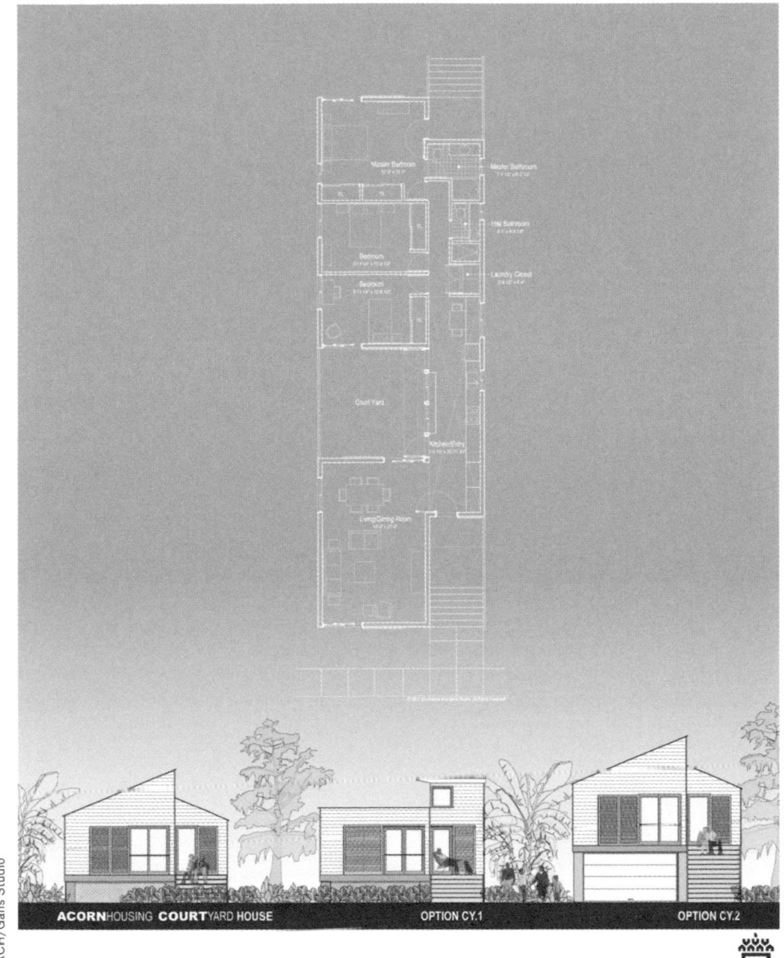

DARCH/Gans Studio

CourtYard House, L9W Rising, sales tear sheet

the market's ability to pay, even at our price point, without subsidies well beyond what the Louisiana Recovery Authority (LRA) or MasterCard could offer. Given the Mean Affordability Index, rent to own became the only viable model with the capacity to achieve both conditions. ACORN Housing, for reasons unknown, refused to consider such a model.

MISSING THE GROUND

While construction of the houses advanced and the houses themselves even reached some of the goals we had set for their performance and cost, the main objective of our planning-grant study, the reactivation of a performative field in which the new homes would be sited, remained elusive. We had clustered the scattered lots as best we could, concentrating first on those closest to Claiborne Avenue's higher ground for development and sale. ACORN Housing attempted to acquire additional

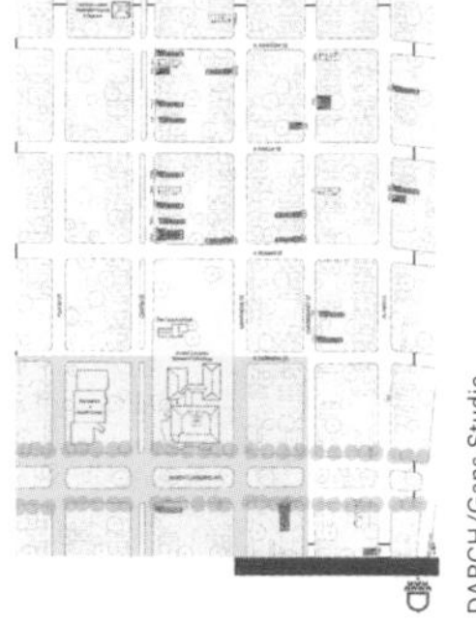

DARCH/Gans Studio

Clusters, L9W Rising site plan

adjacent lots from neighbors willing to sell and to reach out to others who might want us to build a house on their lot. These efforts, however, did not yield the kind of density or critical mass that reviving the neighborhood required. We ended up with only the possibility of a cluster of four houses on Caffin Avenue—and a cool design for a construction sign. Neither the houses nor the sign were built. The potential of community, the first requirement of repositioning in place, failed to materialize, creating little incentive for residents to return.

Just as significantly, the project had no impact in repositioning the neighborhood's infrastructure. Despite cordial and supportive meetings with various agencies and authorities, the relationship of houses and lots to the larger field that we articulated in our grant study was met with sympathy but no shift in the repair/replace-in-kind strategies of these beleaguered and underfunded entities. Had the houses and cisterns that we designed been built, LEED-certified or state-of-the-shelf green, they would have risen on the same fractured and vulnerable ground.

CODA

This is one story among many about the degrees of success and failure (in our case, success on paper, failure on the ground) among relatively small-scale efforts at recovery after the nation's greatest (or at least most abrupt) natural and civic disaster. These efforts operated in the near total absence of coordinated planning at *any* credible scale at *any* level of government. Perhaps it's too obvious to mention, but New Orleans's planning crisis was around long before Katrina and only partly accounts for the failure of most of our efforts, even in aggregate and despite heroic levels of civic activism, to achieve the scale of response warranted by disasters such as Katrina—or suburban sprawl.

Even as we acknowledge that the Adjudicated Properties Project took building houses as its urgent and primary mission, the scattered lots of our devastated neighborhood clearly demanded a more global approach. The district planners who led the Unified New Orleans Plan (UNOP), the Office of Recovery Management (ORM), the Public Works Department, the Sewerage and Water Board, and even Entergy New

Orleans may have liked our ideas about soft streets and solar panels, but no mechanism, policy, or budget exists to incorporate these strategies into the recovery effort, even as millions flow for street, drainage, and utility work. Nor did our politically freighted, strapped-for-cash, not-for-profit developer/client consider this within its scope of work. Development models in which architecture is conceived as more or less autonomous cannot address the environmental (or the social) challenges of New Orleans's devastated neighborhoods. In a place where inches of topological difference can be critical, design strategies on scales ranging from the house lot to the levee system that knit house, lot, street, and levee into larger performative fields are of no small importance.

The wasting of Detroit or the slo-mo collapse of governance in California, as much as Katrina or the Great Recession, are dead canaries: indicators all of the *absence* of the capacity needed for planning at *any* critical scale. Reductive development models may be the consequence of a general governance crisis, or a radically privatized recovery effort based on the individual citizen, or a fractured and fractious array of public agencies and political jurisdictions. Though we rush to fill the void with our good ideas, best practices, and community-based initiatives, we soon confront this absence at the end of our streets, and very little scales up.

POSTSCRIPT

On April 1, 2010, ACORN ceased national operations and filed for bankruptcy after more than a year of alleged scandals and relentless embarrassment in the press. ACORN Housing relinquished its development rights to the tax-adjudicated properties it had been awarded in New Orleans, transferring the few lots to which it had clear title to a local not-for-profit; the remaining lots retain their tax-adjudicated status. None of the originally awarded lots have been redeveloped. ACORN Housing continues to operate nationally but has changed its name to Affordable Housing Centers of America. It does not maintain an office in New Orleans.

GREEN.O.LA: A MODEL BLOCK FOR HOLY CROSS

MATTHEW BERMAN and ANDREW KOTCHEN

The Sustainable Design Competition (2006) for New Orleans, sponsored by Brad Pitt and Global Green USA, set out to create affordable, efficient, and healthy housing that could become a prototype for the rebuilding of the entire hurricane-damaged Gulf Coast region. From among 125 entries submitted by an international group of architects, Matthew Berman and Andrew Kotchen's firm workshop/apd was selected in August 2006 to design a model block for the Holy Cross neighborhood of New Orleans. The envisioned mixed-use development was to include an eighteen-unit multifamily building, five single-family homes, and a community center with services for working families, such as daycare and retail. In Berman and Kotchen's design, the community center anchors the site and also functions as a resource center where residents can learn more about sustainable design and green building practices. Additionally, the "educational transect" linking the project to the Mississippi riverfront provides an outdoor recreation area for the entire neighborhood. It is hoped that the model block will act as a catalyst for every scale of rebuilding: the neighborhood, the city, and beyond. Anthony Fontenot interviewed Matthew Berman and Andrew Kotchen on May 16, 2011.

FONTENOT: How did your office first get involved with doing work in New Orleans following Hurricane Katrina?

BERMAN: Right after the disaster, most people wanted to help New Orleans, either financially or physically, by participating in the cleanup efforts. Our ability to make a financial contribution was limited, and we couldn't leave our office for a long period of time. While waiting for the right opportunity to contribute, we became aware of a competition that was sponsored by Tulane University and *Architectural Record* called "High Density on the High Ground." It challenged designers to examine an industrial area on the high ground along the river and to develop strategies for multifamily housing. Given that it was an "ideas" competition, we were free to pursue more radical ideas and fortunately were selected as one of five commended projects. We traveled to New Orleans and could not believe what we saw. Eight months had passed since the

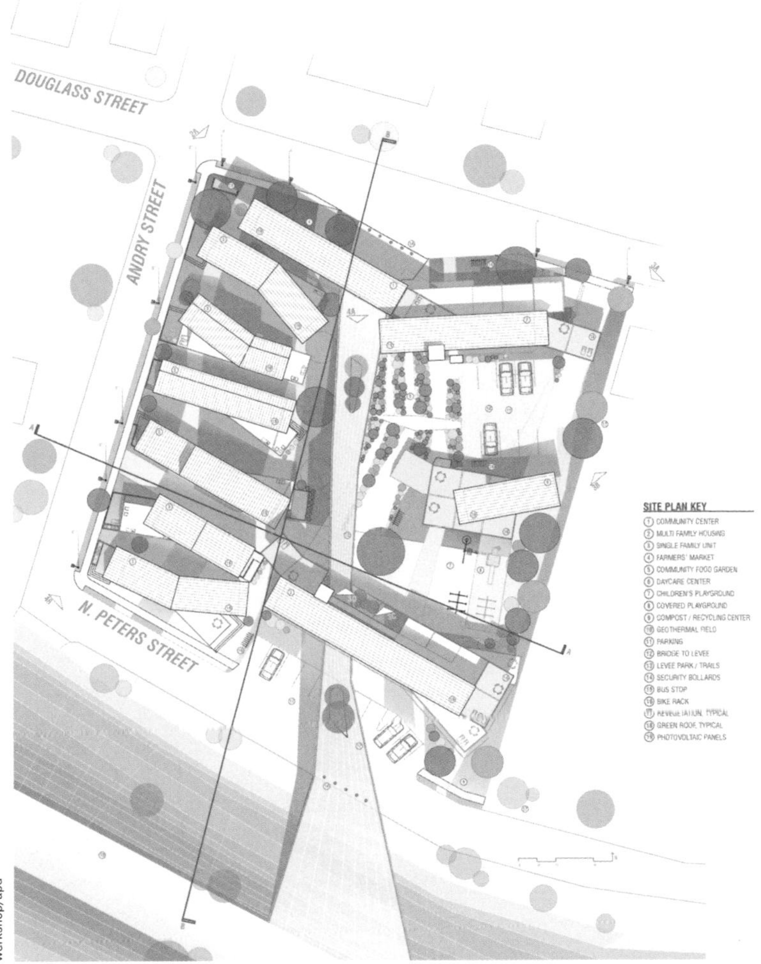

wcrkshop/apd

A plan showing the architects' site competition-winning strategy for a single block and the massing and configuration of housing units and community buildings on it.

disaster, and many areas were still covered with debris. The city was still crippled, and we knew that more help was needed.

When Global Green USA and Brad Pitt announced the Sustainable Design Competition for New Orleans, we saw an opportunity to take our work a step further. It was a multistage competition that asked participants to address the multifamily component and the sustainable goals first, followed by a second stage that addressed the single-family houses. Our original proposal featured a landscape sloping up to the levee, with building components sliced into the terrain. We were selected as one of six semifinalists. However, although the seeds of some good ideas were there, and the design jury liked the direction, the technical jury tore us apart, turning many of the assumptions that we had made on their proverbial heads. Humbled, we followed their advice and continued to develop the project.

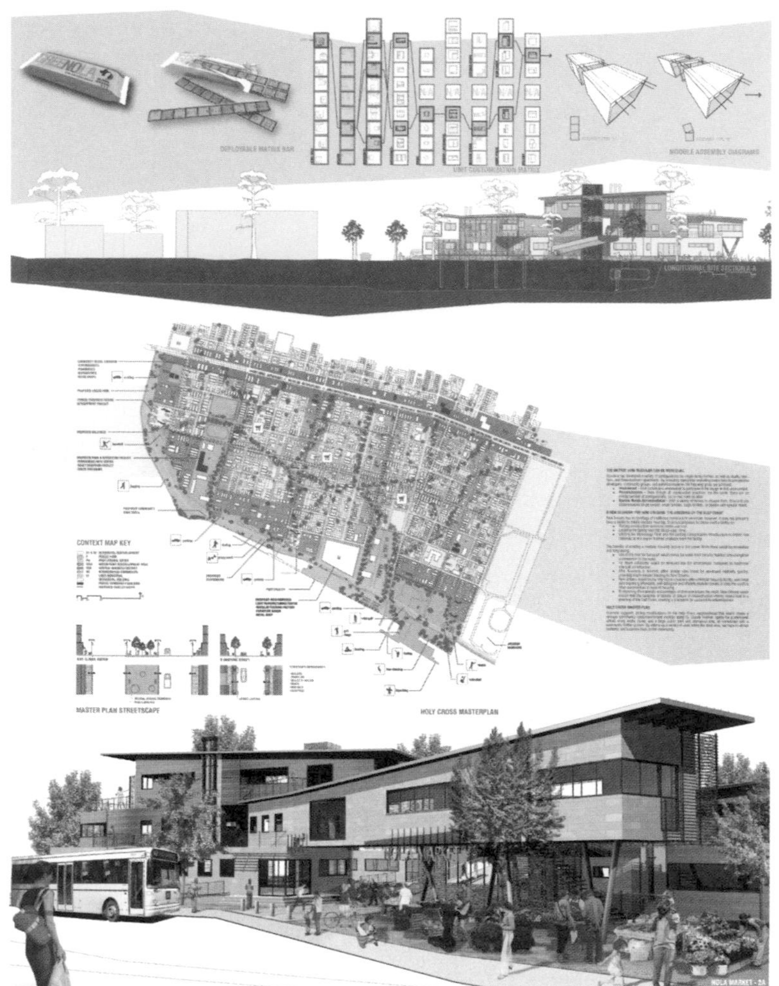

Holy Cross Farmers' Market, illustrated at the top left of the Holy Cross neighborhood block plan

workshop/apd

Following those jury reviews, over a period of six weeks, semifinalists each made several trips to New Orleans to present their ideas to community groups and get feedback. These meetings were invaluable and gave us an opportunity to listen and educate, spending a lot of time discussing the merits of pursuing a more progressive vernacular instead of simply re-creating what had been destroyed. It was very important for us to understand the fundamental strengths of the local architecture. It was also important for the future of New Orleans that the community allow us to develop the local architecture in a way that could be carried forward. We were told that one of the reasons we won the competition was that we listened and responded thoroughly to what the community had to say. With any project, one is always balancing one's own interest and what one feels most strongly about with the feedback one gets from

workshop/apd

Exterior of the completed Global Green house

the client. This project has come a long way. It doesn't look exactly like what we originally designed or what won. The first house has some great qualities, but at a high cost. The other houses are good examples of how to achieve a similar look but on a much more responsible budget. At the end of the day, what excites us about this project is not one building but rather the power of the entire complex to create a new sense of place within the community.

FONTENOT: Where does the project currently stand? How many houses have been built so far? And what aspects of the project are you most excited about?

BERMAN: The Community Center is looking really sharp. It meets the budget and was approved by HDLC [Historic District Landmarks Commission]. It incorporates a corner store with a canopy, offices for Global Green, a local bank or credit union, and a cistern system shrouded in a metal mesh that glows at night. The back of the building abuts the "rain garden," which stretches out toward the levee and separates the backs of the houses from the more public gathering spaces. If the apartment building is built, the site will be more like a campus with various conditions of a domestic edge, a community edge, and a more multiuse edge. Although many of the details have changed, the overall planning strategy is still very much the same.

FONTENOT: It appears to me that this project is unique in many ways compared with other projects that were proposed and built following Katrina. How do you think this project distinguishes itself from other reconstruction projects in New Orleans?

KOTCHEN: Most of the press about our project has focused on the green story. While that's a great story to tell, it is one-dimensional. There should be more of a discussion about the evolution of design and how one can create a "progressive vernacular" that relates to a particular context but doesn't copy it. I think that is a more interesting story and deals with the history and future of the city. We spent a lot of time trying to understand that context, and the houses we designed reflect that. You could take any one of them and put it in another New Orleans neighborhood, and there would be a contextual relationship to the broader New Orleans fabric. I don't think that can be said of all of the new homes being built in New Orleans today.

FONTENOT: Can you talk a little bit more about what you believe are the fundamental contextual relationships that the designs are responding to?

KOTCHEN: One is proportion. Many New Orleans homes are narrow and long, and our homes are similar. Additionally, on the interior the proportions create a succession of spaces, causing occupants to move through rooms to get from one to the next. Front porches and roof planes are also essential to maintaining a connection to the neighborhood at ground level and from a distance. For us, it was extremely important to create an architectural language grounded in the history of place that could also move New Orleans forward into the next century.

FONTENOT: It is interesting to position your work among the various models of reconstruction that were offered following Katrina, such as the traditional model of replicating what existed, on the one hand, and the far-out contemporary model, on the other.

KOTCHEN: Unfortunately, no one talks about this. Each one is being developed in its own vacuum. Six years later, we should take a very critical look at what has been and is being done and create a positive forum for discussing the merits of each model proposed for reconstruction so that more learning can happen instead of everyone doing their own thing.

BERMAN: The other big difference is that, although we have completed five houses, our project is still a work in progress. The community center is set to begin construction this year, and it will be a huge addition to the site. This was always meant to be a model block. One of the big differences between this project and some of the others is that this is about more than replacing lost housing. Global Green wanted to create a new core that would enable the community to thrive. We defined this as "Live, Work, Play"—a community had to provide all three of these elements to its residents, instead of depending on the larger city for them. Our goal was to suggest ways that the neighborhood could be more self-sustaining. A neighborhood needs to serve the needs of its people, especially considering that many lack private transportation.

FONTENOT: The implication of your model block is particularly interesting because it deals with so many pressing issues simultaneously. As it keeps accumulating more elements, it becomes larger than itself. It is really unfortunate that there has not been more discussion about that aspect of the project so far. I also think it is unfortunate that the client will not attempt to replicate this model in other parts of the city, especially given that it has now been engineered to the point where it is feasible. The last houses are being built for a fraction of what the first house cost, which is an amazing accomplishment. It would be really unfortunate if it just stopped there. Why do you think other people have not picked up on the project as a relevant model for other parts of the city?

KOTCHEN: Replicating the concept, as Make It Right did, requires investment. Their infrastructure is built to enable development. Global Green, on the other hand, is not a developer. To their credit, this was a huge undertaking at the time. Ours was the first Global Green house.

BERMAN: It certainly should be possible to package up the set of drawings with the specs and offer them to anybody who wants to build.

KOTCHEN: That is kind of what [the firm's online platform] RightFrame is intended to do. The goal of RightFrame is to do the whole house as one package.

BERMAN: RightFrame came out of the New Orleans project. As we went through this process, from competition to reality, we continually evaluated materials and products that were outside of the high-end world that we had been operating in. The budget was extremely tight, so we had to look for novel ways to achieve our design and performance goals. We learned quickly that affordability and sustainability were unfortunately at odds with one another. It was very frustrating because we wanted state-of-the-art but could only afford state-of-the-shelf. We also learned that there was very limited access to clear information. What was available was mostly confusing and oftentimes contradictory. There are a lot of good products out there that people should know about, and there are a lot of practical green solutions that do not cost a fortune. RightFrame's goal is to get better design to more people and empower the consumer in the process.

FONTENOT: How did your office and Global Green go about establishing the "green" agenda for the first house?

BERMAN: The goals for the first house resulted after about a year of discussions and research with many consultants. Each was charged with the task of looking for the best solution to something, from building systems, to cooling systems, to energy generation, and so on. This research yielded suggestions for implementation, and some were feasible and others were not. Additionally, as the project advanced toward becoming a reality, it became even more important to focus on what could be done now, with the technology that existed, and not get sidetracked by what might exist in the future. One of the main goals of this project was to make it repeatable. If it could not be replicated, it would be of little value to the local community. The first house was a proving ground for many advanced ideas, but ultimately it was not replicable. The second set of houses was much more so, and now, finally, we have a third set of houses that are very replicable. Cost, products, and construction all align, and one can be built for a reasonable market price; it is very "state-of-the-shelf."

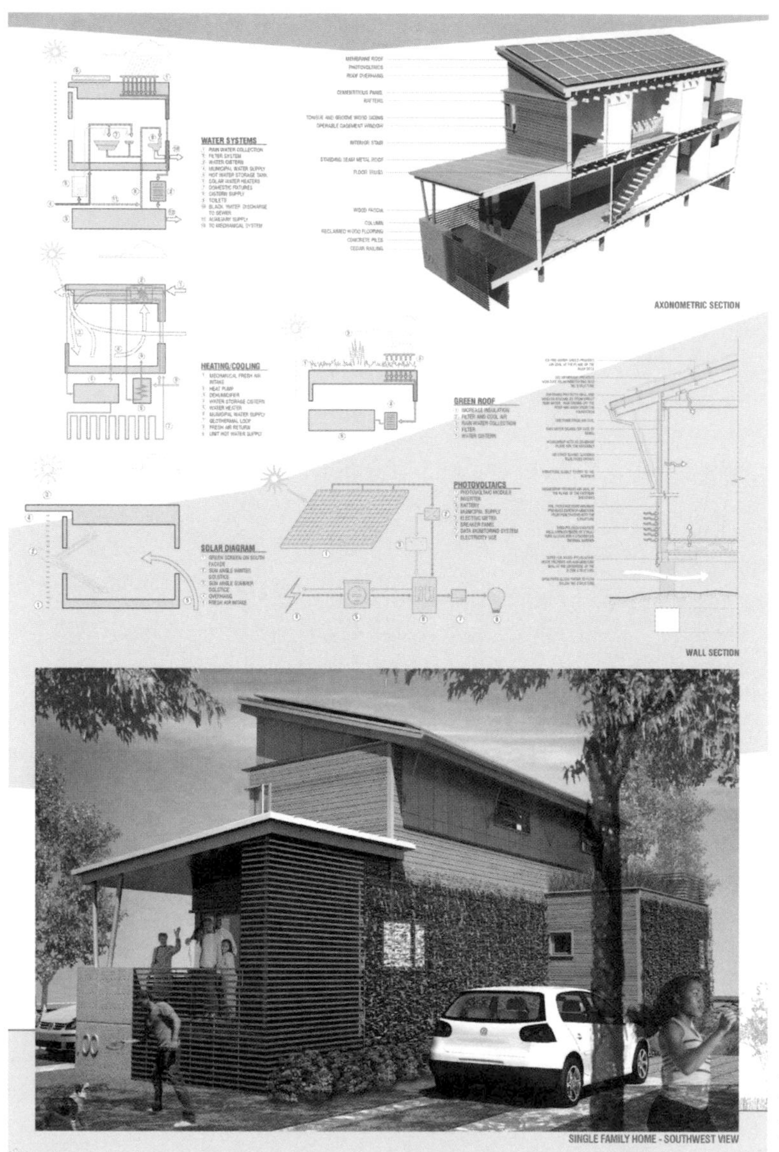

workshop/apd

Competition submission depicting the environmental systems of the Global Green house

To the incredible credit of Global Green, their team was determined to create an affordable, sustainable, and replicable model while educating the trades and local providers along the way. For example, a plumber who had never installed an on-demand hot water system might ask a premium to do it. Although it is not a complicated system to install, lack of knowledge drives the price up. This project sought to eliminate that type of obstacle to using new systems, so that the local community could reap the benefit. Now plumbers routinely connect these systems—and there are many other local tradespeople who know how to execute systems that had been previously unfamiliar. They have raised the level of the shelf.

FONTENOT: As I mentioned before, now that a model for a "green house" has been figured out and packaged in a way that it can be reproduced, I am astounded that—especially given the primary goals of the project—there are no developers who see this as a gold mine. It is a system that has been proven to be feasible and cost effective.

BERMAN: It will take time and money.

FONTENOT: But all the parts have been figured out. If someone came to you and said, "I would like to build one of these houses," would you be able to honor that wish?

BERMAN: Ultimately Global Green would have to make that decision.

FONTENOT: Is this the [intellectual] property of workshop/apd or of Global Green?

BERMAN: It is a jointly owned product.

FONTENOT: If someone in New Orleans, or anywhere for that matter, wanted to build one of these houses, would they be able to use the existing plans?

BERMAN: We discussed that possibility at the very beginning, and we are all open to it. We just need to figure out the logistics. It would be a joint effort between our office and Global Green. I think we would all be very excited if someone wanted to do this work on a significant scale.

FONTENOT: Given the various proposals that were put forth following Katrina, this project may be one of the only examples of urban reconstruction based on a model master plan of a complete urban block. It is extremely exciting to witness it move from a proposal to actualization and to see how it will change the context of the neighborhood.

BERMAN: It will either work very well or not. At least it does not just re-create a pattern that was there, but instead attempts to rethink a pattern that can complement the context while challenging some of the current notions about development. This project is a great opportunity to understand the impact that architecture can have on the evolution of a plan. Now we can study many different plans and typologies that have been put in place in New Orleans post-Katrina and begin to evaluate what impact those typologies have had on the city, whether it be the Duany/Plater-Zyberk model, the Make It Right model, or our model. Many years later, we are now able to begin testing a compatibility or reaction and discuss the effects that each model has had on the city. Can we start looking with hindsight at these projects in a way that gives us a big enough picture to understand the relationships of each to the city, or is it still too soon? Can we step back and look at, say, three or four different typologies of post-Katrina—the Duany/Plater-Zyberk cottages, Tulane's URBAN Build projects, Make It Right, and our progressive vernacular—and be able to discern their long-term value for the city?

FONTENOT: Did you coin the term *progressive vernacular*?

BERMAN: No. Allen Eskew coined it. We think it is a brilliant term and have used it ever since we first heard it. For lay audiences, the word *vernacular* makes them feel comfortable, but *modern* and *contemporary* scare many people. The word *progressive* gives us a little leeway to do what we want to do. It very accurately describes the type of work we are interested in developing.

FONTENOT: It is particularly interesting to me to hear your enthusiasm about the term and that you find it so useful. Along with other architects in New Orleans, for many years Allen Eskew has been developing these ideas in an effort to establish a critical practice that can respond to the specific conditions of the city. I think it is important for the development of New Orleans that architects engage with broader critical ideas outside the region. In that way, one can begin to produce a particular method that is useful for thinking not only about New Orleans but about other contexts as well. In fact, many of the current experiments in New Orleans might prove to have a kind of universal relevance. What are some of the key lessons you have learned about the role of sustainable architecture and urbanism in the twenty-first century by working in post-Katrina New Orleans?

BERMAN: I think the biggest lesson might be that there is a still a very wide knowledge gap between what most people think can be accomplished using state-of-the-shelf materials and how much actually can be. This project and our current work with RightFrame seek to change that.

PROJECTS
MULTI-UNIT HOUSING

New Orleans is not a town of multiple dwellings—beyond the ubiquitous "doubles" that in varying stylistic dress populate all of the city's neighborhoods. Indeed, before the storm the most visible multiple constructions were the series of federally financed housing projects that provided homes for more than 5,000 families. Federal and local officials had long wished to see these units expunged. Following federally mandated integration and ensuing white flight, they were overwhelmingly occupied by African Americans, and, after Katrina, HUD boarded them up and prevented their residents from returning, despite the fact that these sturdy buildings had survived the storm almost unscathed. The scandal of this forcible eviction raised two key questions regarding apartment buildings in a radically depopulated city: who would live in them and what the role of density would be in a shrinking environment.

For the most part, post-Katrina proposals for multiple dwellings have been based on a logic of concentration that is not specific to New Orleans, rather on a more general idea of the social and environmental benefits of urban density. Little attention has been paid to the hot potato of public housing, perhaps because it is such an overwhelmingly non-architectural matter. For now, HUD continues along the path laid out and followed before the storm, converting the housing projects under its jurisdiction into mixed-income developments in classic Hope VI–style misdirection, the "mix" to be obtained by simply throwing 90 percent of the poor out of their homes.

The designs included here are particularly attuned to opportunities that reflect special attractors for density: sites along the river and atop the levees. Reconstituting the city to take advantage of such "natural" opportunities makes sense if it can be done within a larger context of equity and access.

Global Green USA Competition, Sustainable Design for New Orleans:

ECO-SHELLS

SOFT SHOE STUDIO

Forest Hills, New York

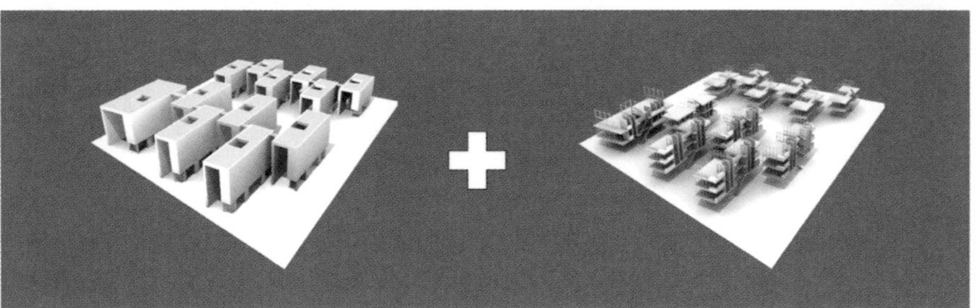

eco-shells adaptive occupancy

Principal: Francis Hur
Designers: Francis Hur, Aya Maeda

As its name suggests, the eco-shell is an external envelope, designed to withstand New Orleans's environmental challenges and allow several life cycles of residents to create spaces fulfilling their needs and preferences. Imagined as a long-term infrastructural investment, the eco-shell has a permanent outer structure of double-wall, insulated, unit masonry with openings spaced to receive joists and beams at any level, allowing for maximum adaptability in the interior. The green roof provides rainwater filtration and storage.

Global Green USA Competition, Sustainable Design for New Orleans:

LOCAL GREEN, LIVE WORK PLAY

CP+D WORKSHOP

Charlottesville, Virginia

Principal: Judith Kinnard, FAIA
Designers: Judith Kinnard, FAIA; Maurice Cox, Justin Laskin, Pete O'Shea, Leigh Wilkerson, Giovanna Galfione, Kenneth Schwartz, FAIA; Kathleen Mark

Local Green was created for New Orleans's Holy Cross neighborhood. The proposal integrates the levees that border Holy Cross into the fabric of the neighborhood by reshaping them as gently sloping parks rather than sharply defined barriers. Housing designs draw on the historical precedent of narrow street frontage, and spaces between and atop homes are available for urban farming and forestry. All elements are designed to be sustainable, with homes planned for maximum energy efficiency and with a water management system that supports farming and does not rely on the city's decaying infrastructure.

ECOLOGICAL CROSSINGS IN NEW ORLEANS

GRADUATE SCHOOL OF ARCHITECTURE, PLANNING, AND PRESERVATION

Columbia University, New York City

Instructor: Laurie Hawkinson
Designer: Huey-Jye Kahn

This community development plan for New Orleans's Gentilly neighborhood, based on studies of the typical residential block, links prefabricated houses using a "green" system of communal pathways and open spaces. The houses and greenways are elevated to help them withstand severe flooding, and rooftop gardens provide additional, more personalized outdoor space.

Architectural Record Competition: High Density on the High Ground

FEMANATOR: CAN A TRAILER PARK EVOLVE?

m2d

Brooklyn, New York

can a trailer park **evolve?**

Principal: Matthew Dockery

This project proposes a new kind of trailer park that is able to fill the immediate and long-term needs of a post-disaster city. Inspired by the problematic fact that the federal government ordered 300,000 trailers to the New Orleans region after Hurricane Katrina yet lacked the capacity to deploy and maintain these shelters, this scheme provides shelter, security, services, and community developed over time. *Femanator* imagines a series of phased interventions that would help an emergency trailer park evolve into a stable and secure residential environment.

RESILIENT TOPOGRAPHIES: ASCENDING GARDENS

SCHOOL OF DESIGN

University of Pennsylvania, Philadelphia

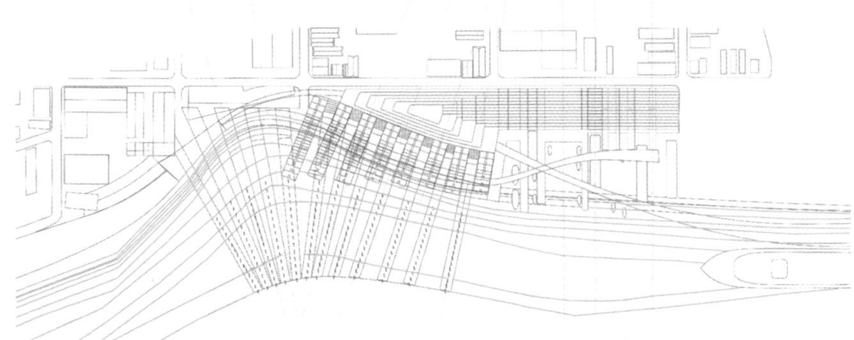

Instructor: Marion Weiss
Designers: Chin Ming Chang, Diego Pacheco

This project proposes a high-density, multiple-unit housing complex with adjacent commercial and cultural buildings—a museum of hydrology, a market, and a ship terminal. The differentiated levels of the roofs of the complex can be planted as individualized green spaces specific to each unit or group of units. The project is sited on the riverbank, east of downtown New Orleans.

DENSITY AND THE ARCHITECTURE OF EXCHANGE

SCHOOL OF ARCHITECTURE

Tulane University, New Orleans

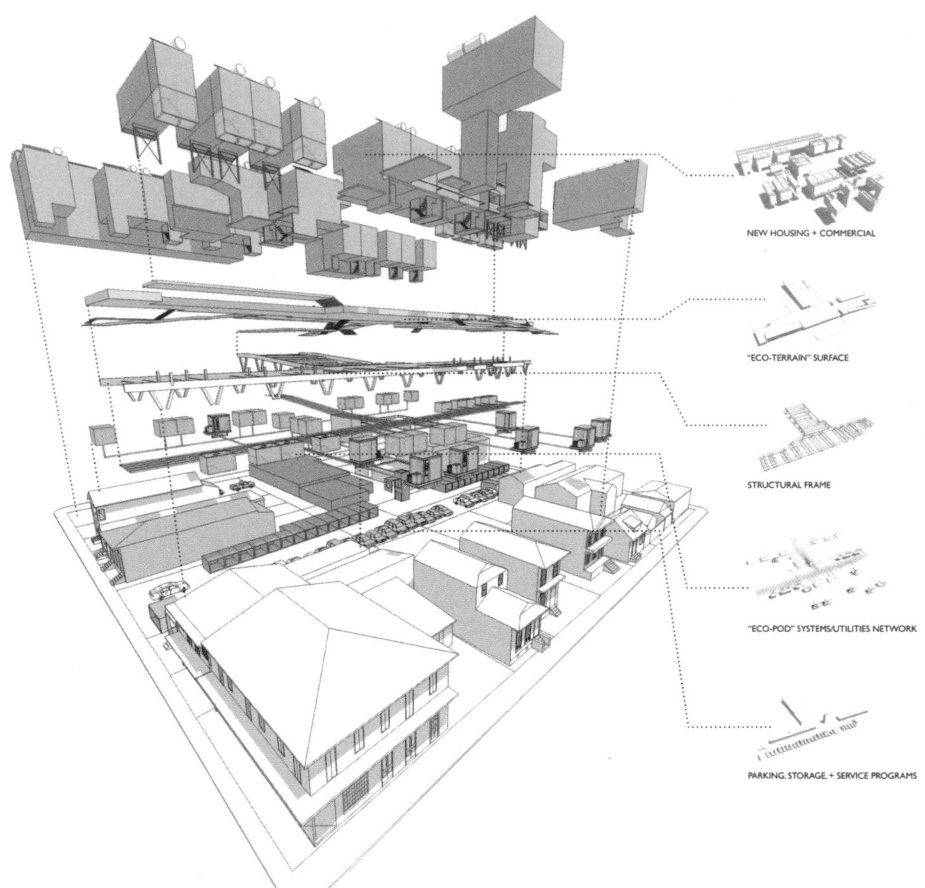

Instructor: Doug Harmon
Designer: Blake Fisher

Responding to arguments urging a decreased footprint for post-Katrina New Orleans, this proposal explores a sustainable neighborhood model for higher density on high ground that could be inserted in the existing built fabric, avoiding wholesale demolition. The design uses the "leftover" spaces of the interiors of typical city blocks, building into them structural frameworks on which housing units are stacked. The ground-level area of this layered scheme provides for parking, storage, day-care facilities, and utilities.

PART V
RECONSTRUCTING THE PUBLIC SPHERE

REINVENTING THE CRESCENT
R. ALLEN ESKEW

Reinventing the Crescent is a joint effort of the New Orleans Building Corporation (NOBC), the Port of New Orleans, and the City of New Orleans to transform the relationship between the city and the river. In September 2006, the NOBC board of directors announced a competition to design a redevelopment plan for a six-mile strip along the Mississippi River, stretching upriver from Poland Avenue to Jackson Avenue. A team led by Allen Eskew of Eskew+Dumez+Ripple (EDR, New Orleans), with Alex Krieger of Chan Krieger Sieniewicz (Cambridge, Massachusetts), George Hargreaves of Hargreaves Associates (San Francisco), and Enrique Norten of TEN Arquitectos (New York and Mexico City), was selected to produce a master development plan. Phase I of the plan, which includes public recreational amenities downriver from the French Quarter, is currently under way, led by EDR, with David Adjaye Associates (London), Michael Maltzan Architecture (Los Angeles), and Hargreaves Associates. Anthony Fontenot interviewed Allen Eskew on June 15, 2011.

FONTENOT: Reinventing the Crescent is particularly interesting because it seems to function somewhat outside the "official" reconstruction efforts currently going forward in New Orleans.[1] Who initiated the project and what was its primary goal? Perhaps you could explain the significance of changes in the design team over time. Also, was it just coincidence that, following Katrina, Reinventing the Crescent emerged as a major redevelopment project at approximately the same time that a master plan for the city was being developed?

ESKEW: Katrina hit during the third year of Mayor Ray Nagin's term. If one goes back to 2002, when Nagin was elected, he appointed a young, local, and stylish developer named Sean Cummings, who had been very supportive of his mayoral candidacy, as CEO of the New Orleans Building Corporation, one of several benefit corporations that handle various portfolios of properties for the city. Sean, who owns a series of hotels

1 See reinventingthecrescent.org.

and apartment buildings in the city, was always interested in the larger development of the New Orleans riverfront. So as a representative of the city he began working with the port on a cooperative endeavor agreement. One of the things that stymies New Orleans in any kind of best-practice riverfront development is the fact that the state owns the port—all appointments to the Board of Commissioners of the Port of New Orleans are made by the governor. In typical Louisiana fashion, the operations of the port are under the domain of the state, but the residual land is owned by the city of New Orleans, and a sort of dysfunctional relationship exists. Neither the city nor the state has complete authority over the port's activity or the real estate. For years in New Orleans, every time developers tried to do something on the riverfront, they would start negotiating with one, eventually start negotiating with the other, and would never be able to close the loop. It was Sean Cummings who called that into question and then proceeded over a couple of years to negotiate with the port to create a cooperative-effort agreement that is now prescriptive to a six-mile stretch of the port, which is gradually being decommissioned.

I will put it very simply: A formula was developed for sharing the revenues, so that if a place on the riverfront were to be turned into a for-profit commercial development, the port would get a percentage of the revenues and the city would get another percentage. It was predetermined so that the developer did not have to negotiate ad nauseam to the point of throwing in the towel and walking away from the project. So Sean got the public-policy work done, and then Katrina happened. After Katrina we were all focusing on saving the city and rebuilding. Sean realized that if in the rush to rebuild the city and in the rush for a new master plan the riverfront were ignored—not as a recovery project but as what he called an "advancement project"—an opportunity would be missed. So he put together some funds from the New Orleans Building Corporation and published an international call for teams. I would say there were maybe twenty international teams that were formed and submitted requests for proposals. Five teams were shortlisted, one from Daniel Libeskind and a number of teams from Europe.[2] I put together a collection of distinguished players whom, according to our strategy, EDR would lead. I invited George Hargreaves—we were already working with him—Alex Krieger and Lawrence Chan for urban design, and Enrique Norten for the architectural component. So it was the four of us, plus ten or so technical consultants. I asked three of them to fly in for the interview, and in the end we won the day. In about eight months of work we produced a master plan, what Sean called a "development plan." That was then used by the city of New Orleans under the direction of Mayor Nagin, who had been reelected, to get a federal community development block grant

2 New Orleans Building Corporation, "New Orleans Riverfront: Reinventing the Crescent. Preliminary Framework and Concepts," 2007.

Fifteen special places along the river from Jackson Avenue, upriver, to the Holy Cross neighborhood, downriver

of 30 million dollars to support Phase I, which is what we call Crescent Park. When they announced Phase I, they put out another call for international teams. Since it is a public project, everything has to be totally transparent. A number of teams submitted, and I used the opportunity to slightly adjust my team because our prior team had been selected only to prepare the master plan. I did not ask Enrique Norten to move forward with us, but I invited David Adjaye and Michael Maltzan to join. So that addresses the second part of your question.

FONTENOT: So this collaboration is not an equal partnership. Eskew+Dumez+Ripple is the head of the team?

ESKEW: Yes, we are the executive architects in association with George Hargreaves, the design lead for the park. Michael Maltzan is an associate architect, as is David Adjaye, and Alex Krieger is an urban design consultant.

FONTENOT: Is Krieger still part of the team?

ESKEW: Krieger is still on, but his work has been very minimal in Phase I. He was much more involved in the initial master plan.

FONTENOT: Why did you select Adjaye and Maltzan? What aspects of their work were you most interested in as relevant to this project?

ESKEW: I appreciated the fact that Sean Cummings's motivation was to really use the post-Katrina "creative disruption" of the city as a way to try to set a high mark for expectations along the riverfront. Sean was not interested in developing a conservative plan. He was interested in something that was comparable to the best practices in the country. I love to collaborate and I sought out people who would spice up our team. Sean was certainly looking to put charisma and celebrity status on whatever team he and the selection committee chose. I was lucky enough to call it correctly that they were looking for some additional international cachet. I selected

Eskew+Dumez+Ripple

View looking upriver from the intersection of the Mississippi River and the Industrial Canal. Holy Cross Levee Promenade is in the foreground and Bywater Point and the Port of Embarkation redevelopment appear in the middle ground.

David Adjaye, the Tanzanian-born architect from London. I thought an African architect would be an interesting fit. We had met David right after Katrina. Like us, he was among the first thirteen architects working on the Make It Right project. I brought Maltzan to the table because I think he is one of the most interesting architects in the country at the moment. I love his work, and I thought he would be a good addition.

FONTENOT: What role do you think Reinventing the Crescent plays in the larger scheme of the reconstruction of New Orleans?

ESKEW: For me, the role it initially played was that it got out in front of all the neighborhood planning. The riverfront was being marginalized because whichever neighborhoods touched the river were considering it in their individual plans. The riverfront was being chopped up into increments, and there was no larger conceptual framework to take it into account. I started working on the riverfront in 1980, for the 1984 World's Fair, so I have been involved in riverfront projects in this community for approximately thirty years. And in that time what I observed was that only little bitty incremental interventions were proposed. There was not a big vision for what that six-mile stretch should be. I really applaud Sean for giving us the opportunity to create one. Although it is a development plan and does not have the force of law, it was well done because we did it with the input of the community over the course of at least twenty public meetings. Now the official city planners—as New Orleans moves forward with a master plan that does have the force of law—are adopting many of the things that we identified and articulated in renderings and brought to life in the development plan. So I guess my quick answer to you is, concerning the development plan, we had a client who allowed us to create a vision for six miles rather than just to take parochial views along the riverfront, neighborhood by neighborhood.

FONTENOT: Are there relationships between Reinventing the Crescent and the various neighborhood plans that were incorporated into the city's master plan? In other words, are there specific connections between the way the master plan treats various neighborhoods that front on the river and aspects of your plan, or are the two separate and unconnected?

ESKEW: I always describe it as a very organic set of events. What happened was traumatic, no matter how you cut it. Whether you say there are seventy-two neighborhoods or there are the original set of neighborhoods, the planners bundled them into thirteen planning districts as a way to manage recovery planning all over the city. Reinventing the Crescent was not a recovery plan, except economically; it certainly was not envisioned to repair stuff that had been torn out in the storm. I think that almost all of the planners who took part in creating the official master plan for the city acknowledged the work that we did. David Dixon, the chief planner for Goody Clancy, the Boston firm that led the master planning in New Orleans, asked to review our progress on the riverfront development plan every time he saw me because he thought it was such a good document. He was able to absorb it into his process, and it served as a kind of plug-in document for his own work.[3] Our development plan is very well respected in the city, and it is still posted on the city's website. I think we captured the community's imagination.

FONTENOT: What were some of the main concerns raised about this plan, and how have you addressed them moving forward?

ESKEW: I have learned through many years of design and planning work in the public realm that complications in communications and process get in the way of design intent. Reinventing the Crescent has generated a lot of public conversation, as we hoped it would. During the planning process we had more than twenty public meetings and countless smaller focus-group meetings to ensure that community and neighborhood input was valued. Kristina Ford, who served as executive director of city planning and of the NOBC, duly noted the criticisms of the city's planning process and regulatory protocols in her recent book, *The Trouble with City Planning*.[4] The other major dynamic during our planning process was the leadership of the official client, NOBC, which Sean Cummings led. Because of Sean's commercial real estate background, community activists sometimes challenged his objectives for the project. However, I saw his leadership to be clear and focused on maximizing this special riverfront real estate for the public good.

3 On the final post-Katrina master-planning effort, the outcome of which was "Plan for the 21st Century: New Orleans 2030," see David Dixon's essay in Part II of this volume.

4 Kristina Ford, *The Trouble with City Planning: What New Orleans Can Teach Us* (New Haven, CT: Yale, 2010). Ford served as the executive director of the New Orleans City Planning Commission from 1992 until 2000, under mayors Sidney Barthelemy and Marc H. Morial. Mayor Morial named Ford executive director of NOBC in 2000, a post she held until 2002, when Ray Nagin assumed the mayoralty and named Sean Cummings in her stead. Under Mayor Mitchell J. ("Mitch") Landrieu (elected in 2010), Ford returned to New Orleans to serve as a key aide to Cedric Grant, Landrieu's deputy mayor of Facilities, Infrastructure, and Community Development. Grant's portfolio includes the executive directorship of the NOBC. Ford left her most recent post with the city in June 2011.

FONTENOT: During the eighteenth and nineteenth centuries in New Orleans, there was a much more integrated relationship between the city and the river. Then in the twentieth century, infrastructure interventions introduced a series of levees and massive concrete walls. A kind of Berlin Wall phenomenon emerged in New Orleans, separating the city and the river—for example, along Tchoupitoulas Street upriver from the French Quarter. The city is surrounded by water, but residents have very little access to it. The goal of this project seems to be to undo that history of separation and bring the city back to the river by offering a series of new public spaces. In addition to the linear parks, what types of programs and urban spaces are being proposed? What are, say, three key ideas that are being developed?

ESKEW: Let me preface my response by saying that your observations about New Orleans being disconnected from the river are true. However, this is an ordinary situation in U.S. cities. The classic American riverfront strategy is to use the river's edge as an industrial corridor. I would say that it has only been since the 1980s that American cities have started looking to their waterfront as an area ripe for development and that there has been a renaissance. Even in Manhattan there is not a consistent or comprehensive waterfront master plan. There are some wonderful isolated projects in Manhattan, but they are not connected. New Orleans should not be overcriticized. I think we are fortunate in that we do not have manufacturing along the river. We have benign warehouses.

So to address your point about three big ideas, I would say that the biggest was the way that we found to establish a linear path of six miles of public space along the waterfront and use it to offer a string-of-pearls experience. We started from Jackson Square, which is right in the middle. We have an overlook, which is our ceremonial ground zero. Then downriver, at the Governor Nicholas, Esplanade Avenue, and Mandeville wharfs, we've developed plans for what could arguably become the largest sheds for riverside public festivals. New Orleans probably has more festivals than any other city in the country. Currently the riverfront is an underperforming venue, with potential for hosting many more events. Ten acres of covered festival decks right on the side of the Mississippi River, with sun and rain protection, makes our hosting of festivals near the French Quarter and at the edge of the Marigny a very dependably lucrative business model. So that is another big idea. Finally, we envisioned a complete rethinking of the area upriver at Jackson Square near Canal Street and Poydras Street that includes the possibility of taking down the old World Trade Center building.[5] I have been championing its site for our tricentennial, which will be in 2018. I think of the riverfront as our front porch—a series of front porches for the city. I think it is part of the culture of the city, a city with a great personality.

5 The International Trade Mart, designed by Edward Durell Stone in 1959.

Eskew+Dumez+Ripple

Michael Maltzan's bridge connection to the event area under the Mandeville Wharf Shed

Eskew+Dumez+Ripple

Event area under the Mandeville Wharf Shed

FONTENOT: The pavilion designed by Frank Gehry for the 1984 World's Fair in New Orleans was located directly along the river. Many people were very excited by this space because one could watch performances with a dramatic background of boats moving along the river. There was great disappointment when it was demolished. The project offers an interesting precedent: It featured innovative work by a prominent architect and also exposed the potential for developing new types of spaces in the city.

ESKEW: Yes, absolutely.

FONTENOT: The mid-twentieth century saw contributions to modern architecture in New Orleans that were recognized nationally and internationally. New Orleans has not occupied that position for quite some time. Given the infusion of national and international architects and planners working in the city since Katrina, to what degree do you think New Orleans might now be able to reengage an international dialogue about contemporary architecture and planning?

ESKEW: You are right that since the heyday of the 1960s, when Arthur Davis and Buster Curtis were practicing, New Orleans has not been performing up to its full potential. There was a period when Curtis and Davis, although based in New Orleans, also had offices in New York and Berlin. They won more progressive architecture design awards in one

Eskew+Dumez+Ripple

David Adjaye's Piety Street Bridge connection to Piety Wharf and Gardens

ten-year period than any other firm in the country. In addition, Charles Colbert practiced here, and so did James Lamantia. A number of practitioners working in this city were committed to modern architecture. Arthur Davis and I are good friends, and I am very fond of listening to him tell stories about how he and Buster just decided that, given a chance, they were going to do nothing but practice contemporary architecture—that was where they hung their hats.

You are also right that no other firm filled that role in the 1970s, 80s, and 90s. Our firm has been working very hard, and there are a number of people in the city who now acknowledge that we are the first one since Curtis and Davis to have arrived at a similar level of national recognition based on a portfolio of work that is unabashedly modernist. I am proud to not only talk about that but actually to produce it. One of the strategies I employ to produce more contemporary architecture in New Orleans, in addition to our work, is to invite collaborators who arrive with portfolios, credentials, and celebrity status that can add more contemporary muscle to our efforts. This is a hell of a tough place to do contemporary architecture. I believe that the community is in many ways held hostage to the historical fabric. I talk about it in terms of authenticity. We have one of the finest, most truly authentic historical fabrics of any city, but replication and fake historicism are running amok; I include New Urbanism and all that comes with it in this judgment. I feel that we have an obligation to further develop the architecture of this city. The more we bring in and collaborate with great designers such as Adjaye, Maltzan, and Krieger, the more I think we help our portfolio and the city.

FONTENOT: I recently interviewed Matt Berman and Andrew Kotchen about their work in New Orleans, and they spoke quite a bit about the idea behind *progressive vernacular*, a term Matt claimed that you coined.

He was quite excited by the idea and said it had proved very helpful for them in thinking about their own work both in New Orleans and beyond.[6]

ESKEW: Matt is being very gracious. I have been working on that expression for a couple of years because I have found in my public advocacy that *vernacular* is a safe term. It is a bit academic, but when one says it, most citizens understand it as a reference to our historical urban fabric. When one tags *vernacular* with *progressive*, it is a safer way of saying *contemporary*—a word that has become so contaminated that the easiest way to derail a constructive conversation in New Orleans is to say that you will do something contemporary. Calling your plan progressive vernacular is a more strategic way of approaching the matter.

FONTENOT: What are the unique aspects and qualities of the projects in Reinventing the Crescent that most excite you?

ESKEW: I get asked this often, and I have to be careful, but I never back away from giving the same answer. We believed that in the development plan we needed to put forth images of hypothetical architecture that clearly said, "Given a chance to build on the riverfront, we, or whoever builds there, should build in a contemporary vocabulary and not continue to replicate and distort by wrapping buildings in historical costumes." Many still want to clothe our buildings in Victorian or Arts and Crafts dress. What we create in New Orleans now must be smart buildings, full of technology, able to accommodate air conditioning, etcetera—all the things that historic architecture was not. Every time we have an opportunity to show renderings or block-up massing on the riverfront, we present our ideas in a contemporary (or progressive vernacular) way. As you know, Anthony, anything in New Orleans over three stories is considered a high-rise. In terms of architectural taste, we have a very provincial community.

FONTENOT: I have a three-part question, and this will be my final question. I want to hear your thoughts on some of the larger issues that the city is currently facing. What were some of the most difficult urban issues that New Orleans was struggling with before Katrina? What, in your opinion, are some of the most devastating long-term consequences that Katrina has had on the city? And finally, what do you say to those critics who argue that we should be building houses—not parks—and securing the infrastructure to bring people back to the city?

ESKEW: For me, the biggest and most complicated issue post-Katrina is that our population peaked in 1962. A series of social reengineering episodes ensued, such as desegregation and white flight, and we also annexed New Orleans East, which added 50 percent to the footprint of the city. The African-American upper and middle classes moved to New Orleans East and, consequently, the city's historical core emptied. Concurrently, the white upper and middle classes moved to the surrounding, neighboring parishes of Jefferson and St. Bernard and also

6 See Anthony Fontenot's interview with Berman and Kotchen in Part IV of this volume.

Eskew+Dumez+Ripple

Piety Promenade and Gardens

across the lake to St. Tammany Parish. So between 1962 and 2005, our population decreased from 625,000 to 455,000, but our footprint increased by 50 percent. We had a significant loss in population density but not in historical fabric. This population shift created lots of vacant buildings in the core of the city, and that produced blight. What I learned a number of years ago was that one of the reasons New Orleans looks so Southern Gothic—funky and ruined—is that even before Katrina the city had a significant number of blighted properties.[7] We had a lot of empty space and a lot of people rattling around in the carcass of a city—not nearly as bad as Detroit, but the population was eroding. In 2005, our numbers were not declining at the same fast rate, but they weren't picking up, either. So that was the biggest issue we had before Katrina. How in the world can we make New Orleans a quality city when so much of it is blighted and we do not have the population to fill it?

The biggest tragedy after Katrina was a lack of leadership with the integrity and honesty to tell people that there are places in the city that are too dangerous to reoccupy. Instead, Mayor Nagin played the race card; he avoided taking responsibility and allowed people to start moving back. We lost that six-month window of opportunity when we really could have envisioned change based on our moral responsibility to address topographical hazards. The real tragedy was to allow people to rebuild in New Orleans East, to put their lives and life savings at risk. And, yes, it would have been difficult, and, yes, it would have been heartwrenching, but I think if it could have been done with social justice and fairness, it would have been the right thing to do.

7 The number of blighted homes and empty lots in New Orleans was estimated to be 35,700 in March 2013, while in September 2010, the estimate was 43,755; Claire Garofalo, "City launches website to track blighted properties," October 11, 2013, NOLA.com. See also Allison Plyer and Elaine Ortiz, "Benchmarks for Blight: How much blight does New Orleans Have?", August 21, 2012, gnocdc.org.

To address your last question, about not building houses and building a park, my answer is that we are building a community, and we have to have quality of life, and we have to aspire to not just hitting the replay button, which is to say, we need to advance forward. I think it is a both/and situation; it is not either/or. We should be able to build great public spaces and recover neighborhood housing. It should not be a choice and should not be put to the community as a choice. We should be responsible for building the public realm and, at the same time, for building the proper housing infrastructure.

PROJECTS
PUBLIC BUILDING

Like so many of the proposals made after Katrina, those for public facilities were intended not simply to address the damage the storm had done but also to redress deficits it had exposed. Following the almost total collapse of the public realm in Katrina's wake, many ideas were offered for the restoration of the city's conviviality and styles of association and for the distribution of public benefits to the historically and newly disenfranchised. Hospitals, schools, and other pillars of public culture and services were savaged by the storm, and much of this crucial infrastructure has yet to be restored.

The majority of the projects that we have collected here are not simple engagements to restore missing elements of the city's public function. Rather, these works seek to offer incentives for recuperating a thriving and enfranchised public. Focused on schools, libraries, gathering spaces, and the revival of key cultural practices like cooking, eating, music making, and fine and craft art, they propose architectural agents that can help reestablish human connections and re-create rituals based on communal diversity.

THE HILL: MARTIN LUTHER KING SCHOOL

MVRDV

Rotterdam

A child's drawing of people climbing a hill in the rain inspired MVRDV's design for a new elementary school, to be located in New Orleans's Central Business District near the Superdome, where stranded citizens sheltered when the city flooded. The architects have envisioned a building constructed as a grass-covered "hill," giving the public a viewpoint overlooking the city and providing an island of safety, with all programmatic elements situated above sea level. These elements protrude from the protecting hill like tubes and also form verandas, a common feature of Southern homes, inverting the enclosed courtyard of the traditional school.

SCHOOLS WITHIN SCHOOL PROTOTYPE FOR PUBLIC SCHOOLS: TO LEARN, MUST NEW ORLEANS EMBRACE ITS BIGGEST FEAR?

GRADUATE SCHOOL OF ARCHITECTURE, PLANNING, AND PRESERVATION

Columbia University, New York City

Instructors: Scott Marble, Eric Ng, Kelvin Sealey
Designer: Christopher McAnneny

This project proposes a new school sited alongside the London Street Canal, one of the outflow canals that breached in the aftermath of Katrina. The bridges from the school's property spanning the canal would symbolically and literally link neighborhoods and connect students with the bridged communities. The building itself incorporates not only spaces for the school's use but also spaces for the use of the general public, as well as areas where students and the general public can interact. The school becomes a focal point in celebrating community life and the rebuilding of the damaged city.

NEW ORLEANS NEIGHBORHOOD CENTER

HARVARD UNIVERSITY
Cambridge, Massachusetts

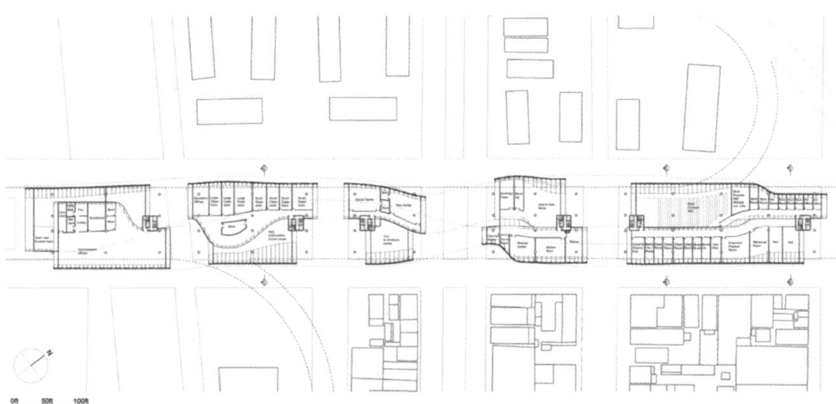

Level 2 Plan

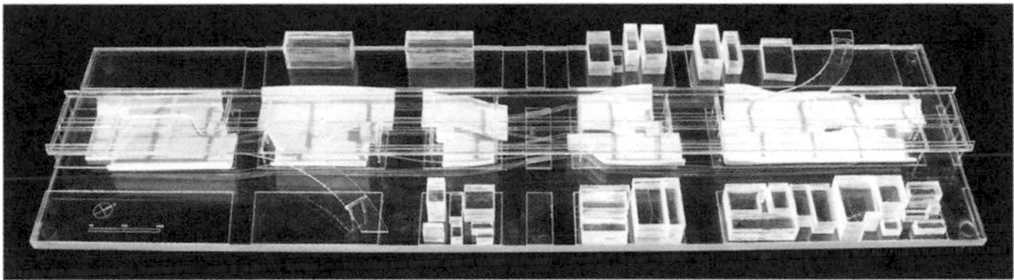

Photograph of a Site Model of the proposal

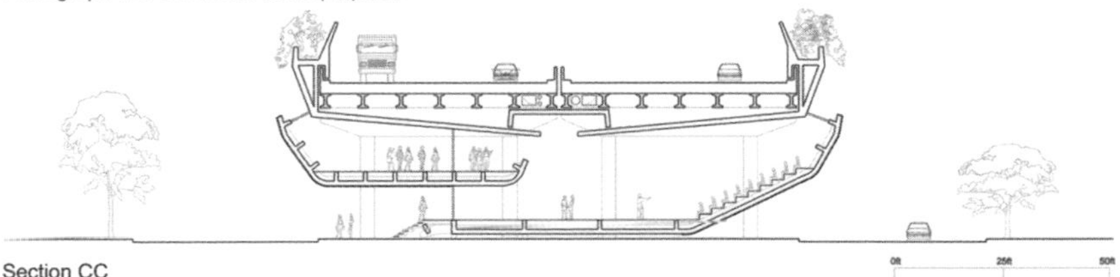

Section CC

Photograph of a Sectional Model of the proposal

Instructor: Fred Schwartz
Designer: Jerry Tate

The aim of this project is to reclaim Claiborne Avenue, which today lies beneath the elevated interstate highway I-10, in the Tremé and Lafitte neighborhoods, as "neutral ground" and a space for community events. The project also provides a hurricane facility beneath the raised concrete deck of the highway structure; the underbelly of the deck is clad with precast concrete components to reduce the traffic noise and fumes. At the ground level, prefabricated timber components serve as venues for cultural activities.

CLASSROOM PROTOTYPE FOR PUBLIC SCHOOLS: THE URBAN SALVAGING SYSTEM

GRADUATE SCHOOL OF ARCHITECTURE, PLANNING, AND PRESERVATION

Columbia University, New York City

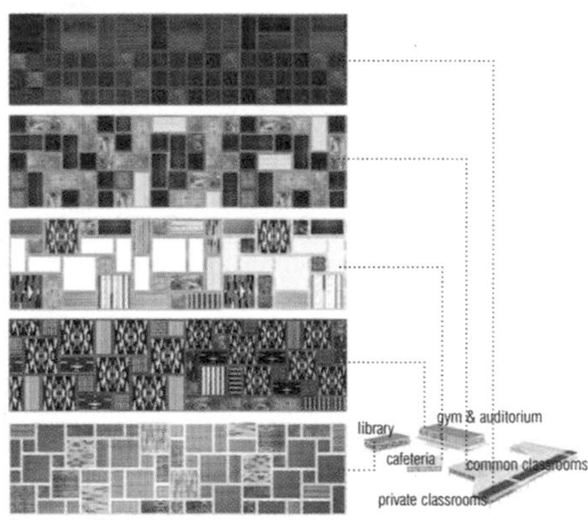

Instructors: Scott Marble, Eric Ng, Kelvin Sealey
Designer: Yooju No

The Urban Salvaging System is proposed as a solution for New Orleans's Edward Henry Phillips Junior High School, where flood heights caused by Katrina reached approximately six feet. Recognizing that the second floor and concrete structure remained viable, the designer proposes to open the ground floor as a public plaza, retain the second floor as the foundation for a new school and use architectural waste—concrete, glass, masonry, siding panels, and other debris—as material for wall components.

NOLA MoFAD, MUSEUM OF FOOD AND DRINK

SCHOOL OF ARCHITECTURE

Clemson University, Clemson, South Carolina

Instructor: Virginia San Fratello

Designers: Miranda Beystehner, Jane Ann Bolin, Isaiah Dunlap, Ryne Hawkins, Lee Henderson, Jeremy Hughs, Kevin Hyslop, Kathleen Lilly, Sarah Lyman, Jason Mobraten, Tim Takacs, Dwight Troyer

Planned for the Lower Ninth Ward along the Poland Street Wharf, the Museum of Food and Drink is a celebration of the culinary history of New Orleans, geared to attract cultural tourism. In creating their building, the designers sought inspiration in the relationship between culinary and architectural creation. They investigated the processes involved in making, serving, and consuming gumbo, crepes, and po'boys. Their analysis informed the process of designing their building; they studied their construction materials as they had their cooking ingredients and proportioned and combined them into the ideal museum for one of New Orleans's most famous traditions: great cuisine.

NATIONAL JAZZ CENTER AND PARK

MORPHOSIS

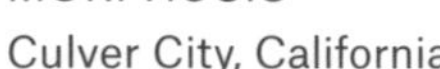

Culver City, California

Morphosis designed the National Jazz Center and Park to catalyze New Orleans's cultural revitalization by emphasizing the city's connection to the development of jazz as a musical form. The park and a dynamic, sculptural hall for exhibitions and performances are sited in the Central Business District, at the corner of Poydras Street and Loyola Avenue. The park's green spaces offer outdoor performance venues; they also link the Jazz Center with city administrative buildings, including City Hall, and with other cultural institutions, such as the central public library.

THE PALPABILITY OF LITERATURE AND ARCHITECTURE: A LIBRARY IN NEW ORLEANS

COLLEGE OF ARCHITECTURE AND ENVIRONMENTAL DESIGN

California Polytechnic State University, San Luis Obispo

Instructor: Jonathan Reich
Designer: Caela Beene

Inspired by the notion of palpability—a quality of experience so intense that the bodily senses are affected—the designer has planned a library for North Claiborne Avenue, in the Ninth Ward, as an anchor for the rebuilding of the entire community. The library would serve a variety of community needs, accommodating both individual study and group interaction through a series of "pods." Ideally, the project would lead to the repair not only of other damaged structures but also of the community's devastated spirit.

CULTURAL COMPLEX PROTOTYPE FOR PUBLIC SCHOOLS: WHO GETS TO CALL SCHOOL HOME?

GRADUATE SCHOOL OF ARCHITECTURE, PLANNING, AND PRESERVATION

Columbia University, New York City

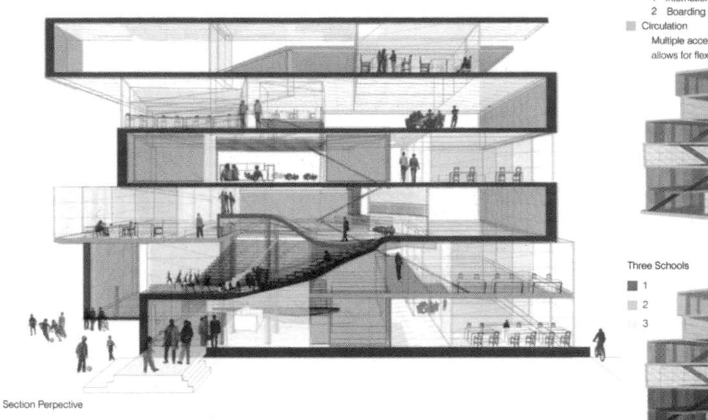

Section Perspective

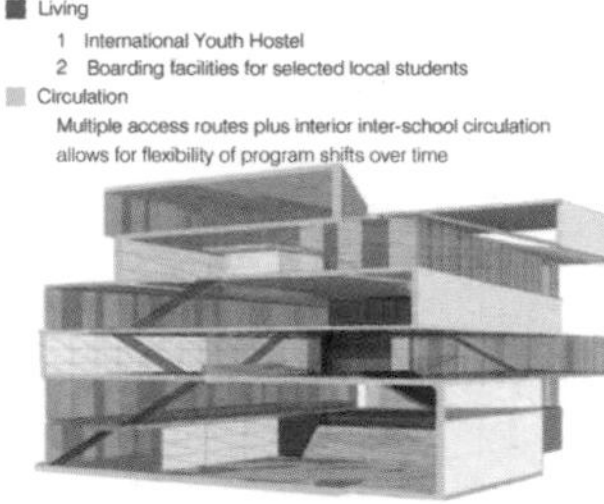

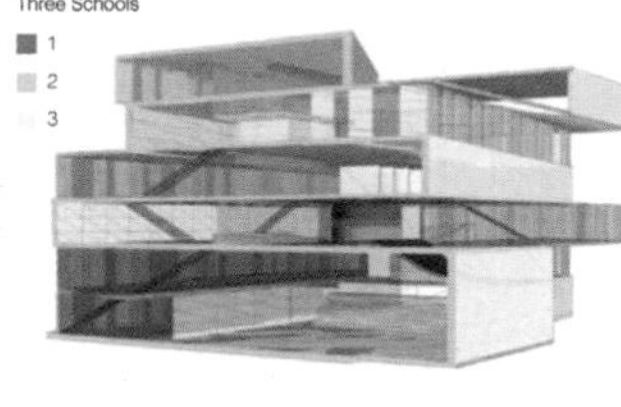

Interior Perspective

Theater Perspective

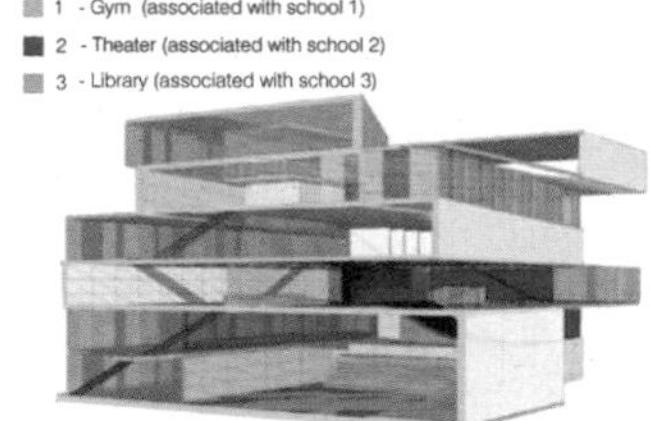

Instructor: Scott Marble
Designer: Xan Young

Intended for Independence Square in New Marigny, this project proposes housing four new schools in one complex, with shared facilities designed to maximize efficiency and minimize redundancy. One of the four schools is envisioned as an international youth hostel that would host exchange programs with other middle schools worldwide and also offer boarding facilities for students from troubled homes. The architectural design of the complex emphasizes the physical bonds among the different schools as well as the intellectual and emotional bonds among their students, in a unique series of interlinked spaces that symbolize cooperative learning.

PART VI
RECONSTRUCTING CULTURAL LANDSCAPES

ARCHITECTURAL ACTIVISM THROUGH MULTIPLE SCALES, VENUES, PROGRAMS, AND COLLABORATIONS

DEREK JAMES HOEFERLIN

From my perspective as a teacher, architect, and activist, I decided that the complex set of circumstances presented by post-Katrina New Orleans demanded a flexible model for architectural practice, a model that blurred common academic and professional distinctions. This model of practice seemed to work well for the city's specific dilemmas —the unprecedented post-disaster situation, the frustration of the citizenry, and the scarcity of funds for professional work. Indeed, much of the productive recovery and rebuilding completed to date has been the work of volunteers, teachers, students, and entrepreneurs.

In this essay, I emphasize what I believe to be an important approach to architectural activism in New Orleans: tackling a broad range of projects on multiple scales, of varied programs, in disparate venues, and with diverse collaborators. Since the spring semester of 2006, I have led a series of Post-Katrina NOLA Architecture and Urban Design Studios. Through these studios, my students in the Sam Fox School of Design and Visual Arts at Washington University in St. Louis have aggressively engaged in design projects with actual clients to address a wide spectrum of needs in the recovering city. Our work has expanded beyond a narrow bandwidth of activism, such as designing housing for a single neighborhood. We have seized dramatically different opportunities to develop designs that we hope will provide models not only for our clients but also for New Orleans's citizens at large. We have responded to specific crises with projects that ranged widely: in scale, from the backyard to the parish; in program, from urban agriculture to water management; and in partnerships, from local to international collaborations. The varied set of projects illustrated here form a loose yet connected network. Each of the projects had a client, but together they served something beyond a specific person, group, or organization. Their common client was the city of New Orleans, considered as a whole.

Participating in the rebuilding of New Orleans was something I had to do. Before Hurricane Katrina, I had acquired more than a decade of academic and professional experience in the city. From 1992 to 1997, I was an undergraduate architecture student at Tulane, and from 1997 to 2003, I worked for the local firm Waggonner & Ball Architects in the

Garden District. Graduate architecture studies at Yale took me away from New Orleans in 2003, and in the summer of 2005, my wife and I ended up back in our hometown of St. Louis. At that time, we intended to return to New Orleans after she completed her medical fellowship.

Only a couple days after Hurricane Katrina made landfall, I began teaching at Washington University in St. Louis. That fall I was pretty much in shock and felt helpless viewing events from afar. I made my first trip to post-Katrina New Orleans in November 2005, hoping to better understand what my role as an architect and educator in the city I loved most could be. Residents had just begun to return to rebuild. Their work went on within the absolute confusion of the citywide recovery and rebuilding effort. I met with my friend David Waggonner, and we discussed ideas for my first Washington University post-Katrina design studio, which I set for spring 2006. I would consult with his practice long-distance, from St. Louis. We were both convinced that rebuilding efforts must be for the long term—must reach beyond the previous status quo—and that architectural proposals would have to deal with the extreme conditions at hand: the city's location within a deltaic landscape.

I was reluctant to jump right into working with a community group or have students build something immediately without really knowing the post-disaster needs of New Orleanians. All I knew about the Lower Ninth Ward pre-Katrina was that it had been a tightly knit community that unfortunately was cut off from most of New Orleans by the Industrial Canal; I thought that wasn't enough knowledge for me to assist with work there. I settled instead on a context that I knew pretty well: Central City's historic Oretha Castle Haley Boulevard corridor, which was in the same planning district (PD2) as the Lower Garden District, where I had previously lived. My studio would research and propose urban design strategies for this part of Central City, which did not flood but had been in desperate need of attention pre-Katrina.[1] Katrina had only added to the preexisting systemic problems of the O.C. Haley corridor and surrounding neighborhood.

My 2006 Washington University studio loosely coordinated its work with the Central City Renaissance Association (CCRA), an umbrella nonprofit for a number of neighborhood nonprofits working there. The students helped identify areas for redevelopment strategies along the corridor, but mostly we were just trying to get our heads around the post-Katrina situation and avoid making too many assumptions. Simple as "dat." Simultaneously, in spring 2006, I served as a consultant to Waggonner & Ball on the recovery and rebuilding plan for St. Bernard Parish—an absolutely devastated area adjacent to the Lower Ninth Ward. This was my first taste of recovery planning.

A little over a year after Katrina, in fall 2006, the Unified New Orleans

1 See Laura Kurgan's essay in Part VII of this volume, "Justice Reinvestment New Orleans," which also focuses on the Central City corridor of Oretha C. Haley.

Plan (UNOP) was kicked off with funding from the Rockefeller Foundation. I became a district plan project manager for planning districts 2 and 13, working with H3 Studio, Inc. in St. Louis, who were chosen as the UNOP consultants for those planning districts. UNOP's goals were to make sense of the previous planning efforts (Urban Land Institute, Bring New Orleans Back, Lambert); to better engage and plan with all of the "wet" and "dry" neighborhoods across the city's thirteen planning districts; to recommend a series of doable recovery and rebuilding projects; and to advocate for a citywide master plan. It was an intense process for everyone, as we attempted to produce our district plans within a ridiculously short time frame. In the end, despite achieving the stated goals, the citywide document that was produced was unwieldy, full of so many recommendations that it was difficult for the public to decipher; it had no clear set of priorities, even though smart and sensible projects were buried within it.

What was amazing about the UNOP process was the phenomenal level of grassroots community engagement. The real work happened—and succeeded—at the neighborhood and district levels. These efforts paved the way for new incremental projects over the years to come. In PD2, this was arguably the first time ever that the Central City and Garden District neighborhoods, separated by the famous St. Charles Avenue and its streetcar line, came together at the same table to plan. I became thoroughly immersed with dozens of community groups and stakeholders within PD2, and I learned how my students could work sustainably in the city's neighborhoods for the foreseeable future.

In spring 2007, the work of my second Washington University design studio for UNOP paralleled H3 Studio's work in the same district. My students conducted thorough research across the transect of PD2, from the Mississippi River, which was well above sea level, to the bottom of the "bowl" (the lower ground between the river and Lake Pontchartrain), which was well below it. Using their knowledge of topographic and land-use conditions, the students worked on urban design proposals and housing prototypes across the Central City and Garden District neighborhoods. Again, this work was not directly engaged with any specific community group or client, but in conversation with the Central City Renaissance Alliance.

In the summer of 2007, however, I made contact with a community group that seemed to offer me and my students an ideal opportunity for collaboration. When Tulane University reopened, in the spring of 2006, its school of architecture had established the CITYbuild Consortium of Schools as an outreach component of Tulane City Center, with a mission to foster partnerships between universities around the country and community groups in the New Orleans region requesting assistance. Through CITYbuild, we were connected with God's Vineyard Community Garden, an urban farm located in the Lower Garden District on Felicity Street.[2] I met with Noel Jones, one of its codirectors, and we agreed that my 2008 spring studio would design and build chicken and goose coops for the farm.[3]

THE FOOD + ECONOMIC DEVELOPMENT + ARCHITECTURE CRISES

Before Katrina struck, many New Orleans communities already lacked access to healthy food and to employment opportunities. Entrepreneurship in the area of food production—urban agriculture—was undeveloped. In 1997, Earl Antwine, Noel Jones, the Sixth Baptist Church, and Parkway Partners founded God's Vineyard Community Garden to tackle these three problems. Their mission was to teach children from the nearby St. Thomas Housing Project how to garden, tend livestock, and produce a saleable product. They wanted to support the farm and use its revenues to fund college scholarships for the volunteers. Pre-Katrina, God's Vineyard had provided poultry, eggs, and vegetables to more than 1,500 people and also produced the kick-ass St. Thomas Seven Hot Sauce.

The garden area was split in two: one half for vegetables—primarily hot peppers for the sauce—and the other half for the animals that supplied eggs, meat, and the fertilizer for the vegetables. Hurricane Katrina had destroyed the crops, damaged the chicken coop, and severely weakened the morale of the volunteers. In order to restore God's Vineyard, the chicken coop had to be rebuilt. Ideally, a design for prefabricated coops could be deployed across New Orleans, promoting sustainable urban agricultural practices and easy access to healthy food, particularly for those without private automobiles.

It was important that the students' design for the coop take into account both the local context and the wider programmatic requirements. New Orleans lies in a subtropical climatic zone, so heat, humidity, ventilation, termites, and hurricanes must be considered no matter what is being designed. Adequate ventilation is especially important for chicken coops, as the buildup of methane gas from droppings can be hazardous. The students' prototype design for the coop used elements made of inexpensive materials, including polycarbonates, corrugated prepainted steel, galvanized steel (for structural parts and fasteners), and treated wood. These readily available elements were packaged together off-site as prefabricated component panels, shipped, and assembled on site within a couple of hours. Taking cues from the local architecture, students created an elevated structure with operable louvers and a sloped roof for ventilation. They selected translucent, insulated wall panels to meet

2 See freewebs.com/godsvineyardnola.

3 Washington University architecture students who participated were Alla Agafonov, Nicholas Berube, Elizabeth Bochner, Claudia Bode, Eric Cesal, Zhan Chen, Leigh Heller, Kathleen Johnson, John Kleinschmidt, Andrew Stern, and Aaron Williams; Leland Orvis provided construction consultation.

Photographs: Derek Hoeferlin. Drawings: Kathleen Johnson and Washington University students in NOLA RECIPE Studio (Spring 2008)

God's Vineyard Community Garden

the chickens' need for adequate, yet diffuse, light. The coop they designed accommodates only roosting and nesting; at other times the chickens roam freely in the surrounding plot. Because the coop has no floor, the chickens can directly fertilize the soil below, allowing on-site soil management.[4] Our group also designed and built a goose coop for God's Vineyard: a series of foldable triangles of treated wood that can be easily configured in various ways for simple shelter. Humble catalysts for recovery, the coops helped to bring the farm back to full productivity, able to attract the necessary volunteers and to achieve its first post-Katrina hot sauce bottling in the fall of 2009.

CITYbuild gave me another critical introduction, to a second community partner in PD2. In the spring semester of 2008 we were able to partner with the Good Work Network, on the O.C. Haley corridor in Central City. The mission of this nonprofit, founded in 2001 by Phyllis Cassidy, is to help new minority- and women-owned community-based small businesses.[5] Around the time that I met Phyllis, in 2007, Enterprise Community Partners announced that in 2008 they would be mounting the annual JP Morgan Chase Community Development Competition in New Orleans, moving it from New York, its venue for fourteen years.[6] The competition sponsors multidisciplinary teams of university students, who, guided by faculty, propose architectural designs and sustainable business development plans for specific projects. First-, second-, and

4 Derek Hoeferlin and NOLA Recipe Studio's *Post-Katrina NOLA Episode III: "Recipe," Volume 01, NOLA Chicken and Goose Coop Prototypes*, 487 pages, can be downloaded from lulu.com.

5 See goodworknetwork.org.

6 See enterprisecommunity.org.

third-place awards of $25,000, $15,000, and $10,000 are given to support the projects developed by the winning teams. Edward Blakely, who headed the Office of Recovery Management under Mayor Nagin, was instrumental in bringing the competition to New Orleans, and Enterprise Partners wrote a brief for the 2008 competition that favored submissions located in one of Blakely's seventeen "target recovery zones." The O.C. Haley corridor was one of those zones, and Phyllis saw in the competition an opportunity for the Good Work Network to win financial support for the rehabilitation of the historic Franz Building on the boulevard, which they had purchased. She was already working with faculty and students from the Department of Urban Studies and Planning at MIT on a project redevelopment feasibility study for the building. But to enter the Chase Competition, she also needed design expertise. Because I had worked on O.C. Haley in both academic and professional situations, I was keen to participate. In April 2008, our Washington University/MIT team submitted a proposal, "The Franz Building: From Recovery to Rebirth" to the competition on behalf of Good Work Network. We placed first, and the $25,000 prize provided seed money to help implement the project.

Our design solution for the Franz Building was deliberately modest, because of budget restrictions and because people wanted to preserve its original architectural character. Built in 1915, the Franz Building, made of load-bearing brick with terracotta detailing, structural ceramic tile, and cypress box trusses, has stood the structural test of time. Hurricane Katrina caused minimal damage to the roof; therefore only minimal alterations to the existing structure were necessary. A comprehensive restoration of the building's exterior was projected in order not only to reintegrate it with the historic O.C. Haley corridor but also to qualify the project for Historic Tax Credits. Programmatically, we designed half of the building's interior to create leasable office or retail spaces; the other half was planned to accommodate the Good Work Network's office needs and to give Good Work a notable public presence on the building's front facade. Features of the design included optimal use of natural day lighting and cross-ventilation strategies; exposure of the existing cypress roof trusses; and advocating for the use of sustainable building materials and on-site water management. The students' drawings and models enabled Phyllis Cassidy to raise significant funds for hiring a local architecture firm to prepare construction drawings. Good Work expects to open the building in 2011.[7]

7 Architecture students at Washington University who worked on this project were Alla Agafonov, Nicholas Berube, Elizabeth Bochner, Claudia Bode, Eric Cesal, Zhan Chen, Leigh Heller, Kathleen Johnson, John Kleinschmidt, Andrew Stern, and Aaron Williams; MIT city planning graduate students Holly Jo Sparks and Lakshmi Sridaran also participated; Karl Seidman of MIT's Department of Urban Studies and Planning served as co-faculty. A PDF of the Franz Building project can be downloaded at practitionerresources.org.

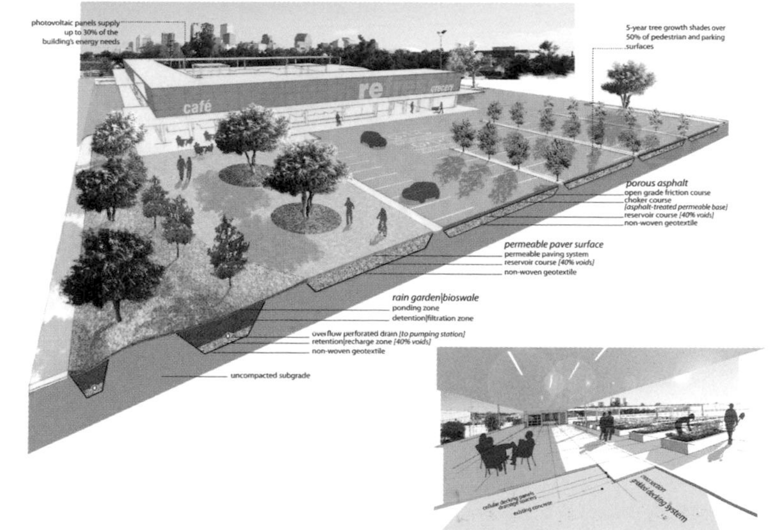

Philip Burkhardt and Brendan Wittstruck, Washington University; Jacquelyn Dadakis and Aditi Mehta, Massachusetts Institute of Technology

Proposed renovation to Robért's grocery store and site

THE FOOD + ECONOMIC DEVELOPMENT + ARCHITECTURE + WATER MANAGEMENT CRISES

In the spring of 2009, my Washington University students and I partnered again with MIT's Department of Urban Studies and Planning to participate in the second New Orleans–based Chase Competition. Broad Community Connections, a nonprofit located in the Mid-City neighborhood and directed by Jeffrey Schwartz was our partner for this project.[8] Our task was to design a renovation and business plan for the vacant historic Robért's grocery store on Broad Street, the neighborhood's main economic and cultural thoroughfare. The students developed a sustainable adaptive reuse design for the store and its blighted site, together with a sustainable business development plan. The project, "Broad Street ReFresh: A Fresh Food Hub for Community, Health, and Economic Development," placed second in the competition, and the $15,000 prize went directly to Broad Community Connections as seed money for the project.

Key features of the Broad Street site redesign included the restoration of the mid-century modern building to its original character and the addition of natural day lighting along the perimeter of the building and top lighting with large light monitors. The existing under-utilized rooftop parking area was transformed into a Community Supported Agriculture (CSA) roof farm to serve the store and the surrounding neighborhood. Additionally, the students redesigned the entirety of the site surface as a model for multimodal transportation, sustainable landscape, and water management strategies, including a bus stop, porous asphalt parking,

8 See broadcommunityconnections.org.

permeable pavers, outdoor seating, bio-swales, rain gardens, and a new tree canopy.[9]

My most recent and ongoing rebuilding project in New Orleans has been a collaborative multiyear studio involving Washington University and the University of Toronto, which we began in the spring of 2009 and named Gutter to Gulf. Hurricane Katrina shed light on New Orleans's failure to design and follow an effective integrated water management strategy. In response, Waggonner & Ball Architects of New Orleans initiated the creation of an international task force of architects, landscape architects, urban designers, hydrologists, and engineers to advocate for a water management strategy designed to be foundational in any post-Katrina planning processes.[10] The mission of their initiative, called Dutch Dialogues, is to create a comprehensive water strategy for the city, "with potential to transform land use by focusing first on water."[11] Our Gutter to Gulf studio has drawn upon and supported the efforts of Waggonner & Ball, resulting in the study "Gutter to Gulf: Legible Water Infrastructure for New Orleans."[12] Studio work in Gutter to Gulf has included extensive research on hydrology and hydraulics in New Orleans; critiques and legible representation of existing, related circumstances and planning mechanisms; and design proposals on scales that vary from the individual lot to citywide infrastructure. This ongoing project provides realizable solutions for the hydrological situation of the New Orleans region, while advocating that water management strategies form the fundamental base layer for intelligent design and planning for the future of New Orleans.

Within the city itself, specifically in Drainage Basin 1, water is mostly hidden below streets or behind floodwalls—in effect, it is out of sight, out of mind.[13] Therefore, Gutter to Gulf students have studied the complex spatial relationships of the water infrastructure in relation to other infrastructures and to the built fabric and ecology of New Orleans. They have made their spatial analyses visible through a series of physical models that overlay varied sets of information, from multiple layers of key infrastructures to historical developments of key waterways and to comparison of the hydraulics and hydrology of New Orleans. Additionally, they prepared

9 Architecture and urban design graduate students who worked on this project were Philip Burkhardt and Brendan Wittstruck of Washington University, and city planning graduate students Jacquelyn Dadakis and Aditi Mehta of MIT; Karl Seidman of MIT's Department of Urban Studies and Planning served as co-faculty. A PDF of the "Broad Street ReFresh" proposal can be downloaded at nola.mit.edu.

10 See the interview with David Waggonner in Part VIII of this volume for a discussion of new water management strategies proposed for New Orleans.

11 See wbarchitects.com.

12 Gutter to Gulf was a collaborative effort between design studios in the John H. Daniels Faculty of Architecture, Landscape, and Design at the University of Toronto, led by Jane Wolff and Elise Shelley, and in the Sam Fox School of Design & Visual Arts at Washington University, St. Louis, led by Derek Hoeferlin; see guttertogulf.com. The project website includes lists of student participants and community advisers over the course of three years, 2009–2011.

13 The New Orleans region is divided into a series of Drainage Basin units. "Drainage Basin 1" is defined by Lake Pontchartrain and the crescent of the Mississippi River and from east to west by the Industrial Canal and 17th Street Canal. The primary research of Gutter to Gulf is on Drainage Basin 1.

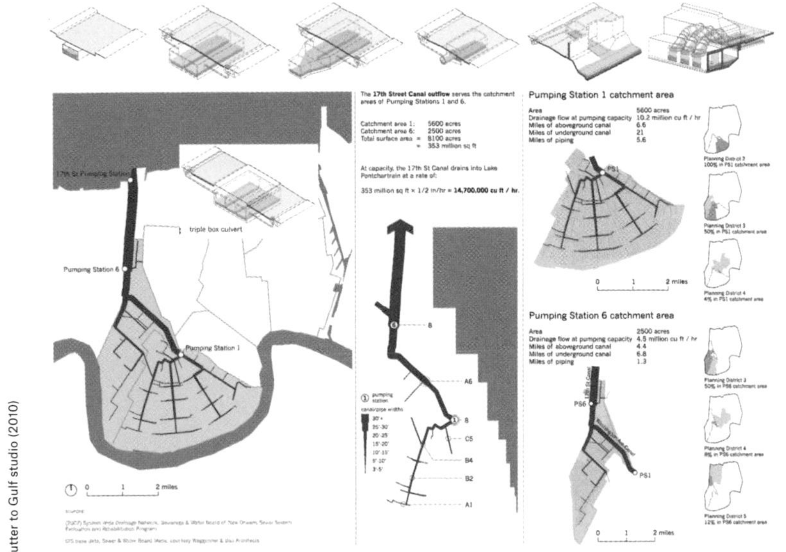

Gutter to Gulf studio (2010)

New Orleans drainage taxonomy

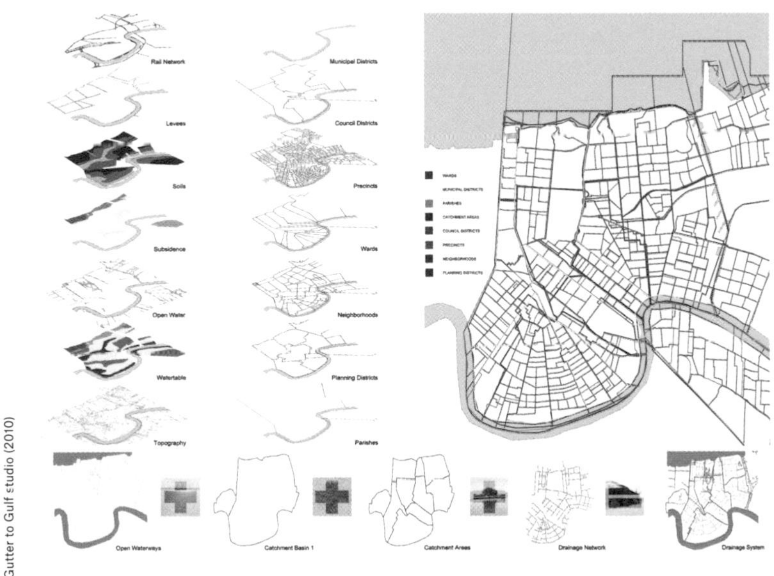

Gutter to Gulf studio (2010)

New Orleans, coterminous with Orleans Parish, physical and political city

"guidebooks" to the water infrastructure to help ensure the efficient conduct of collaborative fieldwork in New Orleans.[14] The studios also worked to visually represent sets of taxonomies in order to make as legible to the public as possible obscure and complicated information concerning the existing drainage and hydraulic systems of New Orleans, including

14 See guttertogulf.com/#1717576/Field-Work to download the studio's guidebooks.

Andy Sternad, Gutter to Gulf studio (2009)

Prototype for Gentilly neighborhood street and neutral ground redesign, with supplementary water management system providing security and amenity

Samantha Stein, Gutter to Gulf studio (2011)

Proposal for reconfiguration of Monticello Canal in Hollygrove neighborhood

the development of canals, navigation waterways, and underground drainage culverts.[15] Additional explanatory research was invested in documenting the city's mostly misaligned physical characteristics and policy boundaries.[16] Armed with the portable models, guidebooks, and

15 See guttertogulf.com/#519603/Water-Today-A-Taxonomy to download the studio's taxonomy studies.

16 See guttertogulf.com/519616/Digital-Model.

analytical drawings, the students presented their findings to local experts and gathered feedback from various neighborhood groups, including groups from Hollygrove and Pontchartrain Park, and from nonprofits with significant ecological outreach programs, such as those of Longue Vue House and Gardens.[17] The design proposals from the studio have been influenced by engineering, economics, ecologies, and politics, and they span the disciplines of architecture, landscape architecture, and urban design. To be able to achieve such multidisciplinary understanding, the proposals have had to operate on multiple scales—from the gutter of a building to the Gulf of Mexico. The studio's work has advocated for the spatial integration of water in the existing character of New Orleans; the studio's projects have attempted to produce water infrastructure that creates civic space and amenity, in contrast to the existing water infrastructure, which creates boundaries and nuisances.

As I reflect on the six years of work I have described here, I believe that the flexible model that blurs the boundary between the academic and the professional, by seeking out a broad range of projects through different scales, venues, programs, and collaborations, is appropriate. And I do not think this approach should be limited to post-disaster settings. But I see grounds for a self-critique definitely emerge as well. First, as much as New Orleans has become a model city for grassroots mobilization, I firmly believe that all of these noble efforts do not add up to a sustainable whole. In other words, as long as big-deal issues—primarily those of comprehensive water management on all scales—are not addressed, all of this incremental work may end up being regarded as deeply irresponsible. *Water* is the big elephant in New Orleans's room, and ultimately should inform most, if not all, design decisions in the city. Second, many of us, as designers—I include myself—have fallen into the trap of responding to disasters with design as hindsight, rather than envisioning design as capable of preventing disasters, that is, design as foresight. I would like to think that this foresight is where the Gutter to Gulf initiative is leading. Most important, I think that this is where the design student—the most important ingredient in all this gumbo—comes into play, gaining the realization that design can be a proactive rather than a reactive agent of change.[18]

17 See longuevue.com.

18 Six of Hoeferlin's Washington University Gutter to Gulf students chose to begin their professional careers in New Orleans: Jessica Garz, Zachary Gong, John Kleinschmidt, John Monnat, Zachary Schwanbeck, and Andy Sternad.

LANDSCAPE AGENCY IN URBAN REVITALIZATION
ELIZABETH MOSSOP

INTRODUCTION

The current condition of New Orleans makes abundantly clear the importance of paying attention to the deep natural systems that underlie cities. The interrelationships between climate, hydrology, geology, and vegetation are inextricably tied to New Orleans's ability to survive the impact of storms and floods in the short term and to create sustainable urban systems in the long term. In reconstructing this city and, more generally, in thinking about the revitalization and development of other cities, we should be informed by an understanding of the key role natural systems play in urbanism: how they influence city structure, the development of infrastructure, and ultimately the formation of urban character and performance.

From this urban ecological standpoint, reflecting on five years of post-Katrina rebuilding in New Orleans, I see three issues of significance largely missing from both the discourse and the actual reconstruction efforts. These are all urban landscape issues: ecological restoration, effective strategies for urban vacancy, and using food production for economic revitalization. This essay discusses three projects that focus on these issues. All three projects illustrate an openness to new ideas that would have been impossible in this context before Katrina. They represent the unique opportunity that currently exists in New Orleans to engage landscaping and urbanism in the solution of intractable and globally relevant problems. The very extreme nature of certain conditions in the city (poverty, urban blight, and lack of effective governance) invites the consideration of solutions that are new to the context. In New Orleans, as in many other places, especially in the developing world, a lack of resources for public infrastructure and facilities can make landscape strategies attractive as solutions to the problems of urban development.

COUTURIE FOREST AND SCOUT ISLAND: RE-CREATING HEALTHY ECOSYSTEMS

One of the little-recognized impacts of Hurricane Katrina was the loss of biomass resulting from the devastation of both natural and cultural landscapes. The loss of canopy trees in urban areas and the loss of thou-

Spackman Mossop + Michaels

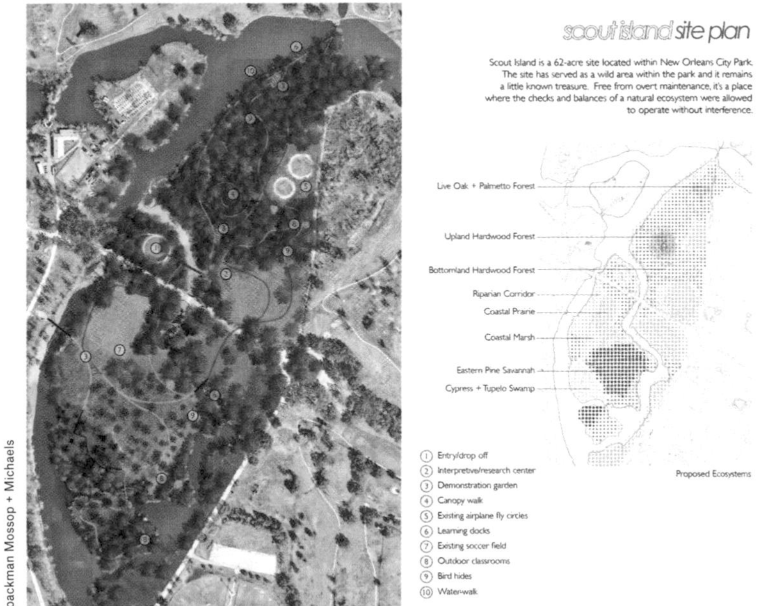

Pre-Katrina locations of existing Chinese tallow trees and other invasive species on Scout Island, in New Orleans City Park

sands of acres of forest and wetland vegetation contributed to the loss of a wide range of the ecosystems' services to habitat, resulting in increased release of atmospheric carbon, worse urban energy performance, decreased landscape amenities, reduced air quality, and damaged hydrological systems.[1] Couturie Forest and Scout Island are elements of a sixty-two-acre site located within New Orleans's City Park that illustrate how replacing biomass through ecological restoration can contribute broadly to the urban landscape. This project focuses on establishing a series of resilient infrastructures and highlights the need for restoring ecological systems as well as educational, recreational, and cultural systems in the aftermath of a natural disaster.

The City Park site has traditionally been a bird-watching and wilderness preserve, but Hurricane Katrina killed approximately 50 percent of the trees and devastated the forest. The entire site flooded to a depth of six feet, destroying much of the ground-level vegetation and displacing many animal species that called the forest home. The forest had recovered from hurricanes before; on these past occasions, through a certain amount of fortuitous neglect the site had been allowed to regenerate slowly. Downed trees provided ground-level shade to help prevent invasive species from sprouting where storms had opened holes in the canopy. The soil was left undisturbed, and the seed bank of native plants was able to outcompete the invasive species to reestablish the canopy.

1 Jeffrey Q. Chambers et al., "Hurricane Katrina's Carbon Footprint on Gulf Coast Forests," *Science* 318 (2007), 1107.

Spackman Mossop + Michaels

Proposed ecosystems to be established in the forest

However, the immediate management response to Hurricane Katrina caused major difficulties for the reestablishment of the site's native ecosystem. Immediately following the storm, most of the downed trees were removed. This opened up the canopy in a significant way, allowing full sun onto areas of the site that had previously been covered. The heavy machinery that was used to remove the trees also disturbed the soil and exposed thousands of dormant seeds of nonnative plants. This has led to a massive invasion of exotic species on the site. In full sunlight, with their seeds exposed to freshly turned soil, such exotic species as Chinese tallow (*Sapium sebiferum*) and ragweed (*Ambrosia spp.*) have outcompeted the native seedlings. Structures on the site were also damaged by the storm. City Park lost more than 50 percent of its staff, who either evacuated and did not return or were not rehired, and with them years of institutional knowledge about the operations and maintenance of the park. Even volunteers who labored on the site were dispersed by the hurricane or compelled to direct their energies toward other, more pressing, problems.

The ecological infrastructure on site, however, faces the most serious threats. Because the two main invasive species described have already outcompeted the site's native plants, eradicating them is a long-term goal, which can only be accomplished by reestablishing native ecosystems enough to limit the opportunities for invasive species to thrive. Planting native seeds and plants and vigilantly managing invasive species over the first five to ten years will give the ecosystems a chance to reestablish themselves. An invasive species removal plan has been implemented and will continue, with native planting and ecosystem establishment to follow. The manipulation of site conditions such as soil and drainage will allow the establishment of a broader range of natural communities than previously existed on the site, creating a more varied habitat and richer visitor experience. Seeds for the establishment of the ecosystems have been collected from the site and other areas in City Park. This will help retain the genetic adaptability of the surviving trees, some of which are more than 150 years old. The establishment of more than twenty-one acres of coastal prairie, representing the severely endangered ecosystem along the Gulf Coast, will not only provide a rich habitat for birds and wildlife but will also contribute to the restoration of other parts of the Gulf Coast by providing a major new seed bank for restoration projects.

The site's existing trails were mostly washed away during Katrina. Because of the community's desire for limited signage in the park, the design team wanted the trail system to serve as an interpretive device within the forest as well as a vehicle for exploring the site. The new trails will represent the variety of ecosystem types, and signage will be incorporated into the pathway. As visitors or school groups move from one ecosystem to another, the path will subtly change, amplifying the experience. Interpretive events will be staged along the path.

GROWING HOME: LANDSCAPE STRATEGIES FOR VACANCY

The combination of historical disinvestment and the devastation caused by Hurricane Katrina has created an extreme form of urban blight, replicating almost exactly the conditions of inner-city Detroit over much of New Orleans. There are massive tracts of vacant land throughout the city that require management in the interim period before reuse becomes viable. Some of these tracts may remain vacant for only a few years, but some are likely to lie empty for decades. There are many creative possibilities for the use of this vacant land that could be productive and stimulate economic growth, but as long as the issues of land tenure and governance remain problematic, broad-scale redevelopment will be time-consuming and economically onerous. Thus it is imperative to develop strategies for the reuse of individual lots.

One public agency trying to address this issue is the New Orleans Redevelopment Authority (NORA), originally created in 1968 as the Community Improvement Agency, which currently owns approximately 4,000 residential lots in Orleans Parish. Like many postindustrial cities, New Orleans had suffered significant urban blight long before 2005, and before Katrina struck had many blighted and adjudicated properties eligible for expropriation by the city. NORA was empowered to acquire these, but the agency only became truly active in the post-storm environ-

Spackman Mossop + Michaels

The Live Garden, part of NORA's Growing Home program, is designed as a series of social spaces.

ment, when the number increased from around 30,000 properties to (by some estimates) well over 100,000. Post-Katrina, NORA was also charged with disposing of or developing the storm-damaged properties that came to the agency through the Road Home Program, which allowed homeowners to sell their properties to the state.

NORA's Lot Next Door program gives eligible homeowners the option to purchase a vacant lot adjacent to their homes and to develop this lot as they see fit. The Growing Home program, which we developed for NORA, is designed to give residents incentive to develop vacant lots as gardens. The program allows Lot Next Door purchasers up to $10,000 toward implementing landscape and garden strategies on their lots. We designed a series of demonstration or model gardens, developed a strategy for awarding the credits toward expenditures, and created a website and a booklet for participants.[2]

The city's aims in the project are to raise property values in neighborhoods by improving the appearance of formerly blighted land; to improve quality of life for residents by reducing public safety risks; and to improve environmental conditions in the city generally. Once participants are accepted into the program, they meet with NORA's landscape architect coordinator to discuss both their aspirations and the site's potential. They are given some help in designing their gardens as well as advice on how to source materials and get help with implementation. NORA is now in the process of making partnerships with suppliers of building materials, plants, and landscape supplies, in order to secure significant discounts on materials for program participants. Many of the city's most blighted areas have a high proportion of elderly and impoverished residents, and so help with implementation is also key to getting these gardens built.

2 A guide to the program can be found at growinghomenola.org.

Therefore NORA is also working to build partnerships with local neighborhood associations, volunteer groups, and organizations like the Salvation Army, all of which are key participants in the city's rebuilding, as well as developing lists of appropriate contractors. Participants have up to nine months from date of purchase to carry out the work.

The model gardens are designed to showcase the full range of possibilities for these gardens rather than representing what any one homeowner is likely to do. "Live" is designed around relaxation and social interaction. It includes a front porch space for watching the street and social spaces with a barbecue, seating, shade, and a small play area. "Work" has a shed and outdoor workspace, large enough for some kind of cottage industry and a productive garden with raised beds and trellises for growing fruits and vegetables. "Play" is focused on making a space for active recreations for children and adults, with swings, a sandbox, basketball hoop, a track for walking, jogging, and riding bikes and tricycles, and a lawn. There are also a barbecue and an outdoor dining area as well as shade, "hanging-out" space, and storage. If NORA, an agency largely remade post-Katrina, can find a way to achieve real cooperation with the city to support this strategy, it has the potential to transform neighborhoods and the life experience of urban dwellers. Over time, the program could also have a significant impact on the environmental performance of areas with high vacancy, so that a high rate of participation would achieve a high return from a relatively low public investment.

VIET VILLAGE: PRODUCTIVITY, FOOD, AND ECONOMIC DEVELOPMENT

Like other communities in the city, the Vietnamese population of New Orleans—the majority of which lives in New Orleans East—is struggling to make the political process work for them and to find a way through the byzantine processes of recovery and development. Mobilizing post-Katrina, without the benefit of consolidated city governance, this unified, self-reliant, strongly led community moved forward more rapidly with its redevelopment agenda than did communities in other devastated parts of the city.

Viet Village, a thriving Vietnamese-American enclave in New Orleans East, was established in 1975, by the earliest influx of Vietnamese immigrants to the city. One of the first things these Vietnamese did was establish home-based gardens to grow traditional fruits and vegetables that weren't available locally. The gardens were informal and widely scattered across the community, in vacant lots, along the edges of canals and levees, in backyards—anywhere that had decent soil and access to water. Before the devastation brought by Katrina, there were more than thirty farmed acres throughout the community. There was also a well-established weekly local market with more than eighty stalls, developed as an outlet to sell produce the local growers did not consume in their homes.

Spackman Mossop + Michaels

Aerial view of Viet Village's farm

The 2005 storm destroyed all of the gardens and displaced many of the gardeners. Most of the gardeners returned (in fact, 95 percent of Viet Village's population has returned, compared to 10 to 20 percent of the population in some other areas), but many found themselves overwhelmed by the prospect of rebuilding their homes and the entire garden infrastructure, especially as the majority of Viet Village gardeners were in their sixties, seventies, and eighties. So in the beginning of the recovery planning process, our vision for this project was a farm that would formalize the gardening and market activities, bringing them together in a single location, and, most importantly, bringing together the different generations within the Vietnamese community through the shared endeavor of the farm. In this way, the traditional skills and practices of the culture brought from Vietnam would be passed down by the elders to younger, American-born generations.

This farm will be a combination of small-plot gardens, for family consumption and the weekly market; larger commercial plots focused on providing produce not only for the market but also for local restaurants and grocery stores in New Orleans; and a livestock area for raising chickens and goats in the traditional Vietnamese way. The perimeter of the site will also be used for a commercial bamboo plantation, which will also buffer the adjoining residential development.

The proposed market on the site will be primarily a regional produce market, providing an outlet for other regional growers as well as locals, and not only serving individual farmers and other local community members but also operating as a central exchange for the larger Vietnamese community along the Gulf Coast. Based on the history of the markets in the area before Katrina, as many as 3,000 people are expected to come to the site for a Saturday market, and more on traditional festival days. The market will be organized into three pavilions: one for fresh produce, one for prepared foods, and one for meat, poultry, and seafood products.

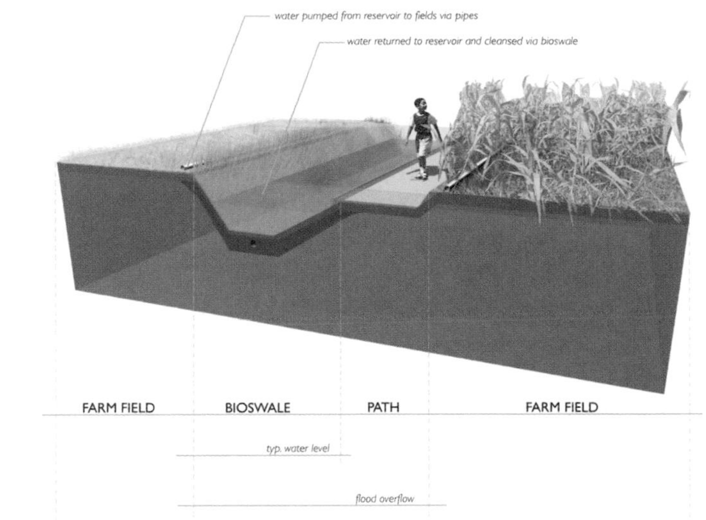

Spackman Mossop + Michaels

The infrastructure of circulation, water, and energy gives structure to the Viet Village farm plots.

The project has always been conceived as engaging the whole community, and so its program will be further enriched by playgrounds; areas for sports, community gatherings, and passive recreation; walking and running trails; and educational activities associated with all aspects of the farm. The site's infrastructure for water management and circulation will provide the key landscape elements that delineate the site and its character. Other aspects of the project that will contribute to its economic sustainability include the establishment of certified organic farming practices (such as integrated pest management, composting, crop rotation, and cover cropping) and the establishment of relationships with area restaurants and grocery stores to provide locally grown produce, a practice of the locavore/Slow Food movement. Moreover, bio-filtration of water resources and alternative energy sources such as wind and passive and active solar power will make the farm and market a model for low-tech, ecologically sustainable site development in the New Orleans area.

CONCLUSION

These three local projects suggest possibilities for the city in general. Through the reestablishment of biomass in parks and all public spaces, including streets and neutral grounds, all of these areas could be redeveloped to perform better both environmentally and socially. Parks and streets could be redesigned to also increase habitat, ameliorate climate, and provide new facilities for recreation and leisure for all city dwellers.

Solving the management problem of the city's vacant lands offers a range of possible new productive uses for gardens, food crops, commercial crops, water management, and so on. The design of new community and public facilities points the way to creating multifunctional landscapes serving a range of community needs while contributing landscape and environmental value. None of these strategies has major implications in terms of capital costs, given how much restoration is being done, but if this work were approached with the right mindset, so much more could be achieved in the urban landscape, and the urban landscape could achieve so much more.

PONTCHARTRAIN PARK + GENTILLY WOODS LANDSCAPE MANUAL

JANE WOLFF and
CAROL McMICHAEL REESE

HOW TO USE THE LANDSCAPE MANUAL

The *Pontchartrain Park + Gentilly Woods Landscape Manual* is the product of Longue Vue House and Garden's partnership with the Pontilly Disaster Collaborative.[1] The PDC is a nonprofit corporation founded in the wake of hurricane Katrina by the Pontilly Neighborhood Association, representing the neighborhoods of Pontchartrain Park and Gentilly Woods, to seek funds and mobilize efforts for rebuilding. Longue Vue House and Gardens is the former estate of Edith Rosenwald Stern and Edgar Bloom Stern. They were New Orleans philanthropists and civil rights activists who developed the "black" neighborhood of Pontchartrain Park, beginning in 1946, to provide opportunities for home ownership in a suburban environment to middle-class African Americans. Lying on Pontchartrain Park's southern edge, "white" Gentilly Woods was developed contemporaneously by the same builder, Hamilton Crawford of Baton Rouge. Following post-integration white flight, Gentilly Woods became more than 90 percent black, and the neighborhoods assumed a joint identity—Pontilly.

The manual has multiple purposes. First, it is intended as a handbook of practical advice for people living in or returning to Pontchartrain Park and Gentilly Woods. Second, it aims to identify neighborhood rehabilitation projects suitable for funding and implementation. Third, it is meant to form the basis for a comprehensive strategy for rebuilding the neighborhoods. Last, and not least, its goal is to help the citizens of New Orleans and southern Louisiana understand their landscape and their own role in its future.

We believe that the future of Pontchartrain Park and Gentilly Woods must be rooted in the neighborhoods' unique history, and so the manual seeks both to explain the past and to make proposals for renewal. It begins with a brief discussion of the neighborhoods' origin and evolution

1 The material presented here was selected from Longue Vue's publication, *Pontchartrain Park + Gentilly Woods Landscape Manual* (New Orleans: Longue Vue House and Gardens, 2009). For a PDF of the manual in its entirety, see longuevue.com.

Longue Vue House and Gardens Archive

West facade of Longue Vue (ca. 1947)

as a cultural landscape and an explanation of the ecological dilemmas inherent in building on low land near Lake Pontchartrain. Next, it provides a review of the issues presented by rehabilitation and a summary of the process we used to develop ideas about how the neighborhoods might change. From these bases, it presents a series of design proposals for rehabilitating the neighborhoods' landscape. These proposals range in scale from individual gardens to the neighborhoods' shared center and treasure, the recreational spaces of Pontchartrain Park and the Bartholomew Golf Course. The proposals aim not only to support the historic image and values that neighborhood residents hold dear but also to broaden and expand the landscape's productive capacities. The design ideas add layers of meaning and function to gardens, streets, canals, and park spaces, which can be restored to their previous social and civic functions *and* become places to store water, mitigate wind damage, grow food, produce income, and educate citizens about the ecological and cultural history of southern Louisiana.

PONTCHARTRAIN PARK AND GENTILLY WOODS: THE HISTORY OF ANOTHER NEW ORLEANS

Pontchartrain Park and Gentilly Woods are emblematic New Orleans neighborhood landscapes. They represent the city's twentieth-century incarnation, and though they may be less famous than New Orleans's older districts they are no less a part of its essential character. Designed separately but built by the same company in the 1950s, Pontchartrain Park and Gentilly Woods are manifestations of a number of mid-century ideas about progress. First, the land they occupy is itself an artifact of progressive faith in technology; until the early 1900s, it was a cypress swamp at the edge of Lake Pontchartrain. It was reclaimed by mechanical pumping a

Longue Vue House and Gardens Archive

Newspaper photograph of model homes in Pontchartrain Park (ca. 1955)

century ago, and once it was drained, the ground was developed without any reference to its basic sogginess. A system of pumps, canals, and levees made its use possible, and its developers, designers, and inhabitants all relied upon the infallibility of that infrastructure, even after the land had subsided to depths as low as eight feet below sea level.

Second, the neighborhoods are ideal Modernist domestic landscapes. Verdant, open, and orderly, Pontchartrain Park and Gentilly Woods are classic examples of postwar U.S. urban design. Although they were built within New Orleans's city limits (coterminous with Orleans Parish), their image was suburban: single-family, ranch-style houses on unfenced lawns lining leafy streets at densities of approximately six dwellings per acre. Relationships between indoor and outdoor spaces were emphasized in the neighborhoods' promotional brochures, and in Pontchartrain Park, at the center of the development, ample facilities for fresh air and sports—including golf, tennis, basketball, and baseball—were provided.

Third, Pontchartrain Park and Gentilly Woods represent the logic of reformist urban planning in the postwar segregation era. They were key projects of deLesseps S. "Chep" Morrison's progressive mayoralty, in which he vowed to "serve all the people regardless of color or creed."[2] Morrison, who took office in 1946, faced a significant postwar housing shortage in New Orleans, one that was mirrored in cities across the United States. He also faced increasing demands from black citizens for equal treatment under the law, and during his first year in office, blacks threatened to sue the city for access to whites-only public golf courses. Following the tenets of segregationist "Jim Crow" legislation that required separate public facilities for blacks and whites, Morrison determined to build a "Negro Park" with an eighteen-hole golf course to

2 Morrison to Norman E. Anseman, May 2, 1950, "Negro Park" file, Morrison Papers, City Archives and Special Collections, Louisiana Division, New Orleans Public Library. Additional papers from Morrison's mayoralty, as well as personal papers of Edgar Bloom Stern, are housed in the Louisiana Research Collection, Special Collections, Howard-Tilton Library, Tulane University, New Orleans.

City Archives and Special Collections, Louisiana Division, New Orleans Public Library. A similar plan book for Pontchartrain Park has not been located.

W.H. Crawford Corporation, *Gentilly Woods Planbook* (ca. 1950), offering thirty-one home styles and floor plans

provide blacks with recreational amenities equal to those open to whites in Audubon and City Parks. He and his advisers, led by Edgar Stern, who served as the chair of his advisory committee, conceived of the new park not in isolation but as the centerpiece of a residential subdivision. This became Pontchartrain Park, which was designed and marketed for middle-class, black home ownership. For the first time in New Orleans, a planned neighborhood of single-family homes provided truly "equal" residential and recreational opportunities to African Americans in the segregated city.

In 1950, Morrison's administration purchased the land for the park and reached an agreement with the Baton Rouge home builder Hamilton Crawford to purchase and develop land for the surrounding subdivision. At the same time, they promoted Crawford's purchase of a tract immediately south on which to build a subdivision for whites; this became Gentilly Woods, which was separated from Pontchartrain Park by the existing Dwyer Canal. Financing was more readily available for construction and loans to home buyers in Gentilly Woods than to buyers in Pontchartrain Park. For that reason, houses were built on most of the lots in Gentilly Woods between 1951 and 1954, while Mayor Morrison, Hamilton Crawford, and Edgar Stern struggled to secure public funds from the city and federal governments to subsidize the adjacent homes in Pontchartrain Park. Finally, with financial assistance from Stern, who incorporated Pontchartrain Park Homes, Inc., in 1954, the Crawford Corporation readied the first houses in Pontchartrain Park for sale in 1955. In 1956, the first nine holes of the golf course opened for play. It is important to stress that within the credo of "separate but equal" the Crawford Corporation provided both neighborhoods with identical subdivision amenities, such as paved, curbed, and lighted streets, and similarly sized lots (generally 60 feet by 120 feet) and housing models. It could be argued, however, that Pontchartrain Park, with its interior recreational facilities and its eighteen-hole golf course, far exceeded the measure of "equality," and indeed it became the nation's preeminent planned community for middle-class and professional African Americans. The extensive public facilities in Pontchartrain Park had tremendous symbolic importance for the African-American community, and black home buyers flocked there. The neighborhood provided its residents a home base of self-respect, and over the years, many residents became prominent civic leaders, artists, activists, and politicians.

Ironically, however, in May 1954, even as the Morrison administration persisted in its reformist, albeit segregationist, urban planning agenda, the Supreme Court handed down its decision in *Brown v. the Board of Education*. This decision eventually served as the legal platform for dismantling "separate but equal" laws in the Jim Crow South. With the passage of the Civil Rights Act and Voting Rights Act by the U.S. Congress, in 1964 and 1965 respectively, New Orleans was forced to integrate public schools and housing developments, as well as parks and other public facilities. White flight to new residential enclaves in Jefferson and St. Bernard parishes ensued, and in the 1980s, Gentilly Woods home ownership shifted predominantly to blacks. The Dwyer Canal ceased to function as a barrier between Pontchartrain Park and Gentilly Woods after north-south streets were connected across it. The neighborhoods, once separated by race, law, and custom, forged a collective identity and founded the Pontilly Neighborhood Association. For the physically and spiritually conjoined neighborhoods, the park formed an essential amenity and point of identification. Even though Pontchartrain Park and Gentilly Woods represented divided, distinct social trajectories in New Orleans for the first quarter-century of their existence, the importance of their more recent shared social and political history cannot be overemphasized as residents return to rebuild their community.

AFTER KATRINA: WHICH WAY FORWARD? A CASE STUDY FOR NEW ORLEANS AND BEYOND

Like all of the neighborhoods built on New Orleans's reclaimed, back-of-town wetlands, Pontchartrain Park and Gentilly Woods were devastated by Hurricane Katrina and its aftermath. They fell victim to the breaking and overtopping of levees and to pump failures. The lowest parts of the area were inundated to depths of eight feet, and the water sat for as long as eighteen days. Houses on the higher ground of Gentilly Woods fared better than those in the "bowl" of Pontchartrain Park, but none escaped significant damage.

The neighborhoods' location on low ground presents real challenges for rebuilding, but many community members are determined to return to their homes. Pontchartrain Park and Gentilly Woods have always been middle-class neighborhoods, and their residents have the resources to come back. Beyond that, the area's cultural significance makes its rehabilitation important. Pontchartrain Park is eligible for nomination to Historic District status on the National Register because it was established more than fifty years ago and because it represents the historic struggle for equity in segregated New Orleans. However, the rehabilitation of both Pontchartrain Park and Gentilly Woods will be impossible without change. Pumps and levees are never infallible, and the infrastructure failures that devastated the low areas of New Orleans could happen again. To reconstruct the area just as it was before Katrina is to invite the next disaster.

What made Pontchartrain Park and Gentilly Woods unique among New Orleans's low-lying neighborhoods—their cultural landscape—offers them the possibility of a sustainable future. That landscape was central to all three of the agendas that shaped both neighborhoods: its domestication meant the triumph of technology over what had been an uninhabitable wilderness; its open character offered light, fresh air, and the promise of good health to modern city dwellers; and its archetypal suburban amenities spelled out the prosperity and social arrival of a community that history had marginalized. Conceived and constructed for public amenity and civic beauty, the streets, gardens, and common spaces of Pontchartrain Park and Gentilly Woods have, in many ways, created the neighborhoods' identity.

However, beauty and amenity alone cannot deal with the environmental issues facing New Orleans today. In the wake of Katrina, the landscape has an urgent new task. The places that community members value for their image must also act as infrastructure to slow and hold water. Pontchartrain Park and Gentilly Woods suffered because their design ignored the paradoxical ecology of southern Louisiana, and addressing that paradox is the only way to restore the neighborhoods to health. Their preservation as cultural landscapes demands their transformation with respect to natural systems.

Every neighborhood in New Orleans, and, to some degree, in almost every city in the United States, faces the questions raised by the revival of Pontchartrain Park and Gentilly Woods. How can the role of urban landscapes as cultivated places be expanded to make them productive places? How can their iconographic value be extended to include ecological value? How can landscape spaces, networks, and systems be reconceived and remade as infrastructure? How can landscape expression serve to educate and remind residents about the fundamental conditions of the places they inhabit? These neighborhoods are an ideal case study for landscape urbanist practice in New Orleans and across the country. Their dilemmas are extreme but by no means unique.

ISSUES FOR REHABILITATION

The biggest dilemmas facing New Orleans—levee failure, coastal land loss, and the future of the Mississippi River—demand government intervention across southern Louisiana, and in the end, the future of Pontchartrain Park and Gentilly Woods rests on regional policy. However, that does not diminish the urgent need for action at the scales of the neighborhood, the block, and the garden. Pontchartrain Park and Gentilly Woods have trouble with water during storms well below the level of a hurricane; because of their soil types and their elevation, parts of the area flood with every heavy rain. Beyond that, the neighborhoods will never escape the risk of another Katrina. They lie below sea level on partly impermeable soils, and the possibility of levee and pump failure will always exist.

Redirecting, slowing, and holding water are ways of minimizing the nuisance of low-level flooding, and they can mitigate damage in a catastrophe. Hydrologically sound strategies for landscape rehabilitation may also become ways to argue for insurance and tax abatements. If, for instance, homeowners can demonstrate that their gardens absorb enough water to prevent damage to their houses, they may qualify for lower-risk premiums than they would otherwise. If the neighborhood can prove that it is not contributing surface runoff to the city's stormwater system, why not request the reallocation of public funds toward other services? Reconsidering these neighborhood landscapes as infrastructure expands the range of their meaning; it gives them practical, ecological, economic, and political value.

Coming to terms with ecological conditions in the reclaimed ground of the back-of-town cypress swamp is essential to the future of Pontchartrain Park and Gentilly Woods. This will mean making changes to the neighborhoods' cultural landscapes, but those transformations can support and enrich that culture's essential qualities. Design in these historically significant neighborhoods has a double mandate: to develop strategies for drainage, planting, and use that will improve the landscape's hydrological performance and to maintain its highly valued image of verdure, openness, propriety, and order.

WORKING METHODS

Longue Vue House and Gardens began its collaborative work with the Pontilly Disaster Collaborative in 2006, after board member and art historian Carol McMichael Reese had made initial connections to the Pontilly Neighborhood Association. In 2007, following work on the restoration and renewal of Longue Vue's historic landscapes, gardener Hilarie Schackai took on the newly created position of garden outreach coordinator. In that capacity, she participated in various park recovery efforts and small-scale garden plantings throughout the neighborhoods. These projects involved working with and coordinating community residents, local and national volunteers, and student and church groups. Establishing a partnership with Pontilly's Committee on Recreation and Open Space

The domestic landscape might also be the means to consider land building. House lots could be raised with dredge spoils from the navigation channel on the Mississippi and with non-toxic construction debris. For approximately $25,000, a typical block in Pontchartrain Park or Gentilly Woods could be raised to eleven feet above sea level, out of reach of the 500-year flood. Land ownership would be preserved. Blocks that remained at their current level could be occupied by elevated houses or by gardens like the ones proposed for uninhabited lots.

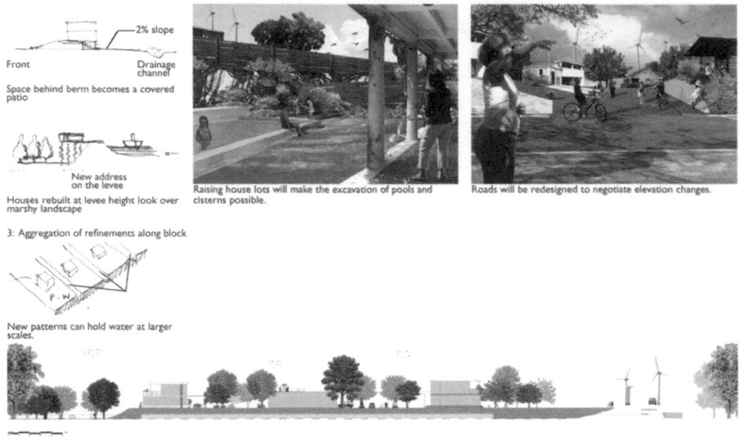

Raised Gardens: Elevating Pontilly

Zara Brown and Jenifer Zell, Louisiana State University, Robert Reich School of Landscape Architecture

was particularly important in realizing these efforts.

In early 2007, Longue Vue asked landscape architect Jane Wolff,[3] who had been Longue Vue's 2004 Catherine Brown Memorial Lecturer, to develop a more comprehensive agenda for rehabilitating the neighborhoods' landscapes. From the beginning, this phase of work was seen as a way to mobilize the talents of all the designers who had participated in the Catherine Brown lecture series. It grew into a collaboration that included not only the Catherine Brown lecturers, Longue Vue's staff, and residents of Pontchartrain Park and Gentilly Woods but also teachers and students of landscape and architectural design and members of the New Orleans planning and horticulture communities.

To get the effort under way, Wolff and Schackai conducted extensive interviews with members of the Pontilly community and with experts on the geography, ecology, and landscape history of southern Louisiana. Two design goals for Pontchartrain Park and Gentilly Woods emerged from those conversations: first, to rehabilitate the neighborhoods' historic landscapes and, second, to increase their ecological and hydrological function. The conversations also identified a range of possible sites for design investigation: typical house lots, occupied and vacant; networks that structured community space, such as streets, drainage canals, and other public rights of way; and the recreational areas of Pontchartrain Park itself, including the Bartholomew Golf Course. To these ends, Longue Vue mobilized resources from its Catherine Brown Memorial Fund in support of the Pontilly Design Weekend, held October 12–14, 2007.

3 Wolff was then on the faculty of the Sam Fox School of Design and Visual Arts at Washington University in St. Louis.

Dwyer Canal is one of the most challenging of the neighborhoods' public rights-of-way. When Pontchartrain Park and Gentilly Woods were built, the Dwyer Canal marked the legal and spatial boundary between blacks and whites. Desegregation nullified the property covenants that differentiated the two neighborhoods, but the canal signifies a painful memory. Renewing the neighborhoods of Pontchartrain Park and Gentilly Woods offers the opportunity to reinvent the canal as a monument to change: it could become a place that unites the two neighborhoods rather than divides them. At the same time, its function as a conduit and reservoir for water can be made more obvious and more beautiful. One strategy for improving Dwyer Canal enlarges the channel and creates a gradual slope up to street level. This increases the channel's capacity, and it also provides space for a public promenade and water garden. If lots adjacent to the canal remain uninhabited, they could be cultivated as entry gardens along the bounding streets.

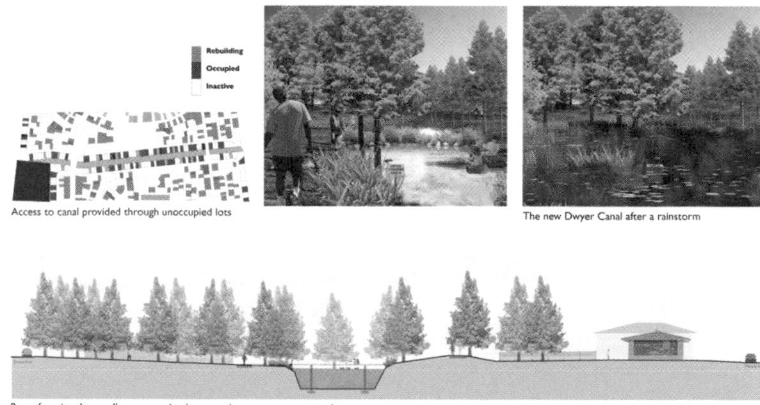

Access to canal provided through unoccupied lots

The new Dwyer Canal after a rainstorm

Reconfuguring the canal's cross-section increases its water storage capacity.

Heather Conn, Louisiana State University, Robert Reich School of Landscape Architecture

Water Storage in the Dwyer Canal

Wolff identified a set of questions to be addressed during the weekend design charrette. In addition, she asked other landscape experts who had participated in Longue Vue's lecture series to join her as the weekend's design advisers and critics; those who participated were Julie Bargmann (University of Virginia), Mia Lehrer (Los Angeles), and Elizabeth Meyer (University of Virginia). They were joined by Hilarie Schackai (Longue Vue); Jasmond Anderson, Jin Lee, Jason Lockhart, Kim Ross, and Archie Tiner (School of Architecture at Southern University, Baton Rouge); Eean McNaughton and Carol Reese (School of Architecture at Tulane University); William Morrish (School of Architecture at the University of Virginia); and Elizabeth Mossop (Robert Reich School of Landscape Architecture at Louisiana State University).

Leading up to the Design Weekend, two graduate design studios, one led by Julie Bargmann and the other led by Elizabeth Mossop, developed comprehensive drawings to describe site conditions in Pontchartrain Park and Gentilly Woods. The students' preparatory work, which documented the area's hydrology, soils, topography, vegetation, demographics, land uses, and culturally significant spaces, provided the basis for collaborative design at the weekend. Joining the UVA and LSU students on working teams for the weekend were architecture and landscape architecture students from Southern University, Baton Rouge and Tulane University. The weekend's design teams were organized to generate ideas for renewing the neighborhoods' landscapes, and community residents and local experts were on hand to advise team members. Four teams studied relevant issues at different scales: the house and garden, the community's public right-of-way networks, and the aggregate recreational spaces of Pontchartrain Park, which included the golf course.

Press Drive could be rebuilt as a boulevard that creates shade, breaks the force of strong winds, and absorbs water. Curb extensions could break the flow of surface water. Lines of mature cypress could take up as much as 200 gallons of water per tree per day. Live oaks in the center of the street could diminish the wind damage to neighboring houses during storms, provide shade to reduce energy consumption, and reinforce New Orleans's lush character.

Curb extensions collect and slow storm water.

Boulevard design offers zones for vehicle, bicycle, and foot traffic.

A New Water Boulevard: Press Drive

Charlotte Paulsen, Louisiana State University, Robert Reich School of Landscape Architecture

The edge of the park could be reinforced by levees, and its center could be excavated to serve as a giant retention basin in case of heavy storms. In that case, the golf course would be redesigned as a series of high berms that stayed dry even if the rest of the park flooded.

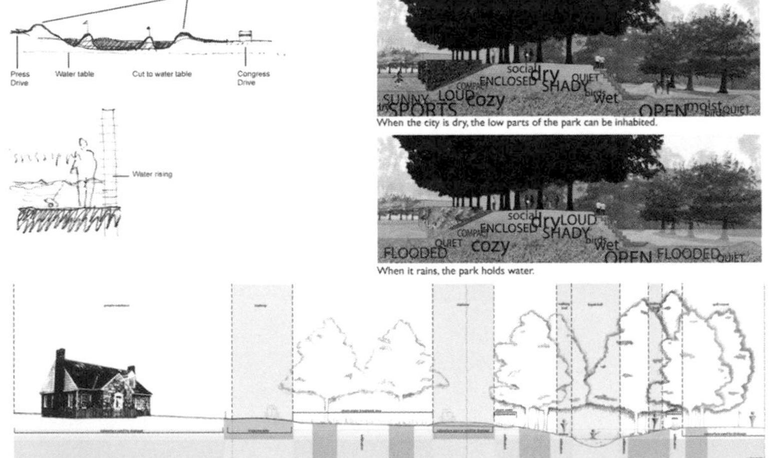

When the city is dry, the low parts of the park can be inhabited.

When it rains, the park holds water.

The park's new character as an emergency retention basin saves the neighbors from flooding.

Park as a Retention Basin – I

Jonah Weiss, University of Virginia School of Architecture, Landscape Architecture Department

The golf course could be rebuilt around a series of ponds that allowed the cultivation of crawfish, the storage of water, and the growth of habitat.

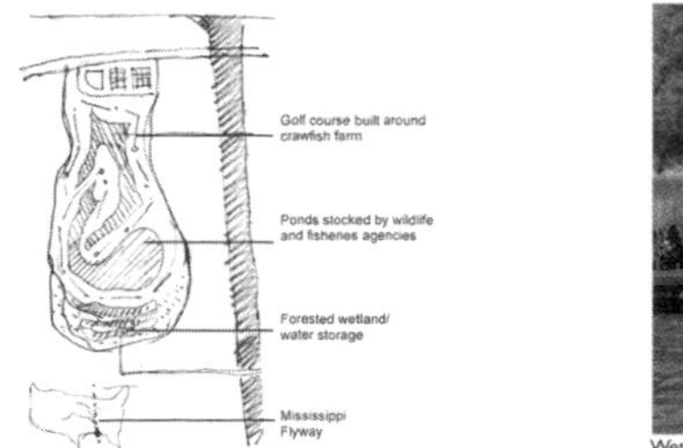

Wetland lakes store water and allow urban fishing.

Crawfish
Fish
Forest wetland

Multiple uses exist together: fishing, farming, water storage, and recreation.

Water hazards for the golf course double as crawfish ponds.

Andrea Kuns and Keera Pullman, Louisiana State University, Robert Reich School of Landscape Architecture

Golfing in a Productive Wetland

At the weekend's close, they presented their strategies to the Longue Vue and Pontilly communities for discussion and comment.

The design ideas generated during the Pontilly Design Weekend were developed further by Professor Mossop's students at LSU and by the students of Professor Bargmann, assisted by professors Meyer and Morrish, at UVA. Working through the remaining six weeks of the fall semester, these two studios provided much of the material that appears in the design "strategies."[4]

CONCLUSION: DESIGN STRATEGIES FOR A PRODUCTIVE LANDSCAPE

The ideas in the landscape manual are the first steps toward an integrated design for the rehabilitation of Pontchartrain Park and Gentilly Woods. Reaching that goal means answering technical, legal, and formal questions. Firm numbers on how much water can be held by plants, cisterns, and green roofs are needed in order to calculate the neighborhoods' ability to manage storms of different levels of severity and to generate more definitive models showing the impact of landscape infrastructure on conventionally engineered systems. New legal structures are needed to hold unoccupied land in trust, because permitting the productive use of the ground while facilitating the right of return is a critical step toward rehabilitation. Some house lots will be developed

4 Jane Wolff's interpretive sketches, which she drew when she attended fall studio reviews at UVA and LSU, appear on several of the student projects published here and in the *Landscape Manual.*

through publicly sponsored projects overseen by the New Orleans Recovery Authority (NORA), which manages such programs as the city's blighted property acquisition and the Real Estate Acquisition and Land-banking Mechanism (REALM), whose powers include the disposition of properties sold to the state in the post-Katrina Road Home program. Other properties, the future of which is still in question, might conceivably be privately administered by a newly constituted Pontilly community development corporation or other nonprofit organization. Furthermore, it is essential to establish a conservancy to administer Pontchartrain Park, because the city of New Orleans currently lacks the resources to bring the park back to a useful, healthy state. Finally, any design idea must be considered in relation to other proposals. That way, a phased agenda for rehabilitation across Pontchartrain Park and Gentilly Woods can be productively and sustainably developed.

PROJECTS
CULTURAL LANDSCAPES

The discipline that frames the physical issues for New Orleans most succinctly is landscape. This book appears in the middle of an academic debate about the proper boundaries of architecture, planning, landscape, urban design, and environmental studies—an intense effort that both participates in the tedious power struggles that are invariable in schools of architecture but that also recognizes a larger shift in the sensibility of design. No discipline can, any longer, remain uninflected by the need to acknowledge all that we have learned about natural systems and about the way in which our professional practices have contributed to the parlous state of the environment. No design can remain indifferent to the urgent need for repair and rebalance.

The projects grouped under the rubric *landscape* are necessarily imprecise as a category, because the idea of landscape now infuses the range of responses to the territorial, from the scale of the sidewalk to the scale of the region. It is time to reconsider the false distinction between human and natural activities that has led us to deny our role in climate change and to justify our attempt to conquer the Mississippi by hemming it in, interrupting the cycle of flooding and silting essential to the region's fertility. Landscape is at the center of all rational efforts to rethink that "dichotomy" and to make things right.

PRECIOUS MEMORIES FLOATING ON A MYSTIC HORIZON

KNOOPS

New York City

Principal: Johannes M.P. Knoops

Knoops's memorial is meant to be haunting and hallucinatory, rejecting the monumental grandeur and illusion of permanence conveyed by most commemorative architecture. Instead of structures, trees are used to mark the lives lost after Katrina struck. The trees, anchored in planters held in position by unseen frames rooted deep in the sea floor of the Gulf of Mexico, seem to float off Louisiana's coast, hovering between the water and the sky.

SITES OF MEMORY

SCHOOL OF ARCHITECTURE

Clemson University, Clemson, South Carolina

Instructor: Ronald Rael

Designers: Rosalind Ashburn, Brad Baxley, Sara Ashley Brown, Amanda Carter, Tony Cates, Beth Copelan, Robert Eleazer, Benjamin Felton, Janis Fowler, Mark Gettys, Blane Hammerlund, Clifford Hammonds, Shana Hyman, Joseph Lane, Jeffrey Lowder, Matthew Rhodes, Eulanda Rogers, Nicholas Svilar, Broderick Whitlock

This memorial project for the Lower Ninth Ward marks the height reached by the floodwaters there with site-specific memorials. These "hydrocaches" serve as reminders of the flood, representing both the destructive and life-giving properties of water, and designate spaces of communal memory, calling forth hope in the face of devastation.

BIG + FIX

HARGREAVES ASSOCIATES

San Francisco

Levee Connector at Levee Park

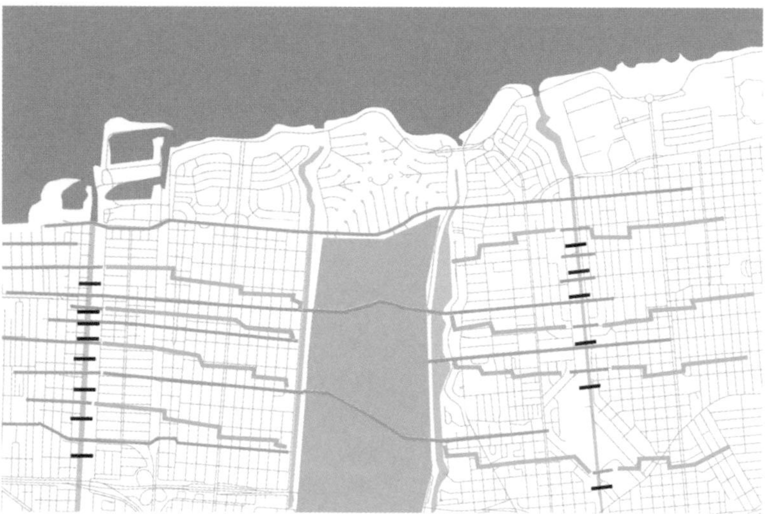

New Network: Connectivity

After Katrina, many outsiders called on New Orleans to shrink in order to survive. Hargreaves Associates recognized that this was not a realistic possibility: Residents were returning after the storm and rebuilding throughout the city. Hargreaves's "Big + Fix" proposal seeks to return the city to its pre-Katrina size with an infrastructural fix that would protect it during another Category 5 hurricane. Stronger pumps, wider and higher levees, and redesigned canals able to handle greater volumes of water would make a safe environment of the whole city, prompting the return of more evacuees and resettlement. A network of greenways planted on vacant lots and providing cross-canal connections between neighborhoods would address the physical and social disjunctures that the canals create.

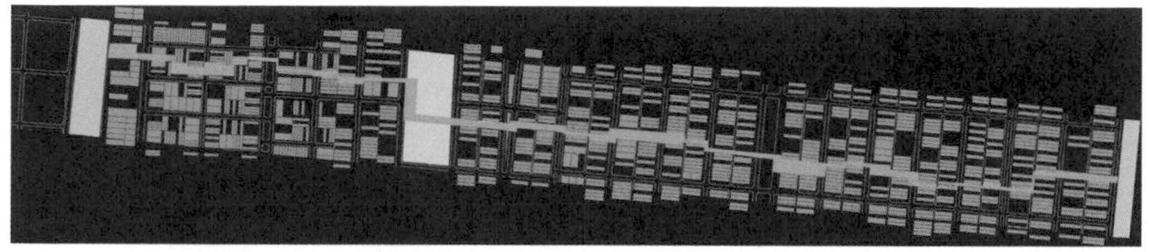

New Parks on Vacant Lots

Big + Fix

LIGHT OF HOPE

TAUBMAN COLLEGE OF ARCHITECTURE

University of Michigan, Ann Arbor

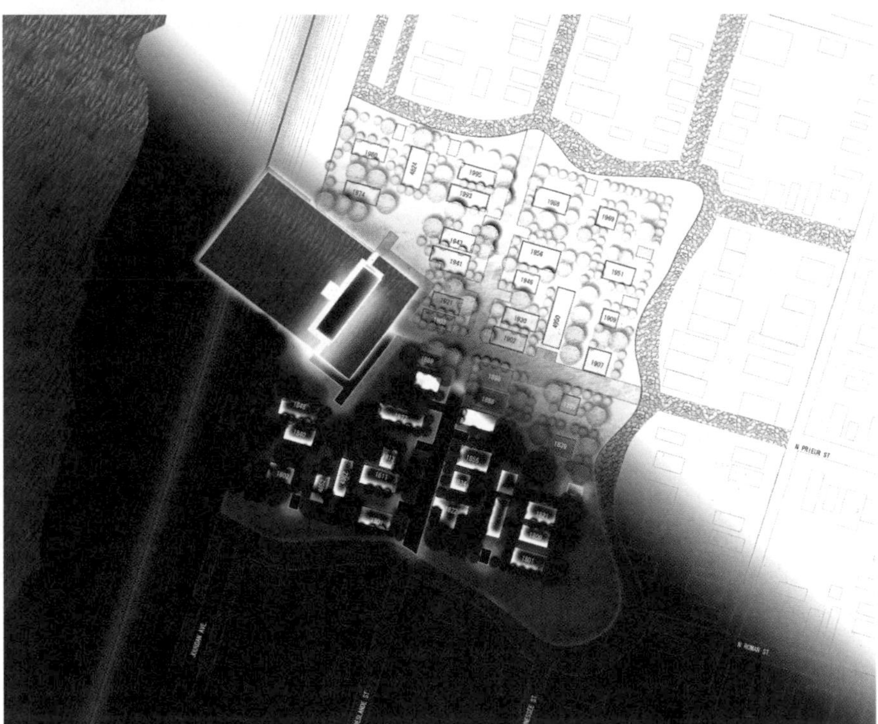

Instructors: Michael Sorkin, Coleman Jordan

Designer: Toshio Yoshimoto

This memorial project for the Lower Ninth Ward proposes a commemorative park with a public building located at the exact point where a barge, untethered when Katrina struck, penetrated the wall of the Industrial Canal, causing catastrophic flooding. The site is designed to focus visitors' attention on the canal and the levee. At night, an exterior lighting system shrouds the building in white light, and colored lights installed in empty lots where other buildings once stood create a dramatic landscape. Fiber-optic lighting within the building is programmed to change throughout the day, giving visitors varied experiences. The project uses light to symbolize the hope of rebirth.

UJAMAA SQUARE: MOVABLE, ELEVATED PATHWAYS

DEPARTMENT OF ARCHITECTURE
Wentworth Institute of Technology, Boston

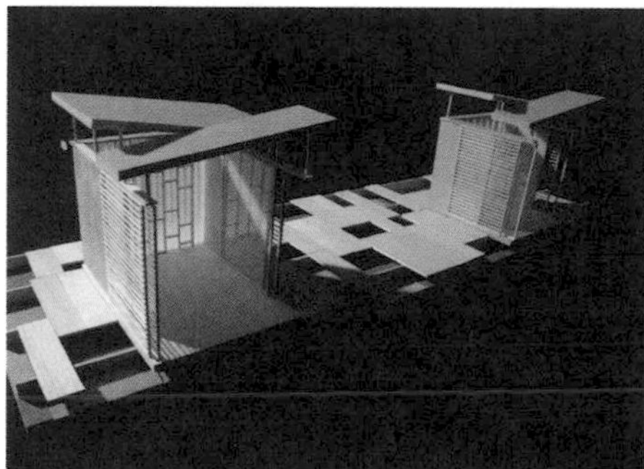

Instructor: Mark Pasnik
Designers: Blaine Abaray and Darin Barnes

The soil in Ujamaa Square in the Tremé neighborhood was found to contain toxins post-Katrina—an issue for many parts of the city that flooded. This project proposes a community center for the site composed of multiple buildings that would house child-care and soil testing facilities and be linked by elevated walkways providing safe outdoor areas for play. The pathways are designed to be moveable, so that areas of the ground could be reclaimed as the soil was remediated. Preexisting shotgun houses on the site would be retrofitted to extend the concept of renovation and reuse. Pavilions with sliding glass panels and wood louvers would connect the houses, providing ventilation as well as energy efficiency.

reGROW: THE LAFITTE CORRIDOR

SCHOOL OF ARCHITECTURE AND PLANNING

Massachusetts Institute of Technology, Cambridge

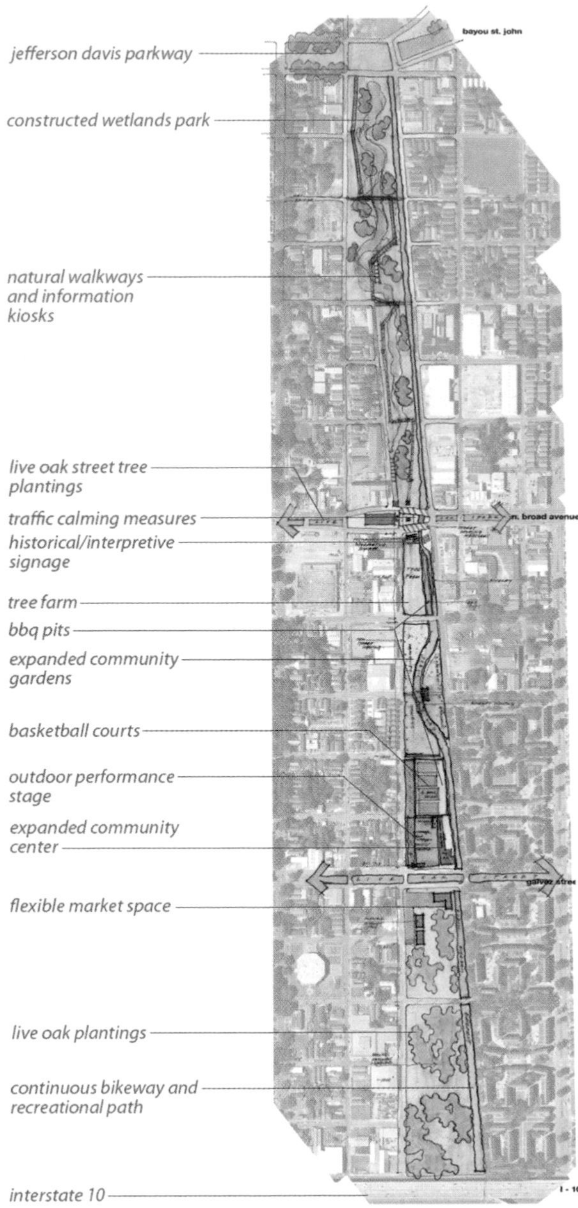

Instructor: Phil Thompson

Designers: Sharlene Leurig, Chris Lyddy, Timothy Terway

This project presents a "green" development plan for the Lafitte Corridor, an area extending between the Tremé and Mid-City neighborhoods. The plan provides for community gardens, wetlands, outdoor gathering spaces, and a continuous pedestrian and bike path. It also proposes basketball courts, a tree farm, flexible market space, outdoor performance spaces, a community center, and the redevelopment of the Lafitte Housing project. By celebrating the cultivation of a new greenway that serves a variety of civic functions, the scheme incorporates environmental remediation with civic and cultural rebirth.

existing conditions

the phytoremediation process...

...leads to active community spaces

community gathering spaces / bbq pits

potential: constructed wetlands park

existing conditions - concrete culvert

STREAMS: CITY PARK

WEST 8

Rotterdam

The creeks of the miniature delta

Principal/designer: Adriaan Geuze

West 8's project *Streams* proposes varied civic functions that New Orleans's devastated City Park could serve during three planned phases of its recovery. In the earliest phase following Hurricane Katrina, the park could usefully become a temporary city of mobile homes for displaced citizens and first responders. As soon as the park was no longer needed as a site for temporary shelter, volunteers could remediate the park's landscape by constructing a new hydrological system, which would help to cleanse its soil, and planting tens of thousands of trees. In the second phase of recovery, the park would begin to function again as a site of recreation and leisure. In the third phase, the park would be significantly redesigned as a place where citizens could engage with the city's culture and ecology. A miniature delta would represent New Orleans's deltaic ecosystem; the Katrina Trace, a watery memorial field, would symbolize the lives lost in the storm; and new pathways would link the park more clearly with routes to the French Quarter and Lake Pontchartrain.

Post-Katrina City Park, flooded

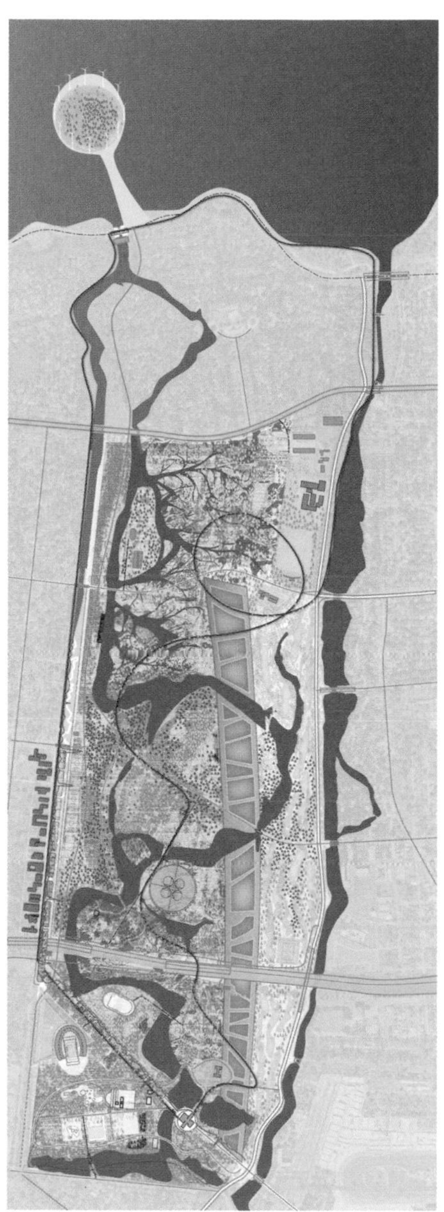

Future City Park, the promise of a miniature delta

The memorial Katrina Trace in City Park

PART VII
URBAN ANALYSIS

HAUNTED HOUSING: ECO-VANGUARDISM AND EVICTION IN NEW ORLEANS

YATES McKEE

> [These projects] seek to house a sense of community, attract attention and activity, and make the landscape visible. They propose a shared space, both physical and mental, around which the city could organize itself in a meaningful manner. And in so doing, they not only suggest an architecture for a Newer Orleans but also point out potential ways for making all of us at home in an increasingly alien world.
>
> —Aaron Betsky, "Sites Unseen"[1]

> To inhabit a house is usually to suppress its nightmares.
>
> —Mark Wigley, "Recycling Recycling"[2]

Integrating postwar cybernetics and Romantic landscape aesthetics, Ian McHarg's *Design With Nature* outlined a physiological diagnosis of the maladjustments between the human organism and its environment, a problem with roots that go deeper than any particular political or economic system. McHarg perceived the pollution, decay, and anarchy in the American metropolis—and the sterility of the car-centered suburbs—as morbid symptoms of a fundamental misunderstanding about the place of man in relation to the "planetary superorganism" of the biosphere. The man-centeredness of our civilization's values, he argued, ensures that those processes essential to man's evolution and survival will be excluded from consideration. Taking himself as the measure and master of things, man was putting at risk his own existence by forgetting his biospheric heritage: "Our phenomenal world contains our origins, our history, our milieu—it is our home. It is in this sense that ecology, derived from *oikos*, is the science of the home."[3] Informed by this sense of deep ecological memory, a designer could bring the built environment into a harmonious equilibrium with organic

1 Aaron Betsky, "Sites Unseen," in Betsky and Reed Kroloff, "A Newer Orleans: Six Proposals," *Artforum* (March 2006).

2 Mark Wigley, "Recycling Recycling," in Amerigo Marras, ed., *ECO-TEC: Architecture of the In-Between* (New York: Princeton Architectural Press, 1999), 48.

3 Ian L. McHarg, *Design with Nature* (Garden City, NY: Natural History Press, 1969), 63–4.

patterns, processes, and cycles of nature, making man a both the "steward" and a "co-tenant" of his terrestrial home.

Aesthetically a cross between a diagram of systematic feedback loops and a phenomenological intuition of the "meaning" of life in all its fragile interdependence, *Design With Nature* reenvisioned human settlements not as self-contained concentrations of artificial structures but as multilayered organisms interacting with larger regional ecologies. Anticipating contemporary GIS technology, McHarg overlaid existing urban maps with a remarkable array of color-coded data sets detailing the naturally occurring topographical, geological, hydrological, and biogeographical features of a particular region. Existing urban "forms" could be judged as to their "suitability" or "fitness" for the specific ecological configuration in which they were situated; on the basis of this visually dynamic knowledge, cities could evolve in and adapt to their proper milieu, growing with nature rather than against it. For McHarg, the stakes of this evolutionary process—the long-term survival of urban life itself—transcended the interest in the realm of politics. Social conflicts such as the ghetto rebellions of the late 1960s seemed to him to be so much entropic "noise," a breakdown in the homeostatic relay between social and environmental systems that would ultimately be resolved through a shift in the "ecological conscience" of urban planners and architects.

Design With Nature is widely acknowledged to have helped inaugurate the discourse on "sustainable development" some fifteen years before the term was officially defined by the report to the UN *Our Common Future* as "development that meets the needs of the present generation without compromising the ability of future generations to meet their own," and it was subsequently adopted by figures such as William McDonough, whose "Principles of Design for Sustainability" calls for "a quality of life and place which depends on the protection ... of our natural home, myriad species, and our own future generations."[4]

Though it has long had a canonical place in bibliographies of "green design," McHarg's work has taken on a new resonance in the aftermath of Hurricane Katrina, which has brought questions of environmental design and the life, death, and survival of cities to the forefront of the architectural discipline. Although McHarg is not cited explicitly, his basic terms—and their depoliticizing implications—are everywhere evident in *New Orleans: Strategies for a City in Soft Land*, the results of a studio and research project undertaken at the Harvard School of Design with the support of the Tulane School of Architecture, carried out during the 2004–2005 academic year but published in December

4 World Commission on Environment and Development, *Our Common Future* (Oxford: Oxford University Press, 1987), and William McDonough Architects, "The Hannover Principles: Design for Sustainability" prepared for EXPO 2000, The Worlds Fair, Hannover, Germany, 1992.

2005, three months into the aftermath of Hurricane Katrina.[5]

In his preface, "The Future of New Orleans: Summary of the New Orleans Studio and Considerations after Katrina," editor Joan Busquets describes the project as "a complete reading of the spatial mechanisms at work in the transformation of the urban and territorial system of this singular deltaic space ... Specific knowledge of the city will then help to interpret the process of giving it form, but above all it may contribute to understanding the why and how behind its reconstruction." As the phrase "deltaic space" suggests, the book positions New Orleans within an expanded scale of regional and ecological processes that are not reducible to—indeed, they underlie—the physical structures of the city itself. Ecological expansion also means a historical deepening, the restoration of a geographical and climatological memory that the city has lost. Indeed, the Katrina disaster was much more than a case of poor engineering or governmental incompetence—it resulted from an arrogant, instrumental way of conceptualizing the relationship of city and river that failed to attend to the inherently fluid topography of deltaic space. In other words, the elaborate hydrological infrastructures built during New Orleans's postwar expansion provided a false sense of security, ignoring the basic ecological dynamics on which the city was originally based. This "excessive faith in the mechanisms of engineering" resulted in "permissiveness in the urbanization of very low areas, such as the Ninth Ward." "Above all," Busquets writes, "the flooding of low-lying areas points to the problems caused by forgetting the city's geographical conditions that cannot be overstepped and must be part of the urban order ... The urban order must be governed by the geographical order." In essence then, the hurricane demonstrated that the pre-Katrina city was poorly adjusted to its environment, yet in its destruction lie the seeds of its "sublime rebirth," giving it a chance at life based on a sustainable "dialogue" with nature rather than a defensive attempt to reverse natural patterns and rhythms. Identifying and adapting to these dynamics requires historical reflection; no future without the past, in other words. The stakes in this task are significant for urbanism as a whole, especially for cities on terra firma, which, Busquets says, "more easily lose the memory of their relation with the location and their seminal topography."[6]

Busquets's call for design to engage site-specific ecological memory may seem benign, but in his positing of a geography as the city's evolutionary determinant, Busquets effaces the memory of those killed and displaced by the hurricane, a disaster whose worst effects were unevenly allocated not only by topographic contingencies but also by race and class, factors that are entirely absent from his analysis. Celebrating the city as the

5 Joan Busquets in collaboration with Felipe Correa, *New Orleans: Strategies for a City in Soft Land* (Cambridge, MA: Harvard University, Graduate School of Design, 2005).

6 Ibid. 13–17.

subject of a unitary historical trajectory, he writes, "I do not intend to speak of the difficulties that occupied the city during the period of emergency ... I refer to the city's urbanistic conditions and its intrinsic values."[7]

Busquets brackets "the emergency" of Katrina as a finite "period" in the overall life of the city, isolating it from historically inherited dynamics of pre-storm inequality and from the ongoing emergency of the displaced survivors. By treating Katrina as essentially a problem of what McHarg described as Values, Process, and Form, he evicts black New Orleanians from the realm of historical representation, a precondition for their permanent material eviction from the future of the city itself. Indeed, the studies in *Strategies for a City in Soft Land* present New Orleans as if it had been depopulated before the storm ever struck.

Busquets's position is given a more dynamic theoretical elaboration by Ila Berman in her essay "Fluid Cartographies and Material Diagrams," which meditates on the inadequacy of conventional architectural procedures when confronted with the fluidity and indeterminacy of New Orleans's topography. Against "the reifications of figuration" that would fix the city as a static thing, the projects outlined in *Strategies for a City* partake of an "evolutionary process" within design itself, one that is informed by "the deep ecological milieu from which the environment of New Orleans emerged." Yet, rather than a purely bio-organic nature such as that imagined by McHarg, the "deep ecology" to which Berman appeals is understood in Deleuzian terms as a "rhizomatic fluvial matrix" that calls for radical diagrammatic strategies capable of layering and transcoding data and landscape, time and space, form and matter in experimental ways. For Berman, the diagrammatic is "interpretative, transformative, and performative," a position she opposes to "critical claims that all is representation—(as the poststructuralists would have us believe that cultural knowledge always precedes and filters our readings of unmediated matter)." Berman thus positions herself as a kind of architectural activist, deploying both scientific and formal rigor to "disrupt habitual modes of envisioning the real" and to "resist the ease of accessibility that accompanies images intended for simple consumption."[8]

Yet Berman's dismissal of "representation" should disturb us—in so-called poststructuralism, this term signals an ethicopolitical attention to the exclusions that govern the spaces of speech and response, the limits to who or what can appear at a given conjuncture, and in what ways. Although motivated by a desire for justice, poststructuralism demands that we remain vigilant about our complicity in violence, even when engaged in the most conscientious of radical aesthetic or political endeavors. These are questions that *Strategies for a City*, despite its eco-vanguardist vocabulary of vectors, fields, and rhizomes, utterly fails to ask, and so the

7 Ibid. 13.
8 Ila Berman, "Fluid Cartographies and Material Diagrams," in Busquets, *New Orleans*, 29–36.

book ends up defining the city as essentially "a floating 'sponge'—a semi-stable ecosystem supported by an intricately entangled biomorphic fabric, a woven living matrix."[9] This definition is offered as "a backdrop to the current and future debates which will govern the rebuilding of the city," which can guard against "the reinstantiation of habitual typological realities and mute development which we already know are unsustainable within this environment."[10] Sustainability is thus understood as a question of aesthetic quality and formal suitability rather than, say, the allocation of environmental risk, spatial resources, and political power.

In its rhetoric of biomorphism, however dynamically machinic it may be, *Strategies for a City* forecloses any discussion of the biopolitical conditions of New Orleans, and thus unwittingly acquiesces to the designs of redevelopment elites such as Joe Canizaro, the real estate mogul who was appointed by the mayor to chair the Urban Planning committee of the Bring New Orleans Back commission and who notoriously remarked, "As a practical matter, these poor folks don't have the resources to go back to our city just like they didn't have the resources to get out of our city. So we won't get all those folks back. That's just a fact." Significantly, Canizaro is a trustee and former chairman of the Urban Land Institute (ULI), the chief think tank and advocacy group for New Urbanism, an aesthetically traditionalist and suspiciously communitarian vision of the revitalized city that is typically framed as the scourge of vanguard architecture, the enemy against which "advanced" practice would define itself.

This position informs what has been perhaps the most prominent response by avant-garde architecture to the situation in New Orleans, a collection of six "visionary" proposals published in the March 2006 edition of *Artforum* in conjunction with the traveling exhibition "A Newer Orleans: A Shared Space." In a tacit acknowledgment that these projects cannot be realized in the current circumstances of the city, the presenters offer them "in the spirit of possibility and in a long-standing tradition of collaborative, idealistic endeavors in the arts, which have in previous eras provided the germ of inspiration for public works."[11] Unlike *Strategies for a City in Soft Land*, with its scientistic agenda of morphological research, "A Newer Orleans" explicitly declares its aspiration to social relevance in the public sphere, under conditions similar to those in post-9/11 New York, when calls for "visionary" architecture were sounded in the name of healing and resurrecting the traumatized metropolis.

In his introduction to the six projects, "After the Flood," Reed Kroloff describes his own walk through the ruined landscape of an unspecified New Orleans neighborhood, which he characterizes as "dead," "almost ghostly," and "spooky": "There's nothing out there. No lights. No people.

9 Ibid. 31.

10 Ibid. 36.

11 Reed Kroloff, "After the Flood," in Betsky and Kroloff, "A Newer Orleans: Six Proposals."

No police. No sound. No horizon. No hope." Yet the pathos of this wasted, indeed terrifying, landscape provides the background against which Kroloff can pose the revitalizing vocation of architecture. Accepting that "New Orleans is going to be a mess for a long time," he writes, "[T]his city needs bright visions to contrast with the bleak present that surrounds us ... We need inspiration and innovation, glimpses into a promising and expressive future." This visionary impulse is resolutely opposed to the New Urbanists, "who would have us believe our only future resides in [the] past" and who offer a "candy-coated dream version" of an architecture that Kroloff denounces as "quaint and predictable but also smart and marketable."[12]

Kroloff's sounding the alarm about the "New Urbanist Svengalis" is laudable, but it is imperative to think about why, how, and in the name of whom or what such forward-looking architectural declamations take place, lest we reproduce the worst aspects of the very thing that critical design—if there is such a thing—would claim to oppose.

The stakes of this criticality—or lack thereof—become evident in the accompanying text by Aaron Betsky, a meditation on how architecture might contribute to the reenvisioning and reconstruction of New Orleans. Unlike *Strategies for a City*, Betsky frames his remarks by criticizing, in a certain way, the politico-economic dynamics of the city:

> The situation in New Orleans is only an extreme instance of the quandary in which architecture in general finds itself—when the economic realities imposed on us by relentless market forces compel the proliferation of nonplaces leached of any individual or social meaning or coherence, how is architecture to respond?[13]

Yet, echoing Berman's claims to resist "habitual typological patterns" and Kroloff's denunciation of "the sugarcoated future" offered by New Urbanism, Betsky's main objection to "market forces" appears to be that they threaten to reduce the aesthetic quality of urban "place." That is, the specific competence of architecture is to be defined through a kind of existential battle against the alienating deprivation of "meaning" and "coherence" in everyday life, a humanist ideologeme that still has surprising currency in contemporary aesthetic discourse.

Betsky acknowledges the question of social housing, but writes that "the provision of adequate dwelling for the displaced is not an activity in which architecture can play a role beyond making sure the houses are safe and more or less aesthetically pleasing. Where, how much, at what price, and who will live there is currently being decided by politicians and no doubt real estate interests." Although Betsky's last point is in one sense true, he cynically takes the domination of the housing discussion

12 Ibid.

13 Betsky, "Sites Unseen."

by elites for granted, narrowly framing it as an unsavory technical part of the reconstruction process from which advanced architecture should be content to keep a distance. Rather than entering into the fractious, interested realm of politics, which he defines in advance as involving only professional politicians, without input from citizens or social movements, architecture should contribute its efforts to a higher end—namely, remaking the architectural image and landscape ecology of the city itself, restoring "meaning" to New Orleans. Betsky complains that "no one seems to be asking why anybody would return to New Orleans in the first place. Every city needs its unique selling points and needs to attract investment. Old New Orleans was in decline. Katrina turned that gradual decay into catastrophe. Why would anyone come back?" Like Busquets, Betsky sees the disaster as an opportunity for urban ecological "rebirth":

> New Orleans is now clearly, in all likelihood irrevocably, one of the world's shrinking cities ... What is interesting is the fact that nature is coming back in many of these areas ... The vast voids left by deindustrialization and depopulation are turning back into forest and field ... As cities still suburbanize, nature is returning into the inner city, and it can draw people back to these burned-out cores ... We believe these elements can also help New Orleans to transform itself into a successful Newer Orleans—a smaller, more compact, and more beautiful city that would use its natural setting and cultural heritage to enhance viable neighborhoods and attract both new businesses and new residents.

Disavowing the unstable, contested status of terms such as *community, heritage*, and *landscape*, Betsky's call for design to contribute to the envisioning of "a smaller, more compact, more beautiful city," echoes with unqualified enthusiasm the basic terms not only of Canizaro and the ULI but also the self-fulfilling forecast by the Rand Corporation completed in January 2006: that just over half of New Orleans's pre-storm population would return in three years.[14] Needless to say, in questioning such a forecast, one should not be glib about the massive obstacles facing the return of displaced people or about the serious ecological and infrastructural issues to be dealt with in low-lying areas of the city. The point is to recognize these as realms of political dispute and negotiation, rather than agreeing to define them as demographic inevitabilities or matters of a sheer technical expertise to which designers should defer. Yet this is precisely what Betsky does, and as a result he is happy to present among his "visionary" projects the "daring, even defiant" plan of Pritzker Prize recipient Thom Mayne/Morphosis for a new "Civic Center, Park, and National Jazz Center" that would redefine New Orleans's

14 Kevin F. McCarthy et al., *The Repopulation of New Orleans After Hurricane Katrina* (Santa Monica, CA: Rand Gulf States Policy Institute, 2006), rand.org.

political node in the Central Business District.[15] According to Mayne, "the city, even three years out, will have lost 50 percent of its population, and given the general assumption of uncertainty, the city realistically can neither rebuild infrastructure nor resume services at pre-Katrina levels ... [C]ontraction can provide an opportunity to radically transform and improve an urban system."[16] Mayne's suggestion that most of the returning population could be concentrated in "Downtown" New Orleans actually goes far beyond the ULI-designed Bring New Orleans Back plan unveiled in January [2006], which was widely criticized for its projected "greenspacing" of poor black neighborhoods such as the Lower Ninth Ward.[17] This unintentionally dystopian vision epitomizes the neoliberal dream of what the Center for Urban Pedagogy has called The City Without a Ghetto, which is to say, a city in which it is not the dynamics of ghettoization that have been eliminated but instead the ghetto residents themselves.[18] This dream, legitimized by an appeal to what McHarg would call ecological suitability, is the nightmare that haunts Betsky's call for a Newer Orleans, a call that concludes as follows:

> These projects seek to house a sense of community, attract attention and activity, and make the landscape visible. They propose a shared space, both physical and mental, around which the city could organize itself in a meaningful manner. And in so doing, they not only suggest an architecture for a Newer Orleans but also a potential way for making all of us at home in an increasingly alien world.

Betsky urges the "housing" of urban community, but only as an eco-phenomenological horizon conceived in the weakly Heideggerian manner of Christian Norberg-Schulz, rather than as a political demand for a human right to housing and its corollary, the right to return declared by organizations such as the ACORN Katrina Survivors Association and the United Front for Affordable Housing Coalition. These rights claims have found one form of expression in the small tent city or Survivors' Village set up outside the barbed-wire fenced premises of St. Bernard Public Housing Development.[19] This housing project, like most others in New Orleans, was evacuated and is still boarded up despite having suffering relatively little damage from the storm. In June 2006, HUD announced

---

15 See Morphosis, "New Orleans Jazz Center and Park," morphopedia.com

16 See Kevin Pratt, "Urban Icon," Morphosis project description in Betsky and Kroloff, "A Newer Orleans: Six Proposals," thefreelibrary.com.

17 For Mayne's ideas about a smaller urban footprint for New Orleans, see Hans Teerds, "Hopeful Images for New Orleans" (February 20, 2006), archined.nl. On the ULI plan for New Orleans, see Christine Boyer's essay in Part II of this volume.

18 The Center for Urban Pedagogy mounted an exhibition (organized by Rosten Woo and Damon Rich) and allied educational events under the title "Urban Renewal: The City without a Ghetto" at the Storefront for Architecture in the fall of 2003 and spring of 2004; see storefrontnews.org; wehavenoart.net; and bombsite.com.

19 See "Survivors' Village," *A Katrina Reader, Readings by and for Anti-Racist Educators and Organizers*, katrinareader.org.

plans to demolish 5,000 units of public housing in order to make way for "mixed-income" redevelopment. This ambiguous term, when left uninterrogated, has often been used to justify programs of aggressive gentrification in the name of "de-concentrating" or "desegregating" the urban poor, whether they are residents of public housing, Section 8, private rentals, or privately owned homes. (It should be remembered that each of these residential situations entails a specific and differential level of vulnerability to the forces of displacement.)

Survivors' Village is designed to remind passing motorists, media outlets, and urban and federal authorities that "public housing residents will continue to fight for the right to return to their homes." A performance intervention in the visual, architectural, and mnemonic landscape of the city, Survivors' Village can be understood as an aesthetic claim on what Jacques Rancière calls the partition of the sensible,

> a delimitation of spaces and times, of the visible and the invisible, of speech and noise, that simultaneously determines the place and the stakes of politics as a form of experience. Politics revolves around what is seen and what can be said about it, around who has the ability to see and the talent to speak, around the properties of spaces and the possibilities of time.[20]

Crucially for Rancière, this partition involves those whose assigned part in society is to have no part, the surplus or remainder of the population whose grievances do not register as such for the agencies by whom they are governed, such as the hundreds of thousands of New Orleans residents still displaced within the city and across the country. Survivors' Village does not simply introduce new elements into a political space whose boundaries and rules are agreed upon in advance—the liberal ideal of "communicative planning" in which different "shareholders" are seated around a common negotiating table—but also marks the exclusions that underwrite that space in the first place. Unsettling Betsky's ideal of a "shared space" properly at home with itself, Survivors' Village shows up as a shadowy apparition of the "old" New Orleans that haunts the imaginary of urban revitalization propounded in distinct, yet kindred ways by neoliberal gentrifiers and avant-garde architects alike.

As a counter to the quiescent or, in some cases, reactionary positions taken by Betsky and his ilk, what other modes of design practice might be invented in response to the ongoing aftermath of the hurricane? The temporary, self-organized, and contestatory structures of Survivors' Village have an obvious appeal for young designers informed by a neo-Situationist desire to reposition their practice within the expanded

20 Jacques Rancière, *The Politics of Aesthetics: The Distribution of the Sensible*, trans. Gabriel Rockhill (London: Continuum, 2004), 8.

networks of activist counterpublicity that have proliferated over the past decade in tandem with the movements of "the multitude" in the U.S. and abroad. But although the Survivors' witness-bearing tactics and the "Solidarity, not charity" program of the Common Ground Collective are important, it is crucial for designers not to fetishize such grassroots spontaneity while neglecting longer-term, larger-scale solutions to the constraints, mediations, uncertainties and inequalities of the reconstruction environment in which social-justice organizations have been struggling to operate.[21]

Indeed, rather than indulging in visionary projections or on-the-ground protest, designers could play a crucial role by attending to the "architecture" of the reconstruction process, which is just as much a matter of bureaucratic agencies, financial flows, media images, scientific data sets, and political claims as it is of buildings, infrastructures, and territories.

This would require a faithful yet critical engagement with two fields that avant-garde aesthetic discourse has not spent much time analyzing: planning theory and information design. Susan Fainstein and others have elaborated on the uncertain status of planning as a form of expertise concerned with the design and coordination of the built environment, operating at the embattled intersection of a) the dynamics of capitalist political economy, b) the techniques and agencies of urban governance, c) a formally democratic electoral system, and d) nonpolitical demands for civic participation and social equity made by inhabitants, users, and in some cases, evictees of the built environment.[22]

Edward Tufte has discussed information design, which involves the translation of various kinds of data sets—often of a technical or quantitative nature—into visual patterns, arrangements, figures, and formats that are cognitively accessible to nonspecialized audiences.[23] Tufte declares that the form in which data is presented crucially shapes its content and the way in which that content is received, judged, and used. His aesthetic insights concerning figure-ground relations; the layering, differentiation, and arrangement of elements; and the use of color and typography are motivated a by transcendental imperative to clarify communication as much as possible in the interests of consensual problem solving in a rational public sphere.

Without indulging in Ila Berman's vanguardist determination to "resist the ease of accessibility that accompanies images intended for simple consumption," we should supplement Tufte's utopian call for formal economy and public legibility with questions about who or what is

21 Scott Crow, *Black Flags and Windmills: Hope, Anarchy, and the Common Ground Collective* (Oakland, CA: PM Press, 2011).

22 Susan Fainstein, *The Just City* (Ithaca, NY: Cornell University Press, 2010) and Naomi Carmon and Fainstein, eds., *Policy, Planning, and People: Promoting Justice in Urban Development* (Philadelphia: University of Pennsylvania Press, 2013).

23 Edward R. Tufte, *Beautiful Evidence* (Cheshire, CT: Graphics Press, 2006) and *Envisioning Information* (Cheshire, CT: Graphics Press, 1990).

authorized to produce "information" in the first place, according to what protocols, and in what ways that information should be mediated before, during, and after becoming an element in the articulation of a political claim. This means understanding specific visual-informational artifacts in relation to the stories that they implicitly or explicitly tell and that are told about them, in all possible institutional, technical, and discursive conditions—a PowerPoint presentation delivered to a planning board, the website of a government agency, an evidentiary demonstration in a courtroom or press conference, a documentary video, a protest banner, or, indeed, a student publication from a school of architecture, planning, and preservation.

This set of questions concerning aesthetics and politics, representation and planning, space and technology, must inform a rethinking of environmentalism in contemporary design. Despite their different ideological inflections, the three dominant tendencies discussed in this essay—diagrammatic biomorphism, New Urbanism, and visionary humanism—are united in their common failure to question the apparent goodness of ecological terms, leading them to treat the city as an organism striving to be properly at home with itself and the world.

This way of thinking authorizes a vision of sustainability, survival, and futurity untroubled by history, understood not as a univocal shared heritage, cultural or biospheric, but as the traces and remainders of violence that mark the living present and prevent it from ever becoming fully itself. It is in this sense that "survival"—life marked by something other than life—can become a claim to biopolitical rights, lodged by the evicted, that at once inhabits and displaces the sense of the term as used by an ecologist such as McHarg, who called for "seeing ourselves in a nonhuman past, our survival contingent on nonhuman processes." Informed by the principles of environmental justice developed by human rights movements around the world over the past fifteen years, any project of "sustainable design" must proactively address the conditions and agencies that continue to deny residents equal access to vital ecological life-support systems such as housing, education, healthcare, and media, while keeping watch over architecture's own disciplinary proclivity for both domestication and eviction.

JUSTICE REINVESTMENT NEW ORLEANS
LAURA KURGAN

PART 1: MAPPING INCARCERATION

Since 2005, the Spatial Information Design Lab has been investigating the geography of incarceration in the contemporary United States. Building on work done jointly by the Council of State Governments, the JFA Institute, and the Justice Mapping Center, the lab's mapping project seeks to focus research and policy attention on the conditions and needs of urban spaces with high rates of incarceration. Rather than examining only the punishment and rehabilitation of individuals, the research identifies particular places and emerging strategies for investing public resources in order to address the urban conditions from which prisoners come and to which most of them return.[1]

A CALL TO ACTION

Hurricane Katrina exposed New Orleans's neglected physical infrastructure and ecological vulnerability. It also highlighted the fragility of civil institutions in the city's poorest neighborhoods, where social life is made even more unstable by the constant displacement and resettlement of people in the criminal justice system. Weeks after the storm, the Spatial Information Design Lab transformed its analytic incarceration mapping project into an action-oriented proposal for justice reinvestment in New Orleans. This resulting document and plan is the product of more than two years of work, countless conversations, and an intricately crafted network of local and national participants dedicated to creating a more just and sustainable future for New Orleans.

THE GROWTH OF PRISONS

The United States has the highest rate of incarceration of any country in the world. Though it has only 4 percent of the world's population, the U.S. is home to one quarter of the world's incarcerated individuals.[2] Since

1 This volume reprints material from Spatial Information Design Lab's report *Justice Reinvestment New Orleans* (New York: Columbia University Graduate School of Architecture, Planning, and Preservation, January 2009), spatialinformationdesignlab.org.

2 Adam Liptak, "Inmate Count in U.S. Dwarfs Other Nations," part of the series "American Exception: Millions Behind Bars," *New York Times*, April 23, 2008.

1970, the state and federal prison population has grown eightfold, to nearly 1.6 million. With another 723,000 people in local jails, a total of 2.3 million Americans are incarcerated. As a 2008 report for the Pew Charitable Trusts documents, for the first time in the nation's history more than 1 in 100 American adults are behind bars.[3]

FROM CRIME MAPS TO GEOGRAPHIES OF INCARCERATION

Crime maps are common instruments for policy makers and urban police forces pursuing tactical approaches to fighting crime. The places where crimes are committed cluster in so-called hot spots at which resources can be targeted. The benefits of this approach are short-lived. The city spaces that are targeted may become safer, but too often crime incidence is simply displaced to other locations.

The geography of crime differs considerably from that of incarceration. When data about the residences of those admitted to prison are mapped, they show that a disproportionate number of the 2.3 million people in U.S. prisons and jails come from a very few neighborhoods in the country's biggest cities.[4] Prison admissions maps can guide urban designers, planners, and policy makers pursuing strategic investments in infrastructure, social capital, and governance that could produce different patterns in our cities.

MILLION-DOLLAR BLOCKS AND NEIGHBORHOODS

In many places the concentration of prison admissions is so dense that states are spending in excess of a million dollars a year to incarcerate the residents of a single city block or particular neighborhood. The terms *million-dollar blocks* and *million-dollar neighborhoods* have been used to describe this pattern.[5] These areas often show a high degree of poverty and disinvestment, as well as neglect of key civic institutions and urban infrastructure. Millions of dollars are spent *on* these neighborhoods, but not *in* them.[6]

SOCIO-SPATIAL ANALYSIS OF INCARCERATION

The U.S. Department of Justice reports yearly on the social and demographic statistics of incarceration. Its data reveal that high percentages of the inmates in American jails and prisons are people of color and male.[7]

---

3 Pew Center on the States, "One in 100: Behind Bars in America 2008," February 28, 2008, pewcenteronthestates.org.

4 SIDL, *Justice Reinvestment New Orleans.*

5 Jennifer Gonnerman, "Million-Dollar Blocks," *The Village Voice*, November 9, 2004. See also Lauren Macintyre, "Rap Map," *The New Yorker*, January 8, 2007, and Amy Zimmer, "Multi 'million-dollar' blocks of Brownsville," *Metro New York*, May 14, 2007.

6 Although the cities analyzed range in size from hundreds of thousands to millions of people, the pattern of incarceration is more or less the same in all of them. See SIDL, *The Pattern* (New York: Columbia University Graduate School of Architecture, Planning, and Preservation, 2008), issuu.com.

7 "At year end 2005, there were 3,145 black male prison inmates per 100,000 black males in the United States, compared with 1,244 Hispanic male inmates per 100,000 Hispanic males and 471 white male inmates per 100,000 white males." Bureau of Justice Statistics, *Prison Statistics: Summary of Findings*, 2005, usdoj.gov.

Analysis of the statistics indicates that high percentages of incarcerated people have (or had) incomes that put them at or below the poverty line.[8] Very little research, however, treats these statistics as indicative of an urban or spatial phenomenon. Using maps as tools, our research has focused on defining the spatial patterns that link poverty, racial segregation, and incarceration and on investigating whether the repeated coincidence of these factors takes on identifiable urban forms.[9]

The patterns suggest that policy responses to urban poverty and racial isolation have systematically abandoned the neighborhoods they were meant to address. This disinvestment has been matched by increased investment in the institutions of the criminal justice system, particularly jails, prisons, and other infrastructures of incarceration. Today, it is those institutions that constitute the primary public investment in many of the nation's most distressed communities.

INFRASTRUCTURE AND EXOSTRUCTURE

Prisons act as part of the public infrastructure of cities. In some neighborhoods they are the best-funded and most significant government institutions. But unlike streets, utilities, communication networks, parks, hospitals, and schools, prisons are often situated outside the cities they serve, sometimes hundreds of miles away. Rather than directing resources toward the neighborhoods, prisons act more like urban exostructures, shifting investment away from their urban constituencies.

REENTRY AND RE-INCARCERATION

As prison costs rise, policy makers look for ways to control them, and they are increasingly paying attention to the 650,000 people who return home from prison each year. The process these newly released prisoners undergo of reestablishing their citizen status in the free world is known as "reentry."[10] Reentry is emerging as a primary site for intervention and innovation.[11] Ninety-five percent of people sent to prison are eventually released, and data suggest that most of them return to the communities from which they came.[12] Nationally more than half of those who return home are readmitted to prison within three years of their release. This cyclical pattern—like a permanent migration in and out of our nation's largest cities—is both costly and spatially concentrated.

---

8 See, among others, Michael Jacobson, *Downsizing Prisons* (New York: New York University Press, 2005), 43.

9 See SIDL, *The Pattern* for documentation of this phenomenon in four U.S. cities. Analysis of data from Phoenix, Wichita, New Orleans, New York City, and other cities revealed that high-incarceration neighborhoods, community districts, and census blocks are overwhelmingly populated by people of color and people living in poverty.

10 See reentry.gov.

11 The Council of State Governments (CSG) created a Reentry Policy Council, and along with the JFA Institute, the Vera Institute of Justice, and others, it is doing pioneering work in this field. See reentrypolicy.org.

12 Joan Petersilia, *When Prisoners Come Home: Parole and Prisoner Reentry* (Oxford: University Press, 2003).

BEYOND CRIMINAL JUSTICE

High incarceration rates take a dramatic toll not only on the prisoners, who shuttle back and forth between cities and remote prisons, but also on the urban communities from which they come. Research conducted by Todd R. Clear suggests that communities can reach a tipping point beyond which increased incarceration undermines the local networks and infrastructures of everyday life.[13] Once past that point, neighborhoods can enter a downward spiral where incarceration perversely leads to increased crime and juvenile delinquency and decreased public health, housing values, and rates of political participation. Incarcerating people in larger and larger numbers not only affects their communities; it also dilutes the overall efficacy of incarceration as a crime-reduction mechanism, while simultaneously increasing its cost. The Vera Institute of Justice has reported that although "increased incarceration rates have some effect on reducing crime," accounting for about one quarter of the drop in crime during the 1990s, "continued growth in incarceration will prevent considerably fewer, if any, crimes than past increases did and will cost taxpayers substantially more to achieve."[14]

CONFRONTING INCARCERATION GROWTH

In 2004, state governments faced the worst budget shortfalls since World War II, with deficits totaling $80 billion. In most states, correctional spending was one of the costliest budget items, totaling over $41 billion nationally. Research conducted by the Council on State Governments (CSG) revealed that incarceration growth in states was driven largely by parole revocation and recidivism, a phenomenon that stemmed from inadequate reentry planning. To cope with extreme fiscal circumstances and failing correctional systems, lawmakers in more than twenty-two states passed sentencing reforms and policy changes that would begin to slow prison growth and reduce costs. The widespread correctional policy changes that ensued led to the passage of the Second Chance Act in 2007, which established a national strategy for prisoner reentry and provided hundreds of millions of dollars in grants to effective programs. State and local governments are now searching for the best approaches to undo the costly economic and social consequences of mass incarceration.[15]

---

13 Todd R. Clear et al., "Coercive Mobility and Crime: A Preliminary Examination of Concentrated Incarceration and Social Disorganization," *Justice Quarterly* 20 (Spring 2003), 33–64.

14 JFA Institute, "Public Safety, Public Spending: Forecasting America's Prison Population, 2007–2011" (The Pew Center on the States, Public Safety Performance Project, rev. June 2007), 24. A PDF can be downloaded from pewcenteronthestates.org.

15 CSG, see reentrypolicy.org.

JUSTICE REINVESTMENT

This report focuses on reentry planning using a new approach known as justice reinvestment, in which public officials identify ways to reduce the growth of the prison population and reinvest those savings in the parts of cities to which most people released from prison return.[16] The states of Connecticut, Texas, Arizona, and Kansas recently passed justice reinvestment laws. In Texas, for example, lawmakers created a $241 million network of treatment and incarceration diversion programs rather than spending $500 million on new prisons. Lawmakers in Kansas mandated a 20 percent reduction in revocation failures and set aside $7 million for reinvestment in high-incarceration communities. The Council on State Governments has provided technical support to lawmakers in half a dozen other states that are considering similar justice reinvestment initiatives. Typical projects include introducing day reporting centers as alternatives to jails and prisons, promoting workforce development and job placement, providing drug treatment and other community-based programs to inmates and parolees, and strengthening family networks as people return home from prison.[17]

AN URBAN STRATEGY

Until now, the institutions supported by justice reinvestment initiatives have remained largely within the orbit of criminal justice and correctional facilities. Although these service-oriented programs are crucial to reducing recidivism, reentry planning must also tackle larger-scale urban problems. Failing schools, chronic unemployment, and laws preventing previously incarcerated people from receiving housing assistance or educational aid are typical of the obstacles facing those who return home from prison.[18] Incarceration as an urban problem is particularly difficult to address because prisons are largely invisible urban institutions. Visualization of the spatial characteristics of incarceration is thus an important first step in implementing justice reinvestment strategies on an urban scale. Recognizing the patterns of incarceration in million-dollar blocks and neighborhoods reveals opportunities to disrupt the cycle of prisoner release and reincarceration.

PART 2: INCARCERATION IN NEW ORLEANS

Crime has been widely cited as a major social, political, and economic obstacle in the rebuilding of New Orleans after Hurricane Katrina. The Criminal Justice Leadership Alliance in Orleans Parish has proposed that the entire criminal justice infrastructure—not just policing—be

16 CSG, see justicereinvestment.org.

17 Erik Eckholm, "New Tack on Straying Parolees Offers a Hand Instead of Cuffs," *New York Times*, May 17, 2008. See also family-justice.org.

18 Jeremy Travis, *But They All Come Back: Facing the Challenges of Prisoner Reentry* (Washington, D.C.: Urban Institute Press, 2005).

rethought to establish a safer city.[19] Some local officials have gone further and suggested that the criminal justice system must be rethought not simply in the interest of crime control but as an essential component of the rebuilding process. Whereas other public and social infrastructures like schools, health, and housing have been transformed, and even linked to one another physically and programmatically, as part of the rebuilding of the city, the criminal justice system has received little attention—at least in the public domain. Moreover, the city's planning process has neglected the obstacles to neighborhood revitalization that mass incarceration creates.

Research conducted in other cities suggests that addressing crime only through increased policing has led to high incarceration levels, resulting in the destabilization of communities as residents cycle in and out of prisons and jails. Focusing on patterns of incarceration rather than on crime, and on particular neighborhoods that disproportionately incur the impact of incarceration, this report outlines a strategy for a safer and more stable New Orleans. The accompanying maps spatialize incarceration expenditures at the scale of the city, neighborhood, and block. They demonstrate that a handful of Orleans Parish neighborhoods contain disproportionate concentrations of the city's incarcerated people. The social and economic viability of New Orleans depends upon the creation of a new urban criminal justice strategy aimed at reducing incarceration rates and undertaking strategic interventions to improve underlying conditions and revitalize neighborhoods.

ORLEANS PARISH: NEIGHBORHOODS AND INCARCERATION

Correlating prison admissions data from 2003 to 2007 with other urban data over the same four-year period, the Spatial Information Design Lab produced a series of maps visualizing incarceration in Orleans Parish's seventy-three neighborhoods. As do maps of other cities in the United States, these maps of New Orleans reveal an uneven distribution of both prison admissions and prison expenditures across the city. Both incarceration and prison expenditures are shown on the maps on a scale that moves from gray to bright red: the brighter the shade of red, the higher the number of incarcerated people and the larger the amount of money being spent on incarceration. Aligning census data from 2000 with criminal justice and other urban data from 2003 provides a picture of Orleans Parish's pre-Katrina condition.[20] After Katrina, and in the years

19 Founded in the fall of 2007, the Criminal Justice Leadership Alliance joined forces with the Vera Institute of Justice to create a fair, efficient, accountable, and effective criminal justice system in New Orleans. Initiatives prioritized by the Alliance include providing a range of sentencing options (for example, community service, drug treatment, and job training) for individuals who do not pose a threat to public safety; enhancing interagency procedures between the New Orleans Police Department and the District Attorney's Office that support early case screening; and developing a problem-solving, community-based approach to municipal offenses.

20 Greater New Orleans Community Data Center (GNOCDC) archives of pre-Katrina statistics, gnocdc.org.

preceding the 2010 census, a lack of accurate data about the returned population of the city made analysis and mapping difficult.[21]

INCARCERATION DEMOGRAPHICS

Before Hurricane Katrina, the state of Louisiana had the double distinction of having the highest incarceration rate in the nation as well as one of the most disproportionately black prison populations.[22] New Orleans residents in particular, most of them African American, were migrating in large numbers between distant state prisons, local jails, and a few city neighborhoods.[23] In 2003, in an effort to address the racial imbalance in the justice system and rethink prison spending as a state investment, the governor convened a task force to consider prison population reduction and high-reentry community investment strategies.[24] In 2003, two thirds of those admitted to prison were arrested for violation of parole, and nearly three quarters of admitted prisoners were due for release in one to three years.[25] Hurricane Katrina halted the task force's efforts and intensified the pattern of migration that the criminal justice system had been supporting for years: Large numbers of people, mostly poor and black, were displaced from the most distressed parts of the city.

COSTS OF INCARCERATION

Orleans Parish was home to 485,000 people prior to Hurricane Katrina. In 2003, it cost $42 million to incarcerate 1,432 of those people. Incarceration expenditures were unequally distributed across the city, concentrated in Planning Districts 2, 4, and 7. The maps and their resulting spatial statistics underscore the overlaps between incarceration, poverty, and race in the city. Census data from 2000 indicates that the percentages of people of color and people living in poverty in PD2, PD4, and PD7 were consistently higher than the citywide averages.

INCARCERATION AND RECOVERY

Data have been mapped to show the citywide density of prison admissions over four years. As of 2007, prison admissions had not yet returned to pre-Katrina levels, but they were rising. Comparing prison admission density maps from 2003, late 2005, 2006, and 2007 reveals how incarceration patterns have shifted and intensified in some areas since Hurricane Katrina, while in other areas prison admissions have decreased. The most striking—if obvious—shift occurs in the 2005 map, just after Hurricane

21 GNOCDC and the Brookings Institute have published estimated population statistics since Katrina based on utility accounts and residential postal deliveries. See brookings.edu.

22 JFA Institute, "Public Safety, Public Spending," iii.

23 On the unusual numbers and conditions of prisoners in Louisiana local jails, see Michael Jacobson, *Downsizing Prisons: How to Reduce Crime and End Mass Incarceration* (New York: New York University Press, 2005), 204.

24 CSG, Criminal Justice Program, "Options for Policy Makers Considering a Justice Reinvestment Initiative in Louisiana," Report submitted to the National Center for Urban Communities at Tulane and Xavier Universities, January 24, 2004; listed but not available. justicemapping.org.

25 Ibid., 14.

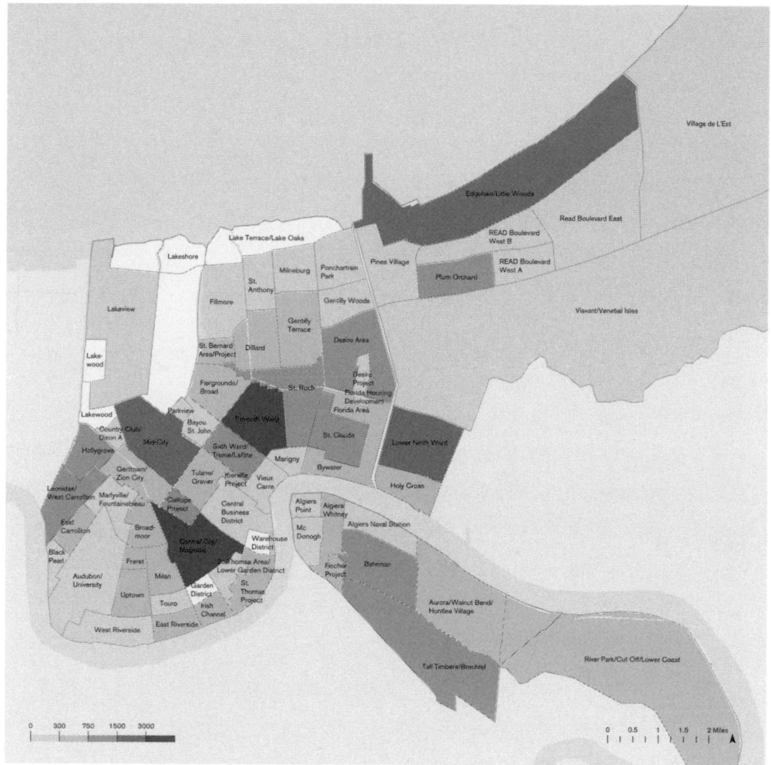

Orleans Parish neighborhoods ranked from lowest to highest incidence of prison admissions, measured by the ratio of percent of prison admissions to percent of total city population. Million-dollar neighborhoods are highlighted in red.

Katrina, when citywide incarceration rates dropped nearly to zero in most areas. The 2006 and 2007 maps clearly show that although some shifts in intensity have occurred, on the whole the reduction was short-lived.

The 2006 incarceration data reflect that incarceration rates began to rebound soon after Katrina. The spatial analysis reveals that incarceration expenditures had understandably shifted toward less damaged and more densely reinhabited parts of the city, such as Central City, while badly damaged areas like New Orleans East experienced far less growth in incarceration costs. By 2007, the citywide incarceration rate was at 57 percent of its 2003 level, and the overall population was estimated at 71 percent of its pre-Katrina figure.[26] Incarceration rates, however, varied from neighborhood to neighborhood, and in some cases exceeded the corresponding rates of population return. Central City, for example, had reached 82 percent of its 2003 incarceration level, even though it had recouped only an estimated 69 percent of the population level it had in 2000. The badly damaged Lower Ninth Ward showed prison admissions

26 Estimated by the Brookings Institute based on the number of households actively receiving mail in the city. See brookings.edu.

down only 75 percent, although its population had fallen by an estimated 85 percent since 2000.

There are, no doubt, many ways to interpret the causes and factors underlying the fluctuations in rates of incarceration in Orleans Parish over this four-year period. More importantly, although the particular neighborhoods facing the highest incarceration rates have shifted since 2005, the pattern of incarceration remains the same as it was before Hurricane Katrina: a small number of neighborhoods are home to disproportionately large concentrations of people in prison. These data and maps suggest that a considerable number of questions are left open in the recovery process. However, despite the prevalence of incarceration in certain neighborhoods, the city has not considered using the neighborhood planning processes to reduce incarceration growth as a means of stabilizing affected communities.

SEEKING A LOWER BASELINE

Orleans Parish criminal justice agencies made their plan for the future of the city's justice infrastructure available to the public in "The Justice Facilities Master Plan," released in September 2007.[27] The master plan projected that incarceration rates would return to pre-Katrina levels by 2017 and proposed refurbishing and expanding the city's justice facilities to meet those demands. The citizens of Orleans Parish voted in 2008 to fund a portion of the construction costs for the first phase of the plan, approving $63.2 million in spending, $41 million of which would go to the construction of a 1,500-bed jail that would be primarily funded by the Federal Emergency Management Agency (FEMA).[28] The facility would nearly double the current Orleans Parish jail occupancy, bringing the total to 4,000 beds, or 57 percent of the pre-Katrina level.[29] The latter phases of the master plan, which have not yet been funded, called for the construction of an additional 3,500 prison beds.

Justice advocates, public officials, and journalists expressed varying opinions about the plan, arguing on the one hand that jail facilities damaged during the storm were in need of repair, and on the other that the expense of the facilities, especially their enlarged size, would necessarily divert funding from other crucial infrastructure and rebuilding priorities. Adoption of the plan suggests that New Orleans voters put building jails ahead of attempting to reduce incarceration levels. However, the choice they were given did not appear to be coordinated with the larger-scale rebuilding plans for the city. Neither the Unified New Orleans Plan (UNOP), which included citizen participation in the design process,

27 Federal Emergency Management Agency, "Justice Facilities Master Plan: New Orleans, Louisiana," September 15, 2007, neworleansbar.org.

28 Bruce Eggler, "Money OK'd for Roads, Parks; $320 Million Slated for City Infrastructure," *Times-Picayune*, October 15, 2008.

29 Laura Maggi, "Jail Bond Proposal on Saturday Ballot," *Times-Picayune*, October 2, 2008.

nor the Office of Recovery Management's Target Area Development Plan incorporated this justice facilities plan in their proposals.

WHAT IF?

As Orleans Parish continues to recover and rebuild, will it reach or surpass its pre-Katrina incarceration rates, even if the overall population size remains at lower levels? Or can the city maintain and even reduce the incarceration rates that have followed Hurricane Katrina? Part 3 of this report suggests an alternative strategy for the city. What if Orleans Parish invested in communities rather than in jails? What if the city confronted the back and forth migration between jail or prison and certain parts of the city? What sorts of projects could interrupt that cycle?

PART 3: JUSTICE REINVESTMENT IN CENTRAL CITY

In July 2006, a team of students and researchers from the Columbia University Graduate School of Architecture, Planning, and Preservation conducted fieldwork in New Orleans with the aim of identifying a pilot site for exploring justice reinvestment strategies. Guided by prison admissions maps, the team focused on sites that had high incarceration rates, less serious damage from Hurricane Katrina, and a significant number of returned residents. The team engaged in a variety of on-site research approaches, attending planning meetings, conducting site surveys of million-dollar neighborhoods, and making maps, drawings, photographs, and diagrams. Exploring possible partnerships, the team presented these findings to community leaders, local groups, nonprofit organizations, and government officials.

Through this fieldwork, the neighborhood of Central City emerged as a prime candidate for justice reinvestment efforts. Maps suggested what residents of the neighborhood confirmed: High levels of incarceration in Central City were the product of systemic social conditions. Central City was a place of concentrated poverty, underperforming schools, limited access to healthcare, lack of job opportunities, disinvestment, and crumbling infrastructure. At the same time, the neighborhood's strong social networks, community groups, and not-for-profit organizations were already engaged with the effects of incarceration, whether or not they were dealing with the issue directly.

A MILLION-DOLLAR NEIGHBORHOOD

Since at least 2003—the beginning year in our data set—Central City has been home to a disproportionate share of people in prison. Even as population numbers plummeted after Hurricane Katrina and then rose in 2006 and 2007, the neighborhood consistently housed about 4 percent of the Orleans Parish population yet more than 11 percent of its prison population. In 2006, only about half of Central City's population had returned, but its disproportionate ratio of prison population to total population remained constant. More recent prison admissions data indicate that this phenomenon is ongoing. In 2006 and 2007, the neighborhood displayed the highest concentrations of prison admissions in relation to the total population in all of Orleans Parish. By 2007, Central City's population was estimated at 69 percent of its pre-hurricane level, yet its incarceration spending had reached 82 percent of its pre-Katrina level, totaling $3.5 million.

SHIFTING PATTERNS OF INCARCERATION

Although Central City maintained consistent incarceration rates on the whole, spatial patterns of incarceration within the neighborhood shifted as a result of the storm. The southeast corner of Central City was not flooded at all, but the flood level rose to six feet in the northwest corner of the neighborhood called the Hoffman Triangle. High levels of flooding in this area were accompanied by a decrease in incarceration, a statistic probably attributable to the fact that those blocks had a small number of returned residents. Conversely, the blocks to the south, which sustained less damage, experienced increases in incarceration spending. Incarceration expenditures seem to have become more concentrated in Central City's core, around Oretha Castle Haley Boulevard and Jackson Avenue.

FORMS OF DISINVESTMENT

In the late 1960s and 1970s, Central City was the site of major urban demolition and building projects that changed the quality of its boundaries and its connections to other neighborhoods. Its northeastern border was altered by the construction of Interstate 10 in the late 1950s and by the completion in 1975 of the Louisiana Superdome, a 72,000-seat stadium. These structures separated the Central City neighborhood—as well as those of Tremé and Lafitte further to the north—from the Central Business District. Until the 1970s, Tremé, Lafitte, and Central City had been centers of New Orleans's African-American business and culture. Because of this separation, however, despite Central City's proximity to the Central Business District and tourist attractions, prior to Hurricane Katrina nearly half of its residents lived below the poverty line. Post-Katrina, the area surrounding O.C. Haley Boulevard in Central City has shown signs of revitalization, yet the overall pattern of public and private disinvestment is visible in the abandoned storefronts and houses lining the neighborhood's streets and in the disrepair of public parks and recreational spaces.

Some forms of neglect are less visible. In 2003, all but one of the public schools in Central City were rated either unacceptable or under warning judged by the nationally standardized criteria of the 2001 No Child Left Behind Act. Approximately 60 percent of the people admitted to prison from New Orleans were between the ages of twenty and twenty-four, and 46 percent of Central City residents had no high school diploma.[30] In too many cases, public education was serving as a pipeline to prison rather than as a public asset. In addition, all three public housing projects in the vicinity of Central City—the C.J. Peete Homes, the B.W. Cooper Homes, and the William J. Guste Houses—were underfunded by the Housing Authority of New Orleans (HANO) before Hurricane Katrina. After the storm, the C.J. Peete and B.W. Cooper homes were closed and condemned, barring many evacuated residents from returning to their city and neighborhood. The buildings are now being redeveloped as mixed-income housing.

ASSET MAPPING

Despite, or perhaps because of, these challenges, Central City as a neighborhood has an extraordinarily strong and diverse array of community-based organizations. These groups provide services related to justice, health, philanthropy, civics, recreation, faith, education, arts, housing, and economics. Their projects range from afterschool programs and cultural events to juvenile justice services and local food establishments. All of them have been forced to grapple with the causes and impact of high levels of incarceration.

Mapping the locations of Central City's organizations and businesses, researching their missions, and conducting outreach formed an initial step toward linking these organizations to one another. Although the success and failure of the work of each organization should be evaluated on its own terms, finding the links between them, addressing what might be common to all in terms of the needs of residents affected by incarceration, formed the heart of our proposal. This technique is called asset mapping.

ESTABLISHING A JUSTICE REINVESTMENT NETWORK

The asset mapping process revealed three concentrations of activity around O.C. Haley Boulevard, Jackson Avenue, and C.J. Peete Homes. This area coincides with some of the highest concentrations of incarceration expenditures in Central City for 2007. An urban corridor links these assets along a central axis running from the intersection of O.C. Haley and Martin Luther King Jr. boulevards south to Jackson Avenue, then west along Lasalle Street to C.J. Peete. The corridor is home to a diverse array of active neighborhood assets, including clusters of small criminal justice and social service nonprofit organizations, an arts and culture center, a café that acts as a training facility for youths recently released from prison, an underfunded community clinic, a newly established charter school, and faith-based organizations. Yet despite their physical proximity, some of these organizations work in isolation. Groups working citywide on issues of health, education, community service, and

30 CSG, "Options for Policy Makers," 3.

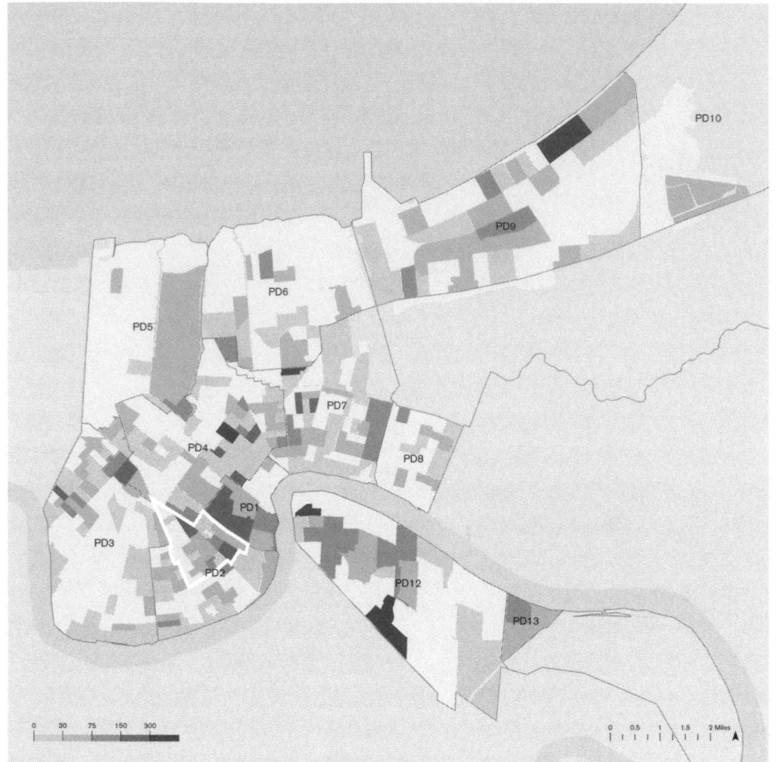

Orleans Parish, showing prison expenditures per block group in thousands of dollars in 2007. Central City is highlighted in white.

economic development were invited to think about expanding their existing programs to new locations in Central City. They were encouraged to examine how their missions might fit into the creation of a broad-based justice reinvestment network that could provide opportunities for reentering individuals and for members of the community at large who by proximity and association are affected by incarceration.

This justice reinvestment proposal for Central City builds on the three recovery and rebuilding plans developed by the city of New Orleans and its residents. The Bring New Orleans Back, Lambert, and Unified New Orleans plans were consolidated into plans for seventeen "target" areas that were to be implemented by the Office of Recovery Management (Edward Blakely's Target Area Recovery Plan).[31] A justice reinvestment network was proposed that would benefit from and reinforce the two target recovery plans projected for Central City, covering South Claiborne Avenue at Toledano and the O.C. Haley corridor. As part of these plans, the city proposed $1.3 million in improvement, development, and expansion projects along the stretch of O.C.

31 Keith I. Marszalek, "City Announces First 17 Target Recovery Zones," *Times-Picayune*, March 29, 2007.

Orleans Parish, showing prison expenditures per block group in thousands of dollars in 2006. Central City is highlighted in white.

Haley Boulevard north of M.L.K. Boulevard. By extending the target area corridor past M.L.K. to the south, the justice reinvestment network could connect these improvements to the areas of the neighborhood with the highest incarceration rates.

ACTIVATING A JUSTICE REINVESTMENT NETWORK

Over the course of this work, the Spatial Information Design Lab team organized a series of meetings with dozens of local organizations. The discussions centered on ways that community groups could, within the limits of mandates not obviously related to criminal justice, nevertheless begin to consider the issues of incarceration and reentry some of their constituents already faced. Many of these groups had worked successfully in Central City for decades; others were seeking local partners. The networking project brought groups and residents together around a common purpose: to create a safer, healthier, and more just community in Central City. Once formalized, a justice reinvestment network could provide opportunities not only to people reentering the neighborhood from prison but also to other members of the community. The ambition was to eliminate disruptive cycles of incarceration and recidivism while simultaneously revitalizing Central City and retaining its residents.

EXISTING JUSTICE REINVESTMENT ASSETS ACTIVE IN CENTRAL CITY, MARCH 2007

JUSTICE

1 Catholic Charities*
2 Family & Friends of LA's Incarcerated Children
3 Juvenile Justice Program of Louisiana
4 Juvenile Regional Services
5 Safe Streets Strong Communities
6 Youth Empowerment Project

HEALTH

7 Booker T. Washington School Based Clinic
8 Central City Mental Health Clinic
9 Edna Pilsbury Clinic
10 Family Dental Clinic
11 Guste Home Clinic
12 NOLA Mission + Homeless Clinic
13 REACH NOLA
14 Senior Citizen Center
15 Tulane Community Health Center *On the Road*

PHILANTHROPY

16 Baptist Community Ministries*
17 Open Society Institute*

CIVIC

18 Allie Mae Williams Multi-Service Center
19 Central City Partnership
20 Central City Renaissance Alliance
21 Urban Impact Community Center

RECREATION

22 A.L. Davis Playground Park
23 Parkway Partners
24 Taylor Center Park
25 Van McMurray Park

FAITH

26 Berean Presbyterian Church
27 Castle Rock Com. Church
28 God Who Cares Tabernacle
29 Israelite Baptist Church
30 Living Witness Ministries + Kids Cafe
31 Mt. Zion United Methodist Church
32 New Hope Baptist Church
33 St. John the Baptist Catholic Church

EDUCATION

34 1st Steps Child Development Center
35 Berean Head Start
36 Booker T. Washington High School
37 Café Reconcile
38 Carter Woodson Middle School
39 Central City Head Start
40 Clear Head Learning Center
41 St. John Community Center + Childcare
42 Dr. MLK Jr. Charter School
43 Dryades YMCA
44 Florence Chester Elementary School
45 High School Signature Center
46 John Hoffman Elementary School
47 Kids Camera Project*
48 KIPP School Central City
49 LA Dept. of Ed. Afterschool Tutoring
50 MLK Head Start
51 Recovery School District*
52 Safe & Smart Afterschool/Summer Camp
53 Sylvanie Williams Elementary School
54 Thomy Lafon Elementary School
55 William J. Guste Elementary School
56 Youth Multi Media Center
57 The Corps Network*

ARTS

58 Ashé Cultural Arts Center

HOUSING

59 B.W. Cooper Homes
60 C.J. Peete Homes
61 New Orleans Area Habitat for Humanity*
62 Neighborhood Development Foundation*
63 N.O. Neighborhood Development Collaborative*
64 William J. Guste Houses

ECONOMIC

65 Central City Economic Opportunity Corporation
66 Good Work Network
67 Hope Credit Union
68 O.C. Haley Business Association*

* not located in Central City or no permanent physical space

Proposed justice reinvestment corridor extends the city's target recovery corridor along O.C. Haley Boulevard, Jackson Avenue, and Lasalle Street, connecting existing neighborhood assets.
Top: Target recovery areas and the proposed justice reinvestment corridor superimposed on prison expenditure map for 2007.

Dozens of organizations within and outside Central City have joined the justice reinvestment network. To enhance communication and supplement face-to-face meetings, social networking tools like Facebook are used to bring unexpected participants into discussions. Reducing gaps between local and distant actors, this online environment has given all of its participants the opportunity to shape project development and the ability to spread news rapidly. As participation continues to expand, social networking software might become a powerful tool for sharing information and coordinating justice reinvestment projects in Central City.

PILOT PROJECTS

The meetings organized by the Spatial Information Design Lab resulted in the establishment of four pilot projects that, if fully implemented, could link multiple organizations into a community-based justice reinvestment network. The projects exemplify a dual approach to justice reinvestment that addresses prisoner reentry and provides alternatives to incarceration, but also addresses the needs of all community residents. Ideally, these and other programs would be funded, at least partially, by the reinvestment of savings gained through the reduction of revocations and recidivism. Although each of the projects originally drew on the expertise of a single field—health, justice, economic development, education—the programs overlap, reinforce one another, and create a network.

1. Tulane University Community Health Center Services

Tulane's Community Health Center "On the Road" program provides weekly health services to Central City residents through a mobile medical unit, addressing the acute health needs of the population regardless of insurance coverage or ability to pay.[32] The unit operates out of the parking lot at Israelite Baptist Church and partners with the church to connect people and resources. The goal is to provide cost-effective, neighborhood-based preventative primary care that is relevant and responsive to the needs of Central City residents.

2. Construction Mentoring Program

Good Work Network, a small-business incubation program for low-income residents, primarily women and people of color,[33] has developed a plan for training formerly incarcerated people to run their own contracting firms. A new tax credit program provides incentive for large developers who agree to mentor small developers; possible partners for the program include the New Orleans Neighborhood Development

32 See tulane.edu.

33 For information about the Good Work Network, see goodworknetwork.org.

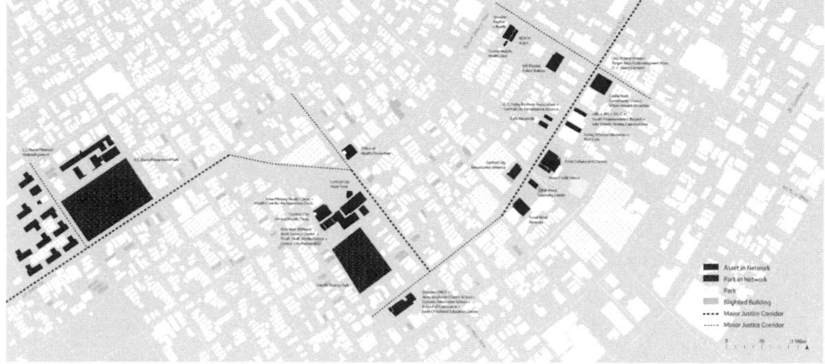

Proposed justice reinvestment corridor, Jackson Avenue and O.C. Haley Boulevard

Collaborative, Café Reconcile, and the Conservation Corps of Greater New Orleans.

3. Central City Day Reporting Center

This day reporting center, funded by the Louisiana Department of Corrections and the Louisiana Office for Addictive Disorders, provides an alternative sentencing program for people with substance-abuse problems or other treatment needs. Participants reside at home but must report daily to a community-based center for drug rehabilitation, education, and community service. Responding to the justice reinvestment networking initiative, the planners of the center decided to locate the project on the border of Central City in order to maximize its local effectiveness.[34]

4. Conservation Corps of Greater New Orleans

The Conservation Corps of Greater New Orleans (CCGNO), a project of the Corps Network, engages young adults, including court-involved youth, in participant-driven service learning projects through seven local programs.[35] Corps projects focus on environmental restoration, energy conservation, and the restoration of historic structures. CCGNO is a vehicle for systems change, viewing youth as assets, employers as primary partners, justice agencies as allies, and education as a vital connection to solutions for community needs. Each corps is charged with formalizing relationships with justice agencies, social service agencies, educational institutions, and potential employers. One of CCGNO's programs, Limitless Vistas, trained students to map the Central City neighborhood block by block to provide information for neighborhood restoration programs.

34 Office of the Governor Bobby Jindal, State of Louisiana, "Governor Jindal Announces New Re-Entry Program," March 18, 2009: "Currently, the only Day Reporting Center in Louisiana is located in New Orleans, which opened in January of this year." See gov.louisiana.gov.

35 Conservation Corps of Greater New Orleans, corpsnetwork.org.

Prison expenditures per block in thousands of dollars in 2007

TWO CYCLES: TWO FUTURES

Justice reinvestment offers an alternative to New Orleans's current cycle of incarceration and reentry. Two choices face residents, community groups, and government officials as they continue to rebuild the city in the aftermath of Hurricane Katrina. They can deepen the current dependence on a criminal justice exostructure that siphons money and jobs away from urban areas and toward prisons, or they can pursue a new strategy, reinvesting these resources in neighborhood infrastructure, networking existing assets and building new ones. All citizens have something at stake in the outcome of this decision.

CONCLUSION

The introduction of a geographic or spatial dimension into the analysis of mass incarceration is important because it identifies specific sites for intervention within the city, so that solutions are not pursued only at the level of citywide policy, services, and programs. Central City in New Orleans is one such site. The work undertaken by the Spatial Information Design Lab has allowed the creation of a neighborhood-based network to catalyze a justice reinvestment initiative in Central City. The four pilot projects established there exemplify ways in which targeted investments could benefit not only reentering individuals but also the community in general. Similar justice reinvestment strategies—funded at least in part through the reinvestment of savings from the correctional system—could grow out of these pilot initiatives and contribute to the ongoing rebuilding of the city.

As a next step, the Central City network needs to formalize, coordinate, and evaluate the impact of these overlapping projects and to enable multiple groups to create a comprehensive plan and programming strategy for justice reinvestment. During this process, the network could collaborate with the New Orleans City Council's Criminal Justice Leadership Alliance, which brings together local government officials and experts to promote correctional policy reform. The alliance, with the support of the neighborhood-based network, could institute policies that would lead to reduced growth in jail and prison expenditures. Guided by the comprehensive plan that addresses this high-incarceration neighborhood, cost savings from the correctional system could be channeled into justice reinvestment in Central City.

By integrating justice reform efforts and community-based participatory programming to coincide with and reinforce the city's rebuilding efforts, the success of a justice reinvestment project in Central City could promote urban, economic, and social revitalization, and serve as a model for other million-dollar neighborhoods.

POSTSCRIPT

Elsewhere, I have used the term *middle-out planning* in describing the sociospatial analyses and community-based participatory programming that the Spatial Information Design Lab undertook in Central City. Presuming that we can be optimistic enough nowadays to say that we can change some systemic problems in the city—education, housing, or incarceration, for example—the question remains: Where do we start? Normative approaches are from the top, working down, or from the bottom, working up. Each choice implies a story.

To an architecture audience, the narrative begins with architects who had bold visions of a new future for the city, proceeds through a story line that links modernism, social change or social engineering, new building types, superblocks, and new construction technologies, and concludes with the demolition of the federally funded Pruitt-Igoe public housing complex (1954–1972) in St. Louis. For many architects, and not only cynical ones, the upshot of the tale is that when architecture has attempted to solve problems of social inequality with bold visions and utopias, it has simply failed. The result has been a position that has now endured for several decades: Architects cannot change the world and so they should stick to forms and materials and stay away from politics, leaving to policy makers and engineers issues of globalization, climate change, and the effects of war and disasters.

To a planning audience, the narrative is different but similar: The history of urban planning teaches that top-down planning probably results in an unjust city. The story travels quickly from the Housing Act of 1949 to urban renewal and then to increased geographic racial segregation (intensified in the wake of legal integration), and ends, again, with the demolition of Pruitt-Igoe. For many planners, the failure of buildings and social environments that is embedded in a top-down planning process raised profound doubts about an approach in which expert knowledge is transformed into and enforced as policy or as code. Many turned to what has come to be known as bottom-up planning, in which members of affected communities themselves are engaged, as another sort of expert voice, in the planning process.

The work I have done in New Orleans (and New York) has led me to question the presumptions that underlie this reversal of top and bottom and to develop different modes of participation in response to a changing sense of community. What notions of community are implied by the emphasis on local expertise and indigenous knowledge? We live in a world of increasing speed, globalization, migration, newly formed slums, and rapid urbanization. Community is perhaps not what it used to be—if it ever was. What are the conditions in which communities are formed in these new environments, what do they look like, and how should processes of design change in response to these conditions? *Middle-out planning* is the somewhat ironic nickname I have adopted for a process that reengineers research and participation to challenge the old notion of The Community. The strategies, processes, and tools that we have developed as planners and designers enable us to engage and comprehend new forms of community.

Although the enthusiasm and optimism of our partners in Central City is infectious, the realities they are up against remain quite grim. One image has emerged that allows us to measure the stakes of the justice reinvestment network in Central City. Directly adjacent to the neighborhood sits the enormous, empty, tragic site of the B.W. Cooper Housing project—evacuated during Katrina; relatively undamaged by the storm but locked up afterward, its residents denied access to their homes; and scheduled for demolition.[36] Across the highway is the site of a vast new prison complex, an expanded version of the existing Orleans Parish Prison, planned, designed behind closed doors without community participation. The proposal referred to the cells as inmate housing, projecting 4,000 units. B.W. Cooper housed almost 4,500 people before Katrina. Thousands of apartments exchanged for thousands of cells, face-to-face across Interstate 10. The symmetry of the substitution is powerful, and it exemplifies for me both the necessity of the networked planning activism and the challenges our partners are facing.

We are back at Pruitt-Igoe, in a sense. But despite the impoverished or cynical imaginations of too many New Orleans officials, there *are* alternatives. From the middle-out position, our partners are proposing new strategies: expanding the reach of the central hospitals into community health clinics, emphasizing disease prevention, and developing alternatives to incarceration. Without a unified community to rely on at the bottom, and with an array of entrenched obstacles, both structural and institutional, at the top, working from the middle out seems not only sensible but also necessary. We should not mourn the disappearance of

36 In a complex that once provided 1,584 apartments, the resident management board was able to accommodate only 300 households in the face of post-Katrina HUD-mandated demolition. See Katy Reckdahl, "B.W. Cooper Resident Management Corp. Head Resigns amid Financial Investigation," *Times-Picayune*, June 1, 2011.

unequivocal expertise, at the top or at the bottom. In the middle, once we learn how to recruit, listen to, amplify, and work with a diversity of the voices, we can discover powerful new opportunities for design, planning, and change in our cities.

THE NEW ALGIERS PROJECT[1]
TERREFORM

New Orleans is at once the creature of the Mississippi and a stranger to it. Buffered by levees, the fabric of the city does not front its river with the gracious parks, promenades, and architecture of so many other river towns. Of course, there is an indisputable logic to this: New Orleans is perpetually at risk from the waterway that enables it to be. As Katrina forcefully revealed, floods here can be biblical.

The reconstruction of New Orleans has forced a deep reconsideration of the relationship between the city and the water, one in which the river has been cast as fundamentally malign. This threatening construct relies on an idea of the Mississippi as the central element in a system that is unnatural. We know that the artifice of barriers exists precisely as an interruption of what the river wants to do: periodically overflow its banks, infuse the soil with silt, and drive cycles of fertility and renewal. By privileging the river's utility as a transportation armature above all, we circumscribe its meaning in both culture and nature.

In truth, it is too late (or far too soon) to radically reconsider the status of the river. Although much of the debate in the wake of Katrina was consumed with ideas of urban triage tinted green—floated on bromides about sustainability and natural process—the real agenda was founded on the logics of race and class or in the actuarial cruelties of the cost-benefit ratio of reconstruction and protection. These arguments were buttressed by their apparent symmetry with discussions about rebuilding the Gulf Coast as a whole and conflated with arguments about logics of withdrawal from the seafront, the restoration of wetlands and barrier islands, and the recovery and renaturalization of the delta. The result of this conflation was to raise the possibility that any territory susceptible to floods would be labeled uninhabitable. This sanctimonious, "natural" risk aversion could then be tailored to do the useful work of more social forms of engineering.

1 Contributors to Terreform's "New Algiers Project" were Michael Sorkin, Director; Robin Balles Cervantes, Nadia Doukhi, Christian Eusebio, Trudy Giordano, Ying Liu, Michela Barone Lumaga, Makoto Okazaki, and Luoyi Yin. For Terreform's complete project, see terreform.info/ios/publications.htm.

But whether or not one reads the city as a natural system with an ecology either comparable or supernumerary to other biomes, it's clear that cities in general are skeins of contingency that invent their demands at a singular pace and scale. New Orleans grew with the unassailable imperative of a port at one of the world's most strategic locations. Whereas the antebellum city was sequestered behind its natural levees and scaled in greater harmony with natural forces, its later development—as with other growing cities along the Mississippi's length—exceeded this harmonizing scale. And, as the city's economy changed to embrace such massively distorting activities as energy and chemical production, the disjunction between the notional and actual bearing capacities of both site and region grew exponentially.

Although, in a sinister kind of serendipity, the city has shrunk and the shrinkage seems likely to be permanent, it still needs to be protected, enhanced, and directed along far more sustainable lines. The embedded patterns of sprawl and coastal destruction are logical areas of resistance and transformation in any rational scenario, and so is a continued investigation of the morphologies of the gradient between habitable land and the river. This investigation must be conducted taking into account threats and changes that are more planetary than local. It is clear, for example, that global warming is producing both a rise in sea level and more numerous and energetic storms and hurricanes that put New Orleans at greater and greater risk. The choice will always be stark: protect or abandon. Since abandonment is unthinkable, protection must be carefully thought out and designed.

This project investigates the form and purpose of a crucial element in the protective regime: the Mississippi River levees. These massive, primitive constructions have proved highly durable; levees have existed as a feature of the world's riverbanks for millennia. Their performance during Katrina, in fact, was much superior to more complexly constructed solutions elsewhere in the city. Indeed, the primary failures in the disaster were of wall-based systems that had been built to solve one of the primary problems of the urban levee: the very high ratio of width to height necessary in the construction of earthen barriers and their consequent enormous space requirements. The kinds of thin concrete membranes that failed so spectacularly along the city's canals had conferred the illusory advantage of deploying for other uses vast amounts of urban real estate.

But what if the levees and their adjacent territories were conceived of not as antithetical but unified? What if the levees could become not simply a piece of necessary infrastructure but a more fully integrated element in a riverine urbanism? And what if because of this reconfiguration levees could become the central component of their own economic sustainability and an armature that offered their adjoining neighborhoods a new apparatus for self-development and self-reliance? Finally, what if such levees became a prototype that could spread beyond the city?

Habitable Levee: master plan, neighborhood scale

This project investigates the form and function of such an occupied levee. It is meant to suggest both a general strategy and a singular one, an idea contoured to a place. The uses it proposes include not simply flood protection but also housing, commerce, industry, movement, and recreation. The proposal even pushes the structure's possibilities by including energy and agricultural production, moving toward a paradigm of local self-sufficiency as a strategy for securing greater neighborhood autonomy and for taking responsibility for key aspects of urban respiration by doing the accountancy much closer to home.

The neighborhood we chose for this proposal, New Algiers, largely escaped Katrina's ravages. Our choice was dictated by the neighborhood's typical low-density fabric, its location opposite the center of the New Orleans (on the opposite bank of the Mississippi River), its embodiment of a number of issues endemic to New Orleans as a whole, and, of course, resonance with the celebrated scheme of Le Corbusier for the city called Algiers. This is important: our scheme is not *sui generis* but rather part of a much longer attempt to imagine the morphology of the modern city in the context of its enabling infrastructures.

In particular, the New Algiers scheme is part of a history of linear city form that has had a special grip on modernist architecture and urbanism, drawn to the search for a rationale for its attenuated morphologies according to logics of function. In the most emblematic of these schemes—including those of Soria y Mata, Chambless, Miliutin, Le Corbusier, and Rudolph—the generative logic sprang from the incorporation of mechanical transportation as the armature for architecture. The speed of the railway and the automobile established a kind of parity among linked sites, and the homogenizing, egalitarian mood of modernism easily translated this into linearity, with its presumption of the abatement of hierarchy. This idea was layered with the possibility of a strict delimitation of the boundaries between city and nature (or between the countryside or the medina) and a strategy of networked colonization with origins as old as the roads of Rome. And—especially in the case of Miliutin—there was a clear idea of the city as a mode of rational production, an assembly line.

Although linearity as a morphological imperative has many consequential sources, its obvious origins are connection and protection—pathways and walls. The possibility of constructing enormous linear artifacts—whether the Great Wall of China or the U.S. interstates—has been a historic preoccupation, to which we can add the worldwide construction of dikes and levees, walls with a particular purpose, forms generated by the natural attenuation of rivers and coasts. And there are linearities that map more specific desires. For example, the walls of buildings that mark the waterfronts of Chicago or Rio were created for their views; it is an immemorial tendency of cities to load the edges of parks, plazas, and shores with the architecture of privilege.

The New Algiers proposal is a frank participant in all of these discourses, seeking to populate the neighborhood's edge as an act addressing both efficiency and desire. The plan occupies a space already exceptional and is intended not as displacement but enhancement, providing uses and conditions meant to enlarge the possibilities of Algiers both through expanding its programmatic content and by establishing a new way for the city to embrace the river. Although contoured to local particulars, it shows the logic of transformative extension both by implication, in the fact that existing levees stretch of hundreds of miles, and suggestion, for the transportation infrastructure depicted might run to Baton Rouge or beyond.

One criticism that might be leveled at a scheme of this magnitude is that it sets up a contest of scales with the texture of the neighborhood behind it. The difference in scales is not necessarily negative and is, in fact, already part of Algiers's morphology. The existing levee is massive, and the discrepancy between what is protected and what is needed to protect it is a truly indigenous condition. Likewise, the scale of the shipping that docks along the Mississippi—and the industry's own supporting infrastructure of cranes and warehouses, rail and trucking spaces—is both native and thrilling to this port city. Moreover, part of Algiers's genius

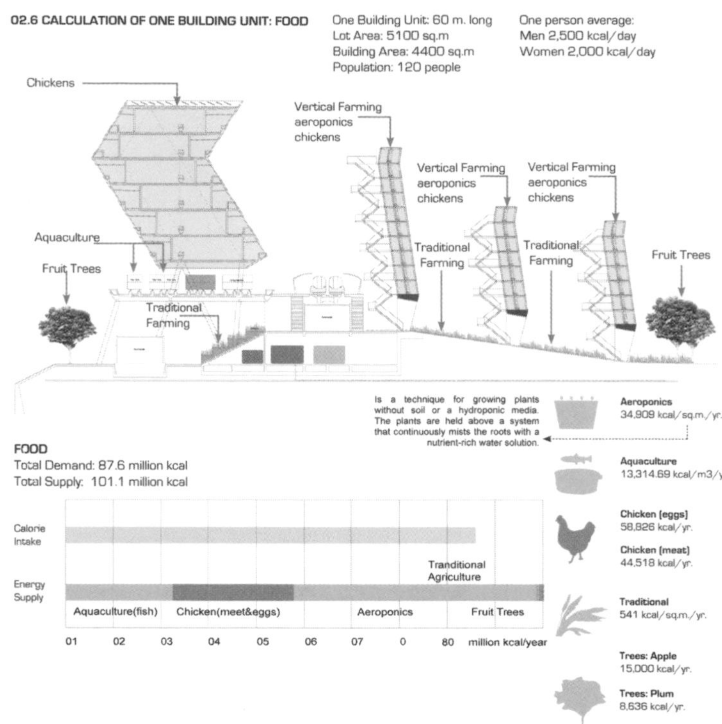

Calculation of one building unit: food

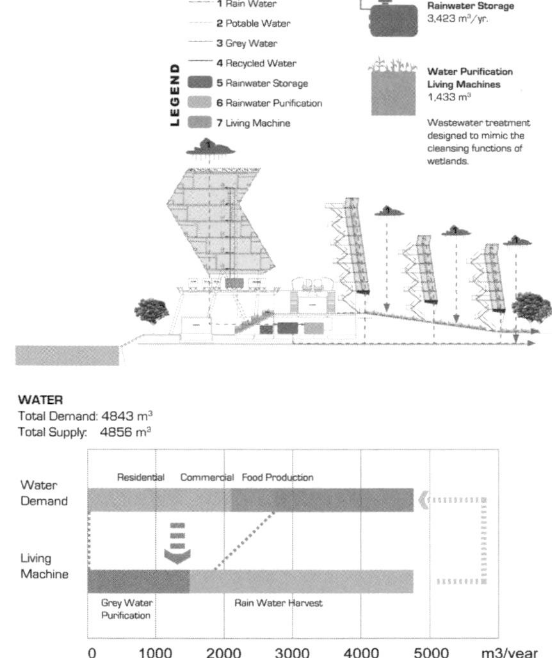

Calculation of one building unit: water

Habitable Levee: bird's-eye-view

loci is its combination of housing types of various scales with considerably larger industrial facilities—the float-building factories of Mardi Gras World and a number of other production sites. Finally, Algiers is home to the very large Navy Support Activity base that is currently being redeveloped into Federal City, a mixed-use project that will include an enormous Marine Forces Reserve Headquarters facility. The reconfiguration of the levee we propose here is meant, among other things, as a form of mediation between already existing discrepancies in scale and a new kind of bridge between them and the river.

More sensitive is the historic Algiers Point district at the bend in the river, and we've striven to appropriately modulate the scale of our additions and to preserve the view shed across the river. We hope, too, that adding diversity of form and use to Algiers as well as greatly enlarging its capacity to sustain itself economically and environmentally will not disrupt but rather enhance its native qualities of place. This effort has three principal aspects. First, the inhabited levee is meant to pay for itself. By including a wide variety of revenue-generating facilities, we can dramatically reduce the costs of flood protection—even eliminate them—using a strategy of programmatic collaboration. This has the additional benefit of providing an armature for a more general elaboration of the mix of uses in a neighborhood with substantial deficits in housing diversity, jobs, transportation, and public facilities. Like other parts of New Orleans, Algiers suffers not simply from the wounds of disinvestment but from the city's widespread "job sprawl," with the attendant challenges that poses for transportation and neighborhood culture.

Second, we have proposed a neighborhood-wide scheme to elaborate and connect green spaces and to deal naturally with runoff. This will not

Habitable Levee: view toward neighborhoods

simply manage potential local flooding, but also improve air quality and the persistent effects of urban heat islands, enhance local recreational possibilities, and enlarge the space of civic culture.

Finally, we have made our scheme the center of a more radical initiative, moving Algiers to a very high level of local autonomy. For example, we have included a series of structures for vertical agriculture, capable of growing enough food to supply all the new residents the new levees will bring. We've also suggested strategies for self-sufficiency in water supply, waste remediation and reuse, energy, local and regional movement, and commerce—introducing, in effect, a third commercial corridor synergistically aligned with the two that already exist. We've also suggested a location for a "nexus" school in line with the excellent policy adopted by the city. In sum, we've offered a proposition in which new construction is designed for complete harmony between its facilities and the needs to which they give rise.

Our hope is that such a scheme can keep a neighborhood and a city secure from floods and at the same time provide a model for a dramatic new form of local responsibility, one that embraces the widest range of urban respiration. And we hope that the living but struggling community of Algiers can be dramatically enriched and invigorated.

Habitable Levee: sectional perspective

Habitable Levee: street view, apartment tower (center) and vertical farm (right)

Habitable Levee: street view, night activity

PROJECTS
URBAN ANALYSIS

***Analysis* is a word that is often used nowadays** instead of *planning*. In the climate of fear that many *bien-pensant* liberal planners have felt since the overturn of the big plans of urban renewal, comprehensive thinking has been reengaged as the less historically freighted and putatively more neutral process of analysis. The upside of analytical thinking is that it can be both "objective" and critical: get the facts on the table and draw out the broad implications for local actions. But analysis can be a prelude to acts of planning that are either wanton or generous. New Orleans has been—and is—the victim of a kind of analytic determinism that leapt from flood maps to the idea that low-lying areas were to be purged.

The projects included in this section sought to do things a little differently. Sometimes this involved an analytic focus that actually suited the issue—that implicated the ravaging of Louisiana's barrier wetlands or the blithe and needless construction of the Mississippi River Gulf Outlet as truly central players in the disaster and suggested that the "problem" was not strictly the city's. Other projects speculate about an "off-shore" New Orleans, about a synergistic consolidation of health services, about community-based recovery strategies, about the real implications of the official analysis and planning done to date.

Perhaps more than other projects proposed post-Katrina, the urban analyses sampled in this section are the record of lost opportunities. The trajectory of sanctioned planning efforts has passed from the draconian to those perhaps least possible to achieve. The vigorous pursuit of additional plans for New Orleans, beyond those proposed in the "official" phases of planning that have now concluded, is a lively gesture of solidarity with a population too often victimized by planning, a population very weary of too much consultation with too few results.

THE BREWERY POD

COLLEGE OF ARCHITECTURE, URBAN DESIGN, AND LANDSCAPE ARCHITECTURE

City College of New York

Instructor: Michael Sorkin
Designer: Chen Heng Chai

This project proposes the rehabilitation of the triangular site in Mid-City where the old Dixie Brewery building sits, at Tulane and N. Tonti streets, as a community and commercial space with a focus on civic engagement. Offering a central point of connection during good times and bad, the site would include a Katrina memorial, an open-air market, a dance theater, a gallery, a child-care center, storage for bicycles, and emergency shelter space. Using the brewing process as inspiration, the design connects the pedestrian with the built environment through a system of ramps and sidewalks. It also works with the existing grid of the typical New Orleans block structure, renovating and enlarging existing housing, to increase the residential density of the area.

CLAIBORNE STITCH

COLLEGE OF ARCHITECTURE, URBAN DESIGN, AND LANDSCAPE ARCHITECTURE
City College of New York

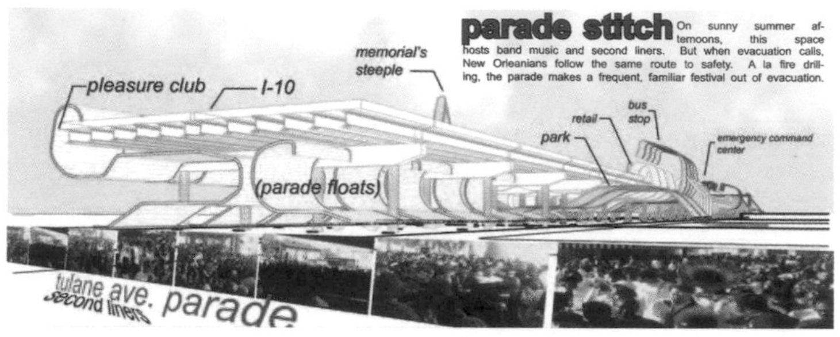

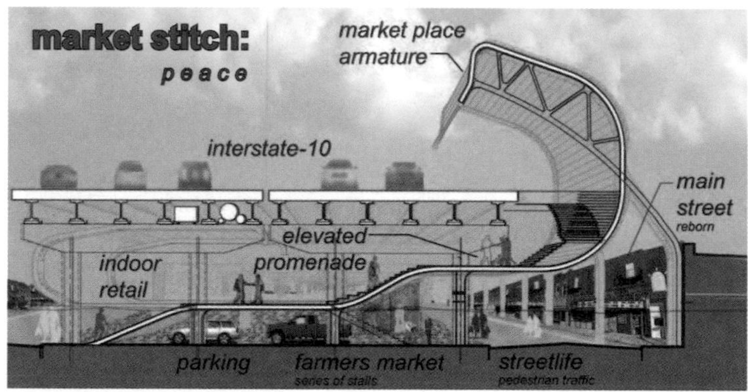

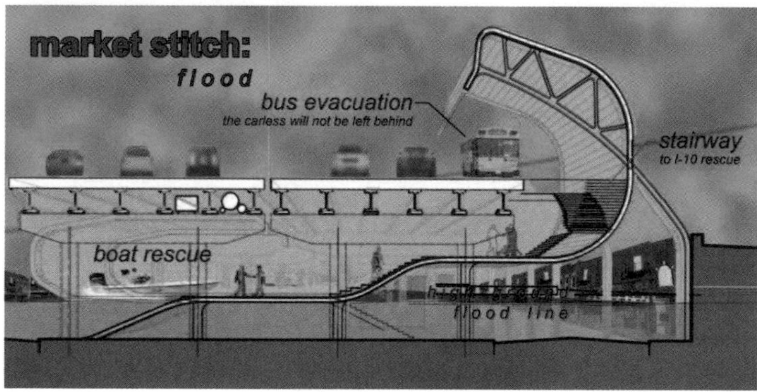

Instructor: Michael Sorkin
Designer: Adam Watson

This redevelopment plan for the Tulane/Gravier neighborhood addresses the possibility of future floods, proposing an infrastructure that accommodates evacuation vehicles and unifies the neighborhood. A system of hatches, catwalks, towers, and scaffoldings, inspired by traditional fire escapes meeting code requirements is added to the elevated structure of I-10, the portion of the highway that provided a refuge for stranded victims of Katrina who did not or could not evacuate. In addition, wavelike multilevel structures are curled over and under the highway that harbor gathering spaces, markets, shops, an emergency command center, and a Katrina memorial. These "stitching" structures connect the two sides of the I-10 corridor, uniting neighborhoods long divided by the cement artery that was built over Claiborne Avenue.

WE ARE ALL PLAYERS IN THE NOLA GAME

SAM FOX SCHOOL OF DESIGN AND VISUAL ARTS

Washington University, St. Louis, Missouri

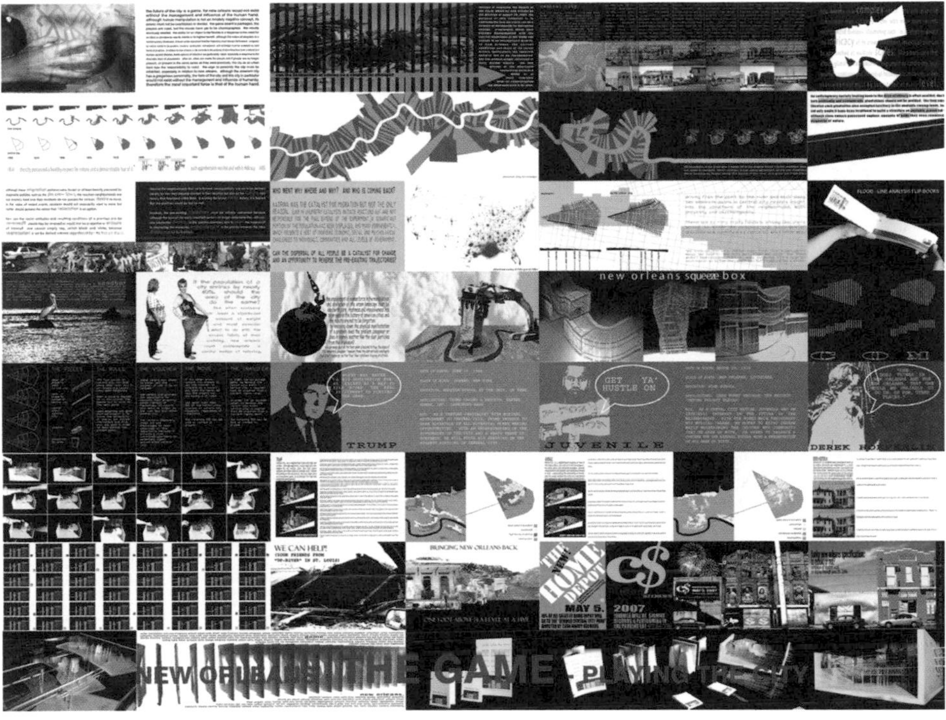

Instructor: Derek Hoeferlin
Designers: Jessica Garz, Kelly Manning

This project proposes that in order to advance understanding of what has been at stake in rebuilding and repopulating New Orleans, the physical space of the city be considered a game board on which property owners and tenants make "moves" by exchanging vouchers related to the real estate that they owned or occupied before the storm. The game focuses on the Central City neighborhood, the lower sections of which flooded badly in Katrina's aftermath. The game's designers hope that those who play it will understand more clearly what residents, and indeed all New Orleanians, might have lost or gained as decisions were made about return and relocation and properties changed hands. The designers propose three imaginary players whose game moves have varied consequences for the neighborhood. "Donald Trump" develops high-rise, mixed-use structures that take advantage of Central City's proximity to downtown but price former residents out of the neighborhood. "Juvenile," an internationally successful musician who grew up in Central City, develops cultural and recreational amenities on lower ground closer to the lake and affordable high-density residential units on the higher ground closer to the river, giving former residents an option to return. "Derek Hoeferlin," a studio critic who admires the low-density fabric that was built in Central City historically, redevelops flood-damaged properties economically, encouraging residents to return. With the goals of preservation and adaptive reuse foremost in mind, he takes an integrated approach to locating recreational, commercial, and cultural activities in the neighborhood.

ENVIRONMENTS OF DESIGN, NEW ORLEANS NOW: PUBLIC HOUSING

GRADUATE SCHOOL OF ARCHITECTURE, PLANNING, AND PRESERVATION
Columbia University, New York City

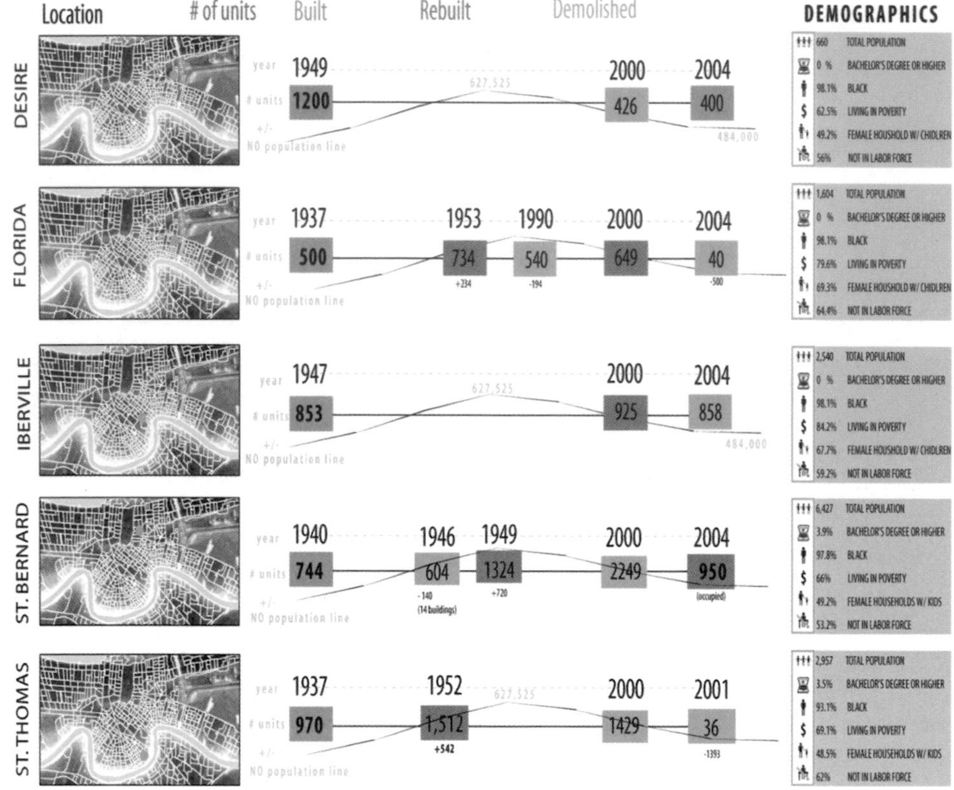

Instructor: Laura Kurgan
Designers: Kay Cheng, Leticia Crispin

This urban analysis examines the state of public housing in New Orleans shortly after Hurricane Katrina. The researchers focus on five of the city's pre-Katrina public housing projects: Desire, Florida, Iberville, St. Bernard, and St. Thomas, documenting their dates of construction (beginning in 1937), the changing numbers of dwelling units that they accommodated as they expanded and contracted, and their demographics as captured in the 2000 census. Post-Katrina, HUD moved quickly to shutter and lock projects, claiming that storm damage had rendered them unsafe. As a result of this federal action, residents who had evacuated were essentially forcibly evicted and denied the right of return to their homes. The students who conducted the research for this study quote a statement from Representative Richard Baker (R-LA, Sixth District) that exemplifies the callous opinion of many New Orleanians: "We finally cleaned up public housing in New Orleans. We couldn't do it, but God did."

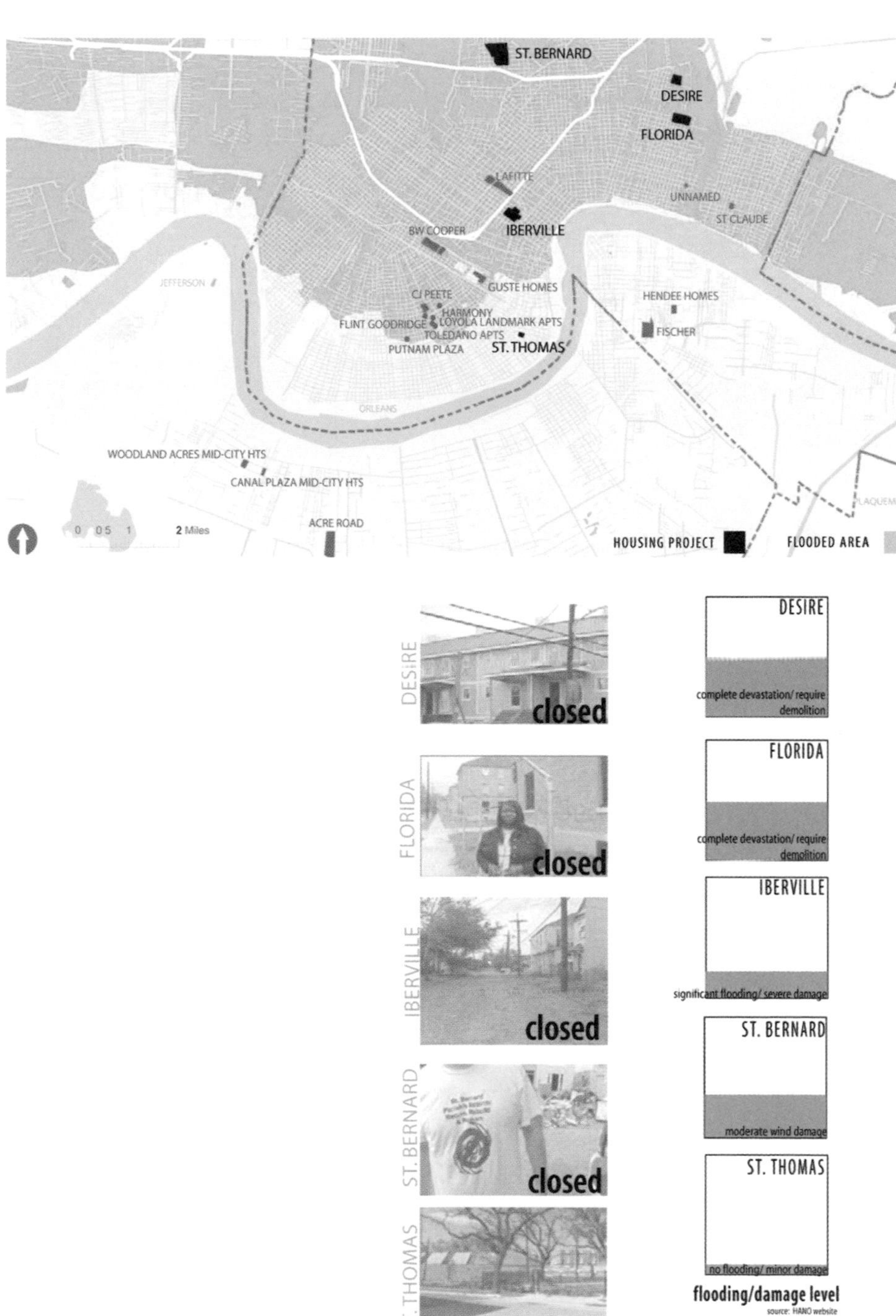
ST. BERNARD
DESIRE
FLORIDA
LAFITTE
UNNAMED
ST CLAUDE
IBERVILLE
BW COOPER
JEFFERSON
GUSTE HOMES
CJ PEETE
HARMONY
FLINT GOODRIDGE
LOYOLA LANDMARK APTS
TOLEDANO APTS
PUTNAM PLAZA
ST. THOMAS
HENDEE HOMES
FISCHER
ORLEANS
WOODLAND ACRES MID-CITY HTS
CANAL PLAZA MID-CITY HTS
ACRE ROAD
PLAQUEMINES
0 0.5 1 2 Miles
HOUSING PROJECT
FLOODED AREA
DESIRE
closed
FLORIDA
closed
IBERVILLE
closed
ST. BERNARD
closed
ST. THOMAS
open
DESIRE
complete devastation/ require demolition
FLORIDA
complete devastation/ require demolition
IBERVILLE
significant flooding/ severe damage
ST. BERNARD
moderate wind damage
ST. THOMAS
no flooding/ minor damage
flooding/damage level
source: HANO website

INTER-LIVING SYSTEM

SCHOOL OF ARCHITECTURE AND URBAN DESIGN

University of Kansas at Lawrence

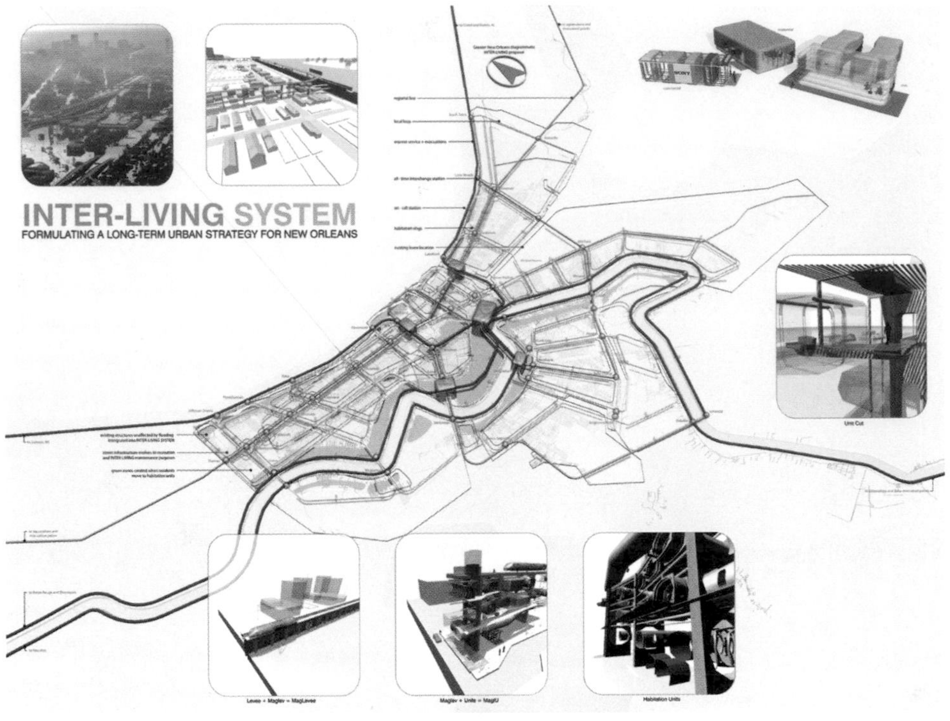

Instructor: Paola Sanguinetti
Designer: Lincoln Lewis

Responding to the city's need for levee protection, regional transportation networks, and housing, this project proposes a new model for land use designed to preserve and protect the fabric of the city. Trains run on a magnetic levitation system along the levees, serving citizens' daily commuting needs and providing evacuation routes to Jackson, Mobile, and Houston. Stacked habitable pods on the routes—the "inter-living" system—provide for mixed use and create a vertical patchwork of urban structure. Residential spaces occupy the higher floors; commercial and civic functions are accommodated on the lower levels. Commercial kiosks and public green spaces are located on rooftops. The inter-living system allows an evolution in the urban fabric that incorporates the cultural and civic needs of New Orleanians.

MEGA MEDICAL CITY

ALEX NG

Los Angeles

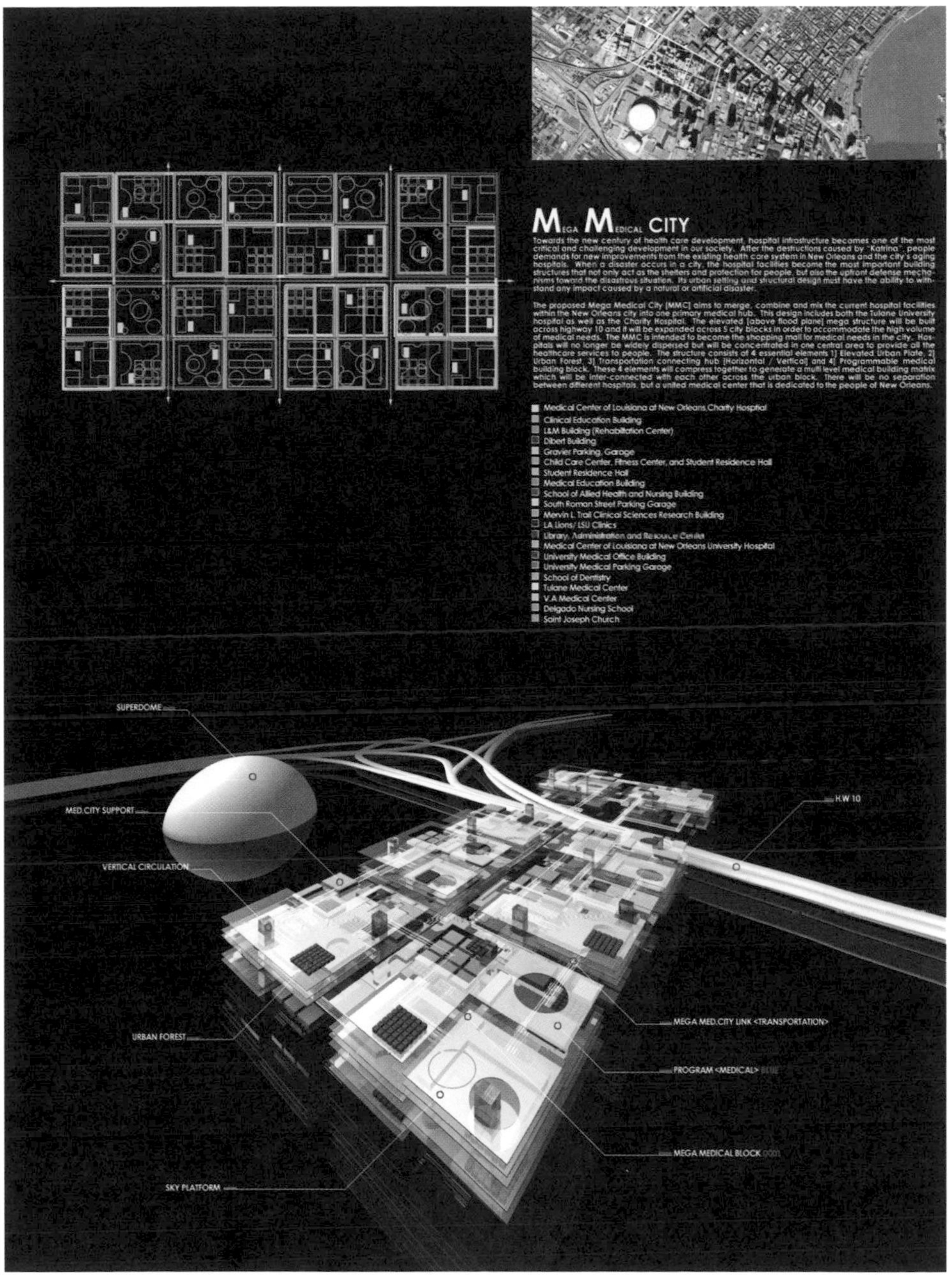

This plan proposes post-Katrina New Orleans as a hub for healthcare industry. Mega Medical City merges the city's existing hospital services into a primary medical hub elevated safely above the floodplain. Stretching five city blocks built across Interstate 10, this complex would be a "shopping mall" for healthcare needs. The multilevel, interconnected matrix would eliminate separations between different hospitals, unifying facilities for the people of New Orleans and the surrounding region in a single medical center.

SEA LEVEL: BALANCING NEW ORLEANS

SCHOOL OF ARCHITECTURE, DESIGN, AND PLANNING

University of Kansas at Lawrence

Instructor: Paola Sanguinetti
Designer: Christina Hoxie

This proposal limits urban growth in New Orleans to areas of the city developed mostly prior to 1900 on ground above sea level. The designer proposes redevelopment at a much higher density than that before Katrina, with residents and businesses repopulating a reduced urban footprint. Habitable structures would align with waterways flowing between the Mississippi River and Lake Pontchartrain. Areas of the city lying below sea level would be maintained as parks, areas of water recreation, and sites of agricultural development. These areas of the new "hydraulic city" could be expanded by the construction of dams and terraces along waterways.

PART VIII
LIVING WITH WATER: FLOOD MITIGATION AND INFRASTRUCTURE

PLANNING AT MULTIPLE SCALES, FROM THE GULF STATES REGION TO NEW ORLEANS NEIGHBORHOODS
ROBERT TANNEN

For more than forty years, Robert Tannen has worked as an economic specialist and planning consultant on design development projects in scales ranging from the entire Gulf Coast region to a neighborhood in New Orleans. He came from the Northeast in 1969 after Hurricane Camille to direct the project group planning the long-term redevelopment of the devastated Mississippi Gulf Coast. The resulting plan, produced for the Governor's Emergency Council, continues to determine development along I-10 in Mississippi. Additionally, he directed the Mississippi Highway 45 Economic Development and Improvement Project, which covered twenty-five counties and produced the Northwest Mississippi Industrial Development Council and Highway 45 Advocacy Group. In New Orleans, Tannen authored a fundamental study that demarcated and named neighborhoods and created the Historic Districts Landmarks Commission. Among other notable civic activities, he collaborated in the planning for the establishment of a National Center for the Mississippi River, a multipurpose institution for research and education. In 1976, he cofounded New Orleans's Contemporary Arts Center, one of the nation's longest-lived alternative art spaces, which provides a venue for both visual and performing arts. Tannen also cofounded the Downtown Neighborhoods Improvement Association, focused on revitalization of the Tremé and adjacent neighborhoods. He currently advocates the creation of a Mississippi River and Estuarial National Park and Wildlife Refuge that would encompass the wetlands along the coast of Louisiana, large portions of which are presently owned by oil companies. Anthony Fontenot conducted this interview on September 24, 2011.

FONTENOT: Given that you have been working as a planner in New Orleans and the region since the end of the 1960s, I would like to begin by asking you to reflect on the way planning methodologies have changed over the past few decades and to discuss your views on planning efforts in New Orleans and Louisiana following Katrina.

TANNEN: When I arrived here, I was working for a water resource planning firm in Cambridge, Massachusetts—Meta Systems Inc., which does not exist anymore. The principal owner and researcher was Dr. Robert Burden, an environmental engineer from Harvard. Much of their work dealt with river-basin planning for which federal funds were available. They also did river-basin planning throughout the world, in India, Egypt, and various places in Asia. After Hurricane Camille in 1969, they had the contract with the state of Mississippi to come up with a plan for reconstruction and to establish a better understanding of how to deal with hurricanes. I think it was the first study of its kind in this region. The document was published as *The Mississippi Gulf Coast Comprehensive Development After Camille*.[1] I was sent by Dr. Burden to be the guy on the ground in Mississippi, dealing with six counties, including Harrison, Hancock, and Jackson on the coast and then the tier to the north [Pearl River, Stone, and George], which Camille had devastated. We made recommendations, for example, for dealing with storm surges and future hurricanes, but few, if any, of the recommendations were actually implemented, because Camille was considered at the time to be a 500-year storm, and therefore the general assumption was, "Why worry about it?"

FONTENOT: It is fascinating to reflect on that history and to think about how those studies were not only right on the mark but could have served as preparation for what would come decades later.

TANNEN: There are two significant differences in planning processes between then and now. One is increased citizen participation; there was very little citizen participation at that time. The other is the change in planning methodologies that NEPA, the National Environmental Policy Act, has brought about.[2] That was passed in 1970, and it required that planning efforts should develop alternative analyses of environmental impacts and include citizen participation. We tried to involve citizens after Camille, but we found that they were not used to being asked to participate in urban and regional planning. The state and federal agencies, which had the responsibility for planning, did not encourage citizen participation because they were opposed to any interference. NEPA changed the whole horizon. It changed the expectations of how planning should be done. But when the federal government initiated citizen participation in federally funded planning efforts, the local agencies—the state, the parish, the county agencies—resisted, and still resist, the involvement of citizens as partners.

FONTENOT: It seems that there are two distinct discussions going on about post-Katrina reconstruction: one concerned with the city and the other with the wetlands. What are your thoughts on how we might begin to consider both of these issues simultaneously as they relate to

1 Mississippi Governor's Emergency Council, *The Mississippi Gulf Coast Comprehensive Development After Camille* (Cambridge, MA: Meta Systems, Inc., 1970).

2 The National Environmental Policy Act (NEPA), was passed during the first session of the 91st Congress and enacted as Public Law 91-190 on January 1, 1970; it was the result of increased appreciation for the environment and growing concerns about human and wildlife well-being, possibly stimulated by the 1969 oil spill off the coast of Santa Barbara, California.

the larger "environment"? How is environmental planning distinguished from urban planning when it comes to citizen participation?

TANNEN: The Environmental Policy Act requires that any [project] involving federal funds—whether it be the construction of a hospital, school, or highway—consider alternatives to the proposed action, including the "no build" alternative. So it was not just set up to deal with the natural environment; it was to be applied to the urban landscape as well. At the same time that NEPA was being developed, other federal agencies, such as the departments of Transportation, Interior, and Housing and Urban Development, demanded that citizen participation be part of their processes of evaluation.

FONTENOT: When we interviewed David Waggonner for our book, he insisted that in discussing planning and participation we have to consider all the various stakeholders, including those who have no "voice"—the fish, birds, and other species that occupy the wetlands. In the urban planning context, we understand what it means to include citizen participation, but what might participation mean in terms of environmental planning?

TANNEN: I do not distinguish between the two. When we talk about citizen participation we are dealing with human beings. The participation of other species in the planning process is more difficult, because of the limitations of communication. Yet there is a sufficient body of knowledge in the biological sciences for dealing with both flora and fauna. Maybe the fish cannot speak to us to indicate their planning preferences, but studying the health of a particular species, the decline of a particular species, or the advancement of an invasive species provides data that is the "voice" of nature. If, for example, the wetlands and the coastal forests begin to disappear, changes in those environments tell us that there is something wrong with what we are doing. The NEPA law requires that whether we are dealing with the natural environment or with the urban or human-made environment, we have to treat them similarly. For example, before you can get a permit to build a canal through the wetlands, you have to be able to demonstrate that this canal will not have negative impacts on the species that inhabit the area, whether they are plants or animals. But of course the oil companies have become very skillful at getting around all that. Taking, for example, the hypothetical case of a proposed canal through wetlands: They work to show that the benefits to be gained by construction will outweigh—and this is the horrible part of how they do this—the loss or destruction of life in the area.

FONTENOT: How do they qualify their argument in terms of "benefits"—economic benefits, I would assume, but certainly not environmental benefits? How should we conceptualize "benefits" in terms of environmental planning?

TANNEN: Different interest groups approach NEPA differently. Those who want to build things, whether within the natural or urban environment, have been concerned about the economic benefits, about being able to demonstrate that their projects will improve economic conditions. But the Environmental Policy Act was not set up with economic benefits in mind. It was set up to require the demonstration of environmental impacts, even for those cases in which human action is disallowed. So, for example, in preparing an environmental impact statement, you have to analyze among the feasible alternatives the alternative of doing nothing. The "no build" alternative provides information about the environmental impact of not going forward with the proposed action. The law is very broad, but unfortunately the people—especially the consultants—writing these documents have been focused more on satisfying the companies that hire them than on looking for alternatives.

FONTENOT: Obviously the industry has become very sophisticated in interpreting the law to satisfy its purposes. As far as environmental agencies are concerned, are there many who have become equally sophisticated in interpreting the law to their advantage? How can industry and environmental groups and organizations form a new kind of alliance to address the myriad challenges of the twenty-first century?

TANNEN: In 2007, America's Energy Coast Alliance was organized; it was a spinoff or outgrowth of America's Wetland Foundation, which started here [in Louisiana, 2001]. It was formed to represent the interest of states where oil production is a major activity. To a certain extent Texas and Louisiana are dominant, but Mississippi participates, and Alabama as well. So these states were trying to work together on cooperative planning efforts, recognizing the oil industry as a player or participant in their discussions.[3]

FONTENOT: In terms of planning, are there relationships between the discussions about wetland reconstruction and those about the reconstruction of New Orleans?

TANNEN: They should be more closely tied together than they are. Wetlands discussions at the state level are not well integrated with the planning going on at the city level, or at the regional level for that matter. One problem that I see is that efforts at the state level need to be better incorporated with activities at the local level. The state has been dealing more with large-scale restoration efforts outside of the city, even though the Corps of Engineers, for example, has been focused on the protection of the city with levees, pumps, and other structures. But I think there is a certain disconnect between the economically driven planning at the city and state levels and the natural-environment issues that the Department of the Interior and other agencies are concerned about.

3 See Jeremy Harper, "LA Seeks Alliance with Gulf States," *The Advocate*, December 1, 2007, reprinted at americaswetland.com. For oil company endorsement, see John Hill, "America's Energy Coast Working Toward New Energy and Ecological Sustainability for the Gulf Coast," forbescustom.com. The Gulf Coast states' need to deal with the disastrous environmental effects of the Deepwater Horizon (BP) Oil Spill, which began in April 2010, seems to have overwhelmed the activities of America's Energy Coast Alliance.

FONTENOT: Could you offer examples of individuals or organizations that are trying to bridge these gaps and form new networks of alliances?

TANNEN: Mark Davis is one example. He is the founding director of the Tulane Institute on Water Resources Law and Policy and a senior research fellow at Tulane University. He was formerly the executive director of the Coalition to Restore Coastal Louisiana.[4] He is interested in establishing better connections between various interest groups. He has been trying to convince the public that our understanding of issues needs to be more broadly based than it currently is. He does not focus so much on regional coastal-state issues; rather, he is more concerned with the oil and gas industries in Louisiana, which own most of the wetlands. More than a million acres of wetlands are owned by the oil companies, which are supposed to be the caretakers and managers of that land. But they have really been poor caretakers in terms of protecting that resource or restoring it. In fact, they are looking to the federal government to pay for restorations after damages that they themselves have caused.

FONTENOT: I am always astounded and wonder how it has been possible that the oil and gas industries have managed to remain so unaccountable for their actions and the long-term destruction they have caused. The wetlands provide very important benefits, protecting against the damage caused by hurricanes and storm surges and supporting the billion-dollar fishing industry and the traditional cultures whose way of life relies on the wetland ecology. Moving on to a different question, what would you consider to be some of the greatest accomplishments in terms of city, regional, and environmental planning since Katrina?

TANNEN: Since the previous Category 5 storm in the area, which was Hurricane Camille [August 1969], I've been dealing with coastal restoration and related planning issues. This has allowed me an opportunity to consider some of these issues over time. The Gulf States—Florida, Alabama, Mississippi, Louisiana, and Texas—form a corridor for major storms. This has historically been the case and will continue to be so. Many of the storms come off the coast of Africa, but some are generated locally in the Gulf of Mexico. Even though hurricanes find their way up the East Coast, Atlantic storms have a high incidence of arriving within the Gulf States, whether crossing from the east coasts of Florida, Georgia, and the Carolinas or making their way through the Straits of Florida. So given that the Gulf of Mexico is a primary target, so to speak, it offers an ideal context to gain a greater understanding of both water and wind issues and their accompanying risks. Though there have been storms this year traveling up the eastern seaboard, by and large the majority of storms arrive in the Gulf

4 See law.tulane.edu/tlscenters/waterlaw; Davis serves on the board of directors of America's Wetland Foundation and on the advisory board of the Coalition to Restore Coastal Louisiana, crcl.org.

States. If you look at the history of hurricanes since they have been documented, you will see that this is the case. In addition to that, because of the warm water coming out of the [Mississippi] river, there is a hot spot, which is more or less focused on the Louisiana coast. So you have the larger context of the five states all being targets over time, but southern Louisiana, given its specific characteristics—its marshes in particular—provides a warmer target area than elsewhere in the Gulf of Mexico. Because of that, Louisiana is the nexus for water- and wind-driven risks. Prior to Hurricane Camille, there was Hurricane Betsy in 1965, which also caused significant damage. I think part of the problem we have had with assessing our responses to Katrina is that we do not think of this continuum. Instead we tend to think in terms of isolated events and responses to those events rather than to the larger landscape and seascape, which should be better understood and better documented.

FONTENOT: What kind of framework would you propose that could advance strategic planning in the specific context of this continuum?

TANNEN: I think there must be a five-state coastal planning effort; this was initiated, in part, by President Obama when he asked Secretary of the Navy Ray Mabus to look at the natural and economic implications of the BP oil spill.[5] But in addition to the study of the oil spill, there should be support for the work of the Gulf of Mexico Alliance and implementation of a regional planning process that involves each coastal county, or coastal parish, in the five states. This would be the basis for developing a large-scale planning tool to better deal with the states' multiple needs, beyond the specific needs of southern Louisiana.[6] NOAA, the National Oceanic Atmospheric Administration, for example, has been maintaining an ongoing file of factors affecting this larger area. NOAA produces studies dealing not only with oceanic issues but also with atmospheric and landside issues.[7] There are several federal agencies—the U.S. Department of the Interior being one—that are looking at this larger landscape and seascape, and consolidating their work might allow us to better understand the planning needs of the five-state area. My point is that while Louisiana may present a complicated case, we should look at our issues in relation to the five-state coastal context.

FONTENOT: It seems to me that this large-scale, five-state approach to planning might help to find common benefits for industry and those concerned with environmental issues.

5 John M. Broder, "Panel Wants BP Fines to Pay for Gulf Restoration," *New York Times*, September 27, 2010.

6 The Gulf of Mexico Alliance was formed in 2004 by the five Gulf of Mexico states to increase regional collaboration and enhance the ecological and economic health of the region. The Alliance is focused on the following areas: water quality, "to ensure healthy beaches and safe seafood"; habitat conservation and restoration; ecosystem integration and assessment; nutrients and nutrient impacts, to establish "criteria for coastal waters and estuaries [to] improve their quality and productivity"; coastal community resilience; and environmental education. See gulfofmexicoalliance.org.

7 See the list of publications concerning integrated ecosystem assessments for the Gulf of Mexico region on NOAA's website, noaa.gov.

TANNEN: The reason I like the five-state approach to planning, as opposed to the localized approach, is that it offers opportunities to better understand the dynamics of these different areas. Certainly the geography and topology of Florida is very different from those of Texas, or of Louisiana for that matter. We need to give more attention to the differences, not only the differences of risk in these various areas but also the differences in how design can be used to improve the quality of the natural and human-made environments. We have to deal with planning at several different scales besides the scales of the city and the region. The federal government, too, is involved. Look at the current effort at coastal restoration, which in Louisiana at this moment is focused more on protecting life and property than on the health of the environment. For example, there is very little effort, and it is considered not feasible, to move people out of harm's way from floodplains to higher ground so that there will be less destruction of life and property in a flood. The federal government, in fact, reinforces the desire to maintain residences and businesses on floodplains by selling flood insurance, which compensates for flood damage. Why is our federal government supporting human habitation in areas that are at continuous risk? This is not just a coastal issue but also a national issue, because flooding occurs not just with hurricane surges but also with river flooding from rain, snowmelt, and so forth.

FONTENOT: As we have recently seen throughout the East Coast following Hurricane Irene [August 2011], flooding is becoming even more extreme as global warming and other factors change weather patterns. It seems to me that there are several ways to approach that issue. One way is to say that we should not live in floodplains. But another way is to say that if we do choose to live in them, we must do so in very particular ways, that is, we must design environments that are responsive and adaptive to the unique conditions of floodplains.

TANNEN: I think the level of severity is the main issue. Floodplains vary in terms of their elevation. A floodplain that is close to or at sea level is at less risk than one that is considerably below sea level, and human habitation can be more easily adapted to it using the means you just described. Whereas a floodplain where you have great risk—and you have to invest in structural improvements to prevent flooding—is where the dilemma is. To protect New Orleans from a 500-year storm, let's say, or a 500-year flooding surge, would require elevating the levees as well as creating other structures that would prevent the inflow of water. So there is a gradient of risk associated with elevation, and I think that has to be taken into account.

FONTENOT: We have built environments in which we rely upon massive forms of infrastructure that offer the illusion of security. When that infrastructure fails, as it did following Katrina, we are reminded in the most brutal way possible of the dynamic forces that act on the landscape, forces that were supposedly "conquered" following the 1927 Mississippi

River flood, when extensive networks of levees and other kinds of infrastructure were put in place.[8]

TANNEN: It was apparent during and after Katrina that federal, state, and local governments, the so-called stakeholders for managing this environment—or at least those who have responsibility for the planning and the funding of activities to better manage it—had failed to provide support and assistance to the city and its residents, in such a way that the residents said, "OK, if the governmental structures at these levels are not doing what we need to have done, then we will do it ourselves." So planning post-Katrina restoration at the neighborhood level became a very local issue and was addressed by very local actions. The federal, state, and city actions were essentially marginal. The immediate federal response was focused more on cleanup and reducing the danger, assisting people who were either injured or potentially at risk, whether that meant helping people out of their houses and out of harm's way or providing some sort of interim or temporary assistance. Eventually, the federal government came to Louisiana with huge sums of money—since Katrina it has spent an estimated $150 billion, but that money was directed more to larger-scale disaster response than to neighborhood interests. Throughout the city, particularly in those areas that were most damaged, existing neighborhood organizations grew stronger and new ones were created. They emerged almost immediately as self-managed entities. It was the neighborhoods, the private sector, volunteers, and nonprofits that really took control of post-Katrina redevelopment, not federal, state, or local governments.

FONTENOT: And now, seven years later, do you think that the kind of neighborhood-based planning structures that emerged following Katrina have been productive and are sustainable? Will these self-organized planning initiatives continue to play a significant role in the future of the city?

TANNEN: I'm thinking about our neighborhood here, Esplanade Ridge, as well as others, where the planning was undertaken more in terms of how individuals could improve their own situations, their homes or gardens or blocks—their immediate neighborhoods. For example, in our neighborhood there were things that we knew needed to be done with schools and health centers and housing; the real work was defining the tasks ahead, even though the resources to get them done were not there. So I think the city is still in a very "at-risk" position. Although the efforts of the federal government—through the Army Corps of Engineers—and some of the state efforts have reduced the threat of future storms and floods, there has been very little redevelopment in the neighborhoods other than the tearing down of public housing and the rebuilding of those "projects" as totally new neighborhoods.

8 For a historical account of the catastrophic flood, see John M. Barry, *Rising Tide: The Great Mississippi Flood of 1927 and How It Changed America* (New York: Simon & Schuster, 1997).

FONTENOT: What about the money that was earmarked for redevelopment, which the city and state became eligible to receive only after the "master plan" was approved? Where is the majority of that money currently being invested in the city?

TANNEN: The money is going to several places. Private developers have used opportunities offered by historic tax credits, "go zone" tax credits, and other related tax incentives to write down or discount costs of development, and by doing that, they are benefiting from federal investments made to stimulate redevelopment. For example, even though more than $30 million is available for the redevelopment of Iberville [a public housing complex], the developers are trying to determine ways to increase the level of funding available to them by identifying additional tax incentives. So the money on the private side has been using the tax advantages provided by the public side from both federal and state sources to reduce the cost of redevelopment. Pres Kabacoff's developments are prime examples of this approach.[9] Privately funded projects that can take advantage of historic tax credits are more numerous than those that cannot. On the public side, most of the rebuilding going on does not deal with basic infrastructure. We have huge below-ground and surface water issues, and yet we don't have the funds to do anything about them. It is estimated that it would cost $5 billion, if not more, to redo the drainage and sewerage and water systems in the city, which are very old, compromised, and inefficient.

FONTENOT: Do we have a historic opportunity to radically rethink the very idea of infrastructure at the city and regional scale and the role it might play in future developments? When considering new ways of thinking about infrastructure, what comes to mind is the idea of soft infrastructure, a concept that uses "living systems," or natural resources such as coastal marshlands, to protect against hurricanes and storm-surge flooding. Compared with traditional hard infrastructure, soft infrastructure is more flexible and adaptive to its environment.

TANNEN: The work that David Waggonner and his associates are doing is along those lines, but the agencies—the stakeholder agencies that fund that kind of work at the federal, state, and local levels—are more interested in hard infrastructure.

FONTENOT: Do you think it is because they are unaware that there are alternatives? What are the main reasons for their resistance to alternative views of infrastructure?

TANNEN: They have a modus operandi that has been in place for many generations, and they are not particularly interested in innovations. They prefer to deal with the environment in the way that they have been

9 Pres Kabacoff is chief executive officer and co-chair of the board of directors of HRI Properties, based in New Orleans. A recent HRI project in downtown New Orleans is the renovation of a historic high-rise office structure at 225 Baronne, which was emptied after Katrina, as a mixed-use building with 192 apartments and 188 hotel rooms.

doing. They adopt ways of thinking and use technologies that are very familiar to them, and they feel that structural solutions are less risky than nonstructural ones. Theirs is a bias in favor of bricks and mortar. And the U.S. Congress is a player in all of this because it funds the Corps's construction of levees and its dredging projects, which are what the Corps focuses on, rather than on coastal restoration. However, there has been a lot of work on both sides of the issue. Although the Corps has not traditionally looked at complicated relationships of systems, there are people in the Corps with whom a systems approach is gaining credibility. In fact, a few months ago I was talking with Major General Michael Walsh, the outgoing commander of the Corps's Mississippi Valley Division, which oversees all of the Mississippi River from Canada to the Gulf of Mexico. He made the point that maybe we should be taking a look at the results of what we have been doing since the Great Flood of 1927 to see if there are other ways of dealing with these issues. So they are slowly beginning to recognize that the practices and strategies that they have utilized since the Great Flood may not be as efficient and appropriate as they once thought.

FONTENOT: As a closing question, I would like to return to an issue that we were discussing earlier. If you could summarize your thoughts, what do you think are the most significant changes that have happened in the planning culture of New Orleans and the region since Katrina?

TANNEN: The first thing is that planning culture is now citizen-driven, whereas prior to Katrina it was driven by federal, state, and local agencies and political organizations, and citizen involvement was negligible, not only in Louisiana but throughout the Gulf South. Now citizens are more engaged. Unfortunately, citizens don't have the power and authority to implement their planning goals—the agencies do, and they are not interested in giving up their territory. There is also a great divide between citizens—essentially laypeople—and "experts," planners and engineers who talk about the fact that citizens may have good ideas but they don't have the technical knowledge to be able to carry out those ideas. There is strong resistance on the part of professionals to engage in conversations or planning efforts with lay people. So that is one thing. The other thing is that we are beginning to think that in order to find solutions that are workable, southern Louisiana may have to become more engaged with the private sector. Private-public partnerships may offer an opportunity to engage not only with the oil companies but with other industries as well. If BP can put up $20 billion to repair the results of one accident, that says something about the extraordinary resources that these companies have. They ought to become more identified with the positive side of redevelopment, rather than just being viewed as criminals who made a mess of things.

FONTENOT: Do you have any thoughts about what types of strategies could be used to encourage new approaches, whether through public-private partnerships or other means?

TANNEN: Well the private sector, as opposed to the nonprofit sector, is less inclined to invest in these issues we have been talking about. A company like BP is more interested in improving its bottom line than in engaging in coastal restoration; even though restoration has a long-term positive benefit, it does not have a short-term potential profit spinoff. I think the private sector has not yet seen an opportunity to be engaged in a way that offers it financial benefits. If a private company were to partner with the federal government on coastal restoration, it would want to be able to identify ways that could benefit not only the environment but also itself as a profit-making organization. If for example a private developer invests in improving the environment, in the long term the enhanced quality of life would add to the property's value, but there might not be any financial advantage in the very short term. And most private companies are more interested in what the return on their investment is going to be in one, two, or three years rather than in ten or twenty years.

FONTENOT: It seems to me that there is a great poverty of imagination when it comes to thinking about innovative ways of investing that could address some of these issues. What we define as a benefit should be more thoroughly and creatively studied. It would be interesting to see a model that identified the overlaps of long-term interests and short-term interests in terms of monetary and environmental profits.

TANNEN: I think the conservation organizations are a good example of how that works. Such organizations are often able to get donations of land, for example, because tax benefits accrue to donors. If there were tax benefits or ways of reducing the tax side of a company's activity, then the company might be more interested in participating in conservation efforts. And there is movement in that direction. The Coastal Restoration Authority is made up of bright people who are trying to figure out the best way to go about restoration, revitalization, and protection.[10] Given the lack of sufficient funding to do the job that needs to be done in the Gulf of Mexico, we need a greater involvement of the private for-profit sector, which includes the oil companies, key developers, the navigation and marine interests, and all of the major industries that are active in this region. They need to find ways, and we need to help them find ways, in which their involvement will benefit them, and benefit the region.

10 The Coastal Restoration and Protection Authority is a state agency, coastal.louisiana.gov. For Louisiana's 2012 Coastal Master Plan, see coastalmasterplan.louisiana.gov.

BEYOND THE LINE
ANURADHA MATHUR and DILIP DA CUNHA

EYEING THE FLOOD

It is hardly the fault of twentieth-century planners and designers in New Orleans that they took levees for granted. Levees are the result of the imaging and imagining of those who made first use of a terrain in the post-Columbian era of the geographic map—the view from above. The vocabulary they gave the place was that of a divided landscape, where the sea is beyond land's edge and land's end, a blue that meets brown across a coastline. Every now and then, this coastline turns in and makes its way up to a source of a flow—a spring or a rill head—before turning back down toward the sea and continuing on its way. As in the case of the Mississippi, where the line reaches into Canada, Ohio, and Montana, this source can be far inland. The foray inland of this line diminishes in fractal fashion as one zooms out. Dwellers around the world share in the experience of the ways in which such a line separates land and water.

The separation between land and water in the Lower Mississippi requires a vast infrastructure to hold it in place. It is an infrastructure that has grown over several destructive events, in particular the great inundation in 1927, after which the lines dividing the Mississippi from land were extended and reinforced by Project Flood. This enterprise of the U.S. Army Corps of Engineers focused on the river basin more than on the river channel. The corps constructed the basin in a scaled, operating, and testable concrete miniature. Then, with the help of the Mississippi Basin Model, the lines dividing water and land were extended along spillways designed to release the pressure within the course to which the river was confined. It is this Project Flood landscape that was wrecked in the wake of Hurricane Katrina.

Levees have lost some credibility through the events of August 2005, but the line separating land and water has not. It carries the weight of the nation's properties, waterways, and waterfronts. An all-seeing eye follows this line. The eye separates before it relates, distinguishes before it unites or divides. It creates a world of articulated things, that is, things that are not only drawn out visually from *stuff* but

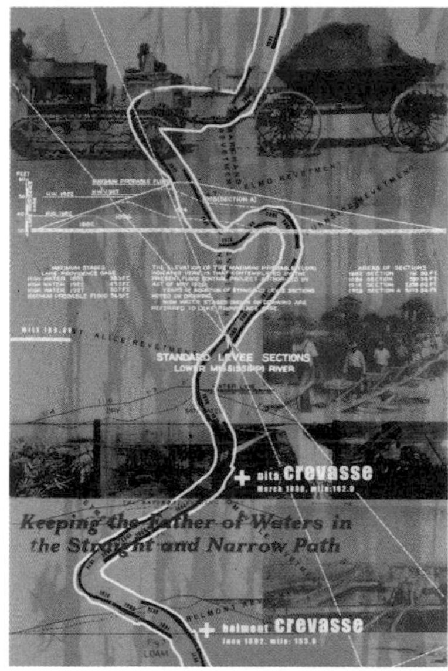

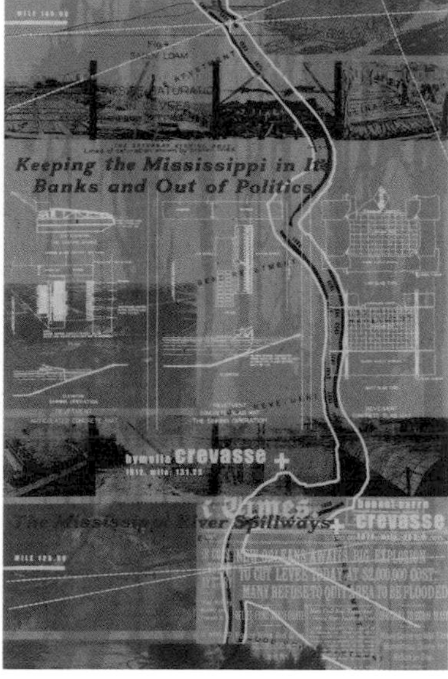

Anuradha Mathur / Dilip da Cunha

The lines that confined the Mississippi River to a singular flow in maps drawn by European settlers have made way for levees that confine it to a channel. Originally low earthen piles heaped and compacted by slaves, today the levees are engineered structures that can top fifty feet. But even as levees have grown in magnitude and importance, so also have the crevasses, the structural breaches that once reduced pressure on levees up and down the river. Since the Mississippi River flood in 1927, the function of the crevasses has been replaced by controlled floodway releases, but they remain both a threat and a last resort.

can also be drawn on paper, on maps, in sketches, or in paintings. Ultimately this eye distinguishes the articulated from the amorphous. It renders much of the Lower Mississippi legible. Only the water beyond land's edge and land's end remains defiant, not providing the legible limits necessary to visual extraction. Bodies of water such as the Mississippi River, Lake Pontchartrain, the Gulf of Mexico, and the bayous are drawn by edges of land, edges that are asserted, constructed, reasoned, and enforced. These edges are sometimes blurred by slopes and pluralized by ecotones to accommodate the restlessness of water—waves, tides, salinity, floods, hurricanes—but the eye that articulates them belongs on land.

In the Lower Mississippi, what the eye sees has contributed to the primacy of the plan, which, like the map, is the view from above, where, beginning with the levee, separations are articulated with clarity. This construction—the levee—reflects the line that was first drawn on paper to contain water to a flow, a line that by default creates flood when water crosses it. Beginning with this separation, though, the eye that sees the flood has reached out to articulate a settlement through many clear and distinct elements—roads, buildings, parks, canals, and so on. These "things" remain the vocabulary of a New Orleans planted in the 1700s between the Mississippi River and Lake Pontchartrain. They represent the development of a City, its River, and its Lake. The seeing eye has placed the first in a bowl, channeled the second, and made a floodway

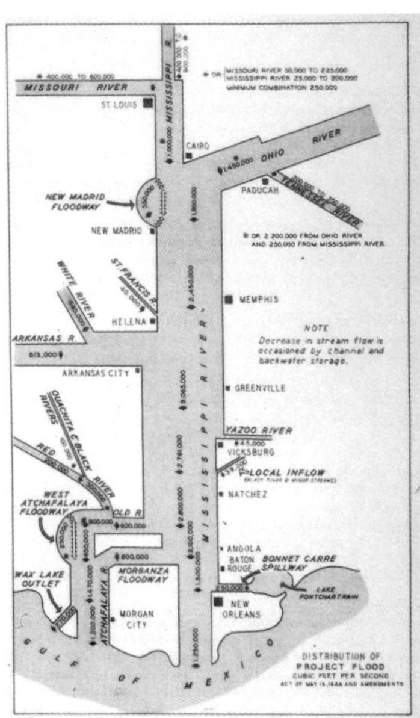

P.A. Feringa and Charles W. Schweizer, *One Hundred Years of Improvement on the Lower Mississippi River* (Vicksburg, MS: Mississippi River Commission, 1952) and Anuradha Mathur / Dilip da Cunha.

The flood of 1927 was notable for encouraging a shift in approach, from engineering a channel to engineering a channel in a basin. Project Flood laid out a system of flows and floodways and, importantly, the control structures at Simmesport, Louisiana, which on an everyday basis keep the Mississippi flowing past Baton Rouge and New Orleans. The system prevents the water from taking a shorter route to the sea through the Atchafalaya swamp to the west.

of the third. The New Orleans that it created waits for the next disaster—water crossing the line of separation—to be tested.

FIELD OF ANCHORS

In the wake of Katrina, New Orleans presents an opportunity not merely to reconstruct a city but also to revisualize a landscape beyond the line we asserted by eyeing the flood. A new visualization can begin with a different understanding of what "settling" means in a delta: the settling of sediment, which is not understood as land formation and consolidation but as anchoring in time.

The place where Jean-Baptiste Le Moyne de Bienville of the French Mississippi Company found himself in 1718 is popularly described by ecologists and historians today as a land between two types of waters: the flowing waters of a river—the Mississippi—and the relatively stationary waters of the swamps. This land between riverfront and backswamp is considered a typical high ground made by waters overflowing a riverbank. These waters lay down heavier sediment in proximity to the stream, raising the land, and spread lighter sediment further away in the swamps. This process continues until the power of the river's meandering flow breaks through this "natural" levee to chart a new course and begin another round of land formation. Historians say that it was in this dynamic terrain, on a piece of relatively stable high ground adjoining the Mississippi River, that Bienville laid out New Orleans, a settlement that has fought ever since to keep its ground separate from water, and has done so primarily with levees.

But seen with a different eye that presents another visualization of land deposition, the place Bienville arrived at was quite different. In this place, sediment does not accumulate to form land so much as maintain its hold with varying degrees of success, sometimes anchoring deep to become rock, other times remaining in suspension, perhaps for years. Land here is not a surface separable from water; it is rather a tenuous anchor in a watery depth. The New Orleans that emerges from this appreciation is imaged and imagined differently. It is not a singular entity—a city—on a space of land, but a field of anchors. The future of this settlement is not warring with water; it is, rather, initiating and nurturing anchors in the water that hold and gather for a period of time, as deposits do.

So how would we rebuild a New Orleans without the image and imagination of a line, a New Orleans that does not have its beginnings on a piece of ground between river and backswamps but rather in a liquid terrain, where deposits anchor in time rather than consolidate to form land? What would it mean to think of human settlements not only in the Lower Mississippi, not only in places "threatened" by water, but everywhere, as acts of anchoring in time rather than forming in space? This is perhaps the most fundamental question raised by Katrina. It urges us to look beyond a spatial divide that has been concretized into historical descriptions and prescriptive design, into maps and other tools of education and administration. The cause of the destructive events of August 2005 does not lie only in the failure of levees; it also lies, more seriously, in the line drawn to separate land from water.

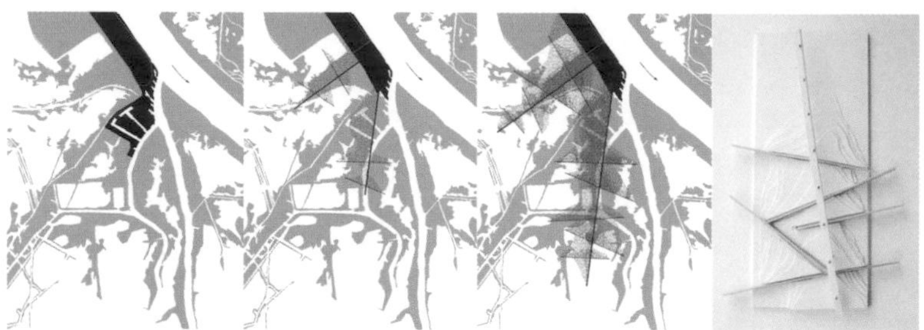

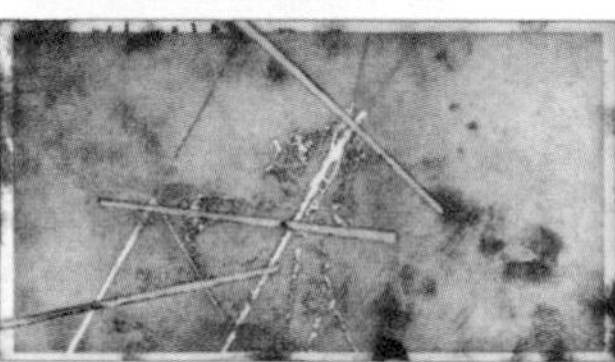

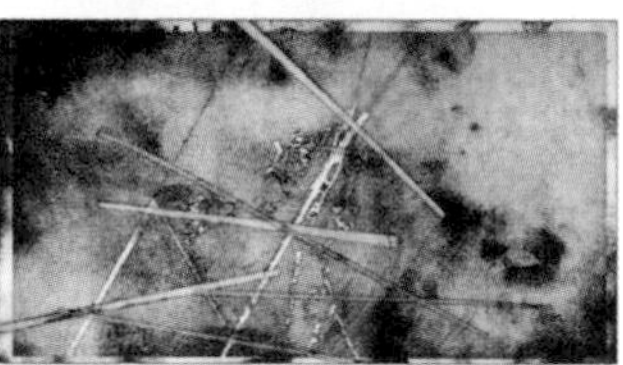

The Lower Mississippi landscape can be seen as Herodotus saw Egypt's: "the gift of a river," an accumulation of sediment brought down from high ground to make land on which humans could settle. It can also be seen, however, as a multiplicity of deposits that anchor in a watery depth. This is not a land surface across the line from flowing water, terra firma across the line from flux, that existed prior to the arrival of the designer/settler; it is rather an undivided field in which each project anchors, gathers, extends, and connects.

Rosalynn Mannion, "Living between Water and Land: Latent Strategies," created for the 2006 University of Pennsylvania design studio "New Orleans: Inhabiting a Fluid Terrain," with studio critic Anuradha Mathur.

GROUND ZERO
J. DAVID WAGGONNER III

The Dutch Dialogues project, of which David Waggonner has been a primary organizer, provides one possible model for the implementation of a planning culture in New Orleans. In a process that has been essential to the development and success of the low-lying Netherlands for centuries, Dutch people come together to talk about physical and social issues (often involving water and its economic impacts); they listen to disparate views, find common ground, and forge agreements. The Dutch Dialogues project was initiated with a delegation to the Netherlands in 2006, and over the course of the past five years it evolved as a series of three conferences and a publication. In the interview below, Waggonner speaks emphatically about the need for a comprehensive water management plan in the region. In short, he believes that in order to maintain a significant settlement in New Orleans, on the unstable and eroding Louisiana coast, space for water must be allotted and an operational water management infrastructure must be developed. Planning efforts must prioritize the building of infrastructure to support the foundation layer of ground and water, in conjunction with programs that promote coastal restoration and improved, dependable levee protection. This is the agenda required to successfully enhance both the safety and the value of the habitation layer. Anthony Fontenot, Carol McMichael Reese, and Maureen Long conducted the interview on August 20, 2010.

FONTENOT: Can you explain how the Dutch Dialogues between Louisiana and the Netherlands first began following Hurricane Katrina? What was your primary goal in initiating these congresses?[1] Also, what do you think we can learn today about planning by studying relationships among water, infrastructure, and the contemporary city?

WAGGONNER: When you and I first started to discuss these issues

1 The dates and locations of the professional exchanges organized by the Dutch Dialogues program are as follows: Dutch Dialogues Delegation, January 2006, the Netherlands; Dutch Dialogues Conference I, March 2008, New Orleans; Dutch Dialogues Conference II, October 2008, New Orleans; Dutch Dialogues Conference III, April 2010. See *Dutch Dialogues: New Orleans-Netherlands, Common Challenges in Urbanized Deltas* (Amsterdam: SUN, 2009).

seriously, in relation to the panel you convened for the "Sustainable Dialogues" symposium in Panama, the categorical idea was about infrastructure.[2] I think we are now starting to realize that this sort of language does not work very well. It appears to me that if we used a more effective term that was able to capture the imagination of the public and hold their attention, this country's infrastructure might not have been allowed to deteriorate so far. There is a problem in the way the message is being communicated, and throughout this country our infrastructure is a mess. My question is, What would be a better conceptual framework? I do not have the answer, but we're certainly thinking about it. One way to approach the problem is to conceive of the ground plane, the earth itself, and water as a primary system of biodiversity. In the Dutch planning model, they tend to talk about the ground and water as the base layer, and the middle layer is infrastructure and the top layer is habitation. We often forget to consider biodiversity as a base system that interacts with multiple layers. There is a serious problem in the message that we put forth, both academically and politically, that stresses differences instead of connections; for the past twenty years we have increasingly differentiated and deconstructed, tearing things apart. If you want to see what the world is like when you tear it apart, when you deconstruct it, then look at New Orleans. What we have found is that the language of planning is pretty damn inadequate. Although certain words stick, I do not think *water management* and *spatial planning* are compelling phrases. How do we move beyond our current inadequate and technocratic language to conceptualize the issues and solutions? I am sure you have heard the quote that circulated after the oil spill: "Louisiana is America's sushi bar, gas station, and toilet bowl." Since we have the fish, it would be only reasonable that we should not only be more aware of, but also have more say about, the upstream/downstream conditions that affect Louisiana directly.

In Rotterdam this year, I made a presentation at the World Estuary Alliance, which is really a program of the World Wildlife Federation, and I also participated in a session of the Delta Alliance congress, which is funded by the Dutch government. I was struck by a comment that someone made at the congress, arguing that when you are considering wetlands and deltas, it is crucial to engage all the stakeholders and get their input. If we are to follow this model seriously, then the Delta Alliance is inadequate, because fish cannot speak, and they are, in the big picture, important stakeholders in deltas. The biodiversity model, which the World Estuary Alliance supports, offers a more compelling and durable overall picture. I think we need to develop something closer to their conceptual framework rather than just thinking about infrastructure,

2 "Sustainable Dialogues II: Panama and New Orleans" was held at the Panama Canal Museum in Panama City on November 15, 2007.

which is a rigid man-made thing that we are not even capable of maintaining. In a developing country, apart from water, infrastructure seems like a good place to invest resources. Given that in many ways southern Louisiana is a developing country, you would think that we would be investing in infrastructure even before investing in community centers. If infrastructure is properly connected to ground and water, it should enable our society to survive and prosper.

REESE: I am reminded of Nan Ellin's book *Postmodern Urbanism*; one of the threads that she followed was the idea of ecology as a holistic understanding of man and nature existing together in the urban sphere and the types of physical decisions that are made if you consider a healthy coexistence, which requires balance and respect.

WAGGONNER: Analyzing the prime rationale for the closed drainage system of New Orleans, which was to prevent mosquitoes and yellow fever, many people today would argue that a solution to the problem [of reopening the drainage canals] could be found by employing biodiversity. Actually, there are two solutions: biodiversity and moving water. Fish and frogs that eat larvae could be introduced. The problem is the lack of complexity, and that shows up all over the place. The complexity that I am referring to grows every day in our own lives, in the compounds in the river and their effects, and in biological matter. Life down here, in many ways, is a science experiment that we need to engage in consciously.

REESE: As one who is working from the outside, where do you see your current work going? Clearly, you are a proponent of education, but in what other ways are you going to deploy your energies, beyond the congresses that you have put together?

WAGGONNER: I am not comfortable being fully inside or outside, and I am happy to be able to go in between. I think most people operate in that way. One feels isolated if one doesn't have a place at the table, but if one never leaves one can feel smothered. One must be able to get away and reflect. By staying inside, one cannot ever know what is going on elsewhere, so it is important to occupy both positions.

We have spent an inordinately long time outside the system, but we are now beginning to engage it more directly. Contact with the U.S. Army Corps of Engineers has been perhaps the most difficult. Recently, we have made a little more contact with the New Orleans Sewerage and Water Board. But if one examines the situation here, it is apparent that we need somebody with authority to do something intelligent about it. I was raised to respect authority, but we need someone who can implement authority effectively. I would argue that since the era of Ronald Reagan we have been told to disrespect the authority of government. I think that part of what we are now experiencing is a byproduct of that, and in my opinion it is not right.

If we are interested in addressing local problems, then this becomes a significant issue. How are we going to get governmental authority to properly respond to the illogical aspects of our system? The most evident problem is the schism between the Sewerage and Water Board and the Public Works Department, which in practice continue to bicker: "A pipe this size is your responsibility. A pipe that size is our responsibility. That's your problem, not mine." If it is an inlet in question, who cleans, who drains, who connects? I can't tell you how often in the UNOP [Unified New Orleans Plan] process, which in many ways was like psychotherapy for the public, citizens would logically point out that the pipes should be fixed before the streets are paved, yet so many times the city would pave the street and then come back and tear it up to fix the pipes. That is a disjunction of authority. Rainwater should be managed by one entity. The mayor, or someone in a position of power, needs to address this dysfunction, and I believe Mayor Landrieu will.

When these discussions happen, we do engage in them, but it is not my job to criticize the Sewerage and Water Board. My job is to describe the physical problem. My interest as an architect is in making a physical world that is beautiful and where we can live without wet feet. If all parties could just agree on a common objective, then we could concentrate on how to best solve the problems. There are entrenched interests that do not appear to be on the same page, insofar as they apparently do not agree that we need civil engineering, for example. At Tulane University there is no school of engineering. Do you really think we can remake this world without engineers? I do not. Having said that, I acknowledge that the engineering community here lacks a progressive attitude about many of the problems we are facing. For example, many do not believe that permeable pavement is a practical solution to address certain problems, and they hold on to old ways, even though those ways have been proven ineffective. We need to build a component into the process that will allow us to test different strategies and understand through experimentation and monitoring how something is going to work.

One cannot stay outside the system, but one should choose what one's role will be. I read that supposedly Steven Holl was going to stop being an architect and run for Congress. He is apparently convinced that buildings do not matter very much in the long run and that there is a bigger problem at hand. If we put more effort into the design of a society, then we might be able to accomplish more than with the design of a building. It is certainly an interesting idea. The way an architect thinks is a point worth noting. I think as a society we have lost the advantages of trying to define the problem first and then attempting to solve it. The role of an architect is to figure out what the problem is and to try to solve it in a way that has some definable measures and limits. We are confronted with many real problems. Water quantity and quality, ground subsidence, rising sea level, and climate change are issues that we need to learn how to address. Heavy rainfall is a problem, as are periods of drought. Many of these issues are quantifiable, and we should find ways to address them. Although I do not think the situation in New Orleans can be properly addressed with only pumps and pipes, we should not abandon them, either. There are other options.

We are products of our experience. What we do is renovate and add to the existing conditions. In common practice, New Orleans is a renovation project. I say that all the time. It is not a clean slate. After the storm, Daniel Libeskind suggested that we rebuild New Orleans around the theme of jazz, and I thought, What the hell does that have to do with the physical structure of the city? Instead of perpetuating fantasies and myths about the place, it is crucial that we address some of the actual and very real conditions here. The fact-based approach, which can describe the way a system actually works, is essential to dispel some of the urban myths, including myths about water and the city. Otherwise, we are dealing with highly emotional responses, such as "I'm gonna drown" or "I'm scared of water," to what has to be a highly engineered environment.

REESE: Speaking of myths, many people actually thought that Pontchartrain Park had been engineered so that the nearby higher, originally white neighborhood, Gentilly Woods, drained into the lower, black neighborhood, Pontchartrain Park. These issues came up recently in a meeting with Intuition & Logic, the engineers from St. Louis who are consultants to Spackman Mossop Michaels for the Dwyer Canal redesign project, which involves Pontchartain Park and Gentilly Woods, which share the canal as a border. The consultants' recommendation to the stakeholders was that just improving the function of the pumps of the larger drainage area beyond the neighborhoods would help control the flooding. It was a really useful exercise because they were able to educate the residents about the actual drainage area for the Dwyer Canal and its relationship to their neighborhoods.

WAGGONNER: Elizabeth Mossop said that the people found the engineering proposal convincing.

FONTENOT: So the engineers were able to dispel misunderstandings through a rational explanation of the way infrastructure works?

REESE: Yes, because they were able to show the actual direction that water drains from the neighborhoods and to explain that the neighborhoods flood during rainstorms because the pump designated to move the water from them to the lake cannot handle it all, and so it backs up into the Dwyer Canal. So that was important for them to hear.

WAGGONNER: Yes, there are so many myths that persist. If one simply looks at the gross pattern of things without examining the specifics, the stories are probably right. But that's not always the case here in New Orleans. I remember Derek Hoeferlin telling me about his experience at a meeting in the Hoffman Triangle area in Central City, when a man in the audience said he believed that the claim that they live below sea level is a conspiracy. So the physical realities of the place are hard to get through to people, because we live in a world of myths and beliefs.

In terms of pipes and pumps, I don't believe there is any long-term solution that would allow us to pump everything successfully. We need to create more canals that can store more water. Marcia St. Martin, the head of the Sewerage and Water board, tells me that New Orleans East did not flood before Katrina. This is understandable, because that area has open canals, which have a huge capacity. A pipe reaches its capacity and then sends water back upstream under pressure; an open canal fills up to its bank and might overflow but doesn't back up. In my opinion, there is something inherently wrong with pumping as the sole solution, yet we cannot jettison that system. Again, our goal in advocacy is to argue that one should not abandon what one has. It is not an either/or situation. Mr. Gorman, a former director of the Sewerage and Water Board, said, "It would be nice to have gone in the direction you are talking about, David, but for more than fifty years we haven't gone in that direction." Now we should be talking about creating a parallel or supplementary system or a complementary system. On the one hand, we should not abandon what we have, but on the other hand, we should not be so committed to keeping it the way it is.

FONTENOT: When we think about large-scale systems—whether we are considering the infrastructure of water, transportation, or energy—a common problem is how to make a transition from one type of system to another. The transitional phase is clearly not a matter of going from black to white. It is one thing to have an ideal plan, and you have outlined what we need. You have also pointed out what we have, so how do we go from what we have to what we need?

WAGGONNER: Five years ago I did not even know about the quasi-science of transition management. There is a slide that I use in presentations that I got from a friend of ours at Deltares named Frans van de Ven.[3] It shows a type of organizational reform where one addresses the problem by working through the organizational system. But there is another approach that he pointed out to me, that of the outsider, in which one acts as an agent of change. That is the approach we are currently following. My claim has always been that one cannot focus in the first instance on organizational reform when an organization has been growing for so long that it has evolved its own imperative to survive, its own set of vested interests to defend. Therefore, it is better to approach the situation by starting with the physical problem. If one starts with the question of the organization or management regime, one might not take the best approach to the physical problem. If one is only looking at the aviation board or the water board—or whatever organization—one is still not looking at the problem, because the problem manifests itself physically.

Of course it is also a social problem. In my experience, New Orleans presents a unique situation. If I were to compare Amsterdam and New

3 Deltares is a research institute based in Delft and Utrecht that focuses on issues of water, soil, and the subsurface.

Waggonner & Ball

Water storage options for the Hoffman Triangle developed during Dutch Dialogues II, compared to existing conditions

Orleans, I'd say Amsterdam is a physical city, functionally beautiful, that depends less on social networks. I would say San Francisco is like that, too. I know that San Francisco's Chinatown has social networks, but New Orleans as a whole is a coded city of very close social networks consisting of family and friends and also relationships involving people who live here and do not live here, all of which create our Southern relationship-based culture. We are even more embedded in it because we have all the rituals that reinforce it. I am not saying we should not respect these types of relationships, but they can blind us. We have to go back and look at the physical problems. If the people in Pontilly think flooding there is just the result of a social problem, they are mistaken. Usually people will wake up if you say, You have to get out of here, the roof is going to fall. At times like these we need to communicate the problem with a sense of urgency. In transition management terms, what we need to remember is that although we need to work outside the system in the beginning, to create a vision that can alter the paradigm, at some point we have to come back inside the system. One cannot stay outside forever and remain the outsider. I know I have said more than once as an architect that an idea is not a good one if it never gets done.

FONTENOT: From your work over the past five years, it is clear that you are interested in addressing very broad issues concerning water. If you had to choose one important project to move forward in the next three years, which project would it be?

WAGGONNER: I am going to answer that in a roundabout way. First, I believe it is important to work with all the different layers, including ground, infrastructure, and habitation. Each layer has its own characteristics. It is no longer easy for me just to say we are dealing with an urban water system alone. I do not think one can continue to ignore the river flow. I don't think one can continue to act as though the flood protection system and coastal restoration are separate discussions. The question that I think you are really asking me is a question concerning scale. For example, one could use three or four abandoned lots in the city and connect them to create a green network that could hold water. That is a small-scale project, but it can serve a valuable function. Furthermore, on one's own property one can disconnect the downspout on the house and create a garden to slow down the runoff toward the street. This is a small-scale intervention that if aggregated can have larger implications. Then there are the middle-scale projects that can have an even greater impact on the city. But I think your question is really concerned with large-scale projects. In my mind it is about the outfall canals and what should happen with them: that is a primary question.

One of the reasons we initiated the Dutch Dialogues was to learn what we could do about the water system. We were interested in thinking about how we could set up a system that incorporated the outfall canals. Once a circulating water system is put in place, many opportunities arise for urban redevelopment. There are 15.5 miles, excluding the Industrial Canal, of outfall canals with unwanted and unnecessary stem walls. That is 15.5 miles of real estate—thirty-one miles, actually, figuring in both sides, and that could be a big deal. The Army Corps will spend a lot of money on the design and construction of massive and permanent pump stations where the outfall canals enter the lake. As far as I know, there are no architects involved in this project, only engineers and contractors. Why Tulane University School of Architecture doesn't make some comment about this issue, I don't know. Why do architects and our press feel the need to talk about strategies that emphasize building little houses

Waggonner & Ball

Existing section of the Orleans outfall canal

Waggonner & Ball

Proposed section of the Orleans outfall canal showing widened public space that can be used for water storage

when there are hundreds of millions of dollars being invested without architects even having a say in the matter or even commenting on the situation? I think that is the big issue.

REESE: Apparently, they have not looked at anything published between 1900 and 1920. During that period, architects loved designing all sorts of major urban infrastructure projects and every mayor in America was engaged in such issues.

WAGGONNER: In the thirties, this is what we reverted to. You are right, our involvement was more pronounced in the Olmsted era. We do not want to engage public space, yet we complain about how ugly the infrastructure and structures are. Sometimes the infrastructure here is not even practical—for example, where a highway dips below a railroad overpass, so that in a flood you cannot get out of the city. Regarding the aesthetics of infrastructure, I like to say we have to create the desire for it. We have to show the public that they should expect more from urban infrastructure and that they should demand beauty in addition to function. The Thames Barrier outside of London had three design criteria: to protect the city from tidal surges, to allow navigation under normal conditions, and to be beautiful. I would call the result a success. The people of London take ownership of that structure, they believe in it, they connect with it, and they pay to maintain it. Can we say the same for our pump stations? Apple knows how to use design to create desire. We

A new water system and public space where Bayou St. John meets the Lafitte Greenway. The bayou appears in the foreground, and the greenway stretches toward downtown.

should learn from them.

FONTENOT: Have you approached or been approached by any of these engineering firms working in New Orleans to collaborate on designs and plans for how water should be managed and how physical space might be organized in relationship to it?

WAGGONNER: Not really.

FONTENOT: Is there an opportunity for such collaboration?

WAGGONNER: It has to do with how one defines success. The metric by which the Corps of Engineers functions is based on time and budget. In their opinion, architects slow things down and cost money. They do not see the cost/benefit ratio, but value judgments have to shift there. If I cannot assure them that I am going to add some sort of benefit, then why should they hire me?

FONTENOT: You were just explaining that there are some fifteen miles of outfall canals to transform. Would that not be seen as a benefit in terms of real estate and the development of public spaces?

WAGGONNER: I think so. Before I got into the morass that is the water issue, we spent a lot of time studying the Claiborne Avenue corridor. For the first time, from our provincial perspective, we realized that Claiborne Avenue in Orleans Parish was the equivalent to Judge Perez Drive in St. Bernard Parish. And just as Jefferson Highway in Jefferson Parish goes through three parishes, Claiborne Avenue goes through the entire city and connects uptown with downtown. There were many interesting parallels. There is a bit of discussion now about certain real estate improvements that would go up alongside the Claiborne corridor if the elevated highway were removed, but there is also concern that redevelopment would bring gentrification, which is probably a long way away. During the BNOB [Bring New Orleans Back] planning process, I presented a related idea to the urban design committee. I suggested that we should advocate for tax increment financing districts along the outfall canals as an incentive to redevelop those swaths of land. The idea did not get much traction, because at that point no one wanted to live near the canals, and most of that area is actually private backyards. It is difficult to speak of public interest where private property is involved.

In the view of those of us who have been thinking about the relationship of the city to water, what we need to do is create a water system for the city and establish district plans based on that system. The water basin district plans need to follow not the boundaries of the city planning commission but hydrologically based boundaries. We then need to identify some key pilot projects to illustrate those districts' potential. The politicians are going to like the pilot projects because those are things they can show and promote. I do not mean that in a cynical way. Pilots can actually test public support. If those projects do not fit with the water system and do not fit with the will of the district, or what residents see as their need, we will never create enough support.

I think the problem with the current round of planning, at least to a degree, which is part of your inquiry, is that it has not put all people in the same boat or provided a unified, desirable vision. The basic common interests of all people have not been talked about. We have heard much more about competing interests. We heard about the competition between Broadmoor and New Orleans East expressed at your conference, for example. But we still have not addressed the most difficult area, New Orleans East, and explained the facts of that situation. The various interests in the area will have to make some sort of decision. This gets into that future world that Kristina Hill describes as a disassemblage of political entities. When the nation-states fall apart, will cities also fall apart? We are evolving into more localized, self-interested groups.

Yet Pontchartrain Park would not be able to operate as an independent entity, because it depends on the London Avenue Canal. To use the same language as spatial planning and water management, each district has a water assignment. Somewhere in the territory a certain amount of water must be absorbed, and each neighborhood should decide where that should happen. These are the basic types of problems we are trying to address. I am fully aware that I am volunteering to have my head knocked around, like the engineers from St. Louis, but this is just about the rainfall. We are not talking about claims of a conspiracy to blow up levees or even about the engineering failures that caused the levees to collapse. Maybe we can quantify overtopping and how much water would come in from the lake during a hurricane, but the bottom line is that each area must be able to handle a certain amount of water during a typical storm. The basic question should be where would that neighborhood like to put it? I think that is the kind of job that this city will have to do next. If we had had the right kind of leadership many years ago, then we would not have wasted so much time, money, and human energy.

REESE: That is precisely what the Greater New Orleans Foundation grant for the Dwyer Canal was targeted to do. Granted the city doesn't yet have the "next" level of a water basin district plan and has not worked out a revised water collection system, but when the engineering consultants met with the Gentilly Woods and Pontchartrain Park neighborhoods, they could point out the conditions within the existing system.[4] Then they could bring it down to the Dwyer Canal and explain the ways in which more water could be held and/or absorbed in the neighborhoods, and the options could be debated, including the idea of introducing water barrels under the downspouts and so on. It became quite interesting when the neighbors said, "OK, we're going to soak up water. How long is the water going to sit there?" If only there were more of these conversations, I really think that people would begin to move toward a more productive discussion that could lead to real solutions. And what about the Lafitte Corridor? I know that you and Jane Wolff were out there over the summer. Could that be a demonstration project?

WAGGONNER: You know we produced a report on Lafitte.[5]

REESE: Did you compete for the build-out of that project?

WAGGONNER: No, we did not compete, partially because of my antiquated sense of ethics. We often do things that are not necessarily in our own self-interest because of what we perceive as ethical. We were doing another study for the Friends of Lafitte Corridor. Austin's Design Workshop had been awarded the contract, but the city had never executed it, and they had to readvertise it. We elected to stand aside. Nonetheless, I have a very strong perspective on this: I don't think water is secondary. I don't think a bike trail matters a whole lot in the grand scheme of things, especially in that particular right-of-way. Small thinking is OK sometimes, but there are situations that demand that we think big, and the Lafitte Corridor is one of them.

FONTENOT: Is water prioritized as an issue in New Orleans's planning offices? At the level of city government, it is important to establish a city's greatest potential and problems. Do you think city officials understand that water is one of the most important issues to consider when thinking about how New Orleans works and how it is organized?

WAGGONNER: No, we repress it. It is a psychological disorder—in

4 See the essay by Jane Wolff and Carol McMichael Reese in Part VI of this volume.

5 A PDF of this report is available on the Lulu website, lulu.com.

Waggonner & Ball

Proposed circulating water system for New Orleans developed during Dutch Dialogues III

fact, a serious psychological disorder. The metaphor is that New Orleans is the land of dreams. Yet in New Orleans we repress the element of dreams, which is water—that is the classical interpretation. We are the land of dreams, but we do not acknowledge that dream element that is all around us. It is delusional. And by living in a delusional condition, one places oneself at risk. Five years ago, we found out how risky our delusion is. We are reminded of that every time it rains hard. Ultimately, what we are giving up is our own economic potential. We do not accept water anywhere in the city. We simply get rid of it. The accumulation of small interventions on higher ground has great significance: the gardens, the rain gardens, the edges of the street, the curbs, and the various ways of dealing with slowing water down become very important downstream. We have an ethical responsibility to deal with the water upslope because these decisions have an enormous effect downslope.

After Dutch Dialogues II, I visited Hal Roark, who was head of the Broadmoor Improvement Association and who has now gone on to Yale Divinity School. He is very bright. I went with Alexandra Evans, who was with the Louisiana Recovery Authority. We presented some ideas, and he was tough. At first he thought we were expecting Broadmoor to solve all of the problems. But when he realized we were talking about holding the water upslope, everything changed. In our vision, in the city we imagine, everyone will do his or her part instead of just shunting all of the water down toward Broadmoor. On a completely different scale, the same thing needs to happen upriver, in Minnesota, Illinois, and Iowa. If you want to go back to talking about planning, the principles really have not been put

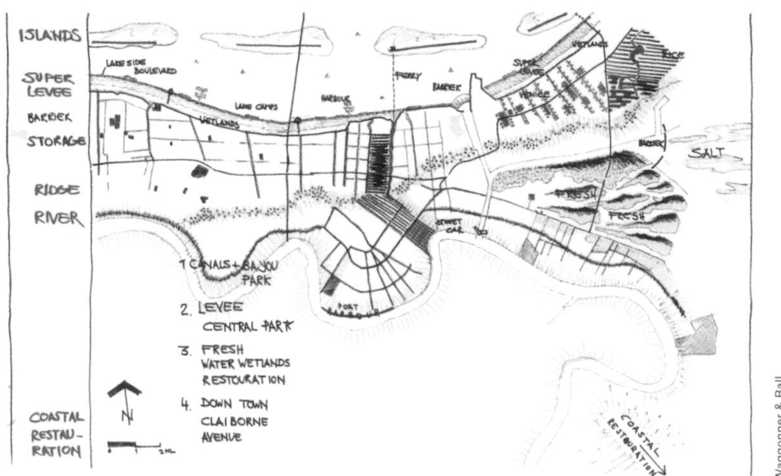

Regional water master plan developed during Dutch Dialogues II

Waggonner & Ball

forth in clear ways. The Unified New Orleans Plan produced, in general, banal principles and projects, such as the right to return. I think the real question is, The right to return to what? The city that used to exist?

FONTENOT: Is there an actual water budget? If so, what agency is responsible for establishing and maintaining that budget for the city?

WAGGONNER: I cannot say for sure, but I do not think there is one. There is also no stormwater management fee.

FONTENOT: Water management exists at the regional scale with the Old River Control Structure, which maintains a thirty-seventy split between the Atchafalaya and Mississippi rivers. It is curious to me that we do not have a similar type of mechanism that would control and redistribute water at the scale of the city.

WAGGONNER: I do not really know what the Sewerage and Water Board figures are. Right now, a drainage master plan is being developed by Camp Dresser & McKee Engineers for the Department of Public Works, but I don't think that is your primary interest. They are basically just trying to get the water into the pipes and figure out what works and what does not work, what the flows are within the existing system, and what levels of flooding occur where in different storm events. As for drainage, I guess the question would be how much is the excess and what is the remainder? The current system cannot handle the rainfall, whether the test is a three-year storm or a ten-year one.

REESE: Thinking of water management on a metropolitan scale, does the system have to be completely reconfigured—not just the pumps and pipes but also the diagram of the system? Is there something usable in the diagram that exists?

WAGGONNER: Sure. But is it perfect? No. Of the limited figures I know for certain, one is the volume of water that flows into the London Avenue Canal versus the volume that flows into the Orleans Avenue

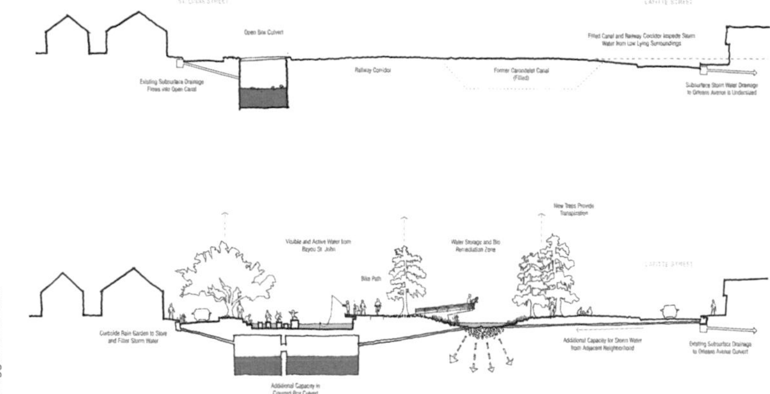

Waggonner & Ball.

Existing and proposed sections through the planned proposed Lafitte Greenway

Canal. The Orleans Avenue Canal has unused capacity, but you need a large culvert from the Broad Street pumping station to redirect the water from where it is currently going, where the system cannot handle it, to where it can. So, there is some degree of redesign required, but again, we must work with what we have. The main areas available to work with, in many cases, are the rights-of-way. The reason that the Westbank Expressway exists where it does is because there was a canal there, so it was a clear public right-of-way. The assemblage of properties is always difficult. The Lafitte Corridor is a possibility because of the assemblage of public land. The difficulty along the outfall canals is that much of the adjacent land is private. And, as you know, there is no public will. "You can't touch what is mine."

FONTENOT: Are there models that consider public-private investment and management that are of interest to you?

REESE: We appropriated an enormous amount of property when we built the interstate highway system. So why can't we just say, hey, it's not cars anymore, it's water. Why can't we transfer that knowledge to address the current problem?

WAGGONNER: We can, but it takes will. One can remain outside the system, but at some point someone inside needs to address the issue of shared benefit. That takes someone who can lead and someone who actually has a vision. The desire for change is one of those things that ebbs and flows. Sometimes there is no appetite for change, but I think there is still an appetite for change in this city.

FONTENOT: Whether the overlap of these systems was consciously planned or not is not clear, but the waterways and interstate highway in southeastern Louisiana coexist. I am thinking about the overlap of the Atchafalaya Basin floodplain and Interstate 10. If one analyzes the existing conditions, it is clear that these things can actually work together.

WAGGONNER: The railroad tracks and road system also coexist. But this level of thinking is rare in addressing issues of the city. All the signs are there telling us that we need to reorganize these systems, but America does not seem to have an appetite for that. We do not want to pay for it, nor do we want to mess with it in our own lifetime. In China, however, that is not a problem. If you want to do something, boom, you do it. That is not exactly an ideal situation, either, but we can learn something from it. I would really hate to think that at the end of the story this will be a place that could not think differently and just got tired, went back to sleep, decided that change was not really of value, and reverted. Down here, one can too easily resort to, "Oh just relax, let's have another drink."

That ties in to another point that I am not afraid to make, which is that one must be willing to compete. New Orleans has not really wanted to compete. We have lost ground for decades to other cities that were more willing. At this point, competition is no longer just local and national; it is global. We cannot ignore it or assume that our city's allure is enough. New Orleans has to accept that for some time it has been in decline. It needs to move forward and find its own niche. It still has a good situation; it does have a place in the world. It still has a very good location. But what are the people of New Orleans going to do to adapt to the difficulties of the site to make it safer and even more attractive? It is an intriguing design problem. It is also a social problem, and one of motivation.

REESE: Do you see any hopeful signs?

WAGGONNER: Yes, I think that the results of the last city election [February 6, 2010] and the degree of support for Mayor Mitch Landrieu look hopeful. I think it's hopeful that when I go into meetings with city officials they actually show some energy about a very difficult problem. They did set up a sustainability initiative. I heard about a young man who works for the mayor talking in a public meeting to a representative of the Sewerage and Water Board, who was explaining to him why they do things the way they do and why it would be impossible to do things differently. The young man apparently had had enough and said, "I've listened to you, and now it is time for you to listen to me. We will not stand down. We refuse to stop inquiring about alternative solutions simply because you claim they will not work." This resistance from officials is typical even when discussing something as simple as cisterns, let alone the big and serious issues. Often, these disputes are over things that we should not be fighting over. It is a brilliant strategy of avoidance to continue to discuss extraneous issues. A good client for an architect is someone who does not spend a lot of time talking about the part of the project that is good. Instead, it is much more helpful to point out the things that are not working quite right and spend time addressing those issues. New Orleans needs to do the same. Water is one of the most critical issues that we are forced to address. And one cannot uncouple water from soil. These are fundamental things that we need to take charge of, because this is our own little piece of the earth.

FONTENOT: Does the new mayor understand how important these issues are for the future development of the city?

WAGGONNER: I think so. Mitch does not own the issues the way Mary [Senator Landrieu, the mayor's sister] does. If you listen to her message on this, she is really good at it. However, she is speaking for the state, and she has to have a statewide perspective. Mitch came to Dutch Dialogues III, and the following Monday morning I heard him address these concerns in a way that showed me that he really understands their importance. He had listened well enough to put Charles Allen in place as director of coastal and environmental affairs. He is a team builder, which I think is great. I hope he understands the priority that we need to give water in the development of the physical city.

I know he understands the issues of safety, crime, and education. It is difficult to prioritize these social systems if one understands that the physical city is in disarray. Furthermore, he certainly understands that the repetitive loss ratios are not good for economic development. He comes from a background of cultural development, which prioritizes tourism. We want tourists, but we are not building the city for them. The city should be for the people who decide to live here.

FONTENOT: Historically, mayors have played an important role in facilitating large-scale public works projects, if for no other reason than to leave behind a legacy. Can the Lafitte Corridor project serve that role for this mayor?

WAGGONNER: I think it could. It is the first project the Landrieu administration has approved. Sometimes I feel that I am so consumed by these issues and so deep into this water world that I might be out of touch with the people who will listen. But the great thing is that people often come back to me with questions. Currently, I am interested in the saline balance, the ratio of brackish water to freshwater, the pH balance, in order to control mosquitoes. That is not something I was interested in five years ago. Recently, I was in Baton Rouge and I showed some slides of our ideas for the Lafitte Corridor, which is organized by water identities. One pH balance characterizes the water in the canal flowing from the end of Bayou St. John, where it is brackish, to pump station No. 2 and Broad Street. Another pH balance occurs in the water flowing from the back of the French Quarter, where it is fresh, and flows in the opposite direction toward station 2. Afterward, people came to me and said they had not thought about the benefits of the brackish water for mosquito control. The idea is not perfect, because our mosquitoes have adapted, but these ideas become obvious if one deals with such issues all the time. Another person asked if brackish water might eventually cause the same problem as the Mississippi River Gulf Outlet, where saltwater intrusion destroys vegetation and erodes the land around it. My response was that the bayou is brackish water, and it is not eroding the landscape. It is all about the degree of salinity. All of this is to say that people do engage these issues. We have found an audience.

REESE: We need a John McPhee.[6] We need somebody who can put these issues into a do-or-die perspective in the compelling way that McPhee did regarding the terror of the California landscape.

WAGGONNER: That is why I keep going back to the urgent issue of the outfall canals. Our ability to engage the Corps of Engineers and access federal money is not going to last forever. There is a legitimate claim against the government on behalf of the city and the destroyed neighborhoods alongside the canals where the breaches occurred. But the neighborhoods do not really know what to ask for. One way that those neighborhoods could be rebuilt is based on the water system, which could include creating a canal system that would be a public benefit. That would be one way to start to regenerate the Fillmore and Gentilly neighborhoods broadly, instead of incrementally, street by street, lot by lot, with more loss than gain. The Corps of Engineers does not want to do that, and they do not want to address internal water drainage. But the Southeast Louisiana Drainage program is a precedent. They might address it, if they had congressional authority.

It is quite an interesting proposition to consider an urban water system for a major city. But does the *Times-Picayune* report on this? Do they discuss the pressing issues that need to be addressed? No. Would it matter if the *Times-Picayune* wrote about this? The press and the public do not seem to understand the extent of our urban infrastructure problems. That is why I say, again half-jokingly, that the word *infrastructure* is wrong. There must be something deadly about that word, because everyone avoids it. We need to find a new word, maybe *networks*. We can learn a lot from others around the world, if we listen. The Italians define infrastructure as something that provides for people without having to provide income. We can improve our messaging, but we need visionary vocabulary. These hidden, forgotten water systems that surround us, that permit our delta settlement, can be our greatest inspiration.

6 John McPhee, *The Control of Nature* (New York: Farrar, Straus, and Giroux, 1989).

MAPPING THE AFTERMATH AND CHARTING NEW STRATEGIES

ANTHONY FONTENOT
with JAKOB ROSENZWEIG

The maps described in this essay were created between 2005 and 2010 and represent a small selection from a larger body of work produced for three different projects: "Exposing New Orleans" (2005), "New Orleans: The Emergence of a New Kind of City" (2008), and "Mississippi River Delta Study: Reviving the Dynamics of the Landscape" (2010–present). In February 2006, the "Exposing New Orleans" (ENO) maps were featured in the exhibition "Newer Orleans: A Shared Space," at the Netherlands Architecture Institute in Rotterdam, accompanied by a symposium organized by the institute, the Tulane University School of Architecture and *Artforum*. They were exhibited again for a symposium and workshop, also titled "Exposing New Orleans," held at Princeton University on March 4, 2006, organized by the author and cosponsored by the Princeton University School of Architecture and the Woodrow Wilson School of Public and International Affairs,[1] timed to coincide with Columbia University's March 3 symposium "Regrounding New Orleans," organized by Carol Reese and Joan Ockman. Thirty-six of the ENO maps were featured in "Resilient Foundations: The Gulf Coast after Katrina," in the Tenth International Architecture Biennale in Venice in 2006. In September 2007, the maps were published in *Neutra*, an architectural journal based in Seville. The work was also featured in a production by ArtSpot Productions and Mondo Bizarro, in collaboration with the Gulf Restoration Network and New Orleans City Park, in their presentation of *Loup Garou*, an "environmental performance" that used the ENO maps as part of a visual installation in their investigation of the relationship between land and culture in Louisiana, which opened October 8, 2009.

The "Exposing New Orleans" project was launched in September 2005, less than a month after Hurricane Katrina hit the city and shortly after I arrived at Princeton University to begin my Ph.D. program. I was joined there by Jakob Rosenzweig and Anne Schmidt, former students of mine

1 Stanley Katz, director of the Center for Arts and Cultural Policy Studies, helped secure support from the latter school.

at Tulane.[2] In the months following the catastrophe, while there was a plethora of discussions about architecture, planning, and the future of New Orleans in the press, there was little debate about the larger systemic issues relating to infrastructure, industry, and ecology that largely controlled the fate of the region. The ENO project attempted to expand the discussion of reconstruction to include the city's relationship to its greater infrastructural and ecological context. To accomplish this, two scales, the city scale and the regional scale, were used to frame the area of study. Positioning New Orleans within the larger context of the delta provided a method of comparison useful for investigating not only the relationship between the city and the region but also the various man-made and natural systems at work at both scales.[3] For example, as we documented the way the extensive network of flood-control infrastructure developed throughout the twentieth century engaged environmental processes at the regional scale, we observed how it operated differently at the city scale.

The ENO maps served as a means of studying the various individual layers, or issues, of the landscape related to infrastructure, industry, geology, urban fabric, demographics, and the social and economic patterns of the region. Yet the main goal of the project was to "expose" and examine the relationships between the various layers and the complex issues arising from their interconnections, which reveal the unique relationships between policy and governance, economy and industry, and culture and landscape. We were also interested in studying the symbiotic relationship between urban and natural processes, exemplified by the symbiosis between New Orleans and the delta region, one of the most peculiar urban and infrastructure situations found anywhere. The original abstract for the "Exposing New Orleans" exhibition expounded on this condition:

> New Orleans and its swampy environs constitute one of the most distinctive cultural, geographic, ecological, and urban sites in the world. Surrounded by lakes, rivers, and wetlands, the city is suspended within a tangled web of extreme man-made and natural conditions. This specificity has inspired highly creative engineering, urban, and architectural responses as well as caused unimaginable difficulties. The peculiar relationship that the city formed with its environment over time moved from working with the successive layers of existing natural processes of a shifting landscape to an act of building as imposition. The natural levees that formed along the river were eventually built upon and fixed, creating a perception of "stability" while producing a

2 Tulane University, like most of New Orleans, remained closed following the storm. Jakob Rosenzweig transferred to Princeton, and Anne Schmidt left her studies in Germany to join our effort to respond to what was happening in New Orleans. Stan Allen, who was then dean of the Princeton's School of Architecture, and Mario Gandelsonas, director of the Center for Architecture, Urbanism, and Infrastructure, offered us great support.

3 For a discussion of planning at various scales, see the interview with Robert Tannen in Part VIII of this volume.

Topographic Elevation
Most of Greater New Orleans is below sea level (dark blue). Only the natural high ground, created by the river and its distributaries, and the levees and landfills, built by man, are above sea level (light green to yellow).

Post-Katrina Flooding
After the failures of federally built levees during Hurricanes Katrina and Rita, 80 percent of Orleans Parish was flooded.

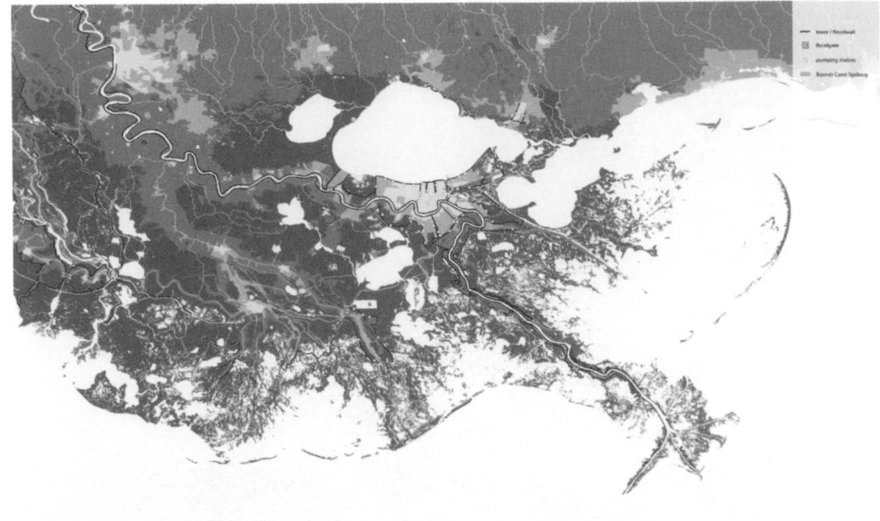

Flood-Control Infrastructure of Southeastern Louisiana
Levees, floodwalls, floodgates, locks, pumping stations, spillways, floodways, and diversions constitute the extensive U.S. Army Corps of Engineering flood-control project that currently dominates the delta region of southeastern Louisiana.

Flood-Control Infrastructure of New Orleans
Like the regional delta, the city of New Orleans is dependent on an extensive network of flood-control systems.

highly tenuous condition. Developments of the eighteenth and nineteenth centuries can be seen as a series of infrastructure interventions provoked by the city's precarious connection to its specific environment; today, however, there is an urgent need to reevaluate, if not reinvent, the relationship between infrastructure, the city, and the larger ecological context in the 21st century. The multiple layers, which constitute a bewildering engineering of the landscape, produce a virtual life support system for the city, on the one hand, while threatening its very existence, on the other. Like a patient dependent on a machine, the city's survival and sustainability depend on the constant maintenance and manipulation of complex mechanical and natural systems.

In pursuing our study, we consciously strove to develop visual representation techniques that could illustrate the complex issues in a way that made them accessible to the general public as well as the scientific community. Although ENO was originally meant to document the rapidly changing conditions of New Orleans and its environs in the aftermath of Hurricane Katrina, the project evolved into an attempt to understand the catastrophic environmental transformations caused by regionally engineered systems, such as the channeling of the Mississippi River, or the international petrochemical industry, while investigating solutions for the long-term viability of New Orleans and the Mississippi River Delta.

It should be noted that in 2005, when the project was being developed, the use of geographic information system (GIS) technology was relatively new, particularly in schools of architecture.[4] In the first few months following Katrina, national and local newspapers, including the *Times-Picayune,* took regular inventories of the city, primarily based on FEMA data and documented their findings in the form of maps, which became an important medium for communicating complex ideas to the general public. In many ways, ENO was engaging with and reacting to post-Katrina data presentation and the maps that had become the new vernacular for describing the ongoing transformations of the city, while "learning from the newspapers" a certain method of collecting and processing public information that circulated in the press. In fact, in some cases we reproduced maps (and their data sources) that we found in newspapers and then redesigned and made graphically consistent to help construct a particular argument.

Three years after the storm, New Orleans remained largely devastated and its future was uncertain. Relying on the 2008 census data, Jakob, Anne and I developed a series of new maps to describe the radically altered urban situation, accompanied by a text, and published it in the spring 2009 issue of *Pidgin*, the journal of Princeton's School of

4 Tsering Wangyal Shawa, a librarian at the Princeton Digital Map and Geospatial Information Center, a.k.a. the maps library, was instrumental in introducing us to GIS and the various forms of data on New Orleans and the region generated by state and federal agencies such as FEMA, NOAA, MMS (now called GOMR), and USGS.

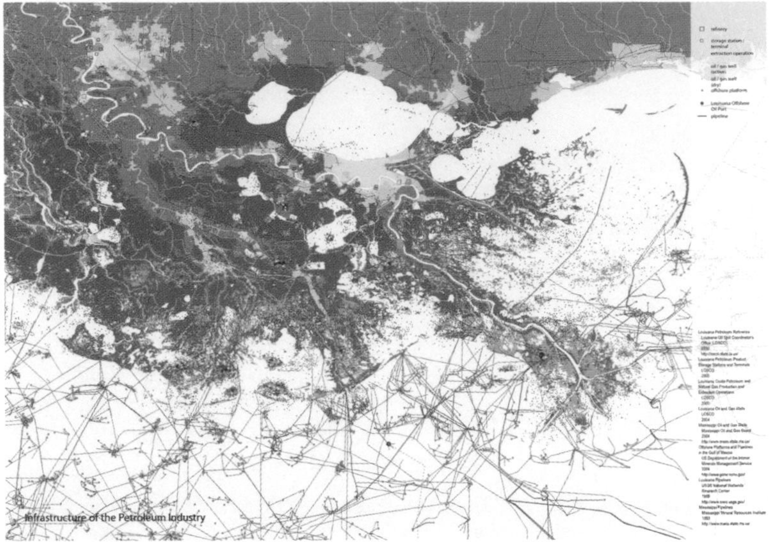

Infrastructure of the Petroleum Industry
The petroleum industry has a broad network of its own: seventeen refineries, hundreds of storage terminals, tens of thousands of wells and platforms, and nearly one hundred thousand miles of pipeline.

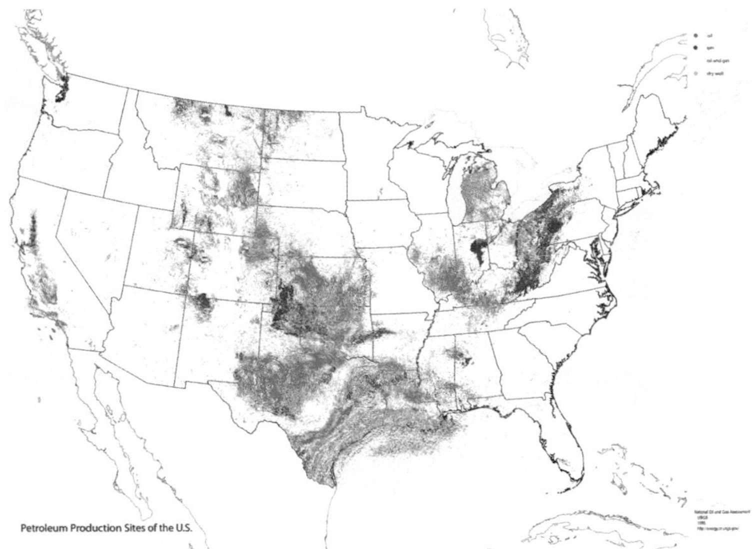

Petroleum Production Sites in the U.S.
The federal offshore oil extraction in the Gulf of Mexico, which begins three miles offshore from each state's coast, accounts for 23 percent of total U.S. crude oil extraction. More than 40 percent of the United States' petroleum refining capacity is located along the Gulf Coast.

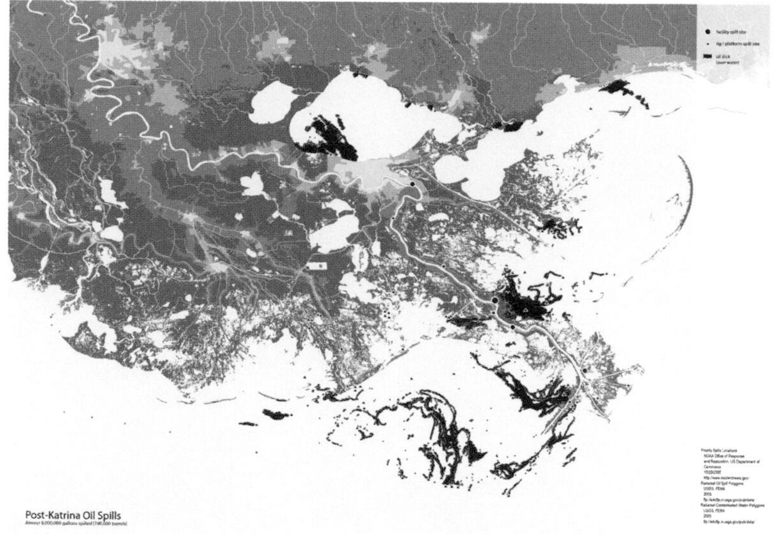

Post-Katrina Oil Spills
Nearly 8 million gallons of oil were spilled in the wake of Hurricanes Katrina and Rita.

Man-made Canals
Thousands of miles of canals and ditches dug by agriculture and industry have carved up the wetlands of the Mississippi River Delta, altering its natural hydrology and exacerbating saltwater intrusion, which devastates a diverse range of fragile wetland ecologies.

Architecture, as "New Orleans: The Emergence of a New Kind of City." The essay described the new demographic configurations of the city and the status of public institutions, especially the crucial changes in education, characterized by a massive move away from public schooling toward privatization in the form of charter schools. Similar neoliberal policies seemed to be guiding decisions about public housing: 4,000 units were demolished and most of the large-scale public housing projects in New Orleans were slated for destruction, to be replaced by "mixed income" developments. Indeed, the thesis outlined by Naomi Klein in *The Shock Doctrine* (2007) appeared to be manifesting itself in New Orleans.[5] A new type of cultural landscape was emerging, defined by a radical shift in real estate values according to the specific topography of neighborhoods. Prices in the lower-lying areas of the city had plummeted and those on higher ground were rapidly soaring. In addition, the data revealed that the long-term consequences of the storm were having a devastating effect on not only the physical but also the psychological progress of the city. Three years after Katrina, the rate of homelessness and suicide in New Orleans had doubled.

Nevertheless, from the scale of the city, with its list of formidable problems, to the scale of the region, with its own set of issues related to a compromised deltaic system, the destruction of New Orleans and the surrounding areas presented a historic opportunity to rebuild in a way that embraced the cultural history and character of the place while developing a progressive vision for the twenty-first century. But reconsidering the region meant addressing the legacy of the extensive network of flood-control infrastructure put into place by the U.S. Army Corps of Engineers after the flood of 1927.[6] This system, designed to contain the Mississippi River and divert excessive flows, severed the river from its distributaries and cut off the seasonal floods that had been the essential means of delivering water and sediment to the delta. Consequently, since the 1930s Louisiana had lost approximately 1,880 square miles of coastal wetlands.

As early as the 1970s, the vulnerability of coastal habitats became the subject of public concern, and legislators and voters began to call for wetland protection with passages of laws such as the Estuary Protection Act in 1970 and the Coastal Zone Management Act in 1972. Since 1990, numerous other plans have been developed to address the widespread problem of coastal erosion.[7]

---

5 See "Disaster Apartheid: A World of Green Zones and Red Zones," the excerpt from Naomi Klein's *The Shock Doctrine: The Rise of Disaster Capitalism* (New York: Picador 2007) in Part I of this volume.

6 The work was authorized by the Mississippi River Commission, which had been established by an Act of Congress on June 28, 1879, as the central organization responsible for conducting surveys and investigations, developing plans to improve the river channel, protect the banks, improve navigation, prevent flooding, and, perhaps most importantly, to promote commerce.

7 These include the Coastal Wetlands Planning, Protection and Restoration Act passed by Congress in 1990, the 1993 Restoration Plan, Coast 2050, Louisiana Coastal Area Comprehensive Plan, and 2007 Coastal Master Plan. The most recent Coastal Master Plan for Louisiana, led by the Coastal Protection and Restoration Authority,, was unanimously approved by the legislature on May 22, 2012.

Median Household Income in New Orleans, 2000
Floodwaters (shown in diagonal hatch) disproportionately affected the poorer areas of the city (shown in white and light gray).

Orleans Parish Schools, 2008
Due to the sudden decrease in the city's population following Hurricane Katrina, many public schools were closed indefinitely and their student populations consolidated into schools that were not vitally damaged by the flood. Charter schools were also introduced.

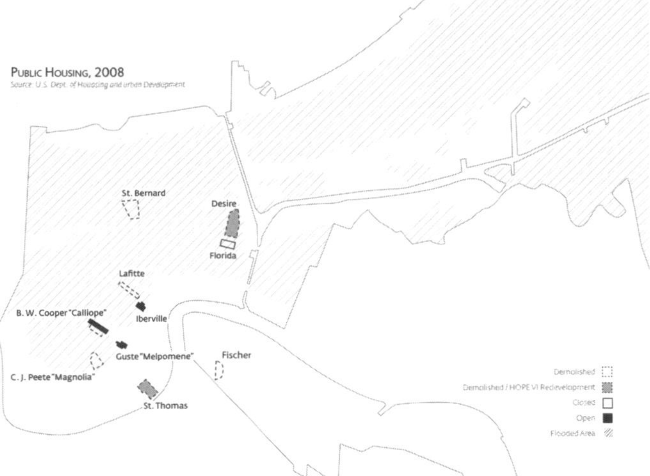

Public Housing, 2008
Following Hurricane Katrina, more than 4,000 public housing units were demolished in New Orleans. Public housing was already transitioning from prewar block-style buildings to subsidized single-family units when Katrina hit. Taking advantage of serendipity, the government speeded up the transformation process, knocking down five of New Orleans's ten historic housing projects within three years of the storm.

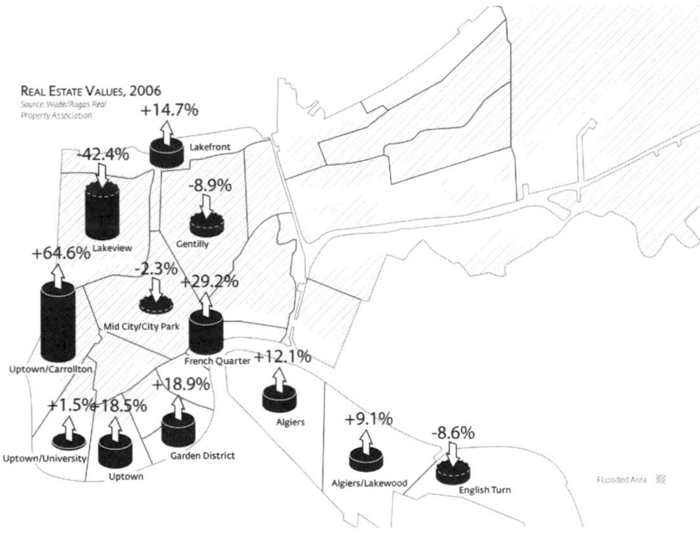

Real Estate Values, 2006
Perhaps because of lost faith in the federal levee system, real estate values changed in the aftermath of Katrina to reflect neighborhoods' vulnerability to flooding.

Given that wetlands have played a vital role in protecting New Orleans and the region from storm surge and hurricane damage, their restoration should be seen as a priority of post-Katrina reconstruction. Yet too many discussions on rebuilding have been conducted exclusively within their respective fields of study. Without an organizational framework for integrating the various disciplines and seeing how their concerns play out at various scales, which is necessary to developing a more comprehensive approach, debates on the reconstruction of the city have mostly been isolated from discussions about the restoration of the wetlands.

In 2010, we had an opportunity to address some of the larger regional-scale issues when we were invited to join Guy Nordenson and Catherine Seavitt, as well as Stephen Cassell and Adam Yarinsky of the Architecture Research Office, and the LSU Coastal Sustainability Studio, to develop a "master plan" for alleviating land loss in coastal Louisiana.[8] Developed in consultation and collaboration with some of the key scientists working on Louisiana coastal restoration, including Dr. Robert Twilley[9] and Dr. Clinton Willson,[10] the project proposed five major freshwater diversions (one extant and four new) placed throughout the delta. These five territories of "growth," based on a projected 50 to 100 years of water and sediment movement and its subsequent land formation, were intended to address the widespread crisis of land loss and rejuvenate the areas over time. The project was presented in the exhibition "The Mississippi Delta: Constructing with Water," featured in "Workshopping: An American Model of Architectural Practice" in the U.S. Pavilion at the 12th International Architecture Biennale in Venice in 2010.

During the same period, Jakob Rosenzweig and I developed an alternative proposal, "Mississippi River Delta Study: Reviving the Dynamics of the Landscape," which was both an outgrowth of and reaction to "Constructing with Water" and served as a means of critiquing what we felt were some of the latter project's shortcomings. We largely agreed with the basic concepts put forth in the group proposal, particularly the idea of using natural forces—such as water—as a means of construction, and appreciated that the proposal had brought together architects, landscape architects, engineers, and coastal scientists to address some of the complex environmental issues affecting the region. Our primary criticism was that the final outcome projected over the next 50 to 100

---

8 See Emily Abruzzo, ed., *Workbook: The Official Catalog for Workshopping: An American Model for Architectural Practice* (Princeton, NJ: Princeton Architecture Press, 2010).

9 Robert R. Twilley's research focuses on ecosystem ecology, management practices, and biogeochemistry of coastal wetlands in the Gulf of Mexico. His publications include *Coastal and Marine Ecosystems and Global Climate Change* (a report he coauthored for the Pew Center for Global Climate Change in 2002), *Confronting Climate Change in the Gulf Coast Region: Prospects for Sustaining Our Ecological Heritage* (2001), and *The Biogeochemistry of Gulf of Mexico Estuaries* (as coeditor, 1999).

10 Clinton Willson, Ph.D., P.E., director of Engineering Design and Innovation at the Water Institute of the Gulf, is an expert in physical modeling systems that test river management proposals.

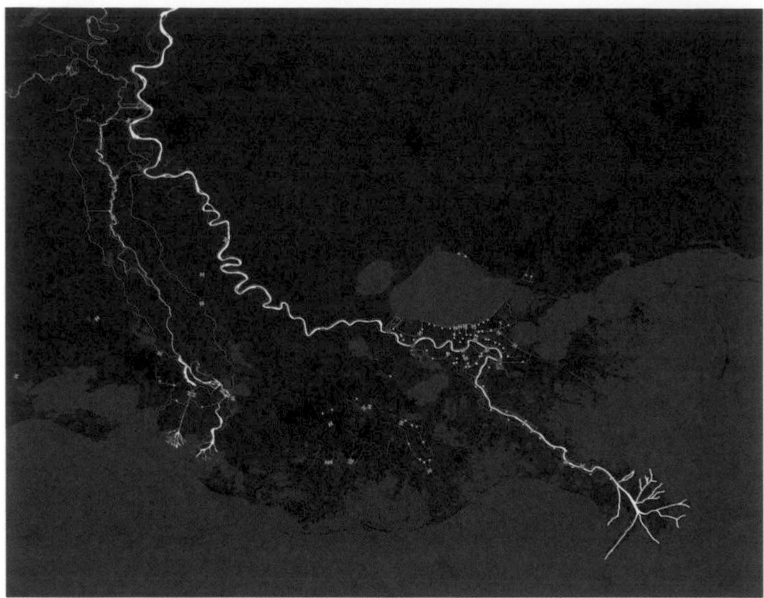

Twentieth-century Infrastructure
This map shows the full extent of infrastructure from the past century that is currently employed in the delta: levees (red), floodgates (green), bifurcations and diversions (pink), and pumping stations (yellow).

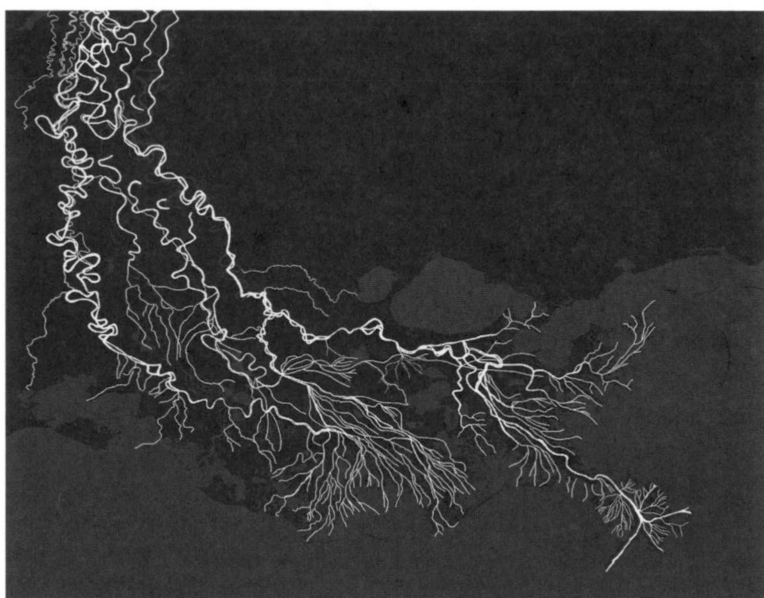

Historical Distributaries of the Mississippi River Delta
This map gives a composite picture of all the historical distributaries of the lower Mississippi River; the Mississippi River Delta was built from the freshwater and sediments that these distributaries carried. Unfortunately, human engineering cut off the large majority of these distributaries, which then dried up. Only two remain today: the Mississippi River itself and the Atchafalaya River.

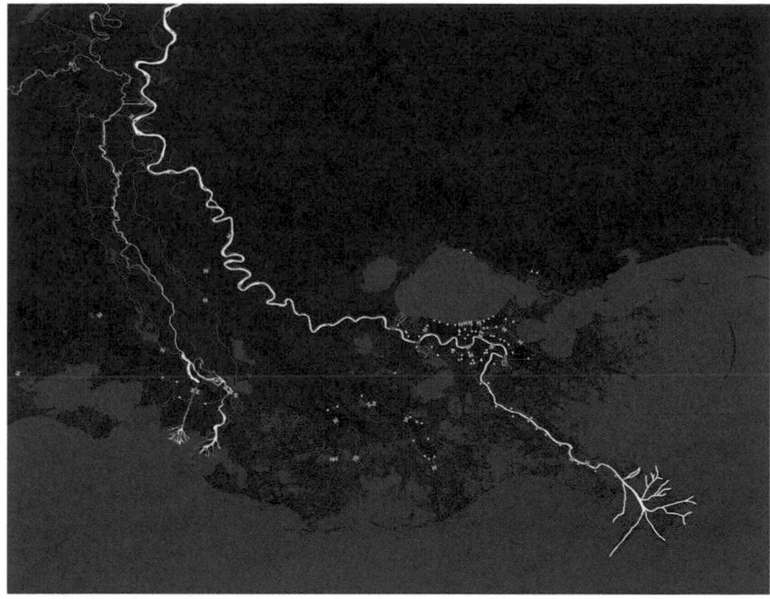

Coastal Land Loss, 1932–1990
Since the 1930s, Louisiana has lost 1,829 square miles of land (shown in fuchsia). Between 1990 and 2001, the wetland loss rate was approximately twenty-five square miles per year. Wetland loss increases year after year.

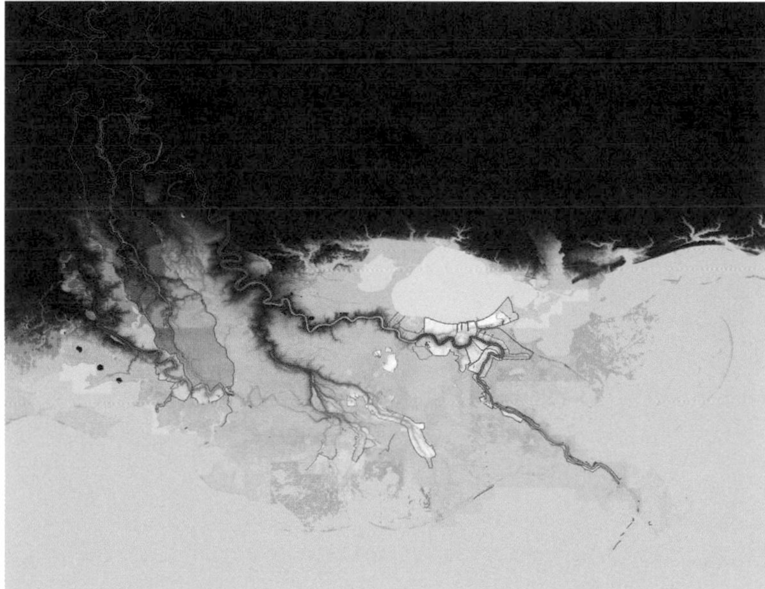

Present-day Elevation of the Delta
This map depicts the present-day elevation of the delta on a spectrum from black to white, with the twentieth century's levees shown in red. Most of the delta is just above sea level (indicated by gray land slightly darker than the gray of the waters of the Gulf); the natural levees left behind by the historical distributaries (indicated in darker grays and blacks) rise above the delta plain. A few urban areas, such as New Orleans and Golden Meadow, have subsided to elevations below sea level (indicated in white).

years did not adequately address the larger territory of the delta as a living system. It lacked both a comprehensive vision and a site-specific approach.

In "Reviving the Dynamics of the Landscape," in place of the centralized model put forth in "Constructing with Water," with its five massive diversions, we proposed a decentralized model consisting of twenty-five diversions that reused five existing infrastructure projects (the Old River Control Structure, Morganza Spillway, Bonnet Carré Spillway, Davis Pond, and Caernarvon freshwater diversions) and added twenty new diversions on the river to divert freshwater and sediment. This plan worked with the specific conditions found in the various basins of the delta, including the Atchafalaya, Terrebonne, Lafourche, Barataria, and Pontchartrain, each with its own watershed and specific ecologies. Moreover, with its network of diversions strategically dispersed throughout the region, the decentralized approach attempted to advance a paradigm shift from "flood control" to "controlled flooding" that avoided urban areas and territories of dense populations.

The later proposal also differed from the former in that it developed a method for moving water along the paths of historical distributaries, where land formations had remained largely intact since the distributaries had been severed in the early twentieth century. Relying on Harold N. Fisk's 1944 report *Geological Investigation of the Alluvial Valley of the Lower Mississippi River*, particularly his extraordinary map "Stream Courses,"[11] the project proposed to reinstate key historical distributaries, including the bayous Lafourche and Fordoche. Furthermore, along with our flood model we proposed a new form of governance that made local and federal agencies jointly responsible for decisions about the control and use of the diversions, including the amount of water and sediment to be moved throughout the year. This model was intended to help dilute the decision-making power of the U.S. Army Corps of Engineers and the state by allowing local agencies with their specific knowledge and concerns to play a vital role in the overall operation of the program.

From the late nineteenth century to the present, the Mississippi River and its delta have been subjected to a long list of extraordinary infrastructure interventions mandated by the U.S. Congress, including the opening of the mouth of the Mississippi River by the implementation of the South Pass jetties (1875–1879) by James Buchanan Eads and the channeling of the river itself.[12] In addition, the endless numbers of canals created by the oil and gas industry have devastated the wetlands by

11 See "Stream Courses," plate 15, sheet 4, in Harold N. Fisk, *Geological Investigation of the Alluvial Valley of the Lower Mississippi River* (Vicksburg, MS: M.R.C. print, 1945).

12 For a history of environmental manipulation of the Mississippi River Delta, see Craig E. Colton, ed., *Transforming New Orleans and Its Environs: Centuries of Change* (Pittsburgh, PA: University of Pittsburgh Press, 2000). For a review of the history of flood-control infrastructure and its relationship to politics, see John M. Barry, *Rising Tide: The Great Mississippi Flood of 1927 and How It Changed America* (New York: Simon & Schuster, 1997).

advancing saltwater intrusion.[13] A critical examination of this history of environmental manipulation would undoubtedly raise questions about allowing such important decisions on managing the "mechanics of the landscape" to remain in the hands of federal and state agencies, which are seldom held accountable for them afterward, whether or not they prove beneficial (or devastating) to the Louisiana's citizens.

The results of these decisions have left their indelible mark on contemporary life in coastal Louisiana. The tenuous conditions of the delta landscape and its people have been studiously documented by the Louisiana photographer and filmmaker Monique Verdin.[14] In the 2011 exhibition "Disappearing Landscapes: The American Delta in Distress," held at the Mesa College Art Gallery in San Diego, the ENO maps were exhibited with Verdin's photographs to show how the various issues highlighted in the maps manifested themselves in scenes of everyday life in the delta. The photographs present a visual catalog of communities living among oak trees dying from saltwater intrusion; networks of pipelines; flooded territories; depleted cypress forests and other signs of the endangered environmental and cultural landscapes of southern Louisiana.

If by "reconstruction" we mean advancing a process of rebuilding that brings what has been damaged or destroyed back to a healthy condition, then the urban, infrastructural, and industrial systems of the region should be reconsidered in terms of their ability to revive the *dynamics of the landscape* and contribute to a sustainable environment. Since Katrina, the work of numerous nonprofit organizations—such as the Louisiana Bucket Brigade, which monitors toxins and their effects on communities across Louisiana—has played an important role in gathering data on the oil and gas industries while examining their impact on the larger environment. For far too long the Louisiana Coast has been firmly established as ground zero for the export of fossil fuels. From the toxic landscapes of "Cancer Alley" to the dead zone in the Gulf of Mexico, which measured about 6,765 square miles in 2011,[15] to the *Deepwater Horizon* oil spill and its apocalyptic ecological devastation that since

13 The historic lawsuit recently filed by John M. Barry, former vice president of the Southeast Louisiana Flood Protection Authority-East, seeks billions of dollars in damages for the massive destruction caused by the canals, pipelines, and wells built by oil and gas companies over the course of generations in coastal Louisiana. See Jeff Adelson, "Levee Board's Suit Could Be Landmark Case," *The Advocate*, August 4, 2013.

14 Verdin's photographs have been exhibited nationally and internationally, and are included in *Ten Wells, The Good Pirates of the Forgotten Bayous* (New Haven, CT: Yale University Press, 2008) and Nonesuch Records' Habitat for Humanity benefit album *Our New Orleans* (2005). *My Louisiana Love* (2012) is Verdin's first documentary film; it investigates the indigenous Houma nation and their complex relationship to environment, economics, culture, climate, and industry in the Mississippi River Delta.

15 The "dead zone," an amorphous area in the Gulf of Mexico where "nothing can live," was inadvertently created by a surplus of nitrate-heavy fertilizer runoff produced by agricultural operations along the Mississippi River. See the NOAA report "Dead Zone: Hypoxia in the Gulf of Mexico," 2009, noaanews.noaa.gov.

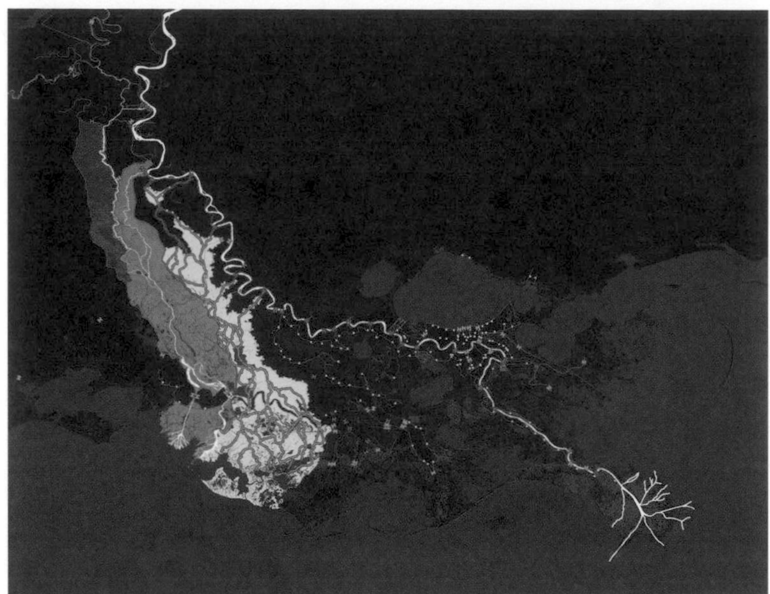

Delta Proposal, Part 3: Terrebonne
This map represents our proposed interventions for Terrebonne Basin, which includes five freshwater and sediment diversions along the Mississippi River (pink). These five diversions allow water to move southward through the basin via the Terrebonne Floodway (yellow), where they eventually combine to form a network of braided streams (blue).

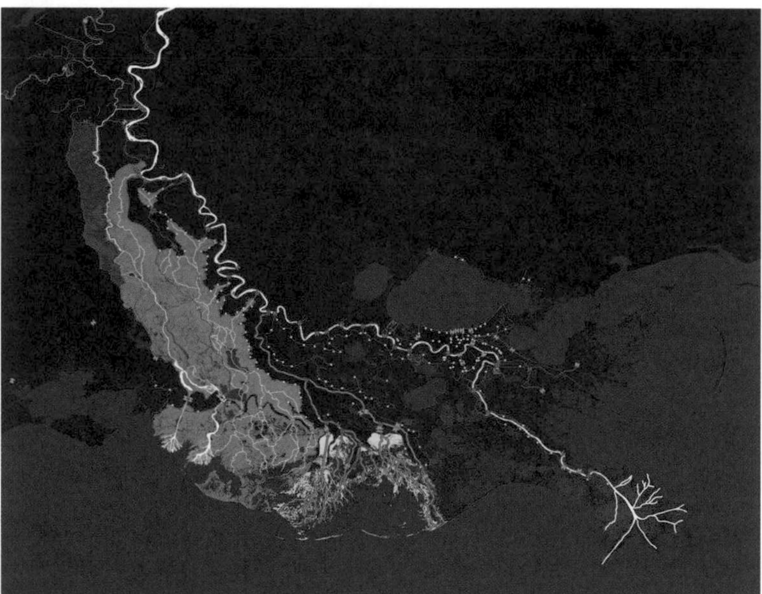

Delta Proposal, Part 4: Lafourche
Bayou Lafourche was a major distributary in the delta for thousands of years until, in 1903, it was cut off from the Mississippi River by a dam constructed at its head in the town of Donaldsonville. In our proposal, this dam is removed and the bayou is restored by creating a mechanical bifurcation at the bayou's head on the Mississippi River (pink) and another bifurcation at Thibodaux (pink). From Thibodaux, two bayous extend toward the coast, and along their paths six diversions (pink) allow them to supply a network of distributaries (blue) carrying freshwater and sediment into wetlands that desperately need replenishment (yellow).

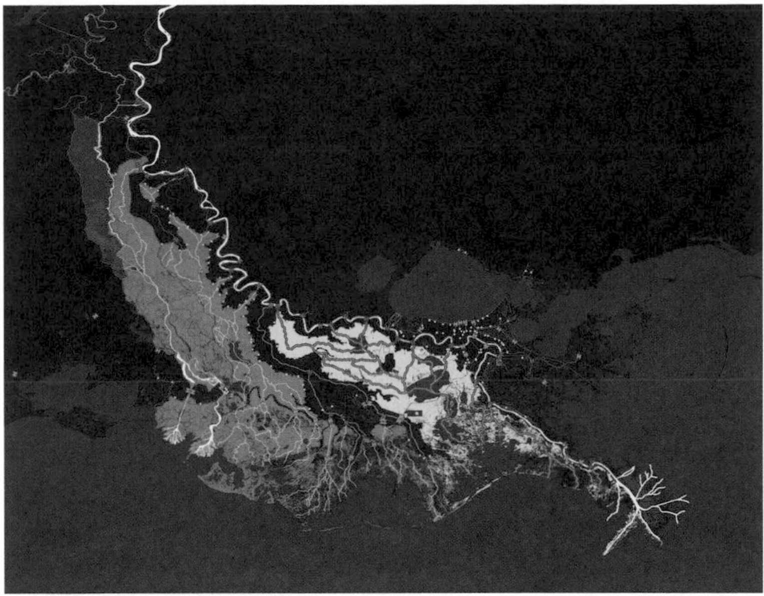

Delta Proposal, Part 5: Barataria
Unlike most of the other proposals on the table that rely solely on the existing Davis Pond Freshwater Diversion Project (2001) to sustain the entire Barataria Basin, our proposal revitalizes the basin with a thorough network of distributaries (blue) by providing nine diversions (pink) along the length of the Mississippi River.

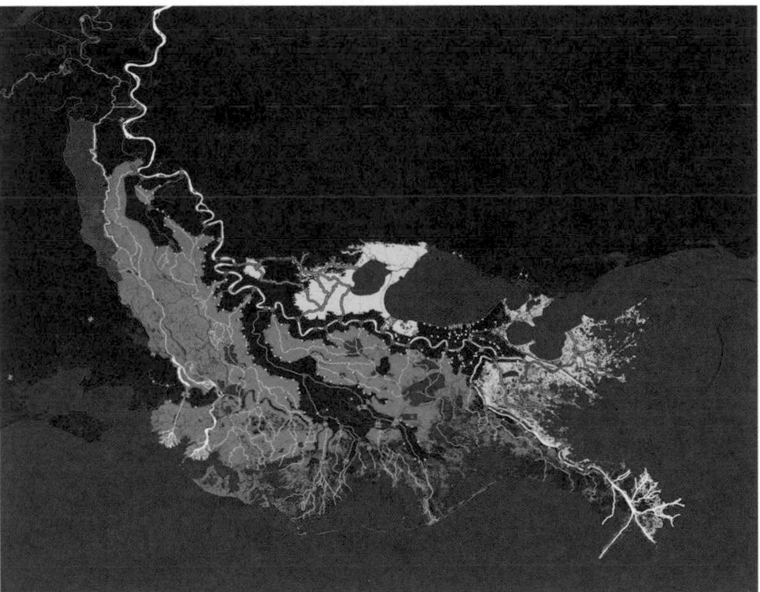

Delta Proposal, Part 6: Pontchartrain
For this basin we employ two existing diversions, the Caernarvon Freshwater Diversion Project (1991) and the Bonnet Carré Spillway (1931) and add four more diversions and one bifurcation, at Poydras. The diversions work together to supply freshwater and sediment to wetlands upriver and downriver from New Orleans, and the bifurcation at Poydras helps deliver a much needed concentration of sediment into the starving wetlands of Chandeleur Sound.

April 2010 has plagued the coast,[16] life in the Mississippi River Delta has become increasingly uncertain.

The situation is grim, but the tireless work of many extraordinary individuals and organizations in combination with the growing number of nonprofits that have recently been established offer hope for rebuilding a more resilient city. But unless the relationship between politics and industry is reformed, it is difficult to imagine how these efforts alone will be able to fulfill the promise of a sustainable reconstruction of the region.

The work presented in the three projects described in this essay is dedicated to the memory of my cousin and lifelong friend, the actor and activist Mark Sanford Krasnoff, who took his own life on September 16, 2006, approximately one year after Hurricane Katrina. In an interview published in November 2005, about a month after New Orleans was submerged in floodwaters and when emotions were still running high, he reflected on the larger social and political situation:

> Look, Louisiana is the same as any exploited oil-rich country—like a Nigeria or Venezuela. For generations the big oil and gas companies have pumped billions out of our bayous and offshore waters, and all we get back is coastal erosion, pollution, cancer, and poverty. And now bloated bodies and dead towns.
>
> People in the rest of America need to understand there are no "natural" disasters in Louisiana. This is one of the richest lands in the world—everything from sugar and crawfish to oil and sulfur—but we're neck-to-neck with Mississippi as the poorest state. Sure, Washington builds impressive levees to safeguard river commerce and the shipping industry, but do you honestly think they give a shit about blacks, Indians, and coonasses [pejorative for Cajuns]? Poor people's levees, if they even existed, were about as good as our schools [among the worst in the nation]. Katrina just followed the outlines of inequality.[17]

For many, it appears that not only is the future of the wetlands and New Orleans at stake but so is the democratic activist tradition of transforming politics to address pressing concerns of citizens. If the process of reconstruction is to serve as a means of ushering in progressive change, it must continue to engender new ways of thinking about infrastructure, urban processes, and ecology at the city and regional scale, while exploring the role of the state and its relationship to innovative forms of sustainable energy, economy, and industry.

16 For an account of the BP oil spill and its environmental impact on the delta, see Rowan Jacobsen, *Shadows on the Gulf: A Journey through Our Last Great Wetland* (New York: Bloomsbury USA, 2011).

17 The interview was published in an essay by Mike Davis and Anthony Fontenot, "Hurricane Gumbo," *The Nation*, November 7, 2005.

PROJECTS
FLOOD MITIGATION AND INFRASTRUCTURE

At the end of the day, Katrina caused a flood. We all know that what is often termed a "natural" disaster was, in fact, a human one, the result of a combination of incompetence, indifference, and hubris. In this final part, we've included several propositions that address the issue of an elaborated hydraulics. These range in scale from regional propositions to manage the Mississippi's flows, to ideas for reconceptualizing the levees as transportation and housing armatures, to remaking houses and highways to facilitate escape and evacuation when the waters break through. These are not Canute-like follies, but serious proposals predicated on our insistence that New Orleans can and must endure.

THE BIG LEAK

Winner of the 2010 Delta Competition
SCHOOL OF ARCHITECTURE
University of Virginia, Charlottesville

Instructor: Jorg Sieweke
Designer: David Wooden

New Orleans's existing drainage network removes stormwater as quickly as possible, pumping it out of the city before it has had a chance to infiltrate and replenish the water table. Conversely, as much as half of the city's clean water may be leaking back into the water table from distribution pipes. This dichotomy inspired the *Big Leak* project, which addresses New Orleans's land subsidence crisis. The proposal calls for surface canals to recharge the city's water table, stopping or reducing the rate of land subsidence through an adaptable stormwater conveyance system. This solution is scalable to the entire city, but the proposal specifically considers the area along the Orleans Outfall Canal, with the Lakeview neighborhood to the west and City Park to the east.

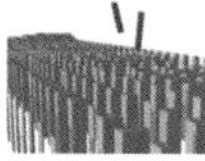

THE BIG LEAK: Orleans Outfall Canal Edge

The edge of the Orleans Outfall Canal creates a continuum of social space with City Park. The abstract models also provided insight into the construction of the ground. Paving systems extend into the ground to provide columnar support and reduce soil compaction.

EXISTING Section 1

EXISTING Section 2

Culverts beneath streets and medians convey storm water from the Lakeview neighborhood.

EXISTING Section 3

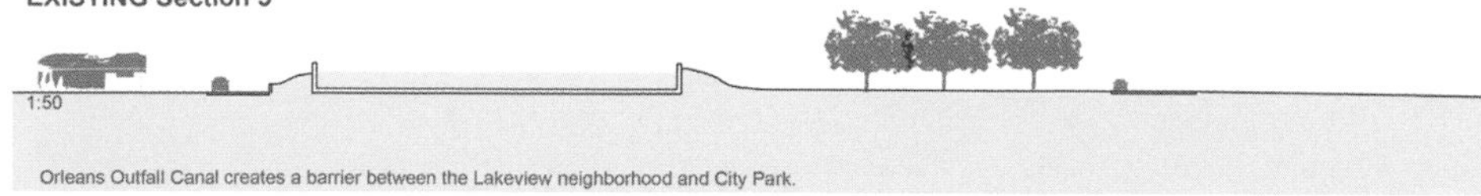

Orleans Outfall Canal creates a barrier between the Lakeview neighborhood and City Park.

THE BIG LEAK: Existing System

NOLA's current stormwater conveyance system. Stormwater flows into below grade culverts and canals. It is then pumped up, into the above grade Orleans Outfall Canal.

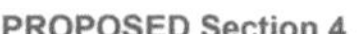

PROPOSED Section 4

1:300
Section 5
Section 6

PROPOSED Section 5

1:50

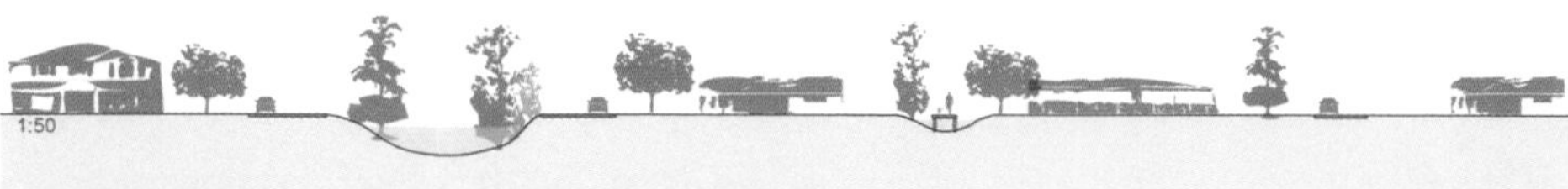

The proposed system converts road medians and alleys into exfiltrating surface canals.

PROPOSED Section 6

1:50

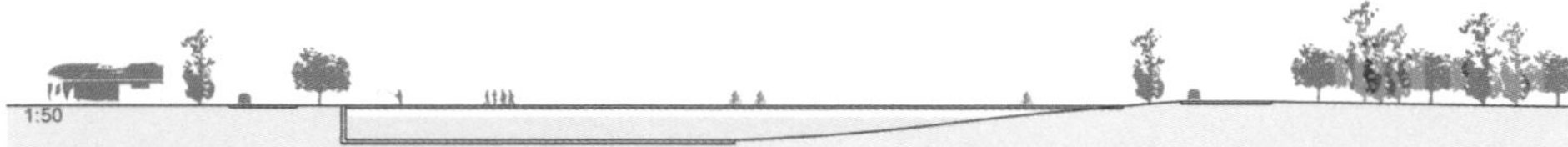

The Orleans Outfall Canal is converted to an expanded surface canal, removing the barrier to City Park, increasing biodiversity and providing a social amenity.

THE BIG LEAK: Proposed System

These sections depict the proposed stormwater conveyance system. Stormwater flows into surface canals. It then flows into the Orleans Outfall Canal as an expanded, surface canal rather than walled, above grade system.

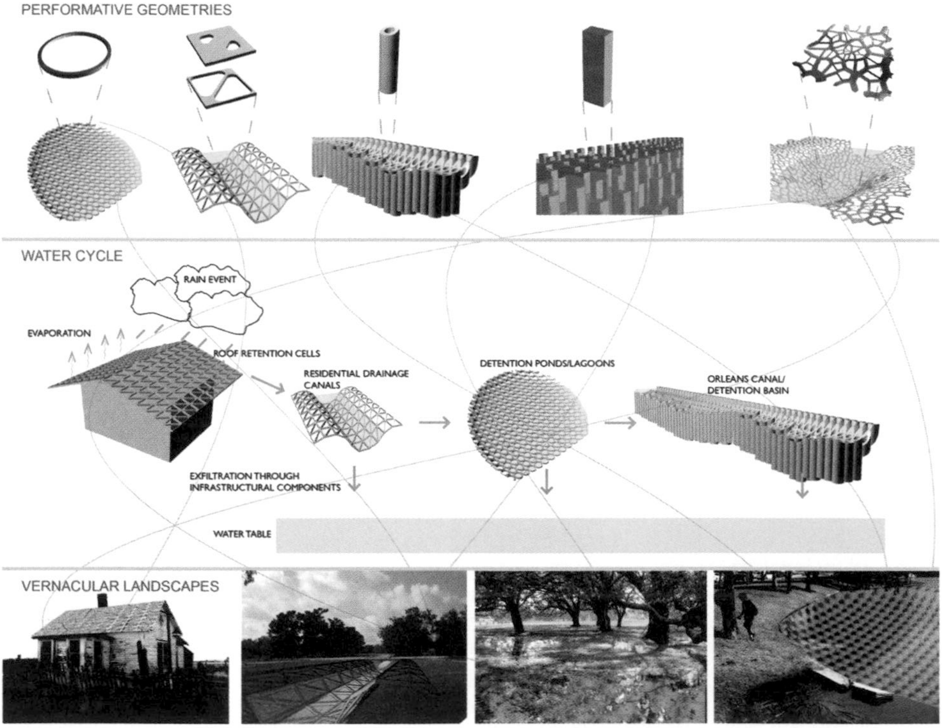
PERFORMATIVE GEOMETRIES
WATER CYCLE
RAIN EVENT
EVAPORATION
ROOF RETENTION CELLS
RESIDENTIAL DRAINAGE CANALS
DETENTION PONDS/LAGOONS
ORLEANS CANAL/ DETENTION BASIN
EXFILTRATION THROUGH INFRASTRUCTURAL COMPONENTS
WATER TABLE
VERNACULAR LANDSCAPES

INHABITING THE FLUID TERRAIN: INHABITABLE REVETMENTS

LANDSCAPE ARCHITECTURE DEPARTMENT, SCHOOL OF DESIGN
University of Pennsylvania, Philadelphia

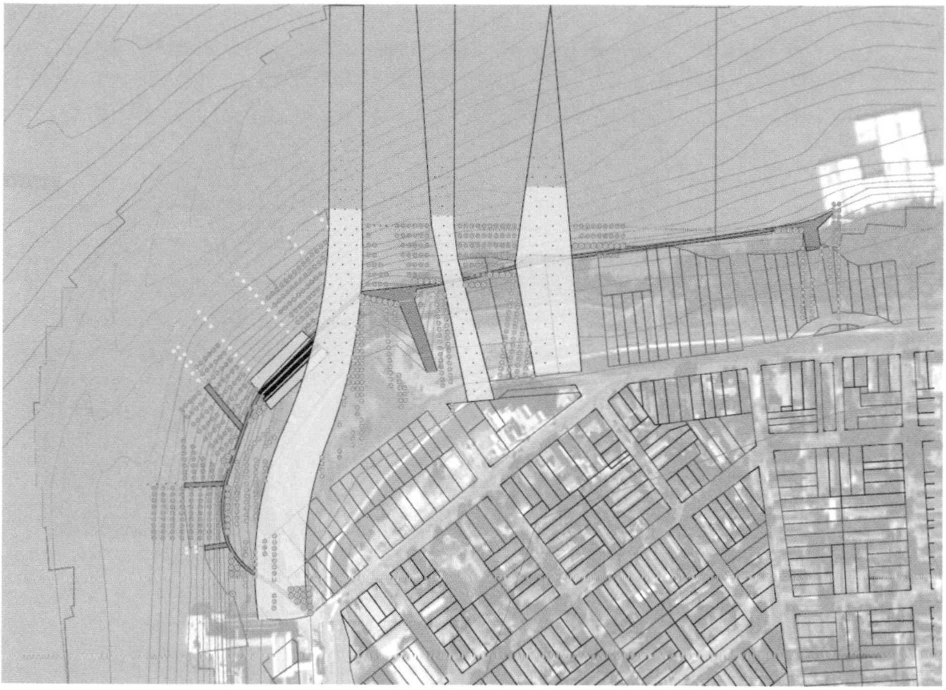

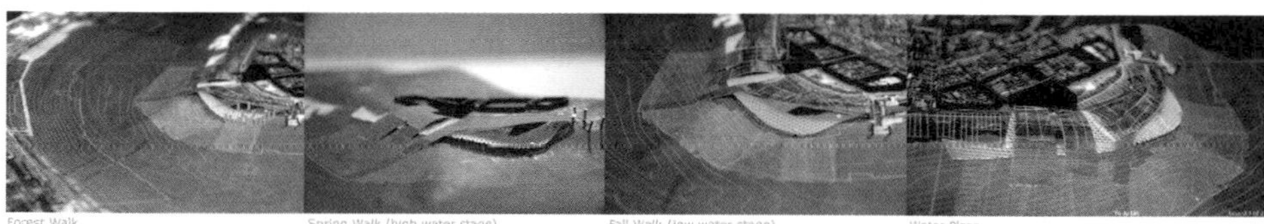

Forest Walk | Spring Walk (high water stage) | Fall Walk (low water stage) | Water Plaza

Instructor: Anuradha Mathur
Designer: Yu-Ju Lin

This project offers designs for site-specific types of revetments along the west bank of the Mississippi River in the Algiers neighborhood, to replace the existing generic concrete-mat type. The proposed high-rise, embedded, and cutting revetment types would respond to the differential force of the river at various points along its course and provide inhabitable terrains. They would bridge the divide that the levees have created between the city and the river.

INHABITING THE FLUID TERRAIN: CONSTRUCTING PERMEABLE LANDSCAPES

LANDSCAPE ARCHITECTURE DEPARTMENT, SCHOOL OF DESIGN
University of Pennsylvania, Philadelphia

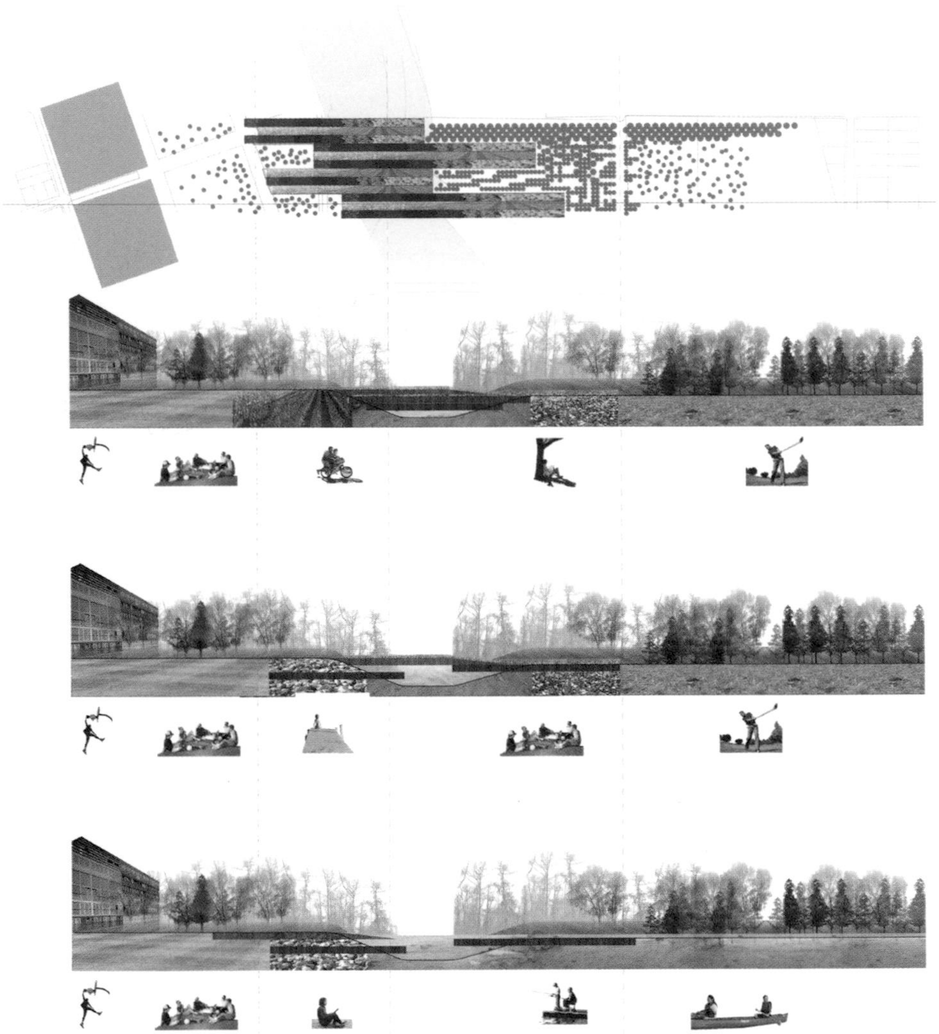

Instructor: Anuradha Mathur
Designer: Miaochi Tsai

Taking as its subject a swath of land extending from the Pontchartrain Park neighborhood near the lake to the Bywater neighborhood near the river, this project proposes a water management system composed of a matrix of locks. These locks could be opened and closed, allowing for flooding in designated areas to control the path of stormwater and to establish a permeable landscape. The system would create wetlands within the city limits that would protect and preserve the higher land deemed suitable and safe for building.

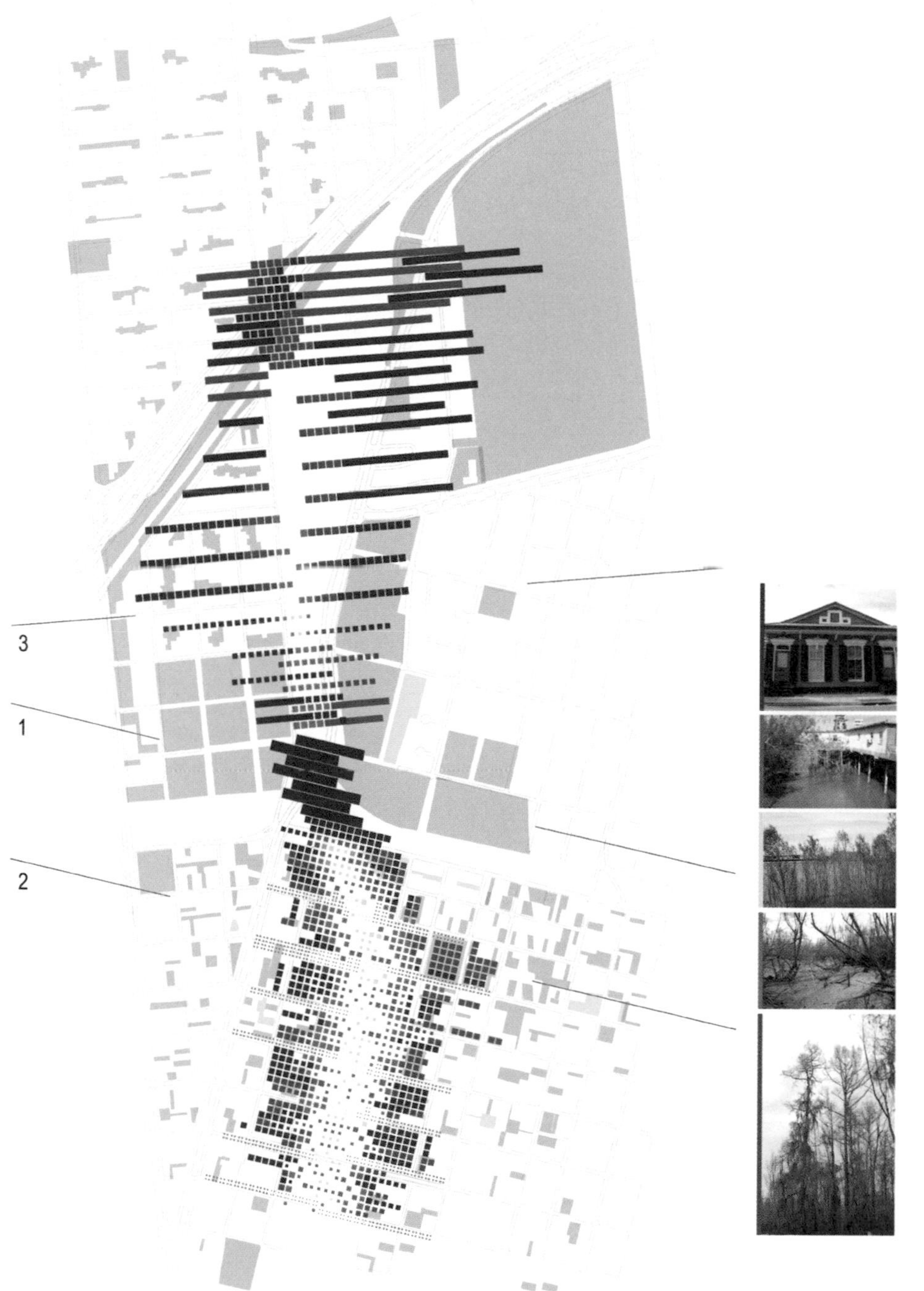
3
1
2

LIQUID URBANISM: NEW HYDRAULIC POCKET GROUND

SCHOOL OF ARCHITECTURE

Pratt Institute, Brooklyn, New York

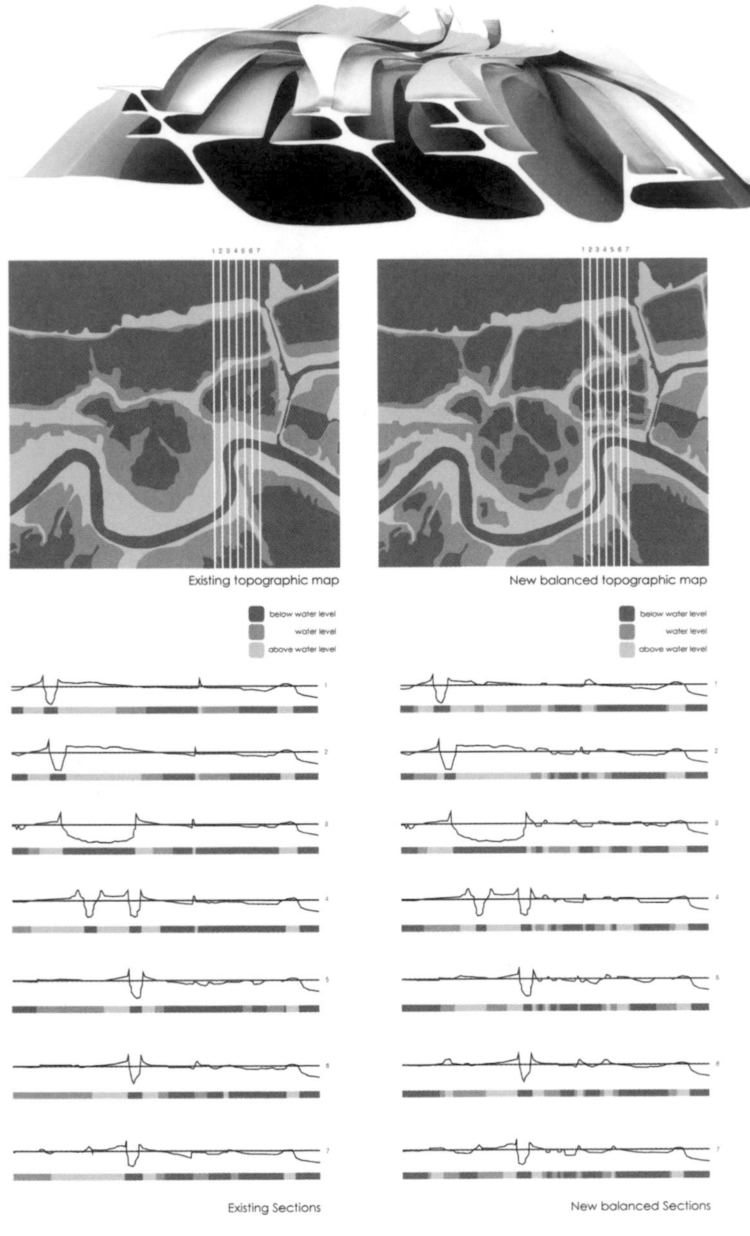

Instructor: Franklin Lee
Designer: Kyoung-Min Seo

This specific proposal for the Marigny neighborhood is intended to create a better method of flood control throughout New Orleans. In contrast to the existing drainage canals, which channel floodwater and direct its outflow to Lake Pontchartrain, the new hydraulic system, would divert floodwater through a branching network of channels and collectors for drainage and absorption. A man-made landscape would "correct" the city's natural topography, providing new higher ground for building and "pockets" for dispersing rain- and floodwater.

NOLA EVACUATION BARGES

TAUBMAN COLLEGE OF ARCHITECTURE AND URBAN PLANNING

University of Michigan, Ann Arbor

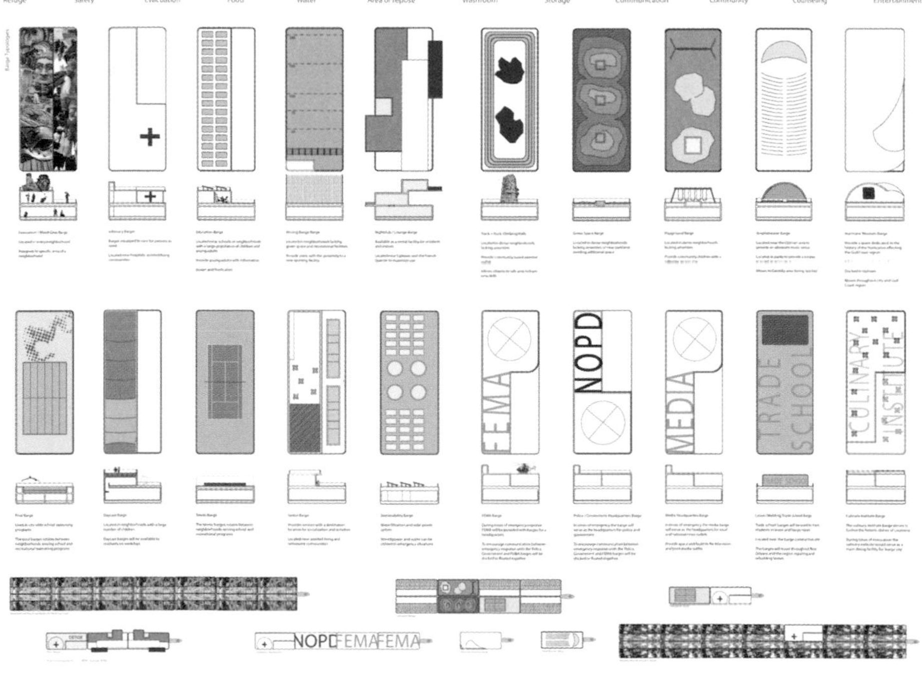

Instructors: Michael Sorkin, Coleman Jordan
Designer: Jenna Gibson

The Mississippi River barge is a ubiquitous feature of the New Orleans urban landscape. This project reinvents the barge as a potential site for community services and amenities. The proposed barges would accommodate various functions ranging from healthcare services to sports and educational activities to child and senior care. They could be moored at sites adjacent to the civic institutions whose programs they extended. In a threatening flood event, they could be deployed to serve as transit vehicles for evacuation.

UPSIDE-DOWN, THE NINTH ISLANDS

TAUBMAN COLLEGE OF ARCHITECTURE AND URBAN PLANNING
University of Michigan, Ann Arbor

Instructors: Michael Sorkin, Coleman Jordan
Designer: Brian Foster

Addressing the dangers involved in building on New Orleans's low-lying terrain, this project proposes the creation of above-sea-level "islands" in the Lower Ninth Ward. Multi-unit housing would be built on the new, higher ground, and existing structures would be moved there as well. The proposal reinvents the neighborhood as an archipelago while preserving aspects of its built environment that have made it a distinctive community.

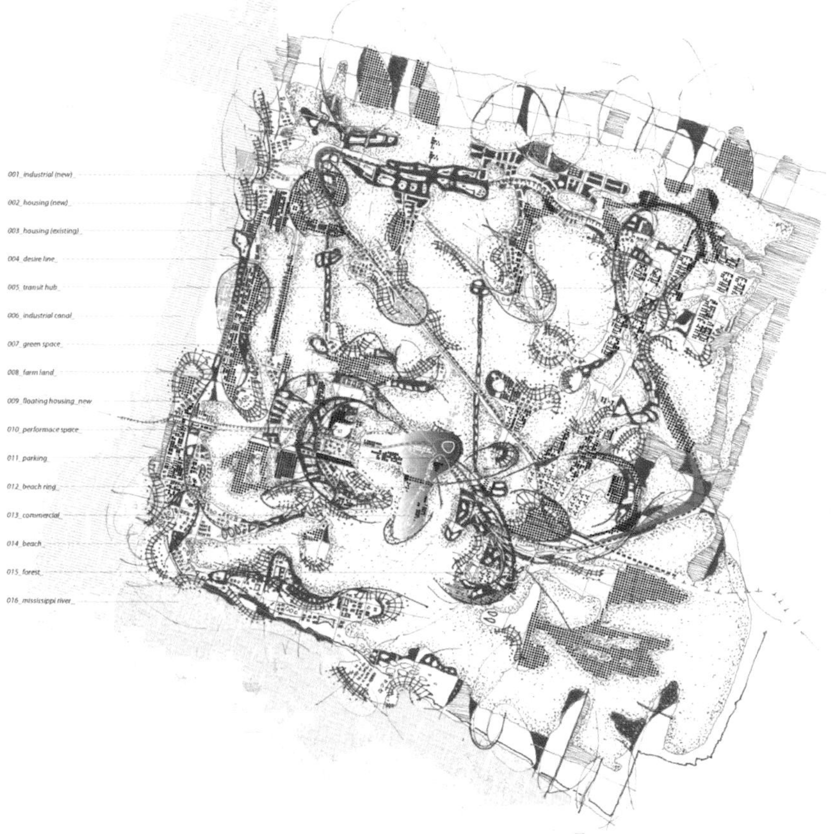

*001_industrial (new)_*
*002_housing (new)_*
*003_housing (existing)_*
*004_desire line_*
*005_transit hub_*
*006_industrial canal_*
*007_green space_*
*008_farm land_*
009_floating housing_new
*010_performace space_*
*011_parking_*
*012_beach ring_*
*013_commercial_*
*014_beach_*
*015_forest_*
*016_mississippi river_*

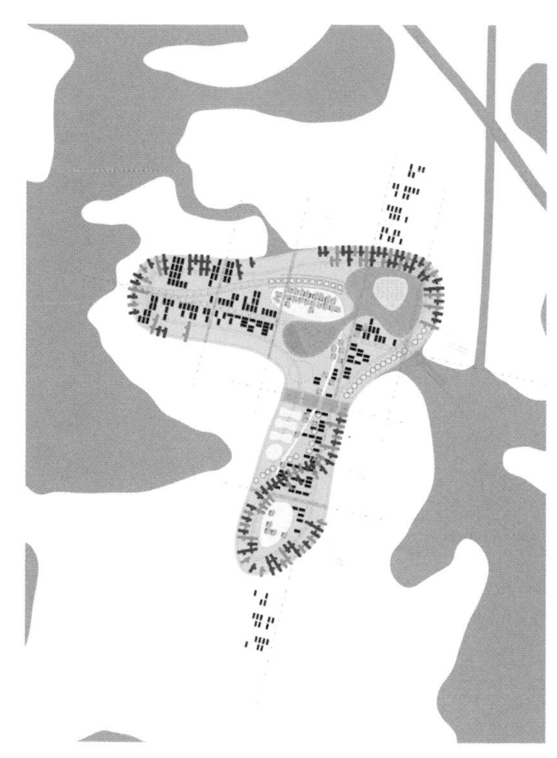

RESILIENT TOPOGRAPHIES: INHABITABLE FOUNDATIONS

ARCHITECTURE DEPARTMENT, SCHOOL OF DESIGN

University of Pennsylvania, Philadelphia

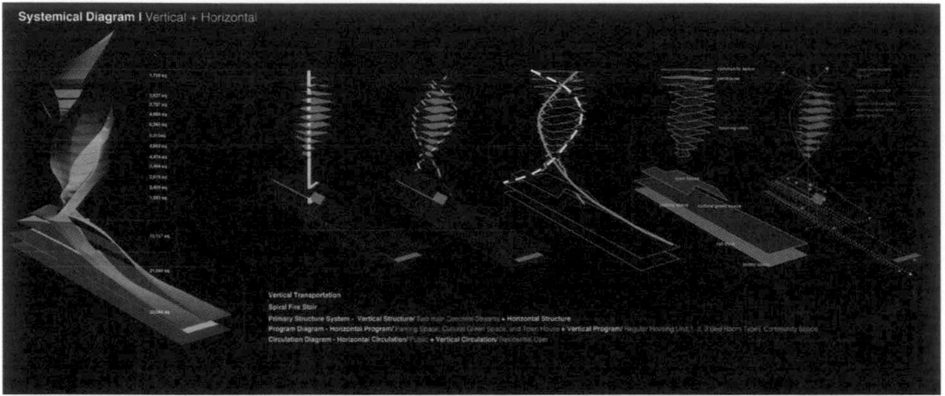

Instructor: Marion Weiss
Designer: So Jung Lee

This design is a response to a project brief that asked students to challenge "the current planning assumptions institutionalized by federal laws and insurance programs and [propose] new prototypes that redefine the relationship between land and water, landscape and home, proposing more contemporary ways of living on a fragile edge." The designer's proposed residential towers use horizontal and vertical structural concrete "streams," the horizontal providing space for parking and public "cultural green" use and the vertical for housing designed as one-, two-, and three-bedroom units. One vertical path provides public access to community spaces on the top floors of the towers; a separate path leads to private residences.

TIMELINE
ALISON N. POPPER

Abbreviations and acronyms (in order of their appearance in the timeline)

Corps	U.S. Army Corps of Engineers
MRC	Mississippi River Commission
SPF	Standard Project Flood
SPH	Standard Project Hurricane
PMH	Probable Maximum Hurricane
HPP	Hurricane Protection Program, a.k.a Barrier Plan
CPC	City Planning Commission
CZO	Comprehensive Zoning Ordinance
FEMA	Federal Emergency Management Agency
ESF-14	Emergency Support Function 14–Long-Term Community Recovery Plan
GNOF	Greater New Orleans Foundation
BNOB	Bring New Orleans Back Commission
ULI	Urban Land Institute
LRA	Louisiana Recovery Authority
NORA	New Orleans Redevelopment Authority
CDBG	Community Development Block Grant
LRC	Louisiana Recovery Corporation
UNOP	Unified New Orleans Plan
NOCSF	New Orleans Community Support Foundation
HUD	U.S. Department of Housing and Urban Development
HANO	Housing Authority of New Orleans
MIR	Make It Right
MRGO	Mississippi River Gulf Outlet
CAEP	City-Assisted Evacuation Plan
NOHSEP	New Orleans Office of Homeland Security and Emergency Preparedness

FLOOD PROTECTION IN LOUISIANA

1928: The U.S. Congress approved the Flood Control Act, which mandated that the U.S. Army Corps of Engineers' (Corps) Mississippi River Commission (MRC) implement flood-control measures, including levee system enhancements and supplemental floodways, on the lower Mississippi River. Established in the late nineteenth century, the MRC is still responsible for the flood-control levees along the Mississippi River.

1929: The U.S. Coast and Geodetic Survey undertaken by the Department of Commerce established the Sea Level Datum, the first national vertical datum, which became the vertical control reference.

1946: Congress authorized the first federal program for levee construction along the southern Lake Pontchartrain shore; the levee was constructed to ten feet above the local mean sea level.

1952: The Corps developed Standard Project Flood (SPF) and Standard Project Hurricane (SPH) policies, producing an engineering manual that established standards for flood protection projects.

1959: The U.S. Weather Bureau described the Probable Maximum Hurricane (PMH), larger than the SPH and with lesser probability for occurrence.

1962: The Corps recommended to Congress the Lake Pontchartrain and Vicinity Hurricane Protection Program (HPP)—a major infrastructural intervention also known as the Barrier Plan, which proposed structures that would meet the criteria for withstanding SPH storm surges.

September 1965: Unprecedented storm surges, levee failures, and flood damage occurred in Louisiana during Hurricane Betsy, approaching those projected for the SPH.

October 1965: Congress authorized the Corps to implement the $65 million HPP, including the construction of levees and the pumping of groundwater—both of which have contributed to soil subsidence in New Orleans.

1977: A federal injunction prohibited the construction of certain elements of the HPP until analyses of their effects on lake salinity and habitat could be conducted.

1980: The Orleans Levee District conducted ten alternative engineering studies to the Barrier Plan, finally promoting the less-costly High Level Plan that provided for SPH protection but with less damage to the environment.

Over the next twenty years, a range of protection studies, technical reviews, and canal redesigns were undertaken. Although many studies recommended the replacement of barrier elements with higher lakefront levees for strengthened protection where New Orleans's outfall canals emptied into the lake, the Barrier Plan continued to be followed with only marginal changes. The revised levees were constructed to less conservative construction criteria and were intended to withstand only short-term impact loading.

1999: During the mayoral administration of Marc Morial, the City Planning Commission (CPC) developed a Comprehensive Master Plan and Land Use Plan, both of which were adopted.

2001: The CPC created a draft Comprehensive Zoning Ordinance (CZO) to update the outdated one from the 1970s and revise zoning districts to coincide with the 1999 master plan, but it was not adopted.

June 2002: The *Times-Picayune*'s "Washing Away" series predicted a storm with deaths and destruction on the scale experienced in the aftermath of Hurricane Katrina.

February 2005: The Corps' annual Budget Justification Sheet included the following statement: "Continuing coastal land loss and settlement of land in the [Barrier Plan] project area may have impacted the ability of the project to withstand the design storm [SPH]. Refinement of existing computer models to assist in determining the impact of these environmental changes on the project will continue."

May 2005: The partially complete Barrier Plan included 125 miles of hard infrastructure—levees, major flood walls, and flood-proofed bridges—although the level of completion on the project varied by parish; its estimated completion date was 2015.

August 2005: The CPC presented the first draft of the Riverfront Vision 2005 to the public. The plan proposed the establishment of multifaceted access for neighborhoods along the riverfront, new parks, mixed-use developments, and new transportation networks, and recommended a public plan review process.

By 2005, the Corps' Southern Louisiana HPP, which included the Lake Pontchartrain and Vicinity, West Bank, and New Orleans to Venice projects, provided 350 miles of protective features of which fifty-six miles were floodwalls.

HURRICANE KATRINA, DAMAGE AND FLOODING

August 26, 2005: Governor Kathleen Blanco declared a state of emergency in Louisiana.

August 27, 2005: President George Bush declared a federal state of emergency, giving the Federal Emergency Management Agency (FEMA) and the Department of Homeland Security full authority to act.

August 28, 2005: Mayor Ray Nagin issued a mandatory evacuation order for New Orleans.

August 29, 2005: Hurricane Katrina made landfall in New Orleans as a Category 3 hurricane, resulting in levee breeches, flood wall failures, and compromised pumping systems.

August 31, 2005: Floodwaters reached equilibrium with Lake Pontchartrain, leaving some neighborhoods under as much as twenty feet of water. It was estimated that pumping the floodwaters out of the city would require a month's time. Approximately 26,000 stranded flood victims sought refuge under horrifying conditions in New Orleans's Superdome; several thousands more sheltered in the nearby Convention Center.

September 1, 2005: Eighty percent of the city was underwater.

September 2, 2005: President Bush visited the Gulf Coast, later signing a $10.5 billion disaster relief bill. Mayor Nagin predicted that parts of New Orleans would be without electricity for three months, and the Corps estimated it would take 36–80 days to drain the city.

September 3, 2005: The last of the refugees in the Superdome and the Convention Center were transported to towns in Louisiana and Texas. Texas officials reported the arrival of over 150,000 evacuees.

September 4, 2005: Serving as a way station, hospital, and morgue, the Louis Armstrong International Airport, housed more than 2,000 people, many with medical problems.

September 5, 2005: The National Guard deployed 16,000 troops dedicated to a search and rescue mission.

September 6, 2005: Mayor Nagin ordered law enforcement officials to evacuate the city, removing anyone who was not involved in recovery efforts.

September 8, 2005: The Rockefeller Foundation announced a $3 million grant to the Greater New Orleans Foundation (GNOF) Katrina Disaster Relief Fund for housing and economic redevelopment.

September 9, 2005: FEMA Director Michael Brown returned to Washington and resigned from oversight of relief operations. U.S. Coast Guard Vice Admiral Thad Allen was appointed director of relief operations.

September 12, 2005: Michael Brown announced his resignation.

Of New Orleans's seventy-two neighborhoods, thirty-four flooded completely and only eight did not flood. Of the 350 miles of protective features built under the HPP (Barrier Plan), 169 miles of structures were significantly damaged and forty-one miles were severely damaged by the Katrina-generated surges and waves. There were a total of fifty major levee breaches and thirty-four of the seventy-one pumping stations in the region were damaged. The diminished capacity of the city's pumps required their rehabilitation as well as the use of temporary pumps and generators that were sent to New Orleans from around the country. Two weeks after the flooding, 40 percent of the city remained underwater, with only forty-one pumps operating to remove water and sludge. The city was not dewatered until fifty-three days after the flooding occurred. Regionally, 90,000 square miles of the Gulf Coast were declared federal disaster areas.

POST-KATRINA PLANNING AND RECONSTRUCTION

September 27, 2005: The city council passed a resolution creating an eleven-person advisory committee to address hurricane recovery.

September 30, 2005: Mayor Nagin announced the formation of the Bring New Orleans Back (BNOB) Commission, a seventeen-member panel, who would be advised by the Urban Land Institute (ULI). BNOB was the city's first official post-disaster planning effort.

October 5, 2005: Mayor Nagin announced the layoff of 3,000 "non-essential" city employees, about half the municipal workforce.

October 17, 2005: Governor Blanco created the Louisiana Recovery Authority (LRA), a twenty-three-member commission to guide state government in the process of rebuilding, headed by Norman Francis and Walter Isaacson.

October 28, 2005: The American Planning Association urged that the CPC participate in the BNOB effort.

November 17, 2005: The House Financial Services Committee held a hearing on the "Baker Bill" (H.R. 4100) introduced on October 20, 2005, by U.S. Representative Richard Baker, R-Baton Rouge, proposing the formation of the Louisiana Recovery Corporation (LRC), a new federal agency for "economic stabilization and redevelopment." To be financed by U.S. Treasury bonds, the LRC would pay liens and acquire properties to promote real estate development. It was never implemented.

November 18, 2005: The ULI published its recommendations to the BNOB in a final report, recommending buyouts of land in the city's lowest neighborhoods.

November 28, 2005: Rejecting the ULI plan, Mayor Nagin reiterated his intention to "rebuild all of New Orleans."

November 28–29, 2005: The Tulane/Xavier Center for Biomedical Research sponsored the conference "Reinhabiting NOLA."

December 2005: The LRA published "Addressing the Challenges of Recovery & Rebuilding from Hurricanes Katrina & Rita," emphasizing the severity of the physical, economic, and social damages in Louisiana and the Gulf Coast states and assessing major needs.

December 13, 2005: Joseph Canizaro, chair of the BNOB land-use committee, proposed a rebuilding plan allowing rebuilding anywhere in the city for three years, after which rebuilding in the lowest areas would not be allowed. To discourage delay, the committee subsequently shortened the proposal's timeframe to one year.

December 15, 2005: The city council passed a resolution stating that all neighborhoods "should get equal treatment and should be rebuilt simultaneously."

December 30, 2005: President Bush signed a spending bill providing $29 billion in recovery funds to the Gulf Coast, including $6.2 billion in Community Development Block Grant (CDBG) funds to Louisiana.

January 1, 2006: The *Times-Picayune* reported that New Orleans's diminished population of 135,000 residents established it as the third largest city in Louisiana, after Baton Rouge and Shreveport. Prior to Katrina, New Orleans was the largest city in the state with a population of 484,000 residents.

January 2006: The major universities in metropolitan New Orleans reopened with enrollment levels that exceeded expectations.

January 7, 2006: President of the National Urban League and former New Orleans mayor Marc Morial called for Category 5 storm protection and a 120 percent buyout program for homeowners.

January 10–11, 2006: Members of the Louisiana planning community, with Governor Blanco and Senator Mary Landrieu, traveled to the Netherlands to form partnerships with the Dutch government and design, planning, and engineering communities.

January 11, 2006: The BNOB land-use committee released its final report recommending a four-month period in which neighborhoods could demonstrate their viability, after which the New Orleans Redevelopment Authority (NORA) would purchase ruined properties and a moratorium on rebuilding in heavily flooded areas would be enforced. $12 billion in recovery funds were designated for property buyouts. New Orleans architect Ray Manning and dean of the Tulane University School of Architecture Reed Kroloff were nominated to lead an urban design committee.

January 15, 2006: Mayor Nagin delivered a controversial speech on Martin Luther King Jr. Day, which stated his intention to rebuild a "chocolate city" with a majority African-American population. He apologized the following day at the BNOB commission meeting, but residents across the city publically spoke out against what they considered the divisive thrust of the speech.

January 19, 2006: Governor Blanco appointed Calthorpe Associates (Berkeley, CA) as regional planning consultant and Andrés Duany (Miami, FL) as neighborhood planning consultant to the LRA and commissioned Raymond Guidroz of Urban Design Associates (Baton Rouge, LA) to create a residential pattern book.

January 21, 2006: Mayor Nagin announced he would not support a rebuilding moratorium. FEMA's Emergency Support Function-14 program held Louisiana Planning Day to solicit input from affected residents. FEMA initiated the ESF-14 Long-Term Community Recovery process to support local and state governments in their efforts to understand and define their needs for recovery. Staffing the ESF-14 effort were 325 FEMA employees, local experts, and national consultants, who led community participation endeavors.

January 26, 2006: The city council's advisory committee on hurricane recovery held its first meeting.

January 27, 2006: BNOB committees concluded their work.

January 31, 2006: The NFL pledged $20 million to repair the Superdome.

February 15, 2006: The Select Bipartisan Committee of the House of Representatives released the "Failure of Initiative" report criticizing pre-storm evacuation preparations and the failures of both Governor Blanco and Mayor Nagin to achieve evacuation, in a disaster situation in which 100,000 citizens lacked private transportation. President Bush announced his intention to request an additional $4.2 billion in federal CDBG funds for Louisiana.

February 16, 2006: The city council designated $2.9 million in CDBG funds to commission Lambert Advisory (Miami, FL) to undertake what would become known as the Neighborhoods Rebuilding Plan or Lambert Plan.

February 20, 2006: Governor Blanco unveiled what would become the Road Home Homeowner Assistance Program. The program was to provide $8.9 billion in assistance to more than 130,000 homeowners toward rebuilding and protecting their homes.

As of March 2006, 100,000 displaced households were temporarily housed in hotels and mobile homes, and 700,000 evacuated households were receiving rental assistance. Property owners awaited FEMA's release of revised flood zone maps that would guide banks in making loans and insurance companies in writing policies and guidelines for building specifications and elevations.

March 10, 2006: After FEMA declined to fund the work of the BNOB urban design committee led by Manning and Kroloff, the LRA pledged $7.5 million to the process.

March 16, 2006: The LRA approved Governor Blanco's Road Home program.

March 20, 2006: The BNOB commission released its final report, which recommended $12 billion for buyouts of private property and $3.3 billion for an extensive light rail system as well as funding for the neighborhood-based planning effort to be led by the BNOB urban design committee. However, the report failed to prioritize specific projects to be funded with CDBG monies, and, lacking mayoral approval, BNOB stalled.

April 7, 2006: Responding to the stalled BNOB process, the city council announced that it had commissioned Paul Lambert and Sheila Danzey to work with neighborhoods devastated by Katrina.

April 12, 2006: FEMA released advisory Base Flood Elevation maps.

April 20, 2006: The Rockefeller Foundation committed $3.5 million to fund the Unified New Orleans Plan (UNOP) to follow the BNOB endeavor and named the Greater New Orleans Foundation (GNOF) to oversee UNOP.

April 26, 2006: The LRA approved the final iteration of the Road Home program.

May 2, 2006: The Joint Legislative Committee on the Budget and the House Appropriations Committee approved the Road Home program.

May 2, 2006: FEMA closed its long-term recovery office in New Orleans.

May 10, 2006: The Louisiana senate approved the Road Home program.

May 20, 2006: Mayor Nagin won a second term, defeating Mitchell Joseph "Mitch" Landrieu.

June 5, 2006: GNOF issued a request for qualifications for planners seeking to participate in UNOP. The New Orleans Community Support Foundation (NOCSF), which had been established to disburse funds designated for planning, hired Concordia Architecture & Planning to staff the review process.

June 14, 2006: Secretary Alphonso Jackson of the U.S. Department of Housing and Urban Development (HUD) announced plans to rehabilitate and reopen 1000 units of public housing within sixty days and to demolish four of the ten Housing Authority of New Orleans (HANO) public housing developments in New Orleans—C.J. Peete, B.W. Cooper, Lafitte, and St. Bernard. Five thousand families were displaced from public housing in the wake of Katrina.

The HUD-HANO plan engendered strong opposition, primarily because rebuilding was to follow federal Hope VI policy guidelines that would replace demolished units with a mix of public housing, affordable rental housing, and single-family homes. Although many of the HANO units suffered damages in Katrina, opponents argued the existing vacant buildings could be improved as viable housing. Opponents claimed that the plan replaced only a third of the public housing units slated for demolition and that rents for new units would be unaffordable for extremely low-income families.

June 15, 2006: President Bush signed the emergency spending bill authorizing an additional $4.2 billion in CDBG for Louisiana.

June 16, 2006: The CPC published the Neighborhood Planning Guide, complementing the UNOP effort by integrating neighborhood groups into the citywide planning process.

July 5, 2006: The LRA, city council, and Mayor Nagin agreed to move forward with the UNOP process.

July 21, 2006: The NOCSF approved a slate of planning teams to lead district planning in the UNOP endeavor.

July 30, 2006: UNOP held its first community meting to establish criteria for the work of planning teams.

August 1, 2006: UNOP-selected planning teams made presentations to neighborhood organizations as a preliminary step to pairing teams and districts.

August 3, 2006: Paul Lambert, in the midst of developing the Lambert-Danzey plan according to district boundaries established by BNOB, denounced UNOP efforts.

Mid-August 2006: The final version of the Orleans Parish ESF-14 plan was released, approximately four months after similar documents were posted for other hurricane-damaged parishes. The plan was never incorporated into New Orleans's planning efforts, but some of the plan's proposals were adopted in eighteen other hurricane-affected parishes.

August 22, 2006: Governor Blanco launched the Road Home program.

August 25, 2006: The city council approved FEMA's flood elevation maps.

August 28, 2006: Mayor Nagin, the city council, and GNOF signed a memorandum of understanding concerning UNOP. The NOCSF announced its slate of board members and assigned planning teams to districts.

August 30, 2006: Global Green announced the winner of its "Sustainable Design" competition for a high-density, net-zero residential project on a 1.25-acre block in the Holy Cross neighborhood of the Lower Ninth Ward.

September 15, 2006: The Bush-Clinton Katrina Fund awarded $1 million to fund the UNOP process.

September 23, 2006: The city council released the Neighborhoods Rebuilding Plan (Lambert Plan) for forty-seven neighborhoods that had been most heavily flooded.

October 27, 2006: The city council unanimously accepted the Neighborhoods Rebuilding Plan.

October 28, 2006: The Project New Orleans exhibition opened at New Orleans's African-American Museum, presenting proposals solicited nationwide from architecture schools and professional offices for rebuilding the city.

October 28, 2006: UNOP held its first community congress.

December 2006: The LRA designated (NORA) the recipient of properties purchased in the Road Home Program.

December 2, 2006: UNOP held its second community congress.

December 4, 2006: Mayor Nagin appointed Ed Blakely, a regional planning and disaster recovery expert, to head the city's recovery office.

Established in 1968 to acquire and expropriate blighted properties, NORA had minimal involvement in large-scale urban redevelopment prior to Katrina. After Katrina, a newly expanded board extended the mission from single-property expropriations to the consideration of neighborhood development, the undertaking of commercial corridor redevelopment projects around the city, and a pilot program under the Lot Next Door ordinance. NORA also took responsibility for land acquisition for Habitat for Humanity's Musicians' Village as well as for the Make It Right (MIR) neighborhood. By 2010, the organization had partnered with eleven community-based organizations to administer $30 million in HUD funding for housing and commercial real estate development.

LONG-TERM RECOVERY

January 20, 2007: UNOP held its third community congress.

June 2007: The New Orleans city council and the LRA approved the completed UNOP.

December 2007: MIR, led by Brad Pitt and GRAFT Architects, kicked off initial fundraising efforts with the Pink Project in the Lower Ninth Ward.

December 13, 2007: The city council unanimously approved HUD's $700 million redevelopment plan to demolish 4,500 public housing units, 3,300 of which were occupied prior to Katrina.

January 2008: FEMA estimated there were approximately 3,400 inhabited FEMA trailers in Louisiana and planned to order evacuations of all occupied trailers by June 2008.

March 2008: The Dutch Dialogues endeavor held its first conference to explore approaches for resilient design and aid New Orleans in the recovery process.

March 2008: MIR, in collaboration with the Clinton Global Initiative, broke ground on its first homes.

April 2008: The New Orleans city council voted to prepare an amendment to the city charter giving the master plan the force of law to guide land-use decisions.

May 2008: Global Green finished its first home in Holy Cross to serve as a Visitor Center where developers, contractors, and residents could find information concerning sustainable building practices.

June 2008: The City Planning Commission selected Goody Clancy of Boston to prepare a master plan, incorporating previous post-Katrina planning efforts and soliciting public participation in the new effort.

June 5, 2008: Congress deauthorized the Mississippi River Gulf Outlet (MRGO) for deep-draft navigation.

The Corps began construction of the seventy-six-mile MRGO in 1958 (completed 1968) to provide a shorter, safer way for ships to navigate from the Gulf of Mexico to the Industrial or Inner Harbor Navigation Canal, (completed in 1923 between the Mississippi River and Lake Pontchartrain) and the Port of New Orleans. MRGO was controversial from the start, and regional groups repeatedly argued that the potential environmental degradation from wetland loss, subsidence, and increased hurricane damage would outweigh benefits. After Katrina, the massive flooding in the region forced the Corps to reevaluate the channel, leading to its deauthorization for deep-draft navigation, the construction of additional surge barriers, and the construction of a rock closure across the channel at Bayou La Loutre (completed July 2009).

August 30, 2008: In response to Mayor Nagin's declaration of a mandatory evacuation in advance of Hurricane Gustav, emergency managers implemented the City-Assisted Evacuation Plan (CAEP) and safely evacuated over 20,000 citizens, 300 pets, and 14,000 visitors from the city.

CAEP was developed by the New Orleans Office of Homeland Security and Emergency Preparedness (NOHSEP) in response to recommendations from a study conducted in 2006 jointly by the U.S. Department of Transit and the U.S. Department of Homeland Security. The program for mass evacuation was designed as a method of last resort for those who could not self-evacuate. CAEP established bus pickup points throughout the city to provide evacuees with transportation to a state or regional shelter.

September 2008: Hurricane Gustav floodwaters overtopped the Industrial Canal.

September 2008: The New Orleans Master Plan and Comprehensive Zoning Ordinance endeavor, led by David Dixon of Goody Clancy, held the first of five citywide public forums that were convened over the ensuing year (September 2008–September 2009) to solicit citizen participation.

October 10–13, 2008: Dutch Dialogues 2 assembled sixty experts to identify design approaches and solutions for New Orleans.

November 4, 2008: New Orleans's citizens voted for the passage of a city charter amendment giving the master plan, then in development, the force of law to guide land-use decisions.

October 2009: NOHSEP opened an Emergency Operations Center in New Orleans City Hall, which was funded with $2 million of city funds leveraged with state and federal homeland security grants.

October 2009: The Bureau of Governmental Research, a private, nonprofit, independent research organization in New Orleans, published their report, "In Search of the Master Plan: Making the New Orleans 2030 Draft Plan Work."

October 23–24, 2009: Project New Orleans hosted the conference "New Orleans Under Reconstruction: The Crisis of Planning" at Tulane, gathering architects, landscape architects, urban planners, scientists, and activists to debate issues that had arisen related to the city's efforts to rebuild.

November 18, 2009: Federal judge Stanley Duval ruled that the Corps was liable for damages to private individuals resulting from the Corps' management of MRGO. A three-judge panel of the Fifth Circuit of Appeals ultimately reversed this decision in September 2013.

January 26, 2010: The City Planning Commission approved the master plan prepared under the direction of Goody Clancy.

February 6, 2010: Mitch Landrieu won the mayoral election, garnering 66 percent of the vote.

April 1, 2010: The Salvation Army announced a $10 million fund to build "green" housing in New Orleans neighborhoods, to be administered in the form of 125 $75,000 grants for new construction and home rehabilitations.

May 3, 2010: Mayor Mitch Landrieu was sworn into office, with an aggressive platform to improve public safety, education, job opportunities, transportation, and the local economy.

July 2010: The New Orleans Master Plan and Comprehensive Zoning Ordinance endeavor held public meetings in the city's thirteen planning districts to solicit reactions to the draft CZO.

August 12, 2010: The New Orleans city council approved the "Plan for the 21st Century: New Orleans 2030," popularly known as the master plan.

September 24, 2010: The U.S. Green Building Council and Salvation Army's "Natural Talent Design" competition announced four residential designs to be built in the Broadmoor neighborhood, which experienced ten feet of flooding. As late as 2009, 20 percent of the damaged and blighted properties in the area had not been repaired or rebuilt.

January 25, 2011: Mayor Landrieu and the Regional Transit Authority announced plans to extend streetcar lines through the French Quarter and the Marigny/Bywater neighborhoods, connecting existing streetcar lines with 2.5 new miles of track and serving the more than 70,000 residents of adjacent neighborhoods.

The last of the temporary housing units, which were commonly referred to as FEMA trailers, were vacated in 2012. At peak levels of housing assistance, FEMA housed more than 92,000 households in temporary units statewide to accommodate the largest housing shortage in the history of the agency.

July 2012: The CPC adopted the Neighborhood Participation Program report, which recommended an organizational plan for resident participation in land use and planning decisions. A key component of the program was the public notification and engagement process, enabling neighborhoods to more effectively review land-use proposals.

February 3, 2013: New Orleans's hosting of the Super Bowl propelled an estimated $1.2 billion in public and private improvements timed to be completed before the game weekend. These included the upgrade of Louis Armstrong Airport, the renovation of the Convention Center, and city street repairs and state road improvements.

June 11, 2013: The City Planning Commission fired executive director Yolanda Rodriguez, who had been appointed to the position in 2004.

August 28, 2013: Eight years after Hurricane Katrina, FEMA reported that the agency had provided nearly $19.6 billion to Louisiana's communities and families, in both public rebuilding assistance programs for individuals and households and preventative assistance to protect against future hazards.

October 2013: The City Planning Commission held the final round of planning district meetings for public discussion of the updated CZO draft, culminating two years of review by the commission, consultants, and citizens.

BIOGRAPHIES

Matthew Berman is a principal of the New York City firm workshop/apd, which he founded with Andrew Kotchen in 1999. Previously, Berman served as assistant editor at *ANY*, an editorial project that addressed architectural and urban issues in the final decade of the last millennium. He received a bachelor of arts degree from Lehigh University and a master of architecture degree from Columbia University and has taught as a visiting professor at Pratt Institute. A former host of Gallery HD's *What the Window Washer Saw*, a weekly television series about the world's most iconic skyscrapers, he now appears regularly on HGTV's *Top Ten*. Berman was coeditor, with Bernard Tschumi, of *Index Architecture* (2003). In 2006, workshop/apd submitted the winning design for Global Green's competition to design a model block in the Holy Cross Neighborhood of New Orleans's Lower Ninth Ward. Based on their experience developing environmentally sustainable and affordable residential options for the Global Green project, Berman and Kotchen created the RightFrame online platform, in order to give prospective residential clients the ability to participate more fully in design considerations. Currently in the beta-testing stage, RightFrame helps those who are building homes according to plans developed by workshop/apd to weigh design options and estimates of construction costs.

M. Christine Boyer is an urban historian whose interests include the history of the city, city planning, preservation planning, and computer science. In 1991, she joined the faculty of the School of Architecture at Princeton University, where she is the William R. Kenan Jr. Professor of Architecture. She was professor and chair of the City and Regional Planning Program at Pratt Institute and has also taught at Cooper Union, Columbia University, and the Graduate School of Design at Harvard University. Boyer has written extensively about urbanism, and her publications include *Dreaming the Rational City: The Myth of American City Planning* (1983); *Manhattan Manners: Architecture and Style 1850–1900* (1985); *The City of Collective Memory* (1993); *CyberCities: Visual Perception in the Age of Electronic Communication* (1995), and most recently, *Le Corbusier, Homme de Lettres* (2011). In 2009, in addition to presenting at the New Orleans Under Reconstruction conference, she gave the keynote address at the interdisciplinary conference "Urban Research and Architecture Beyond Henri Lefebvre," organized by ETH Zurich.

Her recent articles include "Collective Memory under Siege: The Case of 'Heritage Terrorism'" in C. Greig Crysler, Stephen Cairns, and Hilde Heynen, eds., *The Sage Handbook of Architectural Theory* (2012); "'Splendour and Havoc': The Many Maps of Baghdad" in Gillian O'Brien and Finola O'Kane, eds., *Portraits of the City: Dublin and the Wider World* (2012); "Why Do Architects Write? The Case of Alison and Peter Smithson" in Max Risselada, ed., *Alison & Peter Smithso: A Critical Anthology* (2011).

Denise Hoffman Brandt is principal of Hoffman Brandt Projects and director of landscape architecture in the Bernard and Anne Spitzer School of Architecture at the City College of New York. Her work focuses on landscape as ecological infrastructure—the social, cultural, and environmental systems that sustain urban life and generate urban form. Hoffman Brandt has previously worked as senior landscape architect at Mathews Nielsen Landscape Architects and as project landscape architect at Michael Van Valkenburgh Associates. She holds a master of fine arts degree in painting from Pratt Institute and a master of landscape architecture degree from the University of Pennsylvania. As the recipient of a New York Prize Fellowship in the Van Alen Institute's Projects in Public Architecture program, Hoffman Brandt spent her spring 2009 residency working in the systems and ecology area on City Sink, a project that investigated urban planting as an operative program for carbon sequestration. The Environmental Design Research Association recognized City Sink with a Great Places research award in 2010. Working with a team of City College graduate students, she expanded this research to produce a winning entry in the 2010 Build a Better Burb competition sponsored by the Long Island Index and funded by the Rauch Foundation.

Michael A. Cowan is a psychologist, social scientist, and theologian and has been engaged in interracial and interfaith community organizing in New Orleans since 1992. A professor and administrator at Loyola University since 1990, he holds master's and doctoral degrees in psychology from the Ohio State University and a master's degree in systematic theology from the School of Divinity of St. John's University (Collegeville). He currently serves as special assistant to the president of Loyola University. He is a founding leader of three interracial, civil-society organizations: the Jeremiah Group, the New Orleans Industrial Areas Foundation affiliate; Shades of Praise, the New Orleans Interracial Gospel Choir; and Common Good, a network of religious and civil organizations he convened after Hurricane Katrina to seek consensus as a basis for collective action to rebuild New Orleans. He is coauthor of *People in Systems*, *Dangerous Memories*, *Roots for Radicals*, and *The Art of Conversation through Serious Illness*. His articles have appeared in psychology, social science, and theology journals in the United States and Ireland.

James Dart is principal of the New York–based firm dArchitects. His current work includes multiyear, multiphased projects at Bartram's Garden, Philadelphia, the nation's oldest botanical garden: a special collections library and archive center in the former Coach House; the renovation of the Barn and Lath House Addition, which won an AIA Honor Award in 2002; and Bartram Commons, an administrative and garden center. Additional current projects include a multiphased, long-range development master plan—in collaboration with the New York City Department of Parks and Recreation—for Brooklyn's Wyckoff Farmhouse Museum and Educational Center. With colleagues from Pratt Institute, Dart participated after Katrina in a community-based planning and design project for New Orleans East, which was funded by HUD in 2005. In 2006, he collaborated with Deborah Gans on an award-winning submission to "High Density on the High Ground," an international competition for post-Katrina housing sponsored by *Architectural Record* and Tulane University's School of Architecture. For the ACORN Housing Corporation's Adjudicated Properties Project, he and Gans produced designs for prefabricated, modular housing for New Orleans East and the Lower Ninth Ward. Dart has taught design studios at the University of Pennsylvania and Drexel University, both in Philadelphia. He is currently university lecturer and director of the Siena, Italy Studio in the New Jersey School of Architecture at the New Jersey Institute of Technology.

David Dixon, a fellow of the American Institute of Architects (AIA), directs planning and urban design at Goody Clancy, in Boston. His work has won honor awards from the AIA, the American Society of Landscape Architects, the American Planning Association (APA), the Congress for the New Urbanism, the International Downtown Association, and the Society for College and University Planning. In 2007, Dixon received the AIA's Thomas Jefferson Award for Public Architecture for "a lifetime of ... significant achievement in [creating] ... livable neighborhoods, vibrant civic spaces, and vital downtowns." As president of the Boston Society of Architects he organized the First National Conference on Density, and as chair of the AIA's Urban Design Committee he helped shape the institute's response to Hurricane Katrina. He subsequently led teams that undertook recovery planning for roughly one quarter of the city to produce the Unified New Orleans Plan. In 2008, he was asked to lead the team that prepared New Orleans's post-Katrina master plan, which was given force of law in a citywide referendum and in 2010 was awarded the APA's National Planning Excellence Award for a Hard-Won Victory. Dixon lectures and writes frequently about the new generation of opportunities and challenges facing America's cities. He is a coauthor of *Urban Design for an Urban Century: Placemaking for People* (2009).

Andrés Duany, a fellow of the American Institute of Architects, focuses his work on the planning of communities. He and his wife, Elizabeth Plater-Zyberk, founded DPZ, their planning practice, in 1980, when their design of Seaside, Florida, began a debate on alternatives to suburban sprawl. DPZ currently has six partners and employs about thirty persons dedicated to both practice and research, and offers particular expertise in writing urban development codes. The firm has completed more than 200 downtown and new town plans, and received numerous awards, and its writings have been widely published. In 1993, Duany and Plater-Zyberk helped found the Congress for the New Urbanism. They teach traditional town planning at the University of Miami, where Plater-Zyberk served as dean of the School of Architecture from 1995 to 2013. Their coauthored books include *The New Civic Art: Elements of Town Planning* (with Robert Alminana, 2003). Duany's most recent book, *The Smart Growth Manual* (with Jeff Speck and Mike Lydon, 2010), proposes techniques for addressing the development of American cities that are socially, economically, and environmentally sustainable.

R. Allen Eskew is a fellow of the American Institute of Architects and principal of the New Orleans firm Eskew+Dumez+Ripple, which he established in 1986. Eskew has been significantly involved with a number of the post-Katrina recovery planning efforts, beginning with his work for the Bring New Orleans Back (BNOB) Commission. He also served on the planning teams for Planning Districts 3 and 4 in the Unified New Orleans Plan (UNOP) endeavor. Simultaneously, he led the team that secured the commission to prepare a development plan for the riverfront project Reinventing the Crescent, and he now leads the team that is developing the plan's first phase, Crescent Park. Eskew+Dumez+Ripple's recent projects include the designs of the 930 Poydras residential tower, which received a national AIA Housing Award, the Louisiana State Museum in Baton Rouge, and the Paul and Lulu Hillard University Art Museum in Lafayette, Louisiana, and the renovation of the Rosa F. Keller Branch Library in New Orleans, which was heavily damaged in the post-Katrina flooding. Eskew serves on the boards of Unity of Greater New Orleans (an organization serving the homeless), the Contemporary Art Center, and ArtSpot Productions; he is regional director for the central region of the Council for a Better Louisiana, and he was named a Role Model by New Orleans's Young Leadership Council in 2010.

Anthony Fontenot is an associate professor at Woodbury University School of Architecture in Los Angeles. He holds a bachelor of architecture degree from the University of Louisiana, a master of architecture degree from the Southern California Institute of Architecture, and a Ph.D. in the history and theory of architecture from Princeton University. In academic years 2008–2009 and 2009–2010, he was awarded the Woodrow Wilson Scholars fellowship at Princeton, and in 2010–2011, he held a research fellowship at the Getty Research Institute in conjunction with the Pacific Standard Time project. Fontenot has published on the history, devastation, and reconstruction of cities such as Berlin, Beirut, Kabul, and New Orleans. He was a co-curator of the exhibition "Clip/Stamp/Fold: The Radical Architecture of Little Magazines 196X–197X" (2007), and he served as a curator of the 2011 Gwangju Design Biennial in South Korea. He was the principal organizer of "Exposing New Orleans," a conference, workshop, and exhibition at Princeton University in 2006. He organized "Sustainable Dialogues" (2007–2008), a series of symposia on the reconstruction of New Orleans sponsored by the Bureau of Educational and Cultural Affairs of the U.S. Department of State. His research on New Orleans and the Mississippi River Delta was highlighted in the American pavilion at the 2010 Architecture Biennial in Venice as part of a collaborative project titled "Mississippi Delta: Constructing with Water."

Deborah Gans is principal of Gans Studio and professor in the architecture school at the Pratt Institute, where she has chaired the undergraduate architecture program. She has also taught as a visiting critic at Yale University and as an external professor at Dalhousie University. Many of Gans Studio's projects in industrial design and architecture explore forms of social engagement, ranging in scale from a school desk for the New York School Construction Authority to alternative and prefabricated housing and settlements for Kosovo and New Orleans. From 2005 through 2009, she worked in collaboration with James Dart, principal of dArchitects, on housing for New Orleans East and the Lower Ninth Ward, a project that began with a $290,000 HUD grant. Among her publications are *The Le Corbusier Guide*, now in its third edition (2006) and *Extreme Sites: The "Greening" of Brownfield*, which she guest-edited for *Architectural Design* (March/April 2004). She coedited *The Organic Approach to Architecture*

(2003) and *Bridging the Gap: Rethinking the Relationship of Architect and Engineer* (1991), which was honored at the AIA International Book Awards. Her prototype for disaster relief housing, "Roll Out House," was shown at the U.S. Pavilion in the Venice Architecture Biennial in 2008.

Toni L. Griffin's career spans the public and private sectors, combining the practice of architecture and urban design with the execution of innovative, large-scale, mixed-use redevelopment projects and citywide and neighborhood planning strategies. In 2009, Griffin launched her own planning practice, Urban Planning and Design for the American City, and has been working with the city of Detroit on a plan to re-envision the city in the wake of severe population loss. From 2007 to 2009, she served as director of planning and community development for the city of Newark, New Jersey, where she created a centralized and award-winning planning and urban design office. Prior to working in Newark, Griffin served as vice president and director of design for the Anacostia Waterfront Corporation in Washington, D.C., as deputy director for revitalization planning and neighborhood planning in the D.C. Office of Planning, and as vice president for planning and tourism development for the Upper Manhattan Empowerment Zone Development Corporation in New York City. She began her career as an architect with Skidmore, Owings & Merrill in Chicago, becoming an associate partner involved in architecture and urban design projects. Griffin is also an adjunct associate professor at the Harvard Graduate School of Design, teaching option studios and seminars in the urban design and planning department.

Melissa Harris-Perry is professor of political science at Tulane University, where she is the founding director of the Anna Julia Cooper Project on Gender, Race, and Politics in the South, housed at the Newcomb College Institute. She holds a B.A. in English from Wake Forest University, a Ph.D. in political science from Duke University, and an honorary doctorate from Meadville Lombard Theological School. She has served on the faculties of the University of Chicago (1999–2005) and Princeton University (2006–2010). Harris-Perry is the author of *Barbershops, Bibles, and BET: Everyday Talk and Black Political Thought* (2004) and *Sister Citizen: Shame, Stereotypes, and Black Women in America* (2011). She is the host of the *Melissa Harris-Perry* show on MSNBC and a columnist for *The Nation*.

William M. Harris Sr. served as the Martin Luther King Jr. Visiting Professor of Urban Studies and Planning at the Massachusetts Institute of Technology. He is a graduate of Howard University and the University of Washington and currently teaches in the political science department at Augusta State University in Georgia. His research interests focus on black community development, citizen empowerment, and professional ethics. The first African American elected to the College of Fellows of the American Institute of Certified Planners, Harris has served on numerous committees as an advocate for civil rights and the creation of opportunities for African Americans.

Derek James Hoeferlin is a registered architect and urban designer with his own practice. He often collaborates with H3 Studio, Inc. and Ian Caine in St. Louis, and with Waggonner & Ball Architects in New Orleans. Hoeferlin is an assistant professor at the Sam Fox School of Design & Visual Arts at Washington University in St. Louis. From 2006 to 2007, Hoeferlin, as a member of H3 Studio, Inc. served as one of the district plan project managers for Planning Districts 2 and 13 in the Unified New Orleans Plan (UNOP) endeavor. Hoeferlin and his students collaborate with University of Toronto landscape architecture faculty and students on the "Gutter to Gulf" initiative, which advocates for integrated water planning as fundamental to New Orleans's recovery and future. Hoeferlin also participates in the international task force Dutch Dialogues, which is led by Waggonner & Ball Architects, the American Planning Association, and the Royal Netherlands Embassy. He will serve as architect on the recovery and rebuilding plan "Comprehensive Sustainable Integrated Water Management Strategy for St. Bernard Parish and the East Banks of Orleans and Jefferson Parishes," a commission that Waggonner & Ball was recently awarded. In 2009, Hoeferlin and Caine's submission to the

"Rising Tides" competition, which sought solutions for sea-level rise affecting San Francisco, tied for a first place award. Hoeferlin's current research involves the deltas of the Mekong, Mississippi, and Rhine-Meuse rivers.

Naomi Klein is an award-winning journalist, syndicated columnist, and author of the *New York Times* best seller, *The Shock Doctrine: The Rise of Disaster Capitalism* (2007), which has been published in thirty languages and has more than one million copies in print. It appeared on multiple Best of Year lists and was a *New York Times* Critics' Pick of the Year. Klein's first book, *No Logo: Taking Aim at the Brand Bullies* (2000), was another international best seller, as widely translated and also with a printing of more than one million copies. Klein is a contributing editor for *Harper's* and a reporter for *Rolling Stone*, a regular columnist for *The Nation* and the *Guardian*; her editorials are internationally published through the New York Times Syndicate. In 2004, her reporting from Iraq for *Harper's* won the James Aronson Award for Social Justice Journalism. Her writing has also appeared in the *New York Times*, the *Washington Post*, *Newsweek*, the *Los Angeles Times*, the *Globe and Mail*, *El Pais*, *L'Espresso*, and the *New Statesman*, among many other publications. She is a former Miliband Fellow at the London School of Economics and holds an honorary doctor of civil laws degree from the University of King's College, Nova Scotia. She is currently at work on a new book and film on how the climate crisis can spur economic and political transformation.

Andrew Kotchen is a principal of the New York City-based firm workshop/apd, which he cofounded with Matthew Berman in 1999. He previously founded and ran a residential design firm based in Nantucket and New York City. He earned a bachelor of arts degree from Lehigh University and a master of architecture degree from the University of Michigan, where he also received the architecture program chair's Cup Award. He has taught as a visiting professor at Pratt Institute and serves as a visiting critic at the New York Institute of Technology, Columbia University, Lehigh University, Parsons, and the University of Michigan. In 2006, Kotchen and Berman's submission to the "High Density on the High Ground" competition, which *Architectural Record* and Tulane University sponsored to collect housing proposals for flood-ravaged New Orleans, won a Merit Award. Subsequently, Kotchen and Berman submitted the winning design for Global Green's competition for a model block in the Holy Cross neighborhood of New Orleans's Lower Ninth Ward.

Laura Kurgan teaches architecture at Columbia University's Graduate School of Architecture, Planning, and Preservation, where she directs the Visual Studies program and the Spatial Information Design Lab (SIDL). SIDL has collaborated with the Justice Mapping Center on "Graphical Innovations in Justice Mapping," a multiyear research project being carried out in selected states. She pursued this project in post-Katrina New Orleans, documenting "million-dollar blocks" and the urban costs of incarceration. In other projects, she has explored the conceptual, ethical, and political dimensions of digital location technologies; new structures of participation in design; and the visualization of urban and global data. She participated in a collaborative exhibition on global migration and climate change, "Native Land: Stop Eject," at the Cartier Foundation in Paris, and her work has also been exhibited at the Venice Architecture Biennial, the Whitney Museum of American Art at Altria, the Barcelona Museum of Contemporary Art (MACBA), the ZKM Center for Art and Media in Karlsruhe, and the Museum of Modern Art in New York (where it is part of the permanent collection). Her firm, Laura Kurgan Design, blends academic research; design, information, and communication technologies; and advocacy. In 2009, she was awarded a United States Artists (USA) Rockefeller Fellowship. Her articles have appeared in such journals as *Assemblage*, *Grey Room*, *ANY*, and *Volume*.

M. David Lee, FAIA, is a partner in the firm of Stull and Lee, in Boston, where he directs a wide range of planning, urban design, and architectural projects for clients throughout the country. He formerly taught as an adjunct professor of urban planning and design at the Harvard Graduate School of Design and has also served on the faculties of the Rhode Island School of Design and the Massachusetts Institute of

Technology. Lee is a past president of the Boston Society of Architects and a recipient of the Boston Society of Architects Year 2000 Award of Honor. He has served on the Design Arts Overview Panel of the National Endowment for the Arts and was an invited participant in 1992 for "Design and Management Initiatives Toward an Inclusive and Competitive America," a roundtable held in Little Rock, Arkansas, and organized for the benefit of President-elect Clinton's transition team. In 2006, Lee was the designated planner for New Orleans's Planning District 8 in the Neighborhoods Rebuilding Plan project led by the Lambert Advisory. Lee is a graduate of the University of Illinois and the Harvard Graduate School of Design. He holds joint degrees in architecture and urban design.

WM. Raymond Manning, FAIA, is president and CEO of Manning Architects, New Orleans. Before and after Hurricane Katrina, the core of his work has been the development, planning, and urban design of New Orleans. As co-chair of the Urban Planning Committee of the Bring New Orleans Back Commission, he was responsible for spearheading the Neighborhood Recovery Planning process, which led to the funding and organizational structuring of the Unified New Orleans Plan and generated numerous other projects to reinvigorate and restore the city. He was a consultant to the team that developed the Plan for the 21st Century: New Orleans 2030. Manning has frequently lectured at conferences on issues related to urban design, development strategy, community, sustainability, and disaster recovery. Prior to establishing a private practice in 1985, he was a project architect with architectural firms in Louisiana and Michigan, and he also served as a staff architect for the Minnesota Department of Transportation and the Federal Highway Administration. In 2012, Manning served as president of the New Orleans chapter of the AIA.

Anuradha Mathur and **Dilip da Cunha** are principals of the design firm Mathur/da Cunha, based in Philadelphia and Bangalore. A central concern of their practice has been water: how the ways water is visualized and engaged in urban settings lead to conditions of excess and scarcity but also to opportunities for new visualizations of terrain and design. Mathur studied architecture at the Center for Environmental Planning and Technology in Ahmedabad and landscape architecture at the University of Pennsylvania. In 2012, the Department of Landscape Architecture at Penn State University named her its John R. Bracken Fellow. Trained in architecture and planning, da Cunha studied at Bangalore University; the School of Planning and Architecture, New Delhi; the University of California, Berkeley; and MIT. Both Mathur and da Cunha now teach in the landscape architecture department at the University of Pennsylvania School of Design, where Mathur is a professor and associate chair and da Cunha is an adjunct professor. The partners have coauthored several books: *Mississippi Floods: Designing a Shifting Landscape* (2001); *Deccan Traverses: The Making of Bangalore's Terrain* (2006); and *Soak: Mumbai in an Estuary* (2009). They have concentrated on issue-centered investigations, seeking to identify ranges of possibilities and points of departure for transformative projects. Their proposals often take the form of intricate and original visualizations, which they call photoworks and photowalks—sectional drawings and collages that both construct and peel away the many layers of complex landscapes. In 2012, they held an international symposium at the University of Pennsylvania, "In the Terrain of Water," and are developing the outcome for publication; they are also working on a project provisionally titled "The Invention of Rivers," which questions the "natural" status given to rivers and the imaging and imagining that this status has inspired.

Yates McKee is an art critic and activist working in post-Occupy New York City. His writing has appeared in *October*, *South Atlantic Quarterly*, *Grey Room*, *Art Journal*, *The Nation*, and other publications, and on websites, such as *Waging Nonviolence* and *AlterNet*. He coedits the magazine *Tidal: Occupy Theory, Occupy Strategy* and is a founding member of the group Strike Debt.

Elizabeth Mossop is a founding principal of Spackman Mossop + Michaels Landscape Architects, New Orleans. From 2004 to 2010, she served as director of the Robert Reich School of Landscape Architecture at Louisiana State University, Baton Rouge, where she continues to teach. Previously, she directed the Master of Landscape Architecture Program at Harvard University's Graduate School of Design, where she was a faculty member from 1999 to 2004. Mossop is coeditor, with Paul Walton, of *City Spaces: Art and Design* (2001), and author most recently of *Contemporary Australian Landscape Design* (2006). Her work focuses on the design of public landscapes, parks, urban spaces, and infrastructure in Australia and the United States. Her firm has received numerous awards from such groups as the American Society of Landscape Architects, the Australian Institute of Landscape Architects, the Council of Building Design Professions, and the Australian Institute of Architects. Since 2005, Spackman Mossop + Michaels has been active in rebuilding New Orleans, participating in such projects as the redesign of Press Drive and the Dwyer Canal in Pontilly, the combined neighborhoods of Pontchartrain Park and Gentilly Woods, and in the "Growing Home" endeavor of the New Orleans Redevelopment Authority. The firm's designs for the Viet Village Urban Farm in New Orleans East won the 2008 Award of Excellence from the American Society of Landscape Architects, and its work on Couturie Forest and Scout Island Arboretum in New Orleans's City Park was similarly honored in 2009.

Byron Mouton is an architect, designer, craftsman, and founder of bildDESIGN in New Orleans. He studied architecture at Tulane University and holds a master of architecture degree from the Harvard University Graduate School of Design. He is now a professor of practice at Tulane's School of Architecture, where he serves as director of the URBANbuild program and teaches in the new minor degree program Social Innovation Social Entrepreneurship (SISE). In the fall semester of 2005, Mouton directed the Tulane School of Architecture's Hurricane Katrina Satellite Program, "Emergent N.O.," housed at Arizona State University. Recently, bildDESIGN was invited to submit a proposal to Brad Pitt's Make It Right, an opportunity that developed into an URBANbuild studio design and construction project for a housing prototype. Prior to establishing his office in New Orleans (in 1998), he worked in the Vienna ateliers of Hans Peter Worndl and Pichelmann and Co. His active private practice in New Orleans emphasizes residential design, with a focus on craftsmanship as well as on research in building materials and technologies.

Amy Murphy is currently an associate professor in the School of Architecture at the University of Southern California. Before joining the faculty at USC in 1990, she taught at Iowa State University and the Boston Architectural Center. She holds bachelor of fine arts and bachelor of architecture degrees from the Rhode Island School of Design and a master of fine arts degree in cinema production from USC and is currently completing her Ph.D. in critical studies within the USC Cinematic Arts School as well. The broad focus of her academic research is the relationship between media and urban experience from the mid-nineteenth century to the present. Her most recent written work has examined post-apocalyptic narratives in media, particularly in Asian anime, tracking both our changing relationship to nature and our trajectory toward new forms of urban living. She is currently working on an animated digital project, "Measuring the City," a mixed-media work representing how objective dimensions of the city are often redefined by subjective desire and time. Professionally, she has worked in architectural offices in Boston and Los Angeles, and in 1996, she started her own practice, Amy Murphy Projects. She has completed numerous residential and commercial projects in the Los Angeles area, including the restoration and renovation of R.M. Schindler's Yates Studio in Silver Lake.

Jeanne Nathan is executive director of the Creative Alliance of New Orleans (CANO), a network of cultural and creative producers, professionals, businesses, and nonprofit organizations based in New Orleans, founded in 2008. Nathan also cofounded the Contemporary Arts Center in New Orleans, in 1976. As a marketing consultant, she has developed numerous award-winning cultural initiatives integral to the business, community, and commercial development plans of individual clients and organizations, including the City Planning Commission for the Comprehensive Zoning Ordinance and Official Master Plan of New Orleans; the Greater New Orleans Foundation for the Unified New Orleans

Plan; the Bring New Orleans Back Commission; the Louisiana Disaster Recovery Foundation; Global Green USA; the Green Collaborative; the Neighborhoods Partnership Network, the Louisiana Department of Culture, Recreation and Tourism; the Louisiana Disaster Recovery Foundation; Historic Restoration Inc.; the Port of New Orleans; America's Wetlands; the Tulane University School of Architecture; the Ohr-O'Keefe Museum in Biloxi, Mississippi; and the New Orleans Convention and Visitors Bureau. Her many awards and recognitions include being named one of the 2009 *City Business* Women of the Year and a Young Leadership Council mentor in 2010. Nathan received her B.S. in Industrial and Labor Relations, with a minor in economic history, from Cornell University.

Alison N. Popper focuses her work on public interest projects and post-disaster planning. She is currently an associate at Handel Architects, New York City, where she is the project architect and manager for the Idlewild Park Nature Center, commissioned by the New York City Department of Parks and Recreation. She recently served as an adviser for the post-Sandy neighborhood assessment undertaken by the New York Chapter of Architecture for Humanity, and with Emily Sprague she coauthored the publication that documented the project. She has taken an active role in the post-Sandy work done by the Design for Risk and Reconstruction Committee of the New York chapter of the American Institute of Architects and has presented her post-disaster research through such venues as Livable Neighborhoods, a program of the Municipal Art Society of New York. Popper's independent design practice clients have included Creative Time, Egg Collective, Laurel Porcari Architectural Art Glass, Robertson-Tait Design Build, and the Tulane City Center. She has worked with Project New Orleans since 2006, participating first as a curatorial assistant for an exhibition at the New Orleans African-American Museum and more recently as a research and editorial assistant for the book *New Orleans Under Reconstruction: The Crisis of Planning*. Popper graduated cum laude with a master of architecture degree from the Tulane University School of Architecture, and she is currently working toward her architectural license in New York.

Bradford Powers has lived in many locales in the U.S., working for social justice with a particular emphasis on improved legal representation and safer housing. He is currently a pre-doctoral fellow in the interdisciplinary City Culture Community Ph.D. program at Tulane University, where his research focuses on the ways in which market activities and civic institutions can be cultivated, improved, and integrated to regenerate communities. In 2006, he became the founding director of the Jericho Road Episcopal Housing Initiative in New Orleans and served as the program's executive director until 2012. Powers received a B.A. in English from St. Lawrence University in Canton, New York, and a J.D. degree, cum laude, from Vermont Law School. While enrolled at St. Lawrence he studied in East Africa and China, and while in law school he attended a summer program in comparative criminal and civil law at Trinity College, Dublin. After practicing for five years as a criminal defense attorney in various state and federal courts, he took a master of laws degree from the School of Law at the University of Washington. In 2010, Powers completed a one-year fellowship, supported by the Rockefeller Foundation, with the University of Pennsylvania's Center for Urban Redevelopment Excellence (CUREx). In 2011, he completed the Executive Program for Non-profit Leaders at Stanford University's Graduate School of Business.

Carol McMichael Reese is an associate professor and the Mary Louise Mossy Christovich Professor at the Tulane University School of Architecture, where she has taught since 1999. Her books and articles focus on contemporary architecture and urban planning in the Americas. She has written on the relationship of visual imagery and the production of urban identities in early twentieth-century Buenos Aires and Mexico City, and she was a consulting curator for the exhibition "Buenos Aires 1910: Memories of the World to Come," with venues in Buenos Aires, New York City, and Washington, D.C. Her most recent book, coauthored with Thomas F. Reese, is *The Panama Canal and its Architectural Legacy, 1905–1920* (2013), which focuses on the early history of the communities built in the U.S. Canal Zone. Her research on the development of the historically significant Pontchartrain Park neighborhood in New Orleans has opened an investigation of "Jim Crow urbanism," or the ways in which legally bolstered traditions of segregation shaped U.S. urban residential environments in the first half of the twentieth century. In 2009, Reese was one of six finalists for the national Thomas Ehrlich Civically Engaged Faculty award, and the Louisiana Legislative Women's Caucus honored her with their statewide award for Volunteerism and Civic Engagement. Since 2006, Reese has conducted Project New Orleans with co-organizers Michael Sorkin and Anthony Fontenot. Project New Orleans has produced a website; an exhibition documenting plans for the post-Katrina rebuilding of the city, shown at the New Orleans African-American Museum in 2006; and a national conference, "New Orleans under Reconstruction: The Crisis of Planning," held at Tulane in 2009.

Jakob Rosenzweig focuses on the graphic presentation of research, using the tools of GIS and other digital mapping techniques. He received his M.Arch degree from the Tulane University School of Architecture in 2007. His thesis, "Reinventing the Mississippi River Delta," proposed sustainable landscape, infrastructure, and urban design solutions for city life in the unique districts of southeastern Louisiana. He has been associated with Project New Orleans since 2006, when he and Anthony Fontenot, and Anne Schmidt created "Exposing New Orleans" (2006), a set of analytical maps that was widely published and exhibited in prominent venues. including the Netherlands Architecture Institute (NAi) in Rotterdam and the 2006 Venice Architecture Biennial. He contributed graphic analyses of the cultural and topographical conditions of New Orleans's deltaic region to the coauthored studies "New Orleans: The Emergence of a New Kind of City," published in *Pidgin* (Princeton University School of Architecture, 2008), and "Mississippi River Delta Study: Reviving the Dynamics of the Landscape," presented at multiple venues in 2010, among them the Venice Architecture Biennial and the Shanghai World Expo. He has created interpretive maps for nonprofit arts institutions in New Orleans such as Longue Vue House and Gardens and for Prospect New Orleans, the largest biennial of international contemporary art in the United States. He is currently working on an atlas of African-American places of historical importance along Louisiana's River Road for the Louisiana Bucket Brigade.

Denise Scott Brown, member of the Royal Institute of British Architects (RIBA) and 2007 RIBA International Fellow, is an urban planner, architect, and teacher known for her contributions to research and education on the nature of cities and urban development. Scott Brown and her husband and partner, Robert Venturi, of Venturi, Scott Brown, and Associates, in Philadelphia, are regarded as being among the most influential architects and architectural writers of the twentieth century. Together they launched a critique of architectural modernism that led to the development of new strategies for urban design and architecture in the 1960s and 1970s. In the 1970s she and her colleagues at Venturi, Scott Brown, and Associates pioneered preservation planning for historic districts in Galveston, Texas, and Miami Beach. In the 1980s they developed a plan for downtown Memphis. In the 1990s Scott Brown was pivotal in preparing the master plan and schematic design for the Denver Civic Center Cultural Complex; preparing campus plans for Dartmouth College and the University of Pennsylvania; and developing architectural requirements for the Smithsonian Institution's Museum of the American Indian. She has taught at the University of Pennsylvania and Yale University. She has written and advised on urban planning issues related to New York's World Trade Center site, Philadelphia's Penn's Landing, and New Orleans. Most recently, Scott Brown published *Having Words*, a collection of ten essays written between 1969 and 2007. Scott Brown and Venturi were awarded the Design Mind Award by the Smithsonian's Cooper-Hewitt National Design Museum in 2007.

Rebecca Solnit is the author of thirteen books about art, landscape, public and collective life, ecology, politics, hope, meandering, reverie, and memory. They include *Infinite City: A San Francisco Atlas* (2010), a book of twenty-two maps involving nearly thirty collaborators; *A Paradise*

Built in Hell: The Extraordinary Communities that Arise in Disaster (2009), and many others, among them *Storming the Gates of Paradise* (2008); *A Field Guide to Getting Lost* (2005); *Hope in the Dark: Untold Histories, Wild Possibilities* (2004); *Wanderlust: A History of Walking* (2001); *As Eve Said to the Serpent: On Landscape, Gender and Art* (2001); and *River of Shadows: Eadweard Muybridge and the Technological Wild West* (2003), for which she received a Guggenheim Fellowship, the National Book Critics Circle Award in criticism, and the Lannan Literary Award. Her most recent book, coedited with Rebecca Snedeker, is *Unfathomable City: A New Orleans Atlas* (2013), which follows the model that she established with *Infinite City*. As an activist and journalist she has worked on climate change, Native-American land rights, the antinuclear movement, human rights, the antiwar movement, and other issues. She is a proud product of the California public education system from kindergarten through graduate school. She is a contributing editor for *Harper's* and a frequent contributor to the political site Tomdispatch.com and has made her living as an independent writer since 1988.

Michael Sorkin is the principal of the Michael Sorkin Studio, a global design practice working at all scales with special interests in the city and green architecture. The studio has undertaken major projects around the world, including the design of new cities, districts, and buildings in China, Malaysia, Turkey, Germany, Austria, India, and the U.S. Sorkin is founder and president of Terreform, a nonprofit institute dedicated to research into the forms and practices of just and sustainable urbanism. He is president of the Institute for Urban Design and Distinguished Professor of Architecture and director of the graduate program in urban design at the City College of New York. He was previously Professor of Urbanism at the Academy of Fine Arts in Vienna, and has held professorships at Cooper Union, Yale, Columbia, Pennsylvania, Harvard, SCI-Arc, Aarhus, and other schools. Sorkin lectures internationally and is the architecture critic for *The Nation*. He is the author or editor of more than fifteen books on architecture and urbanism, among them *Exquisite Corpse* (1991), *Variations on a Theme Park* (1992), and, most recently *All Over The Map* (2011), a collection of his critical writings that includes work on New York and New Orleans. In 2009, Sorkin was appointed a Fellow of the American Academy of Arts & Sciences, and in 2013, he won the National Design Award as "Design Mind."

Robert Tannen is an economic development specialist, urban design and planning consultant, and conceptual artist. He received a bachelor's degree in Industrial Design and a master's degree in Fine Arts from Pratt Institute. Tannen moved to the Gulf Coast in 1969 to serve as the on-site project director for the Governor's Emergency Council of Mississippi under Governor John Bell Williams, when the council undertook long-range planning for comprehensive development to address the destruction caused by Hurricane Camille. In the New Orleans area, he was responsible for a number of major land-use and transportation projects for DMJM+Harris, now part of AECOM Technology Corporation, including studies to determine the impact of land-based and riverboat casinos on the city, the development of a multimodal transportation center around a renovated Union Passenger Terminal, and the expansion of a high speed rail corridor from Houston to Atlanta. He was integrally involved in the planning for the Riverwalk Project, which redeveloped the site of New Orleans's 1984 World's Fair and which continues to serve as a major downtown festival center and shopping destination. He was also instrumental in planning the mixed-use New Orleans Center, which opened in 1988 adjacent to the Superdome but was heavily damaged during Hurricane Katrina and reconfigured as Champions Square, an outdoor event space. In 2010, Tannen received the Role Model Award from New Orleans's Young Leadership Council for exemplary service to the community. In 2011, he completed a site-specific sculptural installation, *Grains of Sand*: boulders sited on fifteen locations along the trails of the Crystal Bridges Museum of American Art in Bentonville, Arkansas.

J. David Waggonner III is principal of Waggonner & Ball Architects in New Orleans. He was the initiator of a series of workshops known as the Dutch Dialogues and coeditor of *Dutch Dialogues: New Orleans–Netherlands, Common Challenges* *in Urbanized Deltas* (2009). The Dialogues series is a sustained effort to organize a group of experts from the Netherlands and North America, with the support of the Royal Netherlands Embassy and the American Planning Association, to advise the New Orleans region about ways of living with water and building with nature. Waggonner's planning experience includes work in China, notably for the town of Beidaihe, the Chinese central government's summer retreat. After participating in the Bring New Orleans Back Commission's Urban Design Committee, Waggonner led the firm's work in Planning Districts 2, 3, 12, and 13 during the Unified New Orleans Plan endeavor. Waggonner & Ball developed the recovery framework for devastated St. Bernard Parish, and their resulting plan received a 2006 Merit Award from the Louisiana chapter of the American Institute of Architects. Building on the work of Dutch Dialogues, Waggonner & Ball has received a commission to develop a comprehensive water management strategy for St. Bernard Parish and the east banks of Orleans and Jefferson parishes, funded through a Comprehensive Resiliency Program award. The firm is considering ways of utilizing stormwater, waste water, and groundwater; flood-control measures; and water infrastructure, public rights-of-way, and other associated public properties to increase the safety, resiliency, environmental quality, and potential value of the urbanized area.

Jane Wolff is associate professor and former director of the landscape architecture program at the Daniels Faculty of Architecture, Landscape, and Design at the University of Toronto. After studying documentary filmmaking and landscape architecture at Harvard, Wolff pursued a landscape and urban design practice in the San Francisco Bay Area. She has taught at Washington University in St. Louis; Ohio State University; and the California College of Arts and Crafts. In 2006, she served as the Beatrix Farrand Distinguished Visiting Professor at the University of California, Berkeley. Her research interests deal with the hybrid landscapes formed by interactions between natural process and cultural intervention. She is the author of *Delta Primer: A Field Guide to the California Delta*, a book and deck of cards designed to inform broad audiences about the contested landscapes of the California Delta. In the years since Hurricane Katrina, she has worked with several New Orleans organizations, including Longue Vue House and Gardens, the Dutch Dialogues initiative, and Make It Right, to develop strategies for landscape rehabilitation and resilience. She is a partner in the *Gutter to Gulf* initiative, which provides information about urban infrastructure and ecology in New Orleans through the website, guttertogulf.com. Her current projects include an exhibit at the Exploratorium of San Francisco on the cultural landscape of San Francisco Bay and initial studies for an atlas of Toronto's landscape as infrastructure.